C0-ART-739

DISCARD

PYTHON

A STUDY OF DELPHIC MYTH AND ITS ORIGINS

. . . through many a dark and drearie Vaile
they pass'd, and many a Region dolorous, . . .
Where all life dies, death lives, and nature breeds,
Perverse, all monstrous, all prodigious things,
Abominable, inutterable, and worse
Then Fables yet have feign'd, or fear conceiv'd,
Gorgons and Hydras, and Chimeras dire.

MILTON, Paradise Lost, *II, 618–628*

At which the universal Host upsent
A shout that tore Hells Concave, and beyond
Frighted the Reign of Chaos and old Night.

Ibid., *I, 541–543*

GLENDOWER. *I can call spirits from the vasty deep.*
HOTSPUR. *Why, so can I, or so can any man;*
But will they come when you do call for them?

SHAKESPEARE, *1* Henry IV, *III, 1, 53–55*

PYTHON

A STUDY OF DELPHIC MYTH

AND ITS ORIGINS

JOSEPH FONTENROSE

BL
795
.D7
F66
1980

UNIVERSITY OF CALIFORNIA PRESS
BERKELEY, LOS ANGELES, LONDON

TO

JANE, BOB, AND ANNE

WHO LIKE TO SEE THE DRAGON

GET HIS DUE

INDIANA
UNIVERSITY LIBRARY

MAY 4 1984

NORTHWEST

UNIVERSITY OF CALIFORNIA PRESS
BERKELEY AND LOS ANGELES, CALIFORNIA
UNIVERSITY OF CALIFORNIA PRESS, LTD.
LONDON, ENGLAND

© 1959, BY THE REGENTS OF THE UNIVERSITY OF CALIFORNIA
FIRST PAPERBACK PRINTING 1980
CALIFORNIA LIBRARY REPRINT SERIES EDITION 1980
ISBN 0–520–04091–0 PAPER
0–520–04106–2 CLOTH
LIBRARY OF CONGRESS CATALOG CARD NUMBER: 59–5144

DESIGNED BY WARD RITCHIE
PRINTED IN THE UNITED STATES OF AMERICA

1 2 3 4 5 6 7 8 9

kmm
5-4-84

PREFACE TO
THE 1980 EDITION

Of the several books that I have written *Python* has given me most pleasure and satisfaction, and so I am happy to see it appear in paperbound form. Paperbound publication would seem to mean that a scholarly book has met with sufficient approval among educated readers and that its central thesis has stood the test of time.

My method of myth study is thematic. It has met objections, but it seems to me the only method that can be used to show the genetic relationship of several myths to one another and the descent of each with modifications from a common original. It is a kind of structural method, although not Lévi-Straussian. Historical evidence and other methods may supplement it, but this method is indispensable. A single theme may appear spontaneously in several places; a pattern of themes must have a single origin.

The reader should not suppose that the theme list on pages 9–11 is a "prearranged framework," as one reviewer called it, as though I had drawn it up when I began my study of the combat myth, and had then fitted every myth to it. In fact, the themes emerged in the course of study, while I was preparing the first eight chapters; and I did not have all forty-three themes until Chapter VIII was written. After completing the book I placed the theme list after the Introduction for readers' convenience, and inserted references to it in the first eight chapters.

Nor should the reader take my remarks on pages 217–218, as some reviewers have done, to mean that I find the origin of the combat myth in some actual struggle of a prehistoric man with a savage beast or brigand. What I say there is that actual combats suggested the central theme of combat. A storyteller could not imagine a combat if nobody had ever fought one. And these remarks should not be combined with those on page 464 concerning the earliest folk narratives: they are not limited to the combat myth, which could have been a myth to begin with. Certainly the reader should not suppose that the process by which the combat myth was developed was repeated in the development of each variant. That would hardly be consistent with a genetic relationship. Each variant is the myth itself, modified in transmission over space and time and affected by local circumstances.

Python reveals the ways of myth, and it is my hope that the paperbound edition will make these known to many more readers.

Berkeley   Joseph Fontenrose
August 14, 1979

PREFACE

My interest in the Delphic oracle, which began more than twenty years ago, and my interest in Greek mythology, which I have had since childhood, have led me inevitably to a study of the combat of Apollo with the dragon Python, the origin myth of Apollo's Delphic shrine. I have found it a profitable and exciting study. It has carried me to the myths, legends, and folktales of many lands, of Greece, Anatolia, Canaan, Mesopotamia, Egypt, India, China, Japan, Germanic Europe, medieval Christendom, even of Central America and the Pacific Coast.

This book, I hope and believe, will be useful not only to classicists and orientalists, but also to folklorists, anthropologists, and all readers who like myths and folktales. I have therefore tried to suit it to intelligent readers who may have little or no knowledge of ancient or Asiatic languages. In chapters vii, viii, and ix and appendix 3, which deal with Oriental myths, I have cited not only editions of the original text and Orientalists' translations of them into German, French, or English, but also semipopular English translations and summaries. For example, I refer to Donald Mackenzie's books on Babylonian, Egyptian, and Indian myths, which, though the works of a nonspecialist, now outdated in some particulars, are competent, interesting, and not likely to mislead the reader. Such books, moreover, may be found in many public and private libraries; whereas the text editions, commentaries, and specialists' translations are available only in a few university or other learned libraries.

I have usually translated Greek and Latin words, phrases, and sentences quoted in the text, and I have usually written single Greek words in Roman rather than Greek letters. In the text I have spelled Oriental names in a manner that the nonspecialist reader can easily pronounce, provided that he give vowels their Italian values, and that in Indian names he be willing to pronounce *ç* like *sh* and *c* like *ch* in *church* (*Çaci* is pronounced *Shachi*), since I wish to distinguish (in spelling) the palatal sibilant (*ç*) from the lingual sibilant (*ṣ*), for which I use *sh*, and the palatal surd (*c*) from the corresponding surd aspirate, which is commonly transliterated *ch*; in the notes, however, I transliterate the names according to a system which many English and American Indologists employ, and which makes use of diacritical marks.

In this book I have abandoned my former practice of Latinising all Greek names. I have come to believe that such forms as *Cronus, Cadmus, Heracles,* misrepresent the Greek name to English readers (and two of these three names have no existence in Latin literature); and so I now spell them in their directly transliterated forms: *Kronos, Kadmos, Herakles* (I certainly don't believe in *c* for *kappa,* when we have a perfectly good *k* in our alphabet). Then the name is the same whether spelled in Greek or Roman letters (only in special circumstances do I use *ê* and *ô* to distinguish *êta* and *ômega* from *epsilon* and *omicron*). I retain only those Latinised forms which are long established in English (e.g., Aeschylus, Apollo) and which would look very strange if directly transliterated (but if the only difference between the Greek and Latinised forms is *-os* > *-us*, there is no good reason why the name should not be spelled with *-os*, e.g., *Herodotos*). I have also taken care to keep certain authors' names in their Latinised spelling, e.g., Callimachus, since librarians list their works under the Latinised names. But though I write *Lykia* for the country's name, I use the adjective *Lycian;* since the suffix is English, *Lykian* is a hybrid form. However, perfect consistency in this matter is neither possible nor desirable.

I have arranged footnotes, citations, and bibliography in a manner which, I think, avoids cumbrousness without sacrifice of usefulness and clarity. I have tried to cite all relevant sources and all important scholarly works which have dealt with the subjects treated. My own study of the sources has led me to every conclusion expressed in this book, though I may not be the first to have reached any particular conclusion. I have tried to give credit where credit is due; but it may well be that I have overlooked an earlier expression of some view which I have expressed—such oversight has been unintended.

With great pleasure I acknowledge my gratitude to several persons and institutions for assisting me in writing and publishing *Python*. Since my Delphic and Ovidian studies meet in this book, I must thank the American Council of Learned Societies for a fellowship which allowed me to visit the ruins of ancient Delphi as part of my earliest study of the Delphic oracle, Yale University Graduate School for a Sterling Fellowship which allowed me to continue my Delphic studies, and the American Academy in Rome for a senior fellowship in Classics which enabled me to spend a year upon the study of the text of Ovid's *Metamorphoses*. I am grateful to the University of California for research grants which enabled me to pay for photographs and drawings of art works, map-making, typing, and some checking of references; to the British Museum for photographs of art works reproduced in my figures 5, 9, 14, 18, and for permission to publish them; to the Chicago Oriental Institute for a photograph of the seal cylinder reproduced in figure 19, and for permission to publish it; to Viking Press for permission to quote from John Steinbeck's *The Forgotten Village;* to Random House for permission to quote from Robinson Jeffers' *Hungerfield*.

To my colleagues Ivan Linforth, Louis Mackay, and William Helmbold I owe a great debt of gratitude for their careful reading of my entire manuscript and for their many valuable comments and suggestions. My debt is also great to Jørgen Laessøe and Murray Emeneau for reading chapters vii–ix in manuscript and for the help that they gave me in finding or suggesting relevant sources of information. My thanks also to Peter Boodberg and Edward Schafer for help in dealing with Chinese mythology; to Robert Heizer and Jacques Schnier for reprints of articles; to Ben Meritt for a copy of the inscription from Apollo's cave on the Acropolis of Athens; to H. R. W. Smith for valuable help in finding vase paintings and other art works; to other friends who have directed me to material which I might not have hit upon otherwise.

Five young ladies deserve a special word of thanks: Marilyn Sode Smith, Lee Dabney, and Patricia Lawrence for making line drawings and maps; Nancy Helmbold and Anne Pippin for careful typing of a considerable part of the manuscript.

Finally I wish to express my great gratitude to the staff of the University of California Press for helpful assistance from the time of my writing this book until final publication: to Harold Small for directing me to some Paiute and other native Californian myths, and for advice and suggestions; above all, to John Gildersleeve for his careful editing and for his attention to all details of style and arrangement: he has saved me from several lapses and inconsistencies.

JOSEPH FONTENROSE

Kifissia
March 24, 1959

CONTENTS

CONTENTS

ILLUSTRATIONS

[For AW (Art Works) see Appendix 7]

Maps

ABBREVIATIONS USED IN FOOTNOTES

AGV   Auserlesene Griechischen Vasenbilder, edited by Eduard Gerhard. 4 vols. Berlin, 1840–1858.

AHS   T. W. Allen, W. R. Halliday, E. E. Sikes, editors: The Homeric Hymns. 2d ed. Oxford, Clarendon Press, 1936.

AW   Art Works Illustrating the Python, Tityos, Kyknos, and Typhon Combats, Appendix 7.

BCH   Bulletin de Correspondance Hellénique.

BD   The Book of the Dead: An English Translation . . . [See Bibliography: BUDGE (1901)]

BMCC   British Museum Catalogue of Coins.

ÇBr   Çathapatha-Brâhmaṇa.

CIL   Corpus Inscriptionum Latinarum, Academia Litterarum Borussica.

CVA   Corpus Vasorum Antiquorum, Union Académique Internationale.

EM   Etymologicon Magnum.

FD   Fouilles de Delphes, Ecole Française d'Athènes. Paris.

FF   Folklore Fellows Communications. Helsinki.

FR   A. Furtwängler, K. Reichhold: Griechischen Vasenmalerei. 3 vols., 180 plates in 18 folios. Munich: Bruckmann, 1904–1932.

GGM   Geographi Graeci Minores, edited by C. Mueller. 2 vols. Paris, 1882.

HN   Historia Numorum, by B. V. Head. 2d ed. Oxford, Clarendon Press, 1911.

IG   Inscriptiones Graecae, Academia Litterarum Borussica.

J   Felix Jacoby, editor: Die Fragmente der Griechischen Historiker. 3 vols. in 14. Berlin: Weidmann; Leiden: Brill; 1923–1958.

JAOS	Journal of the American Oriental Society.
JHS	Journal of Hellenic Studies.
JNES	Journal of Near Eastern Studies.
LM	Ausführliches Lexikon der Griechischen und Römischen Mythologie, edited by W. H. Roscher.
LSJ	Liddell-Scott-Jones: A Greek-English Lexicon. 9th ed. Oxford: Clarendon Press.
M	C. and Th. Mueller, editors: Fragmenta Historicorum Graecorum. 5 vols. Paris, 1868–1883.
OCD	The Oxford Classical Dictionary. Oxford: Clarendon Press.
P–B	W. Pape, G. E. Benseler: Wörterbuch der Griechischen Eigennamen. 3d ed. 2 vols. Braunschweig, 1863–1870.
RE	Real-Encyclopädie der Classischen Altertumswissenschaft (Pauly-Wissowa).
REG	Revue des Etudes Grecques.
RV	Rig Veda.
SGDI	Sammlung der Griechischen Dialekt-Inschriften, edited by H. Collitz, F. Bechtel. 4 vols. in 5. Göttingen, 1884–1889.
SIG	Sylloge Inscriptionum Graecarum, edited by W. Dittenberger. 3d ed. 4 vols. in 5. Leipzig: Hirzel, 1915–1924.
TS	Taittirîya Saṅhita.

PYTHON

INTRODUCTION

I

Every god has his enemy, whom he must vanquish and destroy. Zeus and Baal, Coyote and Ahura Mazda, Thor and the Lord of Hosts, are alike in this: that each must face a dreadful antagonist. Apollo's enemy was the great dragon Python, whom he had to fight and kill before he could establish his temple and oracle at Delphi. With this myth the present study begins and ends.

Mankind's myths, legends, and folktales are filled with tales of gods and heroes who encounter and defeat dragons, monsters, demons, and giants. So the mere combat is hardly enough to establish a genetic relation between the Apollo-Python myth and any other in which a god fights a dragon. Hence it may seem that the scholar who studies the Python myth has to do no more than find all the literary and monumental sources, distinguish the several versions in which the myth was told, deduce its original form and its provenience, and reveal its relation to Delphic cult. Such a study is valuable and necessary, and part of it has been done. The sources are confined to classical literature and art, and the student seldom has to look beyond those that refer directly to the Python myth and to Delphi.

But if between the Python myth and another myth of combat more points of agreement appear than the combat itself, if the two myths agree fairly well in the antecedents and aftermath of the

1

combat, if, in short, they share what seems to be a common plot, then we may say that the Python myth is genetically related to the other; either that one is derived from the other or that both have descended from a common original, an archetype. So the study of the Python myth enters a second phase: the study of those myths and legends of combat which are nearest to it in place and time.

Hence, in the following study, after reviewing the sources and distinguishing the several versions of the Python myth, I explore several minor legends of combat that cluster about Delphi and the Delphic god: the legends of Tityos, Phorbas, Phlegyas, Kyknos, Sybaris, and some others, to determine what relation they bear to the Python myth. Then I turn to Zeus's combat with Typhon—a myth equally well known to readers of the classics. These were the most momentous of all dragon combats for the ancient Greeks—those which two great gods, Zeus and Apollo, fought with Typhon and Python at peril of their sovereignty and their very lives. Since at first glance several striking correspondences between the two myths can be seen, the question, whether or not they are two closely related variants of one myth, is closely studied and answered.

Furthermore scholar and reader have long been aware that Greece's neighbors to the east and south—the Hittites, Canaanites, Babylonians, and Egyptians—had important myths of combat between god and dragon or similar monstrous enemy; also that the ancient Indians, speakers of a closely related Indo-European language, had such myths, in particular the great myth of Indra's battle with the serpent Vritra. Since the oriental civilisations affected Greece in many ways, both obvious and subtle, it is reasonable to suppose that the Greeks received some myth plots from them. Indeed, scholars have asserted that the Python and Typhon myths were derived from the Asiatic combat myths or influenced by them. But they have confined themselves to pointing out a few coincidences and similarities. A more rigorous study is needed if a genuine relationship is to be proved; and that, so far as it can be undertaken by one who is much more at home in the classical languages and literatures than in those of the Near East and India, is the third phase of the present study. In dealing

with Asiatic myths I have had to rely upon the studies and translations of orientalists; but the work of specialists, after all, is
intended for others' use. Once a comparative analysis has been
made, setting the two Greek myths alongside the relevant oriental
myths, we see that a common pattern underlies the whole group
of myths. A common pattern implies a single origin for all myths
that have it; but should anyone deny that this is so, he must still
grant that the presence of a common pattern, or even of several
striking correspondences, in myths of diverse and independent
origins, is a remarkable phenomenon and worthy of attention. If
it is true that a particular myth pattern was diffused over a great
part of the Old World, from Greece to India and south to Egypt,
if not farther, and manifested in many national variants, then it
must have had an unusual significance to the peoples who told it
and adopted it. So I explore the deeper meanings of the myth:
what were the Asiatics and Greeks trying to say in these mythical
terms and images?

The results of the comparison of oriental myths with Greek
myths—finding a common pattern and exploring its meanings—
make it possible to direct attention once more to Greece and to
determine the relation of heroic legends of combat, those of
Perseus, Kadmos, and Herakles, to the Apollo-Python and Zeus-
Typhon myths. Then I turn back to the Python myth of Delphi
and apply to it the results of the whole inquiry.

Finally I inquire into the relation of the myth to the rituals
that its several variants accompanied, since the combat was often
asserted to be the primeval precedent of certain cult-institutions.

II

At the outset I must make clear that by *myth* I mean a traditional story that accompanies rituals. First of all, I mean a *story*,
something that has a beginning, a middle, and an end—in other
words, a plot. I do not use the term broadly and vaguely to mean
animistic and theological ideas in general. Secondly, I mean a
traditional story, one that was at first orally transmitted. Thirdly,
I mean that kind of story which purports to tell of the occasion on
which some religious institution, a cult or certain of its rites and
festivals, had its beginning, and of the divine acts which set the

precedent for the traditional acts performed in the cult. Even creation myths are generally found to be attached to cults. Other traditional stories, those unattached to cults, are more properly called *legend* or *folktale*, though occasionally I use the term *myth* or *mythology*, as is often done, to include them too. For the same plot may appear among all three kinds of traditional story: it is not plot that makes the difference, and some variants of the combat myth belong to hero tale or fairy tale rather than to genuine myth.

In dealing with the myths of ancient lands we must rely mainly upon narratives, notices, and allusions found in ancient literature, with some assistance from works of ancient art that picture mythical scenes. It was very seldom the purpose of any ancient writer to inform others about the myth—to tell them a story that they didn't already know. This is particularly true of Greek myth. From Babylonia and Egypt myth texts have been recovered that contain the very versions of myths that were associated with the rituals and cults and known to the priesthood and worshippers; but almost nothing of the sort has come to us from Greece. Greek writers were not composing ritual texts; they used mythical materials for their own literary purposes: changing, adding, subtracting, fusing, as they wished. Even when we find a whole mythical narrative, not a summary or fragment or allusion, it is not likely to be precisely the version that was known to the folk, particularly to the folk of those regions in which the myth was attached to a cult. The sources, therefore, are like potsherds, which must be gathered, studied, and combined before the whole vase can be known as it really was.

Many scholars, in dealing with Greek myths, assume that an ancient author received his knowledge of a myth from earlier writers. Hence they are likely to confine themselves to a literary history of the myth and to suppose that any difference encountered must be an innovation of the author in whose work it first appears. Of course later writers were influenced by earlier writers, and of course writers innovated and changed, but often a supposed innovation in a myth, or a feature that appears late in the literary tradition, has a parallel in Greek or foreign cognates of the myth attested by much earlier sources. It is quite possible, sometimes probable, that the author took it from oral tradition, if not from literature now lost: he had the oral tradition all about him. Scholars have tended to neglect the oral transmission of myths, or to assume that it did not exist after some unspecified early date; yet it was surely alive throughout antiquity—in fact, it never disappeared, but took on Christian dress in the Middle Ages. Some traces of the oral tradition can be found in the pages of Pausanias and some in vase-paintings, but in general it must be divined from a comparative study of the myth's sources and the myth's cognates.

Hence in dealing with the Greek myths of combat I make use of all relevant material gleaned from Greek and Latin literature and art, both early and late. Sometimes I get important information from late writers and draw conclusions from it concerning early forms of the myth under discussion. But usually these conclusions drawn from late sources find support in earlier sources. It is also true that later sources of Mesopotamian, Egyptian, and Indian myths offer valuable material, and that conclusions based on them can often be supported by earlier evidence. There survives but little of all that was written in Hellas from the eighth to the fourth centuries or in the Near East during the second millennium. We have no recordings from native informants. The late-appearing version of a myth may very well have appeared earlier in writing, or an orally transmitted version may then have received literary notice for the first time. In short, no evidence can be ignored; all is grist to our mill.

The very permanence of the literary record obscures the fluid nature of the mythical tradition. We are likely to think that Greek myths were always told as Ovid tells them. They most certainly were not. Probably no fifth-century Greek knew any one of Ovid's myths in the form in which he tells it. Any narrative that we find is the version known to one man at one time. A myth or folktale, moving from place to place, passing from one person to another, from generation to generation, is constantly undergoing change; new versions are formed in every region and age. A new *version* appears when details are changed—when a theme or episode is given a somewhat different expression, when something is added or subtracted, when the sequence of episodes is shifted—but the personal and place names remain unchanged. When a particular version in its progress from place to place acquires new names for its persons and places, then a new *variant* has been formed. The variant is essentially the same story told of different gods and men in a different setting. This is the distinction that I make throughout between the terms *version* and *variant,* which many scholars use interchangeably. A type is a traditional plot which appears in several variants. It is a series of episodes, a constellation of themes, that remains fairly well fixed among the variants. There may be changes in sequence; less essential episodes or themes may drop out; new features may be added. But there must be a durable core, observable in all variants, if we are to speak of a type. For example, consider the story type called Potiphar's wife. The Joseph story of Genesis is a Hebrew variant of this type; the Bellerophon, Hippolytos, and Tennes stories are three Greek variants. The Hippolytos variant was told in different ways among the Greeks: each different way can be called a version. The names Hippolytos, Phaidra, Theseus, give unity to the variant; the plot gives unity to the type. The difference between variant and version resembles that between species and variety; the type is the genus.

A traditional plot, on entering a new region, usually becomes attached to the gods or heroes of that region. The names change: a people may substitute, for example, its own weather god for the weather god of the borrowed story. Hence a study of myth diffusion is more concerned with plots and themes than with the divine participants or their names. The origin and development of the myth usually has little or nothing to do with the origin of the gods who appear in a national variant or with the origin of their names.

So this study, in attempting to relate one myth to another, is concerned mostly with narrative themes. By *theme* I mean a recurrent feature or episode of traditional stories. It is an integral part of the story in which it is found; but it is separable in the sense that it may occur in other story types too. Some themes are essential to a type; some may appear in one variant and be absent from another.[1]

The theme is not identically expressed in every variant or version: it constantly changes its outer dress in accord with the national customs or local features of the places where it is found. It may become obscure or disguised; only a trace of it may be left. If it were not for this, all variants would be much alike and common origin would be obvious. But a common origin of the combat myths is not obvious; hence a careful thematic analysis of the several myths is necessary. It may be helpful to point out the sorts of variations in theme that occur.

1. Mutations of role; changes of rank, relationship, class. A hero may replace a god, a giant or lion replace a dragon. A father may become grandfather, uncle, brother, king, tutor; a mother may become grandmother, fostermother, nurse, wife; sister, wife, and daughter interchange frequently.

2. Mutations in action. The mode of combat may change from one variant to another. One kind of punishment or deception may be replaced by another.

---

[1] I choose the term *theme* in preference to Stith Thompson's *motif* (MIFL), and I define it more broadly, because it will thus be more useful to our study. Thompson's motifs are cut a bit too fine: any change in detail or dress of a theme he is likely to list as a separate motif. But I wish to consider as one theme all those story elements that serve the same narrative purpose, those that are logically or practically the same, doing identical work in different tales. My themes will sometimes correspond to Thompson's general motifs that comprise a subclass of motifs; sometimes they will gather together motifs that he has listed under different categories. For example, Th. 3B (see p. 10) indicates the animal shape or component of the god's enemy: he is often a dragon or snake, but he may be conceived as a lion or boar, or his form may be mixed. It makes no difference to the myth: his bestial and savage nature is appropriately emphasised in any of these shapes. Th. 3B sums up the whole of Thompson's B0–B99: our dragons would have to be B11; mixed forms B20 to B29, according to the mixture; fish-forms B80; serpent-demons B91. My Th. 3E, the enemy's transformations, could be anything in the D0 to D699 range. Th. 8D (Venusberg or Siren theme) combines F131.1 (Venusberg), B53 (Siren), F302 (fairy mistress), F302.3.4 (fairies entice men to harm them), G264 (demoness seduces men to destruction), and G530.1–2 (ogre's daughter or wife aids the hero). Th. 9 embraces K811.1 (enemy invited to banquet and killed), K776 and K871 (enemy is captured or killed when intoxicated), K872 (Judith and Holofernes), G521 (ogre made drunk and overcome), K2357 (disguise to enter enemy's camp), K1810 (deception by disguise), and a host of others, all of which perform the same function in the myths to be studied. Again I need but one label for the enemy's deadly visage (Th. 3D): he may destroy with a glance or flash fire from his eyes or breathe fire from his nostrils; so B11.2.11 (fire-breathing dragon), D581 (petrefaction by glance), D2061.2.1 (death-giving glance), D2071 (evil eye), and others must be combined. Use of Thompson's system could not reveal the actual correspondences between stories.

3. A striking feature of one variant may be reduced in another to something less striking, or it may be disguised. Death may be changed to wound, sleep, defeat, exile, disappearance. A deed may become merely the attempt to do it.

4. Deeds or traits may be transferred from one character to another: from the champion to his son or wife or helper, even from champion to enemy and *vice versa*.

5. Themes and roles may be combined or fused. The heroine may play upon the enemy's lust to lure him to destruction: thus Themes 4E, 8D, and 9 (pp. 10 f.) are combined. The dragon's watch over a spring may run together with his habitation in the sea, his damming of waters, his blockade of a road, and his holding of a sacred precinct: Themes 2D, 2E, 4G, 4F, and 2C are thus merged.

6. There may be expansion or doubling of themes, persons, episodes. The champion may split into father and son. A single enemy may become a chief and many subordinates. Several combats may be fought, with several deaths or defeats of either champion or enemy.

Since the likeness of myths to dreams has often been pointed out, we should notice that the modes in which a theme is expressed in actual myths are closely analogous to those in which a dream thought is expressed in the dream content, as Freud has defined them. He points to factors of condensation and displacement. (*a*) Condensation is the converging of several dream thoughts upon a focal point, which becomes a single element in the dream content. One form of condensation may be seen in the composite persons of dreams. Condensation corresponds to the combination and fusion of 5 above. (*b*) Displacement is manifested in the substitution of one idea for another without change of essential meaning, or in the inversion of ideas: transformation into the opposite or something very different. The mutations and reductions of 1 to 4 above are analogous to dream displacements. The doublings of 6 correspond to the doubling that often occurs in dreams.[2]

Such are the changes that themes may undergo. The student must recognise that a theme may assume in one myth a very different dress from that which it has in another. He must often look

---

[2] Freud (ID) 319–397, especially 320–339.

beneath the outer covering to find the theme. He must also realise that mythical thinking is illogical by our standards: in this too it resembles dream thinking. Contraries, contradictories, inconsistencies may and do stand side by side in a single mind and a single narrative. Yet myth is not a jumble of nonsense and absurdities; it has a logic of its own. He who studies myth must try to understand mythical ways of thinking.

In the following pages, *myth*, besides having the meanings defined above, often designates the particular narrative with which we are dealing, the version or variant of the myth type, which may also be called *myth*. The context, I trust, always makes the reference clear.

For the convenience of readers I close this Introduction with a list of the themes that recur in the several myths under study. These themes are constantly referred to throughout by means of the numeral-and-letter symbols which appear beside the theme statements of this list.

THEMES OF THE COMBAT MYTH

1. The Enemy was of divine origin.
   1A. He was son of the primordial mother: chaos demoness or earth goddess.
   1B. He was son of a father god: chaos demon or deposed father god or ruling father god.
   1C. He had a wife or female companion of like origin and character.

2. The Enemy had a distinctive habitation.
   2A. The feature of geographical correspondence: The Enemy lived in a region in which myth tellers were wont to place the dwelling of monsters and demons in general.
   2B. He lived in a cave, hut, or tree.
   2C. He occupied a god's temenos.
   2D. He was guardian or spirit of a spring.
   2E. He lived in sea, lake, or river.

3. The Enemy had extraordinary appearance and properties.
   3A. He was gigantic.

3B. He had nonhuman form: most often that of a snake, but also lizard, crocodile, scorpion, fish, hippopotamus, boar, lion, wolf, dog, horse, bull, eagle, vulture, hawk, etc.; sometimes a mixed form of various combinations of bestial and human members.

3C. He had several heads, arms, legs, etc.

3D. He sent death by fire, glance, or breath: fire from his nostrils, mouth, or eyes, death-dealing glances from eyes or countenance, poison-laden breath from nostrils or mouth.

3E. He could change his shape at will.

3F. He was a death spirit, evil demon, spectre, rising from the lower world.

3G. He was wind, flood, storm, plague, famine, drought.

4. The Enemy was vicious and greedy.

4A. He plundered, robbed, murdered, made war.

4B. He was a despotic ruler or master who oppressed his subjects and imposed tribute.

4C. He carried off the young of man and beast.

4D. He was gluttonous, devouring whole herds, and a man-eater.

4E. He was a lecher and ravisher, demanding that maidens be offered to him.

4F. He commanded a road and killed travelers upon it, often in a contest that he forced upon them.

4G. He blockaded rivers or springs to keep men from water; or he drained rivers in his thirst.

5. The Enemy conspired against heaven.

5A. He wanted to rule the world.

5B. His mother or wife or female companion incited him.

6. A divine Champion appeared to face him.

6A. The weather god or sky god went forth to fight him.

6B. It was his first exploit: he was then a boy or youth.

7. The Champion fought the Enemy.

7A. The Champion, using his favorite weapons, fought and killed the Enemy.

7B. He had to use numerous missiles; for the Enemy was formidable, or had an invulnerable hide.

7C. The other gods were panicstricken: they appeased the Enemy or fled.

7D. The Champion's sister, wife, or mother helped him.

7E. The Champion was helped by another god or hero.

7F. The Enemy fled during the combat.

7G. The combat was the central encounter of a gigantomachy.

8. The Champion nearly lost the battle.

8A. He suffered temporary defeat or death.

8B. The Enemy removed a potent organ from his body or took a potent object from him.

8C. The Enemy overcame him after luring him to a feast.

8D. The Enemy's consort seduced the Champion to his destruction, or entered into a liaison with him (Venusberg theme).

8E. The dead Champion was lamented.

9. The Enemy was finally destroyed after being outwitted, deceived, or bewitched: he was especially susceptible to lures of (*a*) food and (*b*) sex; he was easily taken in by (*c*) disguise; (*d*) magic was employed against him.

10. The Champion disposed of the Enemy and celebrated his victory.

10A. He punished the Enemy, even after killing him, by imprisoning him in the lower world or under a mountain, or by mutilating or cutting up or exposing his corpse.

10B. He celebrated his victory with a banquet and other festivities; he was cheered by gods and men.

10C. He was purified of blood pollution.

10D. He instituted cult, ritual, festival, and built a temple for himself.

APOLLO AND THE DRAGON

In the Homeric Hymn to Apollo we find the earliest known record of Apollo's combat with a dragon at Delphi. Soon after his birth on Delos, Apollo crossed the sea and wandered over the mainland, looking for a good place in which to establish an oracular shrine. He finally chose Haliartos, by the spring Telphusa, and had actually begun to lay foundations, when the spring-nymph Telphusa spoke to him and artfully persuaded him to go instead to Krisa on the slopes of Parnassos. So Apollo went on to Parnassos, and there on the site of Delphi he laid the foundations of his great temple, assisted by Trophonios and Agamedes, who set the stone threshold in place, and by the tribes of men, who erected the temple on the foundations.[1]

It is not clear from the Hymn whether or not this work had been completed when Apollo fought a she-dragon (*drakaina*) beside a spring and killed her with an arrow from his bow. But it is likely that Apollo encountered her while he was at work on the foundations not more than a few hundred yards from her

---

[1] Hom. Hymn 3.182–387. See 298, ἀμφὶ δὲ νηὸν ἔνασσαν ἀθέσφατα φῦλ' ἀνθρώπων, perhaps an allusion to the peoples of the Amphictyony. AHS suggest that the οὐδός, placed by Trophonios and Agamedes, may be the adyton, but are more inclined to think that it means the first courses of the building. For discussion of the Hymn's version see Dornseiff (1933) 16–29. On the myth see Schreiber (1879) 1–9, who does not distinguish the versions as I have done.

spring. She was a monstrous creature, huge and savage, guilty of terrible violence against the people and the flocks of the land. To meet her meant death to any man. She had, moreover, been nurse of Typhaon, Hera's monstrous child, whom the queen of the gods had borne in anger at Zeus, because he had brought forth Athena from his head, and had had no need of her, his wedded wife. Deciding to equal Zeus's feat by producing a child without male help, Hera succeeded, but the child she bore was the monstrous Typhaon, like neither to gods nor to mortal men. She turned him over to the Delphian drakaina, an evil to an evil, κακῷ κακόν.[2]

After a digression of about fifty lines on the story of Typhaon's birth from Hera, the poet returns to Apollo's combat with the dragoness; Typhaon is forgotten, except that Apollo in his speech of triumph tells his dying opponent that now Typhoeus and Chimaira cannot save her from death. The poet merely repeats that Apollo killed the dragoness with his arrow, and gives us no details of the combat. He spends more time on her death throes and on Apollo's speech of triumph, in which and in the verses that follow it we have our first notice of the etymology that derives the place name Pytho from the rotting of the serpent's corpse (πύθειν).[3]

After the combat Apollo went off to punish Telphusa, and then (καὶ τότε δή) bethought himself of providing priests and servitors for his temple. The Telphusa episode completes the Hymn's version of Apollo's combat with a dragon. The female serpent is given no name in the Hymn, but is called Delphyne in later literature. Nor was she guardian of Ge's or Themis's oracular shrine, since the Hymn knows of no shrine at Delphi before Apollo founded his.[4]

---

[2] Hymn 3.354-356,

δῶκεν ἔπειτα φέρουσα κακῷ κακόν, ἣ δ᾽ ὑπέδεκτο·
ὃς κακὰ πόλλ᾽ ἔρδεσκε κατὰ κλυτὰ φῦλ᾽ ἀνθρώπων.
ὃς τῇ γ᾽ ἀντιάσειε , φέρεσκέ μιν αἴσιμον ἦμαρ.

[3] It is better to look on Typhoeus of 367 (v.l. Τυφωνεὺς M) as merely a variant of Typhaon, rather than as the name of a different being. For as we shall see in chapter iv, the names Typh(a)on and Typhoeus (also Typhos) are interchangeable in later literature.

[4] One Scholiast on Apollon. Arg. 2.706 says that some give the dragon the feminine name Delphyne, others the masculine Delphynes. Another Scholiast ibid. says that Callimachus called the Delphian dragon both Delphyna and Delphynes. He is apparently not referring to Call. Hymn 2.100 f. or 4.90-94, where the poet speaks of a male dragon, but gives no name. The same Scholiast also informs us that Leandrios used the masculine

When we next encounter Apollo's combat, the dragon has become male and is called Python. It is from Simonides that we first learn of this form of the tale, the version most often found in later literature, but it is only indirectly that we know what Simonides said. He is cited by the pseudo-Julian concerning Apollo's epithet Hekatos: he received this name, said Simonides, because he vanquished the dragon Python with a hundred arrows. The notice is brief, and we cannot be sure whether Simonides used the name Python or merely referred to a dragon, to whom pseudo-Julian gave the name that had long since become familiar.[5]

In any case the mention of a hundred arrows points to the version that appears to have been most popular after 300 B.C. Apollo, while still a mere boy, came to Delphi while Ge or Themis still ruled the shrine and spoke the oracles. A dragon named Python, who guarded the shrine for the goddess, opposed Apollo on his arrival. The god fought him and after shooting many arrows from his bow finally killed him. Apollo then went to Tempe, or to Crete, to be purified of blood pollution, and thereafter came back to Delphi to take possession. He founded the Pythian games to celebrate his victory over Python.[6]

---

name Delphynes; Schol. on 2.711 says that Leandrios spoke of a female dragon Delphyna. Apollonios himself leaves us in doubt with Δελφύνην πελώριον and nowhere a decisive pronoun. I am inclined to think that he means a dragoness. Likewise ambiguous is Nonn. *Dion.* 13.28. Dionysios Periegetes 441 f. has δράκοντος Δελφύνης (if the text is right). The form is definitely feminine, though its appositive is the genitive of *drakôn*, used either to designate the male of this order or any individual regardless of sex; but a female is *drakaina.* Eustathios *ad loc.* is unsure whether Dionysios meant a male or female dragon. According to John of Antioch (1.20, 4.539 M), there was disagreement whether the Pythian festival concerned the dragon Delphynes or the *hêrôis* Delphyne (p. 377). In FD 3.2.138.25–28, the inscription of an Athenian hymn to Apollo at Delphi, Apollo's enemy is called daughter of Ge; but no name appears among the visible letters. In FD 3.2.137.22, also an Athenian hymn at Delphi, his enemy is certainly a male serpent; here too no name is visible. For the *drakaina* unnamed see also Plut. *Mor.* 414A, 988A. For the masculine *Delphynês* see also Schol. Vet. on Eur. *Phoen.* 232 f.; Suid. Δ 210; Apost. 15.10. It may arise from just such an ambiguity as we see in *Arg.* 2.706. Hesych. Δ 603 calls the male serpent Delphys. For the female Lamia of Delphi see pp. 44 f.

[5] Simonides, frag. 26A Bergk, *ap.* ps.-Jul. *Epist.* 24, p. 395D. AHS state flatly (p. 246) that the name Python is first found in Ephoros' "Euhemeristic version." But I am inclined to think that Simonides used the name. Pseudo-Julian says, διότι τὸν Πύθωνα τὸν δράκοντα βέλεσιν ὥς φησιν (Σιμωνίδης) ἐχειρώσατο. καὶ μᾶλλον αὐτὸν Ἕκατον ἢ Πύθιον χαίρειν προσαγορευόμενον. . . . Apollo's epithet Pythios is often derived from his killing of Python.

[6] Apollod. 1.4.1; FD 3.2.137.21–24; Paus. 10.6.5 f.; Ael. VH 3.1; Poll. *Onom.* 4.84; Men. Rhet. *Epid.* 3.17, p. 441 Sp.; Ovid *Met.* 1.438–451; Stat. *Theb.* 1.562–571, 5.531–533, 6.8 f.; Claud. 2; Sid. Ap. *Carm.* 2.152–155; Argg. 1 and 3 to Pind. *Pyth.*; Vat. Myth.

This is obviously the version Ovid used in the *Metamorphoses*, though he says nothing about Python's guarding the shrine or about the purification of Apollo. But Themis rules over Delphi (1.379), and it is Python, a male dragon, whom the god kills with a thousand arrows. To commemorate his victory the god founds the Pythian festival, naming it after the slain serpent. This derivation of the names Pytho, Pythios, and Pythia from the name Python is characteristic of the second version of the myth; the first, we have seen, derives them from πύθειν.[7]

After the Homeric Hymn and Simonides the earliest literary notice of the combat is found in Euripides' *Iphigeneia in Tauris* (1239–1251). After Leto had given birth to Apollo on Delos she carried the infant god to Parnassos. A dragon lived there, Ge's son and guardian of her oracle. Though still a babe in arms, Apollo killed this monster with his arrows and took possession of the shrine.

This third version of the story is found in some later writers and several works of art. Upon a black-figured lekythos of white background, a work of the early fifth century, and therefore earlier than Euripides' play, we see the infant Apollo shooting his arrows from Leto's arms at a snake of many coils, who appears among rocks in a hollow (fig. 1). Most representations of the Apollo-Python combat in art show this third version: out of

---

I 113, II 19. Casual allusions are too numerous to list here. This was probably the version represented in sculpture by Pythagoras of Rhegion in the fifth century (Plin. NH 34.8.59): the serpent was shown transfixed by Apollo's arrows. It is certainly the version of Call. *Hymn* 2.97–104, though elsewhere Callimachus appears to have told a different version of the story (see note 4). Not all the authors cited have every detail of the story as summarised. Plutarch's remarks on the Septerion festival in *Greek Questions* 12 (*Mor.* 293c) can be referred to this version, but may have a touch of version E too (see p. 21).

[7] In *Met.* 1.439 f., populisque novis terror eras, and 1.459, pestifero ventre, Ovid may be understood to allude to Python as bane of the region, a character that seems to be inconsistent with his guardianship, as Schreiber points out (1879: 7). But *terror eras* is immediately followed by *tantum spatii de monte tenebas*; i.e. it was Python's huge size that struck terror into men. And *pestifero ventre* probably alludes to Python's venom; see 1.444, vulnera nigra veneno. But notice Men. Rhet. *loc. cit.*, where Python, Ge's son, rules over Delphi, plunders the land, and also keeps people from visiting Themis's oracle. In regard to Python's sex, notice Met. 1.439, where an occasional MS has *incognita*, which, if correct, is simply a modifier of *serpens*, a feminine noun, as in 447, perdomitae serpentis. Paus. 10.6.5 and Arg. 3 to Pind. *Pyth.* seem to combine the derivation of *Pytho* or *Pythia* from πύθειν with the second version, but neither names the dragon.

FIGURE 1. APOLLO, LETO, AND PYTHON

thirteen listed in the article "Python" in Roscher's *Lexikon* only the bronze sculpture of Pythagoras of Rhegion and the coin type of Croton (fig. 2) picture another version, probably the second. Pythagoras' sculpture has long since disappeared, and so has the

FIGURE 2. APOLLO AND PYTHON

bronze group of Delphi, described by Klearchos of Soloi, which represented the third version. Leto, says Klearchos, went from Euboean Chalkis to Delphi, carrying the twins Apollo and Artemis in her arms. When she came near Python's cave, he rushed upon them and Apollo killed him. Heliodoros and a poet of the

Anthology seem to refer to this version when they say that Python attacked Leto and was killed by Apollo.[8]

A number of other writers relate a version in which Apollo went to Delphi alone, as in the second version, but expressly to kill Python for having pursued and harried his mother Leto while she was pregnant with him. Servius, Lactantius Placidus, and other commentators say that it was Hera who sent Python to pursue the pregnant Leto and prevent the birth of her son. To this story Lucan alludes briefly, saying that the young Apollo killed Python for pursuing his mother during her pregnancy. Hyginus says that the pregnant Leto, caused to wander by Hera's hatred, was pursued by Python, who wanted to kill her before she could bear her child, since he had learned that Leto's son would kill him. He failed to overtake her and returned to Parnassos, whither Apollo went when he was but four days old and avenged his mother by killing Python with his arrows. Since Hyginus appears to use the same source as the commentators, we may assume that in his account too Hera and Python were leagued together against Leto. An anonymous writer (Bachm. Anecd. 2.351) says that Hera sent the dragon against the pregnant Leto that he might kill her children. As Macrobius has it, Hera opposed the pregnant Leto, and when her twins were born, Python attacked them in their cradles, and Apollo killed him. Lucian limits Hera's role to putting earth (i.e., Ge) under oath not to let Leto bear her children; but Poseidon gave Leto refuge on Delos when the dragon was pursuing her.[9]

---

[8] Klearchos 46, 2.318M; Heliodoros *ap*. Tzetz. *in* Lyc. 208; Anth. Pal. 3.6 and *titulum*; cf. Sen. *Med*. 700; Paus. 2.7.7. For representations in art see AW 1–9 (figs. 1–3, 27); see appendix 7 for list of art works. CVA, France 1, III Dc, pl. 3.12, is a black-figure painting which Pottier interprets as Kadmos and the Theban dragon. Jocelyn Woodward (1932:34–36) argues for Apollo and Python and connects the scene with the throne of Bathykles. Notice that the two (or three?) art works that present the second version are fairly early, none later than 400; whereas of the eleven which present the third version, only one can be dated as early as the fifth century, though the sculptures of Leto fleeing with her children have a fifth-century original.

[9] Lucan BC 5.79–81; Lucian *DMar*. 10; Hyg. *Fab*. 140 (cf. 53.2); Macr. 1.17.50–52; Serv. *Aen*. 3.73; Lact. Plac. *Theb*. 5.533 and *Ach*. 206; ps.-Liban. *Narr*. 25; Schol. on Clem. Alex. *Protr*. 2P; Schol. on Lucan BC 3.177, 5.79, 6.407; Vat. Myth. I 37, II 17, III 8.3; Bachm. Anecd. 2.351. In this version we notice that Apollo, though only a few days old, has already become a *kouros*, an ephebe, and has the appearance of a youth of sixteen years or so (but see p. 24 concerning the art works). For Apollo's rapid growth see Hom. Hymn 3.127–135.

Not only does this version appear to combine the third version, attack of Python

There is also a version, usually called rationalistic or Euhemeristic, in which Python is a man. According to Strabo's brief and incomplete summary of a narrative taken from the historian Ephoros, Apollo, on his way from Athens to Delphi, came to Panopeus, where he encountered and killed the brigand Tityos. The Parnassians then came to him and told him of another brigand in the land, a man called Python or Drakon. Apollo killed him too with his arrows, while the Parnassians cheered him with cries of *Hie Paian* and burned Python's tent—a deed, he adds,

FIGURE 3. LETO, APOLLO, ARTEMIS, AND PYTHON

that was commemorated in later Delphic rites. Pausanias does not mention the brigand's name. After alluding briefly to the story of Apollo's fight with a dragon who was son of Ge, he informs us that another story is told. A certain Krios, who ruled in Euboea, had a lawless son who plundered Apollo's shrine and the whole region around it. When he was on his way to make a second raid, the Delphians asked Apollo to help them. His *pro-*

upon Leto, with the second, but Macrobius and Bachm. Anecd. 2.351 join with it an element from the first: that the rotting of the serpent's corpse gave the place its name Pytho or the god his name Pythios; though Macrobius also tells us that the dragon whom Apollo fought was called Python. He agrees with the third version in saying that the infant Apollo killed Python, but from his cradle, not from his mother's arms.

mantis the Pythia Phemonoe replied in three hexameters, telling them that Phoebus would soon send his arrow upon this bandit and would then be cleansed of blood pollution by Cretans.[10]

There are obvious differences between Pausanias' account and Strabo's summary which make it unlikely that Ephoros was also Pausanias' source. It is true that the incidents and circumstances that are mentioned by one but not by the other could be complementary. But the differences go beyond that. In Strabo's summary the Parnassians met Apollo just after his slaying of Tityos at Panopeus and told him about Python; according to Pausanias Apollo was at his shrine at Delphi when the Delphians appealed to him, for it was the Pythia who answered them. Again, when Apollo, in Ephoros' narrative, killed Python, the Delphians burned his tent, which represented Python's cave, situated at Delphi in the other four versions. Krios' son, in Pausanias' account, did not live at Delphi, but probably in Euboea; he had once plundered Delphi and was on his way to do so again (ἐπεστράτευσε καὶ δεύτερον).[11]

The myth of Apollo against Python was used as *aition* of both Septerion and Pythian festivals (see pp. 453–461). Plutarch, in describing the Septerion, reports a version of the myth which scholars have considered rationalistic and close to Ephoros' version. Actually he says nothing that indicates clearly whether Python is snake or man. He adds to the story two incidents that no other writer mentions: that the wounded Python fled from Delphi to Tempe, whither Apollo pursued him, and that Python, who died before Apollo could overtake him, received funeral rites from his son Aix. Neither incident compels us to believe that his Python is not a dragon: there are many other stories of dragons in flight, and dragons can have sons. And it is no more strange that a dragon receive funeral rites than that the god Apollo be under the need of seeking purification for having killed one. It is only the name Aix that indicates a possible relation to the so-called rationalistic version; for in that, as Pausanias tells it, the father of Apollo's enemy is called Krios. That is, Python who had

[10] Ephoros 31*b*, 2.53 J, *ap*. Strab. 9.3.12, p. 422; Paus. 10.6 f.
[11] Halliday (1928:70) refers Pausanias' account as well as Strabo's to Ephoros without reserve.

a son Goat may be the brigand who had a father Ram. So thin as this is the evidence for supposing that Plutarch's version presents Python as a brigand in human form.[12]

We find, then, in general, five versions of the myth of Apollo's combat with a dragon, each subject to variations of detail or to confusions with other versions:

A. The version of the Homeric Hymn. When Apollo established his shrine and oracle at Pytho, he fought and killed a female serpent that plagued the land. She was sometimes called Delphyne by later writers.

B. The version of Simonides, Apollodoros, Aelian, Ovid, and many others. Apollo came to Delphi and encountered the dragon Python, who guarded the shrine for Ge or Themis. Python attacked him, or barred his approach to the sacred chasm, whereupon Apollo fought him and killed him after a hard struggle in which he used numerous arrows. Apollo then took over the shrine.

C. The version of Euripides, Klearchos, and others. When Leto had given birth to Apollo on Delos, she carried the infant god in her arms to Delphi, where the dragon Python saw her and attacked her. The babe saved his mother by shooting arrows at Python from her arms. Sometimes the infant Artemis is associated with Apollo.

D. The version of Lucan, Lucian, Hyginus, and commentators. Hera ordered Python to pursue the pregnant Leto and destroy her with her unborn son. Leto found refuge on Delos. Later Apollo went to Delphi and settled accounts with Python.

E. The version of Ephoros (E1) and Pausanias (E2). The Delphians sought Apollo's aid against the brigand Python or Drakon, who was plundering the land. Apollo fought him and killed him.

It is apparent that version A, in which Apollo fought the dragoness Delphyne, stands somewhat apart from the other four versions, in which his opponent is the male Python and which are closely related one to another. Version E2 differs from all

---

[12] Plut. *Mor.* 293c, 417f–418b. See Halliday (1928) 69–71. We can attach little weight to the fact that Plutarch, like Ephoros, refers the myth to the Septerion; for it is evident from *Mor.* 417f that the Delphian *theologoi* employed the usual dragon myth as *aition*. Aelian too (VH 3.1), who tells the second version, connects the story with the Septerion. Plutarch agrees with Ephoros concerning the burning of the tent, whereas the linking of his Aix to Krios would establish a connection with Pausanias' account.

others in that Apollo already had possession of Delphi and was operating his oracle when Python came to plunder the shrine. Version E1, on the other hand, says that Apollo was on his way from Athens to Delphi in the course of his travels on his mission to civilise men on earth; this was, so far as we can judge from Strabo's words, his first visit to Delphi, and E1 is consequently consistent with the other four versions in this respect.[13]

At this point we can say only that Apollo fought an enemy at Delphi-Pytho who is usually represented as a snake, but occasionally as a human brigand; who is sometimes represented as male, sometimes as female; but who is otherwise described in much the same terms. Often in the following chapters the name Python will be used merely as a convenient designation for Apollo's opponent without regard to sex or species.

TITYOS

Python was not the only enemy whom Apollo fought and vanquished in infancy or early youth. A giant called Tityos also brought the god's arrows upon himself. He is mentioned in the Odyssey: when Odysseus visited Hades' realm he saw Tityos, a son of Gaia, lying there, stretched out over nine *plethra* of ground; two vultures sat, one on each side of him, and tore his liver, forcing their heads into his belly, and he could not drive them away. He received this punishment because he had maltreated (ἕλκησε) Leto while she was going through Panopeus on her way to Pytho. Alkinoos also mentions Tityos, when he promises Odysseus that the Phaeacians will take him home, even if Ithaca should be farther than Euboea, whither the Phaeacians had made their longest journey, when they took Rhadamanthys to see Tityos, Gaia's son.[14]

So much the Odyssey tells us. We cannot be sure that the poet knew the story as we find it in later writers, but it seems probable that he did. As most of them tell it, Leto, soon after the birth of Apollo and Artemis on Delos, took the babes in her arms and went over sea and land on her way to Delphi. As she passed

---

[13] In Paus. 10.6.6. notice καὶ ἐσύλησε μὲν τοῦ θεοῦ τὸ ἱερόν in reference to Python's earlier raid upon Delphi, and, as mentioned above, the presence of a Pythia at Delphi.
[14] Od. 11.576–581, 7.321–324. See Herzog-Hauser (1930).

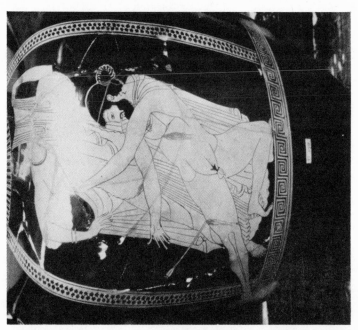

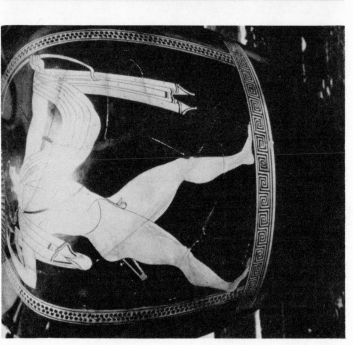

FIGURE 5. APOLLO AND TITYOS

through Panopeus, near the eastern foot of Parnassos—just within Phocian territory as one comes from Boeotia—Tityos saw her, lusted after her, and rushed upon her, and in some accounts actually laid hands on her. In any case the infant Apollo, still in

FIGURE 4. APOLLO AND TITYOS

his mother's arms, shot him down with his arrows. Some accounts say that Artemis too used her bow against Tityos, but Hyginus says that Zeus struck him down with his thunderbolt.[15]

The literary sources, except when describing a sculpture or painting, almost always place Tityos' attack soon after the birth of the twins, while they were still infants. But all vase-paintings, reliefs, and other works of art that represent the incident show the twins (or Apollo alone) full-grown, at least sixteen years old.[16]

[15] Apollo and Artemis together: Paus. 3.18.15, referring to a scene on the throne of Bathykles, 10.11.1, referring to a Cnidian sculpture-group at Delphi (in both art works the twins are full-grown); Call. *Hymn* 3.110 and Schol.; Apollod. 1.4.1; Suid. T696; Vat. Myth. I 13; *App. Narr.* 73, p. 386 West.; *Anth. Pal.* 3.14 *titulum*. See AW 10, 11, 19–21, 26 (see fig. 4). Apollo alone: Apollon. *Arg.* 1.759–762; Anth. Pal. 3.14; Quint. Smyrn. 3.392–398; Serv. *Aen.* 6.595; Lact. Plac. *Theb.* 11.12 (cf. *Theb.* 1.710); Vat. Myth. II 104; Schol. and Eust. on *Od.* 7.324. See AW 12–18, 22–25, 28–32 (figs. 5–7). Pind. *Pyth.* 4.90 f. mentions Artemis only as slayer of Tityos. According to Euphorion *ap.* Schol. *in* Apollon. *Arg.* 1.81, it was Artemis that Tityos tried to seize. Leto alone is mentioned in Hyg. *Fab.* 55. On Tityos see Waser, LM 5.1033–1055 and K. Scherling, RE 6A.1593–1609.

[16] This is true also of art works that no longer exist, but which are described by ancient writers. Apollonios (*Arg.* 1.759–762), speaking of Apollo as βούπαις οὔπω πολλός, is describing an imaginary work of art. The sculptures and coin types that show Leto carrying two infants as she runs are generally taken to represent her flight from Tityos: see Türk, LM 3.3411. Such is a Milesian coin-type of the Roman imperial period (BMCC, Ionia, *Miletus*, nos. 158, 164, pl. 22.13). But AW 8 is referred to Python's pursuit of Leto.

One notices with some surprise that the infant Apollo (or twins) appears in the art representations of the Python story and in the literary sources of the Tityos story; and that the grown Apollo (or twins) appears in the art representations of the Tityos story and in the literary sources of the Python story (except ver-

FIGURE 6. APOLLO AND TITYOS

sion C). It is also apparent that the Tityos story bears a close resemblance to version C of the Python story, and also some resemblance to versions D and E. It is likely that both stories go back to a common original, and this will become more evident in the analysis made in chapter iii.[17]

PHORBAS AND PHLEGYAS

Python and Tityos were not the only scourges of Delphi and Parnassos in Greek myth. Apollo had to fight another brigand, Phorbas, king of the Phlegyans, who from his base in or near Panopeus (Tityos' city), terrorised the Parnassian region and

---

Herzog (1905:990) had information from Theodor Wiegand concerning a relief upon the altar of Artemis Boulaia in Miletos that shows "Leto, von Tityos verfolgte, dargestellt, derselbe Mythos, auf den die Münzen deuten." So far as I know, this relief has not yet been published. Does it really show Tityos? Or, like the coin type, does it merely show the mother (and twins) in flight? If the latter, then Tityos as pursuer is a conjecture of Wiegand or Herzog: if the former, then we have an art work that agrees with the literary versions.

[17] A similarity or relationship between Python and Tityos has been briefly noted by Roscher (1873) 41, Schreiber (1879) 56.

made unsafe the road to Delphi. Like Amykos of Bithynia, he forced the unwary traveller who came his way to box with him (or, as Philostratos has it, to wrestle or race or throw the discus with him). He always won, whereupon his defeated opponent had to forfeit his life, and Phorbas cut off his head and suspended it from an oak tree or added it to a mound of skulls—until one day Apollo came to fight him and killed him with a blow. Then fire from heaven consumed the oak tree. The story, it appears, was known to the Cyclic Poets, and is told in greatest detail by Philostratos; it was the subject of a picture that he describes.[18]

In this legend Phorbas looks very much like a form of Python or Tityos, at least in his character as an enemy of Apollo. But the name Phorbas is also borne by a youth whom Apollo loved, and who was himself a dragon fighter. Yet it is probable that the two are fundamentally the same: for Apollo's enemy was a Phlegyan, the youth a Lapith, and the Phlegyans and Lapiths were the same people (see p. 35); we first meet the Lapith Phorbas as a rival of Apollo in love; and other links between brigand and hero will become clear as we proceed. We have here a reversal of role, a phenomenon that will recur in this study (pp. 174 f., 405).[19]

Phorbas and his Phlegyans, say Ovid and Philostratos, made Apollo's temple at Delphi inaccessible. We learn elsewhere that Phlegyas, eponym of the Phlegyans, attacked and plundered Delphi, and even burned the temple; though the latter touch may be a play on his name. Still other writers, without mentioning a leader, say that the Phlegyans attacked or plundered or burned Apollo's temple at Delphi, but that the god came to the rescue of his shrine and routed the Phlegyans, destroying many of them. According to Pausanias, who does not tell us that the Phlegyans actually plundered Delphi, Apollo destroyed most of them with many thunderbolts and mighty earthquakes, and sent plague upon

---

[18] Cycl. *ap.* Scholl. AB *in Il.* 23.660; Philostr. *Imag.* 2.19; Tzetz. on Lyk. 160.

[19] Diod. 4.69.2, 5.58.5; Paus. 5.1.11; cf. Ovid *Met.* 12.320–326; Plut. *Numa* 4; Polyzelos 7, 3.493 J. That the two are the same is maintained by Roscher, LM 3.2428; and in view of the differing traditions concerning the Lapith Phorbas, his parentage, and exploits, it is probable that other figures of egend called Phorbas are also closely related to him and to Apollo's enemy: see *ibid.* 2424–2430; Johanna Schmidt, RE 20.528–532. See Hom. Hymn 3.211 on Phorbas as Apollo's rival. He was grandfather of Argos Panoptes: Pherek. 66, 1.79 J.

the survivors (according to Pherekydes, Apollo did so at Zeus's command).[20]

It is apparent that Phorbas and Phlegyas are the same person, a legendary ruler and therefore symbol of the Phlegyan people who harassed Delphi. For Phlegyas was no more at first than a name devised for the imagined ancestor of the Phlegyans. He never became a consistently conceived figure of legend; such substance as he had was acquired from Phorbas, with whom he was identified or confused. When Philostratos describes the fallen Phorbas in such words as ὁ Φλεγύας δὲ κεῖται ἤδη (*Imag.* 2.19.4),

FIGURE 7. APOLLO AND TITYOS

it is easily seen how Phlegyas could become the name of the Phlegyan king who was Apollo's enemy.[21]

---

[20] Ovid *Met.* 11.413 f., . . . nam templa profanus/ invia cum Phlegyis faciebat Delphica Phorbas. Philostr. *Imag.* 2.19.1, τὴν γὰρ εὐθὺ Φωκέων τε καὶ Δελφῶν ὁδὸν κατασχὼν οὔτε θύει Πυθοῖ οὐδεὶς ἔτι οὔτε παιᾶνας ἀπάγει τῷ θεῷ, χρησμοί τε καὶ λόγια καὶ ὀμφαὶ τρίποδος ἐκλέλειπται πάντα. Phlegyas: Serv. *Aen.* 6.618; Lact. Plac. *Theb.* 1.713; Vat. Myth. II 128. On Φλεγύας and φλέγειν see Havet (1888) 165. Phlegyans and Delphi: Pherek. 41*de*, 1.74 J; Paus. 9.36.2 f., 10.7.1, 10.34.2. Pausanias has told (9.36.1) of Phlegyas' founding of Phlegya, whence his people continued to plunder their neighbors, until finally they marched on Delphi. One gathers that Phlegyas himself is no longer alive. On Apollo's destruction of them see also Schol. T on Il. 13.302; Socr. *Epist.* 30.8 (Hercher). According to the Scholiast he cast them down to Tartaros. See Schultz (1882).

[21] See Havet (1888) 164: Phlégyas n'est pas un de ces personnages classiques comme Ulysse ou Oedipe, qui, longuement élaborés par le génie des grands artistes, ont fini par acquérir une physiognomie, une biographie, une famille, une patrie, une date. C'est, au contraire, une des figures les plus inconsistantes de la fable, et par conséquent, sans doute

We can already say with some confidence after this brief review of the legends that the names Phorbas, Phlegyas, and Tityos were alike given to a legendary king of the Phlegyans, a composite figure representing the whole people, who was conceived as a gigantic and savage creature, and was for some reason assimilated in character and deeds to Python.[22]

une des moins littéraires. A ce nom de Phlégyas ont été rattachées plus ou moins arbitrairement des traditions decousues.

Authorities differ about his parents and his children, and according to Apollod. 3.5.5, it was Lykos and Nykteus who killed him. Yet all these fragments of tradition may belong to or descend from a larger and older complex of myth: that which is the subject of this study.

According to Serv. *Aen.* 6.618, Phlegyas burned the temple at Delphi, because Apollo had seduced his daughter Koronis, and was punished in Hades for doing so.

[22] On Tityos as Phlegyan see Müller (1844) 185. See chapter iii for analysis of these legends.

॥

KYKNOS AND OTHER BAD CHARACTERS

Python, Tityos, Phorbas, and Phlegyas do not exhaust the list of legendary harrowers of Delphi: several others appear in the sources. But Apollo no longer plays the role of champion; it is Herakles who goes forth to fight and kill the enemy of Apollo's shrine.

KYKNOS

Herakles' combat with Kyknos, Ares' son, was celebrated by three poets before the fifth century: the poet of the *Shield of Herakles* (identified in ancient times with Hesiod), a Cyclic Poet, and Stesichoros. In the fifth century it was alluded to by Pindar and Euripides, and was a favorite theme of vase-painters throughout the sixth and fifth centuries.[1]

---

[1] The principal sources of the Kyknos story are ps.-Hes. *Shield* 57–140, 318–480; Stes. frag. 12 Bergk, *ap.* Schol. Vet. *in* Pind. *Ol.* 10.15(19), 17(21); Cycl. *ap.* Scholl. AB *in Il.* 23.346; Pind. *Ol.* 10.15 f.; Eur. *Her.* 389–393, *Alk.* 501–503; Diod. 4.37.1–4; Apollod. 2.5.11, 2.7.7; Hyg. *Fab.* 31.3, 269; see also Paus. 1.27.6, 3.18.10; Nic. Dam. 54J; Schol. Vet. on Pind. *Ol.* 2.82(147); Arg. 1 to *Shield*. For vase-paintings, etc., see AW 33–49 (figs. 8–11); Vian (1945). There is much resemblance between these and the Tityos representations. Both K. and T. in defeat are seen sitting back upon the ground or kneeling or turning to run away: K. in AW 33, 34, 37–40, 42–46, 49 (figs. 8–11); T. in AW 11, 18–21, 25–31, 54 (figs. 4–7, 12). K. is always in armor as son of Ares in contrast to T's nakedness. In every representation Herakles advances upon his opponent from the left; Apollo occasionally comes from the right (AW 12, 13). H. with drawn sword resembles A. (figs. 6, 8–11). K. and T. vary between being bearded and beardless. T. is almost always bearded; for bearded K. see figs. 10, 11; beardless, fig. 9.

28

In the *Shield* we find a blow-by-blow account of the fight. Herakles and Iolaos, on their way to Trachis to visit King Keyx, encountered Kyknos and his father Ares in the temenos of the Pagasaean Apollo, and Kyknos thought to vanquish Herakles. The contestants left their chariots and fell upon each other. Herakles' spear soon cut through two tendons of Kyknos' neck, and Kyknos fell to the ground. Then Ares advanced upon Herakles, who received his attack. Athena, who had come to give support to Herakles (she had already provided his breastplate) tried without success to hold Ares back, and when Ares' spear struck Herakles' shield, she weakened its force. Ares drew his sword and rushed upon Herakles, but the hero wounded him in the thigh, just as Diomedes did on the Trojan plain, and cast him to the ground. Then Phobos and Deimos, the war god's attendants, picked Ares up, put him in his chariot, and drove off to Olympos. Herakles and Iolaos went on their way to Trachis, and Kyknos' body was buried by Keyx, his father-in-law, and Keyx's neighbors. The river Anauros, however, at Apollo's order, washed the grave away, for Kyknos had robbed pilgrims on their way to Pytho of the hecatombs that they were driving thither.

According to Stesichoros (as reported by the Pindaric Scholiast), Kyknos killed the travelers upon his road and cut off their heads, intending to build a temple to Apollo with their skulls. When Herakles came by, he entered into combat with Kyknos,

FIGURE 8. HERAKLES AND KYKNOS

but fled when he saw Ares supporting his son. He later returned
to the battle, when Kyknos stood alone, and killed him.
But the Cyclic Poet, if quoted correctly by the Homeric Scholiasts, had a quite different story. Herakles, driving the horse
Areion, defeated Kyknos in a chariot race during games that King
Kopreus of Haliartos held in the temenos of the Pagasaean Apollo
near Trachis. There is other evidence that Kyknos entered into
contests.[2]

Apollodoros has two stories about the combat of Herakles with
Kyknos. In one (2.7.7) he met Kyknos, son of Ares and Pelopeia,
at Itonos in Achaia Phthiotis, after defeating the Lapiths and
Dryopes. Itonos is named as the scene by others, and its location
agrees well enough with the traditional story as we find it in the
Shield and Stesichoros. In the other (2.5.11) he met Kyknos, son
of Ares and Pyrene, on the Echedoros River in Macedonia, when
he was on his way to the Hesperides. Ares stood beside his son,
but when Ares had begun combat with Herakles, a thunderbolt
thrown from heaven separated the two. That this thunderbolt
came from Zeus is clear from Hyginus, who appears to follow the
same source. Any doubt that this is the same Kyknos as Herakles'
Thessalian opponent has been removed by Höfer's find of an
entry in the obscure and little-known *Etymologicum Florenti-
num:* Ares and Pyrene (daughter of Himeros, Europs' son) were
parents of Lykaon, king of the Krestones; Lykaon saw Herakles
on his way to the Hesperides and challenged him; they fought
in the grove Pyrene, where Herakles killed Lykaon. This narrative identifies the Lykaon whom Herakles mentions in Euripides'
Alkestis (501–504) as one of three sons of Ares: Herakles had
already killed two (Lykaon and Kyknos) and was on his way to
fight the third (Diomedes). It is plain, therefore, that Lykaon was
the son of Ares and Pyrene whom Herakles fought on the Echedoros, and that he had been displaced by Kyknos in the version
that reached Apollodoros and Hyginus. Even so, the two stories
are very much the same, differing only in the name of Herakles'
opponent and in the scene of combat. Lykaon is essentially the

---

[2] Schol. A's (on Il. 23.346) Τροιζῆνι is obviously a mistake for Τραχῖνι. Schol. B omits
this clause. On Kyknos' contests see p. 60.

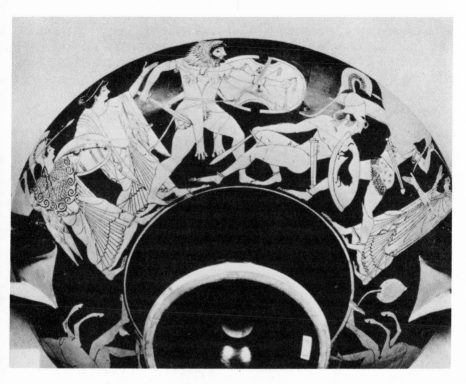

FIGURE 9. HERAKLES AND KYKNOS

same brigand, but localised too far from Delphi to be charged with molesting pilgrims on the way to Apollo's Delphic shrine.[3] Kyknos usually inhabits southern Thessaly, either in Pelasgiotis at Pagasai near the Anauros River (*Shield*, Cycl., Eur.), or at Itonos in Achaia Phthiotis (Diod., Apollod.). Itonos, just north of Mount Othrys, is a more suitable base from which to molest Delphi-bound pilgrims from the north, since it controls the pass from Thessaly over the Othrys range to Malis, Trachis, and Thermopylae. There is also reason to place Kyknos and his legend in Doris-Dryopis (see p. 53), and this must have originally been the residence of Kyknos in his role of robber on the road to Delphi. The location in Thessaly is more suitable to the story of Herakles' journey to Thrace to fetch the horses of Diomedes. In the combat with Kyknos in Thessaly, as in that with Lykaon in Macedonia, a brother of Diomedes hindered the hero on his journey.[4]

The name itself may come from Thessaly. In legend we find another Kyknos, son of Poseidon, in combat with Achilles in Troyland. Wilamowitz thinks that this was the original Kyknos combat and that originally it took place in Thessaly, Herakles later taking the place of Achilles on the original scene. This is very probable. It is also possible that Herakles had previously become opponent of the Parnassian brigand, Phlegyas-Phorbas, son of

---

[3] Apollod. 2.5.11, πορευόμενος οὖν ἐπὶ ποταμὸν Ἐχέδωρον ἧκε. Κύκνος δὲ Ἄρεος καὶ Πυρήνης εἰς μονομαχίαν αὐτὸν προκαλεῖτο. Ἄρεος δὲ τούτον ἐκδικοῦντος καὶ συνιστάντος μονομαχίαν βληθεὶς κεραυνὸς μέσος ἀμφοτέρων διαλύει τὴν μάχην. See Hyg. *Fab.* 31.3. It is not clear from this whether Herakles killed Kyknos. But Apollodoros says that Ares fought H. to exact justice for his son (τούτον ἐκδικοῦντος), which seems to imply that H. had killed him. Probably a clause has dropped out of the text (see Höfer, LM 3.3342). It is possible to reconcile 2.5.11 and 2.7.7 by means of Stes. frag. 12 and Pind. *Ol.* 10.15 f.: i.e., H. first met K. on the Echedoros, but retreated on seeing Ares present; later he encountered K. alone at Itonos. This would suppose that Πυρήνης is a mistake for Πελοπείας, and that ἐκδικοῦν means no more than ἀμύνειν, *defend*. But it is more likely that Höfer's explanation is correct. Frazer (note on Apollod. 2.5.11) believes that there were two Kyknoi who fought H. On *Etym. Flor.* see Höfer, *loc. cit.*, who quotes from E. Miller, *Mélanges de littérature Grecque* (Paris, 1868): Lykaon is called king τῶν Κρητῶν, which Höfer shows must be emended to Κρηστώνων. His abode was placed where he could be imagined molesting the Hyperboreans on their way to Delphi and Delos with their customary offerings. Notice that H. encounters him on his journey to the Hesperides.

[4] Presumably the temenos of the Pagasaean Apollo was at or near Pagasai; and this is confirmed by the *Shield's* placing it near the Anauros River. Schol. T on Il. 23.347 actually says "at Pagasai." But Apollo Pagasaios may have been worshipped elsewhere too: the Cyclic Poet, we have seen, speaks of a Pagasaean Apollo near Trachis.

FIGURE 10. HERAKLES AND KYKNOS

Ares, and that when he replaced Achilles, Ares replaced Poseidon as Kyknos' father.[5]

To look at it another way, Kyknos, like Deukalion and Pyrrha, belonged to the regions on either side of Mount Othrys, regions that are closely interrelated both geographically and traditionally. To the south lie the Spercheios Valley, the mountain mass of Oita, and the related coastal strip: a region that comprises Malis, Trachinia, Ainis, Doris, and eastern Lokris. To the north and northeast lie Achaia Phthiotis and Pelasgiotis. All face the same body of water, that gulf of the sea which is shut off from the open Aegean by the island of Euboea, and which is marked off by Cape Kenaion and the eastward thrust of Othrys into the Euboic, Malic, and Pagasaean Gulfs (Map 1).

In the Kyknos legend Ares is a second opponent of Herakles,

---

[5] Trojan Kyknos: Pind. *Ol.* 2.82 and Schol. Vet.; Ovid *Met.* 12.71–145; Schol. on Theocr. 16.49. Wilamowitz (1895), Commentar p. 31: . . . der schwan, Apollons diener, war früher ein böser könig und feind Apollons, den in seinem dienste der äolische (später der dorische) held erschlagen hat. Notice that the invulnerability of Kyknos, Poseidon's son, is assigned to Ares' son in Sen. HF 485 f. Interesting too is Schol. on Theocr., Κύκνον λέγει τὸν Ποσειδῶνος καὶ Κήυκος. This is probably a mistake for Καλύκης.

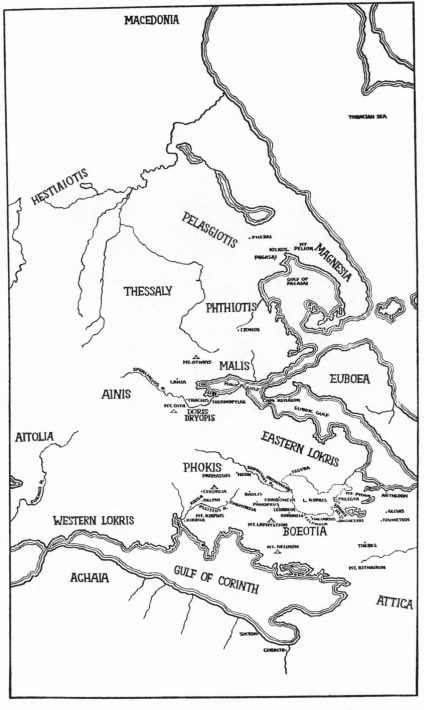

MAP 1. NORTHEASTERN GREECE: PHOKIS, BOEOTIA, MALIA, THESSALY

stepping forward to take his fallen son's place. Naturally, when the myth took this form Herakles could not be allowed to kill Ares. Either Zeus must separate them, or, as in the *Shield*, Herakles must merely wound Ares. But this wounding looks very much like a substitution for killing; and the thunderbolts which fall seem much like those which blast the god's enemy in cognate

FIGURE 11. HERAKLES AND KYKNOS

legends. Both features suggest that originally the hero-god either had only one enemy to deal with, who became divided into two, or had two enemies to face, both of whom he killed (pp. 255–258).[6]

---

[6] For Zeus's thunderbolt see Apollod. 2.5.11; Hyg. *Fab.* 31.3. Though these sources refer to the combat with Lykaon in Macedonia, the intervention of Zeus with a thunderbolt belongs equally to the true Kyknos legend, as is evident from vase paintings, many of which label Kyknos and most of which show details that agree with the *Shield* or Stesichoros, such as the presence of chariots and of Athena; see AW 39–43, 49 (figs. 10, 11). In *Shield* 333–337 Athena expressly limits Herakles to wounding Ares where his body becomes exposed beneath his shield; then he must retire, as it is unlawful for him to do more against A. In *Shield* 458–466 H. wounds A. severely, actually felling him; Phobos and Deimos pick up A's body and carry it off in his chariot. *Shield* 359–367: A. had previously felt H's might, when, in defense of Pylos, he was struck three times by H's spear, badly wounded, and stretched out upon the ground (on A. at Pylos see p. 328). *Shield* 98–101: H. speaks as if A. were his only opponent; see also 70–74, 108–112.

LAPITHS AND DRYOPES

There is a good deal in the legend as we have it to show that Kyknos is a form of the Phlegyan robber-baron who harried Apollo's shrine at Delphi, though it is Herakles and not Apollo who meets him in combat. This conclusion is supported by the close relation of the Kyknos-combat to Herakles' campaigns against Lapiths and Dryopes and his combats with their kings Koronos and Laogoras. According to Diodoros and Apollodoros, whose narratives agree in most particulars, Herakles came with his bride Deianeira through the Dryopian country to Keyx in Trachis. Either Herakles had already aroused the Dryopes to war by killing one of Theiodamas' plough-oxen, or the Dryopes were committing lawless acts against the Delphic shrine (Diod.). From Trachis Herakles went forth with the Malians against them, defeated them, and, according to Diodoros, killed their king Phylas and drove them out of their country.

Immediately thereafter war broke out between the Lapiths and the Dorians, who were then living in Hestiaiotis. Since the Lapiths were superior in might, the Dorian king Aigimios successfully sought Herakles' help, promising him a third of his kingdom and the throne. The allies defeated the Lapiths, and Herakles killed Koronos, the Lapith king, in the battle. It was then, according to Apollodoros, that Herakles killed Laogoras, king of the Dryopes, ally of the Lapiths, as he feasted with his sons in Apollo's temenos. Then, according to both writers, Herakles, passing through Itonos on his way from the Lapith battlefield (going back to Trachis: Diod.), was challenged by Kyknos. After killing Kyknos he went into Pelasgiotis, where he had trouble with King Amyntor (or Ormenos) and killed him too. It looks very much as if different versions of a common original have been conflated, so that Herakles must meet the enemy king four times instead of once.[7]

More than a century ago Karl Otfried Müller showed that Lapiths and Phlegyans were the same people. Hence there is no need to review the evidence that identifies them. I shall point out only that Phlegyas, eponym of the Phlegyans, is a Lapith, father

---

[7] Diod. 4.37; Apollod. 2.7.7.

of the Lapith Ixion, grandfather of the Lapith Peirithoos, and that tradition assigns both peoples to the same regions.[8]

In the Iliad we get an early description of the Lapiths, spoken by Nestor. They were the mighty men of a former generation, far superior in strength and prowess even to the Achaean heroes before Troy. Tradition could soon convert such supermen into giants and brigands like Phorbas and his Phlegyan raiders. They so far surpassed the Dorians in strength that when they went to war with them the Dorians could win only with Herakles' help.[9]

Koronos, the Lapith king whom Herakles fought and killed, has the masculine form of the name of Phlegyas' daughter Koronis, the mother of Asklepios. He and his Lapiths, it is true, do not attack Delphi but the Dorian country in Thessaly, in the only account that we have, that of Diodoros and Apollodoros. Yet they are allies of the Dryopes and Kyknos, who were enemies of the Delphic shrine, and against whom Herakles waged a campaign in Apollo's behalf. This particular story of their war against Aigimios and Herakles probably took shape as the initial part of the Heraclid saga, with which the Delphian priesthood had something to do.[10]

The Dryopes play exactly the same role in this legend as the Lapith-Phlegyan people. They lived about Mount Oita and the upper Kephisos Valley, a region that was then, according to legend, called Dryopis, but later called Doris. Their territory appears to have extended southward to Mount Parnassos, on whose slopes they had a city, neighbor to Lykoreia. They are described in the same terms as the Phlegyans: they were *hybristai*, impious, wicked, forever making war. They plundered the Parnassos region—in particular the very neighborhood of the Delphic oracle (Diod., EM)—and one gathers from Diodoros that they attacked the shrine itself.[11]

---

[8] Müller (1844) 187–191. On the Lapiths see Roscher, LM 2.1851–1865.

[9] Il. 1.260–272; Diod. 4.37.3.

[10] Notice that a Koroneus is the father of another Koronis, who is closely connected with Phlegyas' daughter by Ovid *Met*. 2.569. On the Lapith-Dorian war see Friedländer (1907): 104–107, 147–156.

[11] On the Dryopes, their homeland, and their war with Herakles, see besides Diod. and Apollod. *locc. cit.*, Herod. 8.43; Pherek. 19, 1.66 J; Paus. 4.34.9–11; Strabo 8.6.13, p. 373; Nicander *ap*. Ant. Lib. 32.1; Apollon. *Arg*. 1.1213–1219 with Schol. Vet.; IG 14.1293A. 68–76; Suid. Δ1546; EM 154, 288; Schol. Vet. on Lyk. 479. For Dryopes on

So Herakles went forth against them, as Apollo against the Phlegyans, or himself against the Lapiths. Although Diodoros and Apollodoros attach the Lapith war closely to the Dryopian war, other writers speak only of Herakles' campaign against the Dryopes, making no mention of Lapiths. Some tell how Herakles defeated them and took captive all who were not killed; he made an offering of his captives to Apollo at Delphi (evidence that he undertook the campaign at Apollo's request), and Apollo instructed him to send them to the Peloponnesos, where they founded Asine and Hermione (see p. 41, note 22). Others relate the war to Herakles' offense against Theiodamas: Herakles with his bride Deianeira, his son Hyllos, and a small band of companions, was passing through Dryopis on his way to Keyx in Trachis, when Hyllos became hungry. Herakles asked the Dryopian Theiodamas, then ploughing in his field, for food, which he refused to give them. Herakles thereupon seized one of his oxen, killed it, and with his companions cooked and ate it. Theiodamas ran to the city and roused the Dryopes, who marched against Herakles. Herakles' band was so small that even Deianeira had to put on armor and lend a hand, but they defeated the Dryopes and killed Theiodamas. Apollodoros fits the encounter with Theiodamas into his account of the campaigns against Lapiths and Dryopes: after eating the ox Herakles went on to Keyx in Trachis and then took the field against the Dryopes.[12]

Much the same story is told of Herakles and a ploughman, sometimes called Theiodamas also, encountered near Lindos in Rhodes, as the hero was on his way to the Hesperides. No battle or war followed upon his killing the ox, which in this version he devoured greedily to appease his own hunger. He was only cursed by the ploughman while he ate, which episode served as *aition*

Parnassos see Diod., Paus. (also 5.1.2), Suid., EM, Schol. on *Arg.* 1.1218; Nonn. *Dion.* 35.88–91; Prob. *Georg.* 3.6. Cf. Béquignon (1937) 143–172. Their king Laogoras was *hybristês* (Apollod.); they had no regard for justice, οὔτι δίκης ἀλέγοντες (Apollon. *Arg.* 1.1219; see also Schol. and Suid.), as the Phlegyans were Διὸς οὐκ ἀλέγοντες; they were impious and lovers of war and slaughter (Nonn. Dion. 31.92 f.), λῃστρικὸν ἔθνος (Pherek.). For the same and similar terms applied to the Phlegyans see p. 58, note 45. See Diod. 4.37.1, . . . Φύλαντος τοῦ Δρυόπων βασιλέως δόξαντος εἰς τὸ ἐν Δελφοῖς ἱερὸν παρανενομηκέναι.
    [12] Pherek., Apollon., *loc. cit.*; Call. *Ait.*, frags 24, 25 Pf., and *Hymn* 3.160 f.; Ovid, *Ib.* 485 f.; Prob. *Georg.* 3.6; Suid. B417; *App. Narr.* 28.6, pp. 370 f. West.

for the curses spoken at the beginning of sacrifices to Herakles Bouthoinas in Lindos.[13]

Perhaps the story came from Rhodes to northern Greece, where it was attached to the Dryopian legend as the immediate cause of the war with Herakles. In itself the story may have nothing to do with the combat myth; but (see p. 89) it has been substituted for an original element in that story.[14]

The Scholiasts who call Theiodamas king of the Dryopes are, of course, mistaken. Their king, whom Herakles fought and killed, was Laogoras (Apollod.). Diodoros and Pausanias, however, call him Phylas; but they have apparently confused the king of Dryopis with the king of Ephyra in Thesprotia, whom Herakles killed when he aided the Calydonians against the Thesprotians, and whose story was told in the common source of Diodoros and Apollodoros just before the Dryopian story.[15]

Now Laogoras was feasting with his sons in Apollo's temenos when Herakles, fresh from victory over Koronos, met him and killed him; immediately thereafter, in Apollodoros' narrative, Herakles met Kyknos at Itonos. Kyknos, we recall, also held a temenos of Apollo. Furthermore, Herakles once consumed a whole ox, including the bones, in the house of Koronos. This story was known to Pindar, whom Philostratos cites in alluding to it when he compares Herakles' voracious eating of Theiodamas' ox to his feat as Koronos' guest. We know no more of the tale, but presumably this is the Lapith Koronos. It is probable that Lapith king or Dryopian king is indifferently the subject of a tale in which Herakles killed him at a feast.[16]

Kyknos may have sometimes been the king's name; he may

---

[13] Call. *Ait.*, frags 22, 23 Pf.; Apollod. 2.5.11; Conon 11; Philostr. *Imag.* 2.24; Amm. Marc. 22.12.4; the latter two call him Theiodamas. See Pfeiffer (1949) 29–35, who shows that, for Callimachus, Theiodamas was the Dryopian ploughman, and that the Lindian was anonymous.

[14] See Friedländer (1907) 148 f.

[15] Theiodamas as king: Scholl. on Call. *Hymn* 3.161 and Ovid *Ib.* 488; Prob. *Georg.* 3.6. Notice that the Ephyroi are coupled with the Phlegyans as a very warlike people in Il. 13.301 f. The Dryopian king is also called Phylas in IG 14.1293A.70.

[16] Apollod. 2.7.7, ἀπέκτεινε δὲ καὶ Λαογόραν μετὰ τῶν τέκνων βασιλέα Δρυόπων ἐν Ἀπόλλωνος τεμένει δαινύμενον ὑβριστὴν ὄντα καὶ Λαπιθῶν σύμμαχον. παριόντα δὲ Ἴτωνον εἰς μονομαχίαν προεκαλέσατο αὐτὸν Κύκνος κτλ. Koronos' feast: Pind. frag. 151 Bowra; cf. Philostr. *Imag.* 2.24.2; Schol. on Ovid *Ib.* 488 calls Theiodamas the son of Koronos. This may be a mistake based on the proximity of Koronos to Theiodamas in the source used (cf. Apollod. 2.7.7); yet the very mistake would indicate how near together are Lapith and Dryopian.

have first offered refreshment to travelers before challenging them
to contest or combat (see p. 113). For it is apparent that Laogoras
and Kyknos are the same brigand, both encamped in a precinct
of Apollo, situated either in Thessaly or in Doris-Dryopis, both
working mischief against Delphi, and both encountered just before or after Herakles' visit to Keyx (both afterwards in Diodoros
and Apollodoros).[17]

Dryopis became Doris after Herakles expelled the Dryopes.
Herakles also expelled the Lapiths from the land which they
disputed with the Dorians, a third of which Herakles received as
his reward for helping Aigimios, and which he entrusted to
Aigimios to be kept by him for his descendants. This land, according to Diodoros, was situated in Thessaly; for the Dorians
were then living in Hestiaiotis. But soon afterwards he calls it
Doris; and the historical Doris, homeland of the Dorian people,
was the land that lies about Mount Oita, between the Spercheios
and Kephisos Rivers. Thus the Lapiths alternate with the Dryopes
as the people whom Herakles expelled to make a secure home for
the Dorians, the people with whom he had permanently allied
himself and his descendants; for Aigimios adopted Hyllos as his
own son, and his name was given to a Dorian tribe.[18]

Keyx is also a link between Dryopes, Lapiths, and Phlegyans.
He was, as we have seen, father-in-law of Kyknos, whom he buried
with great honor; yet he was a friend and host of Herakles.
Herakles was on his way to visit him when he encountered Kyknos (*Shield*) and when he encountered the Dryopian Theiodamas
(Apollod.). It was from Keyx's house that he went forth against
the Dryopes and Lapiths (Diod., Apollod.). Against the former
he was allied with Keyx and his Malian subjects, to whom he
gave conquered Dryopis. It is therefore apparent that Keyx and
his Malians play the same part in relation to the Dryopes as
Aigimios and his Dorians in relation to the Lapiths. When we
observe that Herakles and his descendants lived in Keyx's house

---

[17] With Kyknos as κακόξενος (p. 58, note 45) compare Nonn. *Dion.* 35.90 on Herakles'
combat with the Dryopians κακοξείνῳ παρα πέτρῃ.

[18] Doris: Herod. 8.31.2. I do not intend to say that the Dorians did not once live in
Thessaly, as Herodotos says (1.56.3). But the legend of their alliance with Herakles refers
originally to Oetaean Doris; Herakles was then pushed back into earlier traditions of the
Dorian people.

as allies, dependents, and refugees, it becomes apparent that the Malians of the Dryopian legend must be identified with the Dorians of the Lapith legend, and that Keyx is the double of Aigimios; further, as a corollary, the Dryopes must be either the same people as the Lapith-Phlegyans or closely related to them. This becomes more evident when we turn to the tale of Keyx and Alkyone as told by Ovid: Keyx, desiring to consult Apollo, set out by sea for Klaros, since Phorbas and the Phlegyans had blocked the road to Delphi. So the crimes against Delphi of Phorbas, Laogoras, and Kyknos alike are referred to the time of Keyx's reign in Trachis.[19]

Dryops, eponymous ancestor of the Dryopes, was son of Apollo and Dia. Peirithoos, great Lapith king, was son of Zeus (or Ixion) and Dia; Apollo and Stilbe were parents of Lapithes, eponymous ancestor of the Lapiths. Dia, Dryops' mother, was a daughter of Lykaon, who is just as likely to be the brother of Kyknos as the Arcadian hero. Dryope, Dryops' daughter, feminine eponym of the nation, was also a mistress of Apollo.[20]

Dryops means *oak-face,* i.e., *oak-man,* much the same thing as Dryas, who appears among the Lapith warriors that fought the Centaurs. He is probably in origin no different from the Calydonian Dryas, fellow huntsman of the Lapiths Peirithoos and Kaineus. This Dryas was son of Ares, as was a Thracian Dryas, brother of Tereus. It has been conjectured that the Lapith Dryas is eponym of the Dryopes.[21]

---

[19] According to Bacchyl. frag. 22 Snell, Herakles once appeared as an uninvited guest at a wedding-feast in Keyx's house. One thinks of H. *chez* Koronos and Theiodamas, the more since Hylas is called son of both Theiodamas and Keyx; for T. see citations in note 12 to this chapter; for Keyx, Nic. *ap.* Ant. Lib. 26.1. One suspects an ambiguous role: i.e., that in legends now lost Keyx appeared as H's enemy too. Not only was he Kyknos' father-in-law, but he likewise has the name of a water bird. Notice too that Koronos' name appears to mean Crow, a masculine form of the usual noun; also that Phlegyas' daughter is Koronis. See Ovid *Met.* 11.413 f.

[20] Dryops: EM 288; Schol. Vet. on Lyk. 479; Schol. Vet. on Apollon. *Arg.* 1.1218. Peirithoos: citations in RE 19.115. Lapithes: Diod. 4.69.1. Dryops was Spercheios' son: Nic. *ap.* Ant. Lib. 32.1; Pherek. 8, 1.61 J says Peneios, who may represent Poseidon, but it is probably a mistake of the Schol. on *Arg.* 1.1212, who cites him. Arkas as father of Dryops is probably a mistake (Strabo. 8.6.13, p. 373). On Dryope see p. 57.

[21] Lapith Dryas: Il. 1.263; *Shield* 179; Ovid *Met.* 12.290–315, who calls him *saevus* (296). Calydonian Dryas: Apollod. 1.8.2; Ovid *Met.* 8.307; Hyg. *Fab.* 159, 173.3. Thracian Dryas: Hyg. *Fab.* 45.3. Notice Andraimon, husband of Dryope and fosterfather of Amphissos, eponym of Amphissa, and Andraimon, father of Thoas, the founder of Amphissa. Notice also a Lapith Andraimon, son of Koronos and brother of Leonteus: Diod. 4.53.

We find Dryopes or a trace of them wherever we find Lapiths and Phlegyans. Their homelands, we have seen, lay between Thessaly on the north and Phokis and Boeotia on the south. From there, according to the tradition, some moved to Euboea and founded Karystos, Styra, and Oichalia. Others went to northeastern Peloponnesos, where they settled Asine and Hermione. Phlegyas too came to that region to reconnoitre for war and plunder; Koronis came with him and it was then that she gave birth to Asklepios in Epidauros. There were Dryopes in Epeiros at Ambrakia, with which Phorbas is also associated: the heroine Ambrakia was either daughter of Phorbas or of the Dryopian king Melaneus. The name of the Dryopian Theiodamas, we have seen, recurs in Rhodes, where Lapiths settled under Phorbas.[22]

Thus we find the Dryopes always closely associated with the Lapiths, though we cannot identify them with the Lapiths as positively as we can the Phlegyans. They were no doubt a closely related people. Both Dryopes and Lapiths appear to have been early Greek peoples, kinsmen of the Minyans, who held the same Boeotian lands about Orchomenos as the Phlegyans, and from whom, according to Pausanias, who calls them Orchomenians, the Phlegyans separated themselves. For the Phlegyans once held the whole Kephisos Valley and the plain about Lake Kopais. They lived in Orchomenos and Phlegya, and to part of Boeotia gave the name χώρα Φλεγυαντίς (the Phlegyan land). The Lapith-Phlegyan-

---

On Dryas as eponym see Toepffer (1890) 41 f.; Roscher, LM 2.1855. Another connection between Lapiths and Dryopes may be found in Polydora, mother of Dryops and of the Myrmidon Menesthios (Il. 16.173–178; Apollod. 3.13.4), also granddaughter of Aktor, name both of a Myrmidon prince and of a son of the Lapith Phorbas (see LM 1.217 f., 3.2641 f.; Diod. 4.69.3). The Myrmidons, as an early Thessalian people, are closely related to the Lapiths.

[22] More than sixty years ago Toepffer (1890: 41–46) showed that Dryopes appear almost everywhere on the routes of Lapith migrations. With this I agree in spite of the doubts which I have expressed concerning his argument that Theseus was originally a Lapith hero (RE 19.121 f.). Thessalian Dryopis: Plin. NH 4.7.28. Dryopes in Euboea: Diod. 4.37.2; Paus. 4.34.11; see Thuc. 7.57.4: Eurytos of Oichalia was Dryopian. In Asine and Hermione: Herod. 8.73.2; Diod. 4.37.2; Strabo 8.6.13, p. 373; Paus. 4.34.9 f.; 5.1.2; EM 154; Schol. Vet. on Apollon. Arg. 1.1218; according to Steph. Byz. 160 Holst., Hermione was called Dryope; Koronis at Epidauros: Paus. 2.26.3. In Epeiros: Nic. ap. Ant. Lib. 4.3; Plin. NH 4.1.2. Though the story of Herakles and the ploughman may be Rhodian to begin with, it could easily be that Lapith-Dryopian settlers in Rhodes introduced the name Theiodamas into it and that the story went to Dryopis with men returning to the homeland.

Dryopian peoples were therefore Ionians; or perhaps we should say that they were proto-Achaeans, and with the Minyans were the common ancestors of the later Achaeans and Ionians, who had not yet appeared as distinct ethnic groups.[23]

Mention of the Minyans also brings to mind the combat of Herakles with their king Erginos, when by defeating the Minyans of Orchomenos and killing their king he freed Thebes from tribute. On this occasion Herakles received armor from Athena, as before his combat with Kyknos.[24]

Something should also be said about Amyntor and his father Ormenos (Ormenios), one of whom Herakles fought and killed shortly after his meeting with Kyknos. According to Apollodoros, he tried with armed might to prevent Herakles from entering Ormenion. According to Diodoros, Herakles, going through Pelasgiotis from Itonos, came to King Ormenios, whose daughter Astydameia he demanded in marriage. Ormenios refused him, since he was already married to Deianeira; so Herakles made war on him, killed him, and took Astydameia captive.[25]

Ormenion lay in Thessalian Magnesia under Pelion, quite near

---

[23] Paus. 9.36.2. It is true that Strabo (7.7.1, p. 321) classes Dryopes with the Kaukones, Pelasgoi, and Leleges; whence, no doubt, the frequent reference in modern handbooks (such as OCD and Everyman's *Smaller Classical Dictionary*) to the Dryopes as a Pelasgic people. But just what does it mean to call them Pelasgian? The Greeks apparently used the term, when not indicating a definite people who bore the name, to mean *ancient* or *indigenous* and applied it both to pre-Greek peoples and to the earliest pre-Dorian Greeks, who doubtless had become mixed with the aborigines. Notice that Herodotos (1.56–58) considers only the Dorians to be true Hellenes; the Ionians, including Athenians, were Pelasgic. See Munro (1934) on "Pelasgians and Ionians," although I am somewhat doubtful about his conclusions; also Béquignon (1937) 158–167. The Dryopes have a Greek name, and so do the Dryopians Laogoras, Theiodamas, Melaneus, and Eurytos. The Dryopes of Asine, Hermione, Styra, and Kythonos were considered Hellenes. Greeks called *Dryopaioi* were still living in Oitaia in the second century B.C.: IG 9.1.229, 230. Among the Ionians who settled the east Aegaean coast were Minyans and Dryopes: Herod. 1.146.1. Herodotos also mentions Arkades Pelasgoi, by which term he recognises the claim of Arcadians to be autochthones. On the Phlegyan land see Pherek. 41*de*, 74J; Paus. 9.36.1–3; Steph. Byz. 447 Holst.; Scholl. AT on Il. 13.301 f.; Schol. on Od. 11.262, 264. Gomme (1913: 122 f.) has conjectured that Phlegya may be Gla. On Ionians = Minyans see Nilsson (1932) 155–158, Thomson (1949) 197, 390–392.

[24] Erginos: Apollod. 2.4.11; Diod. 4.10. The Phlegyans under Eurymachos also attacked Thebes (p. 317). The vase paintings taken by Engelmann as representing the Herakles-Erginos combat probably do not: see LM 2.1694.

[25] The daughter of Phylas, king of Ephyra, sometimes called king of Dryopes, whom Herakles killed, is also called Astydameia (Diod. 4.37.4), though usually Astyoche; as daughter of either Amyntor or Phylas she became H's captive, upon whom he begot Tlepolemos: Apollod. 2.7.6; Pind. *Ol.* 7.20–24 and Schol. Vet.

Pagasai and Iolkos. The Iliad, however, says that Amyntor lived in Eleon, which the Catalogue places in Boeotia. His neighbor, who robbed him, was Autolykos, resident on Parnassos. And Krates placed Amyntor's Eleon in the Parnassos country. This suggests an exact parallel between Amyntor-Ormenos and Kyknos: each lived near the northeast corner of the Pagasaean Gulf and either on or near Parnassos. They are probably but two guises of the same opponent of Herakles and the Delphian Apollo, whose story acquired different names and details in different sections of the land.[26]

We can also recognise another guise of the same opponent in Eurytos, king of Oichalia, which is usually placed in Euboea. Eurytos was a bellicose Dryopian—son of Melaneus, who was son of Apollo and king of Dryopes in Epeiros—and takes Dryops' place as father of Dryope at least once. Of him too Herakles asked his daughter in marriage and was refused, whereupon Herakles took the city, killed Eurytos, and led the daughter, Iole, away captive. It is also said that Herakles entered into a contest in archery with Eurytos and his sons and surpassed them. Eurytos, like Amyntor, was robbed by Autolykos, who drove off his cattle from Euboea. In another story, perhaps older, it was Apollo who killed him for daring to challenge him in archery. Apollodoros and Diodoros place Herakles' attack on Oichalia immediately after the attack on Ormenion, thereby making it the fifth event in the series that begins with the war against the Dryopes. Finally we find an Oichalia in Trachis, in which region, viz. at Lamia, there stood a *monumentum Euryti*.[27]

It is the brigand who holds the northern approach to Delphi

---

[26] Eleon: Il. 2.500, 10.266; Krates *ap.* Strab. 9.5.18, p. 439. Autolykos: Od. 19.394.

[27] On Eurytos see Apollod. 2.6.1, 2.7.7; Paus. 4.2.2; Hyg. *Fab.* 14.8; Nic. *ap.* Ant. Lib. 4.3. Notice also Skythinos 1, 1.176 J and Lysimachos 8, 3.337 M, who make Eurytos a tribute collector: Skythinos says that Herakles killed him and his sons for collecting tribute from the Euboeans; Lysimachos that he demanded exorbitant indemnity from H. for the murder of Iphitos; this recalls Erginos, who demanded tribute of the Thebans for the death of his father Klymenos, accidentally killed by the Theban Perieres. Eurytos' Oichalia is also located in Thessaly (Il. 2.730; Paus. 4.2.2) and in Messenia (Paus. 4.2.2), where Dryopes settled (Paus. 4.34.9–11). Eurytos as Dryope's father: Ovid *Met.* 9.327–331, 356; Steph. Byz. 160 Holst. says daughter of Eurypylos, which may be a mistake for Eurytos; yet Eurypylos too is a name that enters more than once into this myth complex. See pp. 335, 355, and 482 f. with note 10. On Oichalia and Eurytos in Trachinia see Strabo 10.1.10, p. 448; CIL 3.1.586.

that Herakles meets in his role of divine champion and defender of Apollo's shrine—Laogoras-Phylas is always placed there, Kyknos and Eurytos sometimes—but Apollo meets the brigand who holds the eastern approach. The reason why Herakles appears in Apollo's place as defender of Delphi will be discussed later (pp. 401–405); for the moment it is sufficient to mention that Herakles' interest in the Delphic oracle is manifested in the story of his attempt to carry off Apollo's tripod.[28]

PYRENEUS AND SYBARIS

The eastern road was once held by still another villain, whom neither Apollo nor Herakles fought, so far as we can gather from the only source. This was Pyreneus, a savage (ferox) and wicked tyrant (injustaque regna tenebat), one of the legendary Thracians of Daulis, which he had occupied with his army, thus commanding the road to Delphi. Once the Muses walked that road on their way to Apollo's temple. A storm was raging as they came to Daulis, and Pyreneus offered them shelter, which they accepted. But when the sky had cleared and they started to go, he closed his doors to keep them in that he might force them. They escaped by taking to their wings, and he tried to follow them through the air, but fell from his roof and was killed.[29]

The brigands who harrowed Delphi, Tityos and Phorbas and Kyknos and the others whom I have discussed, correspond to the male dragon, Python. The dragoness too has her counterpart among the spoilers of the region. This was the Lamia called Sybaris, a gigantic beast (θηρίον μέγα καὶ ὑπερφυές), who lived in a vast cave on Kirphis, directly across the Pleistos gorge from Delphi. She went forth every day to seize men and cattle, especially the young. Such a plague was she that the Delphians decided

---

[28] Amyntor as king of Boeotian Eleon is possibly an exception to the placing of Herakles' enemy on the northern road. The site is uncertain, though all indications point to the neighborhood of Tanagra (i.e., eastern Boeotia), rather far from Parnassos. But we have seen that Krates placed Eleon on Parnassos; Demetrios of Skepsis (ap. Strab. 9.5.18, p. 439) said that the Parnassian town was Neon, not Eleon. Neon lay on the northern slopes of Parnassos, and if it had anything to do with Amyntor, a connection that is entirely unattested, then Amyntor also held the northern road. On Herakles and tripod see Apollod. 2.6.2.

[29] Ovid Met. 5.273–293. Daulis, Phlegyan city (p. 51), was traditionally the seat of Thracians in Phokis, the home of Tereus: see Fontenrose (1948) 156 f. with note 80.

to move elsewhere and asked Apollo where to go. He replied that they would find deliverance by sacrificing a Delphian youth to Sybaris. They sorrowfully obeyed, and a beautiful boy, Alkyoneus, was chosen victim by lot. While the priests were getting him ready, Eurybatos Euphemos' son, a young Aetolian hero, chanced to pass by. Struck by Alkyoneus' beauty, he fell in love with him and decided to save him. He dressed himself as victim, went to the Lamia's cave, ran inside, seized her, carried her out, and threw her over the cliff. On hitting bottom her body disappeared, but there gushed forth from the rock a spring that is still called Sybaris.[30]

---

[30] Nic. *ap*. Ant. Lib. 8.

III

PYTHON AND HIS DERIVATIVES

Now that we have reviewed the several myths and legends that cluster about Delphi, it becomes necessary to make a rigorous analysis of them, in order to establish the probability of their close relation to one another and ultimate derivation from a common original. We must notice every theme and feature that occurs either in all the foregoing tales or in several of them, whether plainly or obscurely. I shall state each theme in terms of the Python myth, and then indicate the other legends in which it appears by the name of the divine champion's antagonist: Tityos, Phorbas, Phlegyas, Kyknos, Koronos, Laogoras, Erginos, Amyntor, Eurytos, Pyreneus, Sybaris. The term *Python* includes Delphyne and Krios' son; *Phlegyas* includes the Phlegyan nation; *Koronos* the Lapiths; *Kyknos* includes Lykaon and Ares as Herakles' opponent; *Laogoras* includes Phylas, Theiodamas, and the Dryopes; *Amyntor* includes Ormenos.

If the presence of the theme in a legend is plain enough from the foregoing chapters, this indication by name will usually suffice, though in some instances comment will be necessary. But if the theme is disguised or obscure, or if I have not mentioned it before as part of a legend indicated, I shall subjoin the necessary evidence and elucidation.[1]

---

[1] Here and in chapters v, vii, and viii, features of correspondence are numbered consecutively in narrative order, as nearly as that is possible. After the number, I place the symbol of the theme according to the scheme of themes, pp. 9–11. The corresponding *sigla* of Thompson's motif-index (MIFL) are found in Index A.

1. Theme 1A. Python was son of Ge.[2] Tityos, Phorbas, Phlegyas, Kyknos, Koronos, Laogoras, Erginos, Pyreneus.

Tityos: In the Odyssey and in most later sources his mother is Ge.
But Apollonios and Apollodoros tell us that Tityos' mother was Elara
Orchomenos' daughter. As Apollodoros tells the story, Zeus got Elara
pregnant and in fear of Hera hid her beneath the earth. At the proper
time he brought her gigantic son to the surface. Hence Tityos is sometimes called Ge's fosterson. It may be that Elara herself is a form
of Ge.[3]

Phorbas: No parents are named for the brigand king Phorbas, but
to the Lapith king Phorbas three different mothers are assigned:
Orsinome in Thessalian and Elean legend, Melantho in Argive
legend, Hiscilla (Ischylla) in Rhodian legend.[4]

Melantho may be a name of Ge, since the Greeks often called the
earth *melaina* (black). Even more significant is Melantho, daughter
of Deukalion, wife or mistress of Poseidon, and mother of Delphos,
eponym of Delphi. In other versions Melantho or Melantheia, wife of
Hyamos or Kephisos, was mother of Melaina (Melainis, Kelaino),
who by Poseidon or Apollo was mother of Delphos. Therefore Melantho or Melaina is a consort of Poseidon, who is often the mate of
Ge or Demeter.[5]

Ischylla may refer to Ge as the strong and mighty goddess. Orsinome
is daughter of Eurynomos, a name that also belongs to an underworld
demon who was depicted in Polygnotos' paintings on the walls of the
Cnidian Lesche at Delphi. In the meaning *wide-ruling* his name could

---

[2] Eur. IT 1247; Ovid *Met.* 1.438 f.; Stat. *Theb.* 1.563; Men. Rhet. p. 441 Sp.; Olymp.
on *Phaed.* 201, 240 Norv. The dragoness is called Ge's daughter in FD 3.2.138.

[3] Od.7.324, 11.576, and Scholl.; Lucan BC 4.595 f.; Stat. *Theb.* 1.710 and Lact. Plac.
ad loc.; Lucian *Men.* 14; Quint. Smyrn. 3.396 f.; Nonn. *Dion.* 4.331, 20.77; Serv. *Aen.*
6.595; Schol. Vet. on Apollon. *Arg.* 1.161; notice AW 12, 13, 18–27, 30, 31 (figs. 5–7).
Elara: Apollon. *Arg.* 1.761 f. and Schol. Vet. (Pherek. 55, 1.76 J); Apollod. 1.4.1. See also
Schol. on Od. *locc. cit.* The story was known, it seems, to Hesiod, Simonides, and Pindar:
see EM 60. See Virg. *Aen.* 6.595, Tityon Terrae omniparentis alumnum; Serv. *ad loc.*;
Apollon. *Arg.* 1.762. Schol. on Od. 11.581 calls Tityos son of Zeus and Ge. See RE 5.2235.

[4] Diod. 4.69.2; Schol. Vet. on Eur. *Or.* 932; Polyzelos *ap.* Hyg. *Astr.* 2.14.

[5] Hom. Hymn 3.369, γαῖα μέλαινα. Melantho, Delphos' mother: Epaphroditos *ap.*
Schol. Vet. *in* Eur. *Or.* 1094; Tzetz. on Lyk. 208; cf. Ovid *Met.* 6.120. On Poseidon and Ge
see Apollod. 2.5.11 and Philippson (1944) 25–36, though her proposed etymology of
Poseidon-Potidan as Husband of Earth must be rejected. For Melantho-Melaina see
Mommsen (1878) 10: . . . Meläna oder Melantho, womit nur Gäa γαῖα μέλαινα gemeint
sein kann . . . ; also LM 2.2565. For Poseidon and Demeter see Paus. 8.25.5, 8.42.1;
Ovid *Met.* 6.118 f.; Apollod. 3.6.8; LM 3.2821–2823. Though Demeter and Ge are undoubtedly closely related and probably identical in origin, the etymology "Demeter =
Earth Mother" must also be rejected. Notice Kephisos as consort of Melantho; Poseidon
is closely related to river-gods and alternates with them in myths.

be an epithet of Hades himself; and we find Ge as wife of Tartaros, who is not always distinguished from Hades, and as consort of Zeus Chthonios, the underworld Zeus. Also Ophion and Eurynome (feminine of Eurynomos) take the place of Uranos and Ge in one form of the Greek myth of beginnings.[6]

Thus the names of all three mothers of Phorbas point to Ge. Since he was supposed to have been a real man, it is not surprising that Ge herself ceased to be recognised as his mother.

Phlegyas' mother was named Dotis or Chryse. Dotis is obviously eponym of the Dotian plain in Thessaly, old home of the Lapiths: that is, she is the Dotian earth itself and therefore probably a form of Ge. Chryse is the name of a goddess or nymph of Lemnos, sender of the snake that bit Philoktetes, and also the name of the small island near Lemnos on which Philoktetes was bitten. She was, it seems, an important goddess of the North Aegean area. Her association with the snake suggests that she too is a form of Ge, and her name would suit the earth goddess. She was later called Athena Chryse; but this identification does not appear in Sophocles.[7]

Kyknos' mother is called Pelopeia by Apollodoros and Nicolaus of Damascus. In two vase paintings (figs. 8, 9) we see to the right of Kyknos a woman whose attitude recalls Ge in the Tityos paintings (figs. 5, 6). This suggests that Pelopeia replaced Ge as the mother of the enemy, or that her name is an epithet of Ge's (the Pelopian Earth). In fact, Kyknos is called *Gagenes* (Earth-born) on another vase painting.[8]

Pyrene, mother of Lykaon-Kyknos (p. 30), may very well be a Thraco-Macedonian form of Ge. As Ares' mistress she gave her name to a grove in Macedonia. We also find a Pyrene who was daughter of Bebryx, eponym of the Bebrykes, the name of both a Thracian people in Bithynia and of an Iberian people in the Pyrenees (to which, of course, she gave her name). This Pyrene enters into the Herakles legends. When the hero was on his way to fetch the cattle of Geryon (and so on his way to the western limits of the world as in the Lykaon-Kyknos story), he stopped at the house of Bebryx on the borders of

---

[6] The only other instances of the name Eurynomos in mythology are a centaur (Ovid *Met.* 12.310) and a companion of the Acarnanian Phorbas (see p. 50, note 14); both are opponents of heroes. Tartaros: e.g. Hes. *Theog.* 821 f.; Apollod. 1.6.3; Hyg. *Astr.* 2.15; see p. 78. Zeus Chthonios and Ge Chthonia: SIG 1024.25. Eurynome: Apollon. *Arg.* 1.503–506; see pp. 230–232; cf. Paus. 10.28.7.

[7] Apollod. 3.5.5; Paus. 9.36.1. Dotian plain: Strabo 9.5.22, p. 442. Chryse: Soph. *Phil.* 194 and Schol. Vet. (island: *ibid.* 270). See RE 3.2487–2490; LM 1.901.

[8] Apollod. 2.7.7; Nic. Dam. 54 J. *Gagenes:* AW 48.

Gaul and Spain. There, when overcome with wine, he debauched Pyrene, his host's daughter. In due time she gave birth to a snake and in fright fled from her father's house into the forests. The mother of a snake is likely be Ge. To this story we shall return more than once, for it is intimately related to the group of myths under study. I would conjecture that it was first told in Macedonia and Thrace about the Pyrene who was mother of Lykaon, and that later it was transferred to the country of the Iberian Bebrykes, not only because they were called by the name of a Thracian tribe, but because of their Montes Pyrenaei and the presence at Cabo de Cruz of a shrine of Aphrodite Pyrenaia.[9]

Koronos, Laogoras: Lapiths and Dryopes were descended from Dia: the Lapiths from Stilbe, and the Dryopes from Polydora (p. 41). Dia is an epithet of Earth. Stilbe and Dia both mean shining. Polydora may be a name of Ge as giver of abundance, for Ge has the epithet Pandoros. Dryope herself as a goddess or nymph looks like a faded form of Ge.[10]

Erginos' mother was Buzyge, feminine form of Buzyges, an old Attic agricultural demon.[11]

Pyreneus has the masculine form of the name Pyrene.

2. Theme 1b. Python was a son of Tartaros, i.e., of a great god who was a consort of Earth.[12] Tityos, Phorbas, Phlegyas, Kyknos, Koronos, Laogoras, Erginos, Amyntor, Eurytos, Pyreneus.

Python's derivatives are sons of great gods who appear either as consorts of Ge herself or of a goddess or heroine, e.g., one of those mentioned above, who seems to be a form of Ge.

Tityos was a son of Zeus (p. 47).

Phorbas as Lapith hero was grandson of Apollo, Lapithes' father. But Hesychios says that Lapithes was son of Ares (another link between the Lapith hero and Phorbas-Phlegyas); and as son of Kriasos in Argive tradition Phorbas is either a greatgrandson of Zeus or a descendant of the river god Inachos. The name Kriasos resembles Krios, Euboean dynast, father of the brigand whom Pausanias appears to identify with Python (p. 19). Kriasos was son of Argos, who

[9] Strabo 4.1.3, p. 178; Plin. NH 3.3.22 (see also 3.1.8); Sil. Ital. 3.420–441.

[10] Hom. Hymn. 30.3, χθόνα δῖαν. Notice Dia as a goddess in Phlius and Sikyon, identified with Hebe: Strabo 8.6.24, p. 382; Paus. 2.13.3. Ge Pandoros: Hom. Epigr. 7. Dryope as goddess: Nic. *ap.* Ant. Lib. 32.4 *sq.*; Ovid *Met.* 9.349–393; Virg. *Aen.* 10.551.

[11] Schol. Vet. on Apollon. *Arg.* 1.185; see LM 1.839.

[12] Olymp. on *Phaed.* 201, 240 Norv.

was eponym of the city, but also closely related to Argos Panoptes (p. 483). Pausanias says that Phorbas himself was son of Argos.[13]

There is also a northwestern Phorbas—Thesprotian or Acarnanian —who is probably a variant of the Lapith Phorbas, inasmuch as the northwestern Phorbas is father of Ambrakia, who is also called daughter of Augeias, who in turn is sometimes called son of Phorbas Lapithes' son as we find him in Elean tradition. Like Augeias himself elsewhere, the Thesprotian is called son of Helios, a tradition that manifestly connects him with the Lapith Phorbas of Rhodian legend. The Acarnanian Phorbas is called son of Poseidon: he attacked Athens near Eleusis and was killed by Erechtheus.[14]

Finally, Phorbas appears as son of Triopas in Rhodian tradition; as his father in Argive tradition. Triopas or Triops was probably the epithet of the three-eyed Zeus in Argos; Triopios was Apollo's epithet at Cape Triopion by Knidos, a city that shared with Rhodes the Phorbas-Triopas legend.[15]

Phlegyas was son of Ares (note 7).

Kyknos was son of Ares (p. 28); Kyknos as opponent of Achilles was son of Poseidon (p. 31).

Koronos, Laogoras: Apollo was father of Lapithes and Dryops, ancestors of Lapiths and Dryopes (p. 40). Dryops was also called son of the river god Spercheios (p. 40, note 20).

Erginos' father was Klymenos, whose name is an epithet of Hades (p. 328). The Argonaut Erginos, often identified with the king of Orchomenos (p. 42), was son of Poseidon (p. 479).

Amyntor was sometimes called son of Zeus.[16]

---

[13] Phorbas, Apollo's grandson: Diod. 4.69.1 f. Lapithes Ares' son: Hesych. Λ318. Kriasos: Pherek. 66, 1.79 J; Schol. Vet. on Eur. *Or.* 932. Argos' son: Paus. 2.16.1. Since Pausanias (10.6.6) does not actually name Krios' son, it is possible to identify him with Phorbas or Phlegyas and even to emend Pausanias' text to Κρι⟨άσ⟩ου δυναστεύοντος. But Pausanias himself distinguished his attack on Delphi from that of the Phlegyans: 10.7.1, Ἔοικε δὲ ἐξ ἀρχῆς τὸ ἱερὸν τὸ ἐν Δελφοῖς ὑπὸ ἀνθρώπων ἐπιβουλεύεσθαι πλείστων ἤδη· οὗτός τε ὁ Εὐβοεὺς λῃστὴς καὶ ἔτεσιν ὕστερον τὸ ἔθνος τὸ Φλεγύων. . . .

[14] Phorbas and Ambrakia: Steph. Byz. 54, 150 Holst.; Diod. 4.69.3; Schol. Vet. on Apollon. *Arg.* 1.172, who says that Augeias was son of Helios, but known as son of Phorbas. Attack on Athens: Andron 1, 1.161 J; Hellan. 40, 1.119 J; Hyper. *ap.* Harp. 302 Dind. Notice Agallis *ap.* Schol. T *in Il.* 18.483: a son of Eurynomos is one of Phorbas' followers, and so is a son of the Cyclops Agriopos; this indicates an assimilation of Phorbas' army to the monstrous enemies of the gods.

[15] Son: Hom. Hymn 3.211; Plut. *Numa* 4; Athen. 6.262E. Father: Diod. 4.58.7; Paus. 2.16.1, 4.1.2, 7.26.12. Triopas is also called son of Helios. Three-eyed Zeus: Paus. 2.24.3 f. Apollo Triopios: Herod. 1.144; Thuc. 8.35.3. See Becker (1883) 117–121.

[16] Schol. Vet. on Pind. *Ol.* 7.23 (42).

Eurytos was grandson of Apollo (p. 43). Eurytos-Eurypylos, also associated with the Argonauts, was son of Poseidon.[17]

Pyreneus: Since Ares was father of Tereus, the other wicked Thracian of Daulis, whose crime was similar though more successful, we may conjecture that Pyreneus and Tereus were brothers, sons of Ares and Pyrene, whose other sons were Lykaon, Diomedes, Kyknos, Dryas, and Lakinios (p. 104).

3. Theme 2A. Python lived in Delphi or elsewhere on Parnassos. He also lived in Boeotian Ptoon, came from Euboea and from Thessaly, and sought refuge at the Vale of Tempe in Thessaly. All legends.

a. Delphi, Parnassos, Phokis: Tityos, Phorbas, Phlegyas, Laogoras, Amyntor, Pyreneus, Sybaris.

Tityos: According to the Nekyia of the Odyssey and several later sources, Tityos lived in Panopeus near the eastern foot of Parnassos, where he molested Leto on her way to Pytho. There Pausanias saw Tityos' tomb. Apollodoros merely says that Tityos attacked Leto as she was going to (or into) Pytho. In Ephoros' account (p. 19) Apollo had just killed Tityos at Panopeus when the Parnassians came to him and enlisted his aid against Python-Drakon. Nonnos places Tityos at nearby Daulis.[18]

Phorbas too appears to have waylaid travelers at Panopeus. Philostratos' picture shows Phorbas encamped beside Phocian-Boeotian Kephisos at a place called Dryos Kephalai (Oak Heads), where he held the road to Delphi.[19]

Phlegyas: Pausanias tells us that the Phlegyans occupied Panopeus after leaving Orchomenos. Ephoros says that they inhabited Daulis, four miles from Panopeus, at the eastern foot of Parnassos and at the very entrance to the narrow defile that leads from Orchomenos and the lower Kephisos valley to the *Schistê Hodos* (Cleft Way), where it joins the road from Thebes through Lebadeia and the *Stenê Hodos*

---

[17] See p. 482. Melaneus, father of Eurytos, suggests Hades, as does Eurypylos, sometimes father of Ormenos and Dryope.

[18] Apollod. 1.4.1, ἐρχομένην εἰς Πυθώ, probably no more than a translation of Od. 11.581, Πυθῶδ᾽ ἐρχομένην. See also Quint. Smyrn. 3.392 f. Daulis: Nonn. *Dion.* 3.331.

[19] *Imag.* 2.19.1, 4. The only Dryos Kephalai definitely known was situated in the pass over Kithairon near Eleutherai. It is evident that this name like others could have been applied to several localities, so that there is no need to suppose a confusion. Originally designating a fine grove of oaks, the name was probably later explained by the story that there on an oak Phorbas hung the heads of his victims. That the place commanded the road to Delphi is evident from the words τὴν γὰρ εὐθὺ Φωκέων τε καὶ Δελφῶν ὁδὸν κατασχών.

(Narrow Way), and where both become one road to Delphi. Daulis and Panopeus command the road from Orchomenos and are within easy reach of the road from Thebes.[20]

Laogoras: The Dryopes lived on the northern slopes of Parnassos, where they had a city, and molested Delphi (p. 36).

Amyntor's city of Eleon was sometimes placed on Parnassos (p. 43).

Pyreneus also lived at Daulis (p. 44).

b. Boeotia: Tityos, Phorbas, Phlegyas, Erginos, Amyntor.

Python, Tityos: Tegyra in the Phlegyan country claimed—against Delos, Ephesos, and Lykia—to be the birthplace of Apollo and Artemis, pointing to the springs called Palm and Olive, and to nearby mountains, one called Delos, the other Ptoon, where they said Apollo's combats with Python and Tityos took place.[21]

Phorbas was father of Boeotian Tiphys.[22]

Amyntor's city was identified with Boeotian Eleon (p. 43).

c. Euboea: Tityos, Phorbas, Phlegyas, Laogoras (p. 41), Eurytos.

Python: Krios, father of the Parnassian brigand, was a Euboean ruler, and the oracle which Pausanias quotes (p. 20) calls his son the Euboean robber (Εὐβοεὺς λῃστής). Klearchos of Soloi (p. 18, note 8) tells us that Leto was on her way from Euboean Chalkis to Delphi when Python attacked her.

Tityos: One passage of the Odyssey (7.323 f.) that mentions Tityos places him in Euboea (p. 22). According to Strabo, on the island there was a cave called Elarion, named for Tityos' mother, and an *hêrôon* of Tityos.[23]

Phorbas: Euboia was the name of the wife of the Lapith Phorbas, Kriasos' son.[24]

---

[20] According to Paus. 9.36.3, 10.4.1, the Phlegyans who settled in Panopeus were the remnants of those who escaped Apollo's punishment after their attack on Delphi. That is, Phorbas' depredations would be separate from and later than the Phlegyan attack. This is simply another instance of the confusions and inconsistencies of the Phlegyan legend. It is plain from the extent of the Phlegyan dominion in Boeotia and the Kephisos Valley that Panopeus and Daulis belonged to an area that the Phlegyans ruled from Orchomenos and Phlegya. Daulis: Ephor. 93, 2.65 f. J. See map 1, and Frazer and Van Buren (1930), maps ix, x.

[21] Plut. *Pelop.* 16.3 f.

[22] Hyg. *Fab.* 14.9, 18; see p. 478.

[23] Strabo 9.3.14, p. 423. This is an indication that the story of Elara is Euboean, whereas Ge as mother of Tityos belongs to the Phocian tradition.

[24] Schol. Vet. on Eur. *Or.* 932.

Phlegyas: According to manuscript A of Apollodoros' *Library* (3.5.5), Lykos and Nykteus, after killing Phlegyas, fled from Euboea, a reading that has been unnecessarily questioned, since Phorbas, the Dryopes, and Tityos have Euboean associations. This is another link between Phorbas-Phlegyas and Krios' son.[25]

d. Oitaia and Spercheios Valley: Kyknos, Laogoras, Eurytos.

Python's flight to Tempe, marked by the Pythian Way, went through Doris, Malis, Ainis, and Oitaia.[26]

Kyknos: Euripides describes Kyknos as the inhospitable resident of Amphanaia. This was the name of a Thessalian town or village very close to Pagasai, but it was also the name of a city said to be Dorian by Stephanos of Byzantion, who cites Hekataios and Theopompos. This presumably means a city in Doris. We need not suppose that Stephanos made a mistake; for he expressly says that the Thessalian Amphanaia is different. Now a seat in Doris was more desirable than Itonos for a brigand who plundered hecatombs on the road to Delphi. Moreover we are told that Herakles was on his way to Keyx in Trachis when he met Kyknos (p. 29), and also that he passed through Dryopis-Doris on his way to Trachis from Akarnania and Aitolia (p. 35). It would be very strange for him to pass through Pagasai or Itonos on his way from the west to Trachis. Again, Keyx, Herakles' host in Trachis, was Kyknos' father-in-law, who took charge of his dead body. And it was a king of Boeotian Haliartos, Kopreus, who held the games in which Herakles defeated Kyknos. There can be little doubt that one version (probably Delphian) of the legend placed him in Dorian Amphanaia, so that Kyknos joins Laogoras and Eurytos on the northern road to Delphi.[27]

---

[25] See note 13, p. 50. Wagner in the Teubner edition follows Heyne in rejecting ἀπὸ Εὐβοίας, but Frazer accepts it.

[26] Ael. VH 3.1.

[27] Eur. *Her.* 392 f., ᾿Αμφαναίας οἰκήτορ' ἄμεικτον (᾿Αναύρου παρὰ πηγάς, 390). Hekataios 3, 1.8 J, and Theopomp. 56 Grenfell-Hunt, *ap.* Steph. Byz. 57 Holst., Πόλις Δωρική . . . ἐστι καὶ χωρίον Θετταλίας. See RE 1.1884. Notice Schol. A on Il. 23.346, ἐν τῷ τοῦ Παγασαίου ᾿Απόλλωνος ἱερῷ, ὅ ἐστι πρὸς Τραχῖνι (see p. 30, note 2). In view of the frequent coincidence of names in different sections of Greece, due to the movements of peoples in early times, it would not be surprising that Amphanaia of Doris should also have or be near a shrine of Apollo Pagasaios. This may be the shrine of Apollo in Dryopis-Doris mentioned by Nic. *ap.* Ant. Lib. 32.4. At Eur. *Her.* 389 MSS read τάν τε Πηλιάδ' ἀκτάν; the adjective suits the region of the Anauros River and Thessalian Amphanaia, but the phrase has been emended in most recent texts to ἄν τε Μηλιάδ' ἀκτάν. If the emendation is correct, it may mean that Euripides, perhaps unsure of the geography of northern Greece, confused rival locations of the combat. Such a confusion may be present in Diod. 4.37.4: on his way back to Trachis after defeating the Lapiths, Herakles was challenged by Kyknos at Itonos and killed him; then after going forth from Itonos, he went through Pelasgiotis.

Eurytos: For Trachinian Oichalia and Eurytos' monument at Lamia see p. 43.

e. Thessaly: Phorbas (p. 47), Phlegyas, Kyknos, Koronos, Laogoras, Amyntor, Eurytos.

Python came down to Delphi from Thessaly, according to Lucan, and thither he fled from Apollo to the Vale of Tempe, where he died of his wounds.[28]

Phlegyas and the Phlegyans (under that name) are located in Thessaly as well as in Boeotia and Phokis. Phlegyas was father of Ixion and Koronis, who were Thessalian Lapiths, and of Gyrtone (or brother of Gyrton), eponym of Thessalian Gyrton, where the Phlegyans once lived.[29]

Laogoras: As Apollodoros has it (p. 35), Herakles met Laogoras between the Lapith battlefield in Hestiaiotis and Itonos.

Eurytos: Eurytos' Oichalia is sometimes placed in Thessaly (p. 43, note 27).

4. Theme 2B. Python lived in a cave or hut.[30] Tityos, Phorbas, Phlegyas, Sybaris (p. 44).

Tityos: The Elarion, Elara's cave on Euboea, was undoubtedly Tityos' birthplace in the local tradition. He is also said to lie in an underground cavern.[31]

Phlegyas too lies under *cava saxa* in the lower world.[32]

Phorbas: In Philostratos' picture (p. 25) the Phlegyans are tenting on the Kephisos. A skull-hung oak tree serves as statehouse of the Phlegyan nation.[33]

5. Theme 2C. Python occupied or guarded a sacred temenos of Apollo (p. 15). Kyknos (p. 29), Laogoras (p. 35).

6. Theme 3A. Python was gigantic, a creature of monstrous size.[34] Tityos, Phorbas, Kyknos, Koronos, Sybaris.

---

[28] Lucan, *BC.* 6.407–409. See p. 20.

[29] Hom. Hymn 16.2 f.; Apollod. 3.10.3; Schol. Vet. on Apollon. *Arg.* 1.57, 3.62; Steph. Byz. 143 Holst.; Scholl. AT on Il. 13.301 f.

[30] Eur. *Phoen.* 232 and Schol. Vet.; Ephor. 31*b*, 2.53 J; Klearchos 46, 2.318 M; Plut. *Mor.* 418A; Claud. 2.14.

[31] Sen. *Thy.* 9.

[32] Stat. *Theb.* 1.713.

[33] Compare Kyknos' mound of skulls (p. 29).

[34] Eur. IT 1248, πελώριον τέρας; Call. *Hymn* 4.91, ὄφις μέγας; Ovid *Met.* 1.438, *maxim(us)*, 1.459; Lucan BC 6.407, *maxima serpens*; Men. Rhet. p. 441 Sp.; Hyg. *Fab.* 140.1, *draco ingens*; Stat. *Theb.* 1.562, 569, 5.531 f.; Oros. *Hist.* 6.15, *magnus*; Claud. 2.2; Isid. *Etym.* 8.11.54. For the dragoness see Hom. Hymn 3.302, 374; Apollon. *Arg.* 2.706.

Tityos was a giant. Lying outstretched on the floor of Hades he covered nine *plethra* (*jugera*), and his tomb at Panopeus measured two hundred feet in circumference.[35]

Phorbas, according to Philostratos, was taller than all men (μέγας παρὰ πάντας). When Apollo's fatal blow stretched him upon the ground, he covered a vast expanse of ground.[36]

Kyknos was mighty and huge. He fell like an oak or crag.[37]

Koronos: Gigantic size is dimly reflected in the Lapiths' martial strength that was far superior to that of Aigimios and the Dorians (p. 35).

Sybaris was excessively huge.[38]

7. Theme 3b. Python was a snake (δράκων, ὄφις, ἑρπετόν, serpens, anguis).[39] Tityos, Phorbas. Kyknos, Koronos, Laogoras, Pyreneus, Sybaris.

Tityos is always described in literature as human in form, and is so represented in ancient art. But in the Gigantomachy on the frieze of the great altar of Zeus and Athena at Pergamon the giant who opposes Leto has been identified by some scholars with Tityos. I am inclined to agree, since the giant has fallen back upon the ground in a half-sitting posture that is very similar to that shown in several vase-paintings depicting Apollo's victory over Tityos (cf. figs. 5, 6). A snake grows out of this giant's back and seems to represent a tail in serpent form (fig. 12). Of course, in this Gigantomachy, as in several others, many giants are pictured with serpent members: often from the waist down they are snakes (p. 242). It is not, therefore, surprising that Leto's opponent, whether Tityos or not, should be partly serpentine. But it is significant that Tityos is sometimes

---

[35] Apollod. 1.4.1, ὑπερμεγέθης; Apollon. *Arg.* 1.761, and Schol. Vet., who says he was so huge that Elara died in bearing him; Quint. Smyrn. 3.396, πολυπέλεθρος; Lucian *Rhet. Pr.* 13. On Hades' floor: Od. 11.577; Lucr. 3.985–989; Virg. *Aen.* 6.596–600, *Aetna* 60; Prop. 3.5.44; Tib. 1.3.75; Ovid *Amor.* 3.12.25, *Met.* 4.457 f., *Ibis* 179 f.; Stat. *Theb.* 6.753, 11.12–15; Lucian *Men.* 14; Hyg. *Fab.* 55; Claud. 35.337–339. Tomb: Paus. 10.4.5. Compare Tib. 1.3.75, porrectusque novem Tityos per jugera terrae, and Ovid *Met.* 4.457 f., novemque jugeribus distractus erat (Tityos), with Stat. *Theb.* 1.568 on Python, centum per jugera campi, and Ovid *Met.* 1.459, tot jugera ventre prementem (Pythona).

[36] *Imag.* 2.19.4, ὁπόσον μὲν ἐπέχει τῆς γῆς ποιητής ἐρεῖ.

[37] *Shield* 106 (κρατερόν τε μέγαν τε), 421 f.

[38] Nic. *ap.* Ant. Lib. 8.1, θηρίον μέγα καὶ ὑπερφυές.

[39] See e.g. Simon. frag. 26a Bergk; Eur. IT 1245; FD 3.2.137.22; Call. *Hymn.* 2.102; Apollod. 1.4.1; Lucian *Astr.* 23; Ael. VH 3.1; Anth. Pal. 3.6.1; Clem. Alex., *Protr.* 1, 2 P; Prop. 4.6.36; Ovid *Met.* 1.439, 447, 454; Lucan BC 6.407; Stat. *Theb.* 6.359, 7.96. Version E is an exception; but since other animals than serpents enter into the makeup of dragons and monsters, notice that the brigand Python has a father Krios.

included among the Gigantes in literature, and that Python too is sometimes associated with them. Giant and dragon interchange as opponents of god or hero in folklore; in the gigantomachies we have evidence of their near-identity.[40]

ΛΗΤΩ

FIGURE 12. LETO AND TITYOS IN GIGANTOMACHY

Frieze from the Altar of Zeus at Pergamon

Phorbas, as described by Philostratos, had human form, but was boarlike in appearance (συώδης τὸ εἶδος). With this compare Ephoros' description of the brigand Python as beastlike in nature (θηριώδης τὴν φύσιν). A boar is hardly reptilian, but Philostratos' phrase at once recalls the Tegyraean tradition that a boar frightened Leto on Mount Ptoon, when she was about to give birth to Apollo. In speaking of this myth Plutarch adds in the same sentence that the Tegyraeans

---

[40] On the Pergamene frieze Leto opposes the giant in person, whereas Apollo fights Tityos in the vase paintings. In the Gigantomachies each god has a giant opponent: on the frieze Apollo and Artemis are occupied with Ephialtes and Otos; Tityos, as one of the giant company, is properly opposed by Leto. Of other Gigantomachies extant none includes Leto among the gods, although in the Siphnian frieze her presence is conjectured in a missing section; hence nothing about her opponent can be known: see Vian (1952) 110. In Nonn. *Dion.* 2.307 f. Typhon, boasting that he will start a new war of Titans and Giants against the gods, says that he will wed Leto to Tityos. Waser and Scherling (p. 65, note 68) identify the Pergamene opponent of Leto with Tityos; others with Alkyoneus or Porphyrion: see Mayer (1887) 380; Vian (1951) 19–23, no. 38, does not name him. He has wings also, on which see p. 82. Tityos among Gigantes: Lucan, BC 4.592–597; Sen. HF 976–978, *Thy.* 805–812; Vat. Myth. I 13. Python: Lucan *BC* 7.145–150. For association of either with Gigantes, though not in Gigantomachy, see Lucian *Salt.* 38; Ephor. 31a, 2.52 J.

claimed the stories of Python and Tityos for their neighborhood. Recalling Python's pursuit of the pregnant Leto and Tityos' attack on her, we may conjecture that Python took boar form in the Tegyraean myth. And since Tegyra was situated in the Phlegyan region of Boeotia, apparently very near to Phlegya itself, it is probable that Python-Tityos took the name of Phorbas there, at a time, of course, after the legend of the lawless and marauding Phlegyans had arisen.[41]

It is also striking that in Sikyon a river called Sythas or Sys (Hog River) was closely associated with a panic which seized Apollo and Artemis when, as Pausanias tells the story, they came to Sicyonian Aigialeia, seeking purification for the killing of Python.[42]

Kyknos (Swan) is the name of Herakles' opponent, and it is to be expected that he would become a swan at his death. This is certainly true of Achilles' opponent Kyknos, but not quite so certain of his namesake. According to Boio, Ares changed Kyknos into a bird. This is certainly Herakles' opponent, who was a son of Ares. It is conceivable that Kyknos acquired his bird nature and his name from the bird component of many monsters and dragons (p. 152). Notice the wings upon the figure identified with Tityos on the Pergamene frieze (fig. 12).[43]

Koronos (Crow) too has the name of a bird (p. 40, note 19).

Laogoras: Dryope, female eponym of the Dryopes, was impregnated by Apollo; he had first taken the form of a tortoise, which she picked up and placed within her garments; then, transforming himself into a snake, he had his pleasure of her, whereupon she ran in fright to her father's house and later bore Amphissos: a tale similar to that of Herakles and Pyrene (p. 49). The Dryopes, therefore, in part at least, were descended from a snake; a tradition that perhaps reflects a snake antecedent of Laogoras as Herakles' opponent.[44]

Pyreneus started to fly, but failed; he is but the sorry shadow of a winged dragon.

Sybaris is called a beast (ϑηρίον, p. 44, note 38).

---

[41] Philostr. *Imag.* 2.19.4; Ephor. 31a, 2.52 J. Plut. *Pelop.* 16.4, καὶ γὰρ τὸ Πτῷον ἐγγὺς, ὅθεν αὐτὴν ἀναπτοηθῆναι προφανέντος ἐξαίφνης κάπρου λέγουσι, καὶ τὰ περὶ Πύθωνα καὶ Τιτυὸν ὡσαύτως οἱ τόποι τῇ γενέσει τοῦ θεοῦ συνοικειοῦσι. See also Steph. Byz. 40 Holst.; Schol. Vet. on Lyk. 265; both of whom say that the boar appeared when Leto was on the point of giving birth. A folk etymology derives *Ptoon* from πτοεῖν, the fright given to Leto.

[42] Paus. 2.7.7 f.; for the name Sys see Ptol. *Geogr.* 3.14.28. It is interesting to observe that immediately after concluding the Sicyonian myth Pausanias says that in Apollo's temple at Aigialeia Meleager consecrated the spear with which he had killed the Calydonian boar; see p. 384.

[43] Ares's son as swan: Boio *ap.* Athen. 393E. Trojan Kyknos: Ovid *Met.* 12.144 f.

[44] Nic. *ap.* Ant. Lib. 32.2 *sq.*

8. Theme 4A. Python was a savage and violent brigand who plundered the land, robbed pilgrims, murdered inhabitants and travellers. Even as guardian of Ge's shrine he inspired terror.[45] All legends.

9. Themes 4A, 7G. Python made war on his neighbors (version E2). Phorbas, Phlegyas (p. 25), Koronos (p. 36), Laogoras (p. 36), Erginos (p. 42), Amyntor (p. 42), Eurytos (p. 43).[46]

Phorbas: The Acarnanian Phorbas and Eumolpos attacked Eleusis with two armies. Phorbas was killed by Erechtheus. The Lapith Phorbas as ally of Alektor, king of Elis, went to war against Pelops' kingdom and won a realm thereby.[47]

10. Theme 4E. Python attacked the goddess Leto. Tityos, Phorbas, Pyreneus (p. 44).

Tityos' attack on Leto was in all accounts lustful. Though Euripides and Klearchos (p. 18, note 8) seem to imply that it was as guardian of Ge's oracle that Python attacked Leto, Heliodoros uses words Λητὼ βιάζοντα which may mean "making a violent attack on Leto," i.e., with intent to drive away, kill, or rob, but may also mean

---

[45] On Python's plundering see Men. Rhet. p. 441 Sp.; Paus. 10.6.6–7.1, where as Krios' son he is called *sintês* and *lêstês*. See also Hom. Hymn 3.302–304, 364–366. Compare Pherek. 41*de*, 1.74 J, and Paus. 9.36.1–3, concerning the Phlegyans. Tityos was *lêstrikos*: Eust. on Od. 11.575, p. 1699; cf. Ephor. 31*b*, 2.53 J.

For whatever the evidence may be worth, we must observe that the same opprobrious epithets recur among these ogres: (*a*) Python or brigand is called an arrogant and overbearing transgressor (ὑβριστής, ὑπερήφανος, ὑπερφίαλος). Python: Paus. 10.6.6. Tityos: Quint. Smyrn. 3.392. Phorbas: Cycl. *ap.* Scholl. AB *in Il.* 23.660. Phlegyas: Hom. Hymn 3.278; Hesych. Φ587. Laogoras: Apollod. 2.7.7. (*b*) Savage, cruel, terrible, violent (ἄγριος, βάρβαρος, βίαιος, ὠμός, χαλεπός, *ferox, dirus*). Python: Ephor. *loc. cit.*, Hom. Hymn 3.302 (*drakaina*). Tityos: Ephor. and Eust. *locc. cit.* Phorbas: Philostr. *Imag.* 2.19.1 (ὠμότατος τοῦ ἔθνους), 4. Pyreneus: Ovid *Met.* 5.274, 277. Sybaris: Nic. *ap.* Ant. Lib. 8.1*sq.* Iliad 13.302 calls the Phlegyans μεγαλήτορες, which may mean either high-spirited or insolent. (*c*) Lawless, unrighteous (ἄνομος, παράνομος, ἀθεμιστός, ἄδικος, *injustus*). Tityos: Ephor., Eust., *locc. cit.*; Schol. on Od. 7.324. Laogoras: Apollon. *Arg.* 1.1219 and Schol.; Suid. Δ1546. Pyreneus: Ovid *Met.* 5.277. (*d*) Impious (ἀσεβής, δυσσεβής, Διὸς οὐκ ἀλέγων, *impius, sacrilegus, profanus*). Phorbas: Ovid *Met.* 11.413. Phlegyas: Hom. Hymn 3.279; Euphorion *ap.* Serv. *Aen.* 6.18; Hesych. Φ587. Laogoras: Nonn. *Dion.* 31.92. (*e*) Inhospitable (κακόξεινος, ἄμεικτος). Kyknos: Stes. frag. 12; Eur. *Her.* 393. Laogoras: Nonn. *Dion.* 35.88–91. Amyntor: Apollod. 2.7.7. (*f*) Generally wicked, destructive, wanton. Python was νοῦς ἄτακτος, a demon of disorder: Olymp. on *Phaed.* 240 Norv. The *drakaina* was κακὸν πῆμα, κακὸν δήλημα: Hom. Hymn 3.304, 364. Tityos was μάργος καὶ ἀφροσύνῃ μεμεθυσμένος: Anth. Pal. 3.14; θρασύς: Nonn. *Dion.* 4.331. The Phlegyans were δεινορέκται: Schol. T on Il. 13.302.

[46] Phlegyas was called πολεμιχώτατος τῶν τότε: Paus. 2.26.3; cf. 9.36.

[47] Attack on Eleusis: Agallis *ap.* Schol. *in Il.* 18.483; Hyper. *ap.* Harp. 302 Dind. *et* Suid. Φ584. War on Pelops: Diod. 4.69.2.

sexual attack, since the same term is used for Tityos' amorous attack.[48]

Phorbas: The Thesprotian Phorbas offered violence to Demeter and was in consequence struck down by Zeus's thunderbolts.[49]

11. Theme 4F. Python held the road to Apollo's shrine and made it unsafe for visitors; whosoever travelled that road met his death. Tityos, Phorbas, Phlegyas, Kyknos, Amyntor, Eurytos, Pyreneus.

Python: The Homeric Hymn says of the dragoness, ὃς τῆγ' ἀντιάσειε, φέρεσκέ μιν αἴσιμον ἦμαρ (3.356), "whosoever met her, the day of doom carried him away." The theme of death to anyone met suggests that she, like Phorbas, forced men into a contest with her, so that she may be compared to the Sphinx (p. 310). Again, the tradition that the Pythian games commemorated Apollo's victory over Python may have been suggested by a form of the myth in which Python forced wayfarers to fight with him.[50]

Tityos, Phorbas, Phlegyas, Pyreneus: All held Panopeus or Daulis or both, and so commanded the eastern road to Delphi. Indications are that Tityos and Pyreneus were as dangerous to all wayfarers as was Phorbas-Phlegyas.[51]

---

[48] Heliod. *ap.* Tzetz. *in* Lyc. 208. The verb is most often used in middle forms, but the active voice appears to have the same range. Notice Anth. Pal. 3.6.3, σκυλᾶν γὰρ ἐθέλει πινυτὰν θεόν. The verb σκυλᾶν means *despoil, strip*, and is usually used of stripping armor from a dead body; applied to an attack on Leto it may possibly indicate sexual attack. Tityos' attack: Nonn. *Dion.* 4.433, βιαζομένης Λητοῦς; Quint. Smyrn. 3.392 f., Λητὼ βιάζετο; Lucian *Jov. Conf.* 17, ἠθέλησε βιάσασθαι τὴν Λητώ; Schol. on Call. *Hymn* 3.110, βιασάμενος Λητώ.

[49] Anon. Myth. 5, p. 347 West. This brings Phorbas into relation with Iasion, Iasios, or Iasos, who lay with Demeter in a thrice-plowed field: Od. 5.125–127; LM and RE s.v. *Iasion.* Notice Iasos, son of Triopas and grandson of Phorbas: Paus. 2.16.1; Schol. Vet. on Eur. *Or.* 932. Demeter was a willing mistress of Iasion in Od.; but in another story he did violence to her image: Hellan. 23, 1.113 J; Apollod. 3.12.1; Strabo 7, frag. 50, p. 331.

[50] Cf. Philostr. *Imag.* 2.19.2 on Phorbas, τοὺς δὲ βαδίζοντας ἐς τὸ ἱερὸν λαμβάνων . . . τοὺς μὲν καταπαλαίει, τοὺς δὲ ὑπερτρέχει, κτλ., κεφαλάς τε ἀποκόπτων ἀνάπτει τῆς δρυός. . . . Cf. Cycl. *ap.* Scholl. AB *in Il.* 23.660. Only the able-bodied were so treated by Phorbas: children and the aged he sent to the *koinon* of the Phlegyans to be robbed and ransomed.

[51] Compare Ovid and Philostratos as quoted p. 26, note 20, concerning Phorbas' effect on Delphi, with Men. Rhet. p. 441 Sp., on Python's, οὕτως ἀβάτους μὲν ἐποίει Δελφοὺς τοῖς ἅπασιν, ὥκει δὲ τὸν τόπον οὐδείς, ἦν δὲ τὸ Θέμιδος μαντεῖον ἔρημον; and with Plut. *Mor.* 414B on the dragoness's, τοῦτο δὴ τοὐναντία . . . ὑπὸ θηρίου χαλεποῦ δρακαίνης πολὺν χρόνον ἔρημον γενέσθαι καὶ ἀπροσπέλαστον. . . . These words immediately follow upon mention of Tegyra and Ptoon. MSS read δήπου ἐνταῦθα, corrected to the above reading by Haupt. Hence the sentence was formerly taken to refer to Ptoon, but since the oracle referred to is called oldest in time and most famous in reputation, Plutarch must have meant Delphi. In Modern Greek ἐνταῦθα always means *here*, and it often means *here* in ancient Greek, so that even without emendation I should refer the words to Delphi.

Kyknos too, it seems, in some versions of his story, forced whoever came his way into contests with him. Not only does the Cyclic Poet say that Herakles defeated him in *hippodromia,* but Pausanias has a story very like that of Phorbas: Kyknos challenged men to single combat for prizes, and killed many, including the Thracian Lykos, until Herakles came along, fought him, and killed him. According to Hyginus, Kyknos killed a man in armored combat at the funeral games of Pelias. Something of this theme appears to be present in the *Shield:* no mortal man could face Kyknos in combat before Herakles and Iolaos did so.[52]

Eurytos challenged men to contests with the bow, which Herakles and Apollo entered, bringing him his doom directly or indirectly (p. 43).

12. **Theme 5A. Python fought Apollo for dominion over Delphi** (p. 15). **Phlegyas, Koronos, Laogoras, Erginos, Amyntor, Eurytos, Pyreneus.**

Phlegyas actually attacked Delphi, and his people were driven from their land by Apollo (p. 25).

Koronos, Laogoras: They fought Herakles and his Dorian or Malian allies over disputed land, and in consequence lost all their realms to him (p. 39).

Erginos, Amyntor, Eurytos, lost their dominions to Herakles as a result of war (pp. 42 f.).

Pyreneus had taken Daulis with his army (p. 44); his death presumably brought an end to Thracian rule at Daulis and made the road safe for Muses and pilgrims.

13. **Theme 5B. Hera incited Python to attack Leto** (p. 18). **Tityos, Phlegyas, Kyknos, Erginos.**

Tityos: Hyginus tells us that Hera ordered Tityos to attack Leto after she had lain with Zeus, an exact parallel to version D of the Python myth.[53]

Phlegyas: There may be a reminiscence of this theme in Servius' statement that Phlegyas attacked Delphi because he wanted to avenge

---

[52] Cycl. *ap.* Scholl. AB *in Il.* 23.346; Paus. 1.27.6. Hyg. *Fab.* 273.11, Cygnus Martis filius armis occidit †Pilum Diodoti filium. *Pilum* can hardly be right. Cf. *Shield* 72–74. Notice that the Boeotian Lykos killed Phlegyas: Apollod. 3.5.5. Observe too, concerning the Cyclic version, that in the *Shield* both Herakles and Kyknos were in chariots when the combat began (61–65, 321–324, 338–348). See AW 35, 41, 43, 45. In 41 Herakles has a winged horse, possibly Areion.

[53] Hyg. *Fab.* 55.

Koronis. This fragment may be the remnant of a tale in which Koronis, a great goddess as mother of Asklepios, wronged by her mate Apollo as Hera was wronged by Zeus, incited a kinsman against him.[54]

Kyknos: No goddess incited Kyknos to evil courses in the extant sources; but Ares, his father, aided and abetted him. In a vase painting (fig. 8) a woman, probably his mother Pelopeia, takes the place of Ares as seen in other paintings (figs. 9–11), and so corresponds to Ge in the Tityos paintings (figs. 4–7).[55]

Erginos: Hera sent madness upon Herakles immediately after his victory over Erginos, a hint that she had supported Erginos against Herakles.[56]

14. Theme 6A. Apollo appeared as champion to fight Python. All legends.

Tityos was killed by Apollo, or by the twins together, according to most sources; Artemis alone is named by Pindar (p. 23, note 15), and Zeus by Hyginus (p. 23).

Phorbas: Zeus sent fire from heaven to consume Phorbas' oak tree (p. 25). With this compare the burning of the brigand Python's tent (p. 19).

Phlegyas: At Zeus's command Apollo destroyed the Phlegyans (p. 26). Poseidon, enraged at the impious Phlegyans, dwellers on an island (Rhodes, Kythnos?), destroyed them with his trident.[57]

Kyknos: Against Kyknos and the other enemies of chapter ii (except Pyreneus and Sybaris) Herakles takes Apollo's place as champion. Yet in our earliest source (p. 29) it was Apollo who sent Herakles against Kyknos.[58]

Athena told Herakles that Zeus granted him victory over Kyknos, and Iolaos told him that Zeus and Poseidon were delivering Kyknos into his hands that he might win great glory. Also notice Achilles as opponent of Kyknos (p. 31).[59]

Eurytos: Apollo once takes Herakles' place as the slayer of Eurytos (p. 43).

Pyreneus: In an earlier version, very likely, he could fly, and a god,

---

[54] Serv. *Aen.* 6.618.

[55] See AW 34–36, 38–43 (figs. 9, 10).

[56] Apollod. 2.4.11.

[57] Euphorion *ap.* Serv. *Aen.* 6.618; Nonn. *Dion.* 18.36–38.

[58] A vase painting (AW 43) shows Apollo to the left behind Ares and Kyknos, rushing, like Poseidon opposite him, to the center. Apparently the two gods are coming to Zeus's aid in parting Ares and Herakles.

[59] *Shield* 328 f., 103–107.

Zeus or Apollo, struck him down. As it is, we are to understand that heaven caused his folly, probably Zeus as father of the Muses.

Sybaris was killed by the hero Eurybatos. Here, strangely, Apollo through the Pythia appears to have acquiesced in the Lamia's depredations, or even to have favored them; for he did nothing more for the Delphians than instruct them to make human sacrifice to her (see pp. 101–105).

In the derivative myths Apollo may be replaced by Herakles or another, sometimes Zeus. That is, it is a great god or hero who stands forth to face the enemy.

15. Theme 6B. Apollo fought Python in his infancy, boyhood, or early youth (pp. 15 f.). Tityos, Phorbas, Erginos, Sybaris.

Tityos likewise was killed by Apollo when the god was extremely young (p. 23); several writers place his encounters with Python and Tityos in close sequence, and either Tityos' death or Python's may be first.[60]

Phorbas: Apollo came to fight Phorbas in the likeness of a stripling (μειράκιον) with unshorn hair.[61]

Erginos: Herakles fought Kyknos rather late in his career. In the *Shield* he is accompanied by Iolaos, a full-grown nephew of his twin brother. According to Diodoros and Apollodoros (p. 28, note 1), he encountered Kyknos after his twelve labors and marriage to Deianeira. They also place his adventures with Koronos, Laogoras, Amyntor, and Eurytos just before or after the Kyknos episode. This is a consequence of attempts to reduce Herakles' manifold adventures to a system. However, in the Erginos-legend, obviously a variant of those just mentioned, the champion retains his early youth; for this combat appears in Diodoros and Apollodoros as one of the earliest of his exploits.

Sybaris: Eurybatos was young (νεὸς ὤν) when he killed Sybaris.

16. Theme 7A. Apollo fought and killed Python with his arrows (p. 15). All legends.

Python, Tityos: There is some allusion to other weapons, sword and spear.[62]

---

[60] Apollod. 1.4.1 and possibly Lucian *Salt.* 38, put Python before Tityos. Ovid (*Met.* 1.441 f.) emphasises the slaying of Python as Apollo's first martial exploit. But others put Tityos first: Ephor. 31*b*, 2.53 J; Men. Rhet. p. 441 Sp.

[61] Philostr. *Imag.* 2.19.3.

[62] In several vase paintings Apollo, after wounding Tityos with his arrows, closes in with a sword: AW 28–31 (figs. 6, 7). In one (AW 11) Artemis brandishes a spear against

Phorbas: Apollo killed Phorbas with his fists (p. 25); this is perhaps an introduction of the Amykos-theme into the story. For Zeus's lightning against Phorbas see 14 above.

Phlegyas: Apollo used thunderbolts, earthquake, and plague (= his arrows in Il. 1.48–52) against the Phlegyans (p. 25). Poseidon used his trident (= earthquake) against them (see 14 above).[63]

Kyknos: According to the *Shield* and several vase-paintings Herakles killed Kyknos with a spear. Other paintings show Herakles with a sword, either closing in on Kyknos, as Apollo against Tityos, or preparing to move against Ares, having delivered the fatal stroke to Kyknos (figs. 8–11). In two representations he wields his familiar club, and in another a huge stone. But according to Euripides he killed Kyknos with arrows. For Herakles' chariot, used either in battle or contest against Kyknos, see pp. 29 f.[64]

During the combat Zeus thundered above and sent down bloody raindrops, words which recall the thunderbolts that consumed Phorbas' oak tree or Phorbas and Tityos themselves (pp. 23, 25). In a simile Kyknos' fall is compared to that of a tree or crag which Zeus's thunderbolt has struck. In other accounts Zeus really did throw a thunderbolt down from heaven to part Herakles and Ares, and I have conjectured that originally he threw this thunderbolt not as peacemaker but as combatant (p. 34).[65]

Koronos, Laogoras, Erginos, Amyntor: The precise weapons used in these combats are not mentioned; but since they were combats between champions fought during a battle of armies, such as we find in the Iliad, we can safely assume that spear and sword were Herakles' weapons.

Eurytos: The same assumption can be made concerning Herakles' combat with Eurytos; but Apollo's arrows reappear in this story, and Herakles defeated Eurytos in a contest with bow and arrows (p. 43).

Pyreneus was struck with madness, probably a late substitution for heaven's bolt.

---

him. Notice fig. 5: Tityos has two arrows visible in his body, and Apollo is taking the last arrow from his quiver. This recalls *Met.* 1.443, *mille gravem telis exhausta paene pharetra*, concerning the arrows that Apollo used against Python.

[63] Apollo is probably ὁ θεός of Paus. 9.36.3, though it could be Zeus. Pausanias' account agrees pretty well with Pherek. 41*de*, 1.74 J, who says that Apollo destroyed them at Zeus's command.

[64] Spear: *Shield* 416–420; AW 34–36, 43, 46. Sword: AW 37–40, 42, 44, 47, 49 (figs. 8–11); cf. AW 28–31 (figs. 6, 7). Club: AW 33, 48. Arrows: Eur. *Her.* 389–393. See AW 40: Herakles holds a bow in his left hand, a sword in his right; also AW 42, 48; cf. *Shield* 129–134.

[65] *Shield* 383–385, 421 f.

Sybaris: Eurybatos used his bare hands to seize her and hurl her over a cliff.

This summary shows that a difference between legends concerning the champion's weapons has little significance: almost any weapon may be found in any legend. It also shows that the weapon tends to be determined by the champion: Apollo used his bow and arrows; Herakles his sword, spear, and club; Zeus his thunderbolt; Poseidon his trident. But some interchange is seen: Apollo with sword, thunderbolt, and earthquake (= trident); Herakles with arrows. In any case the battle was won and the enemy was slain.

17. Theme 7D. Apollo was helped by his sister Artemis (p. 21). Tityos (p. 23), Phorbas, Kyknos, Laogoras, Erginos.

Kyknos: In the *Shield* and several vase paintings we find Athena supporting Herakles against Kyknos and Ares, and providing him with armor. Athena as Herakles' sister can be likened to Artemis in the Python and Tityos myths.[66]

Phorbas: Athena helped Erechtheus to ward off the Acarnanian Phorbas' attack on Athens (p. 50, note 14), though on that occasion Ares too took the Athenian side.

Laogoras: Deianeira put on armor and fought beside her husband against the Dryopes (p. 37).

Erginos: Athena provided Herakles with arms for this combat (p. 42).

18. Theme 10A. Python was punished after death. Tityos, Phlegyas.

Python: Though nothing is said about Python's being cast down into the lower world, a doom that befalls the dragon in cognate tales, there are some indications that he was thus disposed of. Ampelius says, dii immortales Pythonem digna poena affecerunt; though in this passage he is confusing Python with Typhon. But in the exposure of Python's corpse, left to rot upon the mountainside, we probably have a diversion of the punishment theme for the sake of a folk-etymology. Similar is the tradi-

---

[66] *Shield* 125–127, 325–344, 443–450, 455 f.; AW 36–39, 41–43, 45, 49 (figs. 7–11).

tion that Apollo flayed the corpse and hung the hide upon his tripod.[67]

Tityos became one of the standard sinners who receive punishment in Hades—one with Tantalos, Sisyphos, Ixion, and the Danaids. Though it was Apollo who killed him, it was Zeus who imposed the punishment.[68]

Phlegyas too received punishment in Hades. Apollo imposed it upon him, and he also cast the Phlegyans down to Tartaros.[69]

19. Cf. Theme 10D. Python received a tomb (pp. 374–377). Tityos (pp. 51, 52), Kyknos (p. 29), Eurytos, Sybaris.

Eurytos had a tomb in Andania, the Messenian Oichalia, and a memorial in Lamia.[70]

Sybaris: The spring that gushed up marked the spot where her body disappeared and was equivalent to her tomb.

We have, therefore, nineteen features that the Python myth shares with all or several combat tales that appear in chapters i and ii. Not all are equally important for establishing a common descent. The champion, the combat, and the dragon's defeat (14, 16), as nuclear themes, are to be expected. But a correspondence in features 1, 2, 5, 10–13, 15, 17–19 is especially significant.

The analysis is presented graphically in tables 1 and 2, where one may see the interrelations of all twelve tales. In table 1 the symbol

---

[67] Ampel. 2.10. Exposure of corpse: Paus. 10.6.5; Macr. 1.17.50, 52; Suid. Λ210, Π3138; EM 696; Scholl. AB on Il. 9.405; Arg. 3 to Pind. *Pyth.*; see p. 14. Corpse flayed: Serv. *Aen.* 3.90, 3.360, 6.347; Lact. Plac. *Theb.* 1.509. See fig. 27.

[68] See p. 22. The descriptions of and allusions to Tityos' punishment are numerous. See e.g. Od. 11.576–579; Lucr. 3.984–994; Virg. *Aen.* 6.595–600; Apollod. 1.4.1; Ovid *Met.* 4.457 f.; for other citations see Waser, LM 5.1035–1040; Scherling, RE 6A.1593–1598. Zeus imposed the punishment: Anth. Pal. 3.14; Lact. Plac. *Theb.* 11.12; cf. Od. 11.580: Tityos had attacked Διὸς κυδρὴν παράκοιτιν. Apollo appears to be the punisher in Stat. *Theb.* 1.709 f., though the poet may be merely merging Apollo's victory with the consequent punishment. The lines that follow mention Apollo's victory over Python and the punishment of Phlegyas in Apollo's behalf (ultrix tibi torva Megaera).

[69] Virg. *Aen.* 6.618–620; Stat. *Theb.* 1.712–715; Val. Flacc. *Arg.* 2.192–195. According to the last two, he received the punishment that others assign to Tantalos, although Virg appears to assign it to Ixion and Peirithoos. Some editors have assumed a lacuna wherein Tantalos was mentioned. But Havet (1888) believes that lines have been misplaced and that Virgil too, whom Statius and Valerius undoubtedly follow, meant the unattainable feast and tormenting Fury to be the punishment of Phlegyas. Schol. T on Il. 13.302, Φλεγύαι . . . ὑπὸ 'Απόλλωνος κατεταρταρώθησαν, if this means anything more than that he destroyed them.

[70] Paus. 4.2.2; see p. 43.

TABLE 1

CORRESPONDENCES BETWEEN PYTHON MYTH AND ITS DERIVATIVES

Feature number		Python	Tityos	Phorbas	Phlegyas	Kyknos	Koronos	Laogoras	Erginos	Amyntor	Eurytos	Pyreneus	Sybaris
1		X	X	x	x	x	x	x	x			x	
2		X	X	x	X	X	x	x	X	X	x	x	
3	a	X	X	X	X			X		x		X	X
	b	X	X	X	X				X	X			
	c	x	X	x	x			X			X		
	d	x				X		X			X		
	e	x		x	X	X	X	x		X	x		
4		X	X	X	x								X
5		X				X	X						
6		X	X	X		X	x						X
7		X	x	x		x	x	x				x	x
8		X	X	X	X	X	x	X	x	x	x	X	X
9		X		x	X		X	X	X	X	X		
10		X	X	x								X	
11		X	X	X	X	X				x	x	X	
12		X			X		x	x	x	x	x	x	
13		X	X		x	x				x			
14		X	X	X	X	X	X	X	X	X	X	x	X
15		X	X	X					X				X
16		X	X	X	X	X	X	X	X	X	X	X	X
17		X	X	x		X	X		X				
18		x	X		X								
19		X	X			X					x		x

X indicates that a feature, designated by its number in the above sequence, appears clearly and prominently; the symbol x indicates that the feature appears obscurely, rarely, or uncertainly in the legend concerned. Since each feature is stated in terms of the Python myth, the statement may not always be literally true of another myth in the group, and yet the feature may be considered to appear clearly therein. For instance, feature 14 is Apollo as champion, though in the Kyknos tale and some others the champion is called Herakles, and in the Sybaris tale Eurybatos. Table 2 shows the relation of each legend to each of the other eleven; the upper numeral in each square indicates the total number of features shared between the two

TABLE 2

INTERRELATIONS BETWEEN PYTHON MYTH AND ITS DERIVATIVES

Myth	Python	Tityos	Phorbas	Phlegyas	Kyknos	Koronos	Laogoras	Erginos	Amyntor	Eurytos	Pyreneus	Sybaris
Python 19/18	...	16/14	14/8	12/8	13/9	12/5	9/5	11/7	8/5	9/3	10/5	9/7
Tityos 16/15	16/14	...	13/8	10/7	11/8	8/3	7/4	9/6	6/4	7/3	9/5	9/7
Phorbas 14/8	14/8	13/8	...	9/5	10/5	10/2	8/4	9/4	7/3	7/2	9/4	8/7
Phlegyas 12/9	12/8	10/7	9/5	...	8/6	8/4	8/5	9/5	8/5	8/3	8/4	5/4
Kyknos 13/10	13/9	11/8	10/5	8/6	...	10/5	7/4	7/4	6/4	7/3	7/3	6/4
Koronos 12/6	12/5	8/3	10/2	8/4	10/5	...	9/3	8/4	7/4	7/3	7/1	5/2
Laogoras 9/5	9/5	7/4	8/4	8/5	7/4	9/3	...	7/3	7/3	7/4	8/3	5/4
Erginos 11/7	11/7	9/6	9/4	9/5	7/4	8/4	7/3	...	7/5	6/3	6/1	4/3
Amyntor 8/5	8/5	6/4	7/3	8/5	6/4	7/4	7/3	7/5	...	8/3	7/1	4/2
Eurytos 9/4	9/3	7/3	7/2	8/3	7/3	7/3	7/4	6/3	8/3	...	6/1	4/2
Pyreneus 10/5	10/5	9/5	9/4	8/4	7/3	7/1	8/3	6/1	7/1	6/1	...	5/3
Sybaris 9/7	9/7	9/7	8/7	5/4	6/4	5/2	5/4	4/3	4/2	4/2	5/3	...

legends concerned; the lower indicates the number of clear and prominent correspondences. The upper number beside each legend name on the left side indicates the total number of features which appear in that legend; the lower, of those which appear clearly.

It is clear that these twelve stories are very closely related to one another, and that the Python tale is the center of them all. The correspondences are more numerous and significant than the differences, which lie only in superficial details. One might point to Erginos' imposition of tribute (p. 42) as a theme both different and important; but it is shared by the Eurytos-legend (p. 43, note 27), and may well be a variation on the plunder theme or the blockading of a road. Again, Eurytos refused to give his daughter to Herakles in marriage; but so did Amyntor and perhaps Phylas (= Laogoras), whose daughter Herakles took after his victory (p. 38): thus the theme not only occurs in three out of the twelve legends, but may be a transformation of the theme of sexual attack (10, Th. 4ᴇ)—i.e., Herakles' enemy tried to take his wife from him—for in the Nessos and Acheloos legends we can see stages that lie between Python-Tityos' attack on Leto and the enemy king's refusal of his daughter. So if one asks whether any of the other eleven legends contain an important episode or feature not found in the Python myth, the answer must be no. The fact that eight stories show only from eight to twelve of the nineteen features is mainly due to the scanty information that we have about them.

It is plain that Tityos and Phorbas are very closely related to Python, who likewise appears in human form as a giant brigand. The ancients often linked Python and Tityos as enemies of Apollo. Phorbas and Phlegyas (see p. 26) are two names for one and the same brigand-king of the Phlegyans. Phorbas-Phlegyas strikingly resembles Tityos, and sits at the same place on the road to Delphi. Kyknos too is obviously a scion of the same stock. The stories of the combats of Herakles with Lapith, Dryopian, and Minyan kings (Koronos, Laogoras, Erginos, Amyntor, Eurytos) are very similar to one another and closely related to the Kyknos and Phorbas-Phlegyas legends. In Pyreneus, Tityos and Phorbas appear to be repeated, and in Sybaris we can see Delphyne, the female Python.[71]

It appears that the dragon took on human form in course of time, even at Delphi (p. 19), though the dragon form remained dominant in Delphian lore. He became a giant and brigand and in that character took on different names in other localities. The brigand, for whatever reason, became identified with Lapith and Dryopian kings, perhaps rulers who fought for possession of Delphi and lost (pp. 36 f.). That is, Python became historicised, and his myth was joined to actual events (see p. 424).

It is also apparent that Delphi was not the only shrine concerned with the Python myth complex. It was early localised at

---

[71] Python and Tityos linked: Ephor. 31b, 2.53 J; Strabo 9.3.12, p. 423; Stat. *Theb.* 1.709–711, 7.349–353; Apollod. 1.4.1; Lucian *Salt.* 38; Men. Rhet. 441 Sp. Stat. *Theb.* 1.709–715 links Python, Tityos, and Phlegyas together as enemies of Apollo. See p. 65, note 68.

other Apolline shrines—e.g., Itonos, Pagasai, Ptoon, and probably at shrines of Herakles or Zeus—but Delphi clearly became the peninsular center about which the Python myth and its cognates clustered. Now we must leave Delphi and its neighborhood for Cilicia, center of the Zeus-Typhon myth.

IV

ZEUS AND TYPHON

Zeus, father of gods and men, also had a critical fight with a dragon—for we may properly call Typhon a dragon, though his body was not entirely reptilian and included more than one snake within it. We may also call him monster or ogre; but the Greeks called him *drakôn* and I shall henceforth use the term *dragon* broadly to mean any kind of monster of animal or mixed shape. Typhon was a supergigantic figure, anthropomorphic from the hips up, serpentine below; his legs, in fact, were simply snakes (fig. 13). Such is Typhon's primary pattern, often elaborated by poets or painters (p. 80; figs. 14, 15). He was dragon, giant, and monster in one, good evidence in himself of the folkloristic identity of every kind of ogre.[1]

His name appears in several forms: *Typhôn, Typhāôn, Typhôeus, Typhôs*. We hear of him first in a simile of the Iliad: when the Achaean host advanced, "the ground rumbled under foot as it does when Zeus the thunderer in his wrath lashes the earth about Typhoeus among the Arimoi, where, men say, are the couches of Typhoeus." The *when* clause has its verb in the subjunctive (ὅτε . . . ἱμάσσῃ), indicating a present-general condition.

---

[1] On the Typhon myth see Seippel (1939); also J. Schmidt, LM 5.1426–1454; R. Holland (1900), Teipel (1922), Cornford (1952) 218–220, Worms (1953). The term *dragon* is applied to mixed forms like Typhon and to monsters of little or no reptilian component by Siecke (1907), Elliot Smith (1919) 76–139, Witzel (1920) 167–208, Van Buren (1946). See Grimm (1875) 457–460, 574 f.

FIGURE 13. ZEUS AND TYPHON

Therefore the lines do not refer to Zeus's combat with Typhoeus, but to subsequent expressions of the god's enduring wrath: from time to time he hurls thunderbolts about the place where Typhoeus' body lies. The Arimoi, it seems fairly certain, are the Aramaeans, and the country is either Syria or Cilicia, most likely the latter, since in later sources that is usually Typhon's land.[2]

Hesiod (or his interpolator) has the earliest extant narrative of Zeus's combat with Typhon. After Zeus had defeated and cast out the Titans, their mother Gaia bore to Tartaros her youngest child Typhoeus, a monstrous being. He would have taken heaven and ousted the Olympians on that day, if Zeus had not seen him in time and begun battle against him. The god first hurled thunderbolts from heaven, then came to earth and struck the monster from nearby, and burned all his hundred serpent heads. Typhoeus fell aflame in mountain glens and Zeus hurled him down to Tartaros.[3]

---

[2] Il. 2.781–783. Arimoi: Strabo 13.4.6, pp. 626 f., 16.2.7, pp. 750 f.; Hommel (1926) 190, note 3; Schmidt, LM 5.1431: Seippel (1939) 26. I cannot agree with von Mess (1901:169) and Worms (1953:38 f.) that originally the Arimoi land was a mythical locality only later identified with Cilicia or Syria. It may be true that Homer and Hesiod had no clear idea of its whereabouts, but certainly the name must have been the Greek version of *Aramaeans.*

[3] Hes. *Theog.* 820–868: if an interpolation, it was made early enough. See Solmsen (1949) 53, note 172, and citations there. Against the bracketers, I would point out that Ge's *phradmosynai* of 884 are those of 626–628, and that though Ge's prophecies foretold Olympian victory, she may very well have been incensed at the Olympian treatment of her sons. There are several parallels in Greek mythology.

Hesiod's Typhon also appears to have lived among the Arimoi; for he mated with the monstrous Echidna, who lived there in a cave and became by Typhaon (as he is called in this passage) the mother of Orthos, Kerberos, Hydra, and Chimaira.[4]

The Homeric Hymn to Apollo has information of great significance concerning Typhon, though nothing about his combat with Zeus. The poet, at variance with the Hesiodic tradition, surprises us with a narrative in which Hera is the mother of the monster, when in anger at Zeus's androgenesis of Athena, she decided to counter his performance (p. 14). Going apart from the gods, she struck the earth with the flat of her hand, and called upon Gaia, Uranos, and the Titans to grant her a child mightier than Zeus. Her prayer was granted and she bore Typhaon, mighty enough, yet hardly as admirable as Athena. He was unlike either gods or men, an evil creature who did great harm to mankind. Hera at once handed him over to the Delphian dragoness, who reared him. At this point the poet drops Typhon from the narrative. He is mentioned but once again (367 f.).[5]

Similar to the Hymn's tale of Typhon's birth is a narrative quoted by a Scholiast, wherein Ge, angry because the gods had destroyed the Gigantes, slandered Zeus to Hera. In anger Hera went for help to Kronos, who gave her two eggs smeared with his semen, telling her to bury them underground; for from them would spring a *daimon* to usurp Zeus's throne. So Hera buried them in Cilicia among the Arimoi, and in due time Typhon came forth. But by now Hera had become reconciled to Zeus and warned him, whereupon Zeus easily disposed of Typhon.[6]

Aeschylus has much the same version as Hesiod. Typhon was born of Ge and lived in Cilician caves, a destructive monster who opposed the gods. He wanted to end Zeus's reign, but Zeus's thunderbolt came down upon him and blasted his whole mighty frame. Now he lies under Etna. Pindar follows the same version. He describes Typhon much as Aeschylus does and definitely

---

[4] Hes. *Theog.* 295–325, 869–871.

[5] Hom. Hymn 3.305–355. Stesichoros too, it seems, called Typhoeus son of Hera; but perhaps the lexicographer who cites him made a mistake: Stes. frag. 60 Bergk, *ap.* EM 772. But see Dornseiff (1933:18–23), who believes that the author of the Hymn was later than Stesichoros, from whom he took this story.

[6] Schol. B on Il. 2.783.

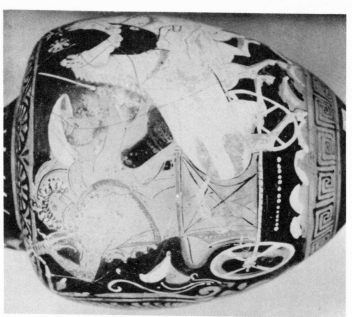

FIGURE 14. ZEUS AND TYPHON IN GIGANTOMACHY

places him in the "Cilician cave of many names" (Κιλίκιον θρέψεν πολυώνυμον ἄντρον), i.e., the Corycian Cave; but he barely alludes to the combat, saying only that Zeus destroyed Typhon among the Arimoi (presumably in Cilicia) and that he lies in dread Tartaros under Etna. He is the earliest author to mention the flight of the gods before Typhon, when they took animal forms to escape him.[7]

In the version of the combat found in Hesiod, Aeschylus, and Pindar, Zeus has no great difficulty in overcoming Typhon, formidable though he is: he moves straight to victory without a setback. Most later writers adhere to this simple view of the victory, and such differences as they have concern the preliminaries or the aftermath of the battle.[8]

A more complex story is told by Apollodoros. After the gods had defeated the Gigantes, Ge in anger mated with Tartaros and bore Typhon, a huge monster of mixed form. He attacked heaven, hurling flaming stones and belching fire from his mouth. The gods fled before him to Egypt, where they took animal forms to escape his notice—all except Zeus, who stood against him. At first Zeus pelted him with thunderbolts from a distance. Then he moved in with an adamantine sickle with which he wounded Typhon, who fled to Mount Kasios in Syria. Zeus followed him thither and grappled with him, a move that gave Typhon a chance to entangle Zeus in his coils. Taking Zeus's sickle from him, Typhon severed his sinews and carried the god, thus rendered impotent, over the sea to Cilicia, where he laid him in the Corycian Cave. The sinews he hid in a bearskin and set the dragoness Delphyne to guard them. But Hermes and Aigipan (Goat Pan) recovered the sinews and restored them to Zeus, who renewed battle, mounting his chariot and once more hurling thunderbolts. Typhon fled to Nysa, where the Moirai deceived him

---

[7] Aesch. *Pr.* 353–374, *Sept.* 511–517; Pind. *Pyth.* 1.15–20, 8.16, *Ol.* 4.7 f., frags. 81, 240 Bowra. Von Mess (1901) derives the version of Aeschylus and Pindar from an epic that perhaps belonged to the Hesiodic school: see Usener (1901), Solmsen (1949) 131, Worms (1953). There is such striking correspondence of phrase between Pindar and Aeschylus that it is quite likely that one was influenced by the other or that both used the same source.

[8] See Nic. *ap.* Ant. Lib. 28; Strabo 16.2.7, pp. 750 f.; Opp. *Hal.* 3.15–25; *Titanomachia ap.* Schol. *in* Opp. *Hal.* 3.16; Nonn. *Dion.* Books 1, 2; Ovid *Met.* 5.319–331, 346–358; Hyg. *Fab.* 152; Claud. 26.62–66; Lact. Plac. *Theb.* 2.595; Schol. B on Il. 2.783; Schol. Rec. on Aesch. *Pr.* 351; Pherek. 54, 1.76J.

with ephemeral fruits, telling him that to eat thereof would increase his strength. He fled thence to Thrace, where he made another stand and heaved whole mountains at Zeus. The god's thunderbolts thrust all his missiles back upon him, and he lost much blood from the wounds he received—hence Mount Haimos (Bloody Mountain) in Thrace—and as he fled across the Sicilian Sea, Zeus cast Mount Etna upon him and so pinned him down.[9]

This version impresses one as earlier than Hesiod's, an impression that will be confirmed. Significant are the features of Zeus's temporary defeat, his great difficulty in attaining final victory, the tricking of Typhon, and Typhon's flight. In the Hesiodic version Zeus also comes down from heaven after hurling thunderbolts, closes in, and strikes Typhon; immediately thereafter he achieves victory. Obviously Hesiod or his source has omitted the defeat and maiming of Zeus as inconsistent with his power and majesty; in this respect most later writers followed Hesiod.

Yet two distinctive features of the Apollodoros version, the tricking of Typhon with Pan's help and his flight, recur in other writers. According to Oppian, Pan aided Zeus by cooking fish on the shore, thus luring Typhon from the Corycian Cave into the open, where Zeus could strike him down. According to a Scholiast, Pan caught Typhon in nets.[10]

Nonnos' long-winded account, though granting Zeus a fairly easy victory once the combat begins, since Typhon is, after all, no match for Zeus, plainly shows a watering-down of the Apollodoros version: it is a late and highly embellished example of the sort of process which resulted in the Hesiodic version. Undoubtedly Nonnos made many changes himself, but some peculiarities of his narrative must have come to him from tradition, since they reflect themes found in cognate myths. Zeus, pursuing an amour with the maiden Pluto, who became by him mother of Tantalos, hid his weapons (thunderbolt, etc.) under a rock in Cilicia,

---

[9] Apollod. 1.6.3.
[10] Opp. and Schol. *loc. cit.*; Schol. Vet. on Soph. *Ajax* 695. For convenience I shall use the term "Apollodoros version," a designation which should lead nobody to suppose that I consider the handbook author (the pseudo-Apollodoros) to have done anything more than report the story as he found it in his source. Furthermore, I do not mean that Nonnos learned this version from the handbook when I say that Nonnos plainly knew it.

whence Typhoeus stole them—to this feeble pass has the severing of Zeus's sinews come. Armed with Zeus's weapons, Typhoeus set out to take Zeus's place and rule the world. Zeus was momentarily at a disadvantage, being without his arms; but he saw Kadmos, who was wandering through Cilicia in search of his sister Europa, and enlisted his help against Typhon. Kadmos, assisted by Pan and Eros, dressed himself as a herdsman and beguiled Typhon so successfully with music of syrinx that Zeus could steal unobserved into the cave and recover his weapons.[11]

Strabo (see p. 73, note 8) mentions the wounded Typhon's flight, in the course of which he plowed the channel of the Orontes as he desperately sought escape underground. Strabo's source places the Arimoi in Syria.

The flight of the gods before Typhon and their change into animal forms, an episode known to Pindar, was introduced as a result of the identification of Typhon with Egyptian Set (p. 177); thus the Greeks explained the animal forms of Egyptian gods. The Pindar fragment does not mention Egypt, but for all later writers (e.g., Nicander, Ovid, Nigidius) who speak of the flight and transformation Egypt was the scene. Yet, it seems, both Zeus's defeat and the tricking of Typhon were absorbed into this episode. For Ovid and perhaps Pindar (who says πάντας τοὺς θεούς), Zeus also fled and turned himself into a ram (Ammon). According to Nigidius, the gods, on Pan's advice, tricked Typhon by taking animal forms, so that they could move about him without his recognising them.[12]

So, in contrast to the Python myth, we find but two main versions of the Typhon tale, and the later, which appears first in the ·extant literature, and which we may call Hesiodic, differs from the earlier mainly in omitting an episode discreditable to Zeus. Some writers who follow Hesiod in this respect (Oppian, Non-

---

[11] Nonn. *Dion.* 2.356–563: Typhon no match for Zeus. 1.145–156: stealing of weapons. 1.362–2.5: Kadmos beguiled Typhon. Notice that sinews (νεῦρα) of Zeus are mentioned in 1.510–516: Kadmos beguiles Typhon into giving them to him as strings for his lyre. These *neura* were those τάπερ χθονὶ πῖπτε Τυφαονίῃ ποτὲ χάρμῃ. But nothing has been said about them previously, and as yet Zeus has not encountered Typhon. Perhaps Rose (Loeb edition of Nonnos, *ad loc.*) is right in saying that Nonnos introduced the sinews without understanding the meaning of the episode of their severing.

[12] Nigid. *ap.* Scholl. BS *in* Germ. *Arat.* 289; cf. Hyg. *Astr.* 2.28, Ampel. 2.10.

nos), nevertheless include distinctive features of the earlier version in their narratives, either in original or emasculated form. It may be more correct to say that the Typhon myth of the Greeks had only one form, the narrative as found in Apollodoros, and that some authors chose to leave out the central and most significant part of the story.

V

TYPHON AND PYTHON

It is now time to inquire whether there is any closer relation between the Typhon and Python myths than the obvious fact that in both a great god meets and kills a monstrous enemy. The mere encounter between god or hero and dragon or giant might occur in folktale anywhere, one would say (though in fact not everywhere). A true relation, i.e., derivation from a common source, can only be established by showing common themes from beginning to end and also geographical connections, just as in the study of the relation of the Python myth to the myths of Tityos, Phorbas, and others. So I must set the Typhon myth against the Python myth, pointing out that *Python* now subsumes the eleven derivative figures of chapters i–iii.[1]

1. Theme 1A. Typhon was son of Ge (Python 1, p. 47).[2] So all authorities say, except the Homeric Hymn to Apollo, a Scholiast on Iliad 2.783 (p. 72), and Hyginus. In the Hymn Ge helped Hera to conceive Typhon; the Scholiast says that Ge set in motion the course of events that ended in the birth of Typhon, and that

---

[1] The similarity of the two myths has, of course, been noticed, and a common origin has been conjectured: see Siecke (1907) 42 f.; Gruppe (1906) 102, 812, 1255–1259; Kerényi (1951) 26–28, 136. But no real proof has been offered.

In the following analysis I shall not cite authorities for statements that are obvious from the previous chapters. Occasional cross-references will be sufficient.

[2] "Python 1," "Python 2," etc., placed in parentheses in the following analysis, mean features of the analysis of chapter iii.

the eggs from which he sprang were hatched in earth; and Hyginus says that his mother was Tartara, no doubt Ge herself under a name which designates all that lies beneath the surface of the earth. Typhon's birth underground recalls the birth of Tityos underground (p. 47).[3]

2. Theme 1B. Typhon's father was Tartaros (Python 2, p. 49), who, according to Olympiodoros, was also father of Python and Echidna, Ge being the mother of all three. Only the Homeric Scholiast just cited differs, in that he derives Typhon from two eggs smeared with Kronos' seed.[4]

3. Theme 1C. On the dragoness, associated with both Typhon and Python, see chapter vi.

4. Theme 2A. Typhon's home was the Corycian Cave near Korykos (Corycus) in Cilicia.

There is also a Corycian Cave on the slopes of Parnassos above Delphi (Python 3, a, p. 51), which had something to do with Apollo's combat. For, according to Apollonios, the Corycian nymphs cheered Apollo's victory over Delphyne with cries of Iéie (Paian). The coincidence of name is not accidental (see pp. 407–412). Moreover Typhon is positively associated with Delphi by the Homeric Hymn: his nurse was the dragoness of Pytho, which means that he was reared there. Again, Plutarch speaks of "Tityoses and Typhons and that Typhon who held Delphi and upset the oracle with wickedness and violence." In view of the other evidence which connects Typhon with Delphi there is no need to suppose a scribe's mistake for Python. There is also the strange statement of a commentator that on the advice of a Delphian, Nero stopped the oracle by throwing Typhon's head into the temple (chasm?).[5]

Typhon is associated with Boeotia too (Python 3, b, p. 52), where there was a mountain called Typhaonion. When Zeus was on his way to visit Alkmene, says the poet of the Shield, he went

---

[3] See Hyg. Fab. 152.1.

[4] Olymp. on Phaed. 201, 240 Norv. Plutarch (Mor. 355F) means the Egyptian Typhon (= Set) when he says that he was son of Kronos (Seb or Geb); he (Mor. 362B) also mentions Phrygian writings which said that Typhon was son of Aiakos or Alkaios Herakles' son; but the text is very uncertain.

[5] Apollon. Arg. 2.711 f.; FD 3.2.191.27 f.; see also Arg. 3 to Pind. Pyth.: the Parnassian nymphs rewarded Apollo; Claud. 2.11–13. See Usener (1901) 184 f. on Corycian Cave and Delphyne in both Typhon and Python myths. Plut. Mor. 945B; Proleg. in Aristid. Or. 3.740 Dind.

quickly from Olympos to Typhaonion, whence he stepped to the top of Phikion (Sphinx Mountain), and from there went to Thebes. This seems to place Typhon Mountain north of Sphinx Mountain and farther from Thebes. Dion Chrysostom, however, places it near Thebes, when he speaks of a mountain of two peaks, one called Basileios (Royal), sacred to Zeus Basileus (King), the other Tyrannike, known as Typhon's peak. If this is not pure fiction (for Dion makes this mountain the scene of the choice of Herakles), then this mountain may well have been considered a battleground of Zeus and Typhon. In any case there was a Mount Typhon in Boeotia, in the Phlegyan country, perhaps near Tegyra. And Boeotia claimed Typhon's body: the Pindaric Scholiast cites authorities who say that Typhon's body lay beneath the mountain in Boeotia (he apparently means Typhaonion), from which there were exhalations (*anadoseis*) of fire. There are no volcanoes in Boeotia; if any credit can be given to the Scholiast's statement the *anadoseis* were probably ground-fires such as are attested near Trapezos on the lower slopes of Mount Lykaion in Arcadia.[6]

Finally, I have already mentioned Boeotian Phikion, mountain of the Sphinx, who is sometimes called daughter of Typhon and Echidna.[7]

Just as Typhon appears in Python's territories, so Python appears in Typhon's. The Python combat was localised in two cities of Asia Minor, Phrygian Hierapolis and Gryneion in the territory of Myrina; and in these regions, Phrygia and Lydia, the Typhon combat was also placed in obviously local traditions.[8]

5. Theme 2B. Typhon lived in a cave (Python 4, p. 54).

6. Theme 2D. For the association of both Typhon and Python with springs see Appendix 6.

7. Theme 3A. Typhon, says Apollodoros, was the biggest of

---

[6] Typhon mountain: *Shield* 32; Dion Chrys. 1.67; Hesych. T1698; Schol. Vet. on Pind. *Ol.* 4.7(11), *Pyth.* 1.16(31). Ground fires: Paus. 8.29.1; see Fontenrose (1945) 105 f. Perhaps this is the mountain of Hes. *Theog.* 860, where Typhon fell flaming. Some editions read Αἴτνης, but ἀϋδνῆς is right: see Mazon *ad loc.* and on *Shield* 32.

[7] Sphinx: Apollod. 3.5.8; Hyg. *Fab.* 67.4, 151.1, praef. 39. Her parents were Orthos and Echidna, according to Hes. *Theog.* 326 f.

[8] AW 9; *Acta Philippi* 113; *Miraculum a S. Michaele Chonis Patratum* 1 (*Acta Bollandiana* VIII, pp. 289 f.); Serv.-Dan. *Ecl.* 6.72. On Typhon in Phrygia and Lydia see pp. 110, 160.

Ge's children (Python 6, p. 54). He overtopped all mountains and his head brushed the stars; when he stretched out his arms laterally his hands reached to the eastern and western limits of the world.

Similar expressions are used of Python, e.g., by Menander Rhetor: Ge brought forth a dragon unspeakably and unbelievably huge, so that he actually hid Parnassos from sight with his coils, while his head towered above the mountain to the very sky.[9]

Like Tityos, spread over so many acres in Hades, is Typhon, who in death lies outstretched under the whole of Sicily. His immensity exhausts the Greek and Latin store of adjectives that designate great size. His strength, furthermore, was in proportion to his size. He is numbered among or associated with the Gigantes oftener than is Tityos or Python.[10]

8. Theme 3B. Typhon's body had both serpentine and human members (Python 7, p. 55). Hesiod's description is not entirely clear, but his Typhoeus apparently had an anthropomorphic body, from the shoulders of which grew a hundred serpent heads. Apollodoros says that a hundred snake heads grew from his arms, but that he had human form above his hips, snake form below; for legs, in fact, he had coils of vipers (*echidnai*) that could reach upwards to his head. He had, it seems, a human head surmounting his manlike trunk, for Apollodoros speaks of his unkempt hair and beard. In post-Hesiodic literature his snake legs and hundred snake heads remain fairly constant. His serpent nature is always emphasised, and sometimes, like Python, he is called

---

[9] Men. Rhet. p. 441 Sp.; Claud. 2.3 f., (Python) qui spiris tegeret montes . . . sanguineis tangeret astra jubis; *id*. 26.66, lamberet attonitas erectis anguibus arctos. Man. 2.876 f.: Typhon was as big as his mother Ge. For Typhon see also Nonn. *Dion.* 1.184–189, 258–260, 2.53 f., 128 f., 348 f.; for Python, Ovid *Met.* 1.440, 459; Stat. *Theb.* 1.562–569, 5.531 f., 7.349 f.; cf. *Theb.* 11.12–15: the very vultures who tear his liver are amazed at the *immensa membra* of Tityos. See fig. 15 for Typhon in Gigantomachy.

[10] Under Sicily: Pind. *Pyth.* 1.17–19; Ovid *Met.* 5.346–355; Nonn. *Dion.* 2.622–624. On Tityos see p. 55. As one might expect, many of the same adjectives were applied to Python, Tityos, Phorbas, etc.; see pp. 54 f., notes 34–38. Notice, e.g., *immani magnitudine*, applied to both Typhon (Hyg. *Fab.* 152) and Tityos (*ibid.* 55); compare Lact. Plac. *Theb.* 2.595 and Sen. *HOe* 1733 on Typhon with Lucr. 3.987 on Tityos. Other passages on Typhon's size: Hes. *Theog.* 845, 856; Nic. *ap.* Ant. Lib. 28.1; Ovid *Fasti* 4.491; Nonn. *Dion.* 1.297, 421 f., 2.549, 561, 22.141, 30.58, 34.183, 48.77 f.; Val. Flacc. *Arg.* 2.23 f., 3.130; Suid. T1228. Typhon among Gigantes: Hyg. *Fab.* 151.1, *Astr.* 2.28, 2.30; Philostr. *Imag.* 2.17.5; Solin. 38.8; Sid. Ap. *Carm.* 15.19; Nonn. *Dion.* 1.176, 263, 299, and many other verses.

simply *drakôn*. Both Typhon and Python were poisonous and
had particolored bodies, in which bright reds and greens were
prominent.[11]

From his hundred heads, says Hesiod, issued the voices and
cries of all sorts of creatures: bulls, lions, dogs, snakes, gods. A

FIGURE 15. ZEUS AND TYPHON

Frieze from the Altar of Zeus at Pergamon

Scholiast says that he had a hundred heads representing every
kind of wild beast. Nonnos too gives him heads of several kinds of
animals—leopards, lions, bulls, boars, wolves, bears, dogs, and
snakes—all of which had snaky locks. His description is character-

---

[11] *Theog.* 823–825,

> οὗ χεῖρες μὲν ἔασιν ἐπ' ἰσχύι ἔργματ' ἔχουσαι,
> καὶ πόδες ἀκάματοι κρατεροῦ θεοῦ. ἐκ δέ οἱ ὤμων
> ἦν ἑκατὸν κεφαλαὶ ὄφιος, δεινοῖο δράκοντος.

He apparently imagined one snake with a hundred heads, whereas Apollod. 1.6.3 uses
the plural δρακόντων, imagining a hundred snakes. See Nic. *ap.* Ant. Lib. 28.1; Man.
4.581; Hyg. *Fab.* 152.1; Lact. Plac. *Theb.* 2.595; Claud. 26.65 f.; Nonn. *Dion.* 1.184,
415; 2.30 f., 36, 141, 562; 13.496. See AW 50–65 (figs. 13–15). Called *drakôn;* Strabo
16.2.7, p. 751; Nonn. *Dion.* 1–2 *passim.* Typhon's poison: Nonn. *Dion.* 1.162, 268, 508 f.;
2.31, 142, 520, 612; Python's: Ovid *Met.* 1.444; Stat. *Theb.* 1.565 f.; Claud. 1.188, 2.9;
Isid. *Etym.* 8.11.54. Typhon's color: Suid. T1226, 1227; EM 772; Python's: Eur. IT
1244–1246; Stat. *Theb.* 1.502, 711; Claud. 2.9. On Set's red color see p. 185.

istically overdrawn, but the mixture of several beasts' heads in Typhon's form is supported by the Scholiast just cited, somewhat by Hesiod, and by several allusions to Typhon's complex form. In the Pergamene Gigantomachy (fig. 15), Typhon has the horns and ears of a bull. Typhon's boar heads recall the boar that frightened Leto, and Phorbas' swinish appearance.[12]

The art works usually picture Typhon with wings (figs. 13, 15). Apollodoros says that his whole body was winged or feathered, Nicander that he had many wings. This puts birds also into Typhon's makeup; and we may recall the winged Tityos of the Pergamene frieze (fig. 12), the names of Kyknos and Koronos, and Pyreneus' attempt at flight.[13]

Typhon appears once in entirely human form, like the brigand Python: Typhon was king of Egypt and gave his name to a species of snake. This is Egyptian Set, with whom Typhon was identified and whose various forms will be dealt with later (pp. 185–188).[14]

Finally, Typhon's shagginess can be compared with the shaggy Tityos seen in a vase painting (fig. 4).[15]

9. Theme 3c. Typhon had not only a hundred heads, but also, according to some authors, a hundred arms; or, as Nicander has it, numerous arms and wings. Euripides calls him three-bodied (trisômatos), a word that is elsewhere applied to Geryon, Kerberos, and Chimaira. As a dragon, he had huge coils and countless scales.[16]

Python, as a thoroughly Hellenised dragon, lost the many heads and arms, but retained the many coils. He ringed Parnassos with nine

[12] Hes. *Theog.* 826–835; Schol. Rec. on Aesch. *Pr.* 351; Nonn. *Dion.* 1.156–162, 2.42–47, 250–256, 281–290; Eur. *Her.* 1271 f.; Plat. *Phaedr.* 230A with Schol. Vet.; Suid. T1227.

[13] AW 50–65. I have listed only representations of combat, and only those combats in which it is fairly certain that Typhon is pictured. For Typhon or Typhonlike figures not engaged in combat see Schmidt, LM 5.1450; Mayer (1887) 275–280; Vian (1952) 12–16. Vian shows that Gigantes with snake legs were unknown before the fourth century B.C. But earlier figures are not necessarily Typhon, for Boreas and Kekrops, among others, were pictured in this way. If the creature also has wings it is likely to be Typhon. In Apollod. 1.6.3 (πᾶν δὲ αὐτοῦ τὸ σῶμα κατεπτέρωτο) *feathered* is perhaps a better translation, since the word is predicated of his whole body. But see Nic. *ap.* Ant. Lib. 28.1. See also Man. 4.581: simply wings on shoulders.

[14] Plin. NH 2.25.91.

[15] Pind. *Pyth.* 1.19; Apollod. 1.6.3 (unkempt hair and beard).

[16] Nic. *ap.* Ant. Lib. 28.1; Apollod. 1.6.3; Ovid *Met.* 3.303; Claud. 26.64 f.; Nonn. *Dion.* 1.297, 2.342–344, 512 f., 620 f. Nonnos is not content with fewer than two hundred arms. See Eur. *Her.* 1271 f. and LSJ s.v. τρισώματος.

coils, says Callimachus; Delphi with seven, says Statius; other writers simply say that they were numerous. The number one hundred recurs in the number of acres that Python's corpse is said to have covered.[17]

10. Theme 3D. Typhon, as a proper dragon, spouted fire from his mouth and flashed fire from his eyes. The fire belched forth by Etna (or whatever volcano he was placed under) was attributed either to this property or to his catching fire from Zeus's thunderbolts.[18]

Python appears to have done even less fire-breathing than the Reluctant Dragon: no ancient author endows him with that power. Yet a hint of fire-breathing appears in the earliest record of the Kyknos combat. The poet says that Ares flashed fire as he faced Herakles at Kyknos' side, and that the whole grove of the Pagasaean Apollo gleamed with the brilliance of his armor and body. Again, Kyknos and Ares advanced like fire and whirlwind. The names of Kyknos' mother Pyrene, of the villain Pyreneus, and of Phlegyas, suggest fire demons.[19]

11. Theme 4A. Needless to say, Typhon was as thoroughly wicked a character as Python, Tityos, and the others, and it is important to observe that he is described in the same or very similar terms: e.g. ὑβριστής, βίαιος, ἄνομος, ἀσεβής impius, ferus. According to Olympiodoros, Typhon, Echidna, and Python were equally spirits of disorder.[20]

The Homeric Hymn says of Typhon, in nearly the same words used concerning his dragoness fostermother, that he did much harm among the tribes of men (Python 8, p. 58): he filled land and sea with his wickedness; he ravaged and destroyed crops, meadows, and woods.[21]

---

[17] Call. *Hymn* 4.93; Stat. *Theb.* 1.563 f. (cf. 1.568, hundred acres covered); Men. Rhet. p. 441 Sp.; Claud. 2.3; Sid. Ap. *Carm.* 2.155; Dion. Per. 443; cf. AW 1–3, 7 (figs. 1–3).
[18] Hes., Aesch., Apollod., Ovid: see pp. 71–74, notes 3, 7–9.
[19] *Shield* 70–72, 345 f.
[20] ὑβριστής: Hes. *Theog.* 307; Plut. *Mor.* 945B. βίαιος: Diod. 1.21.2; Plut. *Mor.* 945B. σμερδαλέος: Opp. *Hal.* 3.19. terribilis: Ovid *Fasti* 2.461. *ferus;* Sen. *Oct.* 238. δεινός, ἀργαλέος: Hes. *Theog.* 307; Hom. Hymn 3.352. ἄνομος: Hes. *Theog.* 307. ἀσεβής, *impius;* Diod. 1.21.2; Nigid. *ap.* Schol. B *in* Germ. *Arat.* 289. πῆμα: Hom. Hymn 3.352; κακόν: *ibid.* 354. Notice ἀκάματος applied to both Typhon (Hes. *Theog.* 824; Quint. Smyrn. 6.261) and Tityos (Quint. Smyrn. 3.394). See Olymp. on *Phaed.* 201, 240 Norv.
[21] Hom. Hymn 3.355; Plut. *Mor.* 361D; Nonn. *Dion.* 2.42–93.

12. Themes 4A, 7G. Typhon made war on the gods, and is often associated with the Gigantes in their attack on heaven (Python 9, p. 58).[22]

13. Theme 4D. Typhon swallowed beasts of the forest, birds of the air, and cattle of the fields. Python devoured whole herds.[23]

14. Theme 4E. Typhon, in Nonnos' account, intended to take Hera from Zeus and make her his own wife (Python 10, p. 58). The nymphs ran before him in fear of his lust, and Nike in Leto's form feared for the virgin goddesses Athena and Artemis. That Typhon's lechery is not merely Nonnos' fancy is indicated by earlier allusions to Typhon's pursuit of Aphrodite.[24]

15. Theme 4G. Both Typhon and Python drained whole rivers in their thirst.[25]

16. Theme 5A. Typhon wanted to overthrow Zeus and take his place as sovereign of the world, just as Python fought Apollo for lordship of Delphi (Python 12, p. 60).[26]

17. Theme 5B. As Hera incited Python-Tityos to pursue Leto (Python 13, p. 60), so Ge bore Typhon for the express purpose of attacking Zeus and the gods. In Nonnos' account it was she who induced Typhon to steal Zeus's weapons.[27]

18. Theme 6A. Zeus stood forth as divine champion to meet Typhon (Python 14, p. 61). But Apollo or Herakles sometimes appear as opponents of Typhon; their role will be discussed later (pp. 90 f.).

19. Theme 6B. Zeus was still very young when he fought Typhon (Python 15, p. 62). He had just established himself on the throne of heaven and earth after defeating the Titans when Gaia raised up Typhon against him, according to Hesiod; or he had experienced only the Gigantomachy between his accession and Typhon's attack, according to Apollodoros.

20. Theme 7A. Zeus, using his favorite weapon, the thunder-

[22] Typhon as *letifer:* Lucan *BC* 6.92.

[23] Typhon: Nonn. Dion. 2.42–52. Python: Men. Rhet., p. 441 Sp.

[24] Nonn. *Dion.* 1.471, 2.113–148, 210 f., 232–236, 316–333, 585 f. Pursuit of Aphrodite: Ovid *Fasti* 2.461–464; Man. 4.580 f., 801; Diognetos *ap.* Hyg. *Astr.* 2.30.

[25] Typhon: Nonn. *Dion.* 1.259, 2.53 f. Python: Men. Rhet. *loc. cit.;* Stat. *Theb.* 1.565 f., 7.349 f.; Claud. 2.3 f.

[26] Hes., Aesch., Nic., Ovid, Hyg., Nonn.: see pp. 71, 73, notes 3, 7, 8.

[27] Apollod. 1.6.3; Man. 2.875–877; Jul. *Or.* 2, p. 56D; Nonn. *Dion.* 1.154–156; Schol. B on Il. 2.783.

bolt (= his arrow: Nonn. *Dion.* 1.151), fought and defeated Typhon (Python 16, p. 62). He also used a *harpê,* a sicklelike sword, against him, closing in with it, like Apollo or Herakles against Tityos or Kyknos (p. 63, figs. 6, 7). He pursued Typhon in a chariot, drawn by winged horses, and he hurled Mount Etna upon him. A black-figured hydra from Vulci shows two warriors attacking Typhon with spears. The gods tore the Egyptian Typhon to pieces with their hands.[28]

21. Theme 7B. Zeus had to hurl many thunderbolts at Typhon (p. 73).

Apollo likewise had to use a great many arrows to kill Python (p. 15): Simonides said a hundred, Ovid a thousand. Apollo also hurled numerous thunderbolts upon the Phlegyans.[29]

22. Theme 7D. Zeus had Athena's help against Typhon (Python 17, p. 64). She alone stood beside him when the gods fled.[30]

23. Theme 7E. Zeus was assisted by his son Hermes, son or grandson Pan, and brother-in-law Kadmos, just as Apollo was assisted by his father Zeus and son Philammon against Phorbas-Phlegyas (p. 88), and Herakles by his brother Apollo (or Apollo by Herakles) and nephew Iolaos against Kyknos.

24. Theme 7F. The wounded Typhon fled. Both before and after Zeus's defeat Typhon fled before the god, as Apollodoros tells the story (p. 73).

The flight of the wounded Python to Tempe, pursued by Apollo, is remarkably similar (p. 20).

25. Theme 8A. Typhon temporarily overpowered Zeus and rendered him impotent by removing his sinews (p. 73): that is, he killed Zeus, whose sojourn in the Corycian Cave, where he lay completely strengthless, means death and descent to the dead (pp. 248–253).

This episode of the champion's defeat, so prominent in Apollodoros' version of the myth and dimly seen in Nonnos' version, does not appear in any extant narrative of the combat between

---

[28] AW 52; Nigid. *loc. cit.* (see p. 83, note 20). For Herakles' use of horses and chariot against Kyknos see pp. 29 f.

[29] Simon. frag. 26A Bergk; see p. 63 with note 63. For evidence of many arrows against Tityos see p. 63, note 62.

[30] Nic. *ap.* Ant. Lib. 28.2; cf. Val. Flacc. *Arg.* 4.237 f.

Apollo and Python. Yet there is evidence that Apollo too was temporarily overcome by the dragon.

The most direct testimony is found in Porphyry's *Life of Pythagoras*, where it is said that Pythagoras once went to Delphi and inscribed an elegy on Apollo's tomb, in which he said that Apollo was son of Silenos, had been killed by Python, and was buried at the so-called Tripod, which had received this name from the three daughters of Triopas who mourned for Apollo there. This strange and surprising statement is made by a late neo-Pythagorean author, though there can be no doubt that he received it from the Pythagorean tradition. But, as A. B. Cook has said, it should not be disregarded as merely a Pythagorean vagary, since the traditions of that school often contain elements of ancient lore. Cook proceeds to offer arguments which are mainly concerned with Pythagoras as Apollo's son and the analogy between his golden thigh and Pelops' ivory shoulder. There are better proofs, however, that Porphyry's testimony is essentially sound in respect to Apollo's death from Python.[31]

Most important is the Sicyonian tradition referred to in chapter iii (p. 57). After killing Python, Apollo and Artemis came to Sicyonian Aigialeia for purification; but a great terror came upon them in the place now called Phobos, and they fled to Karmanor in Crete. Then a plague fell upon Aigialeia, which afflicted it until at the instructions of seers the city sent seven boys and seven maidens to the Sythas River to propitiate the twins and persuade them to come back. They succeeded and the Sicyonians afterwards built a temple of Persuasion (Peitho) at the spot where the twins first reappeared.

Schreiber believes that two legends are here combined. In one the twins sent a plague upon Sikyon in anger and abandoned the city, but were induced to return. The other localised the Python combat in Sikyon; after killing the dragon Apollo had to go to Crete for purification, since the blood-polluted could not be purified in the land where he had killed.[32]

There can be little doubt that Schreiber is partly right. I do not

---

[31] *Vit. Pyth.* 16, ὡς δὲ πλέων (Πυθαγόρας) Δελφοῖς προσέσχε, τὸ ἐλεγεῖον τῷ τοῦ Ἀπόλλωνος τάφῳ ἐπέγραψε δι᾽ οὗ ἐδήλου ὡς Σειληνοῦ μὲν ἦν υἱὸς Ἀπόλλων, ἀνῃρέθη δὲ ὑπὸ Πύθωνος, ἐκηδεύθη δ᾽ ἐν τῷ καλουμένῳ Τρίποδι, ὃς ταύτης ἔτυχε τῆς ἐπωνυμίας διὰ τὸ τὰς τρεῖς κόρας τὰς Τριόπου θυγατέρας ἐνταῦθα θρηνῆσαι τὸν Ἀπόλλωνα. MSS of the *Vita* do not show the words δὲ ὑπὸ Πύθωνος ἐκηδεύθη, which appear in the quotation of this passage by Cyril *Contra Jul.* 10.342A. See Cook (1925) 222. That Apollo was killed and buried is also asserted by Mnaseas 16, 3.152 M, if Fulgentius can be trusted, and by Euhemeros, T 4*f*, 1.301 J; see p. 381.

[32] Schreiber (1879) 44 f.

believe, however, that he needed to assume a combination of two different myths. Rather, it seems to me, Pausanias' account shows one myth either garbled by the natives or wrongly reported. The terror (*deima*) and the subsequent flight to Crete represent Apollo's defeat by Python. The plague (*nosos*) represents the dragon's devastation and the blight upon the land. The people mourned for the fallen Apollo and performed ritual acts for his return; Apollo came back from the dead, renewed combat with the dragon, and killed him. It is very likely more than a coincidence that in Apollo's temple to which he returned were once placed, so the story went, the flutes of Marsyas, whom Pausanias also calls Silenos.[33]

In the Delphic myth, as told by Plutarch, Apollo fled to Tempe after killing Python. The Delphians were divided, he says, about the reason: some said that Apollo went to Tempe to be purified, others that he pursued the wounded and fleeing Python thither, and arrived only to find that Python had already expired.[34]

In the ritual of the Septerion which was supposed to commemorate Apollo's victory the boy who acted Apollo's part fled from Delphi with his companions after setting the dragon's hut on fire; there is no hint of a ritual killing of the dragon before this flight. The boy then wandered and underwent ritual servitude, finally receiving purification in Tempe. He thus reënacted Apollo's flight and servitude of nine years. If we set this Delphian tradition beside the Sicyonian, we can perceive that Apollo's flight and servitude do not represent expiation and purification (or not that only) in the earliest myth, but the god's defeat and death. According to Anaxandrides, Apollo had to serve Admetos after killing the dragon at Pytho. Admetos is the invincible, a form of Hades, as several scholars have recognised. Apollo's servitude means his sojourn among the dead.[35]

---

[33] Artemis' part in the myth will be clarified by oriental myths that will be studied in chapters vii–ix. The merging of the god's death with his purification will recur (pp. 198–200). See p. 57, note 42. On Marsyas-Silenos see pp. 384–386.

[34] Plut. *Mor.* 293c, οἱ μὲν γὰρ φυγεῖν ἐπὶ τῷ φόνῳ φασὶ χρῇζοντα καθαρσίων, οἱ δὲ τῷ Πύθωνι τετρωμένῳ καὶ φεύγοντι κατὰ τὴν ὁδὸν ἣν νῦν ἱερὰν καλοῦμεν ἐπακολουθεῖν, καὶ μικρὸν ἀπολειφθῆναι τῆς τελευτῆς. For the flight to Tempe see also Ael. VH 3.1; Arg. 3 to Pind. *Pyth.* For purification of Apollo in Crete or Argos see Paus. 2.7.7, 10.6.7, 10.7.2; Stat. *Theb.* 1.569 f. and Lact. Plac. *ad loc.*

[35] Plut. *Mor.* 293c, 418B, 421c; Anaxandrides 5, 3B.299 J. See Philippson (1944) 69–73. For Hades ἀδάμαστος see Il. 9.158; Croon (1952) 70. Usually Apollo's servitude to Admetos is said to be punishment for killing the Cyclopes, Zeus's smiths: Eur. *Alk.* 5–9; see pp. 325–327. But the Cyclopes are also ogres. On Apollo as herdsman Arg. 1 to Pind. *Pyth.* says, ἔρχεται τοίνυν εἰς Δελφοὺς ὁ Ἀπόλλων Πυθῶνι τὰς βοῦς νέμων (this was soon after his birth). This has been interpreted, e.g., by Schreiber, to mean that Apollo tended cattle for Python, then lord of Delphi (τότε κυριεύσαντος τοῦ προφητικοῦ τρίποδος). However, Πυθῶνι may be locative of the place-name.

In a Pindaric fragment it is said that Ge wanted to cast Apollo into Tartaros after he took possession of Delphi.[36] Another hint of Apollo's death at Python's hands occurs in the story that Philammon came with an Argive army to help Delphi against the Phlegyans and met his death in the battle. Philammon was Apollo's son in legend, and the traditions of his musical skill and of his instituting choral dances at Delphi and maidens' choruses in general suggest that he was a form of Apollo himself.[37] Again, Phlegyas' burning of Apollo's temple was probably suggested by a play on his name and substituted for the god's defeat.

In the story of Sybaris we notice that Apollo appeased the Lamia (Th. 7c) during her depredations, and that the beautiful youth Alkyoneus narrowly escaped death from her; in Eurybatos' invasion of her cave we see a pale reflection of descent to the lower world.[38] Herakles as champion fled at first from Kyknos, according to Stesichoros and Pindar (p. 30); he later returned to vanquish him.

In a strange story of the sort called Euhemeristic, Herakles, while pursuing Acheloos, who had fled on horseback, was wounded in the breast by an arrow that Acheloos shot from his bow. Then Herakles' arrow hit Acheloos as he was crossing the stream called Phorbas, into which he fell, thus changing its name to Acheloos. Herakles died a few days later from his wound. In the usual accounts the river and the river god, Herakles' enemy, were always one and always called Acheloos. Here we learn that Phorbas was also a name of this river, which flowed through northwestern Greece, where we have already encountered a Phorbas who attacked Demeter and fought the hero Erechtheus (pp. 58 f.). So Acheloos and Phorbas appear to be two names of one river god, who in this version of the tale dealt Herakles a mortal wound in combat.[39]

It is apparent, therefore, that the theme of the champion's defeat and death had its place in the Python myth and that Porphyry's tes-

---

[36] Frag. 261 Bowra: the verb is ταρταρῶσαι, which may mean simply *kill*.

[37] Pherek. 120, 1.92 J; Paus. 9.36.2 (his death), 10.7.2; Ovid *Met.* 11.316 f.; Hyg. *Fab.* 161, 200.1; Herakl. *ap.* Plut. *Mor.* 1132A. Philammon's son Thamyris also suggests Apollo in his great musical skill and youthful beauty: Apollod. 1.3.3.

[38] See pp. 44 f. Notice that *Alkyoneus* is the masculine form of Alkyone, wife of Keyx, who represented herself as Hera: Apollod. 1.7.4.

[39] Kedalion 7, 2.445 J. Notice too that there was an Admetos son of Augeias, therefore grandson of Phorbas: Paus. 10.25.5. In Kedalion's story Herakles has also the name Polyphemos, which means an identification of H. with the Argonaut Polyphemos, who also loved Hylas, searched for him, and stayed behind: Apollod. 1.9.19; Schol. Vet. on Apollon. *Arg.* 1.1207. Hylas was a Dryopian, son of Theiodamas, taken captive by Herakles when he defeated the Dryopes: Schol. Vet. on Apollon. *Arg.* 1.1212; *App. Narr.* 28.6, p. 371 West.

timony can be accepted. If Apollo was killed by Python, obviously he came back to life and renewed the battle. The only hints of how his return came about are the supplications of the Sicyonians to secure Apollo's return and the mourning of Triopas' daughters. These allusions to supplication and mourning suggest some sort of ritual that helped to bring Apollo back to life.

26. Theme 9. Typhon was tricked by means of food. The Moirai induced him to eat of the ephemeral fruits, telling him that they would increase his strength (p. 74). But in spite of his throwing whole mountains immediately afterward, they apparently had the opposite effect, enabling Zeus at last to overcome him. In Oppian's version it was Pan, whom Hermes had taught the fisherman's art, who lured Typhon forth by cooking fish upon the shore.

We noticed that in the Python myths Laogoras was feasting with his sons in a precinct of Apollo when Herakles came upon him and killed him, and that the feast theme was also present in the Koronos legend (p. 38). Again, Herakles' eating of Theiodamas' ox reflects the episode of a meal enjoyed by Herakles at the house of the enemy king, as will be evident later (p. 113), although it is apparent that Herakles' notorious voracity captured the feast scene in the Lapith-Dryopian story.[40]

Typhon was also tricked by disguise. Kadmos, dressed as a herdsman by Pan, beguiled Typhon on the shepherd's pipe, so that Zeus could recover his weapons (p. 75). Eros too helped Zeus on this occasion by putting into Typhon's soul a readiness to be charmed by Kadmos' music. Pan was again the trickster in the Greco-Egyptian form of the myth of Typhon-Set: it was he who advised the gods to assume animal forms (p. 75).

In the Phorbas legend Apollo met Phorbas as if he were just another traveler on the road whose fate would be to box with Phorbas and so meet his death. Phorbas, it is plain, did not recognise a great god in his opponent. Undoubtedly this is an earlier form of the Kyknos story too: he did not realise that the man he took for just another victim had a power greater than human. So, though the tricking of the dragon disappeared from the Python story proper, as far as we know, it clung to the Lapith-Dryopian offshoots of the myth.

---

[40] The Theiodamas and Koronos tales are clarified by the story of Syleus (p. 112).

27. Theme 10A. As the story is usually told Typhon was punished by having a volcano placed upon him—Etna or one of the Lipari group (Python 18, p. 64). In being sent underground and pinned beneath a mountain he was considered to have been cast down to Tartaros like the Titans and Gigantes: e.g., Horace includes him among those giants whom Zeus's thunderbolt hurled down into Orcus.[41]

28. Theme 10B. Zeus exulted over the fallen Typhon and taunted him. His victory was celebrated with notes of salpinx and dance.[42]

Apollo made a taunting speech of triumph over the fallen dragoness in the Homeric Hymn. The fifth part of the Pythian nome, the *katachoreusis,* represented his dance of victory. His victory was cheered by the Delphians, Corycian nymphs, and his mother Leto, with the *paianismos,* cries of *Hie Paian,* and the singing of the paean.[43]

The foregoing comparison shows twenty-eight features shared by the Typhon and Python myths. Of these, 1, 3, 4, 7, 8, 11, 12–17, 19, 21, 25–27 are especially significant correspondences.

So alike are the two dragons in most respects that no surprise need be occasioned when Ampelius uses the name Python instead of Typhon for the dragon who was born in a cave on Tauros and who pursued the gods to Egypt. Typhon and Tityos are several times named together as sons of Ge, as associates of Gigantes, or as troublemakers. Of greater significance than confusion of similar monsters or the obvious linking of two of them together is the appearance of both Apollo and Herakles as opponents of Typhon.[44]

Apollo killed Typhoeus in the Gigantomachy, according to Sidonius Apollinaris; Zeus killed Enkelados. As early as Herodotos, Apollo was identified with Horos, who fought and killed Typhon-Set after the latter had killed his father Osiris. According

---

[41] Hor. *Carm.* 3.4.53, 73–76; Sen. *Thy.* 805–809. Teipel (1922) does not see that Typhon in Tartaros and Typhon under Etna mean the same thing.

[42] Nonn. *Dion.* 2.557–636.

[43] Hom. Hymn 3.363–369; Poll. *Onom.* 4.84; Ephor. 31*b*, 2.53 J; Call. *Hymn* 2.97–104; Apollon. *Arg.* 2.711–713; Klearchos 46, 2.318 M; Claud. 2.11–13; Lact. Plac. *Theb.* 8.224; Schol. on Lucan *BC* 5.82; cf. Aristoxenos *ap.* ps.-Plut. *Mor.* 1136c.

[44] Ampel. 2.10. Typhon and Tityos linked: Sen. *loc. cit.*; Lucan *BC.* 4.595 f.; Plut. *Mor.* 945B; Nonn. *Dion.* 48.394–396.

to Nigidius, Apollo killed Typhon with a thunderbolt in a temple in Memphis. It is noteworthy that Apollo-Horos lost an eye to Typhon in this combat. It is true that this is Egyptian rather than Greek myth, but it is important to notice that by the fifth century B.C. Apollo had been identified with the slayer of Set, while Set had been equated with Typhon. This may mean that before the fifth century some Greeks, if not all, called Apollo's opponent Typhon. This conjecture will be strengthened by other evidence (pp. 95, 252).[45]

Herakles too faced Typhon and suffered death at his hands. He was revived by Iolaos, who applied a quail to his nostrils. This was the so-called Phoenician Herakles (= Melqart); but his relation to the Greek Herakles is much closer than mere identification would indicate (pp. 321–323). At any rate Typhon is sometimes numbered among the enemies of the Greek Herakles: e.g., Euripides' Herakles says that he has faced three-bodied Typhons.[46]

So, on the one hand, Apollo or Herakles appears instead of Zeus as champion against Typhon; on the other, Zeus appears instead of Apollo against Tityos (p. 23), stands behind Apollo against Phorbas-Phlegyas, and behind Herakles against Kyknos (p. 61). Taking all the evidence together we can see that the several myths of Zeus against Typhon, Apollo against Python or Tityos or Phorbas, and Herakles against Kyknos and other opponents, are variants of one original myth of god against dragon.

If it is true that these myths have a common origin, it is possible also that the names Typhon and Python are variants of a single name. Assuming that *Typhon* is the earlier name, one may conjecture the process by which the change to *Python* came about: there occurred a metathesis of mutes, dental-vowel-labial to labial-vowel-dental, the initial consonant remaining unaspirated, the final remaining aspirated, i.e., ΤΥΦ > ΠΥΘ. This change

---

[45] Sid. Ap. *Carm.* 6.27; this may be based, however, on Pind. *Pyth.* 8.18, where Zeus and Apollo together are named as killers of Typhos and Porphyrion; but Vian (1952:197) is probably right in saying that in reality Pindar considered Zeus the vanquisher of both. Apollo-Horos: Herod. 2.144.2, 156.4; Plut. *Mor.* 373BC; Nigid. *ap.* Schol. S *in* Germ. *Arat.* 289; cf. Diod. 1.13.4. See pp. 193, 391.

[46] Eudox. *ap.* Athen. 9.392DE; Eur. *Her.* 1271 f.; cf. Virg. *Aen.* 8.298 f., Plut. *Mor.* 341E. Loyen (1940) shows that Virgil meant a real combat between Herakles and Typhon.

was assisted perhaps by a desire to assimilate the dragon's name to the place name Pytho.

It may be objected to this suggestion that *Pythôn* (Πύθων) is accented differently from *Typhôn* (Τυφῶν, Τυφών, Τυφώς). But the place name in the form Πυθών (see p. 87, note 35) has final accent. No statement can be made with certainty about the relation between place name and dragon name, but a connection between the place name *Pytho(n)* and the dragon's name *Python* was certainly assumed in antiquity. The shift of accent may be due to the folk etymology: the dragon was ὁ πύθων, he whose rotting corpse gave the place its name. The etymology could not affect the place name, however, which was already established with final accent. Again, there is some evidence for the accenting of Typhon's name on the first syllable.[47]

As already pointed out, Typhon's name is also found in the forms, *Typhāôn*, *Typhôeus* (Τυφάων, Τυφώευς). It is probable that forms *Pythāôn* and *Pythôeus* (Πυθάων, Πυθώευς) were once used beside *Pythôn;* but I have found no instance recorded. Yet Apollo had a son called Pythaeus (Πυθαεύς), a Delphian who founded the Pythian Apollo's cult and oracle in Argos, and an epithet of the same form, a variant of the usual *Pythios*.[48]

---

[47] See Hesych. T1707, Τύφω, defined as one of the Gigantes; I can also point to Τύφων as a man's name: Paus. 6.3.12. For final acute Τυφών see EM 772 (as name of storm wind) and P-B s.v.

[48] It may be that Tityos is another form of the name Python-Typhon. Perhaps more than an analogy may be seen in the name of the Pisidian city Tityassos, which may be the Pityassos of Strabo 12.7.2, p. 570. According to W. M. Ramsay (1926: 102, 104), variation between initial P and T through TW is characteristic of Anatolian words. He points also to *Perseus* as the hero-founder of *Tarsos* (*Tersos*); see p. 279 below. Since Pisidia lies next to Cilicia, and *Titys* occurs as a variant of *Tityos* upon a vase inscription (AW 28; cf. Tityas in AW 29, fig. 6), this may have been the city of Tityos = Python = Typhon. There was a Titiopolis or Tityopolis in nearby Isauria: see Ramsay (1890) 370; Sundwall (1913) 208; BMCC, Lycaonia, Isauria, Cilicia lx f.; RE 6a.1553; while a Pitaoupolis is attested for Caria (Sundwall 181). But Sundwall's study of Lycian names does not support Ramsay's statement; for in *Tityassos* he sees **tiθθu-wa-(a)za,* while in Pityassos he sees **pita-wa-(a)za* (*ibid.* 209, 181); and he refers *Pitênos, Titênos,* and *Touitênos* to entirely different words (*ibid.* 181, 208, 223). Notice the second consonant in the Lycian form of *Tityassos.* On the city see Ramsay (1890) 408 f.

The form *Tityon* is found in some late Latin authors as a nominative: Lact. Plac. *Theb.* 11.12; Isid. *Etym.* 11.3.7. The nature of these sources would lead one to infer that *Tityon* as a nominative arose from mistaking the accusative *Tityon* in a commentator's lemma for nominative; and the source of the error may be Lact. Plac. *Theb.* 4.538. But ps.-Clem. Rom. *Recogn.* 10.23 has accusative *Tityonem.* AW 20 (fig. 4) has ΤΙΤΤΟΣ, not ΤΙΤΤΟΝ, as once thought. For accent Τίτυος see Men. Rhet., p. 441 Sp.

Notice that *Parnassos* has the variants *Ternesos* and *Larnassos*, according to Eust.

Now that I have made clear the numerous points at which the Typhon and Python myths coincide, we can turn back to the Homeric Hymn to Apollo and see that in the seventh century Python was called Typhon in the Delphic myth: for the dragoness's fosterchild Typhaon was obviously Python himself. In the Hymn, Apollo fought the dragoness. Did he also fight the dragon in the underlying myth? Or has the poet allowed the dragoness to usurp Typhon-Python's place in the combat? To answer these questions requires a study of the dragoness.

---

on Od. 19.466, p. 1872; Steph. Byz. 338 Holst.; Schol. Vet. on Apollon. *Arg.* 2.711; Herodian I 209 Lentz. Eustathios says that the people of the region called it Ternesos in his time (1100 A.D.); but they call it Parnassos today. It is a pre-Hellenic name, also found in Anatolia (p. 408). Notice Pisidian *Termessos* and *Tarbassos*, Boeotian *Permessos* (also called *Termessos*, Paus. 9.29.5), Trojan *Lyrnessos*, Carian-Lycian *Telmessos*. Sundwall's studies forbid deriving them from a common original; yet Parnassos and its two attested variants are very similar to these names. Also it is an interesting coincidence that all these names are found in the same regions as Python, Typhon, and Tityos, and that Parnassos is prominent in the story. Notice too that *Panopeus* has a variant *Phanoteus* (Strabo 9.3.14, p. 423).

VI

DRAGONESS AND LAMIA

Delphyne the dragoness guarded the Corycian Cave of Cilicia for Typhon. The Delphian dragoness who nursed Typhon and fought Apollo is called Delphyne by later writers, though the Homeric Hymn leaves her nameless. Moreover in Apollonios' account it was when Apollo had fought Delphyne that the Corycian nymphs of Parnassos cheered his victory, an indication (p. 78) that the combat was sometimes located near the Corycian Cave above Delphi. In this presence of a dragoness Delphyne and of a Corycian Cave in both myths we see the most remarkable correspondence between them.

Now who was Delphyne? What was her relation to Typhon? In both myths she is called *drakaina,* and Apollodoros adds that she was half beast (ἡμίϑηρ). She was Typhon's nurse in the Hymn and no less wicked than he was. In Apollodoros' narrative nothing more is said than that Typhon set her to watch over Zeus's severed sinews in the Corycian Cave.[1]

ECHIDNA, KETO

From Hesiod and Apollodoros we learn that Typhon had a wife, the monstrous Echidna, by whom he became father of mon-

---

[1] *Beast* is not an especially good translation of θήρ, which covers reptiles and fish as well as quadrupeds, but it is the conventional translation and I can find no better word. *Animal* will not do here, nor will *creature* or *brute.*

strous progeny: Chimaira, Hydra, Orthos, and several others. According to Hesiod she was unlike either mortal men or immortal gods, just what the Hymn says of her mate Typhaon; she was half nymph (i.e., young woman), with bright eyes and fair cheeks, and half snake, dwelling in the depths of earth, eating raw meat. The gods gave her a cave to live in far from themselves and men (near black night, says Quintus of Smyrna); yet she lived among the Arimoi, i.e., in the Cilician Cave. She was immortal and ageless. Hesiod differs from Apollodoros and Hyginus in saying that she bore Sphinx and the Nemean lion to her son Orthos, not to Typhon.[2]

Hesiod doesn't make clear whether Echidna's parents were Phorkys and Keto or Chrysaor and Kallirrhoe; but it is fairly certain that he means the former. Apollodoros agrees with Olympiodoros that she was daughter of Tartaros and Ge; therefore she was Typhon-Python's sister. Epimenides of Crete said that her parents were Peiras and Styx.[3]

It is at once obvious that Echidna and Delphyne are very much alike. (1) Both were of mixed form, upper part woman and lower part snake: for that is plainly Apollodoros' meaning in calling Delphyne at once dragoness and half-beast. (2) Both lived in a Corycian Cave with Typhon. (3) Both were called daughters of Ge (p. 78). (4) Echidna, like Delphyne, killed all men who came her way, as Apollodoros tells us; though it was Argos Panoptes who killed her in an Argive legend in which Argos has the heroic role of Zeus, Apollo, or Herakles.[4]

Yet it seems probable that in Phrygian Hierapolis, where Apollo had an oracle, his dragoness opponent was called Echidna; for coins of the city show that Apollo's dragon combat was localised there. This fact Leo Weber links with the testimony of the

---

[2] Hes. *Theog.* 295–332; Apollod. 2.3.1; 2.5.1, 10 f.; 3.5.8; Hyg. *Fab.* 151.1, praef. 39; *Astr.* 2.15; Val. Flacc. *Arg.* 4.428, 516; Quint. Smyrn. 6.261 f. In one source or another Typhon and Echidna are parents of Orthos, Kerberos, Hydra, Chimaira, Nemean lion, Hesperidean snake, Prometheus' eagle, Sphinx, Gorgon, Colchian snake, Skylla, Harpies. *Theog.* 304 has ἔρυτ(ο), which may be middle voice, "she guarded," or passive "she was confined." Lyk. 1353 f. places her cave by a lake in Lydia. The common noun *echidna* means *viper*, also called *echis*; see Douglas (1928ʙ) 117–120.

[3] Apollod. 2.1.2; Olymp. on *Phaed.* 201, 240 Norv.; Epimen. *ap.* Paus. 8.18.2.

[4] Apollod. 2.1.2, τοὺς παριόντας συνήρπαζεν, with which compare Hom. Hymn 3.356, quoted p. 59 above. In the above comparison occur Ths. 1ᴀ, 1ᴄ, 2ᴀ, 2ʙ, 3ʙ, 4ᴀ, 4ꜰ. On Argos Panoptes as doublet of Herakles see Bayet (1923) 30.

apocryphal *Acta Philippi:* that the pagan Hierapolitans worshipped Echidna and her entourage of snakes, called her sons. In
this Christian legend Saint Philip has ousted Apollo.[5]

Clearly Echidna and Delphyne are two names for the same
monstrous sister-wife of Typhon. That she was also called Keto
is evident from the following considerations. (1) Though Hesiod
calls Keto Echidna's mother, she was Typhon's wife, according to
Euphorion, and bore him many children. (2) Phorkys and Keto
alternate with Typhon and Echidna as parents of the Gorgons
and the Hesperidean snake. (3) Keto was daughter of Ge. (4) Her
name is formed from *kêtos,* a big fish or sea monster, a form that
the dragon of legend often takes. (5) Her husband Phorkys was
also an old sea deity or sea monster, and a son of Ge.[6]

Phorkys is sometimes called father of Skylla, whose mother was
Krataiis or Hekate; Hyginus says that Skylla's parents were Typhon and Echidna; and according to Hesiod, as cited by the
Scholiast on Apollonios, her parents were Phorbas and Hekate.
Some scholars have thought *Phorbas* a mistake for *Phorkys,*
though the Scholiast definitely places Hesiod's testimony against
that of other authorities, among whom is Akusilaos, who say
Phorkys and Hekate. And Phorbas can be accepted as a name of
Skylla's father, since it is an alternative name of Typhon-Python,
as we have seen, and since Typhon alternates with Phorkys as
father of Skylla. In Deimos, also named father of Skylla, we see
Ares-Kyknos.[7]

So Echidna, Delphyne, and Keto are different names for the

---

[5] See Weber (1910) 201–221, and AW 9; also citations on p. 79, note 8. Notice that
Nonnos (*Dion.* 4.318) calls the Delphian serpent "Cirrhaean echidna."

[6] Hes. *Theog.* 237 f., 274 f., 333–336; Euphor. *ap.* EM 396; Apollod. 1.2.6, 2.4.2;
Hyg. *Fab.* praef. 9; see note 2. Pontos was mate of Ge as mother of Phorkys and Keto.
On the various applications of *kêtos* to sea creatures see D. Thompson (1947) 114,
Douglas (1928b) 151.

[7] Phorkys: Akusilaos 42, 1.57 J: Apollon. *Arg.* 4.828 f.; Schol. Vet. on Plat. *Rep.*
588c; Apollod. *Epit.* 7.20; Serv. Aen. 3.420; Schol. on Od. 12.85. Krataiis is another
name of Hekate according to Apollon. *loc. cit.* and Schol. on Od. 12.124. Typhon: Hyg.
Fab. 125.14, 151.1, praef. 39. Phorbas and Hekate: Hes. frag. 150 Rz., *ap.* Schol. Vet. *in*
Apollon. *Arg.* 4.828; for doubts about Phorbas see LM 4.1031. We have already seen
Phorbas as another name for the river Acheloos (p. 88). Deimos: Semos 22, 3b.289 J:
Triton and Hekate were parents of Krataiis, who with Deimos as father bore Skylla. In
Shield 195 f., 462–466, Deimos and Phobos stand beside Ares and Kyknos and drive Ares'
chariot. See p. 329.

same monstrous snake woman or sea monster; she has, moreover, some relation to Hekate, though we cannot yet see precisely what. Typhon and Phorkys are both named as her mate, and it is likely that Phorkys is Typhon as creature of the sea (pp. 142 f.).

SKYLLA

Skylla herself seems to be another form of Echidna-Delphyne. (1) She too was a mixed creature, often represented as a woman from the waist up, a fish below; she had once been a beautiful woman whom Circe or Amphitrite thus transformed. As the Odyssey describes her, she had twelve legs and six terrible heads. (2) She lived in a cave which was just opposite Etna, under which the defeated Typhon lay. (3) She seized sailors who passed through the straits of Messina, and (4) she killed and ate them.[8]

She also came into conflict with Herakles as one of several cattle rustlers who bothered the hero on his way back from Erytheia (p. 338). When Herakles, driving Geryon's cattle, reached the straits of Messina, Skylla carried off some of his herd; he killed her, but her father Phorkys brought her back to life with fire.[9]

This legend is obviously a doublet of the Cacus story (p. 339). Also, except for its conclusion, it has a striking parallel in a story told by Herodotos. There too Herakles was returning from Erytheia, driving Geryon's cattle, but through Scythia rather than Italy. Winter overtook him as he journeyed, so that he went into hibernation under his lionskin, leaving his chariot horses to graze. When he awoke, his horses had disappeared. Searching for them, he came upon a creature that Herodotos calls *echidna*, a woman above her loins but a snake below ($\mu\epsilon\iota\xi\omicron\pi\acute{\alpha}\rho\vartheta\epsilon\nu\acute{o}\nu$ $\tau\iota\nu\alpha$ $\check{\epsilon}\chi\iota\delta\nu\alpha\nu$ $\delta\iota\phi\upsilon\acute{\epsilon}\alpha$), who lived in a cave. Herakles asked her if she had seen his horses; she told him that she had them and would give them back to him if he would tarry there and lie with her. This Herakles did, be-

---

[8] (1) Od. 12.89–92; Apollod. *Epit.* 7.20; Ovid *Met.* 14.51–67; Hyg. *Fab.* 125.14, 151.1; Schol. Vet. on Lyk. 46. See the art works listed in LM 4.1035–1064. Notice Themes 2A, 2B, 2E, 3B, 3C, 4D, 4F. She is described in Od. 12.87 f. as πέλωρ κακόν, whom nobody would rejoice to look upon (Th. 4A); 12.92, her teeth were full of black death (see p. 99, note 13). The Schol. on Od. 12.85 adds that her size was marvelously huge and that she had fiery eyes (Ths. 3A, 3D).

[9] Schol. Vet. on Lyk. 46; Dionysios 12, 1.180 J. Her resurrection was probably introduced to reconcile this legend with Od. 12.

getting three sons upon her: Agathyrsos, Gelonos, and Skythes, eponymous ancestors of three peoples of the steppes.[10]

In this story Herakles takes Zeus's place; that is, he is identified with the Scythian father god, whom Diodoros calls Zeus in a story which he ascribes to the Scythians themselves. In the Scythian land appeared an earth-born maiden ($\gamma\eta\gamma\epsilon\nu\hat{\eta}$ $\pi\alpha\rho\vartheta\acute{\epsilon}\nu o\nu$), who was in her upper body a woman, in her lower body an *echidna*. Zeus mated with her and produced Skythes. This is Herodotos' Herakles story, omitting the theft of horses, and it connects that story with another which Herodotos tells. Targitaos, first Scythian, was son of Zeus and of a daughter of the river god Borysthenes (Dnieper). He had three sons, the youngest of whom became king of all Scythians, since only he could safely approach four golden objects sent down from heaven—when his older brothers approached them fire flamed forth—just as Skythes, youngest of the three sons of Herakles (i.e., last born of triplets), alone could bend Herakles' bow and put on his belt, and so become founder of the Scythian nation and ancestor of its kings.[11]

Herakles appears as ancestor of the Kelts in a variant of the same story. Again, he was on his way home with Geryon's herd and stopped in Gaul, at Bretannos' house, where his host's daughter, Keltine or Kelto, hid the cattle and would not give them back until Herakles lay with her. This he was very willing to do, both because he wanted to recover the herd and because the maid was beautiful. He then left a bow with her, as in Herodotos' Scythian tale, instructing her that if a son should be born to her and on growing up should be able to bend the bow, he should be made king. Keltos, their son, successfully drew the bow.[12]

As Maass points out, there is an inconsistency in the story: if Kelto was beautiful, she had no need to hide the herd in order

---

[10] Herod. 4.8 f. Here the Herakles legend meets the sleeping-bear myth; see Carpenter (1946) 112–156. Notice that the snake woman drives off his horses, not Geryon's cattle as in the Cacus, Skylla, and other variants. This points to variants in which the *cattle* were horses and to an original identity of Geryon's cattle and Diomedes' horses.

[11] Herod. 4.5; Diod. 2.43.

[12] The whole story must be put together from Parth. 30, EM 502, and Diod. 5.24. Maass (1906: 159–164) believes that the story of Herakles-Kelto preceded that of Herakles-Echidna, but I can hardly believe that that is true. According to Diodoros, the woman was a beautiful giantess who bore a son Galates to Herakles.

to induce Herakles to gratify her; only if she was hideous was a ruse necessary. But we need not suppose an inept narrator: the inconsistency is resolved if we suppose that Kelto was a snake-woman like the Scythian *echidna* in the cognate story. As hider of Geryon's cattle from the returning Herakles she is Skylla, beautiful in her womanly upper body, but monstrous in her lower body. Kelto's very name may unite her to Skylla and the evil creatures of the sea; for it may be the name *Kêtô*, suited to a legend of the origin of the Kelts (Κητώ > Κελτώ). Notice that her Scythian counterpart as daughter of Borysthenes was a water nymph.[13]

It was in the same western world that Herakles, when he was still on his way to fetch Geryon's cattle, met Pyrene, who conceived and bore a snake after sexual union with him (p. 49). Höfer is justified in seeing a likeness between her and Kelto. Pyrene is also the name of the mother of Lykaon-Kyknos and likewise of Diomedes. For Diomedes' parents are said to be Ares and Kyrene; and *Kyrênê* is almost certainly, as Höfer shows, a variant or corruption of *Pyrênê*. Diomedes is a doublet of Geryon (see p. 98, note 10), a ferocious and wicked keeper of herds near the ends of the earth—to earlier Greeks Thrace meant the distant north, as Scythia to later Greeks. Höfer points also to Kyrene, mother of another opponent of Herakles, one who also appears in the series of brigands who wished to rob him of Geryon's cattle. This was Lakinios of Croton; a different version says that he refused to receive Herakles, not that he stole cattle (compare Amyntor, pp. 42 f.).[14]

It seems, then, that the same themes and names constantly recur throughout the cluster of stories that group themselves about Herakles' eighth and tenth labors, the horses of Diomedes and the kine of Geryon. In some tales the hero encountered a male monster or brigand, in others a female monster. We shall

---

[13] Monsters in fish form and those in snake form are much alike in folklore and art. See Maass (1906) 160: Griechen und manche Nichtgriechen pflegen sich die autochthonen Wesen ihres Glaubens schlangenfüssig, wie die autothalassen fischfüssig, vorzustellen. For the various forms of fish-tailed monster see Shepard (1940), especially 10–50.

[14] Höfer, LM 3.3341–3345. Diomedes: Apollod. 2.5.8. Thrace = far north: Fontenrose (1943) 282. Lakinios: Diod. 4.24.7; Serv. *Aen.* 3.552. See Croon (1952) 13–66.

come back later to the several forms of his male opponent; here we are concerned mainly with the woman.[15]

LAMIA

Stesichoros called Skylla's mother Lamia, giving that name to the figure whom other poets (of whom only Homer and Hesiod are earlier than he) called Hekate or Echidna. We have noticed Lamia-Sybaris at Delphi; but the commonest legend of Lamia places her in Libya.[16]

In Libya there once lived a beautiful queen. Since Zeus loved her and made her his mistress, she aroused Hera's jealousy and hatred. In consequence Hera destroyed every child that was born to Lamia, until from great grief she turned ugly in body and soul. Because she envied other women their children, she went about seizing infants and killing them. Some say that she tore them to pieces or ate them. Finally she became literally a beast and went to live in a cave. Hera sent insomnia upon her too, but Zeus in pity granted her the power to remove her eyes, which she placed in a basket when she wanted to sleep.[17]

Sybaris, like the Libyan Lamia, was a beast who lived in a cave and went about seizing men and animals (τὰ θρέμματα καὶ τοὺς ἀνθρώπους). The word *thremmata,* which I have translated *animals,* meant originally the young of animals, including human beings; later it became pretty much the equivalent of *creatures.* In any case, since Alkyoneus, who was to be sacrificed to Sybaris, was a *kouros,* a teen-age boy, there can be little doubt that she attacked the young especially.[18]

The tale of Gerana is obviously a variant of the story of the Libyan Lamia. Gerana, also called Oinoe, queen of the Pygmies, became so proud and arrogant because of her great beauty that she refused to honor any goddess. Hera, offended on that account

---

[15] The two Herakles legends show Ths. 1c, 2ʙ, 3ᴀ, 3ʙ, 3c, 4ᴀ, 7ᴀ. Herakles' *echidna* lived in a cave in Scythia, Typhon's Echidna in a cave near black Night, far from gods and men (p. 95); that is, Echidna's cave, when not specifically located in Cilicia or elsewhere, is placed at the ends of the earth. For Scythia as a land of night see Fontenrose (1943) 281.

[16] Stes. *ap.* Schol. *in* Apollon. *Arg.* 4.828 *et in Od.* 12.124.

[17] Duris 17, 2.143 J; Diod. 20.41.3–6; Herakleitos, *Incred.* 34; Schol. Vet. on Aristoph. *Pax* 758; Schol. on Aristid. *Or.* 13, p. 102 J; Isid. *Etym.* 8.11.102. The Libyan Lamia was known to Euripides, who is quoted by Diod. *loc. cit.*

[18] See LSJ s.v. θρέμμα. Probably Nicander, whose narrative Antoninus epitomises, clearly specified the young of men and beasts.

and because Gerana's subjects began to worship their queen instead of the goddesses, changed her into an ugly bird, the crane (*geranos*). Since this transformation caused Gerana to lose her son Mopsos, she kept flitting about the Pygmies' houses, longing for him. The annoyed Pygmies drove her away, thus bringing upon themselves her hostility and that eternal war of cranes against Pygmies which was already part of Greek folklore in Homer's time.[19]

Gerana, like Lamia, was a beautiful African queen who incurred Hera's wrath by becoming her rival; she too was transformed into an animal, lost her children, and grieved for them, thus becoming embittered against men so that she thereafter attacked and killed them.

The identification of Gerana with Lamia is strengthened by Boio's introduction to her legend, as reported by Athenaeus: Kyknos was transformed into a bird by his father Ares and flew to the Sybaris River, where he copulated with a crane that had been a distinguished woman among the Pygmies—then the narrative as told above. The conjunction of Kyknos, Sybaris, and Gerana is striking. Gerana, as mate of Kyknos, lived on the Italian river called Sybaris, on which was situated the city of that name. According to Nicander, the Locrians who colonised Sybaris named the city after the spring below Delphi into which Lamia-Sybaris had been transformed. Though Nicander's statement cannot be accepted as historical fact, since the Locrians did not found Sybaris, yet the Delphian spring, hard by the border of Ozolian Lokris, and the Italian city, neighbor of a Locrian colony, Epizephyrian Lokroi, undoubtedly have the same name, and the legendary connection was at some time established between them.[20]

Another link between Italian Sybaris and Lamia is seen in the tale of Heros of Temesa and his combat with Euthymos the Locrian, an Olympic victor of the early fifth century: the supposed

---

[19] Boio *ap*. Ant. Lib. 16 *et ap*. Ath. 9.393EF, Ael. NA 15.29. See also Ovid *Met*. 6.90–92, whence one gathers that Gerana challenged Hera to a beauty contest, and Iliad 3.3–7. Apparently Gerana also had a daughter Chelone, who became a tortoise; see Boio *ap*. Ath. On the tale and sources see Knaack (1880) 4–9.

[20] Nic. *ap*. Ant. Lib. 8.7. Notice the obscure allusion of ps.-Clem. Rom. *Recogn*. 10.22 to a story in which Zeus took the form of a hoopoe to mate with Lamia.

date of the event is the seventy-seventh Olympiad (472 B.C.). The story was known to Callimachus two centuries later, but can be traced no farther back. It must have been current for some time before Callimachus in order to have become a subject of his verse: probably it achieved its known form before 350. It is an interesting example of legend growth: Euthymos, a real person, has become a son of the river god Kaikinos. Either he vanished from earth like Aeneas at his life's end, disappearing into his paternal river, or he cheated death like Sisyphos and returned to live among men: Pausanias had heard from a trader that he was still living in his time.[21]

Pausanias' story is that Polites, one of Odysseus' crew, had been stoned to death by the people of Temesa for violating a maiden of the town. Thereafter Polites' ghost (*daimôn*) avenged his death by going about without cease and killing townspeople of all ages. Finally the Temesians, having decided to move away, consulted the Delphic oracle. The Pythia, however, would not let them leave Temesa, but instructed them to set apart a temenos and build a temple in Polites' honor, and to offer him every year the most beautiful maiden in Temesa. This was done, and Polites, thereafter called *Hêrôs* (Hero: he was also called Alybas), ceased his murderous raids. One day Euthymos came to Temesa from Locri at the time of the annual sacrifice. When he saw the intended victim he fell in love with her and decided to rescue her. So he entered the tomb (*hêrôon*) of Heros, fought him successfully, and chased him from the land into the sea, where he disappeared. Then Euthymos married the girl.

This is exactly the story of Eurybatos and Sybaris except that monster and victim have exchanged sexes: it is now a male demon and a female victim. The two legends have in common (1) the marauding and murdering demon, (2) the desire of the people to move elsewhere, (3) their consultation of the Delphic oracle, (4) the Delphic Apollo's instruction to appease the demon by sacrifice of a beautiful human victim, (5) the fortunate arrival of

---

[21] Call. frags. 98–99 Pf.; Paus. 6.6.7–11; Strabo 6.1.5, p. 255; Ael. VH 8.18; Suid. E3510. See Rohde (1925) 154, note 115, on the remarkable likeness between this story and that of the Delphian Lamia; oddly enough, in spite of the identity of plot and the recurrence of the names Sybaris and Lokris, he would have them spontaneous and independent creations of the local folk imagination.

a hero, who falls in love with the victim, (6) the hero's invasion of the demon's lair, and (7) his victory over the demon, who (8) disappears in water: we should not fail to notice that Heros descended into the sea in Pausanias' version. Furthermore Temesa lies between Locri and Sybaris, though on the upper side of Italy's toe; Euthymos was a Locrian; and a youth called Sybaris appeared in a painting, a copy of which Pausanias saw, that also showed Heros of Temesa (see Addendum, pp. 119 f.).

Aelian's narrative differs in several respects: the demon exacted money or treasures (Th. 4ʙ) rather than a young woman; it was the hero Euthymos who vanished into water, his father Kaikinos' stream, at the end of his days; the *hêrôs* of Temesa was Euthymos. Probably the story had its beginning in the displacing of one local hero cult by another, an incident of wars between cities or peoples of southern Italy. In different circumstances Euthymos might have been the marauding demon's name; in any case we have here another instance of the ease with which a theme can change its narrative position and its meaning from one version of a story to another.[22]

Perhaps near Italian Sybaris, if anywhere, was the Italian town of Lamia, which is mentioned by the Scholiast on Aristophanes, who probably took his narrative from Duris (see p. 100, note 17). It was named, he says, after the Libyan Lamia, whom Zeus had taken to Italy. Nowhere else is an Italian city of that name mentioned, so far as I know. Duris or the Scholiast probably meant the city of the Laistrygones, where Lamos ruled and which is sometimes called Lamos, variously located in Sicily or the Italian peninsula. According to another source, Lamia was queen of the Laistrygones. This brings us again to Herakles' journey to fetch Geryon's cattle; the hero had to fight the Laistrygones in the course of that adventure.[23]

Not far from Sybaris lived Skylla. We can see now that it was

---

[22] The demon took the victim as his mistress, according to Call. *loc. cit.*; the story throws light upon Sybaris' desire for a beautiful young man; compare the relation of Empusa and male victim (pp. 116, 257). But Strabo agrees with Aelian on the nature of the demon's exactions. Compare Alybas-Heros as tribute exacter with Erginos and Eurytos (pp. 42, 43, note 27). On the displacing of Alybas by Euthymos see Maass (1907) 39–53.

[23] Italian Lamia: Schol. Vet. on Aristoph. *Pax* 758. Laistrygon Lamos and Lamia: Schol. on Od. 10.81; Schol. Vet. on Theocr. 15.40. Herakles and Laistrygones: Lyk. 662 with Schol. Vet.

ancient systematisers who called her Lamia's daughter; in origin
she was Lamia herself. Her father was sometimes called Deimos,
who can be identified with Kyknos (see p. 96, note 7). Even
nearer to Sybaris is Croton, home of Lakinios—simply an Italian
version of Kyknos—son of Pyrene and opponent of Herakles (see
Addendum, p. 120). There are several threads, therefore, that
join Sybaris, Gerana, Skylla, and the Libyan Lamia to one another.

POINE AND PSAMATHE

Argive and Megarian traditions offer us another form of the
same monstrous demon woman—Poine or Ker, whom Koroibos
fought and killed. The extant versions of this story appear to be
derived from Callimachus' *Aitia*, whose version can be reconstructed by combining them with the surviving fragments of his
poem.[24]

When Apollo had killed Python, he went for purification to
Krotopos of Argos. There he seduced his host's daughter, Psamathe, who conceived and bore a son Linos. In fear of her father
she exposed the child; or, as Statius has it, she went out into the
fields, bore him among the sheep-stalls, and delivered him to a
shepherd. One day dogs found the infant outdoors and tore him
to pieces. News of her son's death came to Psamathe, who made
great lament, and in her grief told the whole story to her father.
He refused to believe that her lover had been Apollo, and in his
wrath he put her to death; Ovid says that he buried her alive.
Then Apollo, angry because of his mistress's death, sent a monstrous woman, Poine or Ker, against Argos; she had the upper
body of a maiden with snaky locks upon her head, and talons on
her hands. Statius, who describes her, leaves the reader to infer
that her lower body had nonhuman form. From the Ovidian
Scholiast we learn that she had a serpentine body and human
face. She went about the land, seizing children from the very

---

[24] The most complete narratives are Paus. 1.43.7 f., 2.19.8; Stat. *Theb.* 1.557–668;
Conon 19. See also Call. *Ait.* frags. 26–31 Pf.; Anth. Pal. 7.154; Ovid *Ibis* 573–576 with
Schol.; Lact. Plac. *Theb.* 1.570; Vat. Myth. I 168. On the sources see Knaack (1880)
14–28; Wilamowitz (1925) 230–234. The three principal sources fit together pretty well.
Conon's differences from Pausanias and Statius seem due to careless epitomising by
Photios or himself.

arms of mothers and nurses and eating them. Then the hero Koroibos came to the relief of Argos. He went forth against the monster with a band of chosen youths and killed her. But Apollo's rage mounted now that his avenging agent was killed. He sent a plague upon the land, so virulent that the Argives sent an embassy to ask Apollo at Delphi for relief. He ordered Argos to sacrifice to the slain Poine the young men who had killed her. Then Koroibos appeared before Apollo and asked that he be allowed to die as the sole slayer of Poine, and that the other young men be freed from the penalty. Apollo was completely won over by his courage and spared him; but he forbade Koroibos to go back to Argos. He told him to take a tripod from the temple and to carry it away with him; wherever it should fall to the ground, there he should build a temple of Apollo and stay. So Koroibos took a tripod and carried it until it slipped away from him as he crossed Mount Gerania (Crane Mountain) in the Megarid. There he did as the god had told him. The village that he founded received the name Tripodiskoi from the falling of the tripod. At his death Koroibos was given a tomb in the agora of Megara.

Poine-Ker is plainly Lamia, and indeed a Vatican Mythographer calls her that. Furthermore the story is nearly identical with the Delphian tale of Sybaris and the south-Italian tale of Heros-Alybas-Polites; only the position of certain themes is changed a bit. (1) Poine attacked children; (2) she had a partly animal body; (3) Apollo ordered the sacrifice of young men to her, as he asked for the sacrifice of a youth to Sybaris. (4) Koroibos substituted himself for the Argive youths, as Eurybatos for Alkyoneus and Euthymos for the Temesian maid.[25]

Poine coincides with Echidna in appearance and with the Libyan Lamia in her seizing and eating of children. It is important to observe that her attacks followed upon the loss of Psamathe's child and that it was for Psamathe that she exacted vengeance. Psamathe herself shows some likeness to Pyrene, Kelto, and Herakles' echidna woman; her relation to Apollo was exactly theirs to Herakles. Then Psamathe was like Pyrene in her fear of

---

[25] The three stories share Ths. 3B, 3F, 4A, 4C, 6B, 7A, 8A (the hero as sacrificial victim), 10D.

her father and in her going forth from his house into woods or fields to bear her child; one should recall Dryope too and her relation to Apollo (p. 57).

Argive Psamathe, Krotopos' daughter, appears to be originally the same as the sea nymph Psamathe, Nereus' daughter. This Nereid was wife of Aiakos, who won his bride in the same way as his son Peleus won Thetis. She turned herself into a seal (phôkê) while Aiakos struggled with her, and in due time bore him a son, Phokos. After Phokos was killed by his half brothers Peleus and Telamon, she sent a monstrous wolf against the herds of Peleus. He propitiated her, Thetis supported his prayer, and the wolf was turned to stone.[26]

Psamathe's transformation into a seal, her son's name Phokos, and her character as Nereid suggest that she was a woman with a fish body, a mermaid, i.e., a creature something like Keto or Skylla. Another of her husbands was Proteus, old man of the sea.[27]

The specific introduction of the seal into the story seems to be due to a desire to make her son the eponym of the land Phokis, which folk etymology interpreted as seal-land. In fact, three manuscripts of Apollodoros say that she changed herself into a phykês (wrasse). And her son's name, which appears to be the masculine form of phôkê, is identical with a variant of phôkaina, the name of a kind of dolphin. True enough, dolphins are as much mammals as seals are, but the Greeks didn't know it: they had no doubt that dolphins and porpoises were fish.[28]

This fish-woman, then, lost her son and in wrath attacked cattle through a wolf surrogate. She attacked men too: as Ovid tells the story, men of Peleus' band were killed as they tried to protect the herds from the wolf. The wolf was a monstrous beast (belua vasta); his maw and shaggy coat were smeared with blood; his eyes flashed fire. He ate some of the cattle that he killed; others he wantonly destroyed. These Psamathe meant to be offerings

---

[26] Ovid Met. 11.346–406; Apollod. 3.12.6; Nic. ap. Ant. Lib. 38; Paus. 2.29.9; Schol. Vet. on Eur. Andr. 687. The identity of the two Psamathes is recognised by Gruppe (1906) 90, 98, who does not, however, present the case for it.

[27] Eur. Hel. 6 f.

[28] On phykês see D. Thompson (1947) 276–278, Douglas (1928B) 149. There is also a fish that the Greeks called psamathis; Thompson 294. On phôkaina, defined porpoise in lexica, ibid. 281. On the Greeks' classification of dolphins see Douglas 158.

(*inferiae*) to the dead Phokos, as Poine's victims were offerings not only to Psamathe herself but to her son Linos. Furthermore the Nereid Psamathe was temporarily wife of Aiakos, as Argive Psamathe was Apollo's mistress. Peleus' decision to propitiate the Nereid with prayers and offerings rather than to fight her recalls Apollo's instructions to make offerings to Sybaris and to Poine. It is significant too that Psamathe's wolf raided a hero's herds of cattle, a hero, moreover, whose son fought Kyknos. It is also significant that Peleus was then guest in the house of Keyx in Trachis. There is an interesting coincidence of name between Alkyone, Keyx's wife, who enters into Ovid's narrative, and Alkyoneus, intended victim in the Sybaris story.[29]

We have come once more to the familiar region of Malis-Trachinia, which has within it a city called Lamía. Its name is differently accented (Λαμία) from that of the monster (Λάμια), and probably has nothing to do with it; yet the identity in all but accent caused the Greeks to connect them. There were some who said that the city was named after a queen of the Trachinians (Λάμια). Nothing more is said about this queen anywhere, and reference works always list her as a different person from the monster and from the Lamia who was mother of a Sibyl and daughter of Poseidon. Yet some writers says that the Sibyl who was daughter of Lamia by Zeus or Apollo came from Malis. It is Pausanias who says Zeus, and his authority is much greater than that of Suidas, who says Apollo. Now Zeus's Lamia was the Libyan queen; and Pausanias calls the daughter of Zeus and Lamia the Libyan Sibyl. So we find Lamia, daughter of Poseidon, on the same coast as Psamathe, daughter of Nereus.[30]

Alternatively, the Malian city's name was attributed to Lamios or Lamos, son of Herakles and Omphale. After Herakles had killed Eurytos' son Iphitos, and Apollo had enjoined a term of servitude upon him, Hermes sold him to Queen Omphale of Lydia, who dressed him in women's clothes and set him to spinning and weaving among her maidservants. Yet during his three

---

[29] See Ovid *Met.* 11.363–396.

[30] Trachinian Lamia: Steph. Byz. 271 Holst.; EM 555; Schol. on Paus. 1.1.3. The head of a woman on coins of Lamia has been thought to represent this queen; see LM 2.1819. Lamia, Sibyl's mother: Plut. *Mor.* 398c; Paus. 10.12.1; Clem. Alex. *Strom.* 1.358 P; ps.-Dion Chrys. *Or.* 37.13; Suid. Σ355.

years in her service, though a woman in appearance and a slave in fact, he became her lover, begetting a son upon her, and also fought several combats with fierce or monstrous enemies, vanquishing the Kerkopes, the Itonians, Syleus, and a great snake that had been terrorising Phrygia.[31]

So Omphale appears to be another form of the seductive demoness whom we have encountered in the forms of Echidna, Kelto, and Pyrene: at a time when Herakles was dealing with dragons and brigands he lived with a woman who was both alluring and dangerous. Klearchos tells us that Omphale was extremely wanton and vicious: she invited strangers to her bed and afterwards put them to death. Herakles' servitude and effeminacy represent his temporary death (Th. 8A) and reveal the nature of his cohabitation in love with a demon-woman—this is the Venusberg episode (Th. 8D), an important theme of the combat myth.[32]

Omphale's relation to the demon women whom Herakles met on the way to or from Geryon's land is further revealed by Pausanias' remarks on some huge bones which he saw at Temenothyrai in upper Lydia. His Lydian guides said that they were the bones of Geryon and pointed to a torrent nearby that was called Okeanos, beside which horns of cattle had been found. When Pausanias objected to this identification, the guides said that they were the bones of the river god Hyllos, Ge's son—a statement which Pausanias accepted. It looks as if these bones were sacred objects of great antiquity attributed to some figure of native mythology whom the Hellenised Lydians called Hyllos and identified with the Geryon of the Herakles legend.[33]

The name Hyllos, familiar to us as the name of the son of Herakles and Deianeira, was sometimes given to the son of Herakles and Omphale. It was said that Herakles gave his sons this name because of his gratitude to the Lydian river Hyllos: once when he was sick he was healed by the river's warm waters. The story distinguishes between Hyllos, Ge's son, and Hyllos,

---

[31] Diod. 4.31; Apollod. 2.6.2 f.; Apollon. Aphr. 2, 4.311 M; Hyg. *Fab.* 32.4.

[32] Klearchos 6, 2.305 M; Ovid *Her.* 9.53–118; Lucian *DD* 13.2, who speaks of Omphale's striking Herakles with a golden sandal; Hyg. *Astr.* 2.14.

[33] Paus. 1.35.7 f. Temenothyrai, a Greek name of a Lydian town, means *temenos gates*, and recalls the predilection of Kyknos and Laogoras for a god's temenos (Th. 2c).

Omphale's son, who were probably the same originally, since Omphale may be identified with Ge—i.e., with the Lydian earth goddess who would be called Ge in Greek. The name Omphale appears to be the feminine form of *omphalos* (navel), a word that was often associated with the earth: Delphi, claiming to be earth's navel—i.e., central point—symbolised its claim by means of a stone *omphalos,* and other places that made the same claim also had their *omphaloi.*[34]

The river god whose waters healed Herakles was identified with Herakles' enemy Geryon. May not Herakles' sickness have originally been the wound dealt him by his enemy? For the story recalls another; that in which Herakles, killed by Typhon, was brought back to life by his nephew Iolaos (p. 91). Hyllos and Iolaos seem to be the same name, and Hylas is another form of it; the three forms became distinct persons, respectively the son, nephew-companion, and boy favorite of Herakles. The original Hyllos was the son of Herakles and the demon woman, Omphale or Deianeira—Deianeira's character as we see it in classical legend betrays her demonic origin: from a river spirit who loved her she received the Hydra's poison with which she killed the companion of her bed (and from this death too Herakles recovered: he rose from it to the company of the gods). As Herakles' son, Hyllos became his father's helper and rescuer (see chapter x for the role of the champion's son and for a possible meaning of the water which healed Herakles); as the demon woman's son he became identified with the river spirit who was Herakles' enemy and rival.[35]

The great snake that Herakles killed during his Lydian servitude had devastated the lands around the Phrygian river Sangarios. May he not be the river god Sangarios? May not Sangarios have taken Hyllos-Geryon's place in a Phrygian version of the Omphale legend? And may he not have been identified with

---

[34] On Hyllos see Panyasis, frag. 17 Kinkel; Paus. 1.35.8; Lact. Plac. *Theb.* 8.507. Herakles' son by Omphale is also called Acheles, which name is apparently related to Acheloos.

[35] On Hylas as Herakles' son see Schol. Vet. on Theocr. 13.7; he is usually son of the Dryopian Theiodamas, and Herakles took him captive after killing his father and defeating the Dryopes (p. 37). Notice Iole, whose name seems to be a feminine form of *Iolaos,* as wife of Hyllos. For support of my view of Omphale and Deianeira see Krappe (1945) 148 f. See pp. 354–356.

Typhon? Typhon's combat with Zeus and the Homeric "couches of Typhoeus" were sometimes placed in Lydia or Phrygia: that part of Lydia and Phrygia called *Katakekaumenê* (Burnt Lydia and Burnt Phrygia) was said to have been scorched either by Zeus's thunderbolts or by Typhon's fiery breath during the combat. The Lydian dragon's opponent may have been identified with either Zeus or Herakles. Moreover Typhon's wife, Echidna, had a lair by a Lydian lake. Since her name was given by Herodotos to the snake woman with whom Herakles tarried, and since she was the mother of Geryon, who was identified with the Lydian river god Hyllos, we may say that Omphale is the Lydian Echidna. Those scholars who have interpreted her as in origin a goddess of earth and of the dead have done so with good reason. Her name may join those of Echidna, Skylla, Lamia, and Poine as a regional name of the great dragoness of the combat myth.[36]

She was connected with Malian Lamía, as has been noticed, through her son Lamios, the city's eponym, who seems to be the Malian equivalent of Lydian Hyllos as son of Omphale and Herakles. For the Omphale legend appears to have been localised in both Lydia and Malis. Wilamowitz has pointed out the remarkable correspondence between names found in or associated with the Spercheios region and those that are found in the legend of Lydian Omphale: *Kerkôpôn hedrai* near Thermopylae, Omphalion in the Spercheios Valley, Itonians as the people of Itonos in Phthiotis, Kyknos' town; Syleus lived on Pelion, according to Conon—at Aulis, according to Apollodoros (if Aulis is not a mistake for Lydia: Αὐλίδι < Λυδίαι is a possible scribe's error). In the composite Herakles legend the Omphale episode interrupts the sequence of Herakles' adventures in Trachinia; his Trachinian spouse, Deianeira, resembles Omphale, and her son is called Hyllos.[37]

Lamia is simply the feminine form of Lamios, of which name Lamos is a variant. Lamos and Lamia are the names of the king

---

[36] On Typhon in Lydia see Strabo 12.8.19, p. 579; 13.4.6, 11, p. 628; Nonn. *Dion.* 13.474–478; Schol. Vet. on Pind. *Pyth.* 1.16(31). On Echidna in Lydia see Lyk. 1353 f. and Schol. Vet. On Omphale as death goddess see LM 3.885 f., RE 18.394, where she is also connected with Hera and Deianeira.

[37] Conon 17; Apollod. 2.6.3. See Wilamowitz (1895) I 315 f.; Wernicke (1890) 72.

and queen of the Laistrygones, gigantic cannibals with whom Herakles, as well as Odysseus, had dealings. The Laistrygon king was Poseidon's son, and one of the Lamias mentioned above was Poseidon's daughter. So we may suppose that the Malian Lamios and Lamia were once husband and wife (and brother and sister too), later becoming son and mother—such shifts of relationship frequently occur in folklore. The Malian Lamia had the personal name of Psamathe or Omphale, as the Delphian Lamia had the name Sybaris. The name Psamathe was also used for the Lamia of Megara and Argos; but in the Hellenistic poets' treatment of Argive-Megarian folklore, if not earlier, the god's mistress under the name Psamathe became distinct from the Lamia called Poine or Ker.[38]

In the Argive legend, Linos is son of Apollo and Psamathe and was torn to pieces by dogs in early childhood. He was the eponym of the Linos song, both dirge and reaping song, sung throughout eastern Mediterranean lands and a feature of the Arnis festival at Argos. But Linos takes on a quite different appearance in two other legends. In Thebes they said that he was son of Amphimaros Poseidon's son and the Muse Urania—the greatest musician of his time, whom Apollo killed because he rivalled the god in song, and who had thereafter a tomb in Thebes. So once more the theme of contest between god and mortal man appears (Th. 4F): Linos opposed Apollo in song as Eurytos in archery or Phorbas in boxing.[39]

In another well-known story Herakles killed Linos: as music teacher of the boy Herakles, Linos once chastised his pupil, whereupon the boy in sudden anger struck his teacher over the head with his lyre and killed him. Pausanias attempts to distinguish this Linos from the other; but he calls his father Ismenios, i.e., Apollo, and the scene is Thebes. It was no doubt the buffoon Herakles, prodigiously strong and virile, but uncouth, slow-witted, and anti-intellectual, who gave this comic turn to

---

[38] Od. 10.80–132. In 81 it is doubtful whether Λάμου αἰπὺ πτολίεθρον means "Lamos' town" or "citadel of Lamos" (as name of a town). In later times Lamos was taken to be the king's name; see Hor. *Carm.* 3.17.

[39] Paus. 9.29.6–9. Notice that the parents of Linos are Apollo and Urania in Hyg. *Fab.* 161, where no story is told.

the story. In the background one can see Herakles in Apollo's place, slayer of a Linos who challenged him.[40]

This conclusion is confirmed by the Lityerses legend, since the Lityerses song is often coupled with the Linos song as a lamentation sung by reapers. Lityerses, it was said, was a bastard son of Midas and champion mower of grain in Phrygia. He invited everyone who came his way to eat and drink with him, then forced him to mow in the fields with him, and finally in the evening wrapped his guest in a sheaf and cut off his head. Or, as Pollux says, he challenged men to a mowing contest and flogged those who lost. As you might expect, one day Herakles came that way, mowed with Lityerses, outdid him, killed him, and threw his body into the Maeander. According to one version, Herakles thus rescued Daphnis from death; for the youth had come to Lityerses' house to free his beloved Thalia (or Pimplea) from servitude.[41]

Much the same story is told about Herakles and Syleus, who had a vineyard in Lydia in which he forced strangers to dig. Herakles was sold to Syleus as a field slave to work in his vineyard. After the new slave had torn out vines by the roots, he went to the house and made himself some big loaves of bread, killed and roasted the best ox in Syleus' stalls, broke into the cellar and broached the best cask of wine, and made the field-foreman bring him fruits and cakes. Soon Syleus came upon the scene; he railed at and cursed the supposed slave to no avail; finally the hero killed him. This episode of Syleus' cursing Herakles as the latter devoured his roast beef clarifies for us the story of the Rhodian-Dryopian Theiodamas (pp. 37 f.) and its place in the legend of Herakles' combat with Dryopians and Lapiths. Like Syleus, Theiodamas cursed Herakles as the hero ate one of his oxen. And as in Syleus' house, so in the house of Koronos, Herakles greedily ate

---

[40] Apollod. 2.4.9.

[41] Sositheos *ap*. Ath. 10, 415B *et ap. Script. Rer. Mir. Gr., pp.* 220 *sq.* West.; Schol. Vet. on Theocr. 10.41; Serv.-Dan. *Ecl.* 8.68; Phot. *Lex.* 1.392 Nab.; Suid. Δ626; Poll. 4.54. Serv.-Dan. tells the Daphnis story, which probably comes from Sositheos; see Arg. to Theocr. *Id.* 8. On Lityerses and the rural customs of which his story is *aition* see Mannhardt (1884) 1–57. It seems that contest in song also entered into the Lityerses legend: "regi ferali sopito metendi carmine caput amputavit" is very likely right in the text of Serv.-Dan.; see also Sositheos, *loc. cit.* The story shows Ths. 4A, 4D, 4E, 4F, 7A, 8A, 8C, 9, 10A, 10D. As to 4A and 4D notice that L. was ἄγριος ἰδέσθαι καὶ ἀνήμερος ἄνθρωπος, ἀδηφάγος δ' ἰσχυρῶς, also κακόξενος (Sositheos); see p. 58, note 45.

a whole ox. So the whole story, of which we saw only fragments in chapters ii and iii, becomes clear: The brigand-king, Laogoras-Koronos-Theiodamas-Kyknos, forced wayfarers into a contest with him after entertaining them at a generous meal, and put them to death when they lost. One day Herakles came in disguise, thoroughly enjoyed the dinner after his fashion, beat his host at his own game, and killed him. As has been seen, Syleus was also localised in the same general region as the Dryopian brigand—on Pelion and perhaps also at Aulis.[42]

According to one version of the tale it was while Herakles served Omphale that he met and vanquished Syleus. At the same time, it is said, he killed Syleus' daughter Xenodoke, whose name *guest-receiver* indicates a goddess or spirit of death. However, a fragment of a speech from Euripides' satyr play called *Syleus*, if addressed by Herakles to Xenodoke, as has been conjectured, indicates that the hero took her as his mistress after killing her father. In a story told by Conon she became his mistress, when he was being entertained in the house of Dikaios, Syleus' brother. When he left the country she pined away and died; thus her death from the hero's sword is transformed into death from lovesickness after she, as the enemy's daughter, had helped the hero because of love for him. So, as Lydian mistress of Herakles' house of servitude, as companion of his bed, and as death spirit, she is a form of Omphale. That the hero's encounter with Lityerses was also placed within the Omphale legend is indicated not only by its locale in neighboring Phrygia, but also by the relation of Midas to both Lityerses and Omphale: in Klearchos' narrative (see p. 108, note 32) Midas as Omphale's companion in a life of effeminate luxury appears to be her consort.[43]

To sum up: Poine-Ker, Argive Psamathe's avenging spirit, is Psamathe herself. Through her name, character, and myth she may be identified with (i.e., descended from the same original

---

[42] For Syleus see Eur. frags. 687–694 Nauck²; Cramer *Anecd. Par.* I 7 f.; Apollod. 2.6.3; Diod. 4.31.7; Brommer (1944) for vase paintings. Theiodamas is placed in Lydia by Quint. Smyrn. 1.291–293.

[43] Eur. frag. 694 Nauck²; Conon 17. Notice also the Kerkopes, whom Herakles vanquished during his stay with Omphale (see p. 108, note 31). They robbed everyone who passed their way, and were identified or confused with Alebion and Derkynos: LM 2.1170; see Addendum, p. 120. Their story was given a comic ending. See LM 2.1166–1173.

figure as) the Malian Psamathe, Lamia, Omphale, Echidna, and Xenodoke. Her son Linos is linked by his name to the musician Linos and through him to Lityerses and Syleus, by his fate to Phokos, and by his kinship with Psamathe-Poine to Lamios, Hyllos, and ultimately to Geryon and Typhon. The Omphale legend and the two versions of the Syleus-Xenodoke legend are especially valuable for revealing the demon woman's double nature: she is (1) the enemy's dreadful companion, who wants to destroy the hero, and (2) the beautiful seductress who lures the hero to her bed, and either (a) destroys him or (b) really falls in love with him and helps him. Her two characters become two persons in the Argive-Megarian myth: Poine-Ker is pure Lamia, terrible and unlovely; Psamathe is Apollo's mistress (and immediately after his killing of Python). What our sources give us is a composite legend, derived from Callimachus. An ancient monument, antedating Callimachus and showing Koroibos in the act of killing the monster, was seen by Pausanias on Koroibos' tomb in Megara (the elegiac verses which he saw inscribed upon the tomb were much more recent than the sculpture: they told the composite story). That is the core of the original legend—Lamia, a monstrous woman who had lost her own child, raided the land snatching babes from their mothers and devouring them; an oracle ordered human sacrifice to appease her; the hero, offering himself as victim, succeeded in meeting and killing her. It is much the same story as was told of Sybaris and of Heros of Temesa. With this tale was merged the story of Apollo's love for Psamathe and the vengeance which he brought upon Krotopos for killing her. The Apollo-Psamathe story was either derived from or fitted to a story of the seductive Lamia—the hero entered the demon woman's bed in the demon's house; she aided him against the demon, whom the hero finally killed. In the composite legend Apollo as hero in the second story becomes the appeasing oracular god of the first. His vengeance becomes the Lamia's visitation, which is followed by a plague—the Lamia in another form.[44]

---

[44] The verses assume the conflated legend: Κοινὸν ἐγὼ Μεγαρεῦσι καὶ Ἰναχίδεσσιν ἄθυρμα/ἵδρυμα . . . Only Schol. on Ovid *Ib*. 573, mentions Krotopos' death, saying merely that the sorrowing Apollo killed him and also sent a monster against the land. Conon 19 says that the plague ceased when Krotopos left Argos and settled in Tripodiskoi in the Megarid. He apparently means Koroibos.

The Apollo-Psamathe-Linos legend, thus abstracted from the Koroibos-Poine legend in its composite form, turns out to be much the same as the Apollo-Koronis-Asklepios legend, and the two stories illuminate each other. Koronis lay with Apollo, apparently in or near her father Phlegyas' house, as Psamathe lay with him in Krotopos' house; she conceived, as did Psamathe; in an Epidaurian version, told by Pausanias, she kept her pregnancy secret from her father and exposed her son after his birth, in the fields, where a herdsman found him, very much as Psamathe did; Apollo's love brought death to Koronis as to Psamathe (though not in the same way). Whereas Krotopos attacked Psamathe, Phlegyas in rage attacked Apollo at Delphi, setting fire to his temple; Apollo finally destroyed him, as he destroyed Krotopos. As we have seen, Phlegyas is the same as Phorbas and a form of Python; Krotopos has the corresponding role in the other legend.[45]

The hero Koroibos is remarkably like Herakles. His opponent not only recalls antagonists of Herakles, but her name Ker suggests Herakles' encounter with Thanatos; and like Herakles, Koroibos carried a tripod from Apollo's temple at Delphi. However, he held his place as a Megarian hero, never becoming absorbed into the figure of Herakles, as other local heroes did. The link with Delphi is likely to be fairly late.[46]

EMPUSA, MORMO, GELLO

Koroibos' opponent is rightly called Ker, since she came forth from Acheron, where she was born in the halls of the Erinyes (Stat. *Theb.* 1.597 f.). The Keres were spirits of death and were often evil. In the Homeric poems they carry off the souls of the dead to the halls of Hades. In the description of Achilles' shield a single Ker is seen upon a battlefield in company with Eris and Kydoimos; she drags a slain warrior by his feet through the press of battle. In the pseudo-Hesiodic *Shield* a similar battle scene appears on Herakles' shield. There a band of Keres, dark blue (κυάνεαι) in color, fearful to look upon, fight one another over the

---

[45] See Paus. 2.26.4. Koronis, with her name *Crow*, mother of Asklepios, who is closely associated with snakes, may in some lost narrative have lured the hero into sexual intercourse with her.

[46] See chapter xii on Herakles and Thanatos. Notice that the plague sent upon Argos is personified as *Mors* by Stat. *Theb.* 1.632.

dead bodies, eager to drink their blood. While the dead warriors' souls go down to Hades, the Keres fasten long claws upon their bodies, drink the blood, cast the drained corpses aside, and then go back into the throng of warriors for more.[47]

The Keres of the *Shield* show the cannibalistic traits of Lamiai, Empusai, and Mormones. Empusai were vampires: the bride of Corinth, whose story is told by Philostratos in his *Life of Apollonios of Tyana,* was exposed as an Empusa by Apollonios; she was especially fond of the flesh of young men, whom she lured into erotic relations with her; thus she got them in her power and destroyed them (see p. 108 on Omphale). Philostratos' Apollonios specifically identifies the Empusai with Lamiai and Mormolykiai (= Mormones). Elsewhere we find a woman of Corinth called Mormo, who ate her own children—a more gruesome variant of the Libyan Lamia, in that the woman's cannibalism is not a consequence of losing her children, but the very cause of it. In still another variant a phantom called Gello preys upon children and young girls in revenge for her own untimely death: here the bogey-woman becomes identified with the lost children themselves.[48]

Lamia is identified with Empusa, Mormo, Gello, and Karko. All these names are used in the singular and most of them in the plural. All had a place in the ancient nursery as bogey-names used to frighten children into good behavior in mankind's time-honored and foolish way. But they were plainly much more than nursery bogeys: they had, as we have seen, a place in mythology and folklore, merging with other figures that had little or no place in the nursery. They were spectres, underworld spirits, minions of Hekate, forms of Hekate herself. The Lamiai are called *phasmata* that rose from earth in woods and glens; Empusa is a phantom sent by Hekate; the Mormones are wandering *daimones*. These phantoms and demons are hardly to be distin-

---

[47] On Homeric Keres see e.g. Il. 18.535–538 = *Shield* 156–160; Od. 14.207 f.; *Shield* 248–263. Apollonios calls the Keres *soul-eaters* (θυμοβόρους, *Arg*. 4.1666). On Keres and related demons see esp. Harrison (1922) 165–239; she rightly sees Keres as the genus to which Erinyes, etc. belong.

[48] Bride of Corinth: Philostr. *Vit. Apollon.* 4.25; notice that Apollonios calls her a snake (*ophis*). See Keats's *Lamia*. Mormo of Corinth: Schol. on Aristid. *Or*. 13, p. 102 J. Gello: Zenob. 3.3.

guished from the Keres or from those avenging spirits of death called Poinai or Erinyes. Hence Poine, Ker, and Lamia alike as name of the creature that afflicted Argos.[49]

It was Hekate who sent all phantoms, wherefore they were called Hekataia; and Hekate herself was called Empusa, Mormo, and Gorgo. The splendidly and fearfully described Hekate of Lucian's liar Eukrates is not only identified with or likened to Mormolykeion and Gorgon, but is just such an apparition as Lamia or Empusa. She also resembles Echidna in that she has serpent's feet and gigantic size.[50]

So it is not merely caprice that Skylla's mother is called variously Hekate, Lamia, and Echidna in the tradition. All (including Skylla) were names of one monstrous being, mother or wife of the giant-dragon-monster-demon whom we know best as Typhon or Python. This frightful woman was spectre, ogress, vampire, snake, sea monster, several kinds of beast, and various mixtures of them. Her various forms group themselves about the realm of death, the sea, and the terrible or weird fauna of the earth, especially snakes. The snake was, of course, as an underground dweller and denizen of cemeteries, constantly associated with the dead and the powers of death. I need mention only the snakes of the Erinyes, of Kerberos, and of Hekate herself. Dragon and sea monster meet in the sea serpent; and such figures as Gorgons, Skylla, and Psamathe belong at once to sea and underworld. Psamathe, whom Ovid calls *numen pelagi* (*Met.* 11.392), sent her wolf against Peleus' cattle at noontime (11.353 f.): it was Empu-

---

[49] Lamia = Empusa, etc.; Philostr. *loc. cit.*; Schol. Vet. on Aristoph. *Eq.* 693; Suid. M1252; Basilius Schol. *ap.* Ruhnken, *Tim. Lex. Plat.* 182; Schol. Vet. on Theocr. 15.40; Hesych. K836. As one would expect, Empusa, Mormo, and Gello are mutually identified. In Plut. *Mor.* 1101c we find Empusa linked with Poine. For Empusa as a beautiful woman like Lamia see Philostr. *loc. cit.* and Aristoph. *Ran.* 290 f. Other names for this woman are Akko, Alphito, Babo or Baubo, Gorgo or Gorgyra, Makko, Oinopole or Onopole or Onokole or Onoskelis. See Rohde (1925) 590–595. Nursery bogeys: Aristoph. *Eq.* 693 with Schol. Vet.; Plat. *Phaedo* 77ᴇ; Xen. *Hell.* 4.4.17; Diod. 20.41.4; Strabo 1.2.8, p. 19; Plut. *Mor.* 1040ʙ, 1101c; Lucian, *Philops.* 2, *Phal.* I 8, *Zeux.* 12; Dion Chrys. *Or.* 66.20; Schol. Vet. on Aristoph. *Pax* 474, 758. Phantoms sent by Hekate: Schol. Vet. on Aristoph. *Ran.* 293; Dion. Hal. *Thuc.* 6; Hesych. E2518, Λ251, M1669; Suid. E1049; EM 336; Schol. on Paus. 1.1.3.

[50] Hipp. *Morb. Sacr.* 4; Lucian *Philops.* 22–24, 39; Dion Chrys. *Or.* 4.90; Orph. Hymn Mag. 3, p. 289 Abel; Hymn *ap.* Hippolyt. *Ref. Omn. Haer.* 4.35; Hesych. A5308; Schol. Vet. on Apollon. *Arg.* 3.861; see also citations in note 49. Hekate's names Bombo and Brimo suggest such bogey-names as Babo, Baubo.

sa's habit to appear to men at midday. Psamathe's power of assuming all sorts of shapes, a power which all sea deities enjoyed, belonged also to Hekate, Empusa, Lamia, and the Keres. Her agent was a wolf, whose eyes gleamed with fire, like the eyes of Hekate and Empusa. One name of the spectre woman is Mormolyka (Mormo-wolf), i.e., a werewolf, who was nurse of Acheron; as Gorgyra she was Acheron's wife; whereas Poine-Ker, the Argive Psamathe's avenging spirit, was born in deepest Acheron in the halls of the Erinyes.[51]

Mention of Kerberos and werewolves recalls the dogs that seized and rent the child Linos, thus acting in the manner of Poine-Ker-Lamia. Poine was succeeded by a plague. When we find that a plague-demon once took the form of a dog, we realise that Poine, dog, and plague are three derivatives of one original figure. Hekate was attended by dogs: the liar Eukrates described them as bigger than elephants, black and shaggy. Empusa took the form of a dog as one of her quick changes, and huge Molossian dogs were called *mormolykeia*. Though the Odyssey says no more than that Skylla had a voice like a dog's, vase paintings and later literature often portray her with dogs' heads protruding from her loins (see p. 97, note 8).[52]

There can be little question then, after a review of the weird creatures discussed in this chapter, that an intimate relation exists between dragoness (Echidna, Delphyne), sea-monster (Keto, Skylla), and the underworld demons of female shape (Lamia-Empusa). She has a male partner in her misdeeds—dragon or sea serpent or giant or spectre—to whom she is variously related as

---

[51] On Erinyes, ghosts, etc. as snakes see Harrison (1922) 232–237, 325–331; Küster (1913) 40–42, 62–100. Empusa at noon: Suid. E1049; Schol. Vet. on Aristoph. *Ran.* 293. Change of shape: Orphic Hymn Mag. 3.9; Hymn *ap.* Hippolyt. *loc. cit.*; (Hekate-Empusa) Schol. Vet. on Apollon. *Arg.* 3.861; (Empusa) Aristoph. *Ran.* 288–295; Krates *ap.* Schol. Vet. *ibid.*; Philostr. *Vit. Apollon.* 2.4; Suid. E1049; EM 336; (Lamia) Schol. Vet. on Aristoph. *Pax* 758; (Keres) Sinos *ap.* Stob. III, p. 29 Hense. Fiery eyes: Aristoph., Orph. Hymn, Hippolyt., Schol. on Apollon., *locc. cit.* Acheron's wife or nurse: Sophron *ap.* Stob. I, p. 419 Hense; Apollod. 102, 2.1065 J. For the folk conception of underworld demon as snake or other animal see Kroll (1932) 375. The names Lamia and Karko were given to a kind of large shark, which was also called Skylla: Hesych. Λ251; Schol. on Paus. 1.1.3; D. Thompson (1947) 106 f., 144. A monster of the sea was thus identified with underworld spirits. We have seen too that Lamia as the Sibyl's mother was daughter of Poseidon.

[52] Plague demon as dog: Philostr. *Vit. Apollon.* 4.10. Hekate's dogs: Lucian *Philops.* 24; see Orph. Hymn and Hippolyt. *locc. cit.* Empusa as dog: Aristoph. *Ran.* 292. Molossian dogs: *id. Thesm.* 416 f.

mother, wife, nurse, or daughter. Now it is clear that Ge and
Hera, great goddesses though they be in the cults and myths of
Greece, play the monster-woman role in the group of myths
under study. Ge as mother of Typhon-Python-Tityos incited him
against the gods and supported him in his combat (pp. 73, 84).
She shares with Hekate the title Chthonia, like Hekate sends
dream visions and phantoms, and is associated with the dead in
prayers and offerings. Within her live snakes and ghosts. Hera
too is mother of Typhon, and she incited Python and Tityos
against Leto and Apollo, and several serpents and monsters against
Herakles (pp. 60, 356 f.). Her name appears to be the feminine of
hêrôs. She is the Mistress or the Lady, a title that was probably
once employed to designate the supernaturally powerful ghost of
a dead woman, as *hêrôs* of a dead man, and later replaced by
hêrôinê when Hera had become established as the name of a
great goddess. The hero-ghosts were very likely to be malignant
(e.g., Heros of Temesa), and were also associated with the snakes
and lizards that made their burrows and nests about tombs and
graveyards. It is this character that clings to the Hera of the
dragon myths.[53]

ADDENDUM TO CHAPTER VI

Pausanias (6.6.11) briefly describes a painting that he saw which pictured the demon
that Euthymos cast out. It was apparently a picture of the combat, though Pausanias
is not clear about this. The MSS show νεανίσκος Σύβαρις καὶ Κάλαβρός τε ποταμὸς καὶ
Λύκα πηγὴ πρὸς δὲ 'Ήρα τε καὶ Τεμέσα ἦν ἡ πόλις, ἐν δὲ σφισι καὶ δαίμων ὅντινα ἐξέβαλεν ὁ
Εὔθυμος, χρόαν δὲ δεινῶς μέλας καὶ τὸ εἶδος ἅπαν ἐς τὰ μάλιστα φοβερὸς λύκου τε ἀμπέχετο
δέρμα ἐσθῆτα· ἐτίθετο δὲ καὶ ὄνομα Λύβαντα ἐπὶ τῇ γραφῇ γράμματα. The emendations accepted by Spiro of 'Ήρα > ἡρῷον and of Λύβαντα > Λύκαν τὰ are unnecessary and undoubtedly wrong. Hera as a great goddess of the region, worshipped at Cape Lakinion,
is rightly present in the picture. And the last sentence should be emended to 'Αλύβαν τα
or 'Αλύβαντα ⟨τὰ⟩, as Suidas E3510 makes clear, not to mention the word *alibas*, which
means *corpse*; Plat. *Rep.* 387BC sets *alibantes* beside *Kôkytoi*, *Styges*, and *eneroi*. On the

---

[53] Ge Chthonia: Musaios, frag. 1 Kinkel; Aesch. *Pers.* 628 f. She is one of the rulers
of underworld powers (χθονίων ἀγεμόνες) in *Pers.* 640 f. (cf. Eur. *Hec.* 79) and receives
offerings along with the dead in *Pers.* 219 f. She is called *Chthôn*: Aesch. *Pr.* 207, *Eum.* 6;
Eur. *Hec.* 70, *Hel.* 168. Ge sends *phasmata*: Eur. *Hec.* 71, μελανοπτερύγων μῆτερ ὀνείρων;
IT 1262–1267. She was mother of the Sirens: Eur. *Hel.* 168 f. For Ge = Delphyne see
Kern (1926) 79; Kybele = Echidna, Weber (1910) 211–216. *Hêra* as feminine of *hêrôs*
was first suggested by Müller (1825) 244; see also Laistner (1889) I 259 f., II 423; Wilamowitz (1931) I 237. Jacques Schnier (1947: 78) points out the near universality of the female
dragon.

other hand, there is no record of a spring called Lyka in southern Italy, suitable as the name may be to the story. Maass and Höfer suggest Λεύκα; see Maass (1907) 40–44, LM 4.1610 f.

Sybaris is perhaps the river god: he and Kalabros probably frame the whole scene. I believe that Sybaris and Hera back Alybas-Heros, while Kalabros, Lyka(?), and Temesa back Euthymos. Hera has already been noticed as the instigator of Python and Tityos (p. 60), and her relation to the female monsters of this study has just been discussed.

My conjecture is the opposite of Maass's (45 f.), who places Hera and Sybaris behind Euthymos as supporters of the Greek hero against the aboriginal Italian hero whom Kalabros and Lyka back. But notice that in each of three pairs Sybaris, Hera, and Alybas (δαίμων) are mentioned first. Maass places Temesa in the center beside the combatants without good reason, since in Pausanias' description she is obviously the counterpart of Hera. The order from left to right, or *vice versa*, is, therefore, Sybaris, Hera, Alybas, Euthymos, Temesa, Kalabros and Lyka.

On Sybaris of the painting as *Wassermann*, and so at once spirit of water, death, and nightmare, see Laistner (1889) II 33. He represents, I believe, the watery form that Alybas-Heros took after his defeat. The name remained with the story, passing from female to male monster. For his representation as a youth compare Kyknos (figs. 8–11). The name Sybaris is met again as father of Alia or Halia, who lay with a huge dragon in a grove of Artemis in Phrygia, from which union the Ophiogeneis were sprung (Ael. NA 12.39). From her name she has been interpreted as Sea-Woman (Halia = Leukothea), appropriate for a dragon's consort, and as eponym of the Phrygian city of Alia; see LM 4.1612 f. It is quite possible that both meanings were packed into a single name.

We may suppose that in the painter's version the demonic enemy vanished into the earth and became the Sybaris River or, more exactly, the spring from which it rises; and since the river flows into the sea, Pausanias' statement is consistent enough with the conjectured version of the painter.

Kyknos in bird form flew to the Sybaris River, where he mated with Gerana; also in nearby Croton Herakles encountered the brigand Lakinios, who, like Kyknos, was son of Kyrene-Pyrene (p. 99). Lakinios, as brigand king of Croton, was closely associated with Hera Lakinia: for it was he who built her great temple; see LM 2.1812. Another Italian brigand who tried, like Lakinios, to rob Herakles of Geryon's cattle was called Alebion (or Ialebion), which name may well be a variant of Alybas; see Apollod. 2.5.10: Alebion with his brother Derkynos operated in Liguria.

The demon of the painting was black of skin and frightful in appearance. Pausanias says, "he wore a wolfskin"; that is, the picture did not show a wolf, but a man inside a wolf's hide. We may imagine him represented in the manner of Herakles in his lionskin as we often see him in vase paintings: the unsevered animal head serves him as helmet, and his face peers forth from between the open jaws. Pausanias' words indicate that the demon is a werewolf, not literally a wolf.

Perhaps the painter's version was like Aelian's in that the issue between the contestants was something other than the rescue of a girl. Or it may be that the figure called Temesa represents the girl, and that Aelian's version may be reconciled with Pausanias's: the city from which the demon exacted tribute may be personified as the girl victim whom the demon seized.

Still another version of the tale is evident in Paus. 6.6.10: Euthymos lived to an extreme old age, or by report was still living in Temesa in Pausanias' time, because he had eluded death and come back to live among men. That is, like Herakles or Sisyphos, he fought or bound Thanatos, with whom Alybas-Heros can be identified, to escape from death—the issue was his own life, when Death came to take him.

VII

GOD AND DRAGON IN THE NEARER EAST

HITTITE DRAGON AND DEMON

To most Greeks, it seems, Typhon's land was Cilicia, where he lived in the Corycian Cave, and where he fought, or at least began, his combat with Zeus. There were some who placed dragon and combat in Lydia or Syria, which countries were, like Cilicia, neighbors of the Hittites and at times subject to Hittite kings, so that it is not surprising to find a variant of the tale in Hittite mythology.[1]

The Hittite myth, which was *aition* of the Puruli Festival, is found in two versions. In the first the Weather God and the dragon Illuyankas met in combat at Kiskilussa, and the dragon maimed the Weather God, forcing him to retire from battle. Then the god sought the aid of the goddess Inaras, who prepared a lavish banquet, for which she took care to provide wine and every kind of drink in great abundance. She asked the hero Hupasiyas to help her, and he consented only on condition that he lie with her first, to which terms she readily agreed. Then after concealing him in her house, she invited the dragon and his henchmen to the banquet. They came at once and ate and drank gluttonously, gorging themselves until they could barely move. Hupasiyas then sprang out and tied up the helpless dragon with

---

[1] For Python combat in Asia Minor see p. 79 with note 8.

a rope; whereupon the Weather God came and killed the dragon.[2]

In the other version the Weather God's son by a mortal slave girl married Illuyankas' daughter. Before he went to the dragon's house to negotiate the marriage contract his father said to him, "Demand from them my heart and eyes,"—for the dragon had earlier taken these members from the god, either in combat or by theft. So his son made this demand and recovered the heart and eyes, probably because Illuyankas as Stupid Ogre did not know that he was the god's son, but thought him a mere mortal. Equipped once more with heart and eyes the Weather God went at once to the sea and engaged the dragon, whom he finally killed. His son, apparently dismayed at his unwitting betrayal of his father-in-law's hospitality, asked his father to kill him too, and he did so.

The Puruli myth in one version or the other agrees with the Typhon myth in the following themes.[3]

1. Theme 1c. Illuyankas had a daughter who lived with him (Typhon 3, p. 78).

2. Theme 2b. He lived in a cave (I) or a house (II) (Typhon 5, p. 79).

3. Theme 2e. The house was near the sea (p. 74).

4. Theme 2a. The seaside residence makes Cilicia or northern Syria probable (Typhon 4, p. 78).[4]

5. Theme 3b. Illuyankas was a snake (Typhon 8, p. 80).

6. Theme 4d. His gluttony recalls Typhon's response to the savor of fish frying (p. 74) and both Typhon's and Python's devouring of whole herds (Typhon 13, p. 84).

7. Theme 6a. The divine champion was the Weather God, i.e., the Hittite Zeus (Typhon 18, p. 84).

8. Theme 7a. The Weather God fought the dragon in hand-to-hand encounter in Puruli II and in the initial combat of Puruli

---

[2] Puruli Version I = Text II, translated by Gaster (1950) 326–329; Puruli Version II = Text IV, translated *ibid.* 332–334; synopsis and discussion, *ibid.* 317–324, (1952) 134–143. The quotations that I introduce into my summaries of Hittite myths are from Gaster's translation. See also Pritchard (1950) 125 f.; Levy (1953) 61–64.

[3] The obvious similarities of the two myths have of course been pointed out before: e.g., Porzig (1930), Seippel (1939) 36–40. It is my purpose here to make a complete list of correspondences.

[4] See Seippel (1939) 39. Whether Kiskilussa, scene of the initial combat of Puruli I, was the city of the dragon's residence or beside the sea, it is impossible to say.

I; but the only weapon mentioned is Hupasiyas' rope (Typhon 20, pp. 84 f.). However, a Hittite sculpture shows the god killing the dragon with a spear and wearing a sword in scabbard at his side (fig. 16). Relief portraits of the Weather God show him

FIGURE 16. HITTITE WEATHER GOD AND ILLUYANKAS

Rock Sculpture from Malatia

wielding a thunderbolt and battle-axe with scabbard and sword at his side.[5]

9. Theme 7c. The text implies a flight of the gods (p. 73) or at least their shrinking from combat: The Weather God gathered the gods together and asked their help, but (it appears) only Inaras helped him. Later, after he killed the bound dragon, the gods rallied around him (Puruli I).

10. Theme 7d. The Weather God had the help of Inaras (Typhon 22, p. 85). Inaras as goddess-helper is comparable to Athena as Zeus's aid in the Typhon myth, and as support of Herakles against Kyknos and others.

11. Theme 7e. He also had the help of Hupasiyas in Puruli I and of his son in Puruli II, just as Hermes, Pan, and Kadmos helped Zeus against Typhon (Typhon 23, p. 85). Hupasiyas is the real victor in Puruli I, which reduces the Weather God to a cowardly and ridiculous role, and his presence as hero beside the god brings Herakles forcibly to mind as the Delphian Apollo's

[5] See Gaster (1952) pls. VII, VIII; Levy (1953) pl. IVc.

champion against Kyknos and Laogoras. Puruli II shows the god's son as helper: he recalls Hyllos or Iolaos as helper of Herakles, when Herakles plays the leading role.

12, 13. Themes 8A, 8B. A most striking parallel to the Typhon myth is the god's temporary defeat and loss of bodily parts (Typhon 25, p. 85). In Puruli I he was worsted in the first encounter and remained impotent thereafter until he won the effective aid of Inaras and Hupasiyas. In Puruli II we have a very close parallel: the dragon had taken the god's heart and eyes.[6]

14. Theme 9. Also striking are the ways in which the dragon was deceived. In Puruli I Inaras lured him and his minions to a banquet (Th. 9, a), to which they were only too ready to come, as Typhon was lured forth by Pan's fish dinner on the shore, or was deceived by the Moirai into tasting the ephemeral fruits (Typhon 26, p. 89). Again in Puruli II there occurs a sort of deception by disguise (Th. 9, c), when the dragon appears to think that his son-in-law is merely a mortal.

So in fourteen features the Typhon and Illuyankas myths agree, and are nearly identical in the nuclear themes (8–14), if one allows for the differences of outward dress that are bound to arise among different peoples who speak different languages and have different cultures. In the analysis comparison was made only with the Typhon myth, mainly because of its Cilician scene; except that in features 6, 10, and 11 reference was made to the Python myth complex. In the following two features, which are absent from the Typhon myth, the Hittite myth resembles other myths which we have reviewed (including the Python myth).

Theme 8D. Puruli I shows an interesting variation of the Venusberg theme (p. 108). Here it is not dragoness or Empusa, but the Weather God's helper Inaras, who becomes mistress of the hero Hupasiyas. After the dragon's death Inaras built a house on a rock near Tarugga, in which she placed Hupasiyas, forbidding him to look out of the window during her absence, lest he see his wife and child. But Hupasiyas disobeyed, opened the window, and saw his wife and children. Inaras came back to the house in great wrath: here unfortunately the text breaks off. In this episode Hupasiyas must for a time live apart in the house of an

---

[6] Compare Apollo-Horos' loss of an eye to Typhon-Set (pp. 180, 447).

otherworldly woman, with whom he enjoys sexual relations, like Herakles with Echidna, Kelto, Pyrene, and Omphale. Inaras seems to take on the character of a harmful spirit in this episode.[7]

In Puruli II the god's son lived in the dragon's house with the dragon's daughter as his wife, not only like Herakles himself with several daughters of faded dragons, but also like Herakles' son, Hyllos, who married Iole, daughter of Eurytos. The Weather God's son has, moreover, the same sort of ambiguity as Hyllos. He is the god's son and helper, yet son-in-law of the dragon, with whom he chose to die; Hyllos appears as a son of Omphale or Ge and as a giant who was also called Geryon (p. 108).[8]

Theme 10D. The Puruli texts contain ritual prescriptions which immediately follow each version of the myth. In like manner the Delphic Septerion and Pythian festivals were related to the Python myth; in particular, Pollux shows how each of the five parts of the Pythian nome performed at the Pythian festival correspond to five phases of the combat. The relation of the combat myths to rituals will be discussed in chapter xv.[9]

Like the Greeks, the Hittites had more than one myth of this general type. For them too the enemy takes other forms and other names. The Hittite gods were also attacked by a monstrous demon, Hahhimas (Torpor), who brought death to man, beast, and vegetation. A goddess appealed to the Weather God for aid, apparently to send his sons against the demon, but he could do no more than express his scorn of her sons for not being able to revive men or cattle, and advise her to flatter the demon. Her second appeal also failed to move him. But when Hahhimas' ravages continued unabated until the whole country lay devastated, he was finally moved to summon the Sun God, who could not, however, be found. So he sent out Zababa, god of war, to find the Sun God. "But Hahhimas seized Zababa." Thereafter he sent out the gods Lama and Telipinu in turn, and they too were seized. Then he decided to send the Great Goddess and the Gulses

---

[7] Gaster (1950: 328) believes that Inaras' imprisonment of Hupasiyas was meant to keep him from passing on to mortals the supernatural power which he had gained from sexual intercourse with a goddess.

[8] Notice that Hylas was carried off by water nymphs to be their lover: Apollon. *Arg.* 1.1221–1239; Theocr. 13.43–54; Nic. *ap.* Ant. Lib. 26.3; Apollod. 1.9.19.

[9] See Puruli Texts III, VI, and Appendix, Gaster (1950) 329–332, 334–336, with discussion and commentary; Pollux 4.84.

(Fates) to intercede with Hahhimas. Yet he was afraid lest Hahhimas seize them too, and then be able to demand the Weather God's surrender and abdication. So he sent the mighty brothers of Hasamilis to escort them and warned Hahhimas against laying violent hands on them. There follows a mutilated text which gives some indication that Hahhimas heeded the warning—but nothing is certain. Thereafter the text breaks off, so that we cannot know how the Sun God was found or Hahhimas overcome.[10]

Correspondences with Greek myths occur at every point. Hahhimas, as his very name indicates, is a death demon (Th. 3F), who like Python or Lamia spread death among all creatures (Th. 4A). He "paralyzed the whole earth" and "dried up the waters" (Th. 4G). He attacked the gods themselves, seized and carried off many of them, and seemed about to oust the chief god himself (Th. 5A). The abduction of the gods means their temporary death (Th. 8A); among them was the fertility god Telipinu, and though it is not said, it is probable that the Sun God disappeared because he had been captured by Hahhimas. The Weather God's funk recalls the oracular Apollo of the Sybaris and Temesa legends: he too could only recommend appeasement (Th. 7C), and the only remedy that occurred to him was revival of the victims. Notice too that the Weather God sends other gods who become the demon's captives. His sending out goddesses under armed protection to treat with Hahhimas may reflect an earlier version in which he sacrificed them to the demon's lust: certain it is that Hahhimas was likely to take them (Th. 4E). The Gulses helped the Weather God as the Moirai helped Zeus; the Great Goddess recalls Artemis or Athena as helper of the dragon fighter (Th. 7D). Hahhimas, we learn, fed huge quantities of beef, mutton, and drink to his parents: here we have the gluttony theme (Th. 4D) and a suggestion of the banquet at which the demon is host (Th. 8C). He was aided by his brother, Wind: Typhon's name and activity were and still are often associated with the winds (Th. 3G; see p. 546). Finally, the myth is accompanied by the text of a ritual for which it served as *aition* (Th. 10D).[11]

---

[10] Yuzgat Tablet, Gaster (1950) 344–352, with discussion 337–343.

[11] Apparently present too are Ths. 2A, 6A, 7A, 7E. The demon's seizing of Zababa the war god is parallel to the Aloadai's seizing of Ares (p. 329, note 12).

Closely related to the Hahhimas myth is the myth of Telipinu. For some reason this fertility god left the company of the gods in high dudgeon and disappeared, leaving the world blighted and barren: "men and gods alike were perishing of hunger." The Sun God then summoned the gods to a banquet (apparently he was a hoarder) and filled them with food and drink. At this gathering they instituted a search for Telipinu, but could not find him. An eagle was then sent forth and failed to find him. After that the Weather God searched, but saw Telipinu nowhere. Then the Queen Goddess sent a bee forth to look for Telipinu, and the bee found him lying in a meadow within a forest. When the bee aroused him Telipinu flew into a rage and spread destruction everywhere, killing men and cattle, until the eagle was sent to carry him back. Then the gods began magical rituals and incantations to exorcise Telipinu's anger and with some difficulty finally succeeded; Telipinu went back into his temple and restored fertility to earth.[12]

Here, to be sure, there is no combat; yet there is much in the myth that is relevant to this study. First of all, notice the character of Telipinu, who was son of the Weather God and a great god of the Hittite pantheon, and yet vented his wrath upon all creatures of earth and heaven. He not only blighted plants, sent barrenness and famine upon earth, and caused springs to run dry, but also destroyed men and beasts (Ths. 4A and 4G). It seems that he even overturned the gods (i.e., their images, perhaps a vestige of actual war upon the gods in an earlier version). In all this Telipinu acts much like Python and his brigand derivatives or the male counterparts of Lamia and Empusa, e.g., Heros of Temesa. The ambiguity of his nature is due to his character as a dying-and-rising fertility god—"O Telipinu, thou wast [sick] and art recovered; thou art restored to health" (Th. 8A)—for such gods are closely associated with the powers of death (see pp. 253–255).[13]

Notice too the Sun God's banquet as a device for initiating ways and means of dealing with Telipinu. This seems to be an

---

[12] Gaster (1950) 361–377, with discussion, 353–360; see also *id.* (1952) 99–109, Pritchard (1950) 126–128.

[13] He reminds one of Achilles too in his wrath that caused him to withdraw from the god's company and to refuse to return.

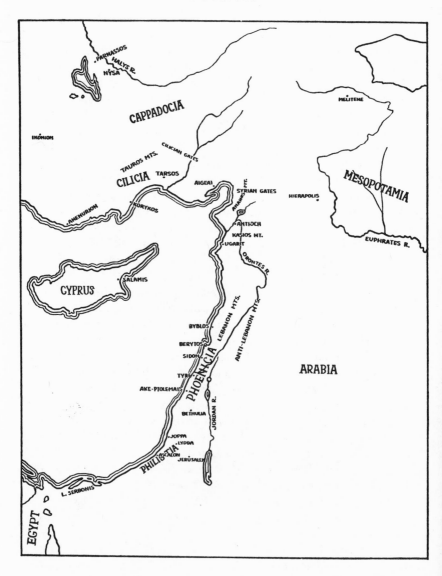

MAP 2. SYRIA, PALESTINE, CILICIA, CAPPADOCIA

echo (or forerunner) of the dragon's feast of the combat myths (Th. 9, *a*). Telipinu was welcomed with a feast upon his return (Th. 10B), the mythical counterpart of the ritual *lectisternium* or *theoxenia,* as Gaster points out. Ritual texts accompany the narrative: the magical ceremonies of the gods are the mythical precedent of the rituals of a festival (Th. 10D). Another correspondence is seen in the help given by goddesses, gods, eagle, and bee to Weather God and Sun God (Ths. 7D and 7E). The Gulses are mentioned in this myth too as present at the welcoming feast. Perhaps in an earlier version Telipinu was not carried over mountains to the gods' city by an eagle's wings, but flew with his own (Th. 3B). Finally, the theme of appeasement (Th. 7c) is dominant here, wholly replacing the theme of combat.[14]

BAAL'S COMBATS WITH SEA AND DEATH

Neighbor of Cilicia to the east and closely associated with her in history and culture is North Syria. On the Syrian coast, not far south of the Syrian Gates and the bend of the coast, just below Antioch and the Orontes River's mouth, lay Ugarit, the modern Ras Shamra, where extremely important texts, written in a Canaanite language, were discovered about thirty years ago. Among them was an apparently connected series of texts that we may call the Baal Series, the Baal and Anat Cycle, or the Poem of Baal. This series has attracted more attention and scholarly controversy than any other Ugaritic text. Much remains uncertain—to what extent the series constitutes a unified whole, the order of the parts, and the precise meaning of many difficult passages—but the uncertainties have diminished steadily over the years. At present it appears that Cyrus Gordon's text is most authoritative and that his translation, Gaster's, and Ginsberg's, though they differ in details, have come nearest to a finally correct interpretation.[15]

---

[14] Implicit too are Ths. 2A, 2c (Telipinu has his city and his temple).

[15] Text: Gordon (1947) part II. Translations: Gordon (1949) 9–56, Gaster (1950) 115–224; Ginsberg in Pritchard (1950) 129–142 and in Mendelsohn (1955) 224–261. Paraphrase: Gaster (1952) 209–234. For citations of earlier publications of cuneiform and transliterated texts and of translations see Gaster (1950) 114, Fontenrose (1951) 139, note 60. See also Engnell (1943) 97–129, Kapelrud (1952), Cornford (1952) 253–256.

El, who has a shadowy supreme authority, granted dominion over earth to Yam (Sea). Aliyan Baal, god of rainfall and fertility, challenged Yam's authority and refused to pay tribute to him, so that Yam sent messengers to El demanding that he surrender Baal and Baal's henchmen to him. The gods trembled before Yam's messengers; El meekly promised that Baal would be Yam's slave and pay tribute to him. Baal, however, went forth to fight Yam, equipped with two magic clubs that the divine smith Koshar-wa-Hasis (Gaster's Sir Adroit and Cunning) gave him, and which could fell an opponent at a distance. Baal threw one club without effect, but with the other he smote Yam upon the head and brought him down. Then Baal took Yam's place as lord of earth and had Koshar-wa-Hasis build him a palace that would befit his high position.[16]

Baal's prosperity had but a short term. Soon a rival appeared in Mot (Death), who would no more submit to Baal's authority than Baal to Yam's. Baal sent messengers to Mot, apparently to ask that he keep to his own realm and never oppose himself to Baal. Mot was in no mood to comply; rather, he invited Baal to descend to his house and dine with him. Baal, in great terror, wanted to refuse this invitation, but finally descended to Mot's realm. This descent means Baal's death: he ate the food of the dead and so had to stay there. Then arose great mourning for Baal in heaven and on earth. Anat, his sister-wife, and Shapash (Sun, a goddess) found his body and buried it on the Mountain of the North (Shapan, Zaphon, which is Mount Kasios), the home of the gods. An inferior god, Ashtar, tried to take Baal's place as lord of earth, and proved inadequate. But Anat wanted to recover

---

I cite the texts according to the translations of Gordon and Gaster. Since the numerical designations assigned to the texts do not correspond to the sequence of texts when presented in narrative order, and since Gaster and Gordon differ somewhat concerning the narrative sequence, I shall cite the Ugaritic texts by reference to the pages of Gordon's and Gaster's translations, which for most readers will be the most convenient means (aside from Ginsberg's translation) of reading the Ugaritic poems. E.g., "*Baal* 11: 133" means "*Baal Series*, Gordon (1949) 11, Gaster (1950) 133."

[16] *Baal* 11–17: 133–140, 153–161. The summary presents the bare essentials of the Baal-Yam episode, and I have confined myself to those incidents upon which the translators agree. There are interesting features in Gaster's translation in passages translated differently from Gordon: e.g., the wounded Yam's survival for a time. But it would be unsafe, for one whose knowledge of Ugaritic is limited to the occasional recognition of a word that his study of Hebrew allows him, to place much reliance upon translations of disputed or unclear passages. For the building of Baal's palace see *Baal* 28–36: 162–182.

Baal's life as well as his body. In a very curious passage she met Mot, attacked him, and subdued him; she cut him, winnowed him, parched him, ground him, and scattered his remains over the fields. This would seem to dispose effectively of Mot; but seven years later he appeared apparently whole and sound, blaming Baal for his humiliation, and once more presenting his own claim to rule over earth. Then Baal, who had in the meantime come back to life, fought Mot in violent and fairly even combat, until Shapash called upon Mot to surrender, warning him of El's wrath. Mot in great terror gave up and Baal entered upon his dominion unhindered.[17]

There is another story of Baal's death, apparently a variant of the foregoing; Gaster calls it *The Harrowing of Baal*. El was Baal's enemy and planned to destroy him. Through a cross between two handmaids and beasts of the desert he procured the birth of some monstrous bovine creatures. Baal saw them while hunting and wanted to capture them. As he chased them, they turned on him, overpowered him, and left his body lying in a swamp (?). Thereupon his brothers searched for him and found his body. Here the text breaks off. Surely Baal rose from death and settled accounts somehow with El.[18]

So there are three myths of combat in the Baal texts: Baal fought Yam, Mot, and El, or at least El's creatures. Rivalry between gods is the central theme of the series, and I have limited my summary to this theme. I have of necessity ignored subordinate episodes such as Baal's effort to acquire the right to build a palace, his building of it, and his dealings with Anat and with other deities. Such subordinate episodes, along with differences of detail, structure, and manner, give the Baal myths an outward appearance that is very different from the Greek and Hittite

---

[17] *Baal* 36–49: 182–205. It must be evident from this summary that much of the Baal-Mot story remains unclear. There are gaps in the tablets and many uncertainties in the visible text. Moreover one cannot help wondering whether the four texts from which the story as summarised is derived really do form a unity. In Text 62 Anat enlists Shapash's aid in a search for the dead Baal: in Text 49 (later in the sequence), presumably after she has found his body and buried it, she again goes out to look for him and again enlists Shapash's aid. But it is within Text 49 that both Anat and Baal subdue Mot; and if Gordon's translation is right, Baal fought and subdued him twice—i.e., three defeats for Mot within one text—so it is possible that within a single poem the goddesses twice looked for the dead Baal.

[18] *Baal* 53–55: 219–222. See Kapelrud (1952) 103, 105 f., 133.

myths which we have reviewed. But analysis shows that they share the same fundamental themes. The following comparison is made between the Baal and Zeus-Typhon myths with occasional reference to myths of the Python group.

1. Theme 1A. Mot is called son of Asherat, El's consort, in Gordon's translation: "Baal seizes the son of Asherah" (Typhon 1, pp. 77 f.). This is consistent with the testimony of Philo of Byblos, who refers his account of Phoenician mythology to a certain Sanchuniathon of Berytos. The Ras Shamra finds have in general confirmed Philo's testimony; but some differences may naturally be expected between Ugaritic traditions and those of Berytos or Byblos. Now Philo says that Muth (i.e., Mot) was son of Kronos and Rhea (i.e., El and Asherat). But Gaster translates, "Baal seizes the sons of Asherat," and interprets the passage to mean that after Baal's resurrection he punished those gods who had supported Mot. In any case Asherat is the mother of deities who opposed Baal.[19]

Asherat-Rhea is daughter of the Phoenician Ge in Philo's genealogy. She is an old mother goddess herself, being mother of numerous gods mentioned in the Ugaritic texts. Her consort El-Kronos was son of Uranos and Ge, according to Philo. She was called Asherat-of-Sea at Ugarit, but her precise relation to Yam is not made known. In Philo's genealogy the sea gods appear relatively late: Nereus, Pontos' father, is third in descent from Uranos and Ge.[20]

2. Theme 1B. Mot is son of El in Ugaritic texts and in Philo's account (Typhon 2, p. 78). Yam, like Mot, is called "beloved of El," and this may mean that he too is El's son, though the texts grant us no certain indication of Yam's parents. According to Philo, Zeus Belos, son of El-Kronos, was father or grandfather of Nereus, Typhon, and Pontos, three gods of the sea who appear to be merged in the Ugaritic Yam.[21]

---

[19] *Baal* 47: 202; Philo *ap*. Eus. PE 38D. Philo (or Sanchuniathon) himself identifies Kronos with El (*ibid*. 36c, 37A, 38A); see Dussaud (1949R) 361, Fontenrose (1951) 137. On Sanchuniathon and the Ugaritic texts see Eissfeldt (1939) 8–12, 75–95.

[20] Philo *ap*. Eus. PE 36c, 37c, 38A. Asherat-of-Sea: *Baal* 28–32: 163–173; 44: 196 f. See Kapelrud (1952) 75–78.

[21] *Baal* 19 f.: 214; 36–40: 186–190; 48: 204; Philo *ap*. Eus. PE 38A, 38D. Philo's Belos is apparently identical with the Zeus Belos who is son of Kronos. He is distinguished from Demarûs, who is Hadad (Had-Amurru), the Baal of the Ugaritic texts: see Kapelrud

3. Theme 1c. Anat, after boasting of her victory over Yam and Mot (for she claims the defeat of Yam too), says that she also crushed Fire, the bitch of the gods, daughter of the god ŽBB, according to Gordon (or herself called ŽBB, according to Gaster). In this creature we may see a monstrous consort of Yam or Mot (Typhon 3, p. 78).[22]

4. Theme 2A. The Ugaritic texts place the gods upon the Mountain of the North (Ṣapân, Zaphôn); it was there that Baal was buried. This must be the highest mountain of the vicinity, Jebel Okrah, which the Greeks called Kasios. Kasios is the name of the mountain to which, in Apollodoros' account, Zeus pursued Typhon and where Typhon overcame Zeus and removed his sinews (Typhon 4, pp. 78 f.). Apollodoros could be referring to either of two mountains called Kasios, Jebel Okrah or Ras Kasaroun, which is on the border of Egypt and Palestine (which the Greeks called Syria) by Lake Serbonis, under whose waters Typhon's body lay, according to Herodotos. But the Typhon of Lake Serbonis is probably Egyptian Set, whereas Jebel Okrah suits the myth of the Greco-Cilician Typhon perfectly. It is situated in northern Syria, which Apollodoros probably means when he says that Kasios is situated above Syria (ὑπέρκειται Συρίας), and northern Syria is the land of the Arimoi (pp. 78 f.); it is on the coast opposite Cilician Korykos, whither Typhon waded through the sea from Kasios; it is near the mouth of the Orontes River, whose channel Typhon plowed up with his coils in a desperate attempt to escape underground from Zeus's thunderbolts, according to a story told by Strabo; and not far to the east, according to other sources, Typhon chased Aphrodite-Astarte, who escaped him by leaping into either the Euphrates or a lake near Hierapolis. Finally, the Baal-Anat poems reveal the importance of this mountain in the religion and mythology of the region: the Mountain of the North was the home of the gods.[23]

(1952) 50–52. Here we see a parallel to Greek myth, wherein Zeus who fought Typhon appears also as father of Tityos. It may be that in one place Yam is called El's son: Baal 26 Gord.; Kapelrud (1952) 103.

[22] Baal 20: 214.

[23] Kasios: Apollod. 1.6.3; Herod. 3.5.2 f. Typhon in northern Syria: Strabo 16.2.7, p. 750; Ovid Fasti 2.459–474; Man. 4.579–582. For Typhon beneath Lake Serbonis see also Apollon. Arg. 2.1215; Herodoros 61, 1.227 J; EM 772.

5. Theme 3B. Either Yam was himself a dragon and had the bynames Lotan (Hebrew Leviathan) and Tannin, or a dragon named Lotan and Tannin was another enemy of Baal, perhaps as henchman of Yam (Typhon 8, pp. 80 f.). Gaster and Kapelrud take the former position. The latter is supported by Philo, who reports the appearance of three sea deities (see feature 2 above). The name of one, Pontos, is a translation of Yam: he fought Demarus, who is Baal; another, Typhon, seems to be Leviathan-Tannin, great dragon or monster of the sea.[24]

Other bestial enemies of Baal were the oxen and buffaloes that El raised against him. The Typhon of the Pergamene frieze (fig. 15) has the horns and ears of a bull, and Nonnos included bulls' heads among Typhon's many heads.

6. Theme 3C. The dragon that Baal fought had seven heads (see note 24; Typhon 9, p. 82).

7. Theme 3D. No mention is made of Lotan's fire-breathing, but we have noticed his ally, the bitch Fire (Typhon 10, p. 83). That she really represents this theme will be evident when we meet Aigis and Kampe (pp. 243–245).

8. Theme 4A. Lotan is called villain (Gaster) or accursed (Gordon) (see note 24; Typhon 11, p. 83). Yam's arrogance is reflected in his messengers' conduct before El.

9. Theme 4D. Mot devours his victims; to die is to enter his mouth; his gaping jaws stretch from earth to sky; Baal was consumed like a lamb or goat (Typhon 13, p. 84; cf. Ths. 3F and 4F). Phorbas and Kyknos, who killed all comers and heaped up their skulls, are plainly forms of the Greek Mot, Thanatos.[25]

10. Theme 5A. Baal fought both Yam and Mot for sovereignty (Typhon 16, p. 84). The dominion that El had granted to Yam was successfully challenged by Baal. Then Mot seriously chal-

---

[24] *Baal* 38 f.: 186 f.: "Because thou didst smite Lôtân, the writhing serpent/Didst destroy the crooked serpent/The accursed one of seven heads." (Gordon). Gaster translates "that Dragon Evasive," "that Serpent Tortuous." See also *Baal* 20: 214, where the name Tannin is found. On Lotan = Yam see Gaster (1950) 186, Kapelrud (1952) 102, 119. Philo *ap.* Eus. PE 38A.

[25] *Baal* 37: 183; 38: 186; 39: 189; 45: 199; cf. Mendelsohn (1955) 241, 250, 255. Perhaps lechery of Yam or Mot can be seen in the episode of Baal's refusal to have windows in his palace; it seems that he fears that an enemy will come through and carry off his daughters (Th. 4E); see *Baal* 34: 176.

lenged Baal's lordship of earth. It was his avowed purpose to rule over all gods and men, and he nearly succeeded in doing so.[26]

In *The Harrowing of Baal* it is plain that El fears Baal: so powerful has the young god become that he threatens to take over the supremacy of El himself.

11. Theme 6A. It was Baal, a weather god, lord of the fertilising rains and of the thunder, "the Rider of Clouds," as he is often called in the Ugaritic texts, who fought Yam and Mot (Typhon 18, p. 84). In character and functions he closely resembles Zeus, and it is well known that the Baals of Syrian cities were identified with Zeus. Philo calls him Zeus Demarus.[27]

12. Theme 6B. Baal appears to be a young god, who has just reached the age when he can successfully challenge Yam (Typhon 19, p. 84). He does not yet have a palace as befits a great god.

13. Theme 7A. Baal fought both Yam and Mot in single combat (Typhon 20, p. 84). He quelled Yam with two bludgeons, Expeller and Driver. These he threw from a distance; it is noteworthy that he avoided coming within Yam's reach. There can be no doubt that Gaster is right in identifying these bludgeons with thunderbolts: they sprang from Baal's hand and "like a vulture with its talons" fell upon Yam. Here the club of Herakles, his favorite weapon, must not be overlooked.[28]

In a combat that Baal fought just after his resurrection, whether against Mot or against the sons of Asherat (p. 132), he also used a club. The final combat with Mot appears to have been weaponless; the combatants gored and bit and kicked. This recalls the weaponless combat of Eurybatos with Lamia (p. 45) and of Euthymos with Heros of Temesa (p. 102). But Baal had weapons of the chase in his hands when El's horned beasts attacked him.[29]

14. Theme 7B. Baal threw the club Expeller and it had no appreciable effect on Yam. It took the second club Driver to bring him down. Though these are not the numerous thunderbolts or

[26] *Baal* 12–16: 135–140, 154–161; 36 f.: 183; 48: 204 f.

[27] Philo *ap.* Eus. PE 38c; Kapelrud (1952); Gaster (1950) 122 f.; LM 6.610.

[28] *Baal* 15 f.: 156–159; see Gaster's note *ad loc.*

[29] *Baal* 47 f.: 202–204; 54: 220 f. Notice that Mot succeeded Yam as Baal's opponent much as Ares succeeded Kyknos against Herakles (p. 29).

arrows of Zeus or Apollo (Typhon 21, p. 85), yet the Ugaritic poet means that Baal overcame Yam with difficulty. He fits the story to the weapons used: a warrior goes into battle with two clubs at most.

15. Theme 7c. As the Greek gods fled before Typhon (p. 73), so did the Ugaritic gods quail before the messengers of Yam and were ready to submit.[30]

16. Theme 7D. Anat, Baal's sister and wife, supported him throughout (Typhon 22, p. 85). She even took part in combat, bringing to Mot his first discomfiture and death; later she claimed for herself victory over Yam, Mot, and Fire (see 3, above). As Baal's sister she resembles Artemis; as a warrior maid she resembles Athena. Shapash the sun goddess helped Anat recover the dead Baal, and finally brought Mot to surrender.

17. Theme 7E. Baal had a god helper in the skilled smith Koshar-wa-Hasis, a Ugaritic Hephaistos, the maker of Expeller and Driver (Typhon 23, p. 85; see 19, below).

18. Theme 8A. The temporary defeat and death of the god-champion are plain to see in the Mot episode, where we can no longer doubt that the combat myth has become thoroughly fused with the myth of the dying-and-rising god (Typhon 25, p. 85). They are again plainly seen in *The Harrowing of Baal*. They were present too in other Canaanite versions of the combat with Yam, as in Philo's account: Demarûs attacked Pontos, but Pontos routed him; then Demarûs vowed an escape offering.[31]

19. Theme 9. Something of the trickery theme (Typhon 26, p. 89) may be seen in the two magic clubs that the divine smith made and gave to Baal (9, *d*). As a crafty god Koshar-wa-Hasis corresponds to Hermes and Pan in the Typhon story.

20. Theme 10B. Baal's victory over Yam (Gordon) or Mot (Gaster) was celebrated with a banquet on the heights of Shapan,

---

[30] *Baal* 13 f.: 138–140.

[31] Philo *ap.* Eus. PE 38A. There are hints of Baal's defeat by Yam in the Ugaritic texts. El promised Yam Baal's submission (*Baal* 14: 139 f.); cf. the Delphic Apollo's role in the Eurybatos story (p. 45). Notice that in the Mot episode Baal offered his own submission: *Baal* 39 f.: 189 f. If Gaster's restorations and translation are right, either Baal or Anat (or both) had to fall back at first before Yam (*Baal* 153 Gast.). The failure of the first bludgeon is perhaps a faded reminiscence of Baal's defeat. Notice that in Philo's account Demarûs was an ally of Uranos, and that his encounter with Pontos occurred before El-Kronos seized and mutilated Uranos.

where "a sweet-voiced youngster" chanted and sang a song in praise of Baal to the accompaniment of cymbals (Typhon 28, p. 90).[32]

In twenty features, therefore, there is correspondence between Baal's combats with Yam and Mot and Zeus's with Typhon. Of these, thirteen (4–6, 8–13, 15–18) are clear, close, and significant; the geographical coincidence (4) is especially striking; and there is a general harmony in the nuclear themes (10–18). There are also interesting parallels to the myths of chapters i–iii and vi.

Theme 4B. Yam exacted tribute from all the gods and demanded that Baal pay tribute. The tribute theme is echoed in the stories of Erginos and Eurytos (pp. 42 f.).[33]

Theme 7C. The appeasement theme is marked (p. 102). El was ready to accede to all Yam's demands and promised Baal's submission. Yam's messengers made no obeisance before El and showed him scant respect. Baal offered his own submission to Mot in nearly the same terms. Compare Apollo's appeasement of Sybaris (p. 45).[34]

Theme 8C. Baal accepted Mot's invitation to dine with him in the land of death and after doing so could not return. Here, plain to see, is the adversary's banquet to which he lures the hero in order to trap him, the reverse of the theme of tricking the adversary with food (9, a). It is the dinner that Lityerses, Syleus, and Empusa served to their guests, it may well be the meal of Laogoras and Koronos, and certainly it is the banquet that Set-Typhon served to Osiris (p. 178).

Theme 8E. Baal's death called forth lamentations from gods and men, as the loss of Apollo caused lamentations among the people of Sikyon (p. 87).

Theme 10C. Anat, after slaughtering partisans of Yam or Mot, purified herself, cleansing herself of blood and dirt with water, as Apollo purified himself after his slaying of Python (p. 15). This means both a literal and a ritual cleansing.[35]

Theme 10D. The Baal poems show throughout that they were

---

[32] *Baal* 17: 210.
[33] *Baal* 14: 140.
[34] *Baal* 12–14: 135–140; 39 f.: 189 f.
[35] *Baal* 18: 212.

designed to accompany rituals (p. 125); they are, says Gaster, the libretto of a ritual drama.[36]

AQHAT

Like Greeks and Hittites, the Canaanites of Ugarit had more than one myth of this kind. Important is the story of Aqhat, subject of a poetic text. Aqhat was son of a chieftain named Daniel, who is no doubt the Daniel of Ezekiel's trio—Noah, Daniel, and Job—who in the time of the Lord's vengeance upon a wicked land "should deliver but their own souls by their righteousness" (Ezekiel 14.14, 20): i.e., like Noah and Job he was a prominent figure in Canaanite folklore. Once Daniel entertained the divine artisan Koshar-wa-Hasis, who was passing through the city on his way back from Egypt to the home of the gods. The god rewarded his host with a wonderful bow, one of a lot that he was carrying with him. Afterwards Daniel gave this bow to Aqhat. The goddess Anat, who coveted the bow, came to Aqhat and promised him riches and immortality, and perhaps her favors too, if he would give it to her. But Aqhat preferred the bow to any goods that Anat could offer, whereupon she went to El and complained. El, submitting finally to her bullying, allowed her to work her will upon Aqhat. First she made a false peace with Aqhat and invited him to feast with her in Abiluma. While Aqhat was eating, Anat and her henchman Yatpan changed themselves into eagles (or griffons) and flew among a flock of eagles over Aqhat's head; then Yatpan swooped down and killed him, apparently contrary to Anat's intention, which was to punish Aqhat and get the bow, but not to destroy him. As Daniel sat in judgement at the city gate, his daughter Paghat observed the flight of eagles overhead, divined that her brother had met with foul play, and told Daniel. Their fears were confirmed by messengers who came to Daniel and told him of Aqhat's death. Daniel then put a curse upon the land that blighted it for seven years, and for that time he and his people kept up a ritual mourning for Aqhat. In the meantime, Daniel with Baal's help recovered Aqhat's remains from the belly

---

[36] Gaster (1950) 49–72, 122–129; Kapelrud (1952) 13–27. Baal's building of a palace after his victory over Yam corresponds to Apollo's building of his temple at Delphi at the time of his dragon combat (p. 13).

of the mother of eagles and buried them. When the seven years had ended, Paghat set out to bring Aqhat back from death. Beneath her fine raiment she put on armor and concealed a sword. Then she went to Yatpan's house, who in great joy at the visit of so lovely a guest invited her to eat and drink with him. As Yatpan drank wine and talked to her, he began to boast of his prowess and openly declared himself the killer of Aqhat. Here the text breaks off, but there can be no doubt that Paghat killed the drunken and unwary Yatpan and that Aqhat was recovered.[37]

At first reading one is struck by the close parallel between the Aqhat tale and the story of Baal and Mot: the names of the leading characters have changed, but the plot remains the same. Baal becomes Aqhat, Anat becomes Paghat; El is now Daniel, and Mot is Yatpan. The actual El and Baal recede into the background as great gods. Anat alone is an important character in both poems, but her role has changed. She is no longer the sister-wife of the dead hero-god, but the mistress and ally of the enemy. Perhaps, as Kapelrud suggests, Aqhat and Paghat were on their way to replacing Baal and Anat as the principal gods of the Ugaritic pantheon, just as Baal and Anat had succeeded El and Asherat. It is especially significant that blight covers the earth while Aqhat is dead, and that a seven-year cycle is mentioned.[38]

Theme 3B. Anat and Yatpan became eagles to attack Aqhat. The word translated *eagle* is also translated *hawk* and *griffon*. The griffon as lion-eagle is closely associated in folklore with the

---

[37] Text: Gordon (1947) 179–184 (see also 161 f.). Translations: Gordon (1949) 85–103, Gaster (1950) 270–313, Ginsberg in Pritchard (1950) 149–155 and Mendelsohn (1955) 262–279. For summary or discussion see Engnell (1943) 134–142, Gordon (1949) 84 f., Gaster (1950) 257–267, (1952) 175–190, Kapelrud (1952) 73–75. *Aqhat* is cited in the same way as *Baal*.

[38] *Aqhat* 94–99: 296–308. Kapelrud's (1952: 74) suggestion is opposed in a review of his book by John Gray (JNES XIII [1954] 204), who also disagrees with those who say that the texts show a conflict between El and Baal, and notes "with satisfaction Eissfeldt's recent rehabilitation of El" (Eissfeldt 1951). To me the texts as translated by Gaster and Gordon show two things: (1) El retains a shadowy final sovereignty; (2) Baal becomes the *de facto* ruler of the world and most powerful god. It is simply the mythical reflection of an historical process: one god gives way to another in popularity or favor, yet retains recognition and something of his former state—hence some confusion in the myths: he is supreme king, yet superseded. There are too many parallels in neighboring mythologies to allow us to ignore the patent indications that all is not well between El and Baal (see pp. 166 f., 179, 213). Nor can we blink the fact that the Phoenician El was identified with Kronos and Baal with Zeus (p. 132); compare Enlil and Marduk (p. 157). After all, Kronos kept a place in worship at Olympia; cf. Paus. 6.20.1.

flying dragon, whose wings are borrowed from eagle or vulture. It may be that in an earlier form of the myth Yatpan and Anat were identical with the father and mother eagles (called HRGB and SML), rulers of the flock to which they attached themselves. These terrible birds that swooped down on Aqhat at dinner strongly recall the Harpies, who belong to the world of Sirens, Erinyes, Keres, Lamias, and Empusas.[39]

Theme 8A. Aqhat's death at Yatpan's hands (or talons) corresponds closely to Baal's death at Mot's hands. As Baal was invited to a meal in Mot's realm, so Aqhat was invited to a meal in Abiluma, city of Mourners, which is the meaning of the name (Semitic root 'BL), and city of the Moon-God. This, Yatpan's city, is plainly the land of death.[40]

Themes 9, 8C. Not only do we find the meal at which the hero was trapped, but also the meal at which the enemy was beguiled: Yatpan in his cups betrayed and delivered himself to Paghat, who herself dealt destruction to him; Inaras of the Hittite myth (p. 121) lured the dragon into an ambush, exactly as Anat lured the hero. Trickery by disguise is also present in the Aqhat myth: for Paghat, having adorned herself as for festivity concealed arms and armor beneath her glad raiment, and Yatpan was not aware that he entertained Aqhat's sister.[41]

Theme 8B. When Yatpan killed Aqhat he took from him his god-given bow, which endowed its owner with supernatural power. It corresponds to Zeus's thunderbolt, which in Nonnos' version of the Typhon myth symbolised Zeus's sinews.[42]

---

[39] *Aqhat* 93: 292–294; 96–98: 300–302.

[40] *Aqhat* 92 f.: 291–294; 99: 304 f. Daniel laid a curse of eternal blindness (Gordon: "May Baal make thee one-eyed") upon Abiluma. This may mean that the city of the dead was a pleasanter place before Aqhat was murdered there.

[41] *Aqhat* 100 f.: 308–313. Gaster perhaps misinterprets Paghat's enterprise when he says (1950: 259; cf. 1952: 184), "Then, at sundown, she set out to raise the posse. And to whom should her steps lead her if not to Yatpan himself— . . ." It seems to me rather that she was pretty well aware that Yatpan was the killer. For that reason she adorned herself with cosmetics and fine raiment and went deliberately to Yatpan's house, presenting herself as an alluring woman visitor (Th. 4E) so as to dine with him and catch him off guard. Apparently she pretended to be gathering helpers against some enemy, so that Yatpan boasted that the hand which had killed Aqhat would smite thousands of the lady's foes. The episode remarkably suggests Judith and Holofernes (see Appendix 2).

[42] It is not clear what happened to the bow. Gaster says that Yatpan dropped the bow and broke it. Gordon says that Anat received the bow; but in his translation Anat says, "Also his bow was not given to me" and "She br[ea]ks the bow." Gordon offers no interpretation of the passage. See *Aqhat* 93 f.: 294 f.; Gordon (1949) 84; Gaster (1950) 259.

Theme 7c. In the Aqhat poem, as in the Baal poem, El gave way to the bullying of a powerful deity. Anat, like Yam, had scant respect for him, though she needed his approval of her design; and she actually threatened him with violence, so that El meekly delivered Aqhat into her hand.[43]

Theme 8d. Plainly Anat coveted not only the bow but the archer too. If Gaster is right, she displayed her charms to him, besides offering him riches, when she tried to coax him into giving her the bow. Later, to beguile him, she apparently offered to become his mistress; if Gaster is right, she pretended to have run away from home to elope with him and live with him in Abiluma; in any case she proposed some sort of intimate relation with him, saying that they would be as brother and sister, which was the relation between her and her husband Baal. Hence Anat behaved very much like the Echidna or Empusa of Greek story. Aqhat in his relation to Anat resembles Orion in his relation to Artemis, both being mighty hunters, now on good terms, again on bad terms with the goddess.[44]

Other correspondences with Greek myths need be mentioned only briefly, since they appear plainly enough in the foregoing summary and discussion. Anat plays the part of dragoness companion of Yatpan (Th. 1c). She is, in fact, the dominant partner, and it is she who sent Yatpan against Aqhat, as Hera sent Python against Leto and Apollo (Th. 5b; see pp. 60 f.). The scene is north Syria as in the Baal poems (Th. 2a). Yatpan and Anat could change their shapes (Th. 3e). Yatpan is boastful, treacherous, intemperate, murderous, ready to kill thousands (Th. 4a). Aqhat was hardly past boyhood (Th. 6b). His sister Paghat aided him most effectively (Th. 7d), and presumably killed Yatpan, as Anat killed Mot. Whether Yatpan came back to life to be slain again by Aqhat cannot be said for sure; but we may suppose that Aqhat had to face some formidable enemy (Th. 7a). The mourning for Aqhat resembles the mourning for Baal (Th. 8e), and there is

---

[43] *Aqhat* 91: 288–290.

[44] *Aqhat* 90–94: 284–295. Anat's role as ogress in the Aqhat poem seems a strange reversal of her part in the Baal poems; yet even there one may notice how she rejoiced in blood and slaughter when she punished the people of the seacoast and west, who had apparently opposed Baal. She waded in gore to her hips and she gathered severed heads and hands (*Baal* 17 f.: 211 f.). She recalls Ker of Il. 18.535–538 and Keres of *Shield* 248–257

evidence throughout that this poem accompanied ritual (Th. 10D).

The Aqhat myth, as a doublet of the Baal myth, is especially noteworthy for revealing the enemy's dam or spouse (p. 118); in the Baal Series she is but dimly seen in the briefly mentioned Fire daughter of ŽBB. The Baal myth is remarkable for revealing the alliance of Sea and Death, Yam and Mot, against Baal: their association is seen both in Mot's succession to Yam as Baal's rival and in El's support of both.

DRAGON AS SEA AND DEATH

It was in the discussion of the dragoness (chapter vi) that sea and death first became prominent in this study. There I showed how remarkably alike are spirits of sea or water and spirits of death; and we saw that death is prior to sea, inasmuch as the sea is identified with either death's realm or the road thither. The bottom of the sea is Davy Jones's locker. I also showed that the dragoness Delphyne-Echidna is intimately associated with powers of sea and death. But in the earlier discussion of Python and Typhon the realms of sea and death were seldom mentioned: they had not yet emerged as important factors in the myths of dragon-combat. For in the surviving versions of the myths Python and Typhon do not show the obvious signs or characteristics of a spirit of either realm. Nevertheless there is sufficient evidence to show that they too were spirits from the vasty deep.[45]

A variation upon Pan's luring of Typhon with fried fish by the seashore is the Scholiast's story that Pan caught him in fishing nets (p. 74); so Tiamat, Asag, and Leviathan were taken, as we

---

[45] Owen Glendower's "I can call spirits from the vasty deep" is itself sufficient answer to a criticism which I have encountered that sea and death do not belong to the same level of concept. There is also the hard fact of Yam and Mot in Ugaritic mythology, whose names mean sea and death. And I have already pointed to the folkloristic view of the sea as realm of death. In fact, concepts of different levels are through personification (or deification) placed on the same level in mythical thinking. Notice the Hesiodic theogony (*Theog.* 116–138): the children of Chaos were Earth, Darkness, Love, and Night. Earth gave birth to Heaven, Mountains, and Sea; Darkness and Night produced Sky and Day; Earth and Heaven mated and produced the twelve Titans, who include Ocean, Law (Themis), Memory, Brightness, along with such figures as Koios and Krios (Ram), who appear to be Titans and nothing more. Here is about every level of concept at once, from the most abstract to the most concrete. On the affinity of dragons to water see Elliot Smith (1919) 77 f., S. Davis (1953) 33.

shall see (pp. 158, 209). In Apollodoros' version we see Typhon walking through the sea with the impotent Zeus upon his shoulders. Again it was while he was making his way through the Sicilian Sea that Zeus hurled Mount Etna upon him (or as other versions have it, it was all Sicily or one of the volcanic islands, Vulcano or Stromboli, p. 90). Nonnos shows Typhon invading the sea in his mad rage of conquest, and his snake members swimming along through the waves, genuine sea serpents. He alternates with the sea monster Phorkys as mate of Keto (pp. 96 f.). I have already told how Typhon became the river Orontes (p. 75); then, exactly like Lamia-Sybaris he disappeared beneath the earth and immediately issued forth as a spring, the river's source. This Syrian Typhon, who is also the river-god Orontes, is Lotan-Leviathan or Tannin, Yam's aid if not Yam's self (Judge River, Lord of Streams). This was not simply a later identification of Greek dragon with Syrian dragon; for the Greeks, we have seen, placed Typhon in exactly this region, Syria-Cilicia. Typhon and Lotan are one and the same. Comparatively early Typhon was identified with Egyptian Set, whom, according to Plutarch, the Egyptians identified with the sea (p. 190).[46]

That Typhon was the same as Python is sufficiently evident from the Homeric Hymn alone (p. 93). Python, after finding his own separate existence on the Greek peninsula, still betrayed his watery nature, as may be seen both in the derivative myths and in his own. Erginos was a son of Poseidon (p. 50) and so was Eurytos-Eurypylos, whose original identity with Eurytos of Oichalia I shall show to be probable (pp. 482 f.). According to one tradition Python's corpse was carried by the sea and cast upon Lokris, where it lay exposed. He was associated with the Castalian Spring and probably also with Kassotis and Delphusa (see Appendix 6), as his female counterpart Sybaris was associated with a spring far down the slope, near the Pleistos River. That Python

---

[46] Apollod. 1.6.3; Nonn. *Dion.* 1.263–293; Strab. 16.2.7, p. 750; Plut. *Mor.* 363DE, 367A, 376F–377A. The Greek and Latin authors who tell of Typhon's pursuit of Aphrodite by the Euphrates or near Ascalon (p. 84, note 24) have preserved a fragment of the Canaanite myth: Yam or Lotan lustfully pursued one of the goddesses, Astarte or Anat, before Baal finally engaged him; see Fontenrose (1951) 132–134, 145. Notice too that Typhon was father of Hydra, the nine-headed water snake (Hes. *Theog.* 313 f.; see p. 356), and of Skylla (Hyg. *Fab.* 151.1). See AW 59 for a fish-legged Typhon.

may have been identified with the Pleistos is suggested by Callimachus, who says that the Delphian snake crawled down from
Pleistos (ἀπὸ Πλειστοῖο καθέρπον) to enfold Parnassos with coils: the
verb prefix suggests that he came from the river's source. Just
across Liakoura, peak of Parnassos, are the sources of the Phocian-
Boeotian Kephisos River and of some of its tributaries. Statius
significantly speaks of *Cephisi glaciale caput*, where Python was
wont to slake his thirst; and according to Claudian, Kephisos
used to foam with Python's poison. Moreover the river-god Kephisos had as a wife Melantho, a name that is borne by a mother of
Phorbas (p. 47). This association with Kephisos is relevant not
only to the combat at Delphi, but also to the combats at Panopeus, Daulis, and Boeotian sites.[47]

Evidence that Python and Typhon were spirits of death is even
easier to find. Both were called sons of Tartaros (p. 78), and to
the depths of earth they returned (p. 90); Tityos and Typhon
literally rose up from the earth in some versions of their myths
(pp. 47, 72, 78). Among the progeny of Typhon and Echidna were
creatures of the lower realm or demons of death: Kerberos,
Orthos, Gorgon, Sphinx, Harpies. Typhon and Python lived in
limestone caverns that penetrated far into the depths of earth
(p. 410). Such caverns were regarded by the ancients as passages
to the realm of the dead—hence, the dragons lived in the lower
world. It was in Typhon's Corycian Cave that the dead Zeus was
laid away, an episode that corresponds exactly to Baal's confinement in Mot's realm.[48]

In both the name and being of Tiphys, nightmare demon, we
may see a form of Typhon (see Appendix 1), and by way of the
helmsman of *Argo* connect him with the boatman of the dead, in
which character we also find Phlegyas (p. 477), in whom we have
seen a form of Python. Notice too the relation of Erginos and

---

[47] Python's corpse: Plut. *Mor.* 294F. Python and rivers: Call. *Hymn* 4.92; Stat. *Theb.*
7.349 f. (cf. 1.565 f.); Claud. 2.9 f.; cf. Antipater *ap.* Macr. *Sat.* 1.17.57. See Hom. Hymn
3.278–280: Apollo came to the city of the wicked Phlegyans who lived ἐν καλῇ βήσσῃ
Κηφισῖδος ἐγγύθι λίμνης. See on Telphusa, pp. 366–374. Poseidon is sometimes put in
Kephisos' place as lover of Melantho (p. 47), another indication of the close relation of
Poseidon to river gods. For sources of Pleistos and Kephisos see Maps 1, 3, and Frazer
and Van Buren (1930) Map x.

[48] Typhon = Tartaros: Plut. *Mor.* 374c. Thus Ths. 2E and 3F can be added to the
correspondences between the Python-Typhon myth and the Yam-Mot myth.

Eurytos to the infernal boatman (pp. 479, 482). Phorbas-Phlegyas and Kyknos lived among skulls: their death-dealing to all comers, their contests in which their opponents always lost their lives, their aspect terrible to look upon, relate them closely to Heros of Temesa, Lityerses, and Syleus. In fact, we can now see, all the spectres, bogeys, and demons of chapter vi are forms of the dragoness and dragon who fought the gods' champion. In some variants of the combat myth the enemy's serpentine character is emphasised, in others his spectral and infernal character.

Coincidence of theme and scene make it probable that the Greek, Hittite, and Canaanite myths discussed are all variants of one story of combat between god and monstrous enemy. It was localised in Syria and Cilicia, whence it went directly to Greece, as the Greek Typhon myth itself shows with its references to Arimoi, Cilicia, Corycian Cave, Mount Kasios, and Orontes River. Yet the story may not have had its origin in that region but farther east.

VIII

GOD AND DRAGON IN MESOPOTAMIA

The Baal poems of Ras Shamra are found on tablets that were inscribed about 1400 B.C. The Hittite documents were written around the same time. Both are therefore older than many of the extant mythical texts of Mesopotamian civilisations, but not so old as the earliest of these: Sumerian tablets that were inscribed about 2500–2000 B.C. and which record a literature that appears to have been already many centuries old. In these Sumerian documents are found the earliest known versions of myths that have become familiar to many of us in the later Assyrio-Babylonian versions. The names of deities differ, though not always—and not much else. This is not surprising when we realise that often a Sumerian text is accompanied by an Akkadian translation: the transmission of myths from Sumerian to Semite was immediate and direct.[1]

THE GOD'S COMBAT

Among the Sumerian myths that were passed on to Akkadian and Assyrio-Babylonian were tales of combat between god and dragon (or similar monster). The hymn series called *Lugal-e,* found in Sumerian and Akkadian texts, tells of a battle between Ninurta and Asag (Asakku). Although translators disagree and

---

[1] See Kramer (1944) 12, 19.

FIGURE 17. GOD FIGHTING ZU

Relief in British Museum

much remains unclear, it seems that the hero-god Ninurta was urged by his weapon Sharur to defend the land against the monster-demon Asag, who with his stone warriors raided the cities. Ninurta went forth to attack and destroy the enemy, but suffered, it seems, an initial setback, and fled. However, Sharur encouraged him, and Ninurta, returning to the attack, succeeded in killing Asag. He received the kingship, which Anu, the father of the gods, had promised him, for killing Asag.[2]

Similar is the tale of the killing of Labbu, known from two fragmentary texts. Labbu was a gigantic sea dragon, fifty to sixty *biru* long (ca. 325 to 390 miles) and one *biru* high (ca. 6 or 7 miles) in one text, or, according to the other, he had a head thirty *biru* high (ca. 200 miles). He raided the plains and cities, killing the folk and beasts, and the gods trembled before him. Then Sin the moon god called upon Tishpak to go forth and fight Labbu, promising him the kingship if he should defeat him. Tishpak refused. A break in the text follows, after which a champion, probably Marduk, has appeared to fight Labbu. Another god, probably Ea, is instructing him to rouse clouds and storm, hold a talisman, the seal of his life, before his face, and attack Labbu. The champion did so and killed Labbu, whose blood flowed forth for three years, three months, a day, and a night.[3]

Very similar is the myth of combat with Zu, the monstrous and terrible stormbird. In its Susan and Ninevite versions, its narrative sequence, aside from its opening, is very like that of the Labbu myth. Zu watched Enlil in his great temple at Nippur and coveted the great god's power, his Enlilship, which was resident in his crown of sovereignty, his robe of divinity, and his

---

[2] Translated by Witzel (1920) 38–40, 50 f., 55, 57–59, with commentary in the intervals; translated in part and summarised by Kramer (1944) 80–82; see also Jacobsen (1946) 146 f., who corrects some of Kramer's renderings and summarises the myth. According to Jacobsen, it is Asag whom the plants and stones proclaim king in Tablet I; but according to Witzel it is Ninurta (Ninib). The same story seems to be present in the hymn series *An-dim gim-ma:* Ninurta fought and killed a sea monster when other gods would not: Witzel 74–84.

[3] Translated by Rogers (1912) 61–63, Witzel (1920) 87 f. (German), Heidel (1951) 141–143; text with German translation, Jensen (1900) 44–47. Heidel's translation, the most recent, appears to be best. Rogers and Witzel believe that Tishpak is the dragon fighter, but his broken-off speech begins in much the same way as those of the gods who declined to fight Zu. Marduk appears in combat with a snake on cylinder seals (fig. 18). For the uncertainty about this snake see p. 153 below. Again, *Enuma elish* I 106 mentions Marduk's curbing of a dragon or griffon.

tablet of destinies. So Zu lay in wait at the temple door, and when Enlil, stepping down from his throne to wash his hands in pure water, laid his crown aside, Zu, seizing the tablet of destinies and the emblems of Enlilship, flew away to his mountain. At once Enlil was struck speechless; his power was gone; and all splendor vanished from his temple. Apparently his authority then reverted to Anu, who is seen calling for a champion to go forth and kill Zu, promising supreme power to whoever does so. The gods summoned Adad, but he refused because Zu's power was too great for any opponent to overcome. Shara, Ishtar's first-born, also refused. Finally, with Ea's help, a god, Marduk or Ninurta or Lugalbanda (there is a break at this point in both versions), went forth to the mountains to fight Zu. He raised storm and winds against Zu, before which Zu's vigor sank. In a tablet from Ashur, Ninurta went forth to fight Zu, but failed; for Zu with the magic power of the tablets of destiny caused his bow and arrows to return to their raw materials. Then another warrior, perhaps Marduk, went forth, presumably to victory.[4]

Probably the most widely known of Babylonian combat myths is the tale of Marduk against Tiamat, an episode of *Enuma elish,* often called *Epic of Creation.* This is a poetic composition written in Assyrio-Babylonian, the author of which has fused several tradiditions, sometimes imperfectly. That much or all of its mythical content goes back to Sumerian mythology seems evident from a Sumerian text, which is, however, as yet imperfectly understood. The latter is a poem whose main content is a Gilgamesh legend to which I shall return later (p. 172); but it begins with a few lines on the beginnings of the world, which contain an allusion to Enki's (Ea's) setting sail for the netherworld—presumably to attack the enemy, the Apsu of the Babylonian myth; for Enki's fight with a monstrous enemy is alluded to elsewhere in Sumerian literature.[5]

---

⁴ For English translations of Susan and Ninevite versions see Pritchard (1950) 111–113 (Speiser); Heidel (1951) 144–147; text with German translation, Jensen (1900) 46–57. Ashur text: Ebeling (1952). Marduk is mentioned elsewhere as slayer of Zu: Langdon (1923) 18, Heidel 147. On Ninurta or Lugalbanda as Zu's slayer see p. 156.

⁵ The most recent English translations of *Enuma elish* are those of Speiser in Pritchard (1950) 60–72 and in Mendelsohn (1955) 19–46, and of Heidel (1951) 18–60; see also Rogers (1912) 3–44, Langdon (1923) 67–211 (with transliterated text); German translation with transliterated text, Jensen (1890) 268–301. Oppenheim (1947) and Frankfort (1949)

FIGURE 18. ADAD-MARDUK AND DRAGON

Cylinder Seal in British Museum

FIGURE 19. GODS FIGHTING A SEVEN-HEADED DRAGON

Cylinder Seal in Chicago Oriental Institute

Enuma elish, often called the Babylonian Genesis, begins with a chaos of waters, which consisted first of two living beings, male and female—Apsu, the male fresh waters, and Tiamat, the female salt waters—then of three, when Mummu, the vizier, joined his parents. Apsu and Tiamat mated and brought forth Anshar and Kishar, heaven and earth, who in turn produced Anu, father and ancestor of the gods, among them Ea. As the gods increased in number, they distressed Apsu and Tiamat, and the crafty Mummu plotted with Apsu to destroy them. When the gods heard of their intention, they were panic-stricken. But Ea saved them by casting a spell upon Apsu that put him to sleep. Then he could seize Apsu's crown and robe, the symbols of his kingship, which apparently transferred Apsu's sovereignty over the fresh underground waters to himself. Anshar seems to have become supreme suzerain of the gods with Anu and Ea as *de facto* rulers under him. Apsu was killed, Mummu imprisoned; Tiamat lived on in her own element.[6]

Then Marduk was born to Ea and his wife, Damkina, growing to gigantic stature in a single day. Ea bestowed a "double equality with the gods" upon him, intending that his son should become mightiest of gods. Marduk's superior qualities soon aroused the jealousy of certain malcontent gods, who, led by Kingu, formed an alliance with Tiamat, whom Marduk's boisterous ways annoyed, and planned war against the reigning gods. Tiamat produced reinforcements, eleven kinds of monstrous creatures, whose very appearance inspired terror: snakes, vipers, two kinds of dragons, great lions, fearful dogs, scorpion-men, storm-demons, dragonflies, bison, and creatures called *lahâmu.* Tiamat married Kingu, intending him for the kingship. When Ea learned of this conspiracy he was afraid; he went for advice to Anshar, who sent him forth against the enemy. When Ea could not face Tiamat

---

182–199 have translation of sections with commentary; Gaster (1952) 52–67, a paraphrase; summaries in Dhorme (1949) 303–308, Cornford (1952) 239–247, Hooke (1953) 65–67, Levy (1953) 107–117, Mackenzie MBA 138–150. For the Sumerian myth see Kramer (1938) and (1944) 37 f., 79; Witzel (1948) 396–405. But Jacobsen (1946: 144 f.) does not believe that the verses concerned refer to Enki's combat. On allusions to his combat in other Sumerian poetry see Witzel (1948) 401.

[6] I follow Oppenheim (1947: 208 f.) in omitting Lahmu and Lahamu, the first-born of Apsu and Tiamat, from the genealogy: they were a failure, he maintains, and lacked the faculty of procreation.

and fled, Anshar sent Anu forth to appease her; but he fled too. Tiamat's face was too terrible to look upon; it may be that her very glance meant death. Ea then advised Anshar to summon Marduk, who agreed to take the field against Tiamat and her hosts on condition that kingship of the gods be the prize of victory. So Anshar had to assemble the loyal gods and induce them to approve Marduk's kingship. They were brought together at a banquet, where they were served food and wine in great quantities, so that when the proposal was put before them, they were in a carefree and lighthearted mood and without a protest conferred the kingship upon him. Then and there he was proclaimed king and given the accoutrements of office.[7]

Marduk provided himself with several weapons, of which he used only the bow and arrows, net, and stormwinds. Mounting his chariot he went forth at the head of the heavenly hosts to meet the enemy. Reaching the field of battle he challenged Tiamat to single combat, and after an exchange of belligerent speeches the battle began. Marduk soon enmeshed Tiamat in his net; she opened her jaws, trying to swallow him, and he sent the stormwinds through her open mouth into her belly. They forced her to hold her jaws open, so that Marduk could shoot an arrow which "cut through her inward parts (and) split her heart." Tiamat fell, and her hosts broke and fled; but the gods under Marduk closed in on them, took them captive, and bound them; and Marduk trampled the "host of demons" underfoot, apparently consigning them finally to the same underworld abode where he imprisoned the rebel gods. Then out of Tiamat's body Marduk created earth and sky, the world order that we know. Kingu's veins were cut open, and from his blood mankind was created. The gods built Marduk a great temple, Esagil, in Babylon, and there Marduk entertained the gods at a banquet, the mythical precedent of the Akitu festival of the Babylonian New Year.

Oppenheim points out that the Ea-Apsu story is basically a

---

[7] Some have it that Tiamat produced eleven individual monsters in *Enuma elish*; but the interpretation that a host of monsters of eleven kinds is meant is supported by Berossos, frag. 12 Schnabel, who lists at least eleven kinds of monsters who were under Omorka's (Tiamat's) rule.

doublet of the Marduk-Tiamat story. There is much the same sequence of events: the gods who disturb the lords of chaos, the plot to destroy the offenders, the gods' dismay, Ea's discovery of the plot and his clever devices, the destruction of the enemy, the acquisition of sovereignty. That Apsu had a more combative role in an earlier version of the myth is hinted in the rebel gods' words to Tiamat, in which they mention Apsu's terrible *shashsharu* weapon.[8]

It is also apparent that the tales of combat between Marduk or Ninurta and Labbu or Zu are doublets of the Tiamat myth; and Asag appears to be the same as Labbu. The myths have in common the monstrous enemy, the trembling of the gods before him, Heaven's (Anu's or Anshar's) quest of a champion, the refusal or failure of at least two gods before the champion steps forth, Ea's help, use of stormwinds against the monster, and other features of correspondence which the following analysis will bring out. Therefore this group of combat myths can be conveniently considered together for the purpose of comparing the Mesopotamian combat myth with the myths of Typhon and Python.[9]

COMPARATIVE ANALYSIS

1. Theme 1A (for Typhon-Python see pp. 77 f.). Asag was son of An and Ki, heaven and earth. Apsu and Tiamat were themselves the parents of heaven and earth. Despite the identification of Tiamat with the salt waters, she seems to be something of an earth goddess; for earth was fashioned from her body. Again, she was Mother Hubur, who fashioned all things. Notice that Ki (Kishar) rose out of the waters in the Sumerian myth, as in Hesiod's *Theogony* Chaos was born first and then Earth. Moreover Tiamat's role corresponds closely to Ge's in Greek myths of beginnings. She was also the mother of the monsters and great-grandmother of the rebel gods who fought Marduk and the loyal gods. Labbu and Zu were probably her children.[10]

---

[8] Oppenheim (1947) 214, 216 f. See note 5 for the Sumerian sources that indicate combat between Ea and Apsu or some monstrous enemy.

[9] For previous discussions of similarities between the Tiamat and Typhon myths see Seippel (1939) 55–59, Cornford (1952) 243–245.

[10] Asag's parents: Jacobsen (1946) 146. An and Ki rose from the waters: Kramer (1944) 40, 73 f. Mother Hubur: *Enuma elish* II 19, III 23, 81.

2. Theme 1B (p. 78). See the preceding paragraph. Apsu was identified with the sea of fresh waters that lay beneath the earth; he was therefore associated with the nether regions. He represents both the waters and the darkness of chaos. As the underworld darkness he is the equivalent of Tartaros.[11]

In one text Enlil is called father of Ninurta's enemy, Asag or Labbu.[12]

3. Theme 1C (p. 78). The pairs Tiamat-Apsu and Tiamat-Kingu resemble Echidna and Typhon. Like Echidna, Tiamat was mother of a monstrous progeny.

4. Theme 2E (pp. 142 f.). Tiamat was identified with the sea, as Apsu with the fresh waters. Of Labbu it was said that the sea brought him forth. Asag seems to be identified with the waters of Tigris. Tiamat's two right eyes were the Tigris, her left the Euphrates.[13]

5. Theme 3A (pp. 79 f.). Tiamat was so huge that earth and sky were fashioned from her body. Apsu was obviously gigantic too. The measurements of Labbu's enormous bulk have been given above in the summary of the myth.

6. Theme 3B (pp. 80 f.). Labbu (and Asag, who was called *labbu*) was certainly a dragon in the literal sense of snake, and is probably the snake seen in conflict with a god in Mesopotamian sculpture and cylinder seals (e.g., figs. 18 and 19). Yet the name means *lion,* and it seems likely, therefore, that Labbu was also conceived as a mixture of lion and snake, the leonine dragon of Mesopotamian art. Put wings on this creature and you have a form very like Zu the stormbird, who was a kind of griffon—an eagle or vulture, usually with the head of a lion but also with that of a dog or horse. Zu can properly be called a winged dragon; for, as Elliott Smith says, the dragon sometimes has the feet and wings

---

[11] See Langdon (1923) 66, note 5; Frankfort (1948) 232, 234; Dhorme (1949) 32, 304. Notice Berossos, frag. 12 Schnabel, Γενέσθαι φησὶ χρόνον ἐν ᾧ τὸ πᾶν σκότος καὶ ὕδωρ εἶναι. I do not agree with Schnabel that σκότος is an interpolation in Polyhistor's text. Berossos' version was obviously not drawn from *Enuma elish,* at least not entirely. It is fitting that Apsu be associated with darkness because of his underworld nature; and certainly the chaos was dark, since light had not yet appeared in the world.

[12] *An-dim gim-ma* III obv. 9, 13 (Witzel 1920: 78).

[13] On Asag see Witzel (1920) 34–37 and *passim;* but cf. Jacobsen (1946) 147. Witzel (75) translates by *Meeresungeheuer* a word that designates Ninurta's enemy. On Tiamat's eyes see text in Ebeling (1931) 35, line 3.

of an eagle (or hawk), the forelimbs of a lion, and a head of either a lion or an eagle.[14]

Many scholars have thought that Tiamat had snake form, and that the dragon against whom a god fights in certain artworks represents Tiamat. Heidel, however, disagrees vehemently, and makes it plain that dragon form cannot be imputed to Tiamat with certainty, although he is not convincing in his attempt to dispose of the horns and tail that she certainly has in one source. But does it make any difference whether or not the Babylonians ever represented Tiamat as a dragon? We have seen that the god's enemy may be conceived as dragon or giant or demon or beast; in some tales, in fact, the enemy assumes various shapes. Tiamat is closely parallel to Labbu and Zu in the combat myths. She brought forth dragons and monsters of many kinds, and their presence beside her as allies in battle probably results from elaborations of the original myth. There is reason to believe that Tiamat was sometimes, not necessarily always, conceived as a dragoness: besides horns and tail she apparently had a hide that weapons could not penetrate, a feature that suggests a dragon's scaly armor. When Marduk went forth to face her, he carried an herb to counteract poison (possibly that of her snake followers). But anyone who feels that the evidence is inadequate must nevertheless realise that Tiamat's role as enemy of the gods is not affected by her shape.[15]

---

[14] On Zu see Fish (1948), Van Buren (1950); also Witzel (1920) 154–156, Langdon (1923) 18–20, Van Buren (1946) 15, 34–37. See further the text in Ebeling (1931) 5 f. Van Buren (1946 *passim*) speaks of dragons of leonine type and of ophidian type; see 23 f. on Labbu as lion-demon. For Zu in art see Rogers (1912) pl. 8; Frankfort (1939) pl. 23*c,g*; Fish figs. 1, 2; Heidel (1951) figs. 6, 7; Gaster (1952) pl. VI; Moortgat (1949) pls. 20, 21, one of which shows a horse-headed Zu (see my figs. 17, 20). Notice that the horses that draw the funeral car of Enmesharra's body are called the death demon (ghost) of Zu: text in Ebeling (1931) 33, line 25. If Van Buren (1950) is right, Zu was sometimes represented as simply an eagle. Yet the identification of the eagle on certain cylinder seals with Zu cannot be considered certain. My colleague, Professor Laessøe, informs me that only in her fig. 8 (pl. XI) is Zu certainly represented. It is apparent that the Mesopotamians had no rigid conception of Zu. For Labbu in art see E. Smith (1919) ch. ii, figs. 2, 9; Heidel (1951) figs. 5, 8 (see my figs. 18, 19). See Witzel's and Van Buren's (1946) end plates for numerous representations of Mesopotamian dragons. On Asag see the citations in note 2 above, especially Witzel 78.

[15] Heidel (1951) 83–88. Among those who think that Tiamat was a dragon are Witzel (1920) 138, 162 f.; Langdon (1923) 12, 221; Gaster (1950) 36, 60; Frazer (1911D) 105–111. In general, Heidel's conception of myth is too rigid; e.g., the snake beside Marduk upon a cylinder seal (Heidel, fig. 1) cannot be Tiamat, he says, because it is merely subdued,

7. Theme 3c (pp. 82 f.). Mesopotamian seal cylinders show gods in combat with seven-headed snakes. One shows a coiled snake who has lost two of his heads: a figure before him holds the two severed heads in his hands. In another two gods attack a seven-headed snake, four of whose heads already hang limp (fig. 19).

Tiamat had two faces, four eyes, and four ears; among her hosts were creatures of four wings and two heads, and also four-bodied dogs.[16]

8. Theme 3F (p. 144). Apsu was identified with the underworld waters; as a person he had his abode in Kur, whither Ea set sail to fight him in a Sumerian poem (p. 148). *Kur* literally means *mountain:* the Sumerians, like other peoples, conceived of the realm of death as a mountain. Asag and Zu lived on a mountain.

There can be little doubt that Zu is an underworld creature, a demon from the realm of death. In an Assyrian text, the story of a king's dream of descent to the netherworld, several demons of Zu-type appear. Noteworthy is Humuttabal, boatman of the dead, who had Zu's head and four hands and feet. The king also saw the *utukku* with lion head, human hands, bird feet; a nameless demon with Zu's head, hands, and feet; another, black as pitch, with Zu's countenance. He saw other kinds of *Mischwesen* too: among them the death god himself with the head of a snake. The list resembles Tiamat's monstrous hosts, especially as they are described by Berossos. In all likelihood they are the same creatures, banished to the underworld after their defeat. As in the Christian tale, the defeated enemy and his followers, cast into the darkness below, became the demons who terrify and torment the dead.[17]

---

whereas Tiamat was killed in *Enuma elish;* Tiamat was not a dragon, because Berossos calls her a woman; and so on. Certainly no figures of Greek myth can be pinned down in this way; and I doubt whether those of Mesopotamian myth can be either. What about Tiamat as Bel-Marduk's nurse? See text in Ebeling (1931) 32, line 19. Nothing of the sort is mentioned in *Enuma elish* and Berossos; yet the evidence cannot be dismissed merely because it is inconsistent with them. In the same text are mentioned Tiamat's horns and tail, and it is said that her death demon is a camel: 36, lines 13 f. On Marduk's herb to counteract poison see *Enuma elish* IV 62.

[16] Ebeling (1931) 32, line 20, 35, line 3; Berossos, frag. 12 Schnabel; seal cylinders in Van Buren (1946) pl. IV, 16, 17; see *ibid.* 19 f.; Heidel (1951) fig. 16, (see also 15). Zu is sometimes portrayed with four wings: Fish (1948) 171; see 8 below.

[17] Heidel (1949) 132–136; Pritchard (1950) 109 f. See Van Buren (1950) 164; Moortgat

Fish relates Zu to Pazuzu, an underworld demon and lord of wind demons, who blew from the mountains (i.e., from Kur). Pazuzu had four wings, a head that was half canine and half human, talons on hands and feet, and a scorpion's tail.[18]

FIGURE 20. ZU ON LIONS

Section of a bas-relief from Lagash

9. Theme 3G (p. 126). As demons of wind and storm, Zu and Asag are very like Typhon, whom Hesiod calls the source of all stormwinds.[19]

10. Theme 4A (pp. 83 f.). On meeting Tiamat, Marduk reproached her for the arrogance of her rebellion against the gods: she sought evil and had proved her "wickedness against the gods." The rebel gods "treat their fathers unjustly." Her monstrous followers inspired terror. Asag is called a base demon, and Zu an evildoer. Both Labbu and Zu were guilty of plunder and robbery. One of Zu's crimes was the blighting of vegetation on earth. Labbu killed the folk far and wide through the cities. Asag was a death dealer from his mountain home.[20]

(1949) 52; Heidel 172. Zu is identified by Van Buren with the fifth creature that the king saw, who had a horned cap, human hands, and bird's feet, and trod upon a snake (or crocodile). Kingu was identified with Enmesharra, an underworld god; so were Asag-Labbu and probably Zu; see Ebeling (1931) 28–31. It may be Zu whom Enkidu saw in his ill-boding dream: a creature with eagle talons that seized him: *Gilgamesh* 7.4.18–22. Cf. Appendix 1 on the infernal boatman.

[18] Fish (1948) 168–171.

[19] Hes. *Theog.* 869–880; Olymp. on *Phaed.* 201 Norv. Wind is brother of Hahhimas, the Hittite demon: Yuzgat Tablet I (Gaster 1950: 344). On Asag as Tigris flood see p. 221, note 3.

[20] *Enuma elish* IV 77–84, I 136–138 (Heidel's translation quoted); *Lugal-e* V; Fish

11. Theme 4D (p. 84). Labbu ate fish in the sea, birds in the air, wild asses upon the plains. He also ate men. Tiamat opened her mouth to swallow Marduk when he had her enmeshed in his net.[21]

12. Theme 5A (p. 84). The struggle for sovereignty is plain to see in these myths. Tiamat wished to make Kingu king over all the gods and she gave him the tablet of destinies. It was this tablet that Zu stole from Enlil. Marduk demanded kingship of the gods as his reward for fighting Tiamat, and received it from Anshar. That Labbu and Zu also aspired to the kingship is evident from Anu's promise of the throne to that god who would fight and kill the enemy. Ninurta received the kingship from Anu because he had killed Asag: he succeeded to Enlil's position as Marduk to Ea's.[22]

13. Theme 5B (p. 84). Tiamat is very like Ge in raising up opponents of the gods. Not only did she produce a host of dragons to fight them, but she encouraged and incited Kingu to take dominion from them.

14. Theme 6A (p. 84). In the long course of ancient Mesopotamian history a number of cities successively rose to prominence and power: Ur, Eridu, Uruk, Nippur (as a religious center), Akkad, Babylon, Ashur, Nineveh, to name but a few. The pantheon was made up of the patron gods of these cities. Hence one god often displaced another in the myths, both in their oral and written forms, whenever one city became supreme over others, or when the myths passed from one city to another. Thus in *Enuma elish,* as we have it, the hero is Marduk, the great Bel of Babylon. It was when Babylon became supreme in Mesopotamia that Marduk became the fighter of Tiamat, Labbu, and Zu. Earlier, under the Sumerians, the champions had been Ninurta of Nippur or Lugalbanda of Uruk. In Assyria, and elsewhere under Assyrian supremacy, the national god Ashur displaced

---

(1948) 166, 170. In the Susan version of the Zu poem, Zu is called "the thief of the Mountain": Pritchard (1950) 111 f. See Van Buren (1950) 168.

[21] See *Labbu,* Assyrian version, Heidel (1951) 143. The passage recalls Typhon's devouring of beasts in Nonnos' account: *Dion.* 2.42–52. Tiamat: *Enuma elish* IV 97.

[22] *Ibid.* I 146–161, II 122–129, III 116–122, IV 1–34; *Labbu* obv. 17–22; *Zu,* both versions (see especially Ninevite, col. 2.1–21, 3.10–16); for *An-dim gim-ma* II, III, and a hymn to Ninurta see Witzel (1920) 75 f., 78–80, 100–102.

Marduk in the Tiamat myth, as a surviving fragmentary tablet shows. Probably before Ninurta and Lugalbanda, the great gods Ea of Eridu and Enlil of Nippur had played the champion role. It is clear, both from Sumerian material and from *Enuma elish*, that Ea fought Apsu. Enlil, Bel of Nippur, where his son Ninurta overshadowed him, was identified with Marduk, Bel of Babylon, and with Ashur, each of whom was called "Enlil of the gods." In the Zu myth it is Enlil whose "Enlilship" Zu coveted; in an earlier version he, like Zeus or Aliyan Baal, may have been his own avenger. It seems certain that the original *Enuma elish* centered upon Enlil.[23]

Enlil was a god of the air, sky, wind, storm, and war; the national gods, Marduk and Ashur, took over his character and provinces when they superseded him. Marduk was identified with Zeus by the Greeks, and Enlil, as a supplanted god, with Kronos. Ninurta was a god of fertilising waters, stormwinds, and war, and was therefore closely parallel to Aliyan Baal of Ugarit. According to Witzel, Lugalbanda was a form of Ninurta. Ea was also lord of fertilising waters.[24]

Especially important as a weather god after 2000 B.C. was Adad, lord of thunder and lightning. He is the same as the Hadad of the western Semites and may have come from the west to Babylonia. It was Hadad whom Syrians and Canaanites called Baal, the title which in the form *Bel* the Babylonians gave to Enlil and Marduk. Adad was identified with Marduk as sender of rain and seems to have also been cast in the role of dragon fighter. He is seen on

---

[23] See Witzel (1920) 125–167; Pallis (1926) 186–189; Dhorme (1949) 26–38, 102–109, 139–150; Frankfort (1949) 146, 156, 183; Moortgat (1949) 93–98. For the Assyrian tablet see Rogers (1912) 53–57. That Ninurta was long recognised as victor over Zu is evident from the text in Ebeling (1931) 33, lines 24–29, 36, lines 20–22, and from cylinder seals: Frankfort (1939) 132–137 and pl. 23c,g; Van Buren (1950) 169, pl. XI 8.

[24] See Witzel, Dhorme, Frankfort, Moortgat, *locc. cit.;* also Frankfort (1949) 153–157, 193 f., 197 f.; Jacobsen (1953) 167. Marduk = Zeus: Herod. 1.181.2, 183.1; Hesych. B565. Enlil = Kronos: Eupolemos *ap.* Eus. PE 9.17; Serv. *Aen.* 1.729. That Ea was also identified with Kronos is indicated by Berossos, frags. 34, 35 Schnabel: it was Kronos who warned Xisuthros (= Utnapishtim) of the coming deluge. *Gilgamesh* XI shows that the informer was Ea, whereas Enlil was very much opposed to the survival of any human beings. Ea was identified with Poseidon too: Hesych. B565. On Lugalbanda's relation to Ninurta see Witzel (1920) 141, Langdon (1923) 19, note 1. Notice that Marduk is Ea's son and Ninurta Enlil's son: so in the west Baal is son of Dagon or El. As El corresponds closely to Enlil, so Dagon corresponds to Ea, who is sometimes represented in fish form (= Oannes or Oes: Berossos, frags. 8, 9 Schnabel); see Fontenrose (1957); for a contrary view of Dagon see Schmökel (1928).

seal cylinders, holding his two-forked or three-forked thunderbolt, either sitting or standing upon a dragon. His position may
or may not indicate victory over the dragon beneath him; but the
god who attacks a dragon with forked thunderbolts on another
seal (fig. 18) is either Adad or Marduk in his Adad character.[25]

15. Theme 6B (p. 84). Marduk in *Enuma elish* was a very
young god, who in a single day had grown to maturity after his
birth. His victory over Tiamat was his first great exploit. He is
remarkably parallel to the Baal of Ugarit in his youthful majesty
and power and in the envy and malice that he aroused in his
brother gods. Ninurta too seems to have been a young god, who
won his first laurels by defeating Asag.[26]

16. Theme 7A (p. 84). Marduk armed himself with quite an
array of weapons before taking the field against Tiamat. He had
the thunderbolt, bow and arrows, a net, and a mace called *abubu*,
which was probably a thunder weapon also, since the word originally means *stormflood*. He filled his body with flame, put on a
coat of mail, and rode a four-horsed chariot. In his mouth he held
a talisman of red paste and in his hands an herb: these were
intended to counteract magic and poison; for Tiamat recited
incantations and cast spells against Marduk when he challenged
her to single combat. He created seven terrible winds to aid him.
This use of wind and stormflood as weapons against the monstrous enemy recalls Nonnos' narrative of the Zeus-Typhon combat, wherein Zeus employed winds, hail, and rainstorm against
Typhon.[27]

Ninurta too had a net or snare in which he caught Asag. He
was armed with bow and arrows and also with two bludgeons that

[25] Adad: Schlobies (1925); Dhorme (1949) 96–102. Adad = Marduk: *Enuma elish* VII
119–121; Deimel (1914) 46. As dragon fighter: Witzel (1920) 154. In art: Van Buren
(1946) 27 and fig. 23. See also the Assyrian relief of a god attacking Zu with thunderbolts
(fig. 17). In the Ashur tablet (p. 148) of the Zu myth it is Adad who goes as messenger
of Ninurta's defeat to Ea and then goes out at Ea's command to invite Marduk (?) to be
champion; see Ebeling (1952) 36–41.

[26] *Enuma elish* I 79–123; *Lugal-e* I.

[27] *Enuma elish* IV 30–104; cf. Nonn. *Dion.* 2.391–552. Despite his overelaborate
treatment and his late date it seems probable that Nonnos, who lived at Panopolis in
Egypt, was acquainted with the mythical lore of the Near East and incorporated much
of it into his epic; see Eissfeldt (1939) 128–151, who shows that *Dion.* 40–43 has Phoenician
sources.

had names and voices, Sharur and Shargaz. Arrows and a mace were his weapons against Zu. Labbu's defeat and death were apparently very like Tiamat's: the god raised a storm against him, held a talisman, the "seal of (his) life," before his face, and shot an arrow. Winds and storm were also raised against Zu. Ea overcame Apsu in *Enuma elish* with magical spells that cast a deep sleep upon him. I have already indicated that in an earlier form of the myth Ea probably had a more violent struggle with Apsu.[28]

So in these Babylonian myths we find not only Zeus's thunderbolt and Apollo's arrows, but also several other weapons that appear intermittently in the Greek combat myths: pike or spear, club, chariot, stormwinds, rainflood. The cylinder seals show gods attacking dragons and monsters with thunderbolts or spears (see p. 153, note 14; p. 158, note 25).

17. Theme 7c (p. 123). The Babylonian gods closely resemble the gods of Greece and Ugarit in their fear and trembling before the enemy. Appeasement is seen in Anshar's attempt, through Anu as his envoy, to calm Tiamat and allay her wrath. After the failure of Ea and Anu the gods despaired of victory, saying that there was no god who could face Tiamat in battle. Likewise the gods cowered before Asag; none dared face him but Ninurta. When Labbu raided the land, they prostrated themselves in helplessness before Sin. In the Zu episode the gods' spirits fell; Adad and Shara refused to face him.[29]

18. Theme 7d (p. 85). In an old Sumerian myth, Inanna (Ishtar) fought an enemy of the gods, perhaps a dragon. Against him she went forth armed with spear, throw stick, axe, and fire. In spite of An's warning against her enterprise she fought and destroyed the enemy. This story is no doubt cognate with the Ugaritic story of Anat's combat with and slaying of Mot (p. 131); perhaps it is the archetype. Therefore we may conjecture that Inanna's combat occurred while her husband-brother was dead. Beltis (*Bêlit*), the Babylonian equivalent of Anat (*Ba'alat* as

---

[28] *Lugal-e* I obv. 25, 43–47; V obv. 1–3, rev. 5–7; *An-dim gim-ma* K38 (Witzel 1920: 82–84); *Labbu*, Babylonian text, rev.; *Zu*, both texts; Frankfort (1939) pls. 23c,g, 28c; *Enuma elish* I 61–65.

[29] *Enuma elish* II 71–91; *Lugal-e* I rev. 31; *An-dim gim-ma* II obv. 7; *Labbu*, Babyl. text, obv. 15 f.; *Zu*, both texts.

Baal's wife), mourned for the dead Bel, as Anat for Baal, and went down to the lower world to seek him.[30]

19. Theme 7E (p. 85). We have seen that the god or hero who fights and defeats the dragon often acts for another, his sovereign, who either has commissioned him to do so or has himself been defeated or maimed by the dragon. At Zeus's command Apollo destroyed the Phlegyans (p. 61), and perhaps Phorbas too; Herakles fought Kyknos at Apollo's command (p. 36); it was Hupasiyas who really mastered Illuyankas (p. 121). Likewise Marduk went out to fight Tiamat at the behest of Anshar on Ea's advice; and it was at Anu's command and on Ea's advice that Ninurta fought Asag, and Marduk or Ninurta fought Zu after the discomfiture of Enlil; and at Sin's command that a champion fought Labbu.[31]

20. Theme 7G (p. 84). While in *Enuma elish* the single combat between Marduk and Tiamat holds the center of the stage, it is nevertheless but one engagement in a battle between the gods and the forces of chaos: monsters and dragons, the issue of Tiamat, allied with rebel gods.

The extant versions of Greek myths in general separate dragon combat wholly from gigantomachy—Typhon and Python had no army about them—yet there are indications that the combats were part of a larger war. We have already seen that accounts of the Gigantomachy sometimes include Typhon and Tityos among the Gigantes (pp. 55, 80). In fact, as early as the fifth century Pindar linked Typhoeus with Porphyrion, king of the Gigantes. Moreover, according to Apollodoros and an Homeric Scholiast, Ge sent Typhon against the gods in wrath for their destruction of the Gigantes; and Hesiod implies that she brought him forth to avenge the Titans. Finally, Diodoros, perhaps euhemerising somewhat, says that Typhon led Gigantes in Phrygia in a war against Zeus.[32]

---

[30] See Kramer (1944) 82 f., Langdon (1923) 34–39; see 21 below. Could this dragon be the sea dragon Hedammu whom Ishtar once sought to allure (p. 175)?

[31] *Enuma elish* II–IV; *An-dim gim-ma* III 15–24; *Zu*, both texts; *Labbu*, Babyl. text.

[32] Pind. *Pyth.* 8.12–18; Apollod. 1.6.3; Schol. B on Il. 2.783; Hes. *Theog.* 820–822; Diod. 5.71.2; Claud. 37.32. Euripides (*Her.* 1272) associates Typhons with Gigantes as enemies of Herakles. Cf. Pergamene Gigantomachy, p. 55, figs. 12, 15. The historicised variants also reflect a gigantomachy: notice Phlegyas, Laogoras, Koronos, Eurytos, and Erginos, commanders of Lapith or Dryopian or Minyan hosts, whose combats with Herakles were incidents of a larger battle.

21. Theme 8A (p. 85). In *Enuma elish* there is a hint that Marduk suffered temporary defeat and death in the episode of Tiamat's opening her mouth to swallow him: for in the parallel Indic myth Vritra swallowed Indra (p. 198). *Enuma elish* shows the theme a little more plainly in the discomfiture of Ea, the former champion. In another text Marduk suffered death and returned to life: Bel, as the god is called, was held captive in the mountain: i.e., the land of the dead; for it is "into the house of bondage" that he descended "from the sun and light." The only stated cause for his descent is that the gods bound him, whereupon "he perished from among the living." Presumably these are the rebel gods of *Enuma elish*, since the text itself, which is full of ritual prescriptions for the New Year festival, prescribes the singing of *Enuma elish*. Belit, Bel's sister-wife, and Nabu, his son, searching for him, descended to the dead. It is not clear how Bel returned to life. Near the end of the text it is said that gods bored holes in the door of Bel's house of confinement and waged battle, presumably with the enemy gods. In another fragmentary text, a hymn to Marduk, it is said that at the Akitu festival Bel sits within Tiamat; in the next line a grave in the house of mourning is mentioned. Ebeling interprets this to mean that Tiamat swallowed Marduk.[33]

Apparently the Babylonian myth had the same episode as the Greek and Ugaritic: Bel-Marduk was overcome by the enemy and held captive in the land of the dead. *Enuma elish*, like Hesiod's *Theogony*, deletes the great god's humiliation as unworthy of him. It also appears that Asag temporarily worsted Ninurta: for Kramer says, "At first, however, he seems to have met more than his match and he 'flees like a bird,'" somewhat as Herakles fled before Kyknos (p. 30). Certainly in the Ashur fragment of the Zu myth Ninurta failed when he encountered Zu, much as Ea before Tiamat, and another champion, probably Marduk, went

[33] *The Death and Resurrection of Bel-Marduk*; text and translation in Langdon (1923) 34–49 (see *ibid.* 50–59 for discussion); see also Hooke (1953) 111–114. Obviously the god who at any time or in any place was called Bel is the central figure of this poem. Before Marduk it was Enlil. For the hymn fragment see Ebeling (1931) 24–26, text and translation into German; see also *ibid.* 30 f. Possibly Marduk was restored by the plant of life, which his spouse succeeded in bringing to him. See Van Buren (1950) 171. Cf. Mot's swallowing of Baal (p. 134).

forth and was victorious. This is the mythical statement of the fact
that one god replaced another in the champion's role. It is probable that in the earliest form of the myth the monster, whether
called Zu or Labbu or Tiamat, swallowed the champion—which
is to say that he despatched him to the realm of death, for the monster's belly was itself identified with the underworld—in later versions the monster simply killed the champion, who then descended
to the dead, and after a sojourn there returned to defeat the monster. Finally it was one god, Ea or Enlil or Ninurta, who suffered
defeat or death, another, Marduk or Ashur, who then went forth
and won the victory.[34]

22. Theme 8B (p. 124). When Zu stole from Enlil the tablet
of destinies and Enlilship, Enlil was at once rendered speechless
and numb and apparently became completely helpless. Enlil's
tablet and crown, therefore, correspond closely to Zeus's fire weapons in Nonnos' version of the Typhon myth as vessels of the
god's power, without which he was impotent: refined versions of
the sinews of the earlier Greek myth or of the heart and eyes of
the Hittite myth. In this respect the Greek and Hittite variants
reflect an earlier stage of the myth.

23. Theme 8E (p. 137). The fragment on the death of Marduk
has much to say about lamentations, prayers, and incantations,
whose object was to bring the dead Bel to life (see note 33).

24. Theme 9 (p. 89). Trickery at a banquet is present in
Enuma elish, but it is not employed to trap the enemy. The gods
were summoned to an assembly for the purpose of making Marduk their king. Since they might oppose giving the sovereignty to
a god so young, and since it might be that many of them felt the
jealousy of Marduk that impelled other gods to league themselves
with Tiamat, they were given abundant food and wine, which
made them carefree and not at all inclined to contest the proposal.[35]

---

[34] Asag: Kramer (1944) 80. Adad, like his west-Semitic counterpart Hadad, also
descended to the netherworld; see Schlobies (1925) 9. In still another story it was Shamash
who died, swallowed or imprisoned by Zu, and Ninurta who rescued him and defeated
Zu; see Van Buren (1950) 170–174. It is a mythical statement of the eclipse phenomenon,
or of the daily setting of the sun: compare the missing Hittite Sun-God (p. 125) and the
Egyptian myth of Ra-Horos against Apep (pp. 186 f.).

[35] *Enuma elish* III 131–138.

Deception at a feast, somewhat in the manner of Paghat's deception of Yatpan (p. 139), may be present in the Zu myth. In a fragment of text concerning Lugalbanda and Zu, if Jensen has translated it correctly and made the right restorations of missing words and phrases, Lugalbanda went to the mountain against Zu, and there invited Zu's wife and son to a feast, apparently with intent to trap Zu. But the interpretation is very uncertain.[36]

Other kinds of cunning are present: e.g., the magic spells that Ea used against Apsu and the irresistible weapon that was given to Marduk to smite Tiamat, much as Baal received two magic bludgeons, which have an even closer parallel in Ninurta's two wonder-weapons, Sharur and Shargaz. And a trick may be discerned in the final stroke against Tiamat: Marduk tricked Tiamat into opening her mouth so that he could send the winds in and force her to keep her jaws open.[37]

25. Theme 10A (p. 90). According to the seventh tablet of *Enuma elish,* Marduk was called Sirsir because he "heaped up a mountain over Tiamat." This seems at variance with the episode in which he fashioned the world from her dead body, but it is probably another version of the myth, wherein Marduk treated Tiamat much as Zeus treated Typhon. Kingu and Tiamat's other companions were bound and imprisoned—presumably in the lower world, for Kingu was counted "among the dead gods." Later Kingu was judged and put to death as creator of strife. Ea imprisoned Mummu, and on Apsu he established his house: i.e., Apsu was confined beneath the earth. Zu was likewise confined underground after being brought to judgement before Ea, and also was dismembered or at least mutilated: his tongue was cut out.[38]

26. Theme 10B (p. 90). The gods praised Marduk's deeds in song and recited all his fifty names at the banquet in his new palace to which Marduk summoned the gods after his victory

---

[36] Jensen (1900) 54–57.

[37] *Enuma elish* IV 30–104.

[38] *Ibid.* I 69–76, IV 111–146, VI 23–34, VII 70; Ebeling (1931) 33, line 27; Van Buren (1950) 173. The existence of land seems to be assumed in *Enuma elish* at the time of Apsu's death, even though this occurs before the making of earth from Tiamat's body. We need not expect consistency, especially when we realise that the Ea-Apsu episode was an earlier and independent combat myth.

and his creation of the world. This banquet recalls that at which Baal entertained the gods after he defeated Yam. When Inanna killed the dragon, she sang a song of exultation and self-praise.[39]

27. Theme 10D (p. 125). The last two tablets of *Enuma elish* make very clear that the Marduk-Tiamat myth served as *aition* for the Akitu Festival. Moreover the text on Bel's death makes explicit in alternate statements the relation of the myth to features of the ritual in this festival.[40]

Like Aliyan Baal, Marduk had a great temple built for him, as befitted his newly won sovereignty: this was the mythical foundation of Esagil, his huge temple in Babylon. Compare the building of Apollo's temple at Delphi (p. 13).[41]

So we find twenty-seven features of correspondence or similarity between the Babylonian combat myths and the Greek Typhon-Python myths. In general, I believe, the former show an earlier stage of this myth type; they have not yet developed very far some themes prominent in the west, e.g., the trickery theme. But the Babylonian myths, especially the Tiamat myth, have two prominent features that are either obscured or absent in western variants: the combat is the climactic episode of the world's beginnings, the event causally precedent to the creation of the present order of things, and it is but one encounter—though the central bout—of a gigantomachy, a primeval war between the heavenly gods and the forces of chaos.

TAMMUZ AND BILULU

Bel-Marduk as a dying-and-rising god suggests the god Tammuz (Dumuzi): it may be, as Moortgat maintains, that he was a synthesis of Enlil, Shamash, and Tammuz. Tammuz, as herdsman, defended flocks and herds against the robber beast. In the earliest tale of Tammuz's death, it may have been a lion that killed him; in later versions the lion (*labbu*) may have become the leonine dragon Labbu; or other kinds of monster may have

---

[39] *Enuma elish* VI–VII. Inanna: Kramer (1944) 83.

[40] *Enuma elish* VI–VII. See p. 161, note 33, and Gaster (1950) 35–37.

[41] *Enuma elish* VI 51–64. Ninurta seems to have won his place in the great temple of Nippur and in other temples after his victory over Asag-Labbu (or Zu?); see the texts in Witzel (1920) 78 f., 100 f.

been substituted. In a Sumerian poem on Tammuz's violent death, the exact nature of his murderer is not clear. Tammuz was killed while pasturing his flocks in the desert (Th. 8A), and the killer drove off his sheep (Th. 4A). When Inanna, his wife, heard of it, she went to the house of the old woman Bilulu, called matriarch, and her son Girgire. With no other weapon than her powerful word she killed the two and their henchman Sirru (Ths. 7A, 7D), changed Bilulu into a waterskin, and all three into spirits of the desert (Th. 3F), there to serve Tammuz by calling him to the offerings made to him (Th. 10A). At this point a lacuna occurs in the text; the poem ends with a lament for Tammuz sung by Inanna and his sister (Th. 8E).[42]

Jacobsen believes that it was Bilulu and Girgire who killed Tammuz; but Kramer maintains that they had nothing to do with Tammuz's death and that Inanna killed them solely for her dead husband's comfort. The identity of the killer must therefore remain uncertain: it could be that a lion killed Tammuz, and that the "man who was not the shepherd" (i.e., not Tammuz), who was seen "returning beside my master's sheep," was an underling. But the Aqhat poem may offer a parallel: after Aqhat's violent death the maid Paghat went forth to the house of Yatpan, deceived him, and killed him in vengeance. If the myths are really parallel in plot, then it was Girgire who killed Tammuz at Bilulu's instigation.[43]

It is evident that Bilulu is very like Tiamat. She is a matriarch, in complete command of her son Girgire and the attendant Sirru, who is "no (one's) child and no (one's) friend" (the parentheses are Jacobsen's), and who recalls Mummu of the chaotic triad in the creation myth. Her transformation into a waterskin looks like a reduction of Tiamat's watery nature, dictated by the special purposes which the Tammuz myth served. To put it another way, the character of Bilulu in the Tammuz myth was modelled upon Tiamat.

Jacobsen suggests that the waterskin was identified with the

---

[42] Jacobsen (1953) has text, translation, summary, interpretation, and commentary. On Tammuz see Moortgat (1949) 9–14, 33–35, 93–98. The Tammuz-Bilulu myth also shows Ths. 1A, 1C, 2E, 3D, 3G, 4A, 6B, 7A, 7F, 9, 10D, some of them obscurely.
[43] Jacobsen (1953) 163 f., 188.

raincloud or thundercloud, conceived "as a huge waterskin floating in the skies." He further points out that the thundercloud
was personified as Imdugud, on the one hand identified with
Ninurta, on the other imagined "as an enormous vulture floating
with outstretched wings in the sky. Because its roar, the thunder,
is like the roar that issues from the lion's mouth it was imagined
with the head of a lion." The lion-headed vulture is Zu, who was
identified with Imdugud. We may therefore look upon Bilulu as
Tiamat in the process of becoming Zu.[44]

According to Jacobsen, Bilulu's name occurs elsewhere only
in *En-bilulu,* a form of the weather god Adad and also of Marduk when he took over Adad's character. Now in another myth
Adad was an ally of seven evil demons that Marduk fought. The
seven are described as both terrible storms and evil-working gods
(Ths. 3G, 4A). Among them were the south wind, a dragon, a
leopard that carried off the young (Th. 4C), a wolf, a terrible
creature called *shibbu,* and something that was enemy to god and
king (Th. 3B). They swept over earth and sky, bringing darkness and destruction (Th. 4A); with them went Adad, and
Shamash the sun god was their helper. They attacked heaven and
beset Sin the moon god, causing his eclipse. There was none to
oppose them. This time it was Enlil, not Anu, who had to find a
champion, for the seven demons were Anu's messengers. As usual
Ea was consulted and sent forth Marduk as champion (Th.
6A). Here the tablet breaks off. There can be no doubt of the
outcome.[45]

If we look upon this as a variant of the Tiamat myth, then
Adad has the role of rebel god. This is another instance of shift
in role: the god who has played the champion's part is displaced
by a new champion and becomes identified with the enemy. Anu
too, the old sky god, is seen here as the lord of the evil demons,
probably the instigator of their attack, a role comparable to El's
in Ugarit (p. 131). Enlil seems to have played the same role
against his son Ninurta. He produced the dragon that Ninurta

[44] *Ibid.* 167–169 with note 27; see Fish (1948), Moortgat (1949) 52. Zu is male in the
texts of the Zu myth; but the Sumerian poem on Gilgamesh (p. 172) places Zu with
nestlings in the crown of an *huluppu* tree; and notice Zu's wife in the Lugalbanda fragment.
[45] Translation in Rogers (1912) 63–67. On Marduk as En-bilulu see *Enuma elish* VII
57–69. The myth also shows more or less clearly Ths. 3F, 5A, [7A], 7C, 7E, 7G.

killed; he quaked in fear on Ninurta's triumphal approach; and Ninurta took possession of his temple.[46]

GILGAMESH

It was Enlil who appointed the monstrous Humbaba to be keeper of a great cedar forest in the "Land of the Living" (Th. 2c) and to be a terror to mortals in the performance of his office (Th. 4A). This brings us to the hero Gilgamesh, the Babylonian Herakles, who resolved to go to the cedar forest and fight Humbaba (Ths. 6B, 7A). Humbaba had the teeth of a dragon, the face of a lion, a roar like the stormflood, a mouth like fire; his breath was death; nobody could escape him (Ths. 3B, 3D, 3G, 4A). With Gilgamesh went Enkidu, his faithful friend and attendant (Th. 7E). In a Sumerian version Gilgamesh also had the help of fifty volunteers from Uruk. He had, moreover, the backing of Shamash (Utu) the sun god, who was lord of the Land of the Living, where Humbaba guarded the cedar forest, and who immobilised seven demons—viper, dragon, snake, fire, flood, lightning, and another—obviously a variation on the seven demons who fought Marduk. Probably it was Shamash who sent Gilgamesh against Humbaba (Th. 7E), for just before the final encounter Gilgamesh said, "I have followed the heavenly Shamash, and have pursued the road decreed for me." The story is closely parallel to the Herakles-Kyknos legend: Humbaba, Enlil's servant, occupied Shamash's domain, as Kyknos, Ares' son, occupied Apollo's precinct; Shamash sent Gilgamesh, assisted by Enkidu, to fight Humbaba, as Apollo sent Herakles, assisted by Iolaos, to fight Kyknos.[47]

---

[46] *An-dim gim-ma* II, III (Witzel 1920: 75 f., 78–80); see also the beginning of *Labbu*.

[47] For the Humbaba story see *Gilgamesh* III–V and a Sumerian text in Pritchard (1950) 47–50. For *Gilgamesh* in English translation see Leonard (1934), Heidel (1949), Pritchard (1950) 73–99 and Mendelsohn (1955) 49–115 (Speiser); summaries in Mackenzie MBA 172–184, Rogers (1912) 81–103, Oppenheim (1948), Gaster (1952) 21–42, Hooke (1953) 68–72, Levy (1953) 123–143; text and German translation, Jensen (1900) 116–265; summary, *id.* (1906) 1–54; German translation, Schott (1934). I quote from Heidel's translation. Gilgamesh may be considered a form of Lugalbanda, his tutelary god; for he was the son of the goddess Ninsun, who was Lugalbanda's wife. The legend makes his father a mortal man, however, so that Gilgamesh can play the part of a mortal hero, subject to death. He was two-thirds god and one-third man, says the epic—a strange biological phenomenon. See *Gilg.* I, col. ii. 1; IIIA 263, 271; IIIB; IX, col. ii. 16; Heidel (1949) 4.

Gilgamesh and Enkidu set out, equipped with axes and swords especially made for them. They crossed seven mountains and finally reached the cedar forest, where they killed Humbaba's watchman. Then Enkidu's hand became paralysed, either because he incautiously placed it upon the enchanted gate of the cedar park, or because the gate slammed upon it (Th. 8B). Soon after this Enkidu became deathly afraid of going into the forest and facing Humbaba, who had an eye of death (Th. 3D). Gilgamesh, however, encouraged him, and they went into the forest to the house of Humbaba. Gilgamesh then cut down a cedar tree as a challenge to Humbaba, who immediately became enraged. Now Gilgamesh's courage was daunted; a panic fear came upon him, and he prayed to Shamash. The sun god raised eight winds that beat against the deadly eyes of Humbaba and blinded him so that he was helpless before the heroes, much as the winds assisted Marduk against Tiamat. The monster begged for mercy in vain: the heroes cut his head off. In the Sumerian version Humbaba fixed his death's eye upon them from within his house. Gilgamesh and his fifty-one companions had to hew through seven cedar trees to reach Humbaba's chamber (Th. 2B), where they cornered him. Gilgamesh struck Humbaba with his hand and loosened his teeth. Humbaba defended himself in vain and was beheaded after futile appeals to the sun god and Gilgamesh.[48]

After the victory over Humbaba, the goddess Ishtar became aware of the beauty of Gilgamesh and wanted him for her husband, promising him riches and power. Gilgamesh refused, pointing out that she had destroyed all her former mates: Tammuz, roller, lion, horse, shepherd-wolf, Ishullanu the gardener (Th. 8D). Then Ishtar in great anger went to her parents, Anu and Antum, and complained against Gilgamesh. Though Anu pointed out that Gilgamesh had rebuked her with justice, he submitted finally to Ishtar's demand and threats (Th. 7c) and created for her the bull of heaven (Ths. 3B, 5B). This monstrous bull

---

[48] The myth also shows, clearly or obscurely, Themes 2A (p. 173), 2E (Humbaba is identified with flood, and his forest is surrounded by ditches "for sixty double-hours on every side") 3A, 3F, 4F (nobody can escape him), 5A, 10B (the good wishes of the elders attend the heroes' departure). For a relief that perhaps shows the victory of Gilgamesh and Enkidu over Humbaba see *Archiv für Orientf.* V (1929) 207 and Hopkins (1934) fig. 4.

descended to earth and killed three hundred men at each snort of his breath (Ths. 3D, 4A), drank the river dry (Th. 4G), and completely denuded the land (Th. 4A) wherever he pastured. Gilgamesh and Enkidu fought him together (Ths. 6B, 7A, 7E). After some vicissitudes—not clearly known, since the text is mutilated—it appears that the bull took to flight (Th. 7F); Enkidu chased him, and catching him by the tail, held him while Gilgamesh, like a matador, plunged his sword "between the nape and his horns." They tore out the bull's heart and reverently offered it to Shamash; for it was at his command that they killed the bull (Th. 7E). Ishtar cursed Gilgamesh as killer of heaven's bull, whereupon Enkidu threw the bull's shoulder at her, crying that he would give her the same treatment if he could catch her. She then gathered the harlots and courtesans and began lamentations over the slain bull. The heroes cleansed themselves in the Euphrates (Th. 10C); Gilgamesh was cheered by the maids of Uruk on his return; and he celebrated his victory with a feast of rejoicing (Th. 10B).[49]

Here we see remarkable parallels to the Ugaritic Aqhat legend (p. 138): the hero rejects the fertility goddess's proposal; she complains to the high god and threatens dire consequences if she cannot punish the hero; the high god submits to her bullying; the goddess then raises a monstrous enemy against the hero (Ths. 1A, 5B). At this point exact correspondence ceases: Gilgamesh did not die. But in the sequel Enkidu died (Th. 8A), because he had killed the bull of heaven.

In this myth Ishtar assumes the roles of dragoness and Lamia, like Anat in the Aqhat myth: no longer is she the loving wife of the champion, but the companion and promptress of the enemy, and deadly seductress of heroes. Though goddess of love, fertility, life, she was also a goddess of death. It was her habit, as Gilgamesh said, to destroy every companion of her couch. This was also the habit of the legendary queen Semiramis, who is in reality a form of Ishtar, and who killed Ninos among her husbands,

[49] *Gilg.* VI, and a Sumerian fragment, Schott (1934) 88–91. Shamash's command: *Gilg.* VII, col. i. 12. It seems that the bull of heaven had some relation to Zu as son or follower; and seal cylinders show him in conflict with a god; see Van Buren (1950) 167 f., pl. XI 7. For the bull component of Typhon see pp. 81 f. and fig. 15.

whence "Ninny's tomb." It was the custom too, as we have seen, of the Lydian queen Omphale, whose ancestry, as given by Herodotos, links her to Babylonian deities: Herakles and Omphale were parents of Alkaios, who was father of Belos, the father of Ninos. And the Libyan Lamia, according to a good source, was daughter of Belos and Libya. The mutual relationship of Ishtar, Semiramis, Anat, Omphale, and Lamia to Bel goes far to confirm a conjecture, based on the deadly erotic character of all five, that they or their legends go back to one original.[50]

The summary and discussion of the bull-of-heaven myth show fourteen clear correspondences to the Greek and Ugaritic myths. Another can be seen in Ishtar's relation to the land of the dead: she has the power to raise the dead (Th. 3F), and it is with the exercise of this power that she threatens Anu. In contemplating Ishtar it becomes easier to understand the identification of Artemis with Hekate, of a goddess of fertility and the hunt with a goddess of ghosts and witchcraft. In the myth of her descent to the lower world Ishtar came back to earth amid a rout of ghosts and demons. Just so did Hekate lead her bands of spirits and bogeys at night (p. 117); and Artemis' band of huntress nymphs that bring death to intruders are the corresponding midday troop, associated with the panic terror of siesta time. Both Hekate and Artemis lead the wild hunt.[51]

The Gilgamesh epic is a composite structure. Its theme is death: how Gilgamesh sought to conquer it. Its successive episodes are variations on this one theme: old myths and legends of combat or of descent to the dead, quite separate variants of the type, and told of others than Gilgamesh, were drawn into the service of this great poem. Again and again Gilgamesh or Enkidu, like

---

[50] Ishtar and her lovers: *Gilg.* VI 42–79. Semiramis: Plut. *Mor.* 753DE; Ael. VH 7.1; Diod. 2.4–20; cf. Fontenrose (1951) 133–136. Omphale's lineage: Herod. 1.7.2–4. Lamia Belos' daughter: Schol. Vet. on Aristoph. *Pax* 758. It is noteworthy that the Lapith Phorbas was an ancestor of Belos and Agenor; and the mother of the latter two was Libya: Schol. Vet. on Eur. *Or.* 932; cf. Paus. 2.16.1. For other connections of Lydia with Semitic lands see Xanthos 11, 1.38 M; EM 493; Schol. A on Il. 2.461. Since both Ishtar and Semiramis were associated with doves, it is noteworthy that in the New Year's festival a dove represented Tiamat: Ebeling (1931) 36, line 19.

[51] Inanna-Ishtar's descent: Kramer (1944) 86–96; Jensen (1900) 80–91; Rogers (1912) 121–131; Contenau (1941) 242–250; Heidel (1949) 119–128; Pritchard (1950) 52–57, 107–109; Mendelsohn (1955) 120–125; summary in Mackenzie MBA 95–98. The bull-of-heaven myth also shows Theme 3A.

Herakles, faces Thanatos. But what was once a story of the conquest of Thanatos in monstrous form—Humbaba or heaven's bull—has been reduced to a preliminary episode, leading up to Enkidu's death and Gilgamesh's journey to the "Far-Away."

Enlil was enraged at the heroes' slaughter of Humbaba and of the bull: such is the transition from these exploits to the death of Enkidu. That the two monsters are linked as equally valuable to Enlil indicates that they are two forms of one original enemy. Enlil himself once more appears as enemy; he demands the death of Enkidu and receives it (Th. 8A). Gilgamesh mourned his friend excessively (Th. 8E); for the first time he realised the fact and certainty of death. So he desired to escape death and gain immortality. He knew that his ancestor Utnapishtim, the flood hero, had won immortal life. To reach him and find the secret he had to go to the ends of the world, through regions of darkness, over mountains and seas, past many dangers, to the paradise where Utnapishtim enjoyed eternal life. That is, Gilgamesh, like Ishtar, went to the realm of death in the hope of defeating death and winning life (Th. 8A). Episodes of the journey were probably once independent stories of conflict with monsters, now reduced to fairly harmless incidents. First he met and killed lions in the mountain passes (Ths. 3B, 7A). On reaching the mountain of Mashu, the gate of night and day, Gilgamesh came to a gate kept by a scorpion man and his wife (Ths. 1c, 2c, 3B). Their bodies flashed with a radiance that terrified Gilgamesh—their very glance brought death (Th. 3D)—but when he found the courage to address them and they learned of his purpose, they let him pass the gate. For twelve days he went through great darkness and came at last to the light and a lovely garden by the sea. There he met Siduri, the divine barmaid, who tried at first to keep him out, then to persuade him to accept death and not to cross the waters. The encounter with Siduri resembles that with the scorpion pair, though elaborated. Siduri is probably a doublet of the scorpion woman, and in her hostel and garden by the waters of death we see the Venusberg (Th. 8D). Finally Siduri directed Gilgamesh to Urshanabi, Utnapishtim's boatman (Th. 3F). For some reason Gilgamesh destroyed the stone images that accompanied Urshanabi in his boat. Without them, punting poles were needed for the crossing; yet Gilgamesh could now cross. So he reached Utnapishtim, only to find that his ancestor's immortality was a special gift of the gods, and that he could not share it.[52]

This is the proper climax of the poem: we would expect Gilgamesh to go back in disappointment. But the epic adds two more attempts made by the hero to escape death. As he was about to leave the "Far-Away," Utnapishtim told him of the plant of life at the bottom of the sea. Gilgamesh dived down and got it: but on the way home he stopped by a pool of cool water to bathe, a snake rose from the water (Ths. 2E, 3B), seized the plant, and ate it (Th. 8B).[53]

Here the epic properly ends as a coherent, though composite, tale. The final tablet is really an entirely different version of Enkidu's death and Gilgamesh's sorrow. It is the second half of a composite story that is now known in its entirety from the Sumerian. There grew on the banks of Euphrates an *huluppu* tree. This the wind uprooted and the river carried off. But Inanna (Ishtar) saw it, took it from the river, and planted it in her garden at Uruk, that later she might make a chair and couch from its wood. But when it had grown big, she could not cut it down. In its roots the snake "who knows no charm" had built his nest, in its crown Zu had built his nest, and in the boughs the demon-woman Lilith had her house (Ths. 1C, 2B, 2C, 3B, 3F). Gilgamesh then came to Inanna's aid (Th. 6B), armed with his mighty axe. He killed the snake (Th. 7A) while Zu and his young flew off to the mountain and Lilith escaped to the desert (Th. 7F). Then Gilgamesh and his companions cut down the tree. From the wood Inanna made a *pukku* and *mikku* (drum and drumstick?), which she gave to Gilgamesh.[54]

So far the Sumerian poem only; the rest is also found in *Gilgamesh* XII. The *pukku* and *mikku* fell into the netherworld, and Gilgamesh could not reach them with hand or foot (Th. 8B).

---

[52] *Gilg.* VII–XI. Notice the long sleep that Gilgamesh has in Utnapishtim's house; thereafter he says that death has already seized his body, and that wherever he walks, there is death. On Siduri = Ishtar see Jensen (1906) 28 with note 5.

[53] *Gilg.* XI 258–308.

[54] Kramer (1938), (1944) 4–10. The cutting of the *huluppu* tree, home of monsters, corresponds to the cutting of Humbaba's cedars. Notice too a certain parallel of Inanna-Gilgamesh to Inaras-Hupasiyas (p. 121) and Anat-Aqhat (p. 138; Th. 8D).

He mourned his loss and called for someone to go down and recover the prized objects. Enkidu his servant offered to descend. Gilgamesh instructed him in the rules that he must observe in order to return. But when he reached the netherworld Enkidu disregarded every instruction—in particular, he used spear, throwstick, and staff against the shades (Ths. 3F, 7A)—so that he was seized and held there, and could not go back to Gilgamesh (Th. 8A). Then Gilgamesh wept for Enkidu (Th. 8E) and went to Enlil for help. But Enlil would not help him, nor would Sin. Ea, however, always helpful, persuaded Nergal to open a hole in the ground, that Enkidu's ghost might ascend and speak with Gilgamesh; but the hero's only gain was to learn about the dismal condition of the dead.[55]

It is in Gilgamesh's journey to the "Far-Away" that we find a topographical link with the myths of earlier chapters. The mountain of Mashu is identified with the Lebanon and Antilebanon ranges, and Siduri's hostelry is placed on the Phoenician coast of the Mediterranean—that is, both are in the region of Mount Kasios (Th. 2A), and therefore of Typhon, Yam, and Mot (p. 133).[56]

The Lebanon ranges and the sea lay to the west of Babylonia, in the region of the sunset: Gilgamesh travelled thither "along the road of the sun." Like Odysseus, he found a region of darkness beyond the sunset. As in the Greek epics the realm of the dead is located either beneath the earth or in the far west at the edges of the world. Now the Land of the Living, where Humbaba held sway, has a name which seems to be a euphemism for the realm of death. He lived in a cedar forest by a mountain: probably the Lebanon range again. Gilgamesh had to cross seven mountains to get there: probably various ranges or ridges of Syria. Shamash was sovereign of the land: therefore it was the land of either sunrise or sunset—the latter, if I have interpreted other indications correctly. Nobody escaped Humbaba: i.e., he was Death himself. Superficially so different, Gilgamesh's two journeys are therefore one and the same.[57]

---

[55] Kramer (1944) 34–37; *Gilg.* XII.
[56] See Heidel (1949) 8 f.
[57] Dhorme (1949: 316) too suggests Lebanon or Amanus as Humbaba's home; see

Before we leave Gilgamesh we must look at still another combat: that which he fought with Enkidu as wild man at the beginning of the epic. In Uruk Gilgamesh ruled as tyrant: his conduct was outrageous (Ths. 4A, 4B). He put all the young men to hard labor, and he took all the young women for himself (Th. 4E). He was two-thirds god, eleven cubits tall, nine spans across the chest (Th. 3A), and he was an invincible warrior. The men of Uruk complained to the gods, who met under King Anu and decided to create an antagonist equal to Gilgamesh. So Enkidu (Eabani) came into being: his body was covered with hair; he lived in the wilderness among wild animals and sucked their milk (Th. 3B); he was prodigiously strong and nearly as tall as Gilgamesh (Th. 3A). He frightened a hunter, who reported the incident to Gilgamesh. The tyrant sent a courtesan into the wilderness to lure Enkidu: a very successful move, for Enkidu spent six days and seven nights with her (Th. 8D). Afterwards the wild beasts shunned him and when he tried to run after them his speed was no longer as theirs: he had become a human being. First he became the protector of herdsmen, catching wolves and lions. Then he went with the courtesan to Uruk, where he blocked the entrance of the temple to prevent Gilgamesh from entering and spending the night with the priestess in an *hieros gamos*. The two fought furiously like bulls, shattering the doorpost as they wrestled. Gilgamesh finally put Enkidu down; but the bout caused each to admire the other. Like Theseus and Peirithoos, they became fast friends. The gods' purpose was served: Gilgamesh became a benefactor of his people.[58]

In this story we cannot tell hero from enemy. Gilgamesh was a tyrant like Erginos, Eurytos, or Yam; he was lustful like Typhon, Tityos, or Heros of Temesa; but he was a divine hero and victor in the combat. Enkidu was at first a savage of fearful aspect, a

---

Clay (1919) 87 f., Oppenheim (1948) 48, Frankfort (1949) 224. Jensen (1906: 13), Mackenzie (MBA 174), and Rogers (1912: 84) speak of Humbaba as king of Elam or Elamite warder; but Clay shows beyond question that Humbaba is an Amorite name and that his cedar forest was among the mountains of Amurru, i.e., Syria.

[58] *Gilg.* I–II. The story also shows Ths. 1A, 1B, 6B. Enkidu's loss of physical prowess from his sojourn with the courtesan recalls Herakles at the court of Omphale (p. 107); see Oppenheim (1948) 26. Again, when he opposes Gilgamesh at the temple door he recalls Herakles opposing Thanatos at the tomb of Alkestis (p. 325), or Euthymos opposing the Temesian Heros at the *hêrôon* (p. 102).

companion of beasts; but he became lion fighter and stood forth to fight the gigantic tyrant king. Evidently the old combat myth has been turned to a new use. Behind the story can be surmised the rival claims of two cities concerning their respective heroes; the conflict was resolved by associating the two, after an initial combat, in the same exploits, as Herakles and Theseus were made friends and occasionally companions. The heroes were given ogrish characteristics in order to motivate the combat, for which the old combat myth served as model.

The courtesan who charmed Enkidu is of course a form of Ishtar; the episode is simply an adaptation of such a story as that of Ishtar's charming of the sea serpent Hedammu, in which the goddess, after careful preparation to enhance her charms, went to the seaside, where she displayed herself nude to the sea serpent, and so captivated him that he was rendered helpless.[59]

The conclusion in reconciliation can also be seen in the myth of Nergal and Ereshkigal. The gods had a banquet to which Ereshkigal, queen of the dead, could not come. So they asked her to send up Namtar, her vizier, to fetch her portion. Namtar came, and all the gods rose and greeted him with respect, except one, perhaps Nergal, who remained seated. When Namtar reported this to his mistress, she sent him back to the gods to demand that they deliver the offending god to her that she might kill him. The gods were willing to comply (Th. 7c). Ea, Nergal's father, encouraged him to go, and gave him an escort of fourteen demons (Th. 7E). Nergal descended to the netherworld (Th. 8A), demanded entrance at once, stationed his fourteen helpers at the fourteen gates of the infernal city, and appeared before Ereshkigal. He at once seized her by the hair and dragged her from her throne to the floor. As he was about to cut her head off, she begged him to listen to her, and, when he did so, proposed that he become her husband and king of the underworld. So Nergal stayed with Ereshkigal (Th. 8D) and became lord of the dead.[60]

---

[59] From a Hittite document: Friedrich (1949); see also Güterbock (1946) 116–118, Otten (1950) 21, note 3, Gaster (1952) 130. It appears to be a Hurrian myth, but it was probably known to Babylonians too. Hedammu was gluttonous and destroyed cities. The text is very fragmentary, but as far as it goes it shows Ths. 2E, 3B, 4A, 4D, 4E, 7D, 9.

[60] Heidel (1949) 129–132, Pritchard (1950) 103 f. (Speiser); text and German translation, Jensen (1900) 74–79. The myth also shows Ths. 1A, 1B, 4c, 8c (obscurely in the banquet that results in Nergal's descent). It is possible that Nergal was not himself the offender, but offered to take his place.

The reader is at once reminded of the Baal poems of Ugarit: Baal's failure to show respect before Yam's envoys, Yam's demand, and the gods' submission; the banquet that Mot did not attend and Baal's subsequent descent to Mot. He is also reminded of Eurybatos entering Sybaris' cavern boldly and seizing her with his bare hands.

Nergal's transformation from demon fighter into death god illustrates remarkably well the union in one person of dragon fighter, dying god, and death god. Gilgamesh too became a god of the dead: he was called both king of the underworld and judge of the dead. Tammuz spent part of every year among the dead. Tammuz, Gilgamesh, and Enkidu were alike protectors of shepherds and fighters of lions, and alike beloved of Ishtar in one or another of her forms. Marduk, Tammuz, and Nergal were brothers as sons of Ea; and the very names of Enkidu-Eabani seem to place him in Ea's circle. Ninurta, Lugalbanda, and Gilgamesh belong to Enlil's circle at Uruk; Nergal is also considered Enlil's son. Ea was lord of the underground waters, successor to Apsu; in the Sumerian poem *Enlil and Ninlil,* Enlil lived and ruled in the netherworld and became father of underworld gods.[61]

Now that the Tammuz, Gilgamesh, and Nergal myths have been considered, we see that many of the themes missing in the Tiamat-Labbu group are present in other Mesopotamian combat myths. In fact, the Mesopotamian material taken as a whole shows all but three or four of the forty-three themes of the theme list (pp. 9–11). The coincidences of specific plots with the Ugaritic poems are especially striking (pp. 159, 169). Altogether the evidence makes clear that the Mesopotamian peoples had much to do with either the origin or the development of the combat myth. But we must also inquire what the other two cradles of civilisation, Egypt and India, contributed to this myth.[62]

---

[61] Gilgamesh as death god: Heidel (1949) 5, Pritchard (1950) 50 with note 4. Marduk-Tammuz: Moortgat (1949) 93–98. Enlil:Kramer (1944) 43–47, Frankfort (1949) 167–170.

[62] The themes lacking in the Mesopotamian myths are not significant: 2D, 3E, 7B (8c is only doubtfully present). Th. 2D is replaced by the identification of the dragon with water, as Asag with the Tigris, or Tiamat-Apsu with all the waters. The others may very well have been present, but missing from the sources extant. As to 3E, Mrs. Van Buren (1950: 163 f.) says that there are hints that Zu could change his shape at will and take on in succession the appearances of man, lion, or bird. We see an approach to 7B in the apparently invulnerable hide of Tiamat.

GOD AND DRAGON IN EGYPT AND INDIA

No later than the fifth century B.C., and probably in the sixth, the Greeks had perceived similarity between their Typhon myth and the Egyptian myth of Set, Osiris, and Horos, and had identified Set with Typhon. In fact, they soon fused the two myths by inserting into the Typhon myth a flight of the gods to Egypt, where they escaped Typhon by assuming animal forms (p. 73)—an *aition* of the images of Egyptian gods in animal form—and Typhon's final resting place was sometimes identified with Lake Serbonis (p. 133). This ancient rapprochement of the two myths is in itself an indication that they were national variants of a common original; and this conclusion is supported by the presence in the Egyptian myth of most of the themes of the Greek myth. It will suffice, I believe, to indicate the themes as they occur in my synopses of Egyptian myths, as in my treatment of the Gilgamesh legends, reserving discussion for only a few especially significant themes: there is no longer need of listing every feature of correspondence.[1]

It is a Greek author, Plutarch, who gives us the most complete

---

[1] The fusion of the Greek and Egyptian myths is already evident in Pind. frag. 81 Bowra; Herod. 2.144.2, 2.156.4, 3.5.3. On the Horos-Set combat see Mercer (1942) 68–78, 93–95, 195.

and connected narrative of the Set combat, an account that has been confirmed in most details by Egyptian documents of 1,500 years earlier—though it is probable that Plutarch has given us a more consistent narrative than the Egyptians ever had. The native Egyptian sources are for the most part inconsistent, repetitious, and lacking in narrative power—Set dies in a confusing variety of ways in one and the same version, and is suddenly alive again—traits determined to some extent by the magical purposes of the texts. Hence I shall first summarise Plutarch's narrative, supplement it from Egyptian and Greek sources, and then turn to the closely related Apep myth.

Plutarch begins with the birth of five deities, children of Geb (Seb) and Nut, whom he identifies with Kronos and Rhea. The five were Osiris, the elder Horos, Set-Typhon (Ths. 1A, 1B), Isis, and Nephthys. Osiris married Isis; Set married Nephthys. Osiris became king of Egypt and a great benefactor of his people; but Set, wicked in nature (Th. 4A) and jealous of his brother, plotted his death with seventy-two confederates, among whom was Aso, queen of Ethiopia (Th. 1C). He had a beautiful coffer made that exactly fitted Osiris; then he invited him to a feast, during which he told the company that he would give the coffer to the guest who fitted it. One after another the guests tried it without success; but when Osiris lay down in it, Set and his band slammed the lid shut and fastened it securely (Th. 8C). Then they threw the chest into the Nile, which carried it out to sea: thus Osiris died (Th. 8A), and Set usurped the throne (Th. 5A). When Isis heard the news, she mourned her husband-brother (Th. 8E) and set out to search for his body. There follows the story of her wanderings and visit to Byblos: a story that is remarkably parallel to the tale of Demeter's wandering in search of Persephone and visit to Eleusis. She recovered the body in Byblos and returned to Egypt with it, hiding it in Buto. Set happened upon it while hunting and cut it into fourteen pieces (twenty-six, according to Diodoros), which he scattered about Egypt. Isis then went about hunting for the pieces. Osiris' ghost came to his son, the younger Horos, and trained him for combat with Set (Ths. 6A, 6B, 7E). Many gods joined Horos, among them Set's concubine Thueris (Ths. 7D, 8D), whom a snake,

no doubt sent by Set, pursued (Ths. 3B, 4E) until Horos'
companions cut him to pieces. Then Horos fought Set for many
days, and finally defeating him (Th. 7A), brought him in
chains (Th. 10A) to Isis. She freed him, and Horos, in disgust,
tore the crown from her head. Now Set took his case to court,
accusing Horos of illegitimacy before the gods (Th. 5A); but
Thoth, identified with Hermes, cleverly pleaded Horos' case
(Th. 7E) and induced the gods to decide for him. After that,
Horos had to fight and defeat Set two more times.[2]

Four times, then, in Plutarch's account, Horos was victor over
Typhon in combat or trial: fewer, however, than the many times
that he must prove himself victor in some Egyptian sources. For
instance, in a text known as *The Contest of Horos and Set,* the
two spend eighty years before the tribunal of the gods (not much
faster than the processes of justice today), contending in a variety
of contests, trials, and combats. This is Plutarch's court episode
just alluded to, in which Thoth acted as Horos' attorney, and the
various combats are included within it as ordeals. The story here
resembles the Baal myth in that the boyish Horos (Th. 6B)
claimed the kingly office against the mighty Set (Th. 5A),
whom Ra favored and appeased (Th. 7C), much as El seemed
to favor Yam or Mot against Baal (p. 142). At one point the contestants changed themselves into hippopotami (Ths. 3B, 3E)
and plunged into the sea to do battle. Isis cast a harpoon into the
water, when she thought that Horos was getting the worst of it
(Th. 7D), but struck him instead of Set. No great harm was
done, it seems, for she loosed the harpoon from his body and
cast again, striking Set this time. But he cried out to her to have
compassion on her brother, and she took the harpoon from his
body too. This so enraged Horos that he cut off her head, whereupon Isis transformed herself into a headless image of flint. Plutarch knew this form of the story, but chose to accept a milder
version in which Isis' crown is substituted for her head. He tells
us that Thoth replaced Isis' crown with a cow-head helmet: obviously a modification of an earlier story in which Thoth placed a
bovine head upon the headless Isis (whence her bovine form, the

---

[2] Plut. *Mor.* 355D–358E; see also Diod. 1.21.2–7, 1.88.4–6. Notice the interesting
variation in Ths. 1A, 1B: it is the father Geb who is earth deity, the mother Nut who
is sky deity.

myth tellers would say). Needless to say, Isis soon reappears quite
sound and whole in the Egyptian text.[3]

Horos, like other champions, met with temporary defeat. Just
after the beheading of Isis, Set defeated him in renewed combat,
removed his eyes, and buried them (Th. 8B). Horos then lay
weeping in the desert (Th. 8A), until the goddess Hathor restored his sight with gazelle's milk (Th. 7D). His power and
life, like the Hittite Weather-God's, resided in his eyes, which the
enemy took from him.[4]

In the *Contest* the theme of tricking the enemy appears in a
variety of forms (Th. 9). Since Set refused to contend in the
tribunal any longer while Isis was present, the gods went to an
island, and Ra instructed the boatman Anti not to ferry Isis
across. But Isis, disguised as an old woman, beguiled Anti with
bread and gold. Once on the island, she used her magic power to
change herself into a beautiful maiden. Set, who was sitting among
the gods as they feasted together on the island, saw her, immediately lusted after her, and left the company of the gods to
pursue her (Th. 4E). Then, taking advantage of Egyptian
homonyms that mean *cattle* and *office,* she tricked Set into affirm-
ing that a living son's claim to his dead father's property is superior to another's. Again, in a rather obscene episode, Isis
succeeded in impregnating Set with Horos' seed, which she had
sprinkled upon the lettuce that Set ate. Since Set's condition was
by Egyptian standards evidence that Horos had humiliated him,
the tribunal's decision went to Horos. As Gardiner points out,
Set ate lettuce to increase his sexual powers, but he became impregnated instead: this recalls the ephemeral fruits that the Moirai gave to Typhon, which enfeebled him when he thought that
they would give him more strength.[5]

[3] English translation of *Contest* in Gardiner (1931), Budge (1934) 444–457, Pritchard
(1950) 14–17 (John A. Wilson). See Plut. *Mor.* 358DE, *Lib. et Aegr.* 6. If Gaster's translation of the Poem of Baal is correct, then Astarte interceded in the defeated Yam's behalf,
as Isis in Set's, and Yam lay upon the shore, imprisoned in a net (also like Set), until
Baal finally killed him (see Gaster 1950: 159–161, 164 f., 167, 179), but Gordon's translation is quite different, and Gaster seems to have changed his mind in his later book (1952:
213).

[4] *Contest* 10.3–11. For Horos' loss of eyes see also the Ramesseum Papyrus 15–20,
25–28, 64 f. (see p. 182, note 8); BD 112.5; Plut. *Mor.* 373E.

[5] *Contest* 5.6–7.13, 11.1–12.12. In Anti, who ferries passengers to an island, we may
recognise the boatman of the dead (Th. 3F); see Appendix 1. Notice too the stone boats
of the next paragraph (cf. p. 487).

In both episodes Set takes on characteristics of the Stupid Ogre. This is even more evident in the contest that follows the lettuce episode. Set, again refusing to accept the gods' decision in Horos' favor, proposed a race in stone boats. He actually provided himself with a stone boat, which sank; but Horos made a boat of cedar wood and plastered it over with gypsum to make it look like stone.[6]

Plainly several versions of the Set-Horos conflict have been combined in the *Contest* text and in other texts too; hence Horos' seemingly futile victories, the different kinds of contest, and the inconsistencies of outcome. In one episode Ra orders the pair to cease wrangling, and they become reconciled for a time. This is the outcome of the Memphite Drama, wherein Geb asks Horos and Set to stop fighting and divides the land between them: Horos gets Lower Egypt and Set Upper Egypt; in the next act Geb gives Horos dominion over united Egypt, and yet the rivals remain reconciled. This recalls the final outcome of the strife between Baal and Mot.[7]

Whereas the *Contest* is framed within the trial scene, and the Memphite Drama is built upon the reconciliation, the Ramesseum Dramatic Papyrus is mainly concerned with Horos' succession to Osiris. It is a ritual program, the Egyptian coronation drama: an important text because of its stage and ceremonial directions; for it makes evident the close relation that the myth bore to cult (Th. 10D). The main outlines of the myth can be recognised. Set killed Osiris (Th. 8A); Isis and Nephthys lamented him (Th. 8E). Horos fought Set to avenge his father and to assert his claim to the kingship (Ths. 5A, 7E). His followers battled with Set's confederates (Th. 7G). He lost his eye to Set (Th. 8B), but later recovered it through Thoth or his followers (Th. 7E). Set and his host were defeated and beheaded, Set being represented by a goat and goose in the ritual; in other scenes he lost his testicles, which Horos fitted to himself, and his thighbone. He was also punished by being forced to carry the corpse of Osiris to heaven on his back (Th. 10A). The play

---

[6] *Contest* 13.3–11. On Set-Typhon's stupidity see Plut. *Mor.* 371BC. Notice the race instead of combat in one version of the Kyknos story (p. 30).

[7] Memphite Drama: text with German translation and commentary, Sethe (1928) 20–77; English translation, Gaster (1950) 407–411.

ends with a banquet of jubilation to which Horos invited the gods (Th. 10b).[8]

So far the opponent of Set has been Horos, son of Osiris. But Set's vanquisher is also identified with the elder Horos, falcon-headed god, and with Horos of Behdet, also falcon-headed and hardly to be distinguished from the elder Horos. As king of Lower Egypt, the elder Horos fought Set, king of Upper Egypt, and having defeated him, achieved the unity of Egypt under one king. But in the Memphite Drama it was Osiris' son who became king of united Egypt. The fifteen major forms and many minor forms of Horos which were distinguished in Egyptian theology were derived from a single god: his different names amount to no more than the several epithets of a Greek god. Different parents were assigned to him in different cities: his father was Ra or Geb or Osiris, his mother Hathor or Nut or Isis or Bast or another; hence the distinction that reappears in Plutarch's narrative between the elder Horos and the younger.[9]

In the Edfu Drama it is Horos of Behdet who fights Set and Set's hosts in his father Ra's behalf. In some scenes Horos, Isis' son, appears beside him as his helper, and is also pictured as hawk-headed on accompanying reliefs (fig. 21). But Horos of Behdet is himself called son of Isis in the prologue. In four other mythical texts on the walls of the Edfu temple Set's opponent is either Horos of Behdet or Horos, Isis' son. Certainly the different forms of Horos were not clearly distinguished in this great center of Horos worship.[10]

Horos was lord of the sky and often identified with the sun, Ra himself. He is not, however, a god of storm; that is hardly to be expected in Egypt's nearly rainless climate, where fertility and growth depend upon the Nile's floods rather than upon rainfall. Rather it is Set or Apep who represent storm and thundercloud.

In the Edfu Drama, Set takes the form of an hippopotamus of

---

[8] Ramesseum Papyrus: text with German translation and commentary, Sethe (1928) 103–243; English translation, Gaster (1950) 384–403.

[9] See Budge (1934) 218–227; Mercer (1942) 117–136, 195 f.; Blackman-Fairman (1942) 32 f.; Gardiner (1944); Černy (1952) 23, 32–34, 46–48.

[10] For the Edfu texts in English translation see Fairman (1935): Myth of the winged disk; Blackman-Fairman (1942–1944): Edfu Drama; see Gaster (1950) 62 f., 144 f. For plates of text and reliefs with description and French translation of parts see Naville (1870). On the elder Horos as son of Osiris and Isis see also Plut. *Mor.* 356a.

gigantic size (Ths. 3A, 3B); he stood in water twenty cubits deep, and the harpoon that Horos used to kill him had a shaft of sixteen cubits, a blade of four cubits, and was thrown on a rope sixty cubits long. Horos had to use ten harpoons (Th. 7B), a spear, arrows, talons, and a net, and he fought from a boat. The divine smith Ptah, the Egyptian Hephaistos or Koshar-wa-Hasis

FIGURE 21. HOROS KILLING HIPPOPOTAMUS-SET

Relief from Temple at Edfu

(p. 130), made his weapons; Isis and Thoth also helped him (Ths. 7D, 7E). Round about this central combat a battle went on between Horos' companions and Set's (Th. 7G). In one scene the latter are represented as snakes (Th. 3B). At one point Set fled into the wilderness (Th. 7F). Finally he was killed, bound, and twice dismembered (Th. 10A). Horos was constantly cheered by Isis and attendant gods, and his victory was celebrated with rejoicing and a feast (Th. 10B).

In Edfu Text A (as Fairman designates it) Ra and Horos of Behdet were sailing in Ra's boat, when they caught sight of Ra's enemies (Th. 7G), who took the form of crocodiles and hippopotami, and opened their mouths to attack the boat (Th. 3B).

Horos, with Ra's permission, took the battle into his own hands
(Th. 7E). He flew up into the sky in the form of a great
winged disk and attacked the enemy host, causing them to lose
their sight and hearing and so to attack and kill one another.
Edfu became Horos' city from that day and his palace received
its name (Th. 10D). Unfortunately the enemy were not yet
disposed of. They reappeared as crocodiles and hippopotami under Set's leadership, and Horos in Ra's boat had to meet them in
several places and inflict defeat and slaughter upon them. Set was
an hippopotamus of red jasper (Th. 3B); at one point he took
the form of a roaring snake and disappeared into the ground
(Th. 7F). But according to Plutarch, Set took crocodile form
on this occasion. Isis and Thoth used magic spells (Th. 9)
against Set to aid Horos (Ths. 7D, 7E). The uraeus goddesses,
Nekhbet and Uto, also helped him.[11]

Apparently Osiris himself fought Set in some Egyptian versions
of the myth. In a hymn he is said to have overthrown and killed
Set. In a chapter of the *Book of the Dead* it was Osiris to whom
Thoth added strength by means of magical words (Th. 9), so
that he might triumph over his enemies. According to Diodoros,
he came from the dead in wolf form to help Horos and Isis fight
Set. But Horos, no doubt, was the original opponent of Set, and
Osiris could never take his place. Osiris' role, extremely important otherwise, became reduced in the combat myth to Set's victim and elder Hamlet, who came from the dead to rouse his son
against the murderer-uncle.[12]

In one story Horos supplants Osiris as dying god: he suffers
greater disaster than the loss of an eye. Set placed Isis in prison,
but somehow she got away and on Thoth's advice hid herself and
her child Horos, accompanied by seven scorpions. In their place
of refuge the scorpion Uhat stung Horos so that he died or lay
near death (Th. 8A). Great lamentation began (Th. 8E); in-

---

[11] Text and English translation, Budge (1912) 56–95; English translation, Budge
(1934) 468–480, Fairman (1935) 28–36; plates of reliefs, Naville (1870) XII–XIX. See
Plut. *Mor.* 371D. On winged disk see Gardiner (1944) 46–52. For other texts on the Set-
Horos combat see Edfu Texts BDE (Fairman 26 f.); BD 173 (Budge 1901: 589–592).
[12] Hymn to Osiris (Budge 1912: 96–105, 1934: 420–424); BD 182.11–13 (Budge 1901:
622); Diod. 1.88.6. On the relations of Horos, Osiris, and Set in myth and history see
Mercer (1942) 65–78, 92–95, 186–190. On Osiris see Budge (1911), Cooke (1931).

cantations were spoken. Finally Thoth came and with his spells brought life back to Horos (Th. 7E). Also according to a chapter of the *Book of the Dead* Horos died in the swamps, and his hands were cut off, perhaps by Isis; but Sebek, the crocodile-god, found them, and Isis restored them. Plutarch too mentions stories of the dismembering of Horos: in one, however, it was his flesh and fat that he lost in punishment for killing Isis. In another story, told by Apollodoros, after Io (= Isis) had borne Epaphos on the banks of the Nile, Hera asked the Kuretes to hide the child. Io then searched for him and found him in Byblos, where the queen was nursing him (contrary to Plutarch's account, in which Isis at Byblos nursed the queen's son).[13]

As the story is told on the Metternich stele, Isis, accompanied by her seven scorpions, came to the house of a woman called Usert, who closed her doors against the goddess. A scorpion named Tefen went into the house and stung Usert's son to death, but Isis pitied the woman's grief and with her magical spells revived the boy. Then the narrator says, "Oh the child shall live and the poison die! Verily Horus shall be in good case for his mother Isis." In the very next episode Horos was stung. In all likelihood these are two versions of one story in which the young god dies from the wound inflicted by the enemy in scorpion form, and which has been reduced to an episode of the developed combat myth.[14]

Set was identified with several animals (Th. 3B) and could take the form of any of them at will (Th. 3E). Whatever his form, he was red in color. His snake form has already been mentioned and will be discussed presently: he was literally a dragon. He also took the form of a crocodile—a reptile that has contributed to the well-known lizardlike dragon of folklore—and, as we have seen, he was frequently identified with that other monster

---

[13] Metternich stele (text and translation, Budge 1912: 156–197, 1934: 491–503); BD 113 (Budge 1901: 338–340); Plut. *Mor.* 358E, *Lib. et Aegr.* 6; Apollod. 2.1.3. See Mercer (1942) 74, 148.

[14] Metternich Stele 53–70 (Budge 1912: 158–165, 1934: 492 f.); I quote Budge's translation. The episode of Anubis' death and exposure is probably a third version of the same tale; see Plut. *Mor.* 356EF. Anubis was the child of Osiris and Nephthys, Set's wife (Th. 8D). Nephthys exposed the child in fear of Set's anger (Th. 8A). Isis learned of this and looked for the child; with the help of dogs she found him, and raised him to be her attendant and protector. Horos was sometimes identified with Anubis: Mercer (1942) 143.

of the Nile, the hippopotamus. This creature, the river horse, both water-dweller and a mammal related to swine, forms a link between the reptilian and piscine forms of the enemy monster on the one hand, and his swinish and equine forms on the other; for Set was also conceived as pig, okapi, donkey, and antelope. According to one story he transformed himself into a black pig, and in that form threw a jet of fire (Th. 3D) upon Horos, causing him to lose his eye (remember the boar form of Python and Phorbas, pp. 56 f., and the boar that killed Adonis, p. 329, note 12). Set as donkey recalls the horse-shaped demons of night, sleep, and death. Empusa (p. 116) had an ass's leg and was called *Onoskelis;* so was Mormo, who, we know for certain, was identified with the nightmare. Notice too the horse-headed Zu (p. 152) and the Centaur enemies of Herakles. Again, in the ritual of the Ramesseum Papyrus a goat and a goose represented Set. Since Set could be a goose, we need no longer be surprised that as Kyknos the enemy took the form of a swan, especially when we recall that Kyknos mated with Gerana (Crane) the Pygmy queen (p. 101): notice Aso, Typhon-Set's Ethiopian queen.[15]

Set's serpent form is attested not only by Edfu Text A, but also by other Egyptian texts. The elder Pliny too, in a rationalised bit of lore, says that Typhon as king of Egypt gave his name to a native species of fiery-colored snake. However, the great serpent enemy of the gods was not Set, but Apep (Apophis), a huge snake, thirty cubits long, with a head three cubits broad (Th. 3A, 3B). He lurks upon the western mountains, where he has a cave (Th. 2B), and attacks Ra's sun-boat as it approaches the horizon. All night the sun god and his crew battle the snake (Th. 7A), and at last with spear or sword or arrows, flame, and magical

---

[15] On the animal forms of Set see Roeder, LM 4.777–784. As crocodile: Plut. *Mor.* 371CD; Ael. NA 10.21. For Set's confederates in crocodile and hippopotamus form see Edfu Text A (Fairman 1935: 29). As pig: BD 112 (Budge 1901: 336 f., 1934: 457–459). As donkey: Edfu Text E (Fairman 27); Plut. *Mor.* 150F, 362F, 363C, 371C; Ael. NA 10.28. Notice that the wild ass was the death demon of Enlil: Ebeling (1931) 36, line 11. Set's red color: BD 182.20 (Budge 1901: 623); Edfu Text A (Fairman 27, 33); Plut. *Mor.* 359E, 362F–363B, 364B; Diod. 1.88.4. Set as goat and goose: Ramesseum Papyrus 44 f.; see Gaster (1950) 390. For possible fish form see Plut. *Mor.* 358B and Roeder, LM 4.781. The unicorn probably has its origin in the rhinoceros, another African beast, which perhaps forms a folkloristic link between hippopotamus or swine and horse. Mormo as nightmare: Theocr. 15.40. Empusa and Mormo as Onoskelis: Suid. E1049; Schol. Vet. on Aristoph. *Eccl.* 1056; Schol. on Aristid. *Or.* 13.102J. See Meyer (1875).

spells (Th. 9) he is overcome, bound, killed, cut to pieces, and imprisoned under the earth (Th. 10A); then the sun-boat emerges in victory from the darkness in the east, where Apep has met his final defeat. He thus represents the darkness of night; he also represents eclipses and dark thunderclouds (Th. 3G), for he may attack the sun-boat by day. He is constantly defeated, but as constantly he comes back to life and tries again.[16]

At first Ra was Apep's opponent and gained the victory in person. Later Horos did the actual fighting under Ra's command: he was in fact often identified with Ra, but usually the texts show Ra and Horos together in the sun-boat (Th. 7E). It is with some surprise that we find Set too as Ra's champion against Apep, either the sole opponent or associated with Horos. That of course is explained by the vicissitudes of Set's role in the course of Egyptian history. He was not only the wicked enemy, but also, especially in certain periods and places, a great god of the pantheon.[17]

Set as enemy was apparently assimilated to Apep. Apep was a roaring serpent, a form that Set once took in his conflict with Horos of Behdet. Apep was a crocodile; so was Set—but Apep's tortoise form may not have been shared by Set. Among Apep's confederates were crocodiles and other kinds of animals; Set's confederates took the form of crocodiles and hippopotami. Apep is the name given to an antelope drawn on papyrus and burned in a magical ritual; Set took antelope form. Both Set and Apep were red in color, poisonous, and fire-spouting (Th. 3D). Both were extremely wicked, evil, ill-disposed, as characterised in the texts (Th. 4A). Both had hosts of demons and monsters to support them (Th. 7G). Horos fought both from the prow of Ra's sun-boat. Horos' eye that Set knocked out is equated with the sun, which Apep as darkness swallows (Ths. 8A, 8B). Isis aided Horos against Apep as against Set (Th. 7D); in the Apep combat we also find the scorpion-goddess Serq, who with magic spell

---

[16] On Apep see Bremner-Rhind Papyrus D: Faulkner (1937) 167–175, (1938) 41–46; Budge (1934) 518–521; part in Pritchard (1950) 6 f.; Metternich Stele 1–8 (Budge 1912: 142–145); BD 7, 11, 39, 40, 108 (Budge 1901: 54 f., 59 f., 167–172, 315 f.); see also Pritchard (1950) 12; Budge (1912) 12 f. See Pliny NH 2.25.91.

[17] Ra against Apep: BD 11, 39; Budge (1912) 12 f.; in Bremner-Rhind Papyrus D, *passim*, Ra alone is spoken of as fighter and victor. Horos: *ibid*. 27.9, 29–31; Metternich Stele 1–8. Set: Bremn. Rh. D 23.21 f., 30.5,10; Pritchard (1950) 12. On Horos = Ra see Mercer (1942) 78–80, 137–140, 191–194.

effectively helped the gods repel the snake. The two demons were distinct, but there was definitely a tendency to fuse them.[18]

In a rather different story Isis placed a venomous snake in the path which Ra travelled in his boat "at the head of his mariners." Ra had become old, and Isis wanted to become "mistress of the earth, and a mighty goddess." This she could do if she could get possession of Ra's secret and ineffable name. She took some of Ra's saliva, moistened dust with it, and fashioned a snake, which she laid in Ra's path. His fang struck Ra as he went by unawares, and the god suffered terribly from the poison. Isis promised to help Ra if he would deliver to her his secret name. He finally consented, and his name, which was also his heart, left his body and passed over to Isis. Ra was now as good as dead; but Isis with an incantation expelled the poison from his body and brought him back to life.[19]

Isis is here a mistress of witchcraft, who, it is said, esteems the spirits even above the gods: that is, she is the Egyptian Hekate. She also creates the snake and incites him against the great god: her role is therefore like Ge's in the Typhon myth. As beguiler of Ra, plotting his destruction and luring him to the surrender of his potency, she seems to be the deadly seductress, a Siren or Empusa (Th. 8D). But since her son Horos as bystander apparently agrees with her, and since we have seen that Ra favored Set over Horos in the *Contest* text, she takes on something of the character of Anat when she helped her brother against El's hostility. Again, she uses magical rituals to bring Ra back to life,

[18] Apep as roarer: Bremn.-Rh. D 22.16; Set's roar was the thunder (Th. 3G): Budge (1934) 24, 280. Apep as crocodile: BD 32.2–7; Budge 141, 516; Faulkner (1938) 52 f., where Apep also appears as antelope; see the last two citations also for Apep's confederates—among them notice the lion-faced snake (cf. Labbu). Apep as tortoise: Bremn. Rh. D 25.19, E 32.26. Apep's red color: Faulkner (1937) 167. Apep's poison: Metternich Stele 3, 8; BD 7.3; Set's poison: Ramesseum Papyrus 33. Apep's fire: BD 32.3, 5 (crocodiles); Set's fire: BD 112.8. Opprobrious epithets are applied to both throughout the texts; see especially "The Names of Apep," Bremn.-Rh. E (Faulkner 1938: 52). Eye of Horos: Bremn.-Rh. D 22.24–23.1, 24.8–16; on his eye as the sun see Mercer (1942) 150–154. Isis against Apep: Bremn.-Rh. D 23.19, 30.9, 31.17 f. Serq: Metternich Stele 3; BD 39.10. See Budge 141, 209, 516; Ortiz (1947) 473 f.; Mackenzie, EML 75, 260; on the fusion of Set and Apep, and Mackenzie 159 on Apep as swallower of the sun boat; also Griffith-Thompson (1904), Magical Papyrus 19.37, where "the face of Set against Osiris" is parallel to "the face of Apop against the Sun."

[19] Budge (1912) 42–55, (1931) 111–117, (1934) 459–463; Mackenzie EML 3–6; Pritchard (1950) 12–14; quotations from Budge. The story contains Ths. 1A, 3B, 3F, 4F, 5A, 5B, 8A, 8B, 8D.

somewhat as Anat or Ishtar performed ritual acts to recover Baal or Tammuz: that is, her role is as ambiguous as Anat's or Ishtar's in relation to the hero and to the enemy. This story of Isis and Ra's name helps us to understand better the episode narrated both in the *Contest* and by Plutarch, wherein Isis saves Set from death, bringing Horos' wrath upon herself, and also to understand better the episode in which she struck Horos with her harpoon. Behind those episodes is the dragoness aiding the dragon against the hero-god.[20]

Nephthys plays much the same part as Isis. She is Set's wife, but also Osiris' mistress and mother of his child, who, like Isis' son, nearly loses his life in an infancy that begins in the swamps. At Isis' side she aids Horos (but also Set) against Apep, and with Isis mourns for Osiris. Plutarch also mentions Aso, the Ethiopian queen who helped Set-Typhon, and Thueris, Set-Typhon's concubine who deserted him for Horos. In Nephthys and Thueris we may see the ogre's wife or daughter who falls in love with the hero (p. 258) and helps him. Isis too may have something of this character in a story in which Horos forces her—that is, he becomes the hero who has his way with the dragon's woman whether she likes it or not, like Herakles or Apollo in the house of Pyrene's or Dryope's father (pp. 48 f., 57)—a mutation of the episode in which the dragoness falls in love with the hero. A love of Isis for Horos may lie behind the story: magical papyri of love spells mention Isis' longing for Horos.[21]

Aso, I believe, has not been identified. Thueris was an important deity, the hippopotamus-goddess, and therefore a fitting consort of Set; however, there seems to be little Egyptian evidence for her association with Set, though there is some. She was in part a goddess of the dead and sometimes considered an evil deity, but in general she was looked upon as benevolent.[22]

Thueris was chased by a snake after she deserted Set for Horos:

---

[20] For her cutting off Horos' hands see p. 185.

[21] See Plut. *Mor.* 356AB, 356EF, 358CD; Bremn.-Rh. A (Faulkner 1936: 122–132), D 31.18. On Horos' violence to Isis see Mercer (1942) 107 and Herod. 2.63.4, where Ares must be Horos. See Magical Papyrus 15.18, 18.17, in Griffith-Thompson (1904).

[22] See Roeder, LM 5.878–882, 888–903. Notice Griffith-Thompson (1904), Magical Papyrus 12.22: Thueris, as sorceress, is called cat (?) of Ethiopia, lady of the uraeus, Sekhmet, lady of Ast. This suggests that she may be one with Plutarch's Aso. This papyrus is very late—third century A.D.—but probably it repeats traditional forms of address.

an episode that recalls Python's pursuit of Leto. Herodotos introduces Leto into the Egyptian myth, by which name he means Uto or Uazit, great goddess of Buto. He says that Leto received the infant Apollo (Horos) from Isis and concealed him on the floating island of Chemmis near Buto, to save him from Set, who was searching everywhere for him to destroy him (Th. 4c); she was not Apollo's mother, but his nurse and protectress. We have already seen Uto as uraeus goddess, protectress of Lower Egypt, helping Horos against the crocodiles and hippopotami in the winged-disk story. Since Thueris had as one of her provinces the protection of infants and mothers, it is probable that she also was assigned the role of Horos' nurse, perhaps in an Upper Egyptian version. Moreover she was sometimes identified with Uto, who has snake form—sometimes winged—and also vulture form. Both she and Thueris are sometimes lion headed.[23]

As Set's snake pursued Thueris, so Set pursued Isis, and in one version held her in prison. The pursuit theme is counterpart of the Siren theme (8D); for the dragon's pursuit usually has lustful intent (Th. 4E). In the famous Egyptian *Tale of the Two Brothers* the sea pursued Bata's wife, having become fired with lust on catching sight of her, and with a cedar's help he took a lock of her hair. Now, according to Plutarch, the Egyptians identified Set with the sea (Th. 2E). There is no evidence of this in native sources; but we have seen Set as hippopotamus and crocodile, fighting or lurking in sea and river: evidence enough that he had something to do with the waters. From Greek and Latin sources we know the tale of Typhon's pursuit of Aphrodite, who saved herself and her son by leaping into either the Euphrates or the lake at Ascalon, where they either took fish form or were saved by fish. It is a Syro-Palestinian story that we have already noticed (pp. 84, 133): Aphrodite is Atargatis or Astarte, and Typhon is Yam or Leviathan. Some classical authors, in their merging of the Greek and Egyptian myths, include Aphrodite's transformation into a fish among the gods' changes into animal form that they effected in Egypt in order to escape Typhon.

---

[23] Herod. 2.156.4 f. On Uto see LM 6.142–144. On Thueris see Roeder, LM 5.902; see Griffith-Thompson (1904), Magical Papyrus 12.22. According to Ant. Lib. 28.3, Leto changed herself into a shrewmouse (*mygalê*) in Egypt to escape from Typhon.

Again, Astarte and Anat became important Egyptian deities—there were many interchanges of cult and myth between Egypt and Syria. In the *Contest,* when the goddess Neith declared for Horos, she proposed appeasement of Set (Th. 7c) by doubling his possessions and by giving him Anat and Astarte, Ra's daughters.[24]

Another Egyptian myth plainly shows influence from Canaan. Sea claimed tribute from the gods as their ruler (Th. 4b), like Yam in the first Baal poem, and they delivered it to him (Th. 7c). The gods sent Astarte with the tribute to Sea, apparently to induce him to take less tribute or none. What happened then is not clear. One is reminded of Paghat's visit to Yatpan (p. 139): but Astarte apparently did not disguise herself, for Sea recognised her at once. After her visit Sea sent a request to the gods, asking that Astarte stay with him, and he kept up his demands for tribute. Astarte received great honor from the gods on her return. That is all: there the story breaks off. Had Astarte, through love's power, persuaded Sea to take less tribute? Or would she catch him off guard on a second visit and put him out of the way altogether? In any case she plays a part opposite the Egyptian dragon, either as the intended victim of his lust (Th. 4e), or as a heroine-siren who turns his lust against him (Th. 8d merged with 9, the Judith theme).[25]

Returning to *The Two Brothers,* we should notice that Bata's wife lived with Bata in the Valley of the Cedar, which represents the realm of death. For Bata lived there bereft of his manhood and of his heart, which now lay on the flower of the cedar; and his brother mourned him in dust and ashes after he had gone there. It was there that his wife, daughter of Ra, whom the gods gave him, walked beside the sea, when he stole a lock of her hair. Once more we see death and sea closely associated: the sea that took her hair is Thanatos himself. The wife's own deadly character is evident from the following episodes. The waves carried the stolen lock to Pharaoh, and when he learned that the owner lived in

---

[24] *Tale of Two Brothers:* Budge (1931) 95–110; Mackenzie EML 45–57; pursuit on pp. 104 and 51 respectively. Set = sea: Plut. *Mor.* 363DE, 364A, 367A, 376F. Aphrodite becomes a fish in Egypt: Ovid *Met.* 5.331; Ampel. 2.12. Neith's proposal: *Contest* 3.1–5. An homosexual turn to Set's lechery may be seen in *Contest* 11.3 f.

[25] Story in Pritchard (1950) 17 f. See Appendix 2.

the Valley of the Cedar, he sent men to fetch her. Bata killed them all. Finally, with costly gifts Pharaoh induced her to come to him. As Pharaoh's wife she told him how to kill Bata by felling the cedar on whose flower his heart lay. So Pharaoh sent soldiers forth with axes; they cut the cedar down and Bata died. This incident recalls Gilgamesh's hewing of the cedar in Humbaba's forest (p. 168): in the folktale perhaps it held Humbaba's life (see p. 172, note 54: of the *huluppu* tree's wood were made objects in which Gilgamesh's power resided). Bata came back to life, after his brother Anpu found his heart in the fourth year of search, took the form of a beautiful bull, and went to Pharaoh's palace, where he found favor in the king's sight. But he was foolish enough to tell the queen, his ex-wife, who he was. While Pharaoh sat at dinner, she induced him to swear that he would do whatever she should ask, and through this mild deception she forced him to kill the bull. But Bata was reborn in two fine trees that grew by Pharaoh's door. Again Bata told the queen of his presence, and again at table she tricked Pharaoh into an oath, so that he was forced to cut the trees down. But a splinter flew into her mouth; she swallowed it, conceived, and so unwittingly brought Bata back to life for the third time in the form of her infant son, who grew up, inherited the throne, sat in judgment on his wife that was, and put her to death. He summoned Anpu to him and made him his heir.

Now all the main characters of this story are gods: Anpu is Anubis, and Bata is a god who was conceived in serpent form, or rather, mixed form—the Bata snake had four human bodies and four pairs of human legs at each end of his body. His wife may be a form of Isis or Nephthys, and Pharaoh may represent Horos or Set. In the story Bata is obviously a dying god like Osiris or Tammuz, or perhaps like Set or Mot, since he is a murderous resident of the land of death. His wife is the seductive and treacherous demoness, made into a Delilah who betrays her husband's weakness: but in flight from Sea she is the hero's wife attacked by a lecherous dragon. It is plain that these themes, which have a large place in Egyptian myth, were carried over into legend and folktale, and used as the narrator wished.[26]

---

[26] Bata snake: Budge (1934) 105. While dealing with the love themes, we should notice that in BD 39.11 the god, gloating over fallen Apep, tells him that now he shall

Before we leave the Egyptian myths we should glance at the roles of Thoth-Hermes and Min-Pan. Thoth was identified with Hermes, and his role in the combat is similar. Without his magic spells and his eloquence Horos could hardly have defeated Set; just as Zeus would have perished utterly but for Hermes' cunning. The god Min was identified with Pan; but though Min plays little part in the Egyptian sources of the combat myth, classical sources give Pan (i.e., Min) an important part in the Horos-Set combat. According to Plutarch the Pans and Satyrs of Chemmis (= Panopolis) were the first to learn of Set's murder of Osiris and spread the news, so that Isis found out. According to other authors it was Pan who advised the gods, after they had fled to Egypt, to assume animal shapes in order to deceive Typhon.[27]

I have already pointed out that the Greeks identified Horos with Apollo no later than the early fifth century (pp. 90 f.). His opponent, however, was identified with Typhon, Zeus's traditional enemy, and his helper Thoth with Hermes, Zeus's helper against Typhon. These identifications point to an earlier form of the Greek dragon myth in which Typhon and Python were not distinguished, and to a time when Apollo rather than Zeus was the principal champion against him.

It is evident that Egyptian mythology, like West-Asiatic mythologies, was pervaded by the dragon combat, and that in Egypt too the myth follows the same general plan.[28]

---

never fulfil his lust for love's pleasures. Since BD 39 concerns the repelling of Apep from the souls of the dead, this may mean that he tries to seize dead women for his pleasure, somewhat as Heros of Temesa came to the tomb for his bride (p. 102). Notice the death spirit in form of crocodile and snake that comes to fetch the young prince in an Egyptian folktale: a giant or spirit, like Herakles, keeps one off, and his wife kills the other; see Budge (1931) 118–127, Mackenzie EML 294–301. The wife lures the snake with bowls of milk and beer, while the prince sleeps; the snake gets drunk and is easily killed (Th. 7H, a). In the legend of the princess of Bakhten, the god Khonsu drives off an evil spirit that has possessed the princess. Notice the feast of reconciliation at the end, with offerings to both Khonsu and the demon. See Budge (1931) 142–148, (1934) 487–490, Mackenzie EML 200–202. Observe Themes 1B, 2E, 3B, 3E, 3F, 4E, 4F, 5B, 7A, 7E, 8A, 8B, 8D, 8E, 9, 10A.

[27] In BD 182 Thoth is given chief credit for repulsing Apep's swallowing of the sun. On Pan's role see Plut. Mor. 356D; Nigid. ap. Schol. B in Germ. Arat. 289; Hyg. Fab. 196; cf. Astron. 2.28 and Ampel. 2.10.

[28] Very few themes are missing. Besides those indicated in text and notes the following are also present: 2A, 4D, 4F. On 4D notice not only Apep's swallowing of Osiris' enemies, but also the fish that swallows Osiris' and Bata's severed members: Plut. Mor. 358B; Budge (1931) 101. On 10D notice that Apep had a tomb, which means a cult; see Bremn.-Rh. D 27.12, 26; 29.19; 31.7.

INDIC MYTHS

Like Greece, Western Asia, and Egypt, India is prolific in tales of dragon combat. And as in those countries, there is one that takes precedence, the myth of Indra's combat with the monstrous dragon Vritra. It is the subject of several Vedic hymns and is alluded to in many more; and it had a vigorous life in later Sanskrit literature.[29]

Vritra was a gigantic snake (*ahi*, Th. 3B), who in the world's beginnings encompassed the waters of chaos and kept them from flowing forth (Ths. 2E, 4G). He was also a boar, lying on the water; so, just as Set or Python-Phorbas, the gods' enemy appears as either snake or boar. Within the waters which he enclosed were the sun and all that the world needed. He was son of Danu (Th. 1A), mother of the Danavas, one of the many names for demons (Th. 3F). According to the *Taittirîya Sanhita* and *Çatapatha-Brâhmana* he was created by Tvashtri (Th. 1B), the divine artisan and creator, from some dregs of soma cast upon the fire; he grew thereafter an arrowshot in all directions until he had forced back the oceans and enveloped the worlds (Th. 3A). As you might expect, Vritra was no better than he should be: he was tricky (*mâyin*), godless (*adeva*), mocking or overbearing (*piyâru*), malicious (*arçasâna*), an insulting demon (*atra mrdha-vâc*) (Th. 4A). He consumed increasingly terrific quantities of food as he grew in size (Th. 4D), and he drained the rivers (= cosmic waters, Th. 4G). Like Egyptian Apep, he lay upon the mountains on the borders of darkness.[30]

---

[29] See especially RV 1.32, 1.52, 1.80, 2.11, 3.32, 4.18, 5.32, 6.17, 8.96, 10.113; TS 2.4.12, 2.5.2 f.; ÇB 1.6.3.1–17, 1.6.4.1–7; *Aitareya Brâhmana* 3.20; *Mbh.*, *Udy.* sects. 9–18; *ibid.*, *Çant.* 342. Other hymns and passages that allude to the combat will be cited in footnotes to the following discussion.

The Sanskrit works, chiefly Vedas and epics, to which I refer in this section, are more readily available to the English reader than the Hittite, Canaanite, Mesopotamian and Egyptian writings of chapters vii-ix. English translations or summaries of *Rig Veda*, *Mahâbhârata*, and *Râmâyana* may be found in any good library. There are also more scholars who read Sanskrit than read ancient Egyptian or Assyrio-Babylonian or Ugaritic. Hence I do not need to cite the pages of editions and translations.

[30] Vritra was *prathamajâ ahînâm*, the firstborn of snakes: RV 1.32.3 f. *ahi* is cognate to Greek *echis*. Danu's son: RV 1.32.9; ÇB 1.6.3.9. Tvashtri's creation: TS 2.4.12, 2.5.2; ÇB 1.6.3.8–11. Boar: RV 1.121.11, 8.77.10; cf. 10.99.6. *mâyin*: RV 1.80.7, 2.11.10, 5.30.6.

Against Vritra the gods had a champion in Indra. He is a weather god, wielder of the thunderbolt (*vajrin*), exactly as Zeus or Baal-Hadad (Th. 6A). Though it is Dyaus (Sky) who has the same name as Zeus, it is Indra who most nearly corresponds to Zeus in character. Indra, like Zeus and Baal, killed his enemy in early youth (Th. 6B): in fact, some hymns have it that he, like Apollo, went forth against the dragon when only a few days old. As in the Canaanite, Babylonian, and Egyptian myths, the god's reward for victory was kingship of the world (Th. 5A). He was called Vritrahan (Vritra Slayer) ever after, as Hermes was called Argeiphontes (Argos Slayer).[31]

It was a terrible battle that Indra fought with Vritra (Th. 7A). He hurled his thunderbolts, apparently many of them (Th. 7B), upon his enemy's back, face, and vulnerable parts. His bolts had a hundred joints and a thousand points each. Or, as some hymns have it, he shot arrows from his bow; but his arrows, each with a thousand feathers, are simply thunderbolts. Thus Zeus's thunderbolts and Apollo's arrows become one. Tvashtri forged Indra's thunderbolts; he corresponds exactly in pantheon and myth to Greek Hephaistos, Egyptian Ptah, and Canaanite Koshar-wa-Hasis. Finally Indra vanquished Vritra, killed him, and freed the waters and the sun—which symbolise the world order—heretofore confined in the waters and darkness of chaos. Vritra was cast into the outer darkness (Th. 10A), the enduring chaos that surrounds or underlies the cosmos, and

---

adeva: RV 3.32.6, 10.111.6; cf. ἀσεβής, δυσσεβής, *impius*, etc., applied to the enemies of Apollo and Zeus (p. 58, note 45; p. 83 with note 20). *piyāru:* RV 3.30.8, and *atra mṛdhavâc:* RV 5.32.8; cf. ὑβριστής, ὑπερήφανος, etc. *arçasâna:* RV 10.99.7; cf. ἄδικος, κακόν, etc. Gluttony: ÇB 1.6.3.11–17; *Mbh., Udy.* 10.3. Vritra is sin: ÇB 11.1.5.7. Encompasser of the waters: RV 1.32.8; 1.52.2, 8; 1.80.3 f., 10; 2.11; 2.14.2; 3.32.6, 11; 4.18.6 f.; 5.30.5 f.; 5.32.1 f.; 8.96.18; 10.99.4; 10.111.8 f.; 10.113.4, 6; 10.138.1. Lies upon mountains: RV 1.32.2, 5.32.2. In his obstruction of the approach to the waters, his blocking them so that they cannot flow (RV 2.11.9, Vritra beleaguered the mighty river), and his lying around them, Ths. 2E, 4F, and 4G are combined (so is 2D: he is keeper of the source of the waters). Since the waters are cows, and also goddesses, whom Vritra holds in thrall, Th. 4E is also involved. See Hillebrandt (1929) 154–187; Macdonell (1897) 158 f.

[31] See RV 6.17.8, "Then the gods placed you, Indra, as their one champion in the van for war; then when the godless foe lay in wait for the gods, they chose Indra to win the light." Indra fought Vritra in infancy: RV 8.45, 8.77. Kingship the issue: RV 1.80, 6.17.8; and see p. 205. On Indra see Hillebrandt (1929) 137–269; also Muir (1870) 77–139, Macdonell (1897) 54–66.

there he remains. For death and banishment to the underworld are the same thing.[32]

Vritra, therefore, is, like Apsu and Tiamat, a spirit of primeval chaos (as W. Norman Brown has shown), after whose death the world that we know came into being. In fact, he may once have been identified with the waters: for there was a version in which he had swallowed the waters, and therefore contained them within him. Since the waters were chaos, containing all elements of the world in them, Vritra was Chaos himself as a living deity. Tvashtri does not appear as his creator before the *Brâhmaṇas;* in the Vedas his mother Danu only is mentioned. As mother of demons she is probably in origin a female chaos spirit, an Indic Tiamat and mate of the dragon, whatever names the pair bore then. It is significant that in *Rig Veda* 1.32, an excellent source, Indra must fight Danu after he has killed Vritra, and her body falls across her son's. In India the male demon took precedence: it was his body that was cut asunder to produce the world. In several hymns it is said that Indra or the Maruts cut Vritra to pieces, just as in the Babylonian and Egyptian myths the dragon may be bound, imprisoned, killed, and cut to pieces, and yet be cast beneath the earth, apparently whole, there to live on and perhaps terrify the dead. Now, according to *Rig Veda* 10.113, Indra rent Vritra to free the waters; in the same hymn he cleft the mountain to let the streams flow forth. Vritra is in fact the same as the mountain which encloses the waters. It was then, the hymn goes on to say, that Indra fixed the vault of heaven in its place and separated heaven from earth. In another hymn his helpers, the Maruts, dismembered Vritra and cleft the mountains or mountain clouds (*paravatâs*); for Vritra's mountains are identified with clouds. Finally, the *Çathapatha-Brâhmaṇa* has it that when Vritra

---

[32] On the battle see citations in note 29, p. 194. Tvashtri forged the hundred-jointed thunderbolt: RV 1.32.2, 6.17.10; TS 2.4.12, 2.5.2 (cf. RV 1.80.12). *Kâvya Uçanâ* is also mentioned as maker: RV 1.121.12. Arrows: RV 8.45.4; 8.77.6 f., 11; 10.103.2 f. Like Marduk and Set, Indra used a net: *Atharva Veda* 8.8.5–8. He went forth to battle in a chariot: RV 1.121.12, 8.96.9. See W. N. Brown (1941), (1942), on the Vedic Vritra myth; he has shown beyond question that this is a myth of the world's beginning. His view reconciles and enlarges the conflicting earlier opinions reviewed by Hillebrandt (1929) 143–147. Therefore Mackenzie (IML 9) is mistaken in asserting that the Indra-Vritra combat, unlike the Babylonian Tiamat myth, had no connection with the creation. For Vritra's fate see RV 1.32.10, "Over Vritra's hidden body, put down in the midst of restless, unsettled currents, the waters spread; in long darkness lay Indra's foe."

fell in defeat before Indra, he asked the god not to kill him, but to cut him in two. This Indra did, and of one part he made the moon, of the other he made bellies for earth's creatures. Putting together these scattered passages, we seem to catch the echoes of a creation myth like the Babylonian (and Norse), in which the whole world is fashioned from the primeval enemy's body, merging, as in Babylonia, with the myth of a watery chaos from which the ordered world is drawn.[33]

As in Babylonia and Egypt, the combat was the main event of a gigantomachy (Th. 7c). Vritra led hosts of monsters and demons, prominent among whom were the several demons who were also formidable opponents of Indra or of a hero, and whom I shall discuss presently. The gods fled in terror before the enemy (Th. 7c), except for a very few who stood by Indra. In one source or another the Maruts, Vishnu, Agni, Soma, Tvashtri, and others helped the champion (Th. 7e). There were efforts at appeasement. In one version Agni and Soma were ready to serve Vritra, until Indra bribed them to help him by offering them a share in sacrifices. In the *Mahâbhârata*, as a prelude to trickery, the gods went at Vishnu's suggestion to Vritra and appeased him with a conciliatory treaty.[34]

Indra, like Zeus or Marduk, is often represented as winning a straightforward victory over the enemy, but there is also evidence that he too suffered defeat and death before final triumph (Th. 8a). In one hymn it is said that Vritra shattered Indra's jaw. According to the *Mahâbhârata*, he fled during the combat and made a truce with Vritra. *Rig Veda* 1.32, however, says that his flight occurred after he killed Vritra: he saw an avenger (*yâtṛ*, "goer after"?) of the dragon and fled in terror across ninety-nine rivers. Who the "avenger" was is not clear. It is probably

[33] Vritra swallowed the waters: RV 10.111.9. See RV 1.32.9. Rending of Vritra: RV 10.113.6; 2.11.2, 18; 8.7.23; 10.138.1; ÇB 1.6.3.17. Cleaving of mountain: RV 10.113.4 f., 8.7.23; cf. 10.112.8; see Hillebrandt (1929) 147, 160–163. It is interesting to notice that in ÇB 1.6.3.16 Vritra, struck down, lay contracted like an empty leather bottle or like a skin bag without barley meal: this recalls Bilulu, who became a waterskin (p. 165).

[34] Gigantomachy: RV 2.12, 2.14, 4.30, 8.96, 10.113.4; TS 2.5.3. Flight of gods: RV 4.18.11, 8.96.7; *Aitareya Brâhmaṇa* 3.20. Indra's helpers: (Maruts) RV 1.80.4, 11; 3.32.4; 8.7.23 f.; 8.96.7 f.; 10.73.1; 10.113.3; (Vishnu) RV 4.18.11; TS 2.4.12.3–7; (Agni and Soma) RV 10.124.6; TS 2.5.2; ÇB 1.6.3.13 f.; (others) RV 1.121.12, 5.30.11, 8.96.15; *Mbh.*, *Udy.* 9.47 f. Appeasement: ÇB 1.6.3.12–14; *Mbh.*, *Udy.* 10. For Tvashtri's help see note 32.

not Danu, who fought Indra after Vritra's death; for she has already been disposed of in this hymn—though it is true that the hymn is not a narrative and does allude to events out of sequence. It has inconsistencies too: the "avenger" is introduced after the poet has said that Indra on felling Vritra found no enemy to stand against him. Perhaps the poet means those enemies mentioned in the *Taittirîya Saṅhita* who threatened Indra after he killed Vritra; then Indra forsook the gods and lost his power. He went far off, feeling that he had sinned, and the gods looked for him. Finally he renewed his strength with certain offerings. It is somewhat different in the *Çatapatha-Brâhmana:* weakness overcame him after he had killed Vritra and he did not realise that he had done so; so in fear he fled to the farthest regions and hid himself. Then the gods had to search for him and inform him that Vritra was really dead. In any case the "avenger" represents the guilt that Indra felt after killing Vritra, who was a Brahman; having committed Brahmanicide, he had to seek purification (Th. 10c). Also, according to the *Çatapatha-Brâhmaṇa*, Indra's strength and vital powers flowed away from his body after he had forcibly taken Tvashtri's soma and drunk it; he was healed by the Açvins and Sarasvati. The long and complex narrative of the *Mahâbhârata* has four versions of Indra's death or discomfiture. First Vritra seized Indra and put him in his mouth to swallow him; the gods at once created Jrimbhika, spirit of yawning, whose power opened Vritra's mouth and allowed Indra to escape. In renewed combat Indra took flight, as mentioned above, but returned to final victory. Then after killing Vritra by guile, he became conscience-stricken, both because he had dealt treacherously with Vritra and because he had committed Brahmanicide when he killed Viçvarupa (p. 204); and so he went off to the edges of the world and lay there in water like a snake, unconscious and unrecognisable. Then the earth became barren, rivers and lakes dried up. The gods found Indra, and at Vishnu's command he purified himself by a horse sacrifice and recovered his powers. But when he went to face a new enemy, Nahusha, tyrant of heaven and earth, he trembled in fear and fled once more to the world's confines to live again in water, this time as a white lotus. Now it was the magic power of incantation in the form of the gods' in-

vocation and glorification of Indra that restored him to his
wonted strength.[35]

The *Mahâbhârata* is later than the Vedas, which say nothing
about the swallowing of Indra or his lying as in death at the
world's end. Yet we should not attribute the epic's elaborations
entirely to the poet's invention—these episodes belong to the
myth of dragon combat. Tiamat tried to swallow Marduk in
Enuma elish (p. 150): in the early folk version, beyond doubt, she
actually did so; for she was herself chaos, the darkness, the realm
of death. Likewise Apep, the darkness, swallowed Ra and his boat
(p. 187) and Mot swallowed Baal (p. 134). Indra lay impotent
like Zeus or Baal, and like the Hittite Sun God or Telipinu he
disappeared from the gods' company to parts unknown. His
disappearance meant blight and barrenness on earth, as when Telipinu, Baal, Marduk, Tammuz, and Osiris disappeared. The
Vedic poets glorify Indra and only hint at his discomfiture, but
they say enough to make it certain that there was a story behind
their remarks.

As early as *Rig Veda* 1.32 Indra fled after Vritra's death. In
later sources his flight and death are combined with his need for
purification of blood guilt. In this the Indra-Vritra myth offers a
remarkable parallel to the Apollo-Python myth in both Delphian
and Sicyonian versions (pp. 15, 20, 86). In the latter, terror seized
Apollo after he had killed Python; he fled to a distant land for
purification, a plague came upon the land, prayers and supplications finally induced him to return. At Delphi the popular story
of Apollo's withdrawal to Tempe for purification was attached
to the Septerion ritual, in which a death of Python before the
flight does not seem at all evident (p. 454), and to the Septerion
myth, in which Apollo pursued the still living Python to Tempe.
Apparently in both India and Greece the purification episode—
originally, as in Babylonian myth (p. 169), representing the ritual
cleansing after shedding of blood—was expanded into a story that
the god incurred guilt which needed expiation through severe
penance for a fixed period, during which he retired from the

---

[35] RV 1.32.14, 4.18.9; TS 2.5.3; ÇB 1.6.4.1–7, 12.7; *Mbh.*, *Udy.* 9–16. From this point
the epics will enter more prominently into the discussion. The reader who is unfamiliar
with them will find Jacobi (1893) and (1903) very helpful.

world. This period of expiation and enforced withdrawal was then confused with the god's temporary death incurred during conflict.

The trickery theme is mainly represented by magical and wonder-working devices (Th. 9, d). So powerful is the enemy that the champion and his helpers cannot rely simply on their own might and valor to defeat him: they must overreach him by other than purely physical means. Maruts or Brahmans sang words of power, hymns that were incantations, to lend Indra might superior to Vritra's. Or sacrificial rituals were performed. Above all, Indra drank soma to give himself the strength needed to face Vritra: for the gods' soma was a nectar of marvelous potency.[36]

In the myth's development magic becomes cunning and deceit, as in the Mahâbhârata's version. We have seen that the gods in defeat struck a truce with Vritra, but only to bide their time and entrap him when they could. Vritra made the gods agree that they must never kill him with wet or dry, stone or wood, close-combat weapon or missile, by day or night. But Indra, seeing Vritra on the shore at twilight, had the good fortune to find a huge mass of sea-foam (neither wet nor dry, stone nor wood, nor a weapon), which he blended with his thunderbolt (into this mixture Vishnu entered according to promise) and blasted Vritra. Essentially the same story is told about the demon Namuci, who had carried off the soma.[37]

In the Vedic myth the soma was especially needed for victory. Usually no more is said than that Indra drank it before the battle, as if he had a supply on hand; but from several passages we learn that he had to get it by force. Either the soma was in Tvashtri's possession, and Indra took it from him, or Indra had to break through a mountain to the milk-giving cows that Viçvarupa, Tvashtri's son, or the demon Vala guarded: the soma is explicitly identified with the milk of the imprisoned cows. Then, rejoicing in the milk-soma, he defeated his enemies. Now

---

[36] Incantations and rituals: RV 2.11.12, 19; 3.32.4, 12; 5.30.6; 6.39.2; 7.104.6; 8.96.5; 10.67.8. Soma: RV 1.32.3; 1.52.2; 2.11.10 f.; 2.15; 3.32.4, 12. It is likely that Tvashtri's thunderbolt had magical properties like the bludgeons made by Koshar-wa-Hasis (p. 130).

[37] Mbh., Udy. 10. Namuci: ÇB 12.7.3.1–4. In this version the cosmic meaning of the myth has been forgotten, yet traces of it cling to the narrative: when Vritra was killed, the world was freed from darkness, and a pleasant breeze came over it.

the waters that Vritra encompassed are again and again called cows, so that the soma-milk must be identical with the waters which Indra cleft the mountains to free. So we have two sequences of events: killing the dragon to win the soma, and seizing the soma to gain the strength needed to kill the dragon.[38]

According to the *Taittirîya-Saṅhita* and *Çatapatha-Brâhmaṇa*, Tvashtri, in anger at Indra for killing his son Viçvarupa, excluded Indra from the soma, which, it seems, he dealt out to the gods. But Indra forced himself into the soma-offering and drank most of the beverage. In fury Tvashtri threw the dregs upon the fire, telling them to grow as Indra's enemy. Thus Vritra came into being.[39]

There and occasionally in the *Rig Veda* Tvashtri is hostile to Indra, though elsewhere he is Indra's helper. In the *Taittirîya-Saṅhita* he changed sides: he feared Vritra after creating him and so made a thunderbolt for Indra. Here we find the same equivocal relationship that we have noticed elsewhere between an older and a younger god: El and Baal, Enlil and Marduk or Ninurta, Ra and Horos. In fact, he is sometimes said to be Indra's father. As Indra's enemy and withholder of the soma he is really *Viçvarûpa* himself; and that name is given to Tvashtri as an epithet in the *Rig Veda*: as creator of all forms he is himself omniform (*viçva-rûpa*). As a primordial being, father of monsters and demons, he, equally with Vritra, can be likened to Apsu. In fact, Tvashtri, Viçvarupa, and Vritra are three names for one being.[40]

Besides Vritra and Viçvarupa there are other demons that Indra fought: Vala, Çambara, Namuci, Çushna, Urana, Pipru, and still others. Like Vritra, they are demons who held back the waters or kept cattle in enclosures. Often, however, the minor demons appear, not as opponents of Indra, but of a hero or minor

---

[38] Soma taken from Tvashtri: RV 3.48.4. Cattle stalls: RV 5.30, 6.17.1–6. Waters = cows: RV 1.32.2, 11 f.; 1.121.2; 2.12.3; 3.30.10; 5.30.4 f., 10. The springs are the mountain's udder: RV 5.32.2. The god Soma as Indra's helper is the power-giving soma personified; notice the story in which Soma at first inclined to Vritra. Soma tells the poet that water teems with healing medicines: RV 10.9.6 f.

[39] TS 2.4.12, 2.5.2; ÇB 1.6.3.1–11; see also *Mbh.*, *Udy.* 9. Indra's irruption into the assembly of soma drinkers recalls Herakles at Koronos' feast (p. 38), and also the tale that he came upon Laogoras at table (p. 35). In this story we have the germ of the banquet form of Th. 9.

[40] Indra's enemy: RV 1.80.14, 3.48.4; and see note 39. Tvashtri *viçvarûpa*: e.g. RV 1.13.10. Tvashtri Indra's father: cf. Macdonell (1897) 57.

god. For example, Trita Aptya fought Viçvarupa; Brihaspati fought Vala; Atithigva or Divodasa fought Çambara; Kutsa fought Çushna; Rijiçvan fought Pipru. The evidence suggests that these combats were once independent myths, variants of an archetype. When Indra became the favorite god of Vedic India, his combat overshadowed all others, so that the demons tended to become Vritra's subordinates—e.g. keepers of his cattle—and the heroes became Indra's allies. Hence the versions in which Indra, assisted by a hero, kills a minor demon in order to free the cows or win the soma, that he may fortify himself to face Vritra.[41]

There is no need to spend much time on these minor demons. But we should notice that Vala had a cave (Th. 2B), in which he kept the cows; Viçvarupa had three heads; Urana had ninety-nine arms; and a demon Araru had four legs (Th. 3C). Like Vritra, Viçvarupa appears as a boar. And there is a significant story in which Namuci stole the soma.[42]

Now the soma drink has the same meaning in the Indic myth as the sinews in the Typhon myth or the tablet of destinies in the Zu myth: it is the vessel of the god's power. It is also called *amrita* (i.e., ambrosia), the drink of immortality. The demon Namuci stole the soma from Indra (Th. 8B) when the god lay powerless from the damage that the soma drink had done him. But the narrative appears confused. For it both identifies Indra's vital powers with the soma and attributes their loss to his having drunk it forcibly. It must be that Indra's power resided in the soma and that he lost it through Namuci's theft. Then either he recovered it himself or the Açvins and Sarasvati recovered it for him.[43]

There was also a story, merely alluded to in the *Rig Veda*, that

[41] *Viçvarûpa:* RV 2.11.19, 10.8.8 f., 10.99.6; *Kâthaka Saṅhita* 12.10. *Vala:* RV 1.52.5, 2.11.20, 2.12.3, 2.14.3, 2.15.8, 6.39.2, 10.67. *Çambara:* RV 1.130.7, 2.12.11, 2.14.6, 4.30.14, 6.43.1. *Namuci:* RV 2.14.5, 5.30.7 f. *Çuṣna:* RV 1.121.9 f., 2.14.5, 4.30.13, 5.32.4, 8.96.17, 10.49.3, 10.99.9, 10.111.5. *Uraṇa:* RV 2.14.4. *Pipru:* RV 2.14.5, 10.99.11. As allies of Vritra: see, e.g., RV 2.11.18–20; 2.12.3 f., 10–12; 2.14; 4.30; 5.30.4–11; 10.99. On these demons see Hillebrandt (1929) 229–249, 254–263, 384–387.

[42] Vala's cave: RV 2.12.3, 10.108. Viçvarupa's three heads: RV 10.8.8 f., 10.99.6; TS 2.5.1; ÇB 1.6.3.1–5; *Mbh.*, *Udy.* 9. *Uraṇa:* RV 2.14.4. *Araru:* RV 10.99.10. Notice the birds that sprang from the severed heads of Viçvarupa: TS, ÇB, *locc. cit.* Viçvarupa as boar: RV 10.99.6.

[43] ÇB 12.7.1.10–14, 3.1–4. Since Zeus's sinews are represented by the thunderbolt in Nonnos' account (pp. 74 f.), I should point out that Vritra was also armed with thunderbolts in his encounter with Indra: RV 1.32.13, 1.80.12.

an eagle brought the soma to Indra in his need. This eagle was Garuda, a powerful and beneficent deity, who carried Vishnu through the air. But the great epic contains a story in which Garuda stole the soma (*amrita*) and came into conflict with Indra and the gods. He was huge as a mountain (Th. 3A), frightful to all creatures; his eyes blazed like lightning (Th. 3D), so that he illuminated the whole world; he had the speed of wind (Th. 3G) or thought. He could take any shape that he pleased (Th. 3E); though entirely eagle in Vedic times, he was represented in partly human form later, e.g., as a human-headed bird (Th. 3B). He could, if he wished, swallow the ocean; he drained ninety times ninety rivers (Th. 4G) to put out the fires that guarded the soma. In his hunger he swallowed the Nishodhas and also a great elephant and tortoise (Th. 4D). It was not so much in hostility to the gods that Garuda took the soma from them—yet the Rishis, who gave him a hundred times Indra's power, so that he might overcome the god, were hostile to Indra for insulting them—as to free his mother from slavery to his cousins, the Nagas (snakes): for the Nagas would free her only if they got the soma in exchange. The gods could not keep him off, nor, within the ring of fire and revolving wheel of razor-edge spokes, could the two great snakes, full of poison, whose eyes and tongues blazed with fire, and whose glance could reduce anybody to ashes (Th. 3D). As Garuda flew off with the soma, Indra hurled his thunderbolt at him, but succeeded only in knocking off a feather. Then Indra made peace with Garuda, and though the latter delivered the *amrita* to the Nagas according to his promise, he aided Indra in cheating them of the prize.[44]

It is not difficult to see the Zu myth in this tale. The eagle Garuda alternates with Namuci (a lesser Vritra) as thief of the soma, whose loss rendered Indra powerless. Garuda received the epithet *vajrijit*, "victor over the thunderbolt wielder" (i.e., over Indra), a name that associates him with Indrajit (victor over Indra), the demon Ravana's son in the *Râmâyana*. Even the theft during ablutions (p. 148) is present, but shifted to the recapture

---

[44] *Mbh., Ad.* sects. 16–34. See RV 1.80.2, 4.18.13, 10.99.8. On *Garuḍa* of mixed form see Hackin AM 64, 200 f. According to another story it was Indra who took eagle form to steal the soma: RV 10.99.8; Macdonell (1897) 152.

of the soma: while the Nagas were performing the ablutions that properly precede the handling of soma, Indra snatched it from the kuça grass on which Garuda had set it.[45]

Two conceptions of Garuda have been fused in the epic narrative: the eagle Garuda who was himself a heavenly god and relentless enemy of snakes, and a terrible and monstrous Garuda who stole the soma and worsted Indra for a time. The same contrast can be seen in Zu, who was also Imdugud, the eagle of Ninurta's emblem (p. 166). According to Mrs. Van Buren, Zu-Imdugud is the eagle of the Babylonian myth in which eagle and snake become bitter enemies—a thesis that the Garuda myth supports.[46]

As yet we have seen nothing of the erotic themes, unless the dragon's lechery may be surmised in his keeping goddesses (= cows or waters) in confinement. The Vedic poets and the writers of *Brâhmanas* were probably aware of the erotic episodes of the combat myth, but deliberately excluded them. They didn't even say much about the dragoness: theirs was a man's world. But they do speak of Ushas, goddess of the dawn, who in some way tried to harm Indra, so that he shattered her chariot, or killed her with his thunderbolt. The story remains unclear, but it is said that she devised evil; and the incident is set within the context of the Vritra myth (Th. 1c). In the epics, however, the erotic themes became prominent elements of the combat myth. In the *Mahâbhârata*, Viçvarupa, Tvashtri's son, though still three-headed, was by no means wicked. On the contrary, he was extremely virtuous, pious, and ascetic, devoting himself to rigid austerities to such a point that he threatened Indra's power—for merit thus acquired bestows divine power upon the agent; and Viçvarupa had heaped up enormous stores of it. So Indra sent the nymphs called Apsarasas to tempt him that he might yield to lust and thus lose merit. But, though their temptations usually succeeded against the saintliest ascetics, the nymphs failed to stir Viçvarupa. So Indra decided to kill him.[47]

---

[45] See s. vv. *vajrijit*, *vajrajit*, in a Sanskrit-English lexicon.

[46] Van Buren (1950); Pritchard (1950) 114–118; Gaster (1952) 71–80.

[47] *Mbh.*, *Udy.* 9; repeated in *Mbh.*, *Çant.* 342. This is really Th. 8D in reverse: the hero's women try to tempt the dragon; but compare Paghat and Yatpan (p. 139). Çaci (see below) may also be compared to Paghat; see Appendix 2. Characters are shifted here:

Very like Viçvarupa at first was Nahusha, Indra's third enemy in the epic narrative. He was also loaded with merit, which was augmented by all the virtues of the Rishis' austerities, which they gave him in order to induce him to take the kingship in Indra's absence. As temporary king he corresponds closely to Ashtar of the Baal Poems, who attempted to rule in Baal's absence. But Nahusha illustrates Lord Acton's axiom that power corrupts; once on the throne he became arrogant and tyrannical (Th. 4B); he forsook virtue and turned to sensual pleasures, surrounding himself with nymphs and song. His might, however, did not diminish on that account, since he still had a great balance of good deeds in his favor and also the Rishi-given virtue. He lusted after Indra's wife and beset her with unwelcome attentions (Th. 4E). She finally took part in a plot (Th. 7D) to beguile him into committing an act that would strip him of his virtue. She went to him privately and promised to yield to him (Th. 9, *b*), if he would come to her in a fine carriage, borne not by commonplace elephants or horses, but by Rishis. Nahusha in his blind folly was immensely pleased by this proposal and soon went forth in a Rishi-borne carriage. The Rishis then involved him in an argument over the authenticity of certain Vedic hymns, which Nahusha foolishly called spurious. So angry did he get that he kicked a Rishi on the head. Thus he committed three atrocious acts—forcing Rishis to be beasts of burden, calling a genuine Vedic hymn spurious, and kicking a Brahman saint—so that all his sum of good deeds evaporated at once. The Rishi Agastya at once condemned him to ten thousand years as an enormous snake (Ths. 3A, 3B, 10A), and Indra regained his throne (Th. 5A).[48]

Very like Nahusha's importunate courting of Çaci was the demon Ravana's wooing of Sita, Rama's wife, in the *Râmâyana*.

---

the god is rather base in motive; the dragon is good; cf. pp. 174, 403, 471. On Ushas see RV 2.15.6, 4.30.8–11, 10.73.6, 10.138.5. On Indra's love for a demoness and submission to her among the Asuras see Macdonell (1897) 57, von Schroeder (1914) 104.

[48] *Mbh.*, *Udy.* 11–17; the story is repeated in *Mbh.*, *Çant.* 342, *Anuç.* 99 f. On the temporary king see p. 393. *Nahuṣa* is obviously a form of Vritra. Not only does he become a snake, in which form he appears elsewhere (*Mbh.*, *Van.* 179), but as king he sent forth poison from his eyes, and so deadly was his glance that even the gods could not look at him (Th. 3D); see *Mbh.*, *Udy.* 16.28, 32. *Nahuṣa* is probably the demon *Nahuṣ* of RV 10.99.7, whose forts Indra shattered.

In fact, the plot of that epic, when boiled down, proves to be our myth of hero against dragon. I shall take time now only to point out its prominent features. The chief demon is Ravana, king of Lanka (Ceylon), a giant who had ten heads and twenty arms (Ths. 3A, 3C). Like the Hydra's, his heads when cut off grew back again. He once fought Indra and the gods. He carried Sita off to his realm and there urged her in vain to submit to him (Th. 4E). He had terrible brothers: Khara, Dushana, Triçiras, and Kumbhakarna (mightiest of demons, who had terrorised the world, greedily devoured beasts and human beings [Th. 4D], and once defeated Indra); and a son Indrajit, who had the powers of becoming invisible and of flying through the air (Th. 3B), had once defeated Indra, and had a serpent noose which he cast about his opponents. There was also the Danava, the terrible Kabandha, who was black, of monstrous size (Th. 3A), headless and neckless; his mouth and single fire-flashing eye (Th. 3D) were in the middle of his body; he devoured lions, bears, and deer (Th. 4D); and his two long arms stretched a league in length and wrapped themselves around their prey—he is clearly modelled upon the octopus. And there was Marica, Tataka's son, a gigantic demon, who took the form of a gazelle (cf. p. 187). These are but the more prominent demons encountered. The dragoness appears in several forms, among them the Empusa-like temptress. Tataka, who attacked Rama and Lakshmana in their boyhood, and whom Rama killed as his first exploit (Th. 6B), was an Indic Lamia: she was hideous to look upon, could change her shape or vanish (Th. 3E), ravaged two realms (Th. 4A), and carried off men for her food (Th. 4D). Later the two princes met Ravana's sister Çurpanakha, another Lamia, who, though misshapen and hideous, could take on the form of a beautiful young woman; it was thus that she tempted Rama and Lakshmana in the forest (Th. 8D), only to have her ears and nose cut off by them. The story is repeated in their encounter with Ayomukhi, a hideous giantess of long fangs, who lived in a cave (Th. 2B), gorging herself on flesh of forest beasts (Th. 4D); she made amorous advances to Lakshmana and likewise lost her ears and nose. Surasa, mother of snakes, took the form of a gigantic demoness and sprang forth from the ocean to swallow

Hanumat (Ths. 3A, 3F, 2E, 4D), but he, like Indra, shrunk him-self to tiny size and thus escaped from her maw. Immediately he was assailed by Sinhika, another dragoness, whose name means *lioness*, as Labbu was a dragon with lion name (p. 152); she too tried to swallow Hanumat, but this time he took advantage of his position in the she-dragon's mouth to tear and mangle her. Demon women of mixed form, with heads or feet of boars, cows, horses, dogs, lions, some one-eyed, some gigantic and others dwarfs, some hideously shaggy, guarded Sita in Ravana's grove. We should also notice Queen Kaikeyi, mother of Bharata, Rama's half-brother, whose hostility to Rama began his sufferings, as Hera's enmity pursued Apollo and Herakles; her husband Dasa-ratha had helped Çambara against Indra (Th. 1c), and she tricked him (much as Bata's wife tricked Pharaoh by inducing him to grant her anything she wished) into dispossessing Rama and raising Bharata to crown prince (Ths. 5A, 5B). Important too is Manthara, Kaikeyi's servant and Bharata's nurse, who was hideous, short-necked, flat-breasted, big-bellied, hump-backed, with legs like a crane's. In character and occupation she recalls Delphyne as nurse of Typhon, and though her appearance was quite different, it was equally monstrous. All the monsters and demons were overcome and killed by Rama, Lakshmana, or an ally. Gigantomachy is present in the war of Indra's forces, al-lied with metamorphosed gods in the shapes of bears and apes under Sugriva and Hanumat, against Ravana's demon hosts (Th. 7G). Garuda appears as Rama's ally, and also the vulture Jatayu, another Imdugud-like figure. The hero's temporary death (Th. 8A) is represented by Rama's long exile in the forest: he and Lakshmana were also twice fearfully wounded in battle, as good as dead, but Garuda's wing and Hanumat's herbs revived them, much as Iolaos revived Herakles when Typhon had killed him.[49]

---

[49] *Râvaṇa* described: *Râm.* 3.32, 7.10. His heads reappear: 6.107. Rape of *Sîtâ:* 3.46–49. Courting of *Sîtâ:* 5.18–24. *Khara, Triçiras, Dûṣaṇa:* 3.19–30, 6.69. *Triçiras,* "three-headed," is another name of Viçvarupa; ÇB 1.6.3.1. *Kumbhakarṇa: Râm.* 6.12 f., 60–67; 7.9 f., 13; he had six-month sleeps in a cave (Th. 2B). *Indrajit:* 5.48, 58; 6.44 f., 86–90; 7.28–30. *Kabandha:* 3.69–73. *Mârîca:* 1.19,30; 3.31–44. *Tâṭakâ:* 1.24–26: she too lost her nose and ears to the heroes; her attack is a doublet of *Çûrpaṇakhâ's* and *Ayomukhî's* without the same amorous motive. *Çûrpaṇakhâ:* 3.17–22. *Ayomukhî:* 3.69. *Surasâ, Sinhikâ:* 5.1. *Sîtâ's* guard: 5.17. *Kaikeyî* and *Manthârâ:* 2.7–12. *Râvaṇa's* death: 6.108. Gigan-

There are many other variants of the combat myth in the mythology and folktales of India. It would be entertaining to talk about Nala and Damayanti, whose story is parallel in many respects to the *Râmâyaṇa*, and about the demon Rahu, who like Apep tries to swallow the sun. But I have dealt with the earliest and most prominent examples, which are sufficient to show that the myth in almost its whole range of themes was well rooted in that land from Vedic times.[50]

Indic mythology illustrates the identity of dragons, underworld demons, sea monsters, and ogres. Vritra and the demons, who are variously known as Asuras, Dasas, Panis, Danavas, and Rakshasas (and by other names too), are again and again conceived as snakes. Their association with the underworld is clear from the Vedas. In *Rig Veda* 7.104, the fiends who are enemies of Indra and Soma live in the underworld depths into which the wicked are cast at death, and have all sorts of animal shapes: snake, dog, owl, eagle, and vulture—just those creatures whose forms the Greek demons take (pp. 117, 352). Among them is a Lamia-like demoness, who roams abroad at night in the guise of an owl, hateful and malicious, and is cast down into bottomless caverns. The Nagas are snake demons who inhabit Patala, a realm of the dead; they are quite often good spirits (p. 491), but many are evil, as the Garuda myth shows. In the same myth we find that the ocean is the home of the same kinds of creatures—Nagas and Asuras live there with sea monsters (*makaras*), tortoises, crocodiles, and gigantic fish that can swallow a whale—there too are subterranean fires and mines of precious stones. It is terrible to all creatures.

tomachy: 6.42–108. *Garuḍa:* 6.50. *Jaṭâyu:* 3.49 f. Rama's exile begins at 2.40. Fall of Rama and *Lakṣmaṇa:* 6.45–50, 73 f. Lakshmana suffered death a third time and was again healed by *Hanumat:* 6.100 f. Notice that Ravana and Kumbhakarna were like Viçvarupa in that they gained great power from ascetic practices; Ravana held gods, sun, sea, fire, Yama himself, in subjection: i.e., he is a derivative of Vritra. Notice too that he molested holy men, as Python molested pilgrims (pp. 58 f.); plundered the gods' sanctuaries (Th. 4A); and carried off goddesses, nymphs, and mortal women to *Laṇka* (Th. 4E). See 1.15 f., 7.9–34. The gods took animal forms on encountering Ravana: Indra became a peacock, Yama a crow, Kubera a lizard, and Varuna a goose: 7.18.

[50] Besides the themes indicated in the text and notes the following are also present in the myths discussed: Th. 2c: Viçvarupa was the gods' domestic priest, according to TS 2.5.1; Th. 3G: Vritra, Vala, etc. are identified with drought; cf. Muir (1870) 95 f., Macdonell (1897) 161; Th. 5B: Çurpanakha incited Ravana, *Râm.* 3.33 f.; Th. 10B: RV 1.52.9, 15; 1.121.11; 2.11.2; 6.17.11; 10.113.8; Th. 10D: *Râm.* 6.112; see pp. 200, 451 f. No doubt, the few themes that remain unmentioned (except 2A) can be found in Indic combat myths. For *Nala-Damayanti* see *Mbh., Van.* 52–79; *Rahu: Mbh., Âd.* 19.

Fish replace birds; otherwise sea and underworld are much alike.[51]

OBSERVATIONS ON ASIATIC MYTHS

We have now traced the combat myth over most of that part of Asia which has had much to do with the origins and development of western culture: through Asia Minor, Syria, Mesopotamia, Egypt, and India. Mention might also be made of the Iranian tale of combat between the hero Thraetaona (Fredun) and the snake Azi Dahaka, who like Typhon was confined beneath a volcanic mountain, and of the struggle between Ahura-Mazda and Ahriman, the central doctrine of the Zoroastrian religion, which no doubt has its origin in the combat myth. But there is no need to multiply examples; and so I shall conclude with a brief review of two myths that have a special interest for people of the Occident, and with a discussion of another that forms an important link in the argument.[52]

Since the ancient Hebrew scriptures have long held a prominent place in our culture, it is worthwhile to point out that the Hebrews also had the combat myth in apparently much the same form as it has in the Ugaritic variant; for the Hebrews and the Canaanites of Ugarit spoke dialects of the same language. Gaster has collected the Old Testament passages which show that Yahweh fought a battle with the sea serpent Leviathan or Tannin or Rahab, Baal's opponent in the Ugaritic texts. Yahweh himself was once addressed as Baal, but only as Adon, which has the same meaning, after the former title had become too closely associated with the gods of the gentiles. He used a net, like several champions we have met, and also harpoons, like Horos: an indication that the Egyptian myth had an influence on the Hebrew variant, a conclusion that is confirmed by the passage on behemoth, the

---

[51] See *Mbh., Ād.* 22; Macdonell (1897) 152 f., 156–164, 169 f.; Hackin AM 137–139, cf. 64; Mackenzie IML 61–75; Hillebrandt (1929) 240–249, 390–393, 402–432; W. N. Brown (1941). *Çeṣa,* king of the Nagas, had seven heads or one thousand; see Hackin 138 with fig. 30; *Mbh., Udy.* 35 f.

[52] See *Avesta, Yaçna* 9.8; *Av., Yaṣt* 19.36 f.; *Bundahiṣ* 29.9; *Dînkard* 7.1.26, 9.21; see Bréal (1863) 113–123, Gaster (1950) 144. The dragon *Azi Dahâka* had three heads (Ths. 3b, 3c) and a thousand magic strengths. He was gigantic (Th. 3a) and very evil (Th. 4a). From his body came forth many harmful creatures. *Thraêta-ôna,* when nine years old (Th. 6b), killed him; and Dahaka was bound and put under Mount Demavend (Th. 10a).

hippopotamus, which precedes the Leviathan passage in Job, where hostility may be implied by "let his maker bring his sword upon (him)" (40.19). Leviathan spouted fire from his mouth and nostrils; he had an invulnerable hide (like Tiamat, Set, Vritra), so that many barbs had to be thrown against him. The gods fled in panic before him (Job 41.17 [25], yāgûrû 'êlîm, translated "the mighty are afraid" in the King James Version). Yahweh no doubt suffered too; but this episode was strictly excluded from the sacred text.[53]

The early Christians adopted a variant of the combat myth, though not the Hebrew variant just mentioned; it appears in Revelations 12. The reader is immediately struck by its close resemblance to version D of the Python myth (pp. 18, 21). The woman who is clothed with the sun and has set her feet upon the moon is suffering in birth pangs. A huge red dragon of seven heads and ten horns, explicitly identified with Satan, came to her out of the sea, ready to swallow the boy child as soon as he was born. But God saved the boy, while the woman fled into the wilderness (as Poseidon rescued the pregnant Leto, and she found refuge on Delos). Then Michael and his angels fought against the dragon and his hosts, defeated them, and cast them beneath the earth. In the sequel, the dragon again pursued the woman, and the earth opened up to save her by swallowing the flood of water that the dragon spewed forth to overwhelm her (again as Delos took Leto from the mainland shore, saving her from Python's pursuit and death in the sea).[54]

---

[53] See Gaster (1950) 145–150, also 73–97. Harpoons: Job 40.31 (41.7), hathmillē' bhesukkôth 'ôrô ûbheçilçal dāghîm ro'shô: "you will fill with barbs his skin and with harpoon of fishes his head." See Psalms 74.13–15, where Yahweh's enemy is called Yam; that the poet does not mean merely "divide the sea," but rather "split Yam," the serpent lord of the deep, is beyond question: it is proved by the parallel structure of Hebrew poetry; Yam is parallel to tannînîm "dragons"; in the next couplet he is called Leviathan; and in the next he is alluded to again in naharôth "rivers": i.e. he is Nahar, "Judge River." The Hebrew evidence shows Ths. 2E, 3A, 3B, 3D, 3G, 5A, 7A, 7B, 7C, 10A, 10B, and perhaps others. Heidel (1951: 102–114) reluctantly grants that Yahweh had a combat with Leviathan, but wants to dissociate it as much as possible from Babylonian and other myths; his argument is not convincing.

[54] The story shows Ths. 2E, 3A, 3B, 3C, 3F, 3G, 4A, 4C, 4D, 4E, 4G, 5A, 6A, 6B, 7A, 7E, 7G, 10A, 10B. Poseidon's rescue: Hyg. Fab. 140.3. In the whore of Babylon who sits upon the seven-headed beast (Rev. 17) and who is drunk with the blood of holy men, we recognise the dragon's seductive companion (Th. 1c). Notice also the beasts of Rev. 13. Diestel (1860) perceives a relation between Satan and Set, though he is undoubtedly mistaken in considering it direct. In drawing the parallels between Python D and this myth, beware

Despite the numerous correspondences of theme and detail between the Greek myths of Typhon-Python and the several Asiatic myths which I have discussed, there are no doubt some readers who will see only interesting coincidences and will deny, or at least question, any genetic relation between Greek and Asiatic mythologies. Their position, however, is rendered untenable by the Hurrian myth of Kumarbi and Ullikummi which has recently come to light. The myth is found in two related texts, each fragmentary and still unclear in parts, written in Hittite. It is not, however, Hittite but Hurrian mythology, as the names of the gods indicate.[55]

The first text contains the tale of the heavenly kingship. At first Alalu reigned over the gods. After nine years Anu revolted and overthrew Alalu, casting him down to the dark earth. After another nine years Kumarbi revolted against Anu. In the combat Kumarbi seized the fleeing Anu, bit off his genitals, and swallowed his seed. Kumarbi rejoiced, but Anu warned him that from the seed he had become impregnated with three terrible gods: the storm god (Teshub), the Tigris, and Tasmisu (Hurrian Hermes). Then Kumarbi tried unsuccessfully to spit out the seed (or he spat out the latter two gods, who nevertheless lived and grew) and then went to Nippur to await the time of birth. After some complications the gods were born. Then Teshub plotted with Anu against Kumarbi, fought him, and overthrew him.

In the second text, the *Song of Ullikummi*, Kumarbi plotted to regain his throne by raising up a rival to Teshub, as Anu had produced a rival to him. He consulted Sea at a banquet, at which they consumed much beer and wine. Sea advised him to pour his seed into a mountain, and told him what would follow from his act and how to make use of it. Kumarbi followed Sea's advice, and in due time was born a boy child of diorite (Th. 1B), whom Kumarbi named Ullikummi and sent off to the Irsirra goddesses

---

of equating the sun and moon with Apollo and Artemis. The man child corresponds to the infant Apollo, Michael to the ephebe Apollo.

[55] Text with German translation and commentary: Güterbock (1946); translated into English by Güterbock (1948), Goetze in Pritchard (1950) 120–125; paraphrased by Gaster (1952) 110–124; new fragments with translation or summary of most of the texts in Otten (1950). I quote Goetze's translation. See Güterbock (1946) 100–105, (1948) 130–132; Barnett (1945); Dussaud (1949A); Lesky (1950) on relation to Hesiod. The date is 1400–1200. Fragments of a Hurrian version have been found; see Güterbock (1948) 123.

with instructions that they should carry him to the dark earth, the abyss beneath sea-bottom (Th. 2E), and place him upon the shoulder of the giant Upelluri, who held up earth and sky. Having been set there, Ullikummi grew at the rate of a cubit or more a day, until he eventually reached a height of nine thousand leagues, towering up to the very city of the gods (Th. 3A). The sun god was the first to notice him as he grew upwards from the sea, and told Teshub and Ishtar, who went to the summit of Hazzi (Mount Kasios, Th. 2A) and looked out across the sea to the stone monster. Teshub was overcome with dismay and wept, but Ishtar stripped herself, made herself as seductive as possible, took harp and *galgalturi*, and went to the seashore to exert her charms upon Ullikummi (Th. 9, *b*). She stirred Ullikummi, who was deaf and blind, no more than the nymphs Apsarasas could stir Viçvarupa. Then the gods went forth under Astabi's (= Ninurta's) command to attack the monster and dislodge him (Th. 7E), but they failed. Now his head towered up into the gods' city of Kummiya, and forced Hebat, Teshub's wife, to flee from her palace (Th. 4E). She then learned that Teshub had been defeated and would have to stay "in a lowly place" until he had completed an ordained term of years (Th. 8A). Teshub and Tasmisu finally went to ever-resourceful Ea for help. Ea went to Upelluri, who was unaware of the monster that stood on his shoulder (aside from a soreness that he felt), and with the ancient bronze knife that once had parted heaven from earth he cut through Ullikummi's feet. Then he sent Teshub and the gods forth against him. As Teshub came against him in his chariot, amidst thunders, Ullikummi vainly boasted that he would destroy Kummiya, drive out the gods, and take the throne (Th. 5A). But once he was loosed from his moorings, the gods had no difficulty in casting him down (Th. 7A).

The parallel between the first part of the myth and the Hesiodic myth of the world's beginning is obvious and striking. The Hurrian myth resembles an earlier and cruder version of the Greek myth. There is a succession of kings, each of whom in turn, except the last, is overthrown by his son: Hurrian Anu, Kumarbi, Teshub; Greek Uranos, Kronos, Zeus. It is true that the Hurrian myth has an earlier step: Anu overthrew Alalu. But Alalu may correspond to Chaos in the Hesiodic myth, since Chaos is a living being: he was born (γένετο, *Theog.* 116), and Erebos and Night were born from him (and probably Ge and Eros too). We should recall the living chaos of Asiatic mythologies: Babylonian Apsu-Tiamat and Indian Vritra, who had to be overthrown. We shall see later (pp. 222–239) that Chaos under several names plays a more important part in Greek cosmogony than Hesiod assigns him. Further, the Babylonian myth presents in Anshar a step between Apsu-Tiamat and Anu; though Anshar, Anu, and Enlil were not violently overthrown by their successors, we still receive the impression of gods who lost power and authority to younger and stronger gods.

Kumarbi is identified with El in a Hurrian text found at Ras Shamra, and with Enlil in a bilingual text found at Boghaz-Keui: both El and Enlil are identified with Kronos (pp. 132, 157). In the Ullikummi myth Enlil appears as a character different from Kumarbi; but one should notice that the stone child was placed first on Kumarbi's knees and then on Enlil's, and that Enlil gave no help when Ea came to him for aid and counsel. Teshub is identified with the Hittite weather god and with Baal. His alliance with Anu recalls the Phoenician myth in which Baal-Demarûs aided "Uranos" against El-Kronos.[56]

More conclusive than correspondence in mere theme of three or four successive reigns and revolts is the correspondence in the very details of how one god succeeded another. Kumarbi's emasculation of Anu differs from Kronos' emasculation of Uranos only in the instrument used; but in this difference the Hurrian myth accounts perhaps better than the Hesiodic for the presence of younger gods within the older god's body. In any case both Kumarbi and Kronos swallow that which then grew up inside them to their hurt. And both Kumarbi and Kronos brought forth a stone. Yet the wives of the god-kings, so important in Hesiod's account, are absent from the Hurrian myth. But we hear about the bronze knife that severed earth from sky, which recalls both Marduk's treatment of Tiamat's body and the Hesiodic story of how Kronos separated Uranos from Ge.

---

[56] Kumarbi = El, Enlil, and Teshub = Baal: Güterbock (1946) 94, 107, 112; (1948) 132 f.; Kapelrud (1952) 37, 88. On Demarûs see Philo *ap.* Eus. PE 38A.

In the story of the stone monster we seem to have a variant of the Typhon myth. Like Typhon, Ullikummi grew to such a height that his head reached the sky. He rose from earth, i.e., from the mountain in which he was sown (Th. 1A). He raised havoc in heaven and on earth, and was beginning to destroy mankind (Th. 4A). He boasted that he would overthrow and supplant the gods. He is greatly different from Typhon, of course, in his stony body, and nothing is said to indicate that he was anything but strictly anthropomorphic. But we have already met Asag's stone warriors (p. 147) and Urshanabi's stone images (p. 171); relevant too are the stone mountains that, being Vritra himself, confined the water-cows of the Indic myth (p. 196); and in Greek myth the sea serpent that Perseus killed was turned to stone (p. 303, note 54). Stone monsters have a place in the myth complex.

Kumarbi raised up Ullikummi to avenge himself upon Teshub and the gods and to restore himself to the throne. It was in wrath at the gods for their treatment of Kronos and the Titans that Ge bore the Gigantes and Typhon. In the Homeric Hymn's version it was Hera who called on the Titans in Tartaros to help her produce a son who would be as much mightier than Zeus as Zeus had been mightier than Kronos. In Nonnos' version Typhon boasted that he would restore Kronos and the Titans, though under his own supremacy. Even closer to the Hurrian myth is the Homeric Scholiast's version, according to which Kronos took part with Hera and Ge in the production of Typhon, in that he gave Hera two eggs smeared with his seed, from which Typhon arose after they had been buried in earth (Ge). Hence the Hurrian myth helps to throw light upon the relation of Typhon to Kronos and the Titanomachy.[57]

Finally, Mount Kasios, whence Teshub and Ishtar looked at Ullikummi, is the mountain on which Typhon overcame Zeus (p. 73), and that on which Baal was buried: Zaphon, home of the Ugaritic gods, hard by Ugarit (p. 133). It appears, therefore, in three variants of the combat myth, told among three different peoples.

---

[57] Apollod. 1.6.1, 3; Hom. Hymn. 3.335–339; Nonn. *Dion.* 1.383 f., 2.228–230, 296–300, 337–341, 565–567, 574–578, 591, 600 f.; Schol. B on Il. 2.783; Claud. 37.28; cf. Hes. *Theog.* 820–822. Egyptian Geb, father of Set, was identified with Kronos: Plut. *Mor.* 355D. Typhon is sometimes numbered among the Titans: see pp. 240 f.

Hence there can be little question that the Kumarbi-Ullikummi myth is closely linked to the Greek creation and dragon-combat myths. On the other side it is obviously linked to Babylonian mythology. Some of the gods who appear in it bear Babylonian names: Anu, Ea, Ishtar, Enlil. Ea plays the same part as in several Babylonian myths (pp. 147–151). Ishtar attempts to lure Ullikummi as in another story she lured the dragon Hedammu (p. 175), or as the courtesan lured Enkidu (p. 174).[58]

As in the Canaanite, Babylonian, and other peoples' myths, we find the sea closely associated with the lower world. The "dark earth" where Upelluri, the Hurrian Atlas, stands, bearing up earth and heaven (though Atlas bears up heaven alone), means the abyss beneath sea-bottom, and the sea is the route thither. After Ea had returned from his visit to Upelluri he reported that he was sad from his sight of the dead strewn about "on the dark earth." The same association—or rather, identification—can be seen in the apocalyptic vision of Revelations to which I have referred, which equates sea with death and Hades in the parallelistic structure that the author has borrowed from Semitic verse.[59]

The Hurrian peoples, the Old Testament Horites, covered upper Mesopotamia and northern Syria through most of the second millennium B.C. They filled the area between Assyrio-Babylonians, Hittites, and west Semites, and they had much to do with all their neighbors politically and culturally. They were especially close to the Hittites and formed a large part of the

---

[58] Other themes of the dragon myth which appear are 3F: "the dark earth"; 4A: Kumarbi plotted evil; 4F: Ullikummi blocked the heavenly threshold, so that Hebat's messenger could not pass; 4D: gluttony of Kumarbi and Sea; 6A, 6B: Teshub as champion in early youth; 7C: gods in terror just before Ea sent them forth; 8C is dimly seen in the banquet at which Kumarbi and Sea plotted Teshub's downfall; 9 in the meal that Teshub and Ishtar provided for the sun god when they conferred upon the present danger (though the sun god refused to eat at first, he finally partook: Otten 1950:20, 24), in the bronze knife of marvelous properties and the magic with which Ea made it effective.

Ullikummi's rate of growth recalls Otos and Ephialtes: Apollod. 1.7.4. Orion too is suggested by Ullikummi's position in the sea, looked upon by the sun, and his being seen there by a brother and sister from a mountain; see LM 3.1037 f., 1042 f.

[59] If indeed the Greek of Revelations is not translated from a Hebrew or Aramaic original. Rev. 20.13,

$$\overset{2}{\varkappa\alpha\grave\iota}\ \overset{1}{\text{ἔδωκεν}}\ \overset{}{\text{ἡ}}\ \overset{3}{\text{θάλασσα}}\ \text{τοὺς νεκροὺς τοὺς ἐν αὐτῇ}$$

$$\overset{1}{\varkappa\alpha\grave\iota}\ \text{ὁ}\ \overset{2}{\text{θάνατος}}\ \text{καὶ ὁ Ἅιδης ἔδωκαν}\ \overset{3}{\text{τοὺς νεκροὺς τοὺς ἐν αὐτοῖς.}}$$

population of the late Hittite principalities of northern Syria, whence they were actually called Hittites by the Hebrews. Their country through its geographical position became an avenue, though not the only one, of folkloristic transmission, and their myth of Kumarbi unquestionably forms an important link in a chain that connects the myths of several nations.[60]

---

[60] On the Hurrians see Goetze (1936) 79–113, Gelb HS 50–91.

X

CHAOS AND COSMOS

It is hardly necessary to speculate upon the combat myth's place of origin. It is sufficient to observe that the national variants show much the same pattern and range of themes. Since our oldest sources come from Mesopotamia, and since that land is centrally located, it may on a working hypothesis be considered the myth's original home; but little stands in the way of supposing that it moved westward from India or eastward and northward from Egypt, or that it radiated out from Canaan and Syria. It will be more fruitful to trace the myth's probable growth and development, wherever it had its start, and then to inquire how and in what form it came to the Greeks—since it almost certainly did not arise in Greece—and how it finally developed into the several Greek variants known to us.

No doubt the combat theme was suggested by actual struggles that men, as herdsmen or as hunters, had with ferocious beasts and dreadful reptiles and sea creatures. In the earliest known mythology, the Sumerian, the divine herdsmen, Tammuz and Enkidu, defended herds and flocks against the attacks of lions and wolves. Adonis, the Syro-Canaanite Tammuz, was killed by a boar while hunting. In Africa and India men were, and still are, sometimes attacked by huge pythons or cobras or crocodiles; from such opponents Vritra, Set, and Apep acquired their monstrous shapes.

Shore-dwellers and seafarers at times had to contend with a shark; other reptiles and marine animals, such as the octopus, usually inoffensive in themselves, were frightening to look upon; and so the sea monster, Leviathan or Kabandha, comes into being. Even more frequently men fought brigands who came to rob them of treasures or cattle: in the very early Bilulu myth Tammuz appears to have been killed by a rustler.

Such combats surely became subjects of conversation long after the event. Then what was at first true narrative passed after a time into the people's store of legend and folktale, receiving increments of the marvelous and supernatural in the process. Such simple tales of encounter between man and beast or brigand certainly arose independently in the folklore of most lands on earth. They were ready at hand in southern and southwestern Asia to suggest the central theme of the complex combat myth. For the myth that has occupied us, though it reaches its climax in the combat and god's triumph, was not intended to be merely an exciting tale of perilous struggle with a happy ending. It had a profounder meaning. It is evident that for Mesopotamians, Canaanites, Egyptians, and Vedic Indians, it was the basic myth of their system, attached to the most significant rituals of the national religion.

THE CHAOS DEMONS

In the earliest records of the combat myth that we know, the Sumerian texts referred to in chapter viii, the combat is already associated with the beginnings of the world. It was just after the emergence of heaven and earth from the waters of chaos and their separation from each other that Enki-Ea set out in a boat to give battle to Apsu. This combat is still seen in the Babylonian creation myth as it is set forth in *Enuma elish,* where it serves as a prelude to the mighty combat of Marduk with Tiamat. And Marduk's triumph over Tiamat was necessary for the creation of our world, since Marduk fashioned it from her body.

The peoples of the Near and Middle East looked upon creation as a process of bringing order out of chaos. But they did not see this process as a philosopher or scientist might see it. They personified and dramatised every part of the supposed series of events—which is to say that the world's beginnings were mythically imagined. Chaos was not merely a dark and watery mass, a confusion of cosmic elements, though it was that too. These peoples saw it as a gigantic and monstrous being; in fact, sometimes as two beings, a primeval pair, male and female (e.g., in Babylonian mythology). To this demon of disorder they opposed the sky god as champion of order, which could not be won until Chaos was vanquished or killed. So the victor god was dragon slayer and creator in the same act.

The chaos demon (or demons) represented not only primeval disorder, but all dreadful forces that remain in the world and periodically threaten the god-won order: hurricane, flood, fire, volcanic eruption, earthquake, eclipse, disease, famine, war, crime, winter, darkness, death. They imagined either that the demon himself came back to life and renewed the combat, or that his progeny continued the war against the cosmos, ever striving for disorder and a return to primeval inactivity. His death amounted to no more than banishment from the ordered world: he was cast into the outer darkness beneath the earth or beyond it, that is, he was thrown back into the primeval chaos from which he came, where he and his minions lived on, ever ready to invade the god-established order and undo the whole work of creation. For the cosmos has been won from the chaos that still surrounds it, as a cultivated plot from the encompassing wilderness.

So in the early Mesopotamian mythology, Apsu, despite his defeat, remains the mass of fresh waters under the earth, and Tiamat remains the ocean of salt waters that surrounds the earth, though her vanquished body was the material with which Marduk fashioned the world—a way of saying that the ordered world came forth from chaos and is still surrounded by it. Apsu and Tiamat are the waste of waters on which no light shines, the realm of everlasting night. There lurk terrible monsters and demons, Zu and Labbu-Asag, eager to burst into the world of men and gods. Their abode is also called the mountain (Kur), since chaos may be conceived as a barren and stony waste, or ringed by a mountain barrier, or, e.g., in both Sumerian and Egyptian

cosmogonies, take shape as a mountain (heaven and earth together in the Sumerian myth) emerging first from the watery
waste.[1]

That Vritra was the Vedic equivalent of Apsu-Tiamat has been
ably demonstrated by W. Norman Brown. As we have seen (p.
194), the ancient Indians imagined him to be a gigantic snake
who confined the waters of chaos, enclosing them in his coils, or,
perhaps earlier, holding them within his body. To bring the
world into being Indra had to free the waters, which contained
the sun and all elements of the ordered world, from Vritra's confinement. But chaos still surrounds the cosmos: beyond the
world's borders lies "a fathomless depth of waters," "an unillu-
mined flood." There in deep darkness and cold Vritra still lurks
with his demon host, the Danavas, the forces of disorder, destruction, and death. Among them is the owl demoness (p. 208), who
roams the earth at night, when the darkness, the demons' own
element, again envelops the world and allows them to wander
abroad.[2]

The Indic myth emphasises Vritra's confinement of the waters
so that they cannot flow forth and become the cosmos, whereas
the Mesopotamian myth begins with a separation of fresh waters
from salt waters, which is followed by a separation from the
waters of the world's parts: heaven, earth, sun, and so forth. But
in both myths the result is the same: out of the chaos spirit's body
came the world. Moreover the confinement theme seems to be
present in the Asag myth. If Jacobsen is right, Asag represents the
wintertime freezing of the waters in the mountains, and Ninurta's
victory is the spring thaw, releasing the waters so that they can
descend into man's world and renew the earth.[3]

---

[1] See Frankfort (1949) 187–199, Kramer (1944) 37–40, Levy (1953) 99 f., 104 f.,
110–119; W. N. Brown (1941) and (1942). It may be objected that, in *Enuma elish* I,
Apsu and Tiamat are annoyed at the clamor and tumult that the gods raise. Actually,
the gods represent the forces of activity, as Jacobsen puts it in Frankfort *loc. cit.*, and
Apsu-Tiamat the forces of inactivity or inertia. The original chaos is a confusion of inert
elements that resist efforts to organise them; the gods, on the other hand, set the processes
of order in motion. The gods' order is the demons' disorder.

[2] W. N. Brown (1941) and (1942), whom I quote. See RV 7.104 = *Ath. V.* 8.4;
RV 10.129. Notice that Vritra or his realm is also identified with stony mountains (p. 196).

[3] *Enuma elish* shows a mixture of theogony and special creation. In fact, heaven and
earth appear three times. First Anshar and Kishar, whose names mean Heaven World
and Earth World, were born, probably from Apsu and Tiamat (I 12). In the next genera-

In Egyptian mythology we find the same primeval chaos of waters, deep, boundless, and dark. It was also conceived as a living being called Nun, or even as eight beings, four pairs of male and female. From this chaos too there emerged a cosmic mountain (Heliopolitan version), which was (or on which was) the god Atun. Out of himself he produced Shu (atmosphere) and Tefnut (water)—i.e., the water is separated from the darkness of chaos—for the sun had not yet appeared to light the atmosphere. Shu and Tefnut in turn produced Geb and Nut, earth and sky, who were united in an embrace until the sun came and separated them. Except that the Egyptians have multiplied the generations, this shows a striking parallel to the Sumerian myth.[4]

The Heliopolitan version is recited twice in the *Book of Overthrowing Apep*. One purpose for which mankind came into being was to make "words of power for the overthrowing of Apep" (Budge). By reciting spells they help Ra when he inflicts blows on Apep and keeps him enchained: that is, Apep, spirit of darkness, is kept from spoiling the work of creation. We have seen that Apep lies upon the horizon, on the borders of the outer darkness, very much like Vritra, where he and his demons attack the sun boat as it passes the western horizon, and menace the dead as they leave the earth for the darkness. It is significant too that Horos or Ra fights from a boat against Apep, who appears as crocodile or tortoise, and against Set, who appears as crocodile or hippopotamus. Tuat (Dewat), land of death, is surrounded by water and intersected by rivers. In some early texts, it seems, Tuat was in the sky, being the waters above the firmament, but in others it was definitely underground. So, in Egyptian myth too, the chaos of waters and darkness still surrounds the world and remains the

tion appeared Anu (I 14 f.), whose name means Heaven, being identical with the first syllable of *Anshar*, and presumably his unmentioned consort Antum, who is identified with Ki (Earth: see Dhorme 1949: 24). Finally Marduk made heaven and earth out of Tiamat's body (IV 137–145).

On Asag see Jacobsen (1946) 147. At the same time Witzel (1920: 34–37) may be right in interpreting Asag as the Tigris in flood, which Ninurta succeeds in controlling. That is, Asag represents the uncontrolled waters, useless or harmful to man and his works, either confined in the ice upon the mountains or raging over the plains. Jacobsen (Frankfort 1949: 194 f.) interprets Tiamat as the spring floods of Mesopotamia, a temporary return to primeval chaos.

[4] See Budge (1912) 2–13, xvii–xxii, (1934) 433–436; Černy (1952) 42–45; Mackenzie EML 1 f.; Bremner-Rhind Papyrus D (*Book of Over-Throwing Apep*: see p. 187, note 16). Concerning Shu as air, notice the Greek association of air with mist and cloud (p. 228).

home of demons and monsters; and, as in the Mesopotamian and Indic myths, the land of the dead is situated there. Set and Apep both represent the forces of disorder: storm, drought, eclipse, plague, black magic, dangerous beasts, and darkness itself.[5]

In Canaanite mythology too the myth of beginnings lies in the background of the combat myth. According to the Psalmist it was when Yahweh brought forth sunlight and fixed the bounds of earth and the seasons that he cleft Yam-Tannin-Leviathan. The Ugaritic-Phoenician Baal fought the same sea serpent, who was identified with the sea itself (*Yam*), and whose ally and successor was the lord of death (*Mot*).

Among the neighboring Hurrians the monster Ullikummi was definitely placed in the theogony as creature of the defeated elder god Kumarbi. The cosmic mountain arising from the chaos of waters has become this huge mass of stone, growing up from the darkness beneath sea-bottom through the waters to threaten earth and heaven above.[6]

Did Typhon and Python have anything to do with Greek theogony and cosmogony? To answer this question we must first look at the Greeks' conception of chaos. I have already pointed out that Hesiod seems to have considered chaos a living creature, who was born and who brought forth other beings (p. 213). Aristophanes too, suiting either the Hesiodic or a similar version of the theogony to his comic purpose, speaks of the birth of Chaos and a mating of Eros with Chaos. Finally, according to Hyginus, whose theogony is probably derived, perhaps indirectly, from the *Titanomachy* of Eumelos (late eighth century B.C., and so little if any later than Hesiod), Chaos was not only a living being, but had a parent Caligo, Darkness, a translation of the Greek *skotos* or *skotia*. Then Chaos and Darkness mated, producing Night,

---

[5] See pp. 185–188 and the citations *ibid.*, notes 15–19. On Tuat (Dewat) and the sun boat see Piankoff (1934): one gathers from the early texts that Nut the Sky Goddess preceded Apep as swallower of the Sun at night, who then came forth from her body in the morning. So Nut seems to be the Egyptian equivalent of Tiamat. See also Budge (1934) 351–379.

[6] The Hebrews and Phoenicians have left us evidence of Canaanite creation myths. The Priestly document (Genesis 1) certainly begins with a dark chaos of waters, which El presently separates by means of the sky, which he places between the upper waters and the lower; then he separates the earth from the lower waters. Chaos is called *təhôm*, cognate to Assyrio-Babylonian *Ti'âmat*. The Phoenician cosmogony, as reported by Philo (*ap.* Eus. PE 33), begins with a chaos of wind and darkness.

Day, Erebos, and Sky (Aither). In effect, we see here a twofold chaos spirit such as appears in Mesopotamian mythology.[7]

The darkness of primeval chaos is emphasised in all Greek theogonies. According to Hesiod, Chaos was born first, then Earth (Gaia) and Love (Eros). From the analogy of other theogonies, Greek and oriental, this means that Chaos was the parent of Earth and Eros, though Hesiod doesn't expressly say so. Then Darkness (Erebos) and Night (Nyx) were born from Chaos. That is, a male and a female spirit of darkness appeared, simply the dual chaos transferred to the second generation. Erebos mated with Night and produced Sky and Day: i.e., out of darkness came light. Aristophanes places Chaos, Night, Erebos, and Tartaros on a par, all equally names of the darkness which filled the world before earth, air, and heaven appeared. When, according to Eumelos' *Titanomachy*, Chaos and ʻDarkness brought forth Night and Day, Erebos and Sky, then light was separated from darkness and the bright sky from the dark sky. According to another cosmogony, Night and Tartaros were the first parents of the world.[8]

---

[7] Hes. *Theog.* 116–125; Aristoph. *Av.* 690–699; Hyg. *Fab.* praef. 1. On Hyginus' version see Rose *ad loc.* and Ziegler, LM 5.1523–1531. *Caligo* is a feminine noun, and may represent a Greek Skotia or Orphnê; while *chaos*, though a neuter noun in Greek, appears to have been considered male as a living being, as Hyginus' second-declension form *Chao* would indicate, as well as the identification of Chaos with Janus (Ovid *Fasti* 1.103). But Chaos as mate of Eros must be either female or hermaphroditic. Aristophanes' four names for darkness may mean either two beings, male (Erebos-Tartaros) and female (Chaos-Nyx), or one hermaphroditic being.

[8] Hes. *Theog.* 119 has commonly been taken to mean that Tartaros came into being along with Earth and Love; so that it is generally said by scholars that Chaos had altogether five children: these three, Erebos, and Night. This means that three of the five would be forms of darkness. Now, while night can be distinguished from darkness, it is very difficult to distinguish between one kind of darkness and another, i.e., between Tartaros and Erebos. They are synonyms throughout Greek and Latin literature for darkness in general (whether personified or not), for the underworld darkness, and for the underworld as land of the dead. Line 119 does not have the masculine singular form *Tartaros*, but the neuter plural *Tartara*. I quote lines 116–120 without stops:

Ἦτοι μὲν πρώτιστα Χάος γένετ' αὐτὰρ ἔπειτα
Γαῖ' εὐρύστερνος πάντων ἕδος ἀσφαλὲς αἰεὶ
ἀθανάτων οἳ ἔχουσι κάρη νιφόεντος Ὀλύμπου
Τάρταρά τ' ἠερόεντα μυχῷ χθονὸς εὐρυοδείης
ἠδ' Ἔρος ὃς κάλλιστος ἐν ἀθανάτοισι θεοῖσι

Lines 118–119 are rejected by many editors as an interpolation. But whether genuine or not, it seems better to take Τάρταρα as a second object of ἔχουσι than as a nominative parallel to Γαῖα and Ἔρος: see Philippson (1936) 8, note 1; Solmsen (1949) 27. The lines express the tripartite division of the world into earth, the common seat of all gods, heaven, and the dark depths beneath the earth. The thought seems unclear or confused at best, and certainly the passage goes much better if 118–119 are excised. Rzach and Evelyn-

Now, Erebos or Tartaros is the darkness that surrounds and underlies the world. That Chaos is but another name for that darkness is already fairly clear from the cosmogonies just cited. Moreover several writers explicitly identify Chaos with Erebos or Tartaros. According to Hesiod, the Titans, cast down into Tartaros, lie in deep darkness, beyond (πέρην, i.e., across a great stretch of, deep within) dark Chaos. According to the pseudo-Platonic *Axiochos,* wrongdoers go down to Erebos and Chaos through Tartaros (i.e., through darkness). Plutarch calls the underworld darkness *orphnê, chaos, Hadês, erebos,* and *skotos.* Virgil, calling upon the underworld gods (Di quibus imperium est animarum umbraeque silentes) to sanction his description of their realm, addresses Chaos and Phlegethon (loca nocte tacentia late) among them. Notice too that Erebos, Chaos, and Hekate are singled out for mention by name from the three hundred underworld gods whom Dido's priestess addresses. Orpheus, singing before Hades and Persephone in Ovid's *Metamorphoses,* calls their realm Chaos. So Chaos is a synonym of Erebos and Tartaros not only as a name of the cosmic darkness, but more particularly as a name of death's realm.[9]

White reject 118, but keep 119, since the late commentator Chalcidius thus quotes the lines. But all earlier *testimonia*, beginning with Plato, *Symp.* 178B, show both 118 and 119 lacking. It seems to me that they stand or fall together.

Elsewhere by *Tartaros* Hesiod means the darkness beneath the earth, except once; he brings Tartaros as a living being into his genealogies in *Theog.* 821 f.: Ge had union with him to produce Typhoeus. Since he uses Tartaros and Erebos interchangeably for the darkness beneath the earth (compare *Theog.* 515 and 669 with 682, 721, 725, 736, 807, 868), it is probable that he employs both names for one and the same spirit of darkness. Notice that Night's mate is called Tartaros in the anonymous cosmogony cited in the text (*ap.* Philod. *Piet.* 137). So Typhon's father enters the *Theogony* at 123. Philippson's effort (1936: 10) to separate Erebos from Hades is unsuccessful.

[9] Hes. *Theog.* 717–745, 807–814; ps.-Plato, *Ax.* 371E; Plut. *Mor.* 953A; Virg. *Aen.* 6.264 f., 4.509–511; Ovid *Met.* 10.29 f. Ovid emphasises the darkness of chaos in his account of creation: *Met.* 1.10 f., 17, 24. Cf. Apollon. *Arg.* 4.1694–1701. The concept of Tartaros as a region beneath Hades in which the wicked are punished is derived from the earlier meaning of outer darkness, and probably begins with the stories that Titans, Gigantes, Typhon, etc. were cast into Tartaros. Notice Il. 8.13–16, where Zeus threatens to cast an offending god "far into dark Tartaros, into the deepest abyss under earth, where are iron gates and bronze threshold, as far below Hades' house as the distance from heaven to earth." Here, I think, Tartaros does not mean just the deep level to which the offender will be cast and where the Titans sit (Il. 8.478–481), but all the darkness beneath the earth. The iron gates and bronze threshold keep the banished out of the ordered world, of which Hades' realm is the lowest part: a later conception, since at first Hades (the invisible ?, i.e., dark ?) was possibly another name for the darkness, whither souls were relegated after death.

There is also evidence that the Greek chaos was watery. Only two centuries after Hesiod, Pherekydes of Syros gave the name *chaos* to water as first principle, taking the term, it seems, from the *Theogony*. Later Zeno the Stoic identified Hesiod's Chaos with water, as did the Stoic Cornutus in his *Theologia Graeca*. There is more in this than an echo of Thales' theory of water as first principle. We now realise, from the labors of Cornford and others, how much Thales and the other early philosophers owed to the mythology that preceded them. There was no sharp break with the past. Subtract the persons and drama from the mythical cosmogonies, leaving the insensate forces, substrates, and materials, and you have passed from mythology to philosophy, from Comte's theological to his metaphysical stage of thought.[10]

In the Homeric picture of the world—which remained the mythical picture, even when men had learned more about the world—earth is encircled by the deep and broad River Ocean. On the farther side lie lands shrouded in deep darkness, whither the sun's rays never reach. Odysseus went there to reach the realm of Hades. Since every river is a god, so is Ocean; and his wife is his sister Tethys. According to Hesiod, they were children of Earth and Heaven and numbered among the twelve Titans. But in the Iliad we are told that Ocean and Tethys are the parents of the gods, and this tradition lingers in verses quoted by Plato from

---

In *Theog.* 720–725, however, Tartaros, into which the Titans are cast, lies as far beneath earth as the distance that an anvil can fall in ten days and nights. About it, says the poet, the gods built a brazen wall (τὸν πέρι χάλκεον ἕρκος ἐλήλαται), and in the wall Poseidon set bronze gates. πέρι should not be taken to mean that the wall encloses Tartaros: that is merely the implication of the English translation "around it." πέρι can mean that the wall goes about the inside of Tartaros, i.e., around the world, shutting it off from the darkness outside. Such at any rate was the earliest meaning, though Hesiod and his contemporaries may have already given *Tartaros* the narrower meaning of infernal prison house, as in Virg. *Aen.* 6.539–627. Notice that the Titans lie in deep darkness, far within chaos, before the bronze gates and threshold, excluded from the gods' world (πρόσθεν δὲ θεῶν ἔκτοσθεν ἁπάντων/Τιτῆνες ναίουσι, πέρην Χάεος ζοφεροῖο), beneath the roots of earth and sea. The place is called a deep chasm, whose floor cannot be reached in a year if one goes within the gates, i.e., passes from the ordered world into the lower darkness. It makes no difference whether Hesiod wrote all the lines cited or not: Mazon, e.g., rejects 721, 731, 736–745, 807–814. If an interpolator inserted them, he was still a Greek expressing a Greek view of the world. Solmsen (1949) 60–62 has some discussion of the topography of Hesiod's Tartaros. In respect to Tartaros = Hades notice a second anonymous cosmogony *ap.* Philod. *Piet.* 137: Hades and Aither were the first parents.

[10] Pherek. Syr. *ap.* Achill. *Isagoge in Arat. Phaen.* 3 *et ap.* Schol. *in* Hes. *Theog.* 116; Zeno *ap.* Schol. Vet. *in* Apollon. *Arg.* 1.498; Corn. *Th. Gr.* 17, p. 28 Lang. See Börtzler (1930), Cornford (1952), Onians (1954).

"Orpheus," according to which Ocean made the first marriage in the world, taking to wife his sister Tethys. In the *Timaeus* Plato appears to combine Hesiodic and Homeric theogonies when he says that Heaven and Earth were parents of Ocean and Tethys, who were in turn the parents of Kronos, Rhea, and Phorkys. Virgil calls Ocean father of the world (*patrem rerum*). Cornutus, or an interpolator, says that everything in the world sprang from the union of Ocean and Tethys (Ocean is called *archêgonos pantôn*). Alexander of Aphrodisias, also citing "Orpheus," places Ocean immediately after Chaos, who is followed in turn by Night, Heaven, and Zeus.[11]

In the Hesiodic theogony, Ocean and Tethys are the parents of all rivers and of three thousand nymphs—of whom the forty-one oldest are named—the Okeaninai, who ranged over land and the depths of the waters. Homer says that Acheloos or Ocean is father of all rivers, every sea (*thalassa*), and all springs and wells (see p. 233, note 21). Virgil's Aristaeus, within his mother's watery home on the bed of Ocean's stream, sees the upper-world's rivers flowing beneath the earth.[12]

Since Ocean and Tethys were the first parents in the earliest Greek theogony known to us, since the world and all waters proceeded from them, and since there is evidence of a watery chaos in Greek mythology, it is plain that Ocean himself is the primeval chaos of waters that envelop the world. We can go as far as to say that Ocean represents the fresh waters and Tethys the salt waters. Tzetzes, for instance, commenting on Lykophron, interprets Tethys as *thalassa*, i.e., the salt sea. If Tzetzes doesn't seem very impressive authority (though he certainly took this from older sources), then one can point to Cicero's translation of Plato's *Timaeus*, in which he renders *Têthys* by *Salacia*, the name of a Roman water goddess, Neptune's wife, who, on the identification of Neptune with Poseidon, became definitely a sea goddess. In Cicero's time her name was connected with *sal* and she was chiefly

[11] The River Ocean: Il. 18.607 f., Od. 10.508–515, 11.13–22, 12.1–4, 24.9–14; *Shield* 314 f.; Ovid *Fasti* 5.81 f. Ocean and Tethys: Il. 14.200–204, 245 f., 301–303; Hes. *Theog.* 132–136; Plato, *Crat.* 402B (Orph. 15 Kern), *Tim.* 40E; Virg. *Georg.* 4.382; Corn. *Th. Gr.* 8, p. 8 Lang; Serv. *Georg.* 4.363; Alex. Aphr. on *Met.* 1091B (Orph. 107 Kern).

[12] Hes. *Theog.* 337–370, 775–777; Il. 21.194–197; Virg. *Georg.* 4.363–367; cf. Himer. p. 367 Bekker.

thought of as goddess of salt waters. Himerios says that from Ocean and Tethys came forth all rivers, lakes, springs, and *thalassa*, the mother of all streams, (ἡ πάντων μήτηρ ναμάτων θάλασσα). That is, the fresh waters and salt waters, formerly united, were separated from each other. Himerios' statement agrees essentially with Homer's derivation of all bodies of water, including the sea, from Ocean; he has simply added a description of *thalassa* as mother of waters and has joined Tethys to Ocean as parent. Elsewhere in the Iliad, Tethys is called Mother Tethys. Hence we may identify her with the mother *thalassa* of whom Himerios speaks. On the other hand, in Hesiod's *Theogony*, only rivers are sons of Ocean, and in later literature we meet river-gods who are his sons. The Homeric and Virgilian verses mentioned above seem to emphasise the fresh waters as Ocean's progeny. The River Ocean was evidently a fresh-water stream: there is nothing in ancient literature to show that salt waters flowed in its streams. It is as though Apsu and Tiamat had changed places: the male fresh waters now surround the world.[13]

Ocean, whose waters ring the world, is closely associated with the encompassing darkness. This is clear enough from the Odyssey. At the "limits of Ocean" Odysseus found the Cimmerian darkness. There he walked along the shore of Ocean until he reached the place where he sacrificed a ram and a black ewe to the dead. On one side of this place was Erebos, whence came the souls of the dead; on the other was the shore of Ocean. In the sources of the myth of Ophion and Eurynome, Ocean and Tartaros are equated. Apollonios and Pherekydes of Syros say that when Kronos and Rhea overthrew Ophion and Eurynome they hurled them into the waters of Ocean; but Lykophron and his Scholiasts, perhaps referring to Pherekydes' version, say that they cast them into Tartaros. According to Hesiod or his interpolator, the three

---

[13] Ocean is identified with the primal chaos of waters in Athenag. *Pro Christ.* 18, 20 (Orph. 57, 58 Kern). Tethys as the sea: Tzetz. on Lyk. 229, 231; Cic. *Tim.* 11, translating Plato, *Tim.* 40ᴇ; Himer. *loc. cit.* Mother Tethys: Il. 14.201, 302. For river-gods as sons of Ocean see Hes. *Theog.* 337–345; Apollod. 2.1.1, 3.12.6. We should notice that Hesiod has a male sea, Pontos, son of Ge without a father, as were Heaven and Mountains; then Ge in union with Heaven produced Ocean, Tethys, and the other Titans; in union with Pontos she bore Nereus, Phorkys, Keto, and other deities of the sea. Then Nereus, Pontos' son, and Doris, Ocean's daughter, mated and produced the Nereids: here is repeated the mating of fresh and salt waters, but with the sexes reversed. (See also Addenda, following Indices.)

hundred-handed giants (Hekatoncheires), who were set to guard the Titans beside the bronze gates (which lie deep within the darkness), live in houses on Ocean's floor (ἐπ' Ὠκεανοῖο θεμέθλοις). There are the springs (πηγαί) of earth, Tartaros, sea, and heaven. In this the poet agrees with the Iliad: the Titans sit at the lowest limits of earth and sea (*pontos*) with deep Tartaros all around them. Finally, Hesychios' lexicon defines Ocean as *aêr*, by which he means, not *air*, but *mist, fog,* or *cloud,* with a suggestion of murkiness, the Latin *caligo* (p. 222); for he adds that this is the *aêr* into which the souls of the dead depart. That is, Ocean is here identified with Chaos and darkness.[14]

At first everything beneath earth's disk belonged to Chaos, into whose dark waters all souls went after death. Later, when Hades became Zeus's brother and part of the Olympian order, his realm was brought within the ordered world. It was brightened a bit, given twilight rather than deep darkness, and the waters now ran in channels. These rivers of Hades are in more than one sense branches of Ocean. Styx is Ocean's daughter, and the Styx River flows off from Ocean with one tenth of his water; Kokytos is an offshoot of Styx and with Pyriphlegethon flows into Acheron, which apparently flows back into Ocean. Three of the four under-world rivers, and Ocean too, bore the names of actual rivers on earth. In Virgil's story, Aristaeus, when on Ocean's floor, saw the

---

[14] Od. *locc. cit.* in note 11; Apollon. *Arg.* 1.506; Pherek. Syr. *ap.* Orig. *Cels.* 6.42; Lyk. 1196 f. with Schol. Vet. and Tzetz. on 1191, 1196; Hes. *Theog.* 734–739, 807–819; Il. 8.478–481; Hesych. Ω108, 109. On Ocean as the primal cosmic stuff see Onians (1954) 247–251, 315–317. In view of my remarks on the Argonauts (Appendix 1) one should notice the shrouding night (νὺξ κατουλάς) that fell upon the Argonauts as they sailed the Cretan sea: Apollon. *Arg.* 4.1694–1701. It was a pitchblack darkness, frightening and deadly (νύκτ' ὀλοήν, which is the Cimmerian night of Od. 11.19), a black chaos (μέλαν χάος) descending from heaven, or a darkness (σκοτίη) arising from the lowest depths. The heroes didn't know whether they sailed in Hades or on the sea. Here, I think, is an echo of the earliest *Argo* tale.

Here too we may notice the Egyptian story cited by Serv. *Georg.* 4.363: boys who had been delivered to the nymphs returned later to report that there were groves beneath the earth and a mass of water that contained everything and in which everything had its origin. Servius identifies this water with Ocean. With this compare Virg. *Georg.* 4.363–367, where Aristaeus on Ocean's floor sees groves and a huge mass of waters.

I cannot see the "polarity," seen by Philippson (1936) and N. O. Brown (1953), between destructive progeny of Chaos and Night and beneficent progeny of Ge and Pontos. Among the "beneficent forces" are such pleasant people as the Gorgons, Harpies, Keto, Phorkys; on the other hand, Night's first children are Aither and Hemera, the Bright Sky and Day. Brown is forced to posit new "polar tensions" among the descendants of Ge. Philippson's contention that Ge does not arise out of Chaos runs counter to all Old-World cosmogonies. See Solmsen (1949) 27–45.

underworld counterparts of all earthly rivers. Socrates, in Plato's *Phaedo,* fitting mythical cosmology to fifth-century philosophy, says that all rivers flow into the chasm of Tartaros and then return to earth, and that among these many rivers are four great streams: Ocean, Acheron, Pyriphlegethon, and Kokytos (Styx is a lake).[15]

So, in the literature preserved to us, we find evidence that the earliest Greek cosmogony began, like the Babylonian, with a dark chaos of waters, embodied in two living beings, called Ocean, the male fresh waters, and Tethys, the female salt waters. As darkness personified, the male Chaos was also called Erebos, Tartaros, or sometimes Skotos, and the female Chaos was called Nyx, Skotia, or Orphne. After creation, Chaos, conceived either as darkness or as water, continued to occupy the outer and lower spaces beyond the walls of the ordered world. In either the darkness beneath the earth or the western darkness beyond the sunset was placed the land of the dead. Here is a striking correspondence with oriental mythologies, whatever the differences due to varying national characters—but so far no combat of god and dragon has appeared: Chaos, Ocean and Tethys, Erebos and Night, are not conceived as monstrous enemies whom the champion god must fight and vanquish; and so far Typhon and Python have had nothing to do with creation.

There is, however, good evidence to prove that they were chaos demons. Both were sons of Tartaros (p. 78), and both, we have seen, had something to do with the waters and with death (pp.

---

[15] Hes. *Theog.* 361, 383, 776 f.; Steph. Byz. 473 Holst.; Od. 10.513–515; Virg. *Georg.* 4.363–367; Plato, *Phaedo* 112A–113c. The Scholiast interprets Od. 10.515 to mean the confluence of Kokytos and Pyriphlegethon. Since this occurs hard by the point at which Odysseus dug his trench, which was near the shore of Ocean, the united rivers must immediately flow into Acheron, just before Acheron meets Ocean, as it must, flowing as near as this. That is, the three rivers virtually flow together into Ocean. Notice the White Rock, *Leukas Petrê* (Od. 24.11), which stands beside Ocean's streams. Is this the same as that lofty rock from which Styx flows, leaving Ocean, in Hes. *Theog.* 777–779, 786 f., 792? In that case the waters of the underworld rivers leave Ocean and return to him at the same place. Odysseus' mother tells him that several rivers lie between the living and the dead, of which Ocean is the first; but Odysseus has crossed Ocean only. In the aforementioned rock we have perhaps an echo of the stony and mountainous chaos (p. 220, note 2), also to be seen in Mountains that Ge bore along with Uranos and Pontos (Hes. *Theog.* 129 f.). Notice Styx's house, roofed with huge stones and supported all around by silver columns that reach towards heaven (*Theog.* 777–779). Recalling Ullikummi, the stone monster, and the dark earth beneath sea bottom where the Hurrian Atlas stands (p. 215), we should notice that Atlas, holding up the sky, stands before the house of Night, which is deep within the chasm of Tartaros (*ibid.* 744–748). For rivers in Crete and Lydia called *Ôkeanos* see p. 108 and Hesych. Ω109.

142–145). Olympiodoros interprets Typhon, Echidna, and Python as spirits or forces of disorder, disturbing the underground waters and air currents. Plutarch characterises Typhon, whom he identifies with Set, in similar terms, explaining him as the disorderly, harmful, destructive, and violent in nature. Both writers, it is true, were interested in philosophical interpretations of old myths; but just as certainly it was Theme 4A of the combat myth that offered them this interpretation of Typhon and Python. That theme expresses the disorderly character of the god's enemy, eager to prevent the formation of the cosmos and ever ready to disrupt it after its formation. This too is the meaning of Theme 5A: the demon of disorder wants to rule the world.[16]

In Hesiod's *Theogony* it was just after the defeat of the Titans and the beginning of Zeus's reign that Ge by Tartaros gave birth to Typhon, and the battle that followed had all the world-shaking effects of the Titan War. Still, the work of creation had been done when Typhon appeared. But Greek mythology had a chaos demon in serpent form, whom a god-champion overthrew in the earliest days of the world. This was Ophion, whose very name reveals his reptilian nature; and Eurynome, Ocean's daughter, was his wife. The god who fought and overthrew him was Kronos. This story was known in the sixth century to Pherekydes of Syros; in extant literature it appears first in the *Argonautica* of Apollonios, who makes it the subject of Orpheus' song on the eve of sailing from Pagasai. It is a song of creation: how earth, sky, and sea were at first mingled in chaos, and how out of the strife of elements they became separated. The first to rule on Olympos were Ophion and Eurynome, Ocean's daughter; but they were forced to yield to Kronos and Rhea, and fell into the waves of Ocean. Later Zeus overthrew Kronos. According to Pherekydes, Ophion and Kronos were leaders of opposing hosts, who agreed beforehand that the victory would go to the host that succeeded in pushing the other into Ocean.[17]

---

[16] Olymp. on *Phaed.* 201, 240 Norv.; Plut. *Mor.* 369A, 371B–E, 376B–377A. Apollod. 1.6.3 pretty clearly shows that Typhon was also conceived as a mountain: like Atlas his head brushed the stars; he hurled whole mountains against the gods; and in death he lay under mountains (cf. p. 290).

[17] Pherek. Syr. *ap.* Orig. *Cels.* 6.42; Apollon. *Arg.* 1.496–511; Lyk. 1192–1197 with Schol. Vet. and Tzetz. on 1191, 1196; Nonn. *Dion.* 2.572–574. There is nothing to prevent

Pherekydes linked this tale to the Titanomachy and Gigantom-achy, and also to the Egyptian myth of Typhon (Set), Horos, and Osiris. According to a Scholiast on the Iliad, Ophion was mighti-est of the Gigantes, Ge's sons, who plotted against Zeus's sover-eignty at Tartessos on the banks of Ocean. Zeus met and defeated the Gigantes, sent them into Erebos, and made his father Kronos their king. On Ophion he put a mountain which was thereafter called Ophionion (Snake Mountain). Nothing more is known about this mountain; but Ophion, we notice, met the same fate as Typhon in being thus pinned down. Furthermore the name re-calls Typhaonion, Typhon's mountain in Boeotia (pp. 78 f.).[18]

The evidence reviewed suggests that Ophion and Typhon were two forms of the same dragon, the antagonist of the combat myth. Ophion's mate Eurynome was very likely a dragoness: that she was a form of Ge has already been suggested (p. 48). A goddess Eurynome was worshipped at Phigalia in Arcadia as a form of Artemis, but Pausanias was inclined to think that she was Ocean's daughter, since her image showed her to be a woman in her upper body, a fish in her lower body (see pp. 97, 283). Fish-goddess, Artemis, and serpent's wife recall the story of Halia (p. 120). She, sea woman and daughter of Sybaris, lay with a dragon in a grove of Artemis in Phrygia and so became ancestress of the people called Ophiogeneis (Snake born), whose name indicates that their ancestor snake was called Ophion or Ophis. The sons of Ophion were called Ophionidai, which means the same thing. Finally, she has the feminine form of the name of Eurynomos, that blue-black demon of Polygnotos' painting, who ate the flesh of corpses. Prob-ably Eurynomos and Eurynome were a husband-wife, brother-sister pair originally, and Eurynomos, as Eurynome's mate, repre-sented Ophion's underworld aspect.[19]

---

our supposing that the Ophion myth is another early version of the Greek theogony, as old and as valid as the Hesiodic, Homeric, and Eumelic. There is no need to consider it especially "Orphic," simply because Apollonios places it in Orpheus' mouth, and because Pherekydes was reputed to be Pythagoras' teacher.

[18] Schol. A on Il. 8.479. Tartessos as the Gigantes' base is perhaps suggested by Tartaros and by the story of Geryon, who was commonly located there (p. 335). Strabo (3.2.12, p. 149) links *Tartessos* with *Tartaros*.

[19] Artemis Eurynome: Paus. 8.41.4–6. Ophiogeneis: Ael. NA 12.39; Strabo 13.1.14, p. 588. Ophionidai: Pherek. Syr. *ap.* Eus. PE 41D. Cf. Ovid *Met.* 12.245, a Centaur named Amycus Ophionides. Eurynomos: Polygnotos *ap.* Paus. 10.28.7: he sat upon a vulture's hide (*derma*) and resembled carrion-eating flies in color.

It is Ophion who links Typhon to Ocean and Chaos. According to a Vatican Mythographer, Ophion, whom, he says, the philosophers also call Ocean or Nereus, was the father of Heaven, who begot Saturn (Kronos), Phorkys, and Rhea. In Nonnos' *Dionysiaca* Hera says that she is going to the house of Ocean and Tethys at the world's end, and from there to the house of Ophion. Here Ophion is Ocean's neighbor and is not identified with him—but Nonnos in his usual manner is showing that he knows a different story, one in which Ophion was the primordial being who still lived at the ends of earth: if one story said Ocean, and another Ophion, Nonnos must have Hera visit both. Lest the Mythographer and Nonnos seem too late or too syncretistic to be of much value, I can point to a passage in Apollodoros in which Eurynome alternates with Tethys as mother of the river-god Asopos. Apollodoros, after saying that Asopos was son of Ocean and Tethys, adds that according to Akusilaos he was son of Poseidon and Pero, and according to others son of Zeus and Eurynome. Poseidon, of course, is the Olympian counterpart of Ocean; and Zeus is Ocean's successor in theogonies that make Ocean the first ruler of the world. According to pseudo-Clement of Rome, Eurynome was the sister of Ocean's wife Europa. Elsewhere both are daughters of Ocean; but notice that Europa was wife or daughter of Phoroneus, a primordial being and son of the river-god Inachos.[20]

Not only is Ocean closely related to river-gods, but he is himself the first and greatest of river-gods. Next to him in majesty was Acheloos, largest of Greek rivers, the Hellenic Father of Waters. In Iliad 21.193–199, as the text stands, Ocean and Acheloos appear to be identified. There it is said that Lord Acheloos is no match for Zeus, nor is mighty Ocean, from whom all rivers, seas, springs, and wells flow: even he fears Zeus's thunderbolt. Now, the verse which introduces Ocean was rejected by the Alexandrian scholar Zenodotos, and it was unknown to Pausanias, who, citing Homer's

---

[20] Vat. Myth. I 204; Nonn. *Dion.* 8.158–161; Apollod. 3.12.6; ps.-Clem. Rom. *Recogn.* 10.21, 23. Daughters of Ocean: Hes. *Theog.* 357 f. According to ps.-Clement, Eurynome was Asopos' daughter. Phoroneus: Schol. Vet. on Eur. *Or.* 932. *Eurynome*, interpreted "with broad pasture," rather than "wide-ruling," may mean much the same thing as *Europa*, "with wide face (i.e. plain)." Women named Eurynome appear as mother of Ankaios (Apollod. 3.9.2; see p. 479), and as wife of Orchamos, descendant of Belos (Ovid *Met.* 4.210, 219).

Iliad, speaks of Acheloos as ruler of all rivers—that is, if Ocean is omitted, the whole passage refers to Acheloos. Acheloos fought Zeus's son Herakles, who is also Zeus's double (p. 357), and a myth of combat between Zeus and Acheloos (or Ocean) may be implied by the verses cited in their allusion to the river-god's fear of Zeus's thunderbolt and dread lightning as the god thunders on

FIGURE 22. HERAKLES AND ACHELOOS

high. One is reminded of Zeus's bolts that lash the couches of Typhoeus (pp. 70 f.). Conversely, an echo of conflict between Ocean and Herakles can be heard in the story that Ocean rocked Helios' boat when it was carrying the hero to the Hesperides, but ceased in terror when Herakles pointed his arrows at him.[21]

---

[21] Schol. T on Il. 21.195 cites anonymous authorities for the identity of Ocean and Acheloos. Il. 21.193–199,

$$
\begin{aligned}
&\text{. . . ἀλλ' οὐκ ἔστι Διὶ Κρονίωνι μάχεσθαι,}\\
&\text{τῷ οὐδὲ κρείων Ἀχελώιος ἰσοφαρίζει,}\\
&\text{οὐδὲ βαθυρρείταο μέγα σθένος Ὠκεανοῖο,}\\
&\text{ἐξ οὗπερ πάντες ποταμοὶ καὶ πᾶσα θάλασσα}\\
&\text{καὶ πᾶσαι κρῆναι καὶ φρείατα μακρὰ νάουσιν.}\\
&\text{ἀλλὰ καὶ ὃς δείδοικε Διὸς μεγάλοιο κεραυνὸν}\\
&\text{δεινήν τε βροντὴν ὅτ' ἀπ' οὐρανόθεν σμαραγήσῃ.}
\end{aligned}
$$

195 (at line 4)

See the critical apparatus of T. W. Allen's edition on 195. See Homeric Scholiasts on 194

In a red-figured vase painting of the combat between Herakles and Acheloos (fig. 22) the river god looks like a human-headed eel (i.e., a snake with a fish's tail); only the horns upon his head suggest his usual bull shape. In Sophocles' *Trachiniae* it is said that Acheloos took three forms: bull, dragon, and bull-browed man. He had, of course, the water-deities' power of changing shape (Th. 3E); but the three forms that he took are significant. There are indications that Ocean too was sometimes conceived in serpent form. In a so-called Orphic cosmogony that may be ultimately derived from Pherekydes of Syros, Ocean was the watery chaos, the first being, who was followed by Earth; then from Ocean was born an hermaphroditic dragon that had three heads (a god's head between heads of bull and lion) and wings. He was called Chronos (Time) or Herakles. He was father of wet (*noteros*) Aither, boundless Chaos, and cloudy Erebos. While this cosmogony certainly contains philosophic syncretism, there is little reason to doubt that the authors have made use of an older mythical theogony, as did Aristophanes when his chorus of birds with comic verisimilitude claimed direct descent from winged Chaos and winged Eros, who was hatched from the egg of black-winged Night. This winged Chaos, as mate of masculine Eros, was apparently hermaphroditic.[22]

That such material as the "Orphic" cosmogony has value as evidence for early myth is illustrated by the Gnostic *Pistis Sophia*, ascribed to Valentinus and written in Coptic. Therein Jesus tells Mary Magdalene that the outer darkness is a huge dragon, who, tail in mouth, encompasses the whole world. In this dragon-darkness are the places for punishment of the wicked, each governed by demons that have the forms of crocodile (who also has his tail in his mouth), cat, dog, snake, bull, boar, bear, vulture, basilisk, among several mixed shapes. It is plain that this is Egyptian cosmology, taken directly from the mythology of the

---

and 195, who speak of Acheloos as source of all waters, seeming to ignore Ocean; and who say (also Serv. *Georg.* 1.8) that the ancients called all water Acheloos. See Gruppe (1906) 344, Onians (1954) *locc. cit.* Ocean was probably identified or confused with other large rivers too: Asopos, Inachos, Peneios, Ladon. Notice that Eurynome the Oceanid is also called daughter of Asopos (see note 20). Herakles *vs.* Ocean: Pherek. Ath. 18a, 1.66 J.

[22] Acheloos-combat: Soph. *Trach.* 9–14. Chronos: Damasc. *De Princ.* 123 (Orph. 54 Kern); Athenag. *Pro Christ.* 18, 20 (Orph. 57, 58 Kern). See Aristoph. *Av.* 695–699.

land in which this Gnostic tract was written, and early cosmology at that: the outer darkness is literally a snake encircling the world, and Hell is located within him, and so is outside the cosmos.[23]

Thus, late esoteric literature preserves early mythology, in which, moreover, the darkness is conceived as a dragon. From Phoenicia, Egypt's neighbor, we hear that the first being was a snake in hawk form, apparently a Zu-like creature, literally a winged Chaos: when he opened his eyes he filled all space with light (Th. 3D); when he shut his eyes, everything was dark. Philo gives us this information on the authority of a certain Epeeis, and says immediately afterward that Pherekydes got his Ophion story from the Phoenicians. Ophion, I am sure, was not a direct borrowing from Phoenician cosmogony; yet we have evidence here that Phoenician and Greek cosmogonies alike began with a chaos-serpent.[24]

From either Greek or Phoenician sources, or both, Lucian could have derived the conception of Ophion as either primal ancestor or one of the world's first beings. In his mock tragedy *Tragodopodagra* his Chorus sing the praises of the goddess Podagra (Gout): Nereus nursed the infant Aphrodite, they say, and Tethys nursed the infant Hera; Zeus brought Athena to birth in his head, and Old Man (*gerôn*) Ophion brought Podagra to birth in his arms (the cradle of the deep?), his first delivery, when dark chaos ceased and bright dawn and the sun's light first appeared. It is hard to say whether Ophion was Podagra's parent or obstetrician: he is subject of the same verb (ἐλόχευσεν) as Zeus, who was both to Athena. Lucian's Podagros (Gouty Man), who hates Podagra, has called her daughter of Kokytos and the Fury Megaira; the Chorus, her votaries, say that her mother was the Moira Klotho, from whose womb, presumably, Ophion received her in his arms. Perhaps Ophion and Klotho are set in contrast to Kokytos and Megaira, whose names suggest the dreadful realm of death; per-

---

[23] Valent. *Pist. Soph.* 287–289 (319–321). For parallel ancient Egyptian descriptions of Tuat see the texts summarised by Budge (1934) 357–379.

[24] Epeeis and Philo *ap.* Eus. PE 41c. Epeeis intimates that the primal hawk-snake was of fiery substance, an indication of a fiery chaos. Easy steps lead from darkness or water to light or fire: darkness or water > mist > air > *aithêr*, the bright sky > fire.

The attribution of Phoenician sources to Pherekydes may be due to a mistake in his nationality. He came from the island of Syros and so was called ὁ Σύριος; in Roman times this may have been referred to Syria.

haps the two pairs are meant to be the same—if any confidence can be placed in this humorous composition. At any rate Ophion was present at the dawn of the world.[25]

To form another link in our chain, Ophion may be identified with Ogygos (Ogyges), an obscure figure who appears both as a Titan and as the earliest ruler of Thebes or Eleusis, and whose name gave to Boeotia and Attica the epithet *Ogygian*, interpreted as *ancient* or *huge*. As a Titan king he helped Kronos, and after Zeus's victory he fled to Tartessos, which was Ophion's base as king of Gigantes. It is also said by a Scholiast that he was first king of the gods. Either statement comes to the same thing: he was a predecessor of Zeus and in due course deposed. He was no doubt looked upon as first father as well as first king, and so plays exactly the part of Ophion or Ocean or Chaos.[26]

In fact, his name is but a synonym of *Ôkeanos*, probably another formation on the same root. An intermediate form is *Ôgenos*, used, for example, by Pherekydes for the Ocean stream into which Ophion fell. It also occurs in the form *Ôgên*, which Hesychios defines as *Ôkeanos*, adding that the *Ôgenidai* are the Ocean nymphs *Ôkeanidai*. Furthermore he defines *ôgenion* as *palaion* (old)—adding the interesting remark that it is also the name of a mountain—it is therefore a synonym of *ôgygion*. Hesiod calls Ogygian the water of Styx, Ocean's daughter. A later source mentions an Ogygias who was child of Eurynome and Zeus. Again, Dionysios Periegetes calls the Ladon River Ogygian; and his commentator Eustathios explains the epithet from the story that Ladon and Ge were parents of the first woman, Daphne. So, if Ogygos is but another name for Ocean, we can surmise the real meaning of the Ogygian flood. From a few postclassical notices we learn of a flood, earlier than Deukalion's, in which Ogygos, the first Boeotian king, was survivor; but the tradition is both scanty and obscure. Since King Ogygos' antiquity is stressed, since

---

[25] Lucian, *Trag.* 1–8, 99–105. There may be some confusion with or play upon *Podargê*, name of a Harpy: liquid metathesis could produce one name from the other. But a goddess of gout is far from being out of the question: in China there are goddesses of smallpox, measles, plague, asthma, boils; see Hackin AM 361. Ophion's epithet of *gerôn* links him to the *Halios Gerôn*, the Old Man of the Sea.

[26] Paus. 9.5.1, 1.38.7; Africanus *ap.* Eus. PE 489BC; Isid. *Etym.* 13.22.3; Thallos 2, 2.1157 J; Kastor 1, 2.1132 J; Schol. on Hes. *Theog.* 806; Hesych. Ω25, 27; Suid. Ω12, 13.

he is called *autochthôn,* sprung from the very earth, and since he was called son or grandson of Poseidon, we can say, in view of the foregoing evidence, that Ogygos was originally not the flood survivor, but the flood itself. This flood and the whole Ogygian tradition are closely linked to Lake Kopais, which is also called Kephisis: we have noticed Python's relation to the river Kephisos, which feeds the lake.[27]

Since the names Ogyges and Gyges occur also in Lydia and Lykia, it should be recalled that the Lydians of Temenothyrai called a river and river god both Okeanos and Hyllos, and that this Hyllos was Ge's or Omphale's son, and was also called Geryon (p. 108).

The chain that connects Chaos, Tartaros, Erebos, Ocean, Ophion, and Ogygos is now complete. Though the surviving literature presents Ocean as a primal deity at peace with the Olympians, we see that under the names Ophion and Ogygos he fought the gods and their champion. Ogygos, king of Titans, who fled to Tartessos after Zeus defeated him, and Ophion, king of Gigantes, who plotted against Zeus at Tartessos, must be one and the same enemy. In Kronos as victor over Ophion we see an

---

[27] Ogenos: Pherek. Syr. *ap.* Orig. *Cels.* 6.42 *et ap.* Clem. Alex. *Strom.* 6.9, p. 741 P; Lyk. 231; Hesych. Ω19–21. Ogygian Styx: Hes. *Theog.* 805 f. Ogygias: ps.-Clem. Rom. *Recogn.* 10.21; there is nothing in the text to indicate that Ogygias was a nymph (see LM and RE s.v.). It may well be a masculine name, a variant of Ogyges or Ogygos; what we have in the *Recognitiones,* after all, is a Latin translation of a lost Greek text. Paus. 1.38.7 reports the disagreement of authorities concerning Eleusis' parents: some said that he was son of Hermes and Ocean's daughter Daeira, others that his father was Ogygos. Ogygian Ladon: Dion. Per. 417 with Eust. *ad. loc.* Ogygos' flood: Varro *Rer. Rust.* 3.1.3; Africanus *ap.* Eus. PE 489BC; Nonn. *Dion.* 3.204–208; Serv. *Ecl.* 6.41; Aug. *Civ. Dei* 18.8; Isid. *Etym.* 13.22.3; Schol. Vet. on Plato, *Tim.* 22A; see Fontenrose (1945) 109 f. The hundred-handed monster Gyges or Gyes probably has another form of the same name: Apollod. 1.1.1. Perhaps the name of the legendary Lydian king Gyges can also be referred to the same root. Whether a king of that name ruled or not, it is certain that the stories told about him are mainly legend. We should notice: (1) The presence in Lydia of a lake called Gygaia, inhabited by a nymph Gygaia: Il. 2.865, Herod. 1.93.5. (2) Gyges' association with a queen who bears a striking resemblance to the legendary Lydian queen Omphale: she killed her husband; she was a sorceress; she had marvelous powers of vision from either a double pupil or dragonstone; she was definitely in command of the situation; see Herod. 1.8–13, and other sources cited by K. F. Smith (1902), with Smith's own searching study of the Gyges legend, especially pp. 367–380. The Lycians, who were related to the Lydians, were called Ogygioi, according to Steph. Byz. 473 Holst. It is quite possible that the Old Testament figures Og, giant king of Bashan (Deut. 3.1–13), and the terrible Gog and Magog (Ezek. 38.2 f.) also have forms of the same name. Ôgygos, Gygês, Gog, are perhaps reduplications of the base seen in Og, Ôgên, Ôkeanos. For etymologies, all disputed, see LM 3.690–694. Finally, we should notice Kalypso's isle Ogygia on the border of Ocean and *thalassa.*

interesting parallel to Mesopotamian mythology, where Enlil or Ea preceded Marduk or Ninurta as champion (p. 157). An additional link between Ocean-Ophion-Ogygos and Typhon-Python is the sea monster Phorkys. On the one hand Phorkys was ruler and maker of the sea, a primal spirit of the deep, called Old Man of the Sea (*Halios Gerôn*), a title that was almost certainly shared by Ophion (see p. 236, note 25). In a theogony known to Plato he was son of Ocean and Tethys; in Hesiod he was son of Pontos and Ge; and the Vatican Mythographer cited above (p. 232) makes him a grandson of Ophion-Ocean, son of Uranos. He was interpreted as the flux of the waters, and Keto as their depth: that is, they were the fresh water and the salt sea, Ocean and Tethys. On the other hand, the mate of Keto and father of many monsters was called either Phorkys or Typhon (pp. 96 f.); Echidna is called Phorkys' daughter by the historian Pherekydes; Skylla and Medusa are daughters of either Phorkys or Typhon (pp. 96, 283). Phorkys was also identified with Erebos-Tartaros: the poet Phanokles says of Orpheus' lyre that it could persuade the hated water of Phorkos, and the poet Euphorion calls the Eumenides granddaughters of Phorkys.[28]

We may conclude after this survey of the evidence that (1) Typhon had more to do with the creation myth, and that (2) Ocean was more hostile to the gods as chaos demon and dragon enemy, than is immediately evident from surviving sources. Originally each played the role of Apsu or Vritra, probably in separate variants of the myth that came independently to Greece.

We also see that both sea and death belong to the myth from the beginning. From the waters of chaos the dragon derives his affinity to the sea, and from the darkness of chaos his habitation in the realm of death or rulership over it. Yet I shall not revise my former statement that death is prior to sea (p. 142). There can be no doubt that long before this myth had begun, the end-

---

[28] Phorkys, ruler of the sea: Od. 1.72; maker of sea: Opp. *Hal.* 2.29–37; *Halios Gerôn*: Od. 13.96, 345. Parents: Plato, *Tim.* 40E; Hes. *Theog.* 237 f. See Schol. on Hes. *Theog.* 270 and EM 798 for Phorkys and Keto as flux and depth, where we may see more than a folk etymology that connects *Phorkys* with *pheresthai*: the interpretations of Keto and the Graiai given by the Scholiast are by no means etymological. Echidna *Phorkynos*: Pherek. Ath. 7, 1.60 J. Phorkys = Erebos: Phanokl. *Erot.* 1.20; Euphorion 52 Mein. We should recall now that both Phorkys and Phorbas are called father of Skylla (p. 96), and that Phorbas occurs as an alternative name of the river Acheloos (p. 88).

less waters of the sea, dangerous to man, and forming the limit of the world that he knew, had suggested the barren as against the fertile (contrary, of course, to the reality of the sea's teeming life), confusion as against order, death as against life. Hence Chaos—a living state of disorder, inactivity, and preëxistent death—was conceived as a waste of waters.

GIGANTOMACHY

Marduk won his kingship by overthrowing Kingu, Tiamat, and their hosts; Indra won his by overcoming Vritra and Vritra's followers. On the analogy of these myths we would expect that Zeus took the throne after defeating Typhon and Typhon's hosts. In the extant sources, however, it was Kronos and the Titans that he had to oust in order to win power for himself and the Olympians; it was only afterward that Typhon menaced Zeus's sovereignty. Yet Hesiod (or his interpolator; the passage is early enough in any case) implies that Ge brought Typhon forth to avenge the Titans. Zeus's combat with him had the same world-shaking effects as the gods' battle with theTitans: earth, sea, and sky rumbled and shook; earth caught fire and the waters seethed; even Tartaros trembled (p. 71, note 3).

We have seen that in the earliest variants of the combat myth known to us, the dragon combat is accompanied by theomachy and gigantomachy (Th. 7G): the dragon pair, leading the forces of Chaos and Old Night, make war upon the gods, whose commander and champion is the weather god. Probably when the myth first took shape it was a tale of single combat: the champion god fought the chaos dragon, or at most a dragon pair, the male and female chaos spirits. But for two reasons the dragon acquired an army. (1) As the original story spread and developed versions and then variants, the dragon acquired different names (and shapes) in different localities. Later, when the version of a capital city became dominant, eclipsing or submerging those of other districts, the provincial dragons became the allies of the capital's dragon, whose name prevailed as the weather god's great enemy. (2) To this story of dragon combat was joined a myth of theomachy, of revolt in heaven. In *Enuma elish* Tiamat commanded an alliance of monsters and rebel gods. In the battle with monsters we have the kernel of gigantomachy; in that with rebel gods we have the kernel of Titanomachy. The older gods hated and envied the vigorous young weather god as he rose to power, and so they revolted against the reigning Anshar. Notice too that their feelings of unease before the waxing Marduk are closely parallel to those of the chaos-demons before the younger gods (p. 149). The welding together of the two kinds of theomachy is expressed in the marriage of Tiamat, the gigantic spirit of chaos, with Kingu, leader of the older gods. It is as though Echidna were married to Kronos.[29]

In Egyptian Set the roles of Kronos and Typhon have coalesced. Set was an honored god of Upper Egypt, and the myth reflects a conflict of cults in early times: one instance out of many in which this myth pattern was employed to dramatise actual events. But Set and his hosts were also portrayed as snakes, crocodiles, boars, hippopotami, and other sorts of beasts; that is, Set was both displaced god and monster.

The dragon-demon Vritra was also a leader of demon hosts that took all sorts of shapes. His combat with Indra was an incident in the unending wars between gods and demons. As in Egypt and Babylonia, the demons seem to be a fusion of hostile gods with dragons and giants. The demons called Dasas have a name that is also associated with the aboriginal inhabitants of India, so that displaced gods can be discerned in them: again the myth has been suited to historical realities. Theomachy is also present in the war of Rama and his allies with the hosts of Ravana.

We have also seen conflict between generations of gods in Phoenician myth (p. 213) and hints of it in Ugaritic myth (p. 131). The Hurrian myth of Kumarbi and Ullikummi, so patently related to the Hesiodic theogony, shows well enough that Kronos and Typhon (or a Typhonlike figure) were allies in an early form of the Greek myth. It also shows that the sequence in the *Theogony* is right: first Zeus overthrew Kronos, and then Typhon arose to avenge Kronos. Hesiod's statement that Typhon was born

---

[29] I employ the term "rebel gods" to designate the older generation of gods, such as the Titans, that fought against the victory-destined younger gods, even though sometimes, as in the Hesiodic Titanomachy, the younger gods are those who revolt. But notice Ovid *Fasti* 3.796 f.: Saturn-Kronos was first deposed; then he roused the Titans to rebellion against the Olympians.

of Ge and Tartaros is consistent with the Homeric Scholiast's story (p. 72) that Typhon was sprung from Kronos' seed smeared upon eggs that had been placed underground (a striking parallel to the Hurrian myth of Ullikummi's birth from Kumarbi's seed sown in a mountain): that is, Typhon was born from eggs in Ge's body and rose from Tartaros, the regions underground. According to the Scholiast, it was "under the Arimon" in Cilicia that Hera placed the semen-smeared eggs, very likely an allusion to a mountain. In a *Titanomachy* to which the Scholiast on Oppian alludes, the story of Zeus's combat with Typhon in Cilicia was told.[30]

So it is not merely late poetic invention when Nonnos interprets Typhon's hypothetical victory to mean a restoration of Kronos and the Titans; nor merely confusion when a Scholiast includes Typhon among the Titans and when Pan's aid to Zeus is referred to the Titan war rather than to the Typhon combat. Typhon really had a part in the story: the chaos demon became the deposed god's ally.[31]

Nor is it confusion that caused some authors to include Typhon among the Gigantes. Among these authors are Pindar and Euripides (p. 160); the association of Typhon with Gigantes is therefore not late. Since I have already dealt with Typhon's part in the Gigantomachy, it suffices now to recall that these authors relate Typhon to the Gigantes in much the same way as others relate him to the Titans: he is numbered among them, even called their king, and it is said that Ge bore him to avenge them after their defeat.[32]

Furthermore certain Gigantes seem to be doublets of the dragon enemy. According to Apollodoros and others, it was Enkelados

---

[30] Schol. on Opp. *Hal.* 3.16. Notice that in Hom. Hymn 3.334–336 Hera calls on Ge, Uranos, and the Titans who live in Tartaros to help her in producing the son who will be Typhon. According to Schol. on Nic. *Ther.* 10 the Titans were beasts (*thêria*), born from the blood of Typhoeus after Zeus struck him down. Compare Hes. *Theog.* 183–185: the Gigantes were born from the blood of Uranos' severed genitals received by Ge. On Typhon in the Titanomachy see Mayer (1887) 135–137.

[31] Nonn. *Dion.* 1.383 f.; 2.228–230, 260–269, 296–300, 314–316, 337–341, 565–567, 574–578, 591, 600 f.; Schol. Vet. on Eur. *Phoen.* 1020; Hyg. *Astr.* 2.28. See Plut. *Mor.* 360F. For an association of Tityos with the Titans see Eust. on Od. 7.324, p. 1581, and 11.575, p. 1699.

[32] On Typhon among Gigantes see Mayer (1887) 215–222, Vian (1952) 197, 234. Dornseiff (1933: 23) places Typhon in the Cyclic *Gigantomachy*.

who was pinned down under Etna when Athena threw the island of Sicily upon him. Porphyrion, whom Pindar links with Typhon in defeat beneath Zeus's thunderbolts and Apollo's arrows, was betrayed by his lust: Zeus put passion for Hera into him and he attacked her during battle (Th. 4E), but Herakles rescued her, killing Porphyrion with his arrows while Zeus cast thunderbolts on him from above (Th. 7E). A similar story is told about Eurymedon, a king of Gigantes in the Odyssey, destroyed along with his people. According to Euphorion, he either actually succeeded in violating the girl Hera or she fell in love with him; after Zeus came to power he learned of this affair and cast Eurymedon into Tartaros. In these sources we can see the shadow of a story in which Hera deliberately lured the enemy to destruction: that is, Hera played the part of Paghat or Ishtar or Astarte, and Eurymedon that of Yatpan or Hedammu or Sea (pp. 139, 175, 191).[33]

From the early fourth century B.C., Gigantes with legs of serpent form, like Typhon's legs, appear in vase paintings and other works of art. Before 400 they are always represented as wholly human in body. There is, moreover, no literary reference to snake-footed Gigantes that can be dated with certainty before approximately 200 B.C. The snake-footed opponent of a god or gods in earlier paintings (figs. 13, 14) is always Typhon, as Vian makes clear. So it is true enough that the Gigantes of Greek art and literature acquired their serpent legs from Typhon. Yet it is more true to say that they regained them—if we are to distinguish, as I have done, between Titanomachy and Gigantomachy, and derive the Gigantes ultimately from such monstrous creatures as gathered around Tiamat, Set, and Vritra. The Greeks of the clas-

---

[33] Enkelados under Etna: Apollod. 1.6.2; Call. frag. 1 Pf. (*ap.* Schol. Vet. *in* Pind. *Ol.* 4.7 [11]); Orph. *Arg.* 1257. Typhon under Etna (or Vulcano), Enkelados under Vesuvius (or Solfatara?): Philostr. *Imag.* 2.17.5; it is hard to tell which lies under which mountain in Sid. Apoll. *Carm.* 6.27 f. Either is under Aenaria (Pithekusai) : Serv.-Dan. *Aen.* 9.712. Porphyrion and Typhon: Pind. *Pyth.* 8.12–18. Porphyrion and Hera: Apollod. 1.6.2. Eurymedon and Hera: Scholl. ABT on Il. 14.295 or 296. Eurymedon's destruction: Od. 7.58–60. Hera, impregnated by Eurymedon, bore Prometheus. Vian (1952: 175 f.) points out the near-identity of theme between this story and four others: (1) Hera's clandestine union with Zeus that resulted in the birth of Hephaistos; (2) Hera's parthenogenesis of Typhon; (3) Porphyrion's attack; (4) Ixion's attempt upon Hera. In each Hera either becomes mother of a fire deity (Prometheus, Hephaistos, Typhon), or the assaulter himself is a fire spirit (Ixion, Porphyrion; cf. Prometheus Pyrphoros). For the "Judith theme" see Appendix 2.

sical period humanised the Gigantes; in general they did not like fantastic monstrosities in their art: there are few representations of Typhon. They assimilated the Gigantes to the Titans (whom, however, they hardly ever pictured), and made the Gigantomachy into a theomachy. For the Titanomachy is simply theomachy, having its ultimate origin, as I have pointed out, in the myth of war between an older and a younger generation of gods.[34]

Vian is no doubt right in maintaining that the Greek Titanomachy and Gigantomachy are independent stories of war in heaven, framed on a common pattern of motives. I would add that the common pattern is that of the combat myth in which dragon and dragoness lead a host of monsters and rebel gods. Titans and Gigantes have each picked up traits from both parties to the alliance; yet, as I have already said, the Titans are the descendants (folkloristically speaking) of the rebel gods, the Gigantes of the monsters. The latter are portrayed as wilder, more savage beings; we have seen that they change places easily with Typhon and that the Typhon figure influenced the Greeks' conception of Gigantes; and, finally, the battle of the Phlegraean Fields, the Gigantomachy itself, in contrast to the battles of the Titanomachy, consisted of a number of single combats, each god facing a special opponent.[35]

Tiamat has by no means disappeared from either war. In the Titanomachy, according to Apollodoros, Zeus first killed Kampe, whom Kronos had set to guard the Cyclopes and Hundred-Handed after imprisoning them in Tartaros: Zeus could not win without them—on his freeing them the Cyclopes gave him the thunderbolts that he needed for victory. Nonnos elaborately describes Kampe. In brief, she was a female counterpart of his Typhon: she had fifty heads of all kinds of beasts, and the body of a woman from the waist up, of a snake from the waist down. That is, she was Echidna under another name, as Nonnos indicates, calling her Echidnaean Enyo, identifying her snaky legs with echidnas, and likening her to Sphinx and Skylla. He also

[34] On snake-footed Gigantes see Apollod. 1.6.1 and Vian (1952) 12–16, 147, 234; cf. Mayer (1887) 274–282; representations in Vian (1951) pl. 48, no. 400 and figures on pls. 51–54. There are no representations of Titanomachy, perhaps because the Gigantomachy adequately occupied the field of theomachy.

[35] Vian (1952) 284–286. For Titans in Centaur form see *ibid.* 10–12.

calls her "black-winged Tartarian nymph" (*nymphê Tartariê melanopteros*), using an epithet that is elsewhere given to Night (p. 234). She sent hurricanes and stormwinds against the gods, and fire blazed forth from her eyes, casting sparks afar.[36]

She has more than appearance in common with Echidna-Delphyne. In guarding the Cyclopes underground she was, like Delphyne in the Corycian Cave, trying to keep Zeus from his sinews. We have seen that in Nonnos' version of the Typhon myth (pp. 74 f.), Zeus's thunderbolts are either identified with or substituted for his sinews. In another version of the Titan war, which Dionysios Leather-Arm said was Libyan, Kampe was killed by Dionysos, who commanded Zeus-Ammon's army against Kronos and the Titans. In this account the Titan war followed the Gigantomachy, and Kampe had a predecessor in Aigis, a frightful earthborn she-monster who breathed forth flames from her mouth. She appeared first in Phrygia and burned up that part of the country that was called Burnt Phrygia. From there she went to the Tauros Mountains of Cilicia and to the Lebanon Range of Syria, burning up all forests as she went; then she went to Egypt and Libya. It is very likely that she is that Fire, bitch of the gods, who is mentioned in the Ugaritic texts (p. 133): she is at least an offshoot of the same stock. As Anat killed Fire, so it was Athena who killed Aigis and flayed her; whereupon Ge in rage brought the Gigantes forth to make war on the gods. Thus did Athena acquire the aegis, her goatskin cuirass. Since the aegis is a talisman, giving Athena or Zeus marvelous power to ward off evil, it has much the same meaning as the sinews or thunderbolts, and like them it was won or recovered by killing the she-monster.[37]

Dionysios' tale is little different from that to which Euripides refers in the *Ion:* Ge bore the Gorgon, a terrible monster, to be the ally of her sons the Gigantes; Athena killed her and took her hide, called *aigis,* for her cuirass (which had upon it the coils of an echidna—*Ion* 993 may be an interpolation, but it is nonethe-

---

[36] Apollod. 1.2.1; Nonn. *Dion.* 18.236–264. Epicharmos (*ap.* Hesych. K614) either called Kampe a *kêtos* or spoke of some kind of sea-beast called *kampê*. See Mayer (1887) 232–234; Vian (1952) 210, 285.

[37] Dionysios Skytobrachion *ap.* Diod. 3.70–72. Aigis may be another name for Chimaira. Her masculine counterpart may be Aix, Python's son (p. 20).

less evidence for a link between Gorgon and the snake called echidna). So the she-monster, whether called Kampe, Aigis, Gorgon, or Delphyne, has in her keeping the instrument of potency, without which the gods cannot defeat their enemies, Titans or Gigantes or Typhon: the three parts of the alliance have broken up among the Greeks into three separate myths.[38]

Alternatively, it was the giant Pallas whose hide Athena took to use as breastplate. But Pallas is also the name of the Gorgon, as is clear from a story interpolated in Apollodoros' text: Pallas was the child Athena's playmate; they once put on armor and started to fight; when Pallas was about to strike Athena, Zeus interposed the aegis, afraid lest she harm his daughter; Pallas took care to avert her eyes before the Medusa's head set upon it, and Athena took advantage of the moment to deal her a mortal blow; then she mourned the loss of her playmate, made an image of her, which was thereafter called the palladium, and garbed it with the aegis. Obviously Athena's defeat of the Gorgon has been reduced to accidental death in girls' sportive combat. Probably the giant Pallas became the source of the aegis after Perseus had become firmly established as Gorgon slayer.[39]

The Titaness Kampe also has her male counterpart. Ovid preserves a story of the Titan war, wherein the Titans are truly rebel gods: Saturn-Kronos aroused them against the gods after Zeus had dethroned him (compare Kumarbi in the Hurrian myth, p. 211). Now Earth had borne a monstrous bull that had the hinder parts of a snake. Styx kept him enclosed within a triple wall amidst dark groves (i.e., in Tartaros, p. 228), since the Fates had decreed that anyone who should burn this creature's entrails would be made strong enough to vanquish the gods. Briareos, whom Ovid mistakes for a Titan (though something might be said for a variant tradition), killed the bull and had almost put the entrails on the fire, when a hawk (*miluus*), at Zeus's command, snatched them up and carried them to Zeus. In this story it is the serpent-bull, in Apollodoros' Titanomachy it is Kampe, that must perish first to give victory to the gods.[40]

---

[38] Eur. *Ion* 987–997; Euhemeros 5, 1.308 J. See Vian (1952) 198–200.
[39] Apollod. 3.12.3. See Mayer (1887) 189–192, Kerényi (1949).
[40] Ovid *Fasti* 3.795–808.

There are strong reminders here of Mesopotamian mythology. The bull recalls Ishtar's bull of heaven (pp. 168 f.), whose heart Gilgamesh tore out and offered to Shamash, and whose shoulder Enkidu tore off and threw at Ishtar. The hawk is plainly Zu-Imdugud-Garuda, seizing the tablet of destinies or the soma, either enemy of the gods or their friend. The hawk, acting on Zeus's orders, is comparable to Indra, when in Garuda's form he seized the soma (p. 203, note 44), or when with Garuda's connivance he recovered the soma that the bird had stolen from heaven. The burning of the entrails is a power-bestowing ritual comparable to the soma oblation of India (pp. 451 f.).

Here the monster whose body holds the needed talisman is distinguished from the guardian dragoness. It is Styx who keeps the serpent-bull confined. Styx, like Ocean, is one of those primordial beings who from Hesiod's time were usually looked upon as friendly to the Olympians. Hesiod says that she sent her children to help Zeus against the Titans, wherefore Zeus gave her great honor. So probably Ovid thought that Styx kept the bull confined for the gods' protection. But Hesiod also tells us that Styx bore these children to the giant Pallas. Also, in an early source, she is Echidna's mother (p. 95). So it can easily be that in Ovid's story she was really keeping the bull from the gods: for Kampe and Delphyne guarded the corresponding instrument of power against the gods. If the Titan called Briareos had any difficulty in reaching the bull, nothing is said about it; rather the gods had to steal the potent entrails (as in the Typhon myth Hermes had to steal the sinews). Notice that in Apollodoros' Titanomachy, Briareos and his brothers have the same position as the bull in Ovid's version: they had the power which the gods needed, and the Titans kept them imprisoned under Kampe's guard.[41]

The serpent-bull, who, as described, looks something like the

---

[41] See Hes. *Theog.* 383–403. Notice that the power instrument is a part of the body of the champion god himself (Zeus), of a female enemy (Gorgon, Pallas), or of a male enemy (Pallas); or a property of a monstrous being who may be considered friend or enemy of the gods (Cyclopes, Hekatoncheires, the serpent-bull); or an external object that neither side possesses at first: the *pharmakon* that Ge wanted the Gigantes to have, but which Zeus seized first by stealth: Apollod. 1.6.1. Compare Indra's seizing of the soma (pp. 200–202). The demoness either possessed the instrument of power (Gorgon, Pallas), or guarded it (Kampe, Delphyne, Styx), or had knowledge of it (Ge).

Acheloos of the vase painting (fig. 22), is none other than the river-god Brychon of Chalcidice, scene of the Gigantomachy. According to Lykophron, ox-horned Brychon was helper of the Gigantes, Hesychios says that Brychos is a river near Pallene, and Suidas defines *Brouchos,* a variant of the name, as *kampê.* This same region has a Giant (Gigas) River, a name that indicates a close relation between Gigantes and river-gods as sons of Earth.[42]

So apart from the occasional inclusion of Typhon among the Titans and Gigantes in the extant sources, and the still more infrequent association of Python and Tityos with them (pp. 55 f.), there is good reason to refer both Titanomachy and Gigantomachy to the myth complex whence came the Typhon and Python myths.[43]

THE DYING GOD

In the encounter of herdsman or hunter with dangerous beast or brigand we have seen a root of the combat myth. The protector and food provider did not always win; sometimes his adversary killed him. So it was but natural that when Tammuz, the herdsman god, became a dying god, his death was attributed to a lion or boar or bandit. He became a dying god when he was identified with a power that brings fertility or promotes the food supply, and that is present for only part of the year. Then the power behind the seasonal phenomena, storm or cold or whatnot, that accompanied his disappearance, was envisaged as the enemy that killed him, and pictured in animal or villainous form.[44]

---

[42] Brychon: Lyk. 1404–1408 (who mentions a Point Titon in the neighborhood); Hesych. B1286; Suid. B562. Gigas River: EM 231. See Mayer (1887) 232–234; Vian (1952) 189–191, 210, 285 with note 9.

[43] In the Gigantomachy Ths. 1A, 1B, 1C, 2A, 3A, 3B, 3C (Kampe), 3D, 4E, 5A, 5B, 6A, 6B, 7A, 7D, 7E, 7G, 9, 10A, 10D, can be clearly seen. Some others are present more obscurely, at least in the extant sources, e.g., 4A, 4D: according to Ephor. 34, 2.53 J, the Gigantes were cruel temple robbers and cannibals. As to 7E, notice that the gods could not defeat the Gigantes without help from Herakles: Apollod. 1.6.1.

[44] Jacobsen (1953: 165–169) identifies Dumuzi (Tammuz) with "the life-giving powers in the milk." The milking season is short on Mesopotamian plains, and it is accompanied by thundershowers, with which Jacobsen associates Bilulu and Girgire (pp. 164–166). Thereafter the short-lived desert bloom disappears, and again the land becomes barren. Here, perhaps, is the source of Tammuz's transition to vegetation god, though Jacobsen does not point it out. In an unpublished myth that Jacobsen mentions brigands killed Tammuz. But earlier it was probably a lion, since he was a lion fighter. Here the reader must be cautioned against supposing that early men consciously personified or symbolised

The sky god, conceived as the bright sky or the summer or the year, or the power resident in them, had to meet the ever-recurring attacks of his antagonist, as winter followed summer, or drought followed the rainy season, or the new year followed the old. As the bright sky he easily became associated with the sun, which disappears at night or goes into eclipse. The sky god was the weather god, sender of fertilising rains, and therefore easily became identified with the god of fertility and vegetation. So it was that Marduk, who took over Adad's functions, tended to merge with Shamash and Tammuz (p. 164). The forces that caused the fertility god's death were identical with the chaotic forces that opposed the sky god and sun god. So the composite god met his temporary death in combat with a monstrous and gigantic enemy, who would in his turn be killed by the reviving god. The barrenness on earth during the god's absence was attributed to the devastation and ruin that the enemy caused during his rule on earth (Ths. 4A, 4B).

Since a lion or panther may eat the body of the man that he kills, and since the enemy is himself the darkness into which the dead go, it is probable that in the earliest form of the myth the enemy swallowed the god (Th. 4D). This form was in any case early: the indications are plain that Baal, Marduk, Indra, and Hanumat were swallowed by Mot, Tiamat, Vritra, and Surasa-Sinhika respectively (pp. 134, 161, 198, 206 f.), and there can be no doubt that Aqhat was swallowed by the mother of eagles (p. 138). Later such an episode was considered uncouth, so that the god immediately escaped the monster's jaws, or the monster swallowed a harmful wind spirit instead.[45]

Very early too was the form in which the enemy killed the god in combat, whereupon the god had to descend to the dead for a term. This no doubt became the usual form of the story, until it was modified to enhance the god's glory. Such, probably, was the version of Bel-Marduk's death that lies behind the text on his death and resurrection (p. 161). Teshub suffered defeat from

---

natural forces and phenomena. On the contrary, these forces were really thought to be living beings. On the merging of dying god with sky-god champion see Levy (1953) 49 f., 79 note 1.

[45] See Oppenheim (1947) 228: Tiamat, opening her mouth to swallow Marduk, swallowed the wind demon instead, as Marduk had planned.

Ullikummi and went to a lowly place for a term of years. We can gather from the *Râmâyaṇa* that Rama had a similar experience in the epic's legendary background: twice Rama fell upon the battlefield, mortally wounded, and only magical herbs could save him (compare the *pharmakon* of the Greek Gigantomachy, note 41), and he spent a number of years in the wilderness—in the epic the descent has become separated from the death in battle. There are indications that Indra too fell in battle before a great enemy (p. 203). So in the Cilician myth that the Greeks adopted, Typhon killed Zeus and sent him into the underworld; and in the earliest form of the Hellenic Python myth, we have good reason to believe, Python killed Apollo, who then had to lie for a period in the tomb.

The god's potency, which is his life, is likely to reside either in one part of his body (Zeus's sinews) or in an external object (Zeus's thunderbolt, Enlil's tablet of destinies). So the episode of the killing of the god is toned down by allowing the enemy no more than the winning of the potency. Thus the Hittite Weather-God lost his heart and eyes, but remained at large to plot the dragon's destruction; Horos lost his eyes in combat with Set; Namuci or Garuda carried off the soma.

Or the god is not killed outright in combat, but is caught by the enemy, like Telipinu or Zababa in the Hahhimas story (p. 125). Or the enemy kills him treacherously, as Set killed Osiris. Or the god is lured into the lower world and then detained there, as Baal by Mot, or Aqhat by Anat.

But the champion may descend of his own free will to the underworld, boldly determined to meet the enemy face to face, or to carry out some design. Such were the descents of Gilgamesh, Enkidu, and Nergal (pp. 171, 173, 175). A weakened form of this variant may be seen in Eurybatos' descent into Sybaris' cave, or in Euthymos' entry into the tomb of Heros, or in the Argonauts' journey to the Colchian land (p. 486). This theme of the hero's voluntary journey to the other world was very much developed in later times (p. 265). It presents a reversal of the original theme: it is no longer the champion's death, but a bold assault on the enemy in his lair. Or, to put it another way, the descent has become merged with an episode that was present from the beginning: the champion's going forth to attack the chaos demon on the demon's own ground, as when Enki set out to fight Apsu, or when Marduk invaded Tiamat's realm, or when Indra broke through Vritra's mountain barrier.

A quite different turn is seen in the stories in which the god or hero merely runs from the enemy at first encounter, as when Ninurta fled before Asag, Indra before Vritra's avenger or before Nahusha (p. 198), Herakles before Kyknos, or Apollo before Python at Sikyon. Similar is the flight of all the gods before the enemy (Th. 7c), a theme which appears early in the myth's development. It has its roots in the gods' fear and submission before the enemy during his reign over heaven and earth, when he shows himself both tyrannical and destructive and they have no champion. But once the god's death has been reduced to something less terrible, or disappears altogether, and the enemy doesn't succeed in winning sovereignty, then the gods are afraid and take to flight when the enemy makes his formidable attempt; in this way the champion god's bravery is emphasised. This is pretty much the situation already in *Enuma elish,* though Mesopotamian literature allows us to see an earlier state of affairs.

In the Typhon myth too it is Typhon's initial onset that puts the gods to flight. But there is a gap in the story as we have it: nothing is said about the government of the world during Zeus's absence in the Corycian Cave. The gods had fled; nobody stood in Typhon's way. Are we to suppose that he didn't take the throne which he coveted? The cognate myths, especially those of Ugarit, Egypt, and India, offer us an answer: this was the period of Typhon's sway.[46]

The conflict of chaos demon with the king of gods, who was likely to be the sky or weather god, may thus become a struggle in which the dragon usurps the sky god's throne, which the god wins back. But the myth of primordial combat is also a myth of recurring combat. The myth not only states what happened when

---

[46] The dragon's tyranny by no means contradicts his desire for chaos and inactivity. His modern counterpart is Hitler, who made use of disorderly elements in the community, and appealed to the antisocial impulses of everyone, so as to overthrow the existing order and win power; then, once he had won it, though he allowed his subjects scope for violence against whatever was left of the old order, he established his own kind of order wherever he held sway, a very rigid order that strictly limited action of all kinds, an order of inactivity and death, should the whole world be won.

the world began, but also what happens at periodic intervals: the renewed attacks of the forces of chaos in their attempts to take over the world. They are the same powers that bring death to the dying god. For this very reason it was easy to add one version (or variant) of the myth to another, when different versions met in one place. Hence the composite narratives that we find in *Enuma elish*, the Baal Poems, and Apollodoros.

It is also due to the merging of different versions or variants, probably, that an older and younger god, often father and son, are allied against the dragon. At first the dead god came back to life, renewed battle, and overcame the dragon. Later his son took up his cause as he lay in the tomb, fought and killed the dragon, and brought his father back to life. Such is the myth of Osiris, Horos, and Set, most obviously an amalgam of different myths: the old rivalry of Set and Horos combined with the death of Osiris. A further complication sets in when the son—e.g., Horos —also suffers defeat, mutilation, or temporary death. In some stories the younger god or hero, who is the real victor, remains subordinate to the older god, who recovers or retains complete power: thus Hupasiyas does no more than help the Weather-God to victory (p. 121); and Gilgamesh acts for Shamash against Humbaba (p. 167). But Horos becomes at least as powerful as Osiris after his victory; and Marduk or Ninurta, after the discomfiture of the older god, Anu or Ea or Enlil, becomes dominant himself on winning the victory, and his father or predecessor retains only a shadowy authority. So Baal ruled after his victories over Yam and Mot, whom El had appeased. Here the theme merges with the usurpations of the theomachy. The overshadowed god may become the displaced god. From the position of Enlil, Ea, and El it is only a step to that of Kumarbi and Kronos; and the former were identified with the latter gods when nation met nation. Hence the Kronos-Kumarbi figure becomes closely associated with the chaotic faction; and it is the younger god, not the monstrous enemy, who overthrows him.

Probably where god and hero are associated against the dragon, though the god remains the dominant figure both as fighter and as sovereign, two variants have been combined, and one champion has been subordinated as helper to the other: Enkidu to Gilga-

mesh (p. 175), Trita Aptya and others to Indra (p. 202), Lakshmana to Rama (p. 206); and in Greece, Iolaos to Herakles in the
Kyknos and Hydra legends (pp. 85, 356), and Hermes to Zeus
in the Typhon myth (p. 73), in which the helper is limited
merely to assistance in tricking the dragon.

But Herakles, as Apollo's helper against Kyknos and the
Dryopes, took over the whole combat, acquiring his own helper
Iolaos in the process, and yet did not displace Apollo as sovereign
of Delphi (but see p. 404). Thus he is closely parallel to the
Hittite Hupasiyas and to Gilgamesh, or to Horos as Ra's champion against Apep or Set (though Horos tends to be identified
with Ra: see p. 187). As Herakles to Apollo, so Apollo to Zeus
in the later history of the Python myth and its subsidiaries. Apollo
certainly acted for Zeus against Phorbas-Phlegyas, and though
Zeus is never explicitly mentioned as Apollo's backer against
Python himself, it is reasonable to suppose that such a view made
its way in step with the belief that Apollo spoke his oracles as
Zeus's mouthpiece.

The concurrence and diffusion on Greek soil of two variants of
the dragon combat, one presenting Apollo as champion, the other
Zeus, may have brought Zeus into the Python myth as Apollo's
backer. But the Homeric Hymn to Apollo shows that there was
more substance to this association round about 600 than merely
Zeus's commissioning of Apollo. With great insight Otto Gruppe
has seen that behind the Hymn lies a story of Apollo's victory
over the dragon while Zeus lay impotent in the Corycian Cave
(and this might very well be the Parnassian cave of that name):
Python or Typhon (it makes no difference which name we use)
had thrown the gods' world into disorder; Apollo, immediately
after his birth, fought and killed him and restored harmony and
order to the world; Zeus was restored to his throne; in the Hymn's
first lines we see the gods celebrating the victory; and Apollo
himself is given a place on Olympos. I find but one fault with
Gruppe's view: he does not satisfactorily account for the female
dragon. Like other scholars, he has assumed that Apollo's dragon
enemy may be indifferently male or female. But to this topic I
shall return (pp. 365–374). We should notice now that the
Olympian gods trembled at the victorious Apollo's approach and

leaped from their seats as he drew his bow, a remarkable parallel
to a Sumerian text in which Enlil and the Anunnaki trembled at
the victorious Ninurta's approach.[47]

Now we should observe that the dragon enemy is also a dying-
and-rising god, inevitably so, if among other things he is the
power behind unpleasant and destructive seasonal phenomena. It
is plain that Baal and Mot take turns in life and death, the original Box and Cox. Drought, ice on the mountains, floods, recur
every year: i.e., Vritra, Asag, Tiamat, return to the attack. As we
shall see (pp. 461–464), this seasonal recurrence has much to do
with the rituals which the myths were designed to accompany and
interpret.

But in Mot we have already seen something more than a destructive demon and lord of death: when Anat killed him, she
cut him into little pieces, which she winnowed, parched, ground
in a mill, and scattered over the fields. Mot is here the grain itself,
or the power within it, that seems to die and later come to life
again. That is, he is a fertility spirit, akin to Tammuz, Adonis,
Attis, and Telipinu.[48]

In Telipinu I have already pointed out an ambiguity of role:
he is in one myth the victim of Hahhimas, and in his absence
vegetation dies; in another he becomes angry with the gods, leaves
them, and deliberately blights the earth (p. 127). With his own
ambiguity he combines that of Zu-Garuda; for on eagle's wings
he returned to the gods. He was himself the soma, so to speak,
self-stolen from the gods and self-returned. That is, he possessed
and controlled the magical potency that caused the land to flour-
ish and the streams to flow: in the time of his anger the springs
ran dry; like Vritra he held back the waters from the earth.

So Telipinu appears to be a transitional figure, crossing over
from demon's victim to demon-enemy. Something of the sort was

---

[47] Gruppe (1906) 1257–1259. See Hom. Hymn 3.1–13 on Apollo's coming to Olympos;
see *An-dim gim-ma* II rev. 7–13 (Witzel 1920: 76): Ninurta is asked not to frighten the
gods when he comes to them. Notice too the fear that the gods felt towards Marduk
(p. 162).

[48] The text shows that Anat scattered Mot's remains over the fields for birds to
consume. We should notice that every use of the grain is referred to in this passage: that
which is ground in the mill to become meal or flour is obviously not that which is sown
in the fields as seed, part of which the birds get; and some of the harvested grain is used
as feed for poultry.

also observed in Gilgamesh and Enkidu. In one legend Gilgamesh showed himself a terrible and despotic king, a character that he may very well have acquired from having become an underworld king and judge. Enkidu, death's victim, was also a savage creature of the wilderness.

It is evident that Lityerses, Syleus, Linos, Bormos, Hylas, and Idmon (pp. 111–113, 480 f.), are dying gods of the same kind as Telipinu and Mot. Lityerses was the corn spirit of Phrygian Kelainai, identified in the myth with both the mowed grain and with the reaper. He was the Old Man, spirit of the grain (John Barleycorn in other words), who enters widely into the harvest customs and lore of Europe, much of which has been gathered and reported by Mannhardt and Frazer. Sometimes he is conceived as an animal, e.g., wolf or dog or boar, and represented as especially dangerous to children. He is killed in the reaping by the person who cuts or binds the last sheaf of grain, and who pays a penalty for being the last, and yet sometimes receives a kind of honor. On the other hand the first person to finish is undoubtedly looked upon as a champion or victor, though the authors mentioned say nothing about him, giving their attention to the loser and his fate. Chance passers and visitors are also taken to represent the corn spirit and must suffer some mild indignity. If we place these customs alongside the Lityerses myth, we see that the loser corresponds at once to Lityerses, his victim, and his killer; the winner to both the hero-killer and to Lityerses as mowing champion; and the chance visitor to victim and, as representative of the corn spirit, also to Lityerses. Thus imperfectly, as we shall see (chapter xv), do the aetiological myths often fit the customs that they are designed to interpret.[49]

So we see that the dying fertility god has a very ambiguous character: he may become champion or victim or the enemy himself. He is champion when he becomes identified with the sky god, as Tammuz with Marduk. Or he may become the sky god's son, as Telipinu of the Weather-God. For this reason, perhaps, we find Zeus as father of Tityos and Amyntor, or Apollo as ancestor of Phorbas, Laogoras, and Eurytos (pp. 49–51): we

---

[49] See Mannhardt (1884) 1–57; Frazer (1912) I 131–150, 214–236, 270–305. Notice death as a reaper in modern symbolism.

should recall at this point the hero worship of Tityos and Eurytos (p. 65) and Phorbas' doubling as dragon slayer and brigand (pp. 24 f.). Or he may be identified with the champion's father (Osiris) or brother (Mot, Dionysos, p. 389). Conversely the sky god receives the victim role from the fertility god. Finally, the fertility god becomes a ruler of the dead from his sojourn in the underworld, and is then likely, though not always (compare Osiris), to take on the character of the demon of death and darkness, and so to become the enemy of the gods. Then the blight that was at first due to his absence becomes the ruin and devastation that he spreads upon earth: the power that gives life is also the power that takes it away. He is thus very different from the sky god, who, if he ever becomes transformed into an enemy at all, does so through becoming the older god in the myth of heavenly usurpation and theomachy (e.g. Kumarbi, Kronos). So the two become enemies; and, as we shall see (p. 388), their opposition or antagonism manifests itself in Greece as the conflict between Perseus and Dionysos, and as the alternation of Apollo and Dionysos at Delphi. For Dionysos plainly belongs to the circle of Telipinu, Mot, and Lityerses.

DEMONESS AND LOVE GODDESS

For some time now it has been plain that the champion was faced with two enemies, whom I have often called dragon and dragoness, regardless of the shape in which any particular representative was conceived. Of the two, the dragoness often appears to be the more formidable, especially in earlier variants such as the Mesopotamian myths of Apsu and Tiamat and of Bilulu and Girgire (chapter viii). In one form or another she remains prominent in most variants, and never entirely disappears from any; but in some, e.g., the Vritra, Typhon, and Python myths, in the forms in which we have them, she recedes into the background, and the dragon takes the spotlight. Or the champion's combat with the dragoness becomes a separate story, as Apollo's encounter with Delphyne, or Herakles' encounter with Skylla (p. 97), or that of Argos Panoptes with Echidna (p. 95).

She is often the wife of the dragon or chaos demon, as Tiamat of Apsu, Echidna of Typhon, Eurynome of Ophion. She is likely to be his sister too: Tiamat and Apsu, as the first two beings in the world, may be considered to be brother and sister; Echidna was Typhon's sister; and Nephthys was Set's sister-wife, though she shows little of the dragoness character. In later variants the dragoness loses the wife-sister role and becomes sister only: such was the relation of Çurpanakha to Ravana. Or she may be the enemy's mother; and this relation too may be seen in *Enuma elish,* since Tiamat was mother or grandmother of Kingu, her second husband. But the incestuous relation is removed sooner when the dragoness is a mother, so that often we find her solely a mother: Bilulu and Danu (pp. 165, 196); and in the Greek myths, as we have seen (p. 119), the dragoness role is played by Ge or Hera as mother of Typhon, or Delphyne becomes the foster mother or attendant of Typhon-Python. Sometimes in Greek legend the dragoness becomes the dragon's daughter: Skylla as daughter of Phorkys or Typhon, Xenodoke as daughter of Syleus (p. 113), and the daughters of Eurytos, Amyntor, Phylas, and Phlegyas, who have become very much transformed (chapter ii).

The close relation of the female chaos spirit, like Tiamat, Tethys, or Eurynome, to the earth goddess and mother goddess has already been indicated (p. 151). Though conceived as a terrible being (except Tethys in her later development), she was also the mother of all the world: gods, men, and lower creatures alike. She was not only deadly and destructive: she was also extraordinarily fecund. So she has a double character from the start: even Tiamat has her gentle side as nurse of Marduk (p. 154, note 15).

Ge and Uranos alternate with Ocean and Tethys as parents of gods and men. Ge's two sides can be seen throughout Greek mythology: she helped the Olympians against Kronos and the Titans, and always held an honored place beside them. But she also raised up Typhon and the Gigantes in wrath against the gods; she made Python the guardian of her Delphic shrine and opposed the coming of Apollo. She was on the one hand *pammêteira,* the All-Mother, and *kurotrophos,* nurse of the young; on the other she was a goddess of death, sender of ghosts and demons, mother of snakes, within whose body lay the land of the dead. Tethys too generally appears as very friendly to the Olympians; she and Ocean took their side against the Gigantes in the mythology of the classical and postclassical periods; but, as we have seen (pp. 229–238), there are indications that they were once conceived as hostile.[50]

As fertility spirit the earth goddess is very like the mother goddesses and love goddesses of the Mediterranean and Near Eastern world: Ishtar-Astarte, Anat, Isis, Inaras, Kybele, Rhea. In fact, it is quite likely that the mother goddess in her several forms was originally identical with the earth goddess. In consequence the mother goddess, as a highly honored member of the pantheon, backs the champion as wife, sister, or occasionally as mother or daughter (Th. 7D): Ishtar as wife of Tammuz, Belit as wife of Marduk, Anat as sister-wife of Baal, Isis as mother of Horos and sister-wife of Osiris, Hera as sister-wife of Zeus, Athena as daughter of Zeus and sister of Herakles, Artemis as sister of Apollo, Leto as his mother. But in her own character, we have seen, she shows a disposition to oppose the champion, as when Ishtar raised the bull of heaven against Gilgamesh, when Anat lured Aqhat to his ruin, when Isis opposed Horos and favored Set, when Hera bore Typhon in anger at Zeus and sent Python to destroy Apollo. In these episodes the fertility goddess betrays her near relation to the demoness of chaos ("Mother Hubur, who fashions all things," p. 151). As goddess of life and love she is heroine; as goddess of death she is the dragoness; in either character she may reveal something of her other side.

Chaos demoness, earth goddess, and mother goddess are alike spirits of fertility. Out of that character arise their amorous propensities, as Dr. Johnson would say, something of which can already be seen in Tiamat's uniting herself to Kingu. So the dragoness puts off her horrid features (or the upper part of them) and becomes a beautiful temptress who helps the dragon by luring the champion to his doom. This is what I have called the Venusberg or Siren theme (Th. 8D). Like the Empusa of Corinth (p. 116) she induces the hero to share her bed that she might destroy him. Or the Venusberg in which temptress and hero live together in dalliance is the realm of death itself, and the hero becomes death's

---

[50] On Ge παμμήτειρα see Hom. Hymn 30; κουροτρόφος in Aristoph. *Thesm.* 299 f.

bridegroom. Thus does her life-giving power, her fecundity and concupiscence, suddenly become converted into its opposite.

We have found this theme variously developed in the myths where it is present. In about every instance it has been modified so that we don't see it in its pristine form. In the Hittite myths it was the Weather-God's son who married the dragon's daughter and went to live with her; or it was the heroine Inaras herself, showing the love goddess's adverse character, who forced the hero Hupasiyas to live apart with her. Anat as Yatpan's accomplice induced Aqhat to elope with her to the City of Mourners. Bata lived with an especially deadly wife in the Valley of the Cedar (p. 191). Behind the episode of Gilgamesh's stop at Siduri's inn we can suspect an earlier amorous tale (p. 171). Ishtar failed to tempt Gilgamesh and Çurpanakha failed to tempt Rama into a love affair with her, stories based upon earlier tales of a demoness successful in her allurements. The theme is especially prominent in the legends of Herakles. Omphale kept him in captivity, she who killed all who came to her bed (p. 108). He tarried amorously with Echidna and Kelto, who had stolen his cattle (pp. 97 f.), and probably had the same relation with Skylla (p. 99). Not much different is the story of Pyrene (pp. 48 f.).

In Zeus's love of Lamia and Apollo's of Psamathe it is possible to see the Venusberg episode of the Python-Typhon myth; since Lamia and Psamathe, as I have shown (chapter vi), can be identified with Echidna and Delphyne. Lamia-Sybaris, the female counterpart of Heros of Temesa, desired young men to satisfy her lust; this was probably also true of Poine-Ker, Psamathe's avenging spirit. In the champion's union with the demonic temptress, as Zeus's with Lamia or Herakles' with Omphale, can be discerned another factor that results in Zeus's becoming the father of such a monster as Tityos.

In Herakles' adventures with Echidna, Kelto, and Pyrene, as we know them, we see a happy outcome for the hero. He wins the love of dragoness or dragon's daughter in the very halls of the dragon. Hence the episode takes a new turn that becomes especially prominent in Greek legend: the enemy's daughter, or his wife, falls in love with the hero and helps him to escape death and to defeat his enemy, a plot that receives its classic expression in the stories of Medea and Ariadne. This development can already be seen in the Egyptian myth when Set's wife Nephthys and his concubine Thueris favor Horos, and when Nephthys becomes the mistress of Osiris and bears him a son (but behind that episode, perhaps, is Nephthys luring Osiris to his doom at Set's hands). It may be present in the Typhon myth in the version in which Hera warns Zeus about Typhon (p. 72). Something of this episode lingers in the friendly giantess of such folktales as *Jack and the Beanstalk*.

In the myth of Nergal and Ereshkigal (p. 175) the disastrous seduction of the hero and his winning of the demoness' love become one: after Nergal's victory over Ereshkigal she proposes with success that he marry her and become lord of the dead. Thus the champion's death becomes the same thing as his victory, and the hero becomes merged with his enemy Thanatos.

Finally, when the champion becomes a lusty hero like Herakles, he simply takes the dragon's daughter and has his pleasure of her. When he was drunk in the house of Bebryx, who can be linked with Amykos and Geryon, he worked his will upon Pyrene, mother of a snake and identical in name with the mother of Kyknos. Herakles took Iole, Eurytos' daughter, against her father's will, and Apollo took Dryope, another daughter of Eurytos, against her own (p. 57). Likewise Herakles carried off the daughters of Amyntor and Phylas (pp. 42, 67 f.).[51]

Conversely, the fertility goddess as heroine exerts her charms upon the dragon in order to entrap him and destroy him. This, the Judith theme (Appendix 2), is the Venusberg theme employed in the hero's behalf. In the earliest and crudest form of the tale the goddess actually gave herself to the monster with the purpose of winning his entire confidence and taking him completely off guard, just as the temptress had no objection to giving herself to the hero. That may be true of the Hedammu myth (p. 175); it is all but explicit in the Egyptian tale of Astarte and Sea (p. 191); and we have a hint of it in the Greek myth of Hera and Eurymedon (p. 242). But it would seem that Paghat succeeded in making

---

[51] This form of the episode may have a root in the myth of heavenly usurpation. Far back in Sumerian mythology Enlil carried off Ki, the earth goddess, after separating her from An: see Kramer (1944) 37 f., 79.

Yatpan drunk and powerless before matters reached that pass; while Çaci succeeded admirably in preserving her chastity inviolate (p. 205). Such is the later story: the heroine accomplished her purpose without loss of her virtue, as Judith in the tent of Holofernes. Isis easily beguiled Set, and Inaras easily beguiled Illuyankas: for I have little doubt that the dinner invitation which she gave to the dragon included a suggestion of carnal pleasures to follow. Finally, the love goddess, like her counterpart, can be allowed to fail, as in Ishtar's attempted seduction of the stone monster (p. 212) or the nymphs' of Viçvarupa (p. 204).

The dragon's lechery (Th. 4E) makes him an easy mark for the heroine's designs. His inordinate lust is the counterpart of the dragoness' erotic nature, and at the same time consistent with his general wickedness. In the next step of the story's progress the heroine becomes the innocent object of his attempt at rape (e.g., Leto, attacked by Python-Tityos, and Sita, carried off by Ravana), or at least of his unwelcome attentions (as Çaci, importuned by Nahusha). The transition can be seen under way in the Gigantomachy in the accounts of Hera's relations with Eurymedon and Porphyrion.

In another development he demands as spirit of death that young women be offered to him; then the heroine, who is to be offered, is rescued by the hero. This is the Alkestis theme, seen most clearly in the story of Euthymos and Heros of Temesa. It becomes prominent in the legend cycle of Herakles and also in the legend of Perseus (see chapters xi and xii).[52]

Whether the dragoness falls in love with the hero and helps him, or the heroine becomes attractive to the dragon, the antagonists become rivals in love. This may be the story that lies behind the Homeric Hymn's allusion (3.211) to Apollo's going wooing with Phorbas Triopas' son. Certainly the immediately preceding verses, expressed in a parallel construction, allude to his rivalry with Ischys for Koronis, here called Azan's daughter, but elsewhere called Phlegyas' daughter. In any case, Herakles becomes

---

[52] Gilgamesh, who, as we have seen, became a ruler of the dead, reflects this character in his exercise of *droit de seigneur* and his cohabitation with a priestess (p. 174), an echo perhaps of ritual. Notice too the princess of Bakhten and the demon that possessed her, p. 193, note 26.

the rival of Acheloos and of Nessos for the love of Deianeira (p. 354).

The dragon's lechery is one phase of his greed. As dragon of chaos he swallows the waters, as darkness he swallows the sun, and as lord of death he swallows all creatures. Hence his reputation as a glutton and man-eater (or cannibal, if he is conceived in human form). So he is beguiled by an offer of food (Th. 9, *a*) as easily as by erotic allurements (Th. 9, *b*). Banquet and sex are combined in Paghat's deception of Yatpan and probably in Inaras' deception of Illuyankas. Isis too employed both food and feminine wiles to trick Set. In addition Paghat and Isis disguised themselves to carry out their designs (Th. 9, *c*) fooling the enemy by pretending to be somebody else. The Typhon myth keeps trickery by food and by disguise (9, *a*, *c*) but drops the erotic deception (9, *b*); yet the latter is still seen in the closely related Gigantomachy, where it is employed against Porphyrion.

The hero, like the dragon, is beguiled either by sexual enticements (Th. 8D) or by an invitation to dinner (Th. 8c). Both kinds of bait were used to catch Aqhat, but a feast only to entrap Baal and Osiris (i.e., in the extant sources). When the hero goes to dine at the house of the enemy, the outcome may be either his own death or the enemy's. In the stories of Lityerses and Syleus the meal was one to which all unwary strangers were invited: when Herakles came he turned the tables, so to speak, on the villain. It is very likely that the feasts of Laogoras and Koronos were of the same kind, and that Kyknos and Phorbas were also hosts at such gruesome entertainment.

Trickery is one way to employ cunning or skill. Hermes' theft of the sinews, or Indra's theft of the soma, shows a use of cunning that is not very different from the deceptions just described. The tricks and thefts, however, belong to nonmagical cunning (except that Hermes has a superhuman ability in thievery). But magical skill (Th. 9, *d*) is the first kind of cunning to appear in the combat-myth. In *Enuma elish,* in Egyptian texts, and in the Vedas and Indian epics, magic is a major factor both in attacking the dragon and in defense against him. The dragon and dragoness too are magicians; but in the end the gods' spells are the more potent. We can see the theme of trickery by disguise arising out of magical change of shape when Isis transforms herself into a beautiful maiden in order to attract Set, and when Çurpanakha did likewise to lure Rama. The earliest nonmagical trick seems to be Marduk's when he enticed Tiamat into opening her mouth so that he could send the winds into her body.

Magic was also a potent means of bringing the dead god back to life: there is mention of incantations, spells, and magical rituals, including lamentations which had a magical purpose. The magical devices of the myths came to them in part from the rituals that they accompanied: from the very incantations and rites that were meant to bring rain, drive winter away, allay storms and floods, banish plague, or rescue the sun from eclipse. This subject will receive more extended treatment in the final chapter.

The banquet, as distinct from the deception for which it is used, is found in earlier variants as a scene of deliberation: the gods gather together at dinner to adopt measures for meeting the crisis, as in *Enuma elish* (p. 150) and the Telipinu myth (p. 127), or to celebrate victory (Th. 10b). A union of banquet and trickery begins to show itself in *Enuma elish* when the gods, reluctant to accept Marduk as king, are plied with food and drink to win them over (p. 162).

SUMMARY

Now the myth type may be outlined in its general features much as it appeared when it entered the Greek world. In saying this I must make clear that the myth did not enter Greece in one fixed form at one particular time. It is evident that several variants, even several versions of the same variant, came to Greece at different times. This was a story that was prone to elaboration and which developed into many different forms.

A) *The Dragon Pair.*—A dragon and dragoness were (1) husband and wife, and/or (2a) brother and sister, or (2b) mother and son (occasionally, father and daughter). Themes 1A, 1B, 1C.

B) *Chaos and Disorder.*—They were (1) male and female spirits of primeval chaos, identified with darkness, water, disorder, death, sometimes stone, mist, fire; and/or (2) they were spirits identified with the violent and destructive phenomena of nature, especially those that recur periodically; and/or (3) they were giants, and/or (4) wholly or partly monstrous and bestial in appearance; and they had (5) violent, wicked, and dangerous characters. Themes 2B, 2D, 2E, 3A to 3G, 4A, 4F, 4G.

C) *The Attack.*—They wished (1a) to keep the chief god (or younger gods) from coming to power, and/or (1b) to overthrow him after he had attained power; and so (2) they gathered their own monstrous progeny and subjects, (3) made an alliance with dissident or deposed gods, and (4) started a war upon the gods. Themes 2C, 5A, 5B, 7G.

D) *The Champion.*—(1) The gods were panic stricken at the enemies' threat, but (2) the sky god, who was very young or had just come to the throne, dared to face the enemies. Themes 6A, 6B, 7C.

E) *The Champion's Death.*—The god (1) was killed by the dragon (or dragoness), being (a) swallowed by him, or (b) overcome by his weapons or strength; or (c) before combat could begin he was lured to his death by the wiles of either dragon or dragoness; and/or (2) he was robbed of that part of his body or of that object in which his power resided. Themes 8A, 8B, 8C, 8D.

F) *The Dragon's Reign.*—While the god was dead and confined in the underworld, the dragon and dragoness ruled the world despotically and destructively, wishing to return it to death, disorder, and desolation: (1) they plundered, murdered, glutted themselves on man and beast, drained rivers of their water, satisfied their lusts; in particular (2) the dragon attacked the god's wife or mother. Themes 4A to 4G, 5A.

G) *Recovery of the Champion.*—(1) The god's wife, sister, and/or mother strove to recover him (a) by use of rituals and magic, or (b) by seduction of the dragon, or (c) by going herself to fight the dragon; and (2) his son helped him (a) by recovering the lost potency, or (b) by taking the champion role upon himself and going forth to fight the dragon and dragoness. Themes 7D, 7E, 8E, 9, 10D.

H) *Battle Renewed and Victory.*—(1a) The god returned to life and renewed the combat, or (1b) his son fought the dragon, and (2) killed the dragon and/or dragoness (perhaps in separate engagements, p. 525) and routed their hosts (3) after a hard struggle in which (4) he was assisted by other gods and goddesses, and (5) had to resort to magic or cunning in order to win. Themes 7A, 7B, 7D, 7E, 7F, 7G, 9.

I) *Restoration and Confirmation of Order.*—The god or his son (1) took or recovered the throne, (2) celebrated his victory, (3) punished the dragon enemies, and (4) established rituals to commemorate the event. The dragons' death and imprisonment were in fact exile to their own element outside the world, where they live on, ever ready to disrupt. Themes 10A to 10D.[53]

In the myths as we find them themes and episodes have become merged, obscured, transformed, transposed, or simply omitted, according to the processes described on pages 5–9. Numerous variants arose, and versions of the variants, many of which interacted on one another. They can be grouped into the following subtypes.

Subtype I: A dragon threatens the gods and the whole world-order. The god goes forth, fights him, and after vicissitudes kills him. The episode in which the god suffers temporary defeat and death tends to become omitted. This we may call the Typhon subtype. Here belong Typhon, Illuyankas II, Yam, Tiamat, Labbu-Asag, Set *vs.* Horos, Apep, Vritra, Ravana, Leviathan, Ullikummi.

Subtype II: This differs from subtype I only in that the god is killed, and his son fights the dragon, recovering his father's life and throne, usually with actual sovereignty for himself. See plot summary under G,2*b* and H,1*b*. This we may call the Python subtype. Here belong Python, Set *vs.* Osiris, Satan (of Rev. 12), Zu; also in certain aspects Tiamat, Labbu, Seven Demons, Apep, Garuda.

Subtype III: The god through death or foul play is confined in the underworld; his sister or wife goes forth either to deal with the dragon directly, and so recover the god, or to recover the god so that he can renew the combat. See summary under E,1*c*, E,2, G,1. This we may call the Mot subtype. Here belong Mot,

---

[53] Theme 2A, unmentioned in the above summary, is simply the symbol of geographical correspondence between the habitats of the dragons of two or more myths. On 10c, purification of the god, see further pp. 198–200.

Yatpan-Anat, Hahhimas, Illuyankas I, Bilulu, Nahusha, the story of Bel's sojourn among the dead, and much of Isis' part in the Set-Osiris myth.

Subtype IV: Chaos, creation, gigantomachy, and dying god have been pretty much forgotten in most variants, so that the basic plot as outlined above is obscured and becomes much as follows: (1) The death god or a demon or a spectre controls and/or terrorises a land; (2) he (the demon may be female, in which case appropriate changes of gender must be made) (a) seizes the young of man and beast, and/or (b) demands that young women be given to him, and/or (c) imposes heavy tribute, and/or (d) kills everyone who comes his road, frequently by forcing him at hazard of his life into a contest with him; (3) the champion (a) through love of the victim, and/or (b) desiring to save the victim, or (c) acting under a superior's orders, or (d) desiring on his own to rid the land of its bane, (4a) descends into the lower world, or (4b) enters into or waits at cave, lair, or tomb, and (5) fights and kills the enemy, accomplishing his purpose. The variants of this subtype can be grouped under two main forms:

Thanatos: Sybaris, Heros, Poine-Ker, Geryon, Nergal-Ereshkigal, Gilgamesh-Enkidu, Bata-Pharaoh, and in certain phases the Rama-Ravana story.

Lityerses: Phorbas, Kyknos, Eurytos, Lityerses-Syleus, Humbaba.

In the version of the Lityerses myth that concerns Daphnis and Thalia-Pimplea, the two forms are combined. Thalia had been carried off by brigands, who were probably in the service of Lityerses: for it was in his house that she was held captive. Daphnis came to deliver her, was challenged by Lityerses, and would have died if Herakles had not appeared to take his place in the contest.[54]

Tables 3 to 8 follow this chapter. Table 3 presents the correspondences among the major combat myths, each indicated by the name of the enemy: Python (including the derivatives), Typhon, Illuyankas, Yam-Mot, Tiamat, Labbu-Asag, Zu, Set, Vritra (including Viçvarupa, Nahusha, etc.), Ullikummi. To these I have added three myths from

---

[54] Serv.-Dan. *Ecl.* 8.68.

more distant parts that are discussed in Appendix 3. The symbol **X**
indicates that the feature appears clearly and prominently; the symbol
x that it appears obscurely or in disguise. Table 4 is to table 3 as
table 2 to table 1, showing the relation of myth to myth: the upper
number in each box shows how many of the themes each shares with
each; the lower number, how many of the shared themes appear
clearly in both myths.

The forty-three themes of tables 3 and 4 have emerged in the course
of our analysis of the several myths as we find them in the sources.
Perhaps a few could be subdivided or merged: perhaps the list could
be enlarged by the addition of a few themes of more infrequent occurrence; the latter have at any rate been mentioned along the way.
Now, putting together the results of our analyses, and of our researches
into the more significant themes, we have arrived at a synthetic pattern, a statement of the whole myth with allowance for possible alter-
natives at each juncture. We now see that a theme sometimes is represented in more than one component of the pattern: e.g., Themes 4A
to 4G emerge from components B and F (and somewhat from E):
again that two or more themes may point to the same component;
e.g., Themes 2c and 5A both point to component C,1. So it may be
worthwhile to present graphically the relation of the thirteen myths of
tables 3 and 4 to the pattern and to one another in terms of the components of the pattern. This is done in tables 5 and 6. Since a theme
may manifest itself in quite different ways from one variant to another
(e.g., Theme 9, which is the essence of component H,5 but also enters
into G,1–2), these tables of synthetic correspondence will show more
clearly the actual resemblance in plot of one myth to another. I omit
components I,2–4, since they do no more than cover the ground of
Themes 10B, 10A, 10D, respectively. The upper numbers in table 6,
like those in table 4, show the features shared by any two myths, the
lower, those that appear clearly in each.

Table 7 presents the correspondences of seventeen myths in respect
to key components of subtypes I and II. In this table *Python* means
the Python myth proper, excluding the derivative tales of Tityos,
Phorbas, and the others; *Yam* is separated from *Mot;* and *Vritra* does
not include the Nahusha tale. Table 8 presents the correspondences
of seven myths of subtype III in respect to key components. The
Python (as in table 7), Typhon, and Tiamat myths are also included
in order to show the relation of subtype III to representative myths
of subtypes I and II. Subtype IV is presented in tables 11 and 12 (pp.
362–364); to it belong several myths discussed in chapters xi and xii.

TABLE 3

CORRESPONDENCES OF THEMES

Theme		Python	Typhon	Illuyankas	Yam-Mot	Tiamat	Labbu-Asag	Zu	Set	Vritra	Ullikummi	Kung Kung	Susanowo	Vucub-Caquix
1A		X	X		X	X	X		X	X	x		X	
1B		X	X		X	X	X		X	X	X		X	
1C		X	X	X	x	X		x	X	x			X	X
2A	a	X	X											
	b	X	X											
	c		X	x										
	d	x	X											
	e		X		X						X			
	f		X						X					
2B		X	X	X				X		X		x	x	x
2C		X						X		x			x	
2D		X	X							X				
2E		x	X	X	X	X	x		X	X	X	X	X	x
3A		X	X			X	X		X	X	X	X	X	X
3B		X	X	X	X	x	X	X	X	X		X	X	X
3C		x	X		X	X	X					X	X	
3D		x	X		x				X			x	X	x
3E								x	X			X		
3F		x	x		X	X		X	X	X	x		X	
3G			x				X	X	X	X		X	X	X
4A		X	X		X	X	X	X	X	X	X	X	X	X
4B		x			X				X	X			X	
4C		x							x			X	X	x
4D		X	X	X	X	x	X			X	x	X	X	
4E		X	X		x				X		x		X	
4F		X			x					X	x			
4G		X	X							X			X	
5A		X	X		X	X	X	X	X	X	X	X	X	x
5B		X	X			X								
6A		x	X	X	X	X	X	X	X	X	X	X	X	
6B		X	X	x	X	X	X	X	X	X	X	X	X	x
7A		X	X	X	X	X	X	X	X	X	X	X	X	x
7B		X	X		x				X	X				

(Continued)

TABLE 3 (continued)

Theme	Python	Typhon	Illuyankas	Yam-Mot	Tiamat	Labbu-Asag	Zu	Set	Vritra	Ullikummi	Kung Kung	Susanowo	Vucub-Caquix
7c	x	X	x	X	X	X	X	X	X	x		x	
7D	X	X	X	X	x	x		X			X	X	
7E	X	X	X	X	X	X	X	X	X	X	X	X	X
7F	X	X						X			X		
7G	x	x			X	X		X	X		X	x	
8A	x	X	X	X	X	X	X	X	X	X	x	X	x
8B		X	X				X	X	X			x	X
8c	x			X				X		x			
8D	x		X					X				X	
8E	X			X	X			X	X			X	
9	x	X	X	x	X	x	x	X	X	X		X	X
10A	X	X			X		X	X	X		X	X	X
10B	X	x		X	X	X		X	X			x	
10c	X			x					X				
10D	X		X	X	X	X	X	X	X			X	

NOTE: Subdivisions of 2A: (a) Delphi, Parnassos, (b) Boeotia, (c) Cilicia, (d) Lydia, Phrygia, (e) Syria, Palestine, (f) Nile Delta. *Susanowo* includes both the two stories in which he is the enemy and the story in which he is the hero against the dragon. *Vucub-Caquix* includes Zipacna and Cabracan.

TABLE 4

INTERRELATIONS OF THE MYTHS OF TABLE 3
(43 themes)

Myth		Python	Typhon	Illuyankas	Yam-Mot	Tiamat	Labbu-Asag	Zu	Set	Vritra	Ullikummi	Kung Kung	Susanowo	Vucub-Caquix
Python	40	...	31	15	28	25	20	16	30	30	18	19	32	15
	27		21	8	13	14	12	10	18	20	11	11	17	6
Typhon	33	31	...	15	23	23	20	16	27	26	17	19	28	16
	29	21		12	16	17	14	12	23	21	12	14	21	8
Illuyankas	17	15	15	...	13	13	12	12	14	14	9	10	16	10
	14	8	12		9	8	7	8	12	11	6	7	12	5
Yam-Mot	29	28	23	13	...	21	18	13	24	23	18	13	24	11
	22	13	16	9		16	15	11	19	18	10	11	18	3
Tiamat	25	25	23	13	21	...	20	14	22	22	15	15	24	12
	22	14	17	8	16		15	11	20	19	11	11	18	6
Labbu-Asag	21	20	20	12	18	20	...	12	19	19	14	15	21	11
	18	12	14	7	15	15		11	16	17	9	12	15	5
Zu	19	16	16	12	13	14	12	...	17	18	10	12	18	13
	16	10	12	8	11	11	11		14	15	7	9	12	6
Set	34	30	27	14	24	22	19	17	...	25	16	18	29	16
	33	18	23	12	19	20	16	14		24	11	15	24	9
Vritra	32	30	26	14	23	22	19	18	25	...	16	15	28	15
	30	20	21	11	18	19	17	15	24		11	13	21	8
Ullikummi	19	18	17	9	18	15	14	10	16	16	...	10	16	9
	12	7	12	6	10	11	9	7	11	11		8	11	4
Kung Kung	21	19	19	10	13	15	15	12	18	15	10	...	19	14
	18	11	14	7	11	11	12	9	15	13	8		15	6
Susanowo	34	32	28	16	24	24	21	18	29	28	16	19	...	17
	28	17	21	12	18	18	15	12	24	21	11	15		8
Vucub-Caquix	17	15	16	10	11	12	11	13	16	15	9	14	17	...
	9	6	8	5	3	6	5	6	9	8	4	6	8	

TABLE 5

CORRESPONDENCES OF PLOT COMPONENTS

Components	Python	Typhon	Illuyankas	Yam-Mot	Tiamat	Labbu-Asag	Zu	Set	Vritra	Ullikummi	Kung Kung	Susanowo	Vucub-Caquix
A, 1		X		x	X		X	X				x	X	X
A, 2a		X			X			X					
A, 2b	X	X			x				X			x	
B, 1				X	X			x	X	x	X		
B, 2	x	X		X	X	X	X	X	X			X	X	X
B, 3	X	X			X	X		X	X	X	X	X	X
B, 4	X	X	X	X	X	X	X	X	X			X	x	X
B, 5	X	X		X	X	X	X	X	X	X	X	X	x
C, 1a	X			X	X			X	X		X	x	
C, 1b	x	X	X	X	X	X	X	X			X		x	
C, 2					X	X		X	X		X		
C, 3	x	x			X			X	X		X	x	
C, 4	x	x			X	X	x	X	X	x	X	x	
D, 1	x	X	x	X	X	X	X	X	X	x		x	
D, 2	x	X	X	X	X	X	X	X	X	X	X	X	
E, 1a				X	X				X				
E, 1b	x	X	X				x	X	X	X			x
E, 1c	x			X				X		x			x
E, 2		X	X				X	X	X			x	x
F, 1	X	X		X	X	x	x	X	X	X	X	X	x
F, 2	X	X		x				X	x	x		x	
G, 1a				X	X			X	x				
G, 1b			X					X	x	X			
G, 1c				X							X		
G, 2a		X	X										
G, 2b, H, 1b	x		x	x	X	X	X	X					x
H, 1a	x	X	X	X	X			X	X	X			
H, 2	X	X	X	X	X	X	X	X	X	X	X	x	X
H, 3	X	X		X				X	X	X			
H, 4	X	X	X	X	X	X		X	X	X	X		x
H, 5	x	X	X	x	X	x	x	X	X	X		X	X
I, 1	X	X	X	X	X	X	X	X	X	X	X	X	

TABLE 6

INTERRELATIONS OF THE MYTHS OF TABLE 5

(32 plot components)

Myth		Python	Typhon	Illuyankas	Yam-Mot	Tiamat	Labbu-Asag	Zu	Set	Vritra	Ullikummi	Kung Kung	Susanowo	Vucub-Caquix
Python	22 11	...	19 10	11 4	17 8	18 8	15 6	12 4	21 10	19 10	16 7	12 8	16 4	11 3
Typhon	23 21	19 10	...	12 11	15 12	18 15	14 10	13 10	21 19	19 16	15 12	12 9	17 8	11 6
Illuyankas	14 12	11 4	12 11	...	10 7	10 8	10 6	9 6	13 11	11 9	10 9	5 5	8 3	7 3
Yam-Mot	22 18	17 8	15 12	10 7	...	18 15	12 9	12 8	20 15	17 14	14 9	12 11	13 5	10 3
Tiamat	24 23	18 8	18 15	10 8	18 15	...	15 13	13 10	22 21	20 18	13 10	15 14	16 8	10 6
Labbu-Asag	16 13	15 6	14 10	10 6	12 9	15 13	...	12 9	16 13	14 11	12 7	11 10	12 5	10 4
Zu	14 11	12 4	13 10	9 6	12 8	13 10	12 9	...	14 11	11 8	9 5	9 6	13 5	9 4
Set	28 27	21 10	21 19	13 11	20 15	22 21	16 13	14 11	...	23 19	18 13	15 13	17 8	13 6
Vritra	25 22	19 10	19 16	11 9	17 14	20 18	14 11	11 8	23 19	...	16 11	14 14	16 7	10 5
Ullikummi	18 13	16 7	15 12	10 9	14 9	13 10	12 7	9 5	18 13	16 11	...	9 7	11 6	8 3
Kung Kung	16 15	12 8	12 9	5 5	12 11	15 14	11 10	9 6	15 13	14 14	9 7	...	12 6	8 4
Susanowo	18 8	16 4	17 8	8 3	13 5	16 8	12 5	13 5	17 8	16 7	11 6	12 6	...	9 4
Vucub-Caquix	13 6	11 3	11 6	7 3	10 3	10 6	10 4	9 4	13 6	10 5	8 3	8 4	9 4	...

TABLE 7

Concordance of Myths, Subtypes I and II

Key component	Python	Typhon	Illuyankas II	Yam	Tiamat	Labbu-Asag	Zu	Garuda	Seven demons	Set	Apep	Vritra	Ravana	Leviathan	Satan	Ullikummi	Kung Kung
A	X	X		x	X		X	X		X		X	X		X		x
B, 1				X	X					x	X	X				x	X
B, 2	x	X			X	X	X	X	X	X	X	X		X	X		X
C, 1a	X			X	X					X		X	X		X		X
C, 1b	x	X	X		X	X	X			X	X			X	X	X	
C, 2					X	X				X	X	X	X	X			X
C, 3	x	x			X					X	X	X	X	X		X	X
D, 1		X		X	X	X	X	X	X	X		X	X	x		x	
E, 1a				X	X						X	X	X				
E, 1b	x	X	X			x				X		X	X			X	
E, 2		X	X				X	X		X		X					
F, 1	X	X		X	X	x	x		x	X	X	X	X		X	X	X
F, 2	X	X								X			X		X	x	
G, 2a		X	X														
G, 2b + H, 1b	x			x	X	X	X		X	X	X				X		
H, 1a	x	X	X		X					X	X	X	X			X	
H, 3	X	X		X						X		X	X	X		X	

TABLE 8

CONCORDANCE OF MYTHS, SUBTYPE III

Key component	Python	Typhon	Tiamat	Illuyankas I	Hahhimas	Mot	Yatpan	Bilulu	Set-Osiris	Nahusha
A	X	X	X			x	X	X	X	
B, 2	x	X	X		X	X		X	X	
C, 1b .	x	X	X	X	X	X			X	X
D, 1	x	X	X	x	X	X	X		X	X
E, 1c	x					X	X		X	
E, 2		X		x			X			
F, 1	X	X	X		x	X			X	X
F, 2	X	X			x	x			X	X
G, 1a			X		X	X		X	X	X
G, 1b				X	x		X			X
G, 1c						X		X		
H, 1a	x	X	X	X		X				x

XI

PERSEUS AND KADMOS

Apollo's combat with a dragon, Python or Delphyne, was the starting point of this study. Then, not far along the way, the combat of Zeus with Typhon was joined with it as another and closely related expression of a common original. The two myths, considered as essentially one, have since shared the center of interest. With them the combat myths of Oriental nations have been compared, with the result that a common pattern, underlying all of them, has emerged. In the Python and Typhon myths, the principal Greek variants of the combat myth, it was a god who fought the dragon, as in the chief combat myths of the Orient. But both in Greece and Asia we have found variants in which heroes rather than gods take the champion role. Some of them became nearly, perhaps fully, as well known as the tales of the god-champion: e.g., the legends of Gilgamesh and Herakles. But in no instance is the hero thoroughly mortal; always there are indications that he was also a demigod or god. We must also remember that the immortal champions can die; the line that separates god from hero is not easy to draw.

We have already studied in some detail those legends of Herakles that are associated with the neighborhood of Delphi, with the Lapith-Dryopian peoples, and with the hero's sojourn in Lydia, and we have glanced at a number of others. We have also referred a number of times to the legends of Perseus and have noticed the appearance of Kadmos in one version of the Typhon myth. There were other Greek heroes too that fought dragons and monsters and brigands: Theseus, Jason, Koroibos, and many another. But the fame of Perseus, Kadmos, and Herakles rivalled that of Zeus and Apollo as dragon slayers. A study of their legends puts them in a class apart from the other hero legends mentioned. Whereas the latter seem to have been fashioned in Greece upon the model of, or under the influence of, the great combat myths that were already upon the ground, the former seem to have come independently and directly (or fairly so) from the same regions that certainly gave the Zeus-Typhon myth to Greece and in all likelihood the Apollo-Python myth too. Therefore we have not had a complete view of the combat myth on its way from Asia to Greece until we have studied with some care the legends of Perseus and Kadmos and a few more legends of Herakles.

PERSEUS

So well known are the legends of Perseus' quest of the Gorgon's head and of his rescue of Andromeda that I need not summarise them. Equally well known are the legends of his birth and of his dealings with Akrisios and Polydektes. Less known, perhaps, are the tales or episodes of his conflicts with Phineus, Kepheus, Proitos, Atlas, and Dionysos; but the substance of them will be made clear in the following discussion. At the moment we can notice that Perseus' enemies are two monsters, a mountain giant, and several kings or rivals for power. In the whole legend cycle of Perseus' adventures I have found all but five of the forty-three listed themes of the combat myth.[1]

---

[1] The only themes missing are 3E, 4F, 4G, 7B, 8B. The principal sources are Hes. *Theog.* 270–283; *Shield* 216–237; Pind. *Pyth.* 10.31–48, 12.6–21; Pherek. Ath. 10–12, 1.61–63 J; Apollod. 2.4.1–5; Dionys. Skyt. *ap.* Diod. 3.52.4–3.55.3; ps.-Erat. 15–17, 22, 36; Lyk. 834–846 with Schol. Vet.; Conon 40; Paus. 2.16, 2.21.5–7, 2.23.7, 4.35.9; Lucian, *DMar.* 14, *Dom.* 22; Palaiph. *Incred.* 31; Herakl. *Incred.* 1, 13; Philostr. *Imag.* 1.29; Ach. Tat. LK 3.6.3–3.7.9; Ovid *Met.* 4.607–5.263; Lucan BC 9.619–699; Manil. 5.538–619; Hyg. *Fab.* 63 f.; Nonn. *Dion.* 25.31–142, 30.264–277, 31.8–25, 47.498–741; Malal. 2, pp. 34–39 Dind.; Serv. *Aen.* 6.289, 7.372; Scholl. ABT on Il. 14.319; ps.-Liban. *Narr.* 35 f.; Vat. Myth. I 73, 130, 157; II 110–114; III 14.1–3. Vase-paintings in Woodward (1937); see figs. 23–25 in this chapter. In the notes on this section sources will be cited by authors' names only with occasionally the addition of a distinctive number or letter unless a more

Even more interesting than the large number of themes represented in the whole Perseus legend is the certain evidence that connects its principal episodes with Palestine, Cilicia, and Lycaonia (Th. 2A). As the Greeks told the story, they often placed Medusa in farthest Libya and Andromeda's sea monster in Ethiopia, i.e., vaguely in distant and fabulous regions that lay to the south, southeast, and southwest. But neither Libya nor Ethiopia is the scene in any known sources earlier than Euripides' *Andromeda*, which is only a century earlier than the earliest known source that places the Andromeda story specifically in Joppa, and is later than known sources which connect Perseus with Egypt and western Asia. Hesiod had placed the Gorgons on the far side of Ocean; and Pherekydes of Athens, so far as we know, was no more specific than that. Pindar, in fact, placed them to the north near the land of the Hyperboreans.[2]

On the coast of Palestine before the old Philistine-Phoenician city of Joppa, on a rocky prominence or island, were shown the marks of Andromeda's chains; either there or in the city the huge skeleton of the sea monster was on display, and near the shoreline a spring of reddish water was said to have got its color from the monster's blood. It was also said that Joppa received its name from Aiolos' daughter Iope, whom some authorities put in Kassiepeia's place as the wife of King Kepheus, who, they say, was king of Joppa or of all Syria. According to Mela, there were altars in Joppa inscribed to Kepheus and his brother Phineus. This Phineus, an Ethiopian prince in Ovid's narrative, and the better-known Phineus of the Harpy story, who cannot be clearly distinguished from him, are both connected with Phoenicia and Baal. Kepheus and Phineus were sons of Belos; the other Phineus was a son of Agenor Belos' son or of Phoinix or of Poseidon. The very name may be a variant of Phoinix, the original Phoenician,

---

specific citation seems desirable. On the Perseus legend, especially for its folktale relations, see Hartland (1894–96), Krappe (1933); see also the articles in LM and RE and Roscher (1879). Hartland's huge work is concerned with tracing the motives of the legend through the world's folklore. Only the third volume is concerned with the combat theme; the first two treat the miraculous birth and the life token.

[2] Eur. frag. 145 Nauck[2] and *ap.* ps.-Erat. 15. The earliest known source that places Andromeda in Joppa is ps.-Skylax, GGM p. 79; see note 3. Hes. *Theog.* 274 f.; Pherek. 11, 1.62 J; Pind. *Pyth.* 10.30 f.

eponymous ancestor of the nation, who is usually son or brother of Agenor.[3]

Now Euripides called Kepheus son of Phoinix or of Belos; there are *testimonia* to support either as father. This is evidence enough that Euripides too connected the story with Phoenicia, if not specifically with Joppa. Herodotos says that Kepheus was son of Belos and cites traditions that connect the Perseus legend with Egypt and Assyria. Hellanikos said that Kepheus ruled over Chaldaeans. Long before the fifth century Hesiod said that Kassiepeia was by Phoinix the mother of Phineus. So from the earliest sources known to us there are indications that the story was referred to the lands about the eastern end of the Mediterranean.[4]

The earliest sources point to Phoenicia, Egypt, or Assyria—without specific mention of a city. And Joppa is not the only place on the coast that was connected with the Perseus legend. A certain Pausanias of Damascus is authority for a story that identifies Perseus' sea-monster enemy with the River Orontes. Though the story is a rationalised version, it is nevertheless significant. Perseus came to the neighborhood of Mount Silpion to visit Ionians who had settled there. During his stay a severe storm came up, which caused the River Drakon, now called Orontes, to overflow and flood the land. Perseus told the Ionians to pray, and their prayers were followed by the fall of a ball of lightning from heaven that stopped the storm and checked the river. We have already become acquainted with the unrationalised version: the Orontes was once called Typhon, having sprung from the earth when Typhon, then a *drakôn*, as Strabo specifically says, fled from the lashings of Zeus's thunderbolts by plowing up the channel of the future river and disappearing into the ground, whence the source immediately gushed forth. Furthermore Mount Silpion

---

[3] Joppa as scene: Strabo 1.2.35, pp. 42 f., 16.2.28, p. 759; Jos. BJ 3.420; Mela 1.11; Plin. NH 5.13.69, 5.31.128, 6.29.182, 9.5.11; Paus. 4.35.9; Conon 40; Steph. Byz. 220 Holst.; Eust. on Dion. Per. 910. Belos father of Kepheus and Phineus: Herod. 7.61.3; Apollod. 2.1.4, who cites Euripides; father of Agenor and Phoinix: Schol. Rec. on Eur. *Phoen.* 247. Phineus son of Agenor: Apollod. 1.9.21; Apollon. *Arg.* 2.178; son of Phoinix, grandson of Agenor: Hes. frag. 31 Rz.; Pherek. 86, 1.83 J. Poseidon father of Agenor and Phineus: Apollod. *locc. cit.* and 3.1.1 (also of Belos). Phoinix Agenor's brother: Schol. Eur. *loc. cit.*

[4] Eur. *ap.* Hyg. *Astr.* 2.9 *et ap.* Apollod. 2.1.4; Herod. 7.61.3, cf. 2.91, 6.54; Hellan. 59 f., 1.122 f. J; Hes. *loc. cit.*

has been identified with a mountain to the south of Antioch. That places it very close to Mount Kasios; and one wonders whether it may not really be this mountain rather than another. Though all mountains were sacred, Kasios was the very home of the gods; and, according to Malalas, it was on Mount Silpion that Seleukos made offerings to Zeus Keraunios, i.e., to Baal as storm god. In any case it is apparent that the local tale of combat between Baal and the serpent Nahar (Yam as "Judge River," "Ruler of Streams") has been Hellenised both as the Zeus-Typhon myth and as the tale of Perseus' combat with a monster of the waters.[5]

Again, a coin type of the Phoenician city of Ake-Ptolemais shows Perseus with Gorgon's head in one hand, his curved sword in the other. Though it appears on coins of the third century A.D., it means that in Ake, as in Joppa and Antioch, the local Baal as dragon fighter was identified with Perseus.[6]

It is probable that the location of the Andromeda tale in Ethiopia arises from its Syro-Palestinian origins or relationships. It is the Erythraean Sea, on whose shores Andromeda was exposed, that links the legendary Ethiopia to Palestine. This name the Greeks gave to the whole Indian Ocean, or at least to the whole Arabian Gulf, including its arms, the Persian Gulf and the Red Sea; the last only has kept the name. Now there are two ways in which the Red Sea could enter the Greek tradition. There was the spring of blood-red water close by the scene of Andromeda's exposure at Joppa; according to Pausanias, there Perseus washed the monster's blood from his hands. Philostratos, describing a painting, says that springs of blood, which arose from the monster's corpse as it lay upon the strand, gave the Red Sea its name. That is, Philostratos has brought the spring of Joppa to the Ethiopian scene. Again, it may be that the Canaanite forerunner of the Andromeda tale came originally out of Arabia, which has the

---

[5] Paus. Damasc. 3, 4.467 f. M. On Silpion see RE 3A.114. The two versions of the Orontes myth illustrate nicely the two sides of the relation between the dragon and the waters. In Strabo's story the waters are released from the ground when Typhon is overcome; in the other Drakon floods the land and has to be restrained. Malal. 8, p. 197 Dind., says that Orontes was also called Drakon, Typhon, and Ophites.

[6] BMCC, Phoenicia, *Ptol.-Ace* nos. 35, 36, p. 134, pl. 17.3; cf. nos. 47, 51–53, pp. 137 f., pl. 17.11.

Erythraean Sea on three sides of it, and that in its new home some versions still retained the name of the sea which the Greeks called Erythraean. Furthermore, for Greeks at least, this name may have seemed to have something to do with Joppa's bloodlike spring. Now, for Greeks, Ethiopia was a land that bordered the Erythraean Sea; in their legends it was a paradise on the edges of the world: on one side ran the Ocean Stream, on whose banks Medusa lived. Their conception of Ethiopia was formed from exaggerated, even fantastic reports of India, Arabia Felix, and the lands to the south of Egypt. There was nothing new in their locating the story there, if the prototype of the Perseus legend had long since been told in Arabia and perhaps on the opposite African shore.[7]

Thus, Perseus' encounter with a sea monster was referred in the earliest extant records to the very regions where Baal fought Yam and Yahweh fought Leviathan, and, as we shall see, seems to be a Greek reflection of the Canaanite myth. But Perseus as slayer of Medusa is associated with Cilicia and Lykaonia, the lands of Typhon and Illuyankas. He was reputed to be founder of Tarsos, a tradition that caused W. M. Ramsay to think that his name could be an alternative form of Terseus or Tarseus as a Greek rendering of Baal Tarz, the Baal of Tarsos (p. 92, note 48). His founding of Tarsos appears to be placed both before and after he killed the Gorgon; in one tradition he launched his flight for Libya from a mountain close to Tarsos. In the Roman imperial

---

[7] Springs of blood: Paus. 4.35.9; Philostr. *Imag.* 1.29.2. Phoenicians on Red Sea: Herod. 1.1.1. Some ancient writers tried to reconcile the Ethiopian and Phoenician scenes in naïve ways: Pliny (NH 6.29.182) says that Syria was part of Kepheus' Ethiopian kingdom; and Strabo (1.2.35, pp. 42 f.) says that there are some who locate the Ethiopia of the story in Phoenicia; while Tacitus (*Hist.* 5.2) says that a band of Ethiopians fled from the tyranny of Kepheus and founded Jerusalem, becoming the Hebrew nation. Some ancient writers saw in *Aithiopê* a cognate of *Iopê*, in which form the name of both city and heroine often appears: see EM 473; Steph. Byz. 220 Holst.; LM 2.294; Tümpel (1888) 139 f. Notice that the name Kassiepeia also has the byforms *Kassiopê* (Ovid *Met.* 4.738; Hyg. *Fab.* 64.1) and *Kassiopeia* (Vat. Myth. I 80, the wife of Oineus): see LM 2.992–996. Kassiepeia and Iope are alternative names of Kepheus' wife, whose beauty rivalled that of the Nereids: and it is inevitable that the Canaanites derived the city's name *Yāphô* from the root YPY "beauty," whether or not that is a correct derivation. Tümpel, in giving the Perseus legend a Rhodian origin, whence it went eastwards to the Levantine coast, has the actual course turned around. If it is true that Perseus was a Philistine hero (see Wainwright 1935: 155), and that the Philistines brought his legend with them from Crete, then it was returning to the east whence its prototype had originally come. For the Minoan Cretans probably got it from Egypt, Syria, or Asia Minor.

period he appears on coin types of Tarsos, alternating with the native Sandon, who was also reputed to be founder of the city, and on coin types of other Cilician cities: Anemurion, Iotape, Karallia, Koropissos. The Koropissos type shows Perseus, Andromeda, and the dead sea monster, the only evidence of this legend in Cilicia. Finally, an inscription of the imperial period shows that the people of Aigeai claimed Perseus as founder of their city.[8]

Perseus' activity in Asia Minor also crossed the Tauros Range. He was reputed to be the founder of Ikonion, so named, it was said, because he set up there an image (icon) of himself holding the Gorgon's head. That this bit of etymological legend arose from the presence of such an image in Ikonion is shown by a coin type whose earliest representatives appear in the first century B.C., considerably earlier than the Perseus types of Cilicia; and it may well be that the image honored Perseus as legendary founder. Thus the Ikonion coin type confirms the value of Byzantine historians as reporters of Anatolian myth and legend: they alone connect Perseus with the foundation of Ikonion; and they add that thereafter Perseus fought and defeated the Cilicians and Isaurians, whereupon he founded Tarsos.[9]

There is early evidence that connects Perseus, not precisely with Tarsos or Ikonion, but with that neighborhood. Aeschylus speaks of the Gorgonean plains of Kisthene, where the Phorkides (Graiai) lived, and near them the Gorgons. It isn't certain where he located Kisthene; apparently he meant a fabulous land near the ends of earth. For beyond the Gorgons one comes to the griffons and the horse-riding Arimaspians who live on Pluto's stream; and beyond them are the springs of the sun and the Ethi-

---

[8] Perseus founder of Tarsos: Lucan BC 3.225; Solin. 38.3; Amm. Marc. 14.8.3; Nonn. *Dion.* 18.291–294; Joh. Ant. 6.18, 4.544 M; Malal. 2, pp. 36 f. Dind.; Cedren. 1.22cD. Set out from Tarsos: Lact. Plac. *Theb.* 3.461, 633; cf. BCH XXVIII (1904) 422, lines 20–23. P. on Cilician coin-types: BMCC, Lycaonia, Isauria, Cilicia, *Tars.* nos. 139–143, 182, 183, 228, 245, 246, 264–267, 304, pp. 185 f., 195, 206, 210, 214 f., 223, pls. 33.11, 36.8, 37.10; *Koropissos*, no. 4, p. 65, pl. 11.12; for Anemurion see *ibid.* p. xli; Karallia, p. 47, note 1; Iotape, p. xxxvii. Inscription of Aigeai: BCH *loc. cit.* In the Byzantine historians cited above Andromeda accompanied P. when he founded Tarsos and Ikonion; but she came from Ethiopia.

[9] Joh. Ant., Malal., Cedren., *locc. cit.*: BMCC, *ibid.*, *Iconium* nos. 1, 4, 5, 15, 16, pp. 4, 6, pl. 1.5, 7, 12. The folk etymology of *Ikonion* is different from that which adheres to the flood myth; see Fontenrose (1945) 116 with note 95.

opians. With Aeschylus' verses one may compare the local tradition of Cilician Aigeai: Perseus on his way to the Gorgons came to
Cilicia, the eastern limit (*terma*) of Asia. It seems to be implied
that this was also the limit of his journey; for there he set up an
image of Athena, his helper. Now, there was a city called Kisthene on the coast of Lykia, which obviously lay on Perseus'
route from Argos to Cilicia, and was admirably situated to be the
home of the Graiai, whom Perseus had to deal with before he
could reach the Gorgons. Those who first received and told the
story in Hellas had little knowledge of distant lands. The Cilician
and Lycian scenes were far away and soon assigned to the bounds
of the world.[10]

Finally, Perseus was associated with Egypt as early as the fifth
century B.C. Herodotos reports that the hero received divine worship in Chemmis. The importance of this testimony will become
clear as we proceed.[11]

Thus there are strong links, some of them early, that attach the
Perseus legends to the eastern coast of the Mediterranean. One
may still doubt whether they prove that the Greeks received the
legend cycle from the Levant and may suppose them to be entirely due to syncretistic identification of Greek with Oriental
figures. But if it can be shown that the Perseus legends not only
reproduce the whole pattern of the combat myth, but bear an
especially close resemblance to precisely the variants that were
told in Canaan and Cilicia, then all doubts should be dispelled.
Therefore we must now study the composite Perseus legend, just
as we find it in the sources, as a variant of the combat myth.[12]

A) *The Dragon Pair.*—In the two best-known tales among the

---

[10] Aesch. *Pr.* 792–809; BCH *loc. cit.* On Lycian Kisthene see Strabo 14.3.7, p.
666; Tümpel (1888) 160 f.; Sundwall (1913) 107; RE 11.524 (where a Mysian Kisthene
is also mentioned).

[11] Herod. 2.91; see also 2.15.1, 6.54. It appears that Perseus was also associated with
Cyprus. Nonnos (*Dion.* 13.461–463) says that Salamis was the city of Perseus *archêgonos*,
for whom Teukros built the city's ramparts. H. J. Rose in his note *ad loc.* says that this
cannot be the hero Perseus, since legend places him several generations before Teukros.
But legend is full of anachronisms, and many local traditions were never fitted into the
system, such as it is, of pan-Hellenic legendary genealogy and chronology. Since P. was
reputedly founder of several cities on the opposite Cilician coast, he might easily have
been attached to the foundation legend of Salamis too. Again, it is possible that in verse
461 the reading ᾧ, translated "for whom," is wrong. It was emended by Koechly to ᾗ;
and I should think that οὗ is also possible; MSS show no iota subscript.

[12] On Oriental elements in the Perseus legend see Hopkins (1934), Wainwright (1935).

legends of Perseus the hero fights a sea monster and kills the Gorgon Medusa. The monster is usually called *kêtos* by the Greeks, *belua* by the Latin writers, a neuter Greek noun and a feminine Latin noun. There can be little doubt, however, that the creature was male in the usual story: the sex is indicated by the maiden victim (p. 304). We have also seen that the monster was identified with Drakon, the river god Orontes, definitely a male deity. Now Medusa seems to have no more to do with Ketos, as we shall call him, than the circumstance that the Andromeda story is usually tacked on to the Medusa story as an incident of Perseus' return. Yet both are related to Poseidon, Medusa as his mistress, Ketos as his subject and minister of his wrath, probably his son (Th. 1B) as a creature whom he raised from the sea to attack Kepheus' land. For Poseidon corresponds to Yam, Philo of Byblos' Nereus; and Ketos corresponds to Lotan-Nahar (Leviathan), Philo's Typhon son of Nereus, but identified with Yam himself at Ugarit (p. 134). To Poseidon Medusa bore Chrysaor, who by an Oceanid became father of the monster Geryon, who lived at Erytheia, a name that in meaning and form recalls the Erythraean Sea. As son and father of monsters, and as son of the sea, it would seem that Chrysaor himself was a monstrous sea creature, so that he and Ketos may be two forms of a single original.[13]

Medusa as the Gorgon of the aegis is that Gorgon-Aigis-Kampe, that mighty companion and protectress of Gigantes or Titans whom Zeus or Athena killed (p. 243): she bore the same relation to the king of the Gigantes, whatever his name, as Delphyne-Echidna to Typhon; he was her dragon consort. On the other hand, Pliny, speaking of the marks of Andromeda's chains at Joppa, adds that the fabulous Keto is worshipped there (colitur illic fabulosa Ceto). He may mean the *kêtos* of the Greek story, or there may be a mistake in the text; but as the text stands it refers to a female sea monster, whom Pliny, by calling her *fabulosa*, appears to identify with that Keto who was mate of Phorkys

[13] For Ketos see Eur. frags. 121, 145 Nauck²; Soph. *ap.* ps.-Erat. 16, 36; Apollod.; Ach. Tat.; Philostr.; Lucian *DMar.*; Ovid 4; Hyg. Poseidon, Medusa, Chrysaor: Apollod. 2.4.2, 2.5.10; Ovid 4.786, 798–803; Hyg. *Fab.* 151.2 and praef. 40. According to Malalas, Andromeda was exposed to Poseidon himself. Roscher considers Ketos to be an eastern variant of the Gorgon: LM 1.347.

and mother of the Gorgons and Skylla. As I have pointed out several times in the course of this study, mother and daughter, father and son, are often two forms of one mythical being that has received different names in different places; the genealogies are attempts at systematising the chaotic materials of popular myth. As a deity worshipped at Joppa, Keto must really be Astarte or Atargatis as goddess of the sea, whose image at Ascalon had fish-form from the waist down, and who on coins of that city was pictured riding on the back of a similarly shaped male figure, who carries a trident. I have elsewhere conjectured that the merman figure is Dagon; but it may be Yam, if indeed the two gods were not sometimes fused. So behind Ketos and Keto we may see Yam and Astarte as consorts. Ketos-Leviathan is the companion or double of Poseidon-Yam, Medusa's mate, as I have already pointed out.[14]

Hence we have reason to see in Medusa the female companion of Ketos (Th. 1c). But the Greek legend as we know it seems to be a composite of the variants of several localities. The Andromeda episode may very well come from Joppa; the Medusa episode probably does not, nor can its original home be conjectured with any like certainty, though it may have been a Cilician city.

Typhon and Echidna were parents of a male Gorgon, according to Hyginus; then Gorgon and Keto were the parents of Medusa and the other two female Gorgons. Gorgon here takes Phorkys' place, though Phorkys and Keto are, as usual, parents of the Graiai. We have seen that the Greeks gave the name Typhon to the Canaanite Yam-Leviathan; also that Phorkys and Keto are hardly more than Typhon and Echidna as denizens of the sea. Finally, no less an authority than Euripides says that Ge was the mother of the Gorgon.[15]

B) *Chaos and Disorder.*—Medusa and her sister Gorgons lived on the far side of Ocean, on Night's side of the stream, at the world's edge, where the rays of the sun and moon never penetrate. To reach them Perseus went through trackless, barren, and stony

[14] Plin. NH 5.13.69. See Lucian *Dea Syr.* 14; Fontenrose (1951) 140 f. with notes 65, 68. Notice Poseidon and Nauplios (p. 481) as ancestors of Polydektes: Pherek. 4, 1.60 J; Argos and Phorbas as ancestors of Akrisios: Paus. 2.16.1 f.
[15] Hyg. *Fab.* 151 and praef. 9, 39; Eur. *Ion* 989.

wastes, whose only vegetation was a scraggly growth of trees. More
specifically, they are sometimes placed in farthest Libya, occasionally beside the fabled Lake Tritonis or near the Atlas Mountains.
Ketos too, according to Euripides, came out of the Atlantic sea
to take Andromeda: another indication of a close link between
him and the Gorgon.[16]

That Medusa and the Gorgons are demons of both sea and
darkness (Ths. 2E, 3F) is therefore clear from the parents assigned
them, from their habitat, and from their very nature. In modern
Greek folklore all nymphs of the sea are called Gorgons, whereas
the Nereids have taken the place of dryads and naiads in field
and wood. That the Gorgons are also death demons is plain from
their likeness to the Erinyes in appearance (fig. 23) and from the
power of Medusa's glance to bring instant death to any man by
turning him to stone. In the desert wastes about Medusa's home
Perseus saw the petrified images of men and beasts: a graveyard
fantasy in which the corpse becomes assimilated to the statue of
the deceased—the Gorgons' realm is truly a land of eternal sleep.
Medusa lay in deathlike sleep when Perseus beheaded her—only
a few of her snakes stayed awake to guard her—and her sisters
slept nearby. She is a Tiamat who wants complete inactivity and
deepest darkness.[17]

It is not strange that the terrible demoness of death should be
thought to dwell at the western limit of the world. To Semites,
Egyptians, and Greeks that would mean the Atlantic shores of
Africa and Spain. Hence Gorgon and Lamia were often placed in
Libya. But Medusa and Lamia have more than residence in common: so many and striking are the parallels between them and
their stories, especially when the scene is Libyan, that they may
be considered two forms, separated not far back, of a single demoness that belonged to a single variant of the combat myth.

1. Each was at first a beautiful woman who later became ugly

---

[16] By Ocean and Night: Hes., Aesch. *Pr.* 796–809, Pherek. 11, Apollod., Ovid 4.
Libya: Dion. Skyt., Paus. 2.21, Ovid 4, Lucan, Palaiph., Serv. 6. See Eur. frag. 145
Nauck²; Philostr.; cf. Diod. 3.70. Palaiph. places the Ethiopians on islands off the west
coast of Libya, which were ruled over by Medusa and her sisters.

[17] Gorgons as sea nymphs: Lawson (1910) 184–190; for a folktale of the Gorgons
and their queen see Legrand (1899) 153–159. Gorgons' sleep: Apollod., Ovid, Lucian
DMar.

as a result of the punishment that a goddess inflicted on her because of a god's love for her. As Hera punished Lamia, her rival
for Zeus's love, so Athena punished Medusa; either because Poseidon lay with her in the very temple of the goddess or because
Medusa boasted that her tresses were more beautiful than Athena's (or simply judged herself more beautiful than Athena),
whereupon the goddess gave her locks of live snakes instead. In
the Medusa tale, rivalry and the god's love have become separated
from each other in the two variations on the theme.[18]

2. Both were queens in Libya. Medusa's very name means
queen, and though she appears as a queen only in euhemerised
sources, one must notice that all sources of the story of the Libyan
queen Lamia show traces of Euhemerism too. Medusa was the
Gorgon queen, still a potent figure in Greek folklore.[19]

3. As Medusa was Poseidon's mistress, so Lamia was sometimes
said to be his daughter (p. 107, note 30).

4. To Lamia Zeus gave the power of removing her eyes, so that
she could sleep. The Gorgons' sisters, the three Gray Ladies
(Graiai), who guarded the approach to the Gorgons' realm, had
one removable eye among them. In some sources, however, it is
the three Gorgons that had but one removable eye, though the
writers who say so may have confused the Gorgons with the
Graiai. However that may be, it is probable that the two sets of
triplet Phorkides were originally identical. The removable eye
of the Graiai seems to have some relation to Medusa's stony eye
(for sometimes the singular is found): each is a version of the
evil eye (Th. 3D). For in a legend that has already been noticed
(p. 237, note 27), the Lydian queen Tudo-Nysia-Habro, wife of
Kandaules and Gyges, a second Omphale, had both a double
pupil and a dragon-stone (*drakontités*) which gave her remarkable powers of vision. But both together are clearly unnecessary,
as K. F. Smith has pointed out. What she had, it seems to me, was
a removable eye of wondrous power. It was an eye that could

---

[18] Medusa: Ovid 4, Apollod., Paus. 2.21, Serv. 6, Schol. Vet. on Pind. *Pyth.* 12.13
(24). Lamia: see p. 100, note 17. Rivalry in beauty has a very close parallel in the story
of the Lamia-like Gerana, pp. 100 f.

[19] Queen Medusa: Dionys. Skyt. *ap.* Diod. 3.55.3; Paus. 2.21.5; Palaiph. Lamia: see
p. 100. The Gorgon queen is also called Lamia of the sea in modern Greek folklore: Lawson
(1910) 176.

penetrate the invisible, so that with it the queen could see the invisible Gyges. The Graiai no doubt penetrated the deep outer darkness with their eye; in any case they were plunged into the darkness of the blind when robbed of it. Moreover Perseus had to get possession of it before he could find the Hades' cap of invisibility that would enable him to approach Medusa unseen. Finally, when Lamia removed her ever-wakeful eyes and went to sleep, her subjects then felt free of her tyranny and did as they wished: it is as though her eyes could see everywhere and hold everyone in thrall. So though Lamia's insomnia may seem utterly opposed to Medusa's eternal sleep, behind both stands a demoness who was plunged into blindness or sleep on losing her potent removable eye.[20]

5. As Lamia became literally a wild beast (p. 100), so Medusa became partly serpentine (Th. 3B).

6. The Lamia lived in a cave in mountains south or southeast of Carthage; the Graiai and Gorgons lived in caves of the Atlas Mountains (Th. 2B).[21]

7. The Gorgons, like Lamia, made destructive attacks upon their Libyan neighbors (Th. 4A). According to Prokles of Carthage, cited by Pausanias, Medusa was a wild woman who came from the desert to harm the people about Lake Tritonis. According to Lucan she brought stony death to the peoples of Ethiopia. Her destructive raids on African peoples suggest Gerana's attacks upon the Pygmies (p. 101). Gerana, the crane-woman, a form of Lamia, was the mate of Kyknos, the swan; Aeschylus says that the

---

[20] Lamia's removable eyes: Diod. 20.41.5; Schol. Vet. on Aristoph. Pax 758. Graiai's one eye: Pherek. 11, Apollod., Ovid 4. Gorgons' one eye: Palaiph.; Scholl. Vett. on Pind. Pyth. 12.13 (24) and on Lyk. 846; Serv. 6; Schol. G on German. p. 147 Breysig. Lydian queen's double pupil and dragonstone: Ptol. Heph. ap. Phot. Bibl. p. 150 Bekk.; K. F. Smith (1902) 367–374. Gorgon's petrifying eye in singular: Nonn. Dion. 8.101, 25.81 f., 30.265, 47.560, 665. In the folk beliefs of Nigeria the sacred pythons' heads carry a precious magical stone that sheds a brilliant light: S. Davis (1953) 36. It is strange that Perseus had to use a mirror to avoid looking directly at Medusa, though she lay asleep and her eyes were closed. But notice that in general Pherek., Apollod., and Ovid (see p. 275, note 1) do not refer to Medusa's eye(s); rather it is her head or face that can turn a man to stone at the mere sight of it (but see Met. 5.241). This suggests that in at least one form of the story her eye(s) gave her unlimited vision rather than petrifying power.

[21] Lamia: Diod. 20.41. Graiai, Gorgons: Ovid Met. 4.772–775; Aesch. frag. 261 Nauck²; Nonn. Dion. 25.59, 31.17.

three Graiai had the forms of swans (*kyknomorphoi*); and the Gorgons were winged creatures (fig. 23).[22]

8. The names Gorgo and Gorgyra appear among the Hekataia (p. 117) along with Lamia, Empusa, Mormo, and Gello. With Hekate and the Erinyes the Gorgons share snaky locks. The wife

FIGURE 23. PERSEUS AND MEDUSA

of Acheron and mother of Askalaphos is known as Gorgyra, Orphne, or Styx; and so the Gorgon is equated with the under-world darkness and waters. That Styx and Hekate are funda-mentally the same powerful goddess of the underworld is plain from Hesiod's *Theogony,* where in successive passages the two are described in similar terms: each a mighty pre-Olympian goddess whose offices and privileges Zeus did not take away, but whom he honors and reveres. And whereas Styx is Ocean's daughter and carries a tenth of his water, Hekate is powerful upon the sea:

---

[22] Prokles, frag. 1, 4.484 M; Lucan BC 9.650 f.; cf. Diod. 3.52.4, 3.54.7.

there she has rights and dominion, and equally with Poseidon she receives the prayers of sailors and fishermen.[23]

9. Aigis—who spread fire through Phrygia, Cilicia, Phoenicia, Egypt, and Libya (p. 244)—is obviously a variant of Medusa, since the corresponding figure in Euripides' version of the tale is called Gorgon, and since the Gorgon's head appears upon the aegis. Hekate and Empusa were also fire demons. Now, since on the one hand Medusa is so closely associated with Cilicia and Phoenicia, and since on the other Lamia is called daughter of Belos and Libya and is thus brought into the Greeks' legendary genealogy of Phoenician kings, and since the Empusa of Corinth was a Phoenician woman, we can conjecture that each is the bitch demoness Fire, transferred to north Africa with the Phoenician colonies that settled there. So Greek legend helps to elucidate an obscure passage in Ugaritic literature.[24]

The Gorgons' dark realm is placed near each of the Greek paradises: the Ethiopians' land to the south and east, the Hesperides to the west, and the Hyperboreans to the north. According to Aeschylus, as we have seen, just beyond the Gorgons live one-eyed Arimaspians, beyond whom live the Ethiopians; but according to Herodotos the Arimaspians live near the Hyperboreans. It is evident that the Gorgons could be placed on any edge of the world; but the Greeks seem in general to have settled finally on west or southwest.[25]

Ketos was also a death demon, as will become clear when I discuss the Andromeda tale as a variant of subtype IV. As a sea monster he is represented in vase paintings as more or less fishlike.

---

[23] Strabo 1.2.8, p. 19, names Gorgo along with Lamia, Mormolyka, and Ephialtes; Hymn *ap*. Hippol. *Ref. Haer*. 4.35 gives Hekate the names Gorgo, Mormo, and Bombo. Lucian *Philops*. 22: Hekate had the frightful appearance of a Gorgon; see *ibid*. 2. Apollod. 1.5.3 names Gorgyra as Acheron's wife. Acheron, Orphne, Askalaphos: Ovid *Met*. 5.539–541. Styx as Askalaphos' mother: Serv. *Georg*. 1.39; Vat. Myth. I 7, II 100. Styx and Hekate: Hes. *Theog*. 383–452. Notice Mormo as horse (Theocr. 15.40) and Medusa as mother of Pegasos (Apollod., Ovid; see p. 275, note 1), and actually shown in Centaur form on a vase relief (Woodward 1937: fig. 3, 650–600 B.C.).

[24] See pp. 118, 133. Hekate, Empusa, and fire: Aristoph. *Ran*. 293 f.; Orph. Hymn. Mag. 3.10; Hippol. *Ref. Haer*. 4.36; Schol. Vet. on Apollon. *Arg*. 3.861. Lamia, Belos' daughter: Schol. Vet. on Aristoph. *Pax* 758. Libya is mother of Belos and Agenor: Apollod. 3.1.1, Hyg. *Fab*. 157.1 (see 149, where Kassiopia is her mother). Phoenician Empusa: Philostr. *Vit. Ap*. 4.25.

[25] Hesperides: Hes., Ovid 4. Hyperboreans: Pind. 10. Arimaspians: Aesch. *Prom*. 803–809; Herod. 3.116, 4.13.2, 4.27.

But the fish monsters of art are often very like snakes in appearance (cf. fig. 22 and p. 231 above); and figure 25 shows a creature that can certainly be called a sea serpent. Yet a sixth-century vase painting (fig. 24) shows Ketos with a mammallike head which

FIGURE 24. PERSEUS AND KETOS

appears more canine than anything else; yet it may also recall Ovid's comparison of Ketos with a fierce boar. Moreover the Perseus legend's dragoness has boar traits: according to Apollodoros, the Gorgons had huge teeth like boars' tusks. Since they have live snakes for hair and are also shown with snakes about their waists, and since they are sea spirits too, they correspond closely to Ketos in their bestial components, if not in superficial appearance.[26]

[26] See Ovid 4.732 f., Apollod. 2.4.2. For representations of Ketos see Woodward (1937) figs. 9, 31–33; LM 3.2053 f., fig. 11. For a thorough study of Greek fish-tailed monsters see Shepard (1940), especially 8, 28–30, 42, 58 f., 78, figs. 38, 39, 64, 78, on doglike and boarlike *kētē:* and pls. 3.4, 10, 12, 16, for snakelike sea monsters. Ketos did not acquire the shape of the familiar, but unclassical, dinosaurlike dragon until the Renaissance; see the paintings of Piero di Cosimo, Rubens, and Lord Leighton. For Gorgons' snakes elsewhere than on head see Woodward, figs. 7, 11, 13, 21. Medusa, like Typhon, is given credit for producing the reptilian class: Apollon. *Arg.* 4.1515–1517; Ovid *Met.* 4.617–620; Schol. on Nic. *Ther.* 11. In the several snake heads of the Gorgons' members we can discern Th. 3c.

The apotropaic use of Gorgons' heads upon Greek temples and other buildings is well known. In this use they resemble those ugly and frightening masks that were called Mormolykeia. The main difference seems to be that the latter belong to costume, the former to architecture and sculpture. In his great work on masks and dragons in Asia, Combaz has found a very close relation between masks and dragon images in symbolism, type, and function. Either sculptured dragon heads or Gorgon-type heads have been used in architecture as antefixes and gargoyles, and as guardian images over doors and openings. Of special interest are the Humbaba and Pazuzu heads of Mesopotamia, which correspond precisely to the Gorgon heads of Greece, as Clark Hopkins too has shown. Beelzebub is used to cast out Beelzebub; and this parallel use of dragon head and Gorgon head reveals still more clearly that dragons too are infernal spirits.[27]

Ketos was gigantic (Th. 3A). According to Pliny, his skeleton, which Scaurus had brought to Rome from Joppa, was forty feet long with a spine that was a cubit thick; and its height was greater than an elephant's. According to Ovid, Ketos was as large as a ship. Medusa too is occasionally described as huge (*pelôros*). Atlas is another opponent of Perseus: he watched over the Garden of the Hesperides (Th. 2c) and tried to drive the hero out of his land; whereupon Perseus turned him into a mountainous mass of stone. Atlas as a gigantic mass of rock and as Perseus' enemy appears to combine in one figure the Upelluri and Ullikummi of the Hurrian myth (p. 212).[28]

In Atlas the stony walls of chaos can be seen. As guardian of

---

[27] Mormolykeia: Aristoph. frag. 131 HG; Hesych. M1665; Suid. M1250; EM 336; Scholl. Vett. on Aristoph. *Pax* 474 and *Thesm.* 417, and on Theocr. 15.40. See Hopkins (1934) 343–351, Combaz (1945), especially 26–33 on Humbaba and Pazuzu, 208–229 on architectural uses, 230–249 for summary. Medusa's deadly visage or eye is connected with this apotropaic use; but the countenance that frightens only demons in architectural superstition is universally potent in myth.

[28] Ketos' size: Plin. NH 9.5.11; Ovid 4; Manil.; Hyg. *Astr.* 2.31. Medusa is *pelôros*, *megas Phobos*: Od. 11.634; *Shield*. Atlas and Perseus: Ovid *Met.* 4.627–662; notice especially 660–662:

> . . . tum partes altus in omnes
> crevit in immensum: sic di statuistis: et omne
> cum tot sideribus caelum requievit in illo,

which can be compared with Ullikummi's growth (p. 212). The story was known much earlier to the poet Polyidos (*ap.* Tzetz. *in* Lyc. 879, *ap.* EM 164), who represents Atlas as a herdsman.

the golden apples he placed a wall of mountains around the gar-den; as himself a mountain range he shut them in—i.e., he is the mountain wall that encloses the soma (p. 200). Furthermore, his mountain range barred the way to the Gorgons: there the guardian Graiai had their post.[29]

Medusa is clearly not far removed from a Tiamat-like chaos hag, a demoness of sea, darkness, and death. Ketos is her male counterpart, modelled upon Yam and Leviathan, yet containing something of Mot too, as we shall see. Both represent not only the primeval chaos, but also those destructive forces that recur at regular or irregular intervals. Ketos is theriomorphic flood: according to some sources Poseidon sent both Ketos and a flood against the Ethiopians. Clearly either sea monster or flood is sufficient. Furthermore, as we have seen, the rationalising Pausanias of Damascus explicitly identifies Ketos-Drakon with a flood of the Orontes. Medusa caused plague and pestilence in Libya. And it seems that Aiolos gave Perseus trouble by sending his winds against him after Medusa's death, much as his Chinese counterpart Fung Po aided Ch'ih Yu (p. 494).[30]

C) *Theomachy.*—The next episode of the combat myth is found mainly outside the Medusa and Andromeda legends. It is in the dealings of Akrisios, Polydektes, Kepheus, and Phineus with Perseus that we find a struggle for the throne (Th. 5A), usurpation, and hints of celestial war (Th. 7G). The well-known story of Akrisios' attempt to destroy the infant Perseus because of a prophecy that Danae's son would grow up to kill him has essentially the same theme as the myth of Zeus and Kronos. In the legend that we know best, Perseus kills Akrisios unintentionally and thereafter gives up the throne of Argos, exchanging it with his cousin Megapenthes for Tiryns and Mycenae. But this turn may be a later pious effort to absolve the revered hero Perseus of parricide; also the legend has probably been influenced by others (e.g., Laios-Oedipus) in which the doom that everyone seeks to

---

[29] Ovid 4, Diod., Lucan. It was a rocky coast on which Andromeda was exposed to Ketos: Achill. Tat., Ovid 4; see citations in note 3, p. 277, *init.*

[30] Ketos as flood: Apollod.; Manil.; Paus. Damasc. 3, 4.468 M. Cf. Mela 1.11: Joppa, where Kepheus reigned, was founded before the flood. Medusa causes pestilence: Lucan. Aiolos' winds: Ovid *Met.* 4.621–626, 663. For association of M. with springs (Th. 2D) see e.g., Ovid *Met.* 5.254–264: her son Pegasos made Hippokrene; see pp. 367–371; for Ketos' springs see Philostr.; Paus. Damasc. *loc. cit.*

avoid comes to pass inevitably. It is only a late and untrustworthy authority, a Vatican Mythographer, who says that Perseus purposely turned Akrisios to stone with the Gorgon's head. He has apparently confused Akrisios with his brother Proitos, whom Perseus thus destroyed in Ovid's narrative; for Proitos then held the Argive throne after taking it from Akrisios. In any case, there was a version in which Perseus intentionally killed the reigning king of Argos; and, according to several authorities, he took the Argive kingship without qualms. Proitos as the twin brother of Akrisios appears to be his double: each, it is said, took the crown from the other. Both were enemies of Perseus; and as Akrisios cast Perseus into the sea, so Proitos' son Megapenthes, in a tradition different from that just mentioned, killed Perseus. Proitos himself tried to kill the hero Bellerophon, who closely resembles Perseus. So the sources still show traces of an earlier story in which Perseus deliberately killed Akrisios and took his throne.[31]

The struggle for sovereignty is repeated in the conflict between Polydektes and Perseus on Seriphos. Polydektes wanted to destroy Perseus and so sent him on a dangerous quest from which he didn't expect him to return. During Perseus' absence his mother and Diktys, his fosterfather, had to take refuge at an altar to escape the king's violence. When Perseus had rescued them and turned Polydektes to stone, he gave the throne to Diktys, who was Polydektes' brother. In another version Polydektes actually married Danae and reared Perseus. When Akrisios came to seize the mother and boy he took their part, and he never made an attempt to get rid of Perseus, who held funeral games in his honor after his death—he has, in fact, pretty much taken Diktys' place. Again,

---

[31] Hesych. A2575 says that among the Phrygians Kronos was called Akrisias. See Krappe (1933) 230 f. Perseus killed Akrisios: Vat. Myth. II 111; he killed Proitos: Ovid 5; Lact. *Narr.* 5.2. Akrisios and Proitos were twins: Apollod. 2.2.1. Megapenthes killed Perseus: Hyg. *Fab.* 244.3. Exchange with Megapenthes: Apollod., Paus. 2.16.3. Proitos and Bellerophon: Il. 6.152–170. Perseus becomes king in Argos: Hyg. *Fab.* 63, Conon, Scholl. AB on Il. Ovid seems to imply that Perseus became king of Argos on killing Proitos. An indication that the Akrisios-Perseus plot came from the Near East appears in Ael. NA 12.21, the only ancient Greek allusion to the legend of Gilgamesh: the king of Babylon learned from soothsayers that his daughter's son would take the kingdom from him; he kept her under strict guard to no avail, since a lover reached her and impregnated her; when a boy was born the guards, in fear of the king's wrath, threw the child from the citadel; but an eagle (Imdugud?) seized him in mid-air and carried him to a garden, where the caretaker was strongly attracted to the beautiful child and reared him, naming him Gilgamos.

Perseus received divine honors on Seriphos, a fact which suggests that he became king of Seriphos in the local legend, and king of the gods in a still earlier myth.[32]

In both Argos and Seriphos the story seems to follow the pattern of the Jason-Aison-Pelias legend or, for that matter, the myths of Marduk-Ea-Kingu and Teshub-Anu-Kumarbi: Perseus' father (or grandfather) was overthrown by his uncle (or father?); later Perseus killed the usurper and recovered the throne, nominally for his father (or grandfather), but in fact for himself. Obviously the Seriphian legend repeats the Argive legend and has been added to it in the composite Perseus legend of classical authors. Yet it has merged with an episode of the original myth: the champion's descent to the lower world.

For Polydektes is not only the displaced king, but clearly the lord of death too. His name, which means "receiver of many," is an epithet of Hades. He had, moreover, some relation to Medusa: it was for her head that he sent Perseus into the darkness, expecting that Medusa would destroy him. So he who is usurping king in the Seriphian legend has become identified in the Argive legend with the death god who awaits the hero at the end of his journey into the other world: for here too the sea into which Akrisios cast Perseus means the realm of death.[33]

In the Andromeda legend too the theme of conflict for sovereignty is reflected. Readers of the *Metamorphoses* will remember how Phineus, Andromeda's uncle, to whom she had been betrothed, disrupted Perseus' wedding feast when he burst in with his companions, claimed the bride for himself, and started a brawl that Ovid describes in the manner of his Centauromachy

---

[32] Pherek. 11, 12; Apollod.; Ovid 5; Hyg. 64. Polydektes married Danae: Hyg. 63; cf. 273.4. On Perseus' worship see Paus. 2.18.1, where it is said that at Seriphos and Athens he received "greatest honors" (*megistai timai*) and had *temenos* and *bômos*. According to Serv. 7, Danae's chest was washed ashore in Italy, where she married a native king and helped found Ardea.

[33] Hades Polydektes: Hom. Hymn 2.9; Cornut. 35, p. 74 Lang; cf. Hades Polydegmon: Hom. Hymn 2.17, 31, 404; Cornut. 35. *Akrisios* too may be interpreted as a name of the death god, meaning that he takes without choosing; Hades is called *akritos:* Orph. Hymn 18.9; Epigr. 204.3 Kaibel. Among the ancestors of Polydektes (Pherek. 4, 1.60 J; Hes. frag. 6 Rz.) are Poseidon, Nauplios (see p. 481), Peristhenes (exceedingly mighty), Magnes (the great, but identified with the eponym of Magnesia), and Damastor (subduer), whose name appears among the Gigantes (Claud. 37.101–103) and recalls Damastes-Prokrustes of the Theseus legend, who as a horrible innkeeper certainly represents Hades.

(Th. 7G). Hyginus says that it was Agenor to whom Andromeda was betrothed; while Conon says that both Phineus and Phoinix wooed her, and that Kepheus decided in Phoinix's favor, but concealing his preference, planned that Phoinix abduct her; whereupon Phoinix carried her off in a ship named Ketos. Though Euhemeristic, Conon's version reveals clearly the alliance of rebel god and dragon.[34]

As Kepheus points out in Ovid's narrative, Phineus merely looked on as Andromeda was chained to the rock, acquiescing in the sacrifice, and didn't lift a hand to save her. The same can be said of Kepheus himself. Again, when Phineus attacked Perseus, Kepheus soon washed his hands of the affair and left the scene. According to Hyginus, he actually took part with his brother against Perseus and plotted to kill the hero secretly; but Perseus discovered the plot and turned the conspirators to stone. And, according to a late Euhemeristic version, which appears to reflect, as such versions often do, earlier phases of the legend, Kepheus invaded Perseus' realm, after the hero had abducted Andromeda; in the ensuing battle Perseus died from looking into the face of his own Gorgon head, which had no effect upon Kepheus, whose blindness from old age was unknown to Perseus. Finally, we are told that Perses, Perseus' son and double, inherited Kepheus' kingdom. Kepheus-Phineus was the grandson of Poseidon, who sent the monster, and the son of Belos (i.e., Baal), the Syro-Palestinian equivalent of Egyptian Ammon, who in Apollodoros' and Ovid's narratives ordered Andromeda's sacrifice. He represents that earlier ruler of the gods, El or Enlil or Kronos, who is now helped by the champion, though diminished in power and glory thereafter, now hostile to him and finally driven from his throne.[35]

---

[34] Phineus: Ovid Met. 5, Apollod., Vat. Myth. I 73. Agenor: Hyg. 64. Phoinix: Conon. Centauromachy: Ovid Met. 12.210–535. Notice that Phineus' supporters include warriors called Phorbas (Met. 5.74–78), Phlegyas (87), Polydegmon (85), Klymenos (98; see p. 328), Erytos Aktor's son (79–84; see p. 483), Halkyoneus (133–139), and Eryx (195–199; see p. 338, note 27). It was truly a gigantomachy.

[35] Phineus' failure to help Andromeda: Ovid Met. 5.19–23. Kepheus' failure to check Phineus: ibid. 43–45. Kepheus vs. Perseus: Hyg. 64; Malal.; Cedren. 1.23B; Joh. Ant. 6.18, 4.544 f. M. Perses Kepheus' successor: Herod. 7.61.3; Hellan. 59 f., 1.122 f. J; Apollod. 2.4.5. MSS of Hyg. Fab. praef. 7 list Cepheus among the children of Pontus and Terra; may this not stand, once we have realised Kepheus' true nature? Ammon ordered sacrifice: Apollod.; Ovid 4.671, 5.17.

The role of Kassiepeia supports my view of the legend. She vaunted her beauty above that of the Nereids, and so committed Medusa's offense against Athena and Gerana's against Hera and Artemis. There is hardly any other legend about her; but she, or at least a woman of the same name, appears also as wife of Phoinix or of Epaphos, and as mistress of Zeus. The evidence, such as it is, makes it very probable that she is a form of Astarte or Asherat, whose ambiguous role has been noticed several times.[36]

In another story Perseus set out to win himself a kingdom: he is the young Baal who must win supreme power for himself. It is significant that he wished to take the Assyrian throne from the sons of Ninos, his uncle, and that he finally succeeded by defeating and killing Sardanapalos, and that during his rise to power he came upon Medusa in Libya and cut off her head. In a related version he led an army against the Gorgon nation that dominated western Libya, or sailed with a fleet against the Atlantic island where Medusa reigned as queen of Ethiopians; there he killed Medusa and seized the potent Gorgon image.[37]

There is also the struggle between Perseus and Dionysos, with which I shall deal in chapter xiii (p. 388). That combat shows better than any other in the whole Perseus cycle that we are not really dealing with heroic legend, but with myths of gods and demons, in short, the combat myth of the Near East. The Perseus legend seems close to the Canaanite myths; and if that is so, it fills in the gaps of the Ugaritic poems and of Eusebios' extracts from Philo of Byblos. It has a powerful dragoness, whose role is slighted

---

[36] On Kassiepeia's mates other than Kepheus see Hes. frag. 31 Rz.; Apollod. 3.1.2; Hyg. *Fab.* 149; LM 2.986–988. According to Schol. Vet. on Eur. *Phoen.* 5, Phoinix married Telephe, daughter of *Epimedusa.* Notice that although Kassiepeia offended the Nereids, it was Andromeda who paid the penalty. Behind this strange feature there may lie a story in part like *Snow-White:* matre pulchra filia pulchrior; consequently the jealous mother wanted to destroy her daughter. It was precisely Andromeda's beauty that arrested Perseus' attention as he flew by: Ovid 4, Lucian *DMar.*, Ach. Tat., Philostr. So at first it was perhaps Kassiepeia against Andromeda; then Kassiepeia, taking over part of the Andromeda role, was replaced by the Nereids, who represent the dragoness as demoness of the waters. Hyginus' statement that Kassiepeia placed Andromeda's beauty above that of the Nereids seems to combine two earlier versions. A link between Kepheus and Medusa may be seen in the obscure tradition that places Kepheus Aleos' son in Arcadian Tegea: he possessed locks of Medusa's hair that ensured the city's invincibility: Paus. 8.47.5.

[37] (1) Malal.; Joh. Ant. 6.18, 4.544 M; Vat. Myth. I 130, II 112, III 14. (2) Dionys. Skyt., Paus. 2.21, Palaiph. Notice the anachronism in Perseus' meeting with Sardanapalos. For wars among Gorgons, Amazons, and Atlantians, see Dionys. Skyt.

in the aforesaid documents; but we should notice that the Andromeda tale, the Perseus legend that can be most directly connected with Palestine, neglects the dragoness, retaining her in only much-disguised forms. The patriarchal Canaanite peoples were likely to make more of the dragon and to diminish the dragoness' role. But the myth that they adopted had a very powerful dragoness, who can still be seen in the Medusa legend, which probably came to the Perseus cycle from the Canaanites' Anatolian neighbors.

The Andromeda legend has not only Andromeda herself as the dragon's daughter, but Kassiepeia, as already pointed out, and the Nereids. The latter have a reduced role that has replaced Kassiepeia's as dragon-queen (see note 36); but it is important to notice that it is they who move Poseidon to attack the Ethiopians (Th. 5B). Hardly anywhere else in the Perseus legend do we find evidence of this theme; only a Vatican Mythographer says that Juno-Hera moved Polydektes to try to destroy Perseus.[38]

D) *The Champion.*—I have already made clear that Perseus is a god: a composite figure, no doubt, as we find him in Greek myth, that has taken traits and deeds from the Baals of several Canaanite, Syrian, and Cilician cities, from the Greek Zeus, and from Egyptian gods. That he was a weather and sky god like Baal and Zeus is already evident in Herodotos' testimony that Perseus had a temple and received worship in Chemmis-Panopolis, a city of the Thebaic nome. That is, he was identified with Min, who was more commonly identified with Pan. Now Perseus is obviously a very different god from Pan, and scholars have been puzzled. But Wainwright has ably demonstrated that Herodotos, or his informants, had good reason to bring Perseus and Min together. For Min was a sky god, sometimes identified with Horos, and wielder of the thunderbolt—and so was Perseus, whose sickle-shaped sword, the *harpē,* is a thunder weapon: Marduk and Zeus were armed with it. This and his boot are combined with a thunderbolt on coins of Ake-Ptolemais in Phoenicia. It was a *harpē* that Zeus held in his hand when he came to close

---

[38] Apollod., Hyg. 64, Vat. Myth. I 157. See the Nereids in fig. 25 on either side of Ketos and mounted on sea beasts. We have already seen the dragoness as the Nereid Psamathe (p. 106).

quarters with Typhon. On the coin types of Phoenicia and Cilicia Perseus has obviously been identified with the local Baal, who is always a storm god. Now the identification of Perseus with Min endured at Chemmis-Panopolis. On a strip of tanned calfskin, dated about 100 A.D., that came from Panopolis, is inscribed a notice of an *agôn* of the heavenly Perseus (Perseus Uranios), which formed part of the Great Paneia festival. So Perseus is a double of his mythical father Zeus; he also had the Cyclopes as his companions and Hephaistos as the maker of his *harpê*.[39]

Perseus' quest of Medusa's head was his first exploit, as is evident from the usual narrative; moreover several sources speak explicitly of his youth (Th. 6B). Like other young dragon fighters he alone dared to face the enemy. Zeus-Ammon himself ordered that Poseidon-Ketos be appeased by offering him the princess (Th. 7c), and so behaved as did the Pythian Apollo when Sybaris, Heros, and Poine-Ker spread terror and destruction through the land. His earthly representative, Kepheus, and all the Ethiopian princes were likewise willing to submit. Again, only Perseus would go to fetch Medusa's head for Polydektes; all other Seriphians gave their king a horse instead. Behind the episode of the feast at which each guest except Perseus promised a horse to the king there lies a phase of the story, one can conjecture, in which Polydektes demanded either a horse or Medusa's head, and Perseus put an end to his tyranny by refusing to give him a horse and setting out to win the Gorgon's head. And behind that phase lies Yam's demand for homage which Baal resisted.[40]

E) *The Champion's Death.*—First of all, as the legend stands,

---

[39] Marduk's *harpê:* Hopkins (1934) 348; Zeus's *harpê:* Apollod. 1.6.3. Perseus-Min: Herod. 2.91; REG II (1889) 165; see Wainwright (1935). Nonnos, who credits Perseus with the founding of Tarsos (see note 8), lived in Chemmis-Panopolis: cf. *Dion.* 47.503 f. on the power of *drepanêphoros Perseus.* Alexander the false prophet posed as Perseus: Lucian *Alex.* 11, 58. See also Paus. Damasc. 3, 4.468 M, and a thirteenth-century inventory in Latin, *De Sculpturis Lapidum* 1.20 (*Arch.* XXX, 1844, p. 450): a stone that shows P. with sword and Gorgon head will protect one from thunderbolt and storm. P. and Cyclopes: Pherek. 12, 1.62 f. J; Hephaistos: ps.-Erat. 22. P. is also another Hermes. Notice that in Pherek. and Apollod. he got his winged sandals from the nymphs, not from Hermes.

[40] Perseus' youth: Eur. frag. 344 Nauck²; Lucian *DMar., Dom.:* Ovid 5.243. Ammon's appeasement: Apollod., Ovid 4.670 f. On Polydektes' *eranos* see p. 299, note 44. The conjectured phase of the legend would immediately precede the version of the latter two sources; it would, of course, be already a humanised form of the old myth in which Polydektes was Thanatos himself.

Perseus met death at the very beginning of his life, when his hostile grandfather threw him with his mother into the sea (Th. 8A). The champion's death in the Perseus-Akrisios conflict has thus been pushed back to Perseus' infancy; but it finds a parallel in the infant Zeus's sojourn in a cave in consequence of Kronos' hostility. The descent into the sea is one form of the dying god's descent to the dead; it is found in the myths of Palaimon, Anios, and the son of Atargatis who was called Ichthys or Eros by the Greeks, all of whom descended into the sea as infants in company with their mothers and reappeared later as gods; and such a story is also told of Dionysos. The infants Zeus and Adonis descended into the earth: the meaning is the same. All, moreover, except perhaps Atargatis' son, were victims of a father's or grandfather's wrath. So the Perseus legend has been influenced by the myths of the infant dying god, in particular those that concern Leukothea and her son, wherein heaven's dynastic turmoil has been combined with the infant fertility god's death.[41]

I have already interpreted Perseus' journey into the outer darkness to get Medusa's head as a descent to the dead that Polydektes forced upon him. Like Eurybatos entering Sybaris' cave, he plunged like a boar into the cave of the Phorkides, says Aeschylus, who may mean either Graiai or Gorgons. His flight during this enterprise should also be noticed, when after cutting off Medusa's head he was pursued by her sisters.[42]

But the Ketos combat shows the champion's death in its most primitive form. There is a version of the story, alluded to by Lykophron and vouched for by his Scholiast, in which Perseus was swallowed by Ketos, and, once inside, killed the monster by hacking or kicking his liver; then he leaped forth to release Andromeda. Thanatos is here identical with his realm: a conception that had already become indistinct in *Enuma elish* and the Vedas. But it was still very much alive in the Canaanite myth of Baal and

---

[41] See Fontenrose (1951). Kadmos cast Semele and Dionysos in a chest into the sea: Paus. 3.24.3.

[42] Aesch. frag. 261 Nauck². Perseus' flight: *Shield* 228–231; Pherek. 11; Ctes. *ap.* ps.-Plut. *Fluv.* 18.6; Apollod.; Paus. 5.18.5; Nonn. *Dion.* 25.53–59; vase paintings in Woodward (1937) figs. 6, 8, 10, 11, 14, 16, 21, 28. An incongruity occurs when the Gorgons' pursuit is combined with P.'s invisibility. According to Ctes. the Gorgons chased P. as far as Mycenae.

Mot—one of several striking coincidences between the combats of Baal-Mot and of Perseus-Ketos.[43]

In Polydektes' *eranos,* the feast that resulted in Perseus' quest of Medusa's head, we can see Mot's feast to which Baal was lured (Th. 8c): both show the challenge that the hero cannot refuse. Again, Perseus' dinner among the Hyperboreans (p. 276, note 2), an otherworldly people, may mean the same thing. It was at a feast in the corresponding paradise, the Ethiopian land, that Perseus was set upon by Phineus.[44]

Evidence of the Venusberg theme (8D) can be seen, not only in the Andromeda tale, as I shall show presently, but also in two sources of the Medusa legend. According to a story told by Pausanias, Perseus marvelled at Medusa's beauty when he looked upon her corpse; just so did he look upon the beauty of the exposed Andromeda. According to the wonder teller Herakleitos, Medusa, an *hetaira,* whose beauty amazed all beholders, fell in love with Perseus, but pined away of unrequited affection.[45]

There is just a trace of evidence that his womenfolk lamented for the temporarily dead Perseus (Th. 8E). In a fragment of Euripides' *Diktys* we learn that Danae wept for Perseus when he went off to Medusa's land. It is furthermore evident that Danae looked upon Perseus' journey as his death: for Diktys says to her, "You think that Hades will heed your tears and free your son, if you lament." [46]

F) *Reign of Dragon and Dragoness.*—That Medusa ruled as queen, and that she and the other Gorgons spread ruin and destruction upon the peoples round about them, is already clear (Th. 4A). Ketos too raided and plundered the Ethiopian land as he pleased, killing and devouring men and cattle (Th. 4D); he held the land at his mercy until Perseus came and killed him. Polydektes was a tyrant (Th. 4B), and Phineus a headstrong brawler.[47]

---

[43] Lyk. 837–841 with Schol. Vet.; cf. Ach. Tat. 3.7.7 and the similar story of Herakles p. 347. Finally, one should notice that Perseus was killed by the Gorgon's head in war with Kepheus (Malal., Cedren., Joh. Ant.; see p. 294, note 35 above) and was defeated by Dionysos (see p. 388). Th. 8B is notably absent, as it is in the Yam-Mot combat.

[44] *eranos:* Pherek. 11, Apollod.; cf. Pind. *Pyth.* 10.

[45] Paus. 2.21, Herakl. 1.

[46] Eur. frag. 332 Nauck².

[47] Ketos' devastation: Philostr.; Soph. *ap.* ps.-Erat. 16; Scholl. BP and G on German.

The dragon's attack upon the hero's wife (Th. 4E), as manifested in the Andromeda tale, will be discussed presently. But it
can also be seen in the relations of Akrisios, Proitos, and Poly-
dektes to Danae. I have already given reasons for supposing
Akrisios and Proitos to be essentially the same character; so when
we learn from one version, which was known to Pindar, that
Proitos debauched Danae, then Akrisios' imprisonment of Danae
acquires an additional meaning—he took her for his bride. The
Hades role is superimposed upon the Kronos role: in this tale
Zeus himself is Akrisios' rival or antagonist. Polydektes wanted
Danae to wife, a desire that both Danae and Perseus resisted.
According to one or two sources, he actually married her. His
attack on her that caused her to fly to an altar and Perseus' rescue
have already been noticed. It is furthermore significant that
Polydektes' attentions to Danae occur just when Perseus is absent
in Medusa's realm. In these episodes the theme of rivalry in love
between champion and dragon is dimly reflected. But it becomes
explicit in the struggle between Perseus and Phineus for Andromeda, when Phineus would kill the hero and take his bride.[48]

G) *Recovery of the Champion.*—Perseus, favored of Zeus, was
carried safely over the waves of the sea. With the help of Athena
and Hermes he came back alive from the outer darkness. There is
little more to say about Perseus' resurrection, but that little is
extremely significant. I have already pointed out those versions of
the Gigantomachy in which Athena fought and killed Gorgon
(pp. 244, 282). That this event was also attached to the Perseus
legend seems evident not only from Athena's hostility to Medusa,
about which Ovid informs us, but also from the testimony of
anonymous authorities cited by Apollodoros, who say that Athena
cut Medusa's head off, apparently because the latter vied with her
in beauty. This is the variant episode of the combat myth in
which the champion's sister goes forth to kill the enemy herself;
and so we discover another link that ties the Perseus-legend

---

pp. 77, 137 Breysig; ps.-Liban. 36. That he was a man-eater is evident from the need
to expose a human victim for him to devour. Polydektes' tyranny: Nonn. *Dion.* 47.553 f.;
cf. Ovid *Met.* 5.242–247; on Phineus see *ibid.* 5.8, 14.

[48] Proitos and Danae: Pind. frag. 296 Bowra; Scholl. AB on Il. Polydektes married
Danae: Hyg. 63; Vat. Myth. I 157, II 110. Phineus-Andromeda: Apollod., Ovid 5, Conon
(Phoinix), Vat. Myth. I 73.

closely to the Canaanite myth—Athena is Anat killing Mot or Paghat killing Yatpan. We have seen that Athena's Gorgon opponent is sometimes called Pallas, and also that her opponent named Pallas is often a male giant (p. 245). So in Athena's killing or beheading of the Gorgon we can see a fusion of Anat's victories over Mot and Fire.[49]

H) *Renewal of Battle and Victory.*—In the Medusa legend and in that version of the Ketos legend wherein Perseus enters the monster's belly, the hero's death has taken the form of a bold invasion of the enemy's land. In the first of these enterprises he was attended and aided throughout by his sister Athena (Th. 7D) and his brother Hermes (Th. 7E). These two were Zeus's principal helpers against Typhon. Eros, who helped Zeus against Typhon (p. 75), attended Perseus in his victory over Ketos.[50]

The theme of trickery can be seen in Perseus' theft of the Graiai's single eye, to force them either to tell him the way to the nymphs, who would give him the articles he needed, or to tell him the way to the Gorgons. Or it was the Gorgons' one eye, the theft of which gave him the power he needed. From the nymphs he got his Hades' cap of invisibility, winged sandals, and the *kibisis* (wallet), in which he would carry Medusa's severed head. From Hermes he got his sickle-shaped sword and from Athena the polished shield which he used as a mirror to guide his stroke. Finally, Medusa's head, once he had it, served as a potent weapon against Ketos, Phineus, Atlas, Polydektes, Proitos, and Dionysos' troop. So the theme is mainly expressed in possession of magic weapons and devices; there is otherwise only the theft of the eye. Hence the Perseus legend shows the trickery theme at about the same early stage as it appears in Canaanite myth.[51]

---

[49] Apollod.; cf. Ovid *Met.* 4.798–803; Vat. Myth. I 131, II 112.

[50] Athena's and Hermes' aid: see especially Pherek. 11, Apollod., Pind., Paus. 2.21, ps.-Erat. 22, Lucian *DMar.*; see Woodward (1937) figs. 4, 6, 8, 11, 13–15 (13 = my fig. 23), 18, 21, 23, 24, 26; cf. *ibid.* figs. 12, 27, for their attendance upon Perseus' dealings with the Graiai and Naiads. Athena helped P. against Phineus: Ovid 5.46 f. For Hermes' attendance at the Ketos-combat see Woodward fig. 30. Eros as helper: Eur. frag. 136 Nauck²; Philostr.; with whom compare fig. 25.

[51] On the theft and magical implements see citations in note 20, p. 286, in particular Pherek. and Apollod., and see vase-painting, Woodward (1937) fig. 27. Gorgon's head used against Ketos: Lucian, Ach. Tat.; against Phineus: Apollod., Ovid 5, Vat. Myth. I 73; against Kepheus: Hyg. 64; against Atlas: Ovid 4; against Polydektes: Pherek. 11, Apollod., Ovid 5.247–249, Hyg. 64, Palaiph., Serv. 6; against Proitos: Ovid 5.240 f.; against Dio-

I) *Restoration and Confirmation of Order.*—If Perseus is Baal
and Zeus, as I am certain that he is, then he returned in victory
to his heavenly throne, which in legend has become the throne of
Argos. His declining the throne of Argos, only to take the throne
of Tiryns, his leaving the throne of Ethiopia to his son-double
and that of Seriphos to Diktys before going back to Argos, are
features that in their present form are due to the systematisers
who brought the different legends together. Yet something lies
behind them. After each victory Perseus leaves the country whose
kingship he has won: Ethiopia, Seriphos, Argos. It was his feeling
of guilt for the killing of Akrisios that prevented his return to
Argos: that is, he expiated his blood guilt before taking the
throne (Th. 10c), just as Apollo and Indra did (pp. 15, 198 f.).
His penance begins in Thessaly, like Apollo's, in the best-known
version of the story. But, as we have seen, it was only in Greece
and India that the theme was thus elaborated; it reflects the
religious requirements for expiation of blood guilt that each country enforced during a certain period of its history. Previously
purification had been limited to a ritual cleansing of hands with
water after the kill, a rite that had its origin in the literal washing
of blood from the hands; it was such simple cleansing as is seen
in the Semitic myths after Anat killed Mot (p. 137) and after
Gilgamesh and Enkidu killed heaven's bull (p. 169). It is another
sign of nearness to Canaanite myth that Perseus cleansed himself
of Ketos' blood in this simple way, and precisely in a version that
placed the scene in Joppa.[52]

Perseus was cheered by the Ethiopians who watched him fight
Ketos (Th. 10b); sacrifices of cattle were made to Hermes, Athena,
and Zeus, followed by a great feast of rejoicing with abundant
wine and milk; the festivities were crowned by the wedding rites
that bound him to Andromeda. Also, as the Corycian nymphs sang

nysos' followers: Nonn. *Dion.* 47.559–593, 665–667. Since the Naiads who had the Hades
cap, etc., are probably doubles of the Graiai and Gorgons, it is likely that in an earlier
version the Hermes-like Perseus stole the token of potency, eye or cap or sword, from the
Gorgons.

A flight of the enemy during combat (Th. 7f) can be seen in Akrisios' flight from Argos
to Larissa before the approach of P.; in Thessaly, no doubt, this meant from Thessalian
Argos to Thessalian Larissa; in the Argolid it meant from the lower city of Argos to the
citadel called Larissa; see Pherek. 12, Apollod., Paus. 2.16. For a flight of Phineus see
Ovid 5.36 f.

[52] Paus. 4.35.9; Ovid 4.740.

Apollo's praises (p. 78), so the Hesperides celebrated Perseus' slaying of Medusa.[53]

Finally, the Perseus legend served as *aition* of cults and rituals in several places (Th. 10D). Mycenae had an *hêrôon* of Perseus and a Perseian spring. Argos had a mound of earth beneath which lay Medusa's head, Danae's underground chamber, and an *hêrôon* of Gorgophone, called Perseus' daughter, but really the goddess Athena. Seriphos had an *hêrôon* of Perseus, the funeral games of Polydektes that Perseus founded, and apparently a stone image of Polydektes. Athens also had an *hêrôon* of Perseus. Probably in all these cities the rites of Perseus or Athena included a flute-played *thrênos,* said to represent the Gorgon sisters' lament for the dead Medusa. I have already mentioned the worship of Kepheus, Phineus, Keto, and Ketos (or their Semitic equivalents) at Joppa.[54]

Clearly the whole pattern of the combat myth is present in the Perseus legend complex, though broken up among the several component legends; and certain episodes receive several expressions. This fragmentation and repetition seems to be due to the merging of several Near-Eastern variants in the cycle and a consequent attempt to systematise them. The Ketos combat seems from the evidence to be most closely and directly related to Canaanite myth. It has, however, perhaps in Greek hands, taken the form of subtype IV, in particular that form which I have called *Thanatos* (p. 265). It has been assimilated, that is, to the plot of the Alkestis, Sybaris, and Heros legends.

In general the sources describe the enemy as a creature of the sea. It is the Nereids who become angry, Poseidon who takes up their cause, and Ketos who punishes the offenders. Yet there is evidence sufficient to show that Ketos was looked upon as a death demon who demanded a bride. In Achilles Tatius' romance *Leukippe and Kleitophon* there is described a painting of Euan-

---

[53] Ovid 4, Philostr. Hesperides: Nonn. *Dion.* 30.277.

[54] Mycenae: Paus. 2.16.6, 2.18.1; cf. Ctes. *ap.* ps.-Plut. *Fluv.* 18.6. Argos: Paus. 2.21, 23. Seriphos: Paus. 2.18.1; Hyg. *Fab.* 63, 273.4; Serv. 6. Athens: Paus. 2.18.1. *thrênos:* Ctes. *loc. cit.;* Pind. *Pyth.* 12. Thessalian Larissa had an *hêrôon* of Akrisios: Pherek. 12; cf. Hyg. 63. Joppa: see p. 276. Th. 10A can be seen in Ketos' petrifaction, parallel to the exposure of Python's corpse: cf. Lucian *Dom.*; and in the severing of Medusa's head, comparable to the cutting-up of Set and Vritra.

thes seen at Pelusion in Egypt in the shrine of Zeus Kasios. It showed Andromeda, chained to the rock, garbed as a bride for Hades (ὥσπερ Ἀιδωνεῖ νύμφη κεκοσμημένη), wearing a white silken tunic that reached to her feet; the rock to which she was bound seemed an impromptu tomb. Manilius says that this was her marriage, when she was arrayed and bound to the rock. Much earlier Euripides seems to have had the same idea: in a fragment of his lost *Andromeda* the heroine laments that she is attended by weeping and dirges rather than by the glad marriage song and the dances of her companions. Surviving vase paintings show Andromeda dressed as a bride (fig. 25). She was in exactly the position of the Temesian maid who was made ready for marriage with Heros and placed upon a bridal couch in his tomb. Now Malalas says that Perseus came upon Andromeda in Poseidon's shrine, where her father had exposed her. Malalas' versions of Greek myths are always important, though late and strange; for he lived in Antioch and was no doubt familiar with the local folklore, then told in terms of the Greek cognates. In Malalas' story Poseidon has completely absorbed his creature Ketos and is himself the death-god bridegroom.[55]

Thanatos-Mot swallows his bride, as his mate swallows her bridegrooms. Thus does everyone descend within his murky realm. Baal says to his messengers, ". . . approach not nigh to the godling Môt, lest he put you like a lamb in his mouth." But the death demons have a special fondness for the young and beautiful. The form of the story in which Ishtar or Empusa kills or eats her lovers after enjoying love's delights is not the most primitive: still earlier the death demon expressed his (or her) love by incorporating his beloved at once.[56]

The Thanatos plot is fused with another, which is akin to the *Lityerses* form of the subtype and to subtype I: the hero, either

[55] Eur. frags. 120, 122 Nauck[2]; Woodward (1937) figs. 29–31; LM 3.2053 f., fig. 11. Cf. Ovid 5.29: Ketos was *certa mors*. It is significant that Euanthes' painting (whether or not painter and painting are Ach. Tat.'s fiction, the romancer has modelled his description upon actual paintings) was placed in Zeus Kasios' temple at Pelusion, near Egyptian Mount Kasios, which like its Syrian namesake was connected with the Typhon combat (p. 133).

[56] The translation from the Baal Poem is Gaster's (1950: 183). The vampire's erotic desires are expressed in his sucking his victim's blood. For the subliminal identification of intercourse with eating see Róheim (1940), Schnier (1947), *passim*. Notice Eur. frag. 121 Nauck[2]: Ἐκθεῖναι κῆτει φορβάν.

in quest of something or wishing to deal with the enemy on his home ground, boldly enters the realm of death and accomplishes his object, sometimes helped by the enemy's daughter. It is the plot of the Jason-Medea and Theseus-Ariadne legends. Here King

FIGURE 25. PERSEUS AND KETOS

Kepheus and the dread Kassiepeia (see p. 295, note 36) correspond to Aietes and Iduia-Hekate, or to Minos and Pasiphae; Andromeda is the ogre's daughter who falls in love with the hero and helps him. But she ceased to be a helper, once she became cast as the intended victim whom the hero must rescue.[57]

At a venture I would say that behind the Perseus legend, as we have it with all its accretions, fusions, and confusions, lies the earliest variant of the combat myth to reach the Aegean area. This was the dragon myth of Crete and Mycenae in the second millennium. In any case it constitutes an important link in our chain. In the several versions of its several episodes we find almost every variation of theme and feature that we have encountered elsewhere. And while it is on the one hand firmly rooted in Argos, Mycenae, and Tiryns, it is on the other closely attached to Phoenicia, Syria, Cilicia, Lykia, Lykaonia, and Egypt.

It is due to the composite character of the Hellenic Perseus legend, to the origin of its parts in separate, though closely related, local variants of the combat myth, that the order of its parts—as presented in Apollodoros, for example—is different from what we might expect. That is, Perseus killed Medusa before he killed Ketos; whereas, as Krappe (1933) points out in dealing with the folktale type, and as we shall see in other variants, the male dragon is killed first, as a rule. The inversion became fixed in the Greek legend through identifying Medusa's head with the token of potency, which the hero used against his rivals for the throne (few sources have him use it against Ketos). But notice that though Apsu was killed before Tiamat, she was killed before Kingu; in that respect the Perseus legend coincides with an early representative of the type.

KADMOS

Kadmos, who helped Zeus trick Typhon, had his own dragon to fight, as everyone who has read Ovid's *Metamorphoses* knows. Having given up his search for his sister Europa, whom Zeus had carried off, and having been forbidden by his father Agenor to

---

[57] Both plots are found in succession in Japanese myth: "Susanowo and the Dragon" is remarkably like the Andromeda tale; then the Land-Master's adventures with Susanowo and daughter in the underworld fall within the frame of the other plot (pp. 500–502).

return home if he failed to find her, he consulted Apollo's oracle at Delphi and was told to follow a cow that he would meet until she should lie down. So he followed the cow to the site of Thebes. There some of his men who went to fetch water were attacked and killed by the dragon, Ares' son, who guarded the spring; whereupon Kadmos fought the dragon and killed him. Then, heeding Athena, he sowed the dragon's teeth in the earth, whence sprung a band of armed men, the Spartoi, who immediately fell to fighting and killing one another until but five were left, of whom Echion (Viperman) has a significant role in the sequent legends. Athena made peace among them, and they helped Kadmos to found Thebes. Then Kadmos married Harmonia, daughter of Ares and Aphrodite.[58]

Such, briefly told, is the story as we find it in most of the sources. As with other myths and legends there are, besides several complete narratives of varying length, many references and allusions, early and late—though not nearly so many as to the Perseus cycle—and a great variety of detail. Like the sources of the Perseus legend, these sources show, in one guise or another, all but a few of the forty-three themes of the combat myth.[59]

The Phoenician origin of this legend is visible on its face. Kadmos, the Greeks said, came from Phoenicia; he has a Phoenician name; he was son of Agenor or Phoinix, king of Sidon or Tyre; he brought the Phoenician letters to Hellas. Probably this variant of the combat myth went directly from Sidon and Tyre to Boeotia in the period when Phoenician traders came to the Greek peninsula.[60]

---

[58] Ovid *Met.* 3.1–137. The other principal sources are Hellan. 1, 1.107 J; 51, 1.121 J; Pherek. 22, 1.67 f. J; Eur. *Phoen.* 5–8, 638–689, 931–941, 1006–1012, with Scholl. Vett.; Derkylos 6, 3в.9 J; Apollon. *Arg.* 3.1176–1187 with Scholl. Vett.; Apollod. 3.4.1 f.; Conon 37; Dionys. Skyt. *ap.* Diod. 4.2.1; Diod. 5.48 f., 19.53.4 f.; Paus. 9.10, 12; Hyg. *Fab.* 178; Palaiph. 3 f.; ps.-Plut. *Fluv.* 2.1; Sen. *Oed.* 712–747; Nonn. *Dion.* 4.285–5.189; Malal. 2, p. 39 Dind. For vase paintings and coins see LM 2.829–872; CVA, France 1, pl. 3.12. These sources will be cited throughout the Kadmos section in the same manner as the sources of the Perseus section have been (see p. 275, note 1). On the legend see Harrison (1927) 429–436.

[59] Missing from the direct sources are 3E, 4B, 4E, 7E, 8B, 8E, 10A. Of these, 4B, 7E, and 10A were probably present in the oral tradition (and in lost sources). The missing 4E is supplied by the Sphinx myth; it is probably also reflected in Zeus's rape of Europa.

[60] Some scholars have doubted that Kadmos and his legend really had a Phoenician origin: they think that some mistake was made about the meaning of *phoinix.* But there are too many connections and associations between K. and Phoenicia. His name is a

Drakon, as we shall call the Theban dragon, was a son of Ares (Th. 1B). His mother, according to a Scholiast, was Tilphossa Erinys, i.e., that naiad Telphusa whom we met in the first chapter; but Euripides says that he was Ge's son (gêgenês, Th. 1A). As we shall see in chapter xiii, Telphusa is but another name for Python's companion. Ares was both grieved and angry when Kadmos killed Drakon, and he avenged himself in ways concerning which the sources differ (compare Ares and Kyknos, p. 29). Ge too, it is said, raised up the Spartoi to avenge Drakon's death, much as she raised up new enemies against Zeus after he had overcome the Titans.[61]

One way in which Ares avenged himself was to send Sphinx (Phix) against the Thebans, although Hera too is said to have sent her (Th. 5B: compare her sending of Python or Tityos against Leto). Still another version has it that Dionysos did so, a version that reminds one both of Dionysos' relation to and manifold dealings with the house of Kadmos and of his conflict with Perseus. At any rate we may see in Sphinx the dragoness or Medusa of the Kadmos myth (Th. 1c). Like Medusa she was sometimes called daughter of Typhon and Echidna, and sometimes given other but equally monstrous parents. She was usually represented as a creature that had the head of a woman, the body of a lion, the wings and talons of an eagle or vulture: a sort of griffoness or female Zu. A Scholiast adds that she had the tail of a snake, which would make her more like Chimaira, who another Scholiast says was her mother by Typhon. Chimaira, whom Bellerophon fought, had the head of a lion, the body of a goat, and a serpentine

---

serious obstacle to these scholars' position; it can hardly be anything but Canaanite, being apparently formed on the root QDM, Hebrew qadm-, qedem, "east"; i.e., Kadmos was the easterner. He was the legendary bringer of the alphabet, which certainly came to Greece from Canaan. Naturally his Phoenician original did not bear that name until Sidon and Tyre became Hellenised. In Roman times K. appears upon their coin types: BMCC, Phoenicia, *Sidon* nos. 218–223, 236–241, 262, 296, 297, 313–315, pp. 180, 183, 188, 194, 197, pls. 23.15, 24.2, 12; *Tyre* nos. 411, *425, 426,* 434, 446, 469, *487,* 488, 489, *496,* pp. 277, 280 f., 283, 285, 290, 293–295, pls. 33.*12;* 34.2, 18; 35.1, 2. The italicised numerals indicate representations of the dragon combat. Compare the nude K. with the nude Herakles-Melqart, *ibid.* no. 427, p. 281, pl. 33.13.

[61] Ares' son: Eur., Derkylos, Apollod., Ovid, Hyg., Palaiph. 3, Nonn. 4, Schol. *Phoen.* 238. Son of Ares and Tilphossa: Schol. Vet. on Soph. *Ant.* 126. Son of Ge: Eur. *Phoen.* 931, 935; Sen. *Oed.* 725 f. Ge's vengeance: Schol. *Phoen.* 934. Schol. *ibid.* 238 calls the Theban dragon Delphynes.

tail, but, so far as I know, is never given wings. Sphinx and Chimaira figures, like those of the Gorgons, had an apotropaic function; and whereas the Lycian Chimaira's form strongly suggests that she came from the Hittites or Mesopotamia, the woman-headed lion obviously came to Greece directly from Egypt.[62]

Sphinx's likeness to Medusa is enhanced by the tradition, assigned to a poet called Peisander (who may be the early epic poet), that she was born in farthest Ethiopia. Also Sphinges, like Gorgons, were numbered among the underworld demons, the Keres, Lamias, and the like. It was Hades that sent her forth, according to Euripides; we may compare the origin of Poine-Ker in the halls of Acheron (p. 115). Aeschylus calls Sphinx a man-eating Ker; in anonymous verses that purport to be Oedipus' reply to her riddle, the hero calls her "evil winged Muse of the dead." Euripides associates her with "lyreless Muse and deadly Erinys." [63]

She closely resembles Lamia in her taste for young men (Th. 4c), though she did not confine herself to the young. She devoured the men whom she seized (Th. 4D), according to the legend. There can be little doubt that her cannibalism represents a primitive and infantile erotic fantasy: she is a dominating mistress (or mother) who takes complete possession of her lover (or son), absorbing his whole being, just as she is interpreted in von Stuck's painting. Her amorous nature can be more directly seen in the tradition that harlots were called Sphinges; and it was said that the gay colors of her wings were meant to allure. A similar inter-

---

[62] Ares sent Sphinx: Schol. *Phoen.* 1064; Arg. 5 Dind. *in Phoen.:* cf. Eur. *Phoen.* 1031 f. Hera: Apollod. 3.5.8; Peisander *ap.* Schol. *Phoen.* 1760. Dionysos: Lykos 1, 3B.249 J; Schol. *Phoen.* 1031. Daughter of Typhon and Echidna: Apollod. 3.5.8; Hyg. *Fab.* 151.1 and praef. 39; of Orthos and Echidna: Hes. *Theog.* 326 f.; of Typhon and Chimaira: Schol. on Hes. *loc. cit.* Her appearance: Eur. *Phoen.* 806–811; Apollod. 3.5.8; Schol. *Phoen.* 1760; cf. Aesch. *Sept.* 791; Soph. *OT* 1199. Palaiph. 4 substitutes dog for lion. According to Schol. Vet. on Lyk. 7, she was a lion in her upper, a woman in her lower body. Chimaira: Il. 6.181; Apollod. 2.3.1. On Sphinx figures in Egypt and Greece see LM 4.1298–1363; apotropaic use, *ibid.* 1401–1407; apotropaic use of Chimaira-figure: LM 1.894.

[63] Sphinx from Ethiopia: Peis. *ap.* Schol. *Phoen.* 1760. Aeschylus' Gorgonean plains of Kisthene were neighbors to the griffons (*Pr.* 803 f.). That Sphinges are nightmare demons is the central thesis of Laistner (1889); he is right about one side of their character at least. Sphinx as Ker, creature of Hades: *Phoen.* 810 f., 1028 f.; Aesch. *Sept.* 776 f.; anon. *ap. Argg. in* Soph. OT, Eur. *Phoen.* Eur. (1028 f.) says that she snatched young men ἄλυρον ἀμφὶ μοῦσαν ὀλομέναν τ' Ἐρινύν. Lyk. 7 calls her "black Sphinx."

pretation of Medusa has already been noticed (p. 299), and Sphinx's likeness to Empusa hardly needs comment.[64]

Like Echidna, who commanded a road, she had a base upon a mountain, whence she could seize men and present them with the riddle that nobody could solve until Oedipus came (Th. 4F). In this respect she is a female Lityerses or Phorbas, the first demoness we have encountered for whom the win-or-die contest is so clearly attested. It was Phikion, Sphinx Mountain, that she held, somewhat northwest from Thebes at the southeast corner of Lake Kopais, and commanding the road to Ptoon (see map 1) and Onchestos, and within easy reach of the road west to Orchomenos and Delphi. It may be that her lair was once placed on the Kadmeia itself, Thebes' citadel; for Euripides places her raids in the area about Dirke, and certainly she perched there when she came on her raids and posed her riddle.[65]

In the surviving literature Sphinx is usually a character of the Oedipus legend. But she was also directly linked to Kadmos and Drakon. According to Palaiphatos, she was an Amazon woman, Kadmos' first wife, who became offended when Kadmos married Harmonia; with a band of followers she took possession of Phikion and made war upon Kadmos and Thebes. Pausanias and a Scholiast also mention a rationalised version in which Sphinx led a robber band that plundered the Thebans (Th. 4A). Pausanias also has a story in which Sphinx knew the oracle given to Kadmos and attempted to control succession to the throne thereby. Finally, as I have mentioned, Ares sent her against the Thebans to get revenge for the killing of his son Drakon, a story that Euripides appears to have known. So once more we have the frequent sequence of the combat myth: first the dragon, then the dragoness, is killed, as is most clearly seen in the Beowulf legend (p. 525).[66]

---

[64] Young men seized: *Phoen.* 1026–1031; Peis. *loc. cit.* (both young and old). Man-eater: Apollod. 3.5.8, Peis. Harlot: Kallias, frag. 23 (1.698 Kock); Anaxilas, frag. 22 (2.270 Kock), whose comic character reveals how closely the Greeks associated prostitutes with she-demons: he mentions *drakaina*, Chimaira, Charybdis, Skylla, Sphinx, Hydra, lioness, Echidna, Harpies, Siren; cf. Plut. *Amor.* (7.133 Bernardakis).

[65] *Phoen.* 806–811, 1026 f.; Apollod. 3.5.8; Paus. 9.26.2; Palaiph. 4. Sphinx is placed on Kithairon by Schol. *Phoen.* 806.

[66] Palaiph.; Paus. 9.26.2–4; Schol. on Hes. *Theog.* 326; see p. 309, note 62. The Sphinx is labeled *Kassmia* on a vase painting, Berlin inv. 3186 = Harrison (1922) fig. 43, p. 210. The form *Kassmos* (= *Kadmos*) appears on a vase painting, LM 2.842, fig. 4.

Drakon lived in a cave (Th. 2B) on a slope of the Kadmeia, guardian of his father Ares' spring (Ths. 2C, 2D), which is identified by Euripides with a spring at the southwest foot of the Kadmeia. Its water flows into the nearby river Dirke; spring and cave overlook this river, which is only a few yards below. But Pausanias identifies Ares' spring with the source of the Ismenos, which flows to the east of the Kadmeia. Drakon's watery nature is seen chiefly in the spring that he guards, but there is more than simile in Ovid's comparison of the charging Drakon to a river in flood (Th. 3G).[67]

Like Python, Drakon was a huge snake, whose reared head overtopped the trees of the grove in which he lived, and, according to Ovid, he was as large as the celestial snake that lies between the two Bears (Ths. 3A, 3B). His eyes flashed fire, and his poisonous breath alone could kill (Th. 3D). When Ovid says that he had three tongues and a triple row of teeth, he may be preserving the traces of a three-headed dragon (Th. 3C). He had a tough hide that made him well-nigh invulnerable and gave Kadmos a hard time.[68]

According to two fourth-century (B.C.) authors, Derkylos and Palaiphatos, Drakon ruled as king of Thebes; Kadmos came from Phoenicia to Thebes, killed Drakon, and took his wealth and kingdom (Th. 5A). These were rationalising authors; yet their date is comparatively early, and a rationaliser usually frames his version closely upon the genuine myth. It is elsewhere said of Kadmos, as of Perseus, that he set out to win a throne for himself. Photios and Suidas say that Kadmos was son of Ogygos. Lykophron calls the Spartoi the people of Ogygos; and Seneca speaks of Thebans, sons of the Spartoi, as Ophion's sons. Ogygos, primeval king of Thebes, we have seen (pp. 236–238), is also a form of Okeanos and Ophion, a Titan king, and first king of the gods. Now the Spartoi were usually considered to be Drakon's sons, and the chief Spartos was Echion, a name that means the same as

---

[67] Cave: *Phoen.* 931, 1010 f., with Schol. on 931; Ovid. Ares' spring: *Phoen.* 658–661, 932, with Scholl. on 238, 657; Eur. *Antiope*, frag. *ap. Hermath.* VIII (1891) p. 47, *vv.* 38–41; Apollon.; Apollod.; Ovid; Paus. 9.10; Nonn.; Phot. *Lex.* 1.302 Naber; ps.-Plut. identifies the dragon's spring with Ismenos' source, which is placed in the Corycian Cave; see also Hyg., who identifies Ares' spring with Castalia; see p. 367. On the location of Ares' spring in Thebes see Frazer on Paus. 9.10.5.
[68] 3A: Ovid (esp. 41–45), Sen. 3c, 3D, 7B: Ovid 33 f., 49, 59–64.

Ophion, and which is the masculine form of *Echidna*. Drakon, would seem, therefore, to be a form of Ogygos, chaos demon and first father-king in preclassical Boeotian mythology, later reduced to king of Thebes, and his father Ares is merely his double as a character in this myth. And Kadmos is his son—the young usurper, the equivalent of Zeus or Apollo.[69]

As with other myths, certain themes and episodes receive several expressions in literature. According to Palaiphatos, Kadmos came to Thebes to contest the throne with his brother Phoinix—presumably to get the means to do so, since Palaiphatos goes on to say that Drakon was then king of Thebes, so that Phoinix, we may suppose, was king in Phoenicia. Now Phoinix is sometimes said to be father of Kadmos. In any case, Kadmos was at odds with his father, Agenor or Phoinix, who banished him from his native land; and this banishment is better motivated as the father's precaution against usurpation than as punishment for failure to find an abducted sister, which hardly seems adequate—unless Kadmos had something to do with the abduction. So Kadmos' exile from Sidon corresponds exactly to that of Perseus from Argos. Agenor, the brother of Belos, corresponds to Kronos, the deposed god who became the chaos-dragon's ally.[70]

Kadmos' character as a weather god (Th. 6A) can be seen in the stone with which, according to most authorities, he killed Drakon. For either unhewn stones or stone weapons, like Thor's Mjölnir, have been considered thunderweapons in Europe and the Near East since neolithic times at the latest; and there is evidence for this belief from ancient Greece and Asia. Only Ovid says that the stone, though it was huge enough and thrown with force enough to shake a city's ramparts, failed to hurt the dragon, and that Kadmos finally dispatched the monster with a spear. But

---

[69] Derkylos, Palaiph. Kadmos' desire for kingdom: Conon, Palaiph.; cf. Malal.; see also Ovid and Sen., who say that K. asked Apollo where he should found a new city. K. Ogygos' son: Phot. *Lex.* 2.272 Naber; Suid. Ω12. Relation of Spartoi to Ogygos-Ophion: Lyk. 1206; Sen. HF 268; to Drakon: Palaiph. 3, and see citations in note 58, p. 307. Echion: Apollod., Ovid; this was also the name of a giant (Claud. 37.104) and of an Argonaut, twin-brother of Erytos (Pind. *Pyth.* 4.179; Apollon. *Arg.* 1.52); the brothers were a guileful pair.

[70] Phoinix Kadmos' father: Conon 32, 37; Schol. *Arg.* 3.1177. Notice that the kingship of Thebes was at issue in the meeting of Oedipus and the Sphinx: Apollod. 3.5.8; cf. Paus. 9.26.3. That K. was very young (Th. 6B) when he became king is implied in the tradition that he reigned for 62 years (Malal.).

according to another version, Kadmos killed Drakon with an arrow, a possible symbol of the thunderbolt (p. 195).[71]

Kadmos is presented as a victor; there is little trace of the champion's defeat and death in the sources. There are his exile, mentioned above, his period of servitude, and a brief retreat before the charge of the wound-maddened Drakon. Besides, there is the interesting passage in Nonnos' description of the battle, when Drakon wrapped himself about Kadmos and caused him to weaken in the struggle: an echo, it would seem, of the primitive myth in which the dragon swallowed the hero.[72]

There is considerably more evidence of the Venusberg theme (Th. 8D). Harmonia corresponds to Andromeda, and she is the enemy's daughter or sister. She was, in most versions, the daughter of Ares and Aphrodite, the Greek Astarte (cf. p. 133); but in the versions of Derkylos and Palaiphatos (see note 69) she was Drakon's daughter; after Kadmos killed Drakon and took his throne, he made her his wife. She was Drakon's sister in those versions in which Ares is the father of both. Her name expresses that order which the divine champion came to wrest from the demon's control and release for the world's good.[73]

We should not forget that Kadmos set out in the first place to find his abducted sister Europa. It was Zeus, as the story is told, who carried her off. But it appears that two roles have been fused: the hero, identified with Zeus, who runs off with the ogre's daughter, and the ogre himself, here conceived in bull form, who carries off a princess. Kadmos takes Zeus's place in a reputedly Sidonian story for which Euhemeros is cited as authority (see note 73): that Kadmos as servant of the king of Sidon ran off with

---

[71] Kadmos kills Dr. with stone: *Phoen.* 662 f., Hyg., Nonn. 4, Scholl. *Phoen.* 238, 662; with spear: Ovid; cf. Nonn. 4.412 f., who says that K. cut off Dr's head with a knife; with arrow: ps.-Plut. On thunder stones see Blinkenberg (1911), esp. 13–27; cf. Paus. 3.22.1. K. uses a stone again when he faces the Spartoi. He wore a lionskin (Ovid), garb that links him with Herakles. He went forth boldly to fight after his companions fled (Th. 7c). Dr. retreated during the combat (Th. 7F): Ovid.

[72] Ovid 81–83; Nonn. 4.365–376, 389. In the related Jason legend there is evidence of a version in which the Colchian snake, also guardian of Ares' sacred grove, swallowed Jason: a vase painting (Vatican) shows Jason in the snake's mouth, Athena standing by; the golden fleece hanging on a tree identifies snake and hero: Harrison (1927) fig. 35, p. 436.

[73] On Kadmos' seizure of Harmonia see also Scholl. *Phoen.* 5, 7 (citing Ephoros, Demagoras); see also Euhemeros *ap.* Ath. 14.658EF.

Harmonia, the king's flute girl. Europa as the demon king's daughter may be seen in the Europa who was wife or daughter of Ocean (p. 232), sister of Eurynome. The name also belongs to a mistress of Poseidon, daughter of Tityos and mother of Euphemos (p. 482). Poseidon is the Olympian equivalent of Ocean; we have seen that in story Poseidon often represents the wild and hostile sea of chaos rather than the orderly sea of the cosmos. And Tityos, as gigantic demon, is another name of the chaos spirit. This Europa can be connected with Agenor's daughter through the Europa who was wife of Phoroneus Inachos' son, Ocean's grandson, and first man, and the Europa who was daughter of Nile (another father of waters) and wife of Danaos, Argive ancestor; for Agenor was a descendant of Phoroneus, uncle of Danaos, and son of Poseidon.[74]

Now Zeus came as a bull to Europa, as most versions have it; but, according to an early version (Akusilaos), he sent a bull to carry her off, and Nigidius says that Poseidon gave this bull of manlike intelligence to Zeus. But most authorities say that Poseidon gave the bull to Minos. Whether sent by Zeus or Poseidon, this was the Cretan bull that both Herakles and Theseus encountered, and that fathered the Minotaur on Pasiphae, Hekate's daughter. The Minotaur's name was Asterion or Asterios, which is a byname of Zeus and also the name of the Cretan king who succeeded Zeus as Europa's mate. One would expect the bull demon's mate to be represented as a cow. Europa, however, never is, though Pasiphae took cow form, which is represented in extant versions as artificially constructed, to copulate with the Cretan bull. It was another mistress of Zeus that became a cow: Io Inachos' daughter, ancestress of Agenor (or daughter of Iasos, Agenor's brother), Europa, and Kadmos, she whom Hermes rescued from the monstrous Argos Panoptes. Another cow appears in the Kadmos legend, she who guided Kadmos to the site of Thebes. She belonged to the herds of Pelagon, a name that ap-

---

[74] Apollod. 2.1.1–5; Paus. 2.16.1. In Argive legend Agenor was father of Argos Panoptes. The appearance of Agenor in Apollodoros' genealogy is due to an effort to reconcile Argive and Boeotian traditions. Notice that either Ocean or Poseidon is the father of the river Asopos: Apollod. 3.12.6. Eurynome appears as Kadmos' daughter in Malal. One tradition brings Europa's abduction nearer to the combat scene: Zeus hid her in Boeotian Teumessos: Paus. 9.19.1.

pears to be formed upon *pelagos* (sea). Now she guided Kadmos to just the place where the dragon lurked, and thus served him much as Telphusa served Apollo. But Telphusa's role must be left to a later chapter. Notice now that the cow was beautiful, and that Pelagon lived in the Phlegyan country, somewhere near the Kephisos River and Panopeus, home of Tityos and Phorbas.[75]

The dragoness is therefore split up among Harmonia, Europa, Sphinx, and the guiding cow. The surviving sources illustrate very well how a mythical figure can change and proliferate, and yet how each new form remains true to the original conception: for the wicked dragoness and the fertility spirit were both implicit in the chaos demoness. Sphinx's concupiscence is all that is left to her of the fertility spirit, and even that is not clearly visible; it must be deduced from her preference for young men, as with Sybaris. She is like Sybaris too in the manner of her death: she leaped from her rock, Kadmeia or Phikion, and killed herself. Though nothing is said about her being transformed into a spring, the spring of Ares that was one of the sources of the Dirke River was also called Dirke's spring, as Euripides makes clear. Dirke, Lykos' wife, was an evil queen, enemy of Antiope and her sons, Amphion and Zethos. When they killed her they threw her body into this spring; or it was Dionysos who transformed her into a spring. Since it is situated below the Kadmeia,

---

[75] Akus. 29, 1.55 J; Nigid. on German. *Arat.* 174 (Schol. BP, p. 74 Breysig); cf. Ampel. 2.2. Euripides (frag. 820 Nauck[2]) seems to have agreed with Akusilaos. Notice his διὰ τοῦ πελάγους and Nigidius' *per pelagus*, when they speak of Europa's journey on the bull's back; cf. the name *Pelagôn* (Apollod., Paus. 9.12). Pelagon, the cow's owner, called *kêritrephês* (Oracle *ap.* Schol. *Phoen.* 638), was son of Amphidamas (*ibid.*); we find an Amphidamas who was son of Eurynome and father of Eurystheus' wife; in his lineage or kin appear Ankaios (p. 479) and Kepheus; another Amph. was son of Busiris; see Apollod. 2.5.11, 3.9.2; LM 1.303. Pelagon also appears as son of Asopos and brother of Ismenos; his sister Aigina was abducted by Zeus: Apollod. 3.12.6. Diod. (4.72.1) calls him Pelasgos, the name of another primordial being and son of Ge: Paus. 8.1.4 f. We should also notice *Pêlagôn*, either the proper name of a Giant or a synonym of *Gigas:* Call. *Hymn* 1.3 with Schol.; Hesych. Π2175; EM 669. Strabo (7, frag. 40, p. 331) says that *Pêlagones* were Titans. Pelagon's home: Ovid, Schol. *Phoen.* 638. On Zeus Asterios see LM 6.605. Asterion: Apollod. 3.1.2–4; Diod. 4.60.2; Paus. 2.31.1. Pasiphae: Apollod. 3.1.4. On Europa as cow see Harrison (1927) 449. On Io see esp. Aesch. *Pr.* 669–681; Apollod. 2.1.3; Ovid *Met.* 1.588–723. Apollod. says that she was daughter of Iasos, on whom see p. 59, note 49. Now Iasion-Iasos, lover of Demeter (or Kybele), was brother of Harmonia, according to Hellan. 23, 1.113 J; Diod. 5.48.2, 5.49.2. Out of Iasion, I think, came the hero Jason, who, like Kadmos, sowed dragon's teeth and raised a crop of warriors; Iasion was K's brother-in-law in Samothracian tradition (Hellan., Diod., *locc. cit.*). Cow's beauty: Ovid 20 f. According to Plut. *Sulla* 17, K. found her at Thurion near Chaironeia.

and since both Sphinx and Dirke had a special relation to Dionysos, besides having in common a wicked character, it may be
conjectured that there was once a story according to which the
spring gushed forth at the spot where Sphinx's body landed.[76]

Such is the evidence for dragoness and Siren episode in the
Kadmos legend. Something of the companion theme, the luring
of the champion to a feast (Th. 8c), may be seen in the dragon's
attack on Kadmos and his men while they were preparing a sacrifice, which would be followed by a communion meal.[77]

Kadmos had the same goddess helper, Athena (Th. 7D), as had
Zeus, Herakles, and Perseus. She is credited by one author or
another with advising him to throw a stone at Drakon and to
throw one among the Spartoi, to sow the dragon's teeth, to abduct
Harmonia, and to take the throne of Thebes. According to Stesichoros, she sowed the teeth herself, as Anat sowed the fragments
of Mot.[78]

In the Spartoi we obviously have the episode of gigantomachy
(Th. 7G). They were considered to be sons of Drakon, from whose
teeth they sprung, and of Ge, from whose body they grew. It is
also said that Ge produced them to avenge Drakon's death (Th.
5B). They are sometimes called Gegeneis or Gigantes; and the
names of the five survivors, Echion (snaky), Udaios (earthy),
Chthonios (earthy), Hyperenor (superman), and Peloros (monstrous), indicate their nature. They are sometimes identified with
Boeotian peoples whom Kadmos had to fight when he first came
to the country. Palaiphatos seems to identify them with Sphinx's
followers who made war on Kadmos. Nonnos in his additive way
places Kadmos' war with Ektenes, Aonians, and Temmikes imme-

---

[76] Sphinx's leap: Apollod. 3.5.8; Diod. 4.64.4. Spring of Dirke: Eur. *Antiope, loc. cit.*
(see note 67); Apollod. 3.5.5; Paus. 9.25.3; Hyg. *Fab.* 7.4 places the *fons Dircaeus*, into
which Dionysos had changed Dirke's body, on Kithairon. Stat. *Theb.* 9.679 calls Kithairon
mons Dircaeus. For Sphinx's connection with Kithairon see p. 310, note 65. Sen. *Oed.*
588 calls the Spartoi a brood born from Dircaean teeth. On Dirke and her resemblance to
Ino, nurse of Dionysos, who killed either her own or her rival's children, see Fontenrose
(1948) 154 f.; Dirke's story is one of the surprisingly few points at which the present myth
complex touches the triangle myths.

[77] According to one version of the oracle given to Kadmos, the sacrifice had to be
made to Ge: Schol. *Phoen.* 638, 662. Other authorities say Athena (Apollod., Schol.
Phoen. 1062, Nonn. 4) or Zeus (Ovid).

[78] Stes. frag. 15 Bergk; *Phoen.* 666–675; Apollon.; Ovid; Hyg.; Apollod.; Nonn. 4;
Schol. *Phoen.* 5, 7, 238, 670, 1062; vase paintings in LM 2.829 f., 837–839, 861 f., figs.
1–3, 5.

diately after the battle of the Spartoi. Now, according to Pherekydes, the Phlegyans under Eurymachos had attacked and destroyed Thebes before Kadmos came and rebuilt it; later
Amphion and Zethos built the walls of Thebes for defense
against Phlegyans: this would seem to imply that Phlegyans were
among the Boeotian enemies of Kadmos. So it may be that the
Spartoi are another mythical reflection of the Phlegyans.[79]

The trickery theme (9) appears only in the Spartoi episode,
when Kadmos hurled among them stones that set them to killing
one another (Pherekydes). For Conon his heaven-taught ruse becomes Phoenician stratagems such as ambushes and use of armor.

Kadmos underwent the same expiatory kind of purification as
did Apollo, Perseus, and Indra (Th. 10c). He had to serve Ares
for eight years before he could become king of Thebes and marry
Harmonia, exactly the period of Apollo's exile and expiation
(p. 456).[80]

Kadmos' triumph was crowned by his marriage to Harmonia
(Th. 10b). The gods came to the wedding feast and gave Harmonia many gifts, among them the famous necklace. The guiding
cow was sacrificed to Athena. Kadmos' wedding and his sacrifices
to several gods appear to be the *aitia* of Theban rituals and festivals (Th. 10d). Pausanias mentions an altar and image of Athena
Onga that Kadmos set up on the spot where the cow lay down,
and a Scholiast adds a temple.[81]

By the source of Ismenos, which Pausanias identifies with
Ares' spring and the scene of the Kadmos-Drakon combat, there
was a tomb of the hero Kaanthos, son of Ocean and brother of

---

[79] Spartoi as earth-born Gigantes: Eur. *Her.* 4, *Bacch.* 1025, *Phoen.* 670, 937–940,
with Schol. on 934, 937 f.; Apollon.; Sen.; Nonn. Ge produced them in wrath: *Phoen.*
937–940 with Schol. Names: Pherek., Hellan. 1, Apollod., Hyg. Kadmos' wars with Boeo-
tians: Conon, Palaiph., Nonn. 5.35–50. Phlegyans: Pherek. 41, 1.74 J. Ares too meant
that the Spartoi should avenge Drakon: Schol. *Phoen.* 934. It was perhaps for this reason
that, according to Hellan. 1 and Pherek., he demanded that K. sow the teeth; and perhaps
Athena supported his demand (Pherek.) because she knew how K. might profit. To
Aietes went half the teeth, which later Jason would sow (Pherek., Apollon.).

[80] Apollod.; Phot. *Lex.* 1.302 Naber; Suid. K17. He also cleansed himself in Dirke's
spring immediately after combat: Nonn. 5.4. It should be realised that other authors,
e.g., Ovid, omit purification altogether.

[81] Wedding-feast: Apollod., Nonn. 5. Sacrifice of cow: Nonn. 5, Schol. *Phoen.* 1062.
Athena Onga: Paus. 9.12.2; Schol. *loc. cit.* See Ath. 11.462b on a tomb of Kadmos and
Harmonia in Illyria; cf. MacKay (1948) 81–88, who, however, reverses the direction
of K's movement.

Melia, whom Apollo carried off. Ocean sent Kaanthos to look for her, and when he found that Apollo had her and would not give her up, he hurled fire into the temenos of Apollo Ismenios. Apollo then killed him with an arrow. Melia bore Teneros and Ismenos to Apollo; Teneros became his father's prophet at Ptoon.[82]

The first part of this remarkable myth closely resembles the Kadmos legend, i.e., up to the point where the hero fails to recover his sister. But the second part is very like the Phlegyas-legend: it is the ravished maiden's kinsman who sets fire to Apollo's oracular shrine. Kaanthos, who starts out like the hero Kadmos to rescue his sister, ends as the god's enemy. There can be no doubt that Kaanthos has something to do with Kadmos; but the precise relation is far from clear. At any rate, Kaanthos as Ocean's son gives support to the rare and rather obscure evidence that Kadmos was son of Ogygos. And Melia the Oceanid is another link that unites the Oceanid Europa to Agenor's daughter. Not only does she play the same part as the latter, but Agenor had a daughter Melia, who married Danaos, whose wife's name is also given as Europa. Notice furthermore that Melia, Ocean's daughter, became Inachos' wife and bore Phoroneus, husband of Europa; that Melia, a Bithynian nymph, became mistress of Poseidon or of Inachos and bore the Phorbas-like Amykos (p. 486); and that a nymph Melia became wife of Silenos and mother of the Centaur Pholos. Finally, one should notice the Meliai, the ash-tree nymphs who were born from Uranos' severed members and were the mothers of the Bronze Men. There appears to be one and the same original behind all these nymphs: the chaos demoness who was first mother of all creatures. Furthermore Melia was nymph of the spring that is Ismenos' source and which was identified by Pausanias with Ares' spring: for it was also called Melia.[83]

---

[82] Paus. 9.10.5; on Teneros see Strabo 8.2.34, p. 413.

[83] Melia Agenor's daughter: Pherek. 21, 1.67 J; Inachos' wife: Apollod. 2.1.1; Ovid *Amor.* 3.6.25 f.; Bithynian nymph: Apollon. *Arg.* 2.1–4; Hyg. *Fab.* 17; Ovid *loc. cit.*; Silenos' wife: Apollod. 2.5.4; cf. Alex. Aet. *ap.* Strab. 14.5.29, p. 681; Meliai: Hes. *Theog.* 187, OD 145; the spring Melia: Schol. Vet. on Pind. *Pyth.* 11.3(5). In the verses cited from Apollon., notice that Amykos is called *agênôr*, which here has the sense of *overweening*. It throws light on *Agênôr*, which was substituted by the Greeks for some Phoenician name.

Another source for the story of Kaanthos has turned up in an Oxyrhynchus papyrus: the first brother murder, it is said, occurred at Thebes when Ismenos killed Klaaitos (which name appears to be a corruption of *Kaanthos,* itself perhaps a corrupt form); both were sons of Ocean who fought over their sister Melia. The Pindaric Scholiast (see note 83) agrees that Ismenos was Melia's brother, not her son, as Pausanias has it. We can be fairly sure that Ismenos was the predecessor of Apollo Ismenios at the Theban Ismenion. In early Theban myth, it appears from papyrus and Pausanias together, Ismenos was successful in rivalry over Melia and killed his brother when attacked by him.[84]

Most likely this myth precedes the Kadmos tale in Thebes. It is probably an offshoot of an early Hellenic version of the combat myth. At any rate, it affected the legends of Phlegyas and Kadmos. It accounts for the shape that the Phoenician myth of Baal's combat with Yam finally assumed in Thebes. Hence the Kadmos legend's unique beginning. It is not a monster, as one would expect, but a god, who has taken the fair maiden that must be rescued; and he who tries to recover her is not the god's enemy, as one would expect, but his friend, himself a divine champion.[85]

The Kadmos legend, then, appears to be another distinct variant of the combat myth, one that came to Boeotia with Phoenician traders and there became mingled with a tale of strife between brothers that was localised at a Theban spring. Like the Perseus-Ketos legend it coincides remarkably with the Canaanite

---

[84] Oxyrh. Pap. X 1241, col. iv. 5–10. As Ismenos is Apollo's precedessor at Ismenion and became identified with him, so Teneros is undoubtedly Apollo's predecessor at Ptoon. This myth, or its archetype, affects the Phlegyas tale in the relation not only of Apollo to Phlegyas, but of Apollo to Ischys as his rival for Koronis' favor. There the parts are shifted a bit: Apollo kills Ischys, but Ischys wins Koronis. Or was each brother equally favored by Melia? The myth of Asopos, Aigina (whose brothers were Ismenos and Pelagon), and Zeus, is another variant of the Kaanthos tale: Apollod. 3.12.6.

[85] It is possibly from Kaanthos, so closely connected with a Theban spring, that Kadmos received his own serpentine character. For the classical Kadmos legend ends with the transformation of K. and Harmonia into snakes among the Encheleis (eel-people) in Illyria: Apollod. 3.5.4; Ovid *Met.* 4.569–603. Ath. 11.462ʙ places this event among the Illyrian Kylikes, a name that recalls K's brother Kilix and his own wanderings in Cilicia; see MacKay *loc. cit.* Another coincidence of K. with Apollo and Herakles is his rivalry with Linos in a contest of alphabets, a subject that we may call Musaean, if not musical, since the Greeks would undoubtedly consider it to belong to the Muses: K., offering his Phoenician letters to the Greeks, came into conflict with Linos, who was teaching his own (Linear B, I suppose), and killed him (to the advancement of literacy); whereupon the backward Thebans expelled K.: Zenob. 4.45; cf. p. 111.

combat myth in a number of features. Now we must return to the hero Herakles, a fighter of many monsters, to see whether a common pattern can be discovered within the chaotic mass of legend that surrounds him.

XII

HERAKLES

It is manifestly impossible to treat the whole legend cycle of Herakles within the limits of a single chapter, however long. A thorough study of Herakles would require another volume at least as large as this, if not more than one. Hence I can only discuss as briefly as possible a few Herakles legends that are especially relevant to the present study and that can augment our understanding of the combat myth in Greece—a few, that is, that I have not discussed as yet. For Herakles is no stranger to this study: he has been with us from nearly the beginning and has stood beside Apollo and Zeus as opponent of the great serpent; he has appeared as victor over brigands and tyrants that seem closely related to Python and as victor over Lityerses and Syleus; and we have noticed his tribulations on his way home with Geryon's cattle.

There can be little doubt that the Herakles who appears upon the pages of Greek and Latin authors, hardly one of whom fails to mention him somewhere, and who is pictured in many ancient paintings and sculptures, is a composite figure. Numerous gods and heroes, Greek and Asiatic, have contributed something to the Hellenic hero—or shall I say god?—for he occupies every point in the religio-mythical spectrum from mortal hero through demigod and chthonian deity to Olympian god. Cicero distinguished six

heroes of the name: the son of Alkmena, the contestant for
Apollo's tripod, and four others whom he calls Egyptian, Idaean
Dactyl, Tyrian, and Indian. Varro, it seems, enumerated forty-
three heroes of the name, even distinguishing a Theban from an
Argive Herakles, and each from a Tirynthian. But it is evident
that most Greeks, even the educated, knew only one Herakles, the
great Theban hero, to whom they referred all tales that used the
name; and they distinguished among the several *Hêrakleis* of the
learned no more than among the several Zeuses or Apollos that
Cicero distinguished in the same work as that in which he distinguished the several *Hêrakleis*. Now it is impossible and unnecessary to know where the name was first used or what local
hero first had it. Suffice it to say that the name itself is Greek and
means "Glory of Hera" or "Glory of the Mistress." I would question Farnell's and Rose's statements that this name, being compounded of a deity's name, proves that Herakles was not a god;
for Dionysos' name seems also to be a compound of which the first
element is the stem of *Zeus* (*Dio-*). Why the original bearer of
the name Herakles was so named we cannot say with certainty:
but an answer may be dimly seen in such a legend as that of the
hero's servitude to Omphale.[1]

Of Cicero's six *Hêrakleis* three are Semitic or Near Eastern on
Cicero's own showing: the Tyrian, who is Melqart, the Egyptian,
and the Indian, whom Cicero calls son of Belos, an indication
that he had more to do with western Asia than with India. Furthermore the great Asiatic giant-and-dragon fighters certainly contributed something to the legend of Herakles: Marduk, Ninurta,
Gilgamesh, Samson, Hupasiyas, Aqhat, and Indra too, as we shall
see. He was also identified with Sandon, god of Lydians, Cilicians,
and Cappadocians. It was this god who was Omphale's lover and
servant in the native Lydian tradition, and there can be little
doubt that the Herakles who died on a pyre was originally Sandon, a god who was burned on a pyre in Anatolian ritual and
myth. According to Ammianus Marcellinus, it was either Perseus
or Sandon who founded Tarsos, while Dion Chrysostom says that
Herakles was founder (*archêgos*); all three appear on coin-types

---

[1] Cic. *Nat. Deor.* 3.16.42; Varro *ap.* Serv. *Aen.* 8.564; see Farnell (1921) 97–103, Rose
(1928) 205.

of the city, as do Zeus and Baal Tarz. Zeus and Perseus seem to be Hellenistic substitutes for the Baal, and Herakles for Sandon, though they are not represented with the attributes of their native antecedents, but in the manner that had become customary in Greek art. The names and attributes are due to the Greeks; yet the identifications can be looked at as reassertions of ancient identities, as a reunion of Greek dragon fighters and dying gods (not of native Greek gods, however, e.g., Zeus, whose origin is not in question) with their Asiatic ancestors or cognates.[2]

Among Herakles' numerous combats can be found parallels to every variant of the combat myth that we have seen. His adventures ring every change upon the experiences and vicissitudes of the divine champion through the whole range of the pattern. But what is central or typical in the Herakles cycle, as I have already suggested (p. 260), is his combat with Thanatos, as we see it in the famous story of how he rescued Alkestis from death.

ALKESTIS AND THANATOS

The Alkestis myth, as we find it in Euripides' play and other sources, is composite. It combines the folktale of the bride's sacri-

---

[2] On Herakles-Sandon see Agath. *Hist.* 2.24; Amm. Marc. 14.8.3; Nonn. *Dion.* 34.191 f.; Joh. Lyd. *Mag.* 3.64; Synk. 290 Dind.; Dio Chrys. 33.47; coin-types in BMCC, Cilicia, pp. 166, 177–230 *passim* (pls. 29, 32–37); figurines in Goldman (1950) nos. 130–168, 194–202, figs. 223–227, 231; cf. Bossert (1932). On Herakles' oriental connections see Levy (1934), Goldman (1949). Miss Levy is unnecessarily troubled by the gulf in time between H. and his Babylonian affinities, and so considers Cilician Sandon the bridge between. Miss Goldman argues against supposing that Sandon can be the original of H. on the ground that Luvian migration to the Aegean area was too early, and Cilicia too far from Greece, to have had any effect upon the formation of Herakles; and she too points to the Greek name. But both ladies misconceive the question. H. is a composite figure, and one should not try to derive him (i.e., his characters, attributes, roles, etc.) *in toto* from any one source. We are concerned rather with particular roles and themes of orally transmitted stories: the tale on entering a country becomes attached to native gods and heroes. Folkloristic transmission does not move on the routes of trade only, but also passes from village to village until frontiers are crossed. Miss Goldman seems to assume that transmission through colonies can occur only at the time of settlement, as though bonds between homeland and colony were broken immediately thereafter. And while Miss Levy is right in supposing no direct relation between Marduk or Gilgamesh and H., she seems to forget that the old myths and festivals of Babylon lived on and influenced their neighbors down to Seleucid times, if not later. Miss Goldman forgets how widespread was Sandon's cult in Anatolia, reaching as it did the eastern shore of the Aegean.

Sandon can be connected with Kadmos too. According to Apollod. 3.14.3, Sandokos, who seems to be Sandon, went from Syria to Cilicia and founded Kelenderis; likewise Kilix, Kadmos' brother, went from Sidon to Cilicia and settled the country, founding cities (Herod. 7.91; Apollod. 3.1.1; LM 2.1185); and Kadmos himself wandered in Cilicia (p. 75).

fice with that of a hero's defeat of Death in combat. Only the latter belongs to the combat myth, which has been combined, as often, with a different type. Several forms of the bride-sacrifice type have been fused in the story as we find it in Euripides or Apollodoros. Each of the three death spirits that must be appeased, circumvented, fought, or caused to relent (Thanatos or Hades, the Moirai, Artemis), represents a different form of the story, as can be judged from studies that have been made of the many variants which have appeared in Europe and Asia. The Artemis who, offended by Admetos' neglect of her, filled his bridal chamber with coiled snakes is Pheraia, the great goddess of Pherai, identified with Hekate. She is that goddess of death, called Persephone in the sources, who relents and releases Alkestis in one form of the myth. The snakes, who in the ancient tale serve only as superfluous omens of coming doom, are adequately accounted for by a modern Rhodian variant of the folktale in which the bridegroom was fated to die of a snake's bite on his wedding day. And, as in so many Greek folktales, this doom was pronounced by the *Mires* (Moirai) at his birth.[3]

It was not difficult to attach the combat with Thanatos to the bride sacrifice as the means by which the bride was rescued from the fate to which she had offered herself. And since Herakles is not the only hero who fought and defeated Death, he may not have been the original rescuer of Alkestis: for it is conceivable that in the earliest story her husband went out to save her. But when Herakles had become the victor over death spirits in numerous stories, it was almost inevitable that he become the hero of the Alkestis story too—I say almost, since he never displaced Eurybatos and Euthymos against Sybaris and Heros. It is important to observe that the Alkestis story is exactly parallel to these: the hero happens along just in time to rescue the victim, whose sacrifice

---

[3] Sources of Alkestis myth: Eur. *Alk.*: Plato, *Symp.* 179BC; Apollod. 1.9.15 = Zenob. 1.18; Hyg. *Fab.* 50, 51, 251.3; Palaiph. 40. For studies of the myth and its folktale cognates see Lesky (1925), Megas (1933), Weber (1936), M. Gaster (1939), Croon (1952) 68–74. Hekate-Pheraia: Philippson (1944) 65–106. Artemis in Alk.-myth: Apollod. 1.9.15. Persephone releases Alk.: Plato, Apollod., *locc. cit.*: Hyg. *Fab.* 251.3 (Parcae). In the sources Thanatos, the popular death figure, is equivalent to Hades, the Olympian lord of death (Th. 3F): see Eur. *Alk.* 260–268, 439 (cf. 871); Apollod. 1.9.15; Aristoph. Gram. *Arg. in Alc.*: Serv.-Dan. *Aen.* 4.694; Charon too is mentioned, *Alk.* 439–441. On Thanatos see Heinemann (1913); Lesky 40, 60 f.; cf. Waser (1898). The coiled snakes are the only evidence of Th. 3B.

will preserve the state; he either waits at the tomb, as Herakles does in the best-known version, or boldly invades the death spirit's own realm, as Herakles does in another version, to wrestle with the demon himself. The rescue of a victim does not enter into many legends of Herakles, since sometimes he fights the death spirit for other reasons; but we have seen it in one version of the Lityerses legend (p. 112), and will see it again in the legend of Hesione.[4]

It is important to notice that several variants of the combat myth surround the Alkestis myth in the literary sources. Herakles was on his way to fetch the horses of Diomedes when he stopped at Pherai and fought Thanatos; nearby at Itonos or Pagasai (Th. 2A) he paused to fight Kyknos and Ares, and further north he met Lykaon. So the Thanatos combat becomes one of a series of four combats: three with sons of Ares, all death-demons, in one of which Ares, a death god, also opposed him; and one with Death in person. Obviously these are variants of a single original. This will become more evident presently when we discuss the combat at Pylos.[5]

When Herakles fought Thanatos to recover Alkestis, he was in servitude to Eurystheus, whose daughter or wife was called Admete. When Apollo tricked the Moirai to recover Alkestis' husband, he was in servitude to Admetos. We have already observed that *Admêtos* (the invincible) is a name that properly belongs to Hades or Thanatos (p. 87). *Admêtê* likewise is properly a name of the queen of the dead. In folklore, as we have seen, the king and queen of the dead are often hostel keepers, hosts who welcome everybody to their house. Now not only is Admetos a host to whose halls come guests from every land, but he is in particular the host of Herakles and of Apollo. And in Euripides' *Alkestis*, as in his *Syleus*, Herakles behaves badly at table and causes his host's servants much distress. So in the fusion of tales that produced the classical Alkestis myth the Admetos who is keeper of the hostelry of death became fused with the husband of

---

[4] Herakles wrestles Thanatos at the tomb: Eur. *Alk.* 837–860, 1140–1142; Apollod., Palaiph., *locc. cit.* He descends to the lower world: Lucian *DMort.* 23.3; Hyg. *Fab.* 51.3; interpolator in Palaiph. 40; cf. Eur. *Alk.* 850–854.

[5] See Eur. *Alk.* 481–506. We have already observed (p. 35) that the Kyknos combat is also a member of the Dryopian series: Koronos, Laogoras, Kyknos, Amyntor, Eurytos.

Alkestis, the self-sacrificing bride; and Alkestis takes the place of the death hostess, Admete or Xenodike or Omphale. As the first two are daughters of the death host, we should notice that Hesychios calls Hekate daughter of Admetos. As the young woman devoted to Thanatos and rescued by the hero, Alkestis would ordinarily become the hero's wife, like Andromeda or the maid of Temesa; but the composite myth could not allow such a conclusion: the bride must return to her husband.[6]

So the underlying combat myth can be discerned: the hero had to enter the house of the death lord because either he had died (Th. 8A) or he had to do penance (Th. 10c), which is just another form of his death, or he entered of his own free will in order to fight Death and conquer him. In any case his sojourn ended with Death's defeat, whereupon he returned to life, bringing a woman with him to be his wife, either Death's own daughter (or wife), who had fallen in love with him and helped him, or a maiden whom he had rescued (Th. 4E). The alternative versions here indicated were all present in the antecedent material of the Alkestis myth: it was truly a composite narrative. Herakles was expiating a murder; he also boldly attacked Thanatos on his own ground. Apollo was undergoing an eight-year purification and expiation for killing either the Cyclopes or Python, merely two versions of one story. For the killing of the Cyclopes is a

---

[6] Admete (Th. 1c): Apollod. 2.5.9; as name of Hekate in Orph. Hymn Mag. 3.3. Admete is a daughter of Ocean and Tethys, according to Hes. *Theog.* 349 and Hom. Hymn 2.421. Persephone is called Δηοῦς θυγατέρ' ἰφθίμην ἀδμῆτ(α): Apollon. *Arg.* 4.896 f. Some scholars oppose connecting Admetos with Hades-Thanatos: Lesky (1925) 5–9, Rose (1928) 160, note 14. But I think that they have confined themselves too much to Admetos' role in the classical Alkestis myth. See Croon (1952) 69–71, who deals with their arguments. One should notice that several verses in Euripides' play are capable of a double meaning. In the text above I have alluded to *Alk.* 747 f.: Πολλοὺς μὲν ἤδη κἀπὸ παντοίας χθονὸς/ξένους μολόντας οἶδ' ἐς 'Αδμήτου δόμους. Cf. 809, 829 f. Hades is called τὸν πολυξενώτατον Ζῆνα τῶν κεκμηκότων, Aesch. *Suppl.* 157 f. Again Admetos says, ζηλῶ φθιμένους, κείνων ἔραμαι, κεῖν' ἐπιθυμῶ δώματα ναίειν./οὔτε γὰρ αὐγὰς χαίρω προσορῶν, κτλ. (866–868). It is hard to believe either that the *double entendre* was not intentional or that an earlier meaning of Admetos has not clung to the story. Notice also that Adm. desires the death of others (Th. 4A): he calls upon the old to die, and he accepts the sacrifice of a young woman (Ths. 4c, 4E, 7c); for Thanatos values especially the death of the young: *Alk.* 55. His father's name was Pheres, masculine form of Pheraia, the great Hekate of Pherai. He was, moreover, the possessor of large herds, a characteristic of Hades: Croon *loc. cit.* Herakles at Adm.'s table (Th. 8c): *Alk.* 747–772. Notice that Alk. had a sister Medusa, according to Hyg. *Fab.* 24.4. It is the husband role that unites the Adm. of the classical story to the death lord; for Death either has a wife (Th. 1c) or desires the to-be-rescued maiden as his bride. Hekate Adm.'s daughter: Hesych. A1156.

sequel to the myth of his love for Koronis, Phlegyas' daughter. The Cyclopes succeed Phlegyas as object of Apollo's wrath; and as the Phlegyans killed his son Philammon, so the Cyclopes killed his son Asklepios, who as slain god doubles for Apollo himself (Ths. 8A, 6B). They had become Zeus's blacksmiths, makers of his thunderbolts, and they killed Asklepios on Zeus's orders (the story shows the hostility between father and son which we have seen elsewhere); but earlier they were also demons of storm, volcanoes, and the lower world: the Cyclops Polyphemos of the Odyssey had nothing to do with Zeus's smithy. So, as in other composite myths, themes are repeated: the enemy is killed twice, and the god dies twice, and his second death is identified with his punishment or expiation for killing the dragon, who in spite of his wickedness was a great and powerful deity and could not be killed with impunity.[7]

HERAKLES AT PYLOS

In the Herakles-Thanatos episode of the Alkestis myth the hero's opponent is simply Death himself, appearing in his own name and form, not transmuted into monster or giant. If the episode is separated from the Alkestis myth, then it appears to be a version of Herakles' combat with Hades at Pylos. There, according to the Iliad, Herakles fought Hades and wounded him fearfully with an arrow, forcing him to flee in dire pain to Zeus's palace on Olympos. Pausanias adds that Hades came to help the Pylians against Herakles, when the hero made his campaign against Elis and Pylos.[8]

---

[7] Cyclopes and Asklepios: Eur. *Alk.* 1–7; Akusilaos 19, 1.52 J; Apollod. 3.10.4. The two last-named authorities say that Apollo's servitude to a man was substituted for casting him into Tartaros (cf. p. 87); i.e., the servitude of the classical story has become distinct from the god's death. The Cyclopes possessed the potent thunderbolt to begin with: Apollod. 1.2.1; cf. p. 243. Notice that during Apollo's servitude to Adm. he performed a dangerous task for his master: he yoked a lion and a boar to a chariot (Apollod. 1.9.15; Hyg. *Fab.* 50); one is reminded of the ordeals of the Land-Master (p. 502) and of the young Maya gods (p. 507). As the classical myth has it, he did so to win Alk. for Adm.; but probably to begin with, the hero won her for himself; for the story is like others in which the hero entered a contest to win the ogre-king's daughter, e.g., Atalanta, Hippodameia; cf. Medea. In the Apollo version the death lord's defeat is reduced to Apollo's deception of the Moirai: he plied them with wine, thus tricking them much as they tricked Typhon (Th. 9a).

[8] Il. 5.395–404, where Hades is called *pelôrios* (Th. 3A); Paus. 6.25.2 f., who also speaks of the unique cult of Hades in Elis.

Now Hades is called euphemistically Klymenos or Perikly-menos, the Renowned; and Herakles' opponent at Pylos is more often called Periklymenos Neleus' son (or Poseidon's; see note 11). Poseidon had granted him the power to change his shape at will (Th. 3E): that power which deities of the sea and dead have in common is here given by the sea lord to the death lord. In combat with Herakles he took the shapes of eagle, lion, snake, bee, ant, or fly (Th. 3B), as we learn from various sources; and either as bee or fly was swatted by Herakles' club on Athena's prompting (Th. 7D), or as an eagle was pierced by his arrow. Apollodoros combines two versions when he pits both Periklymenos and Hades against Herakles.[9]

On that day the hero killed Neleus himself and eleven of his twelve sons (Th. 7G), among whom are found the names Asterios (see p. 314), Tauros, Pylaon (the warder of the gate), Phrasios (see p. 334, note 20), Alastor (Avenger), all of which suggest either death spirits (Th. 3F) or monsters. Their father is the death god too: he is *Nêleus,* the Pitiless.[10]

But Pindar says that it was Poseidon (Th. 2E), Neleus' father, who opposed Herakles at Pylos; then after a brief allusion to Herakles' quarrel with Apollo over the tripod, he adds that Hades opposed Herakles, but could not hold his staff unshaken against him. Like Apollodoros he combines two versions, in each of which Herakles' opponent was differently named.[11]

Finally, in the *Shield* it was Ares whom Herakles fought at Pylos. Four times the hero struck home with his spear and felled the god; the fourth time Ares was grievously wounded in the thigh and would have been stripped of his armor like any slain warrior, had he not been an immortal god. Ares fared just as Hades did; the only difference is spear for arrow. Obviously one version of the Pylos combat called the death god Ares. For Ares, lord of war's slaughter and father of brigands and monsters, was

---

[9] Hes. frag. 14 Rz., and *ap.* Schol. A *in Il.* 2.333; Euphorion *ap.* Schol. Vet. *in* Apollon. *Arg.* 1.156; Apollod. 1.9.9, 2.7.3; Ovid *Met.* 12.549–572; Sen. *Med.* 634–636; cf. Il. 11.690–693; Apollon. *Arg.* 1.156–160. Hyg. *Fab.* 10.2 says that Periklymenos escaped death in eagle form. Herakles can kill the mortal hero, Neleus' son; but Hades he can only wound; yet in the underlying myth there is really no difference: see note 12 below. See further von Schroeder (1914) 100–102.

[10] Apollod. 1.9.9; Schol. Vet. on Apollon. *loc. cit.*

[11] Pind. *Ol.* 9.29–35; Schol. A on Il. 5.392. The Pylian Periklymenos is Poseidon's son (Ths. 1B, 2E), according to Sen. *Med.* 635; cf. p. 479 with note 3.

very likely to be associated with the realm of death; and there is other evidence than the Pylian myth that there were Greeks who considered him the death god. His sons Phobos and Deimos (Fear and Panic) and his sister Eris (Strife) appear among both demons of the battlefield and demons of death. On the other hand those evil underworld spirits called Keres first appear to us upon the battlefield in company with Phobos, Eris, and other war demons (p. 116, note 47). When the Greeks followed the Babylonian fashion of naming the planets after gods, that planet which the Babylonians assigned to the death god Nergal they assigned to Ares (Mars). It may be, after all, that Ares was a death god before he became primarily associated with war.[12]

So the death god who opposed Herakles at Pylos had five different names in the several versions of the tale: Hades, Poseidon, Ares, Periklymenos, and Neleus. A Scholiast says that three gods were allied with Neleus: Poseidon, Hades, and Hera; while two were allied with Herakles: Athena and Zeus (Ths. 7D, 7E). Hera's part in the combat (Ths. 1C, 5B) is mentioned in the Iliad, and also by Panyasis: Herakles struck her in the breast with his arrow.[13]

The combat took place at Pylos, i.e., the gate. Originally it was the gate to Hades' realm; as Nilsson has pointed out, the legend of Herakles' war on Pylos is his combat with Hades-Thanatos

---

[12] Ares at Pylos: *Shield* 359–367. Ares as death-god: Artemid. *Oneir.* 2.34; LM 1.483–485; cf. Farnell (1909) 397, who has a different view. Deimos, Phobos, Eris, among underworld demons: Artemid. *loc. cit.*: Ovid *Met.* 4.485, Pavor and Terror are among the companions of Tisiphone; Virg. *Georg.* 3.552, *Aen.* 6.276, 280; Sen. *Oed.* 594; Sil. Ital. 13.586. The apotropaic images of Phobos can only with difficulty be distinguished from those of the Gorgon: LM 3.2389–2395. Notice that at Aigialeia Apollo and Artemis were overcome by a *deima* and that the place was thereafter called Phobos: Paus. 2.7.7. Nergal's planet: Dhorme (1949) 39. Ares was father of the Argonaut Askalaphos, homonym of an infernal demon: Apollod. 1.5.3, 1.9.16. Notice that Ares' so-called survival in the Kyknos and Pylos combats, when after being severely wounded he was carried off to the abode of the gods, is really no different from the enemy's death in other stories: he is mortally wounded and sent off to another world. In the Adonis-myth Ares in boar form killed the dying god: Scholl. BT on Il. 5.385; Nonn. *Dion.* 41.209–211. Notice that the Aloadai (Otos and Ephialtes) avenged Adonis by imprisoning Ares in a bronze pot, where he lay for thirteen months, nearly dead, until Hermes stole him away from his captors. That is, Ares suffered much the same distress from the twins as Zeus from Typhon: Il. 5.385–391 with Scholl. BT on 385; Apollod. 1.7.4. He has suddenly been converted from enemy into suffering god, whereas the Aloadai shift from avengers of the dying god to the Typhon role.

[13] Il. 5.392–394 with Scholl. ABT on 392; Panyasis *ap.* Clem. Alex. *Protr.* 2.36, p. 31P *et ap.* Arn. *Adv. Gent.* 4.25.

historicised. This interpretation is in fact made by an Homeric
Scholiast, who says that Herakles fought Hades at Hades' gate
(*pylê*) at the time he made his descent to fetch Kerberos. Now at
Hermione the infernal rulers were worshipped as Klymenos and
Chthonia (p. 479, note 3), in whose precinct men could see the
chasm through which Herakles brought Kerberos to the upper
world. Furthermore, in our earliest source, the Iliad, we read that
Herakles struck Hades "at Pylos among corpses," i.e., at the gate
among the dead. The evidence clearly shows that this is a tale of
the hero's bold assault upon the land of death, at the gate of
which the death god tried to bar his way in vain.[14]

ANTAIOS

It was just this combat between Herakles and the death god at
the gate that we find in the Kyknos legend, where Death appears
both as Ares, mounted on a chariot which Deimos and Phobos
drove—Herakles wounded him with his spear, striking deep into
the flesh of his thigh as at Pylos—and as Kyknos, the collector of
skulls (p. 29); then too Herakles fought among corpses. Ares'
son Diomedes also had a mound of skulls, and so did Poseidon's
son (Ths. 1B, 2E) Antaios, whom Herakles fought and killed in
Libya. Like Kyknos, Antaios was using the skulls as building
material: for he roofed over Poseidon's temple with them. His
mother was Ge (Th. 1A), who renewed his strength when he
wrestled: for whenever he felt exhausted, he merely had to fall to
earth in order to recover and even increase his might (Th. 7B).
He challenged all visitors to a wrestling match in which they were
bound to lose their lives (Th. 4F). But when Herakles came that
way, he killed Antaios by lifting him clear of the ground and
crushing him in his arms.[15]

---

[14] Il. 5.397 with Schol. A; also Scholl. BT on 5.395; Paus. 2.35.10. See Nilsson (1932)
203 f., Kroll (1932) 373 f., Croon (1952) 67–87. The historicised tale was located at both
Elean and Messenian Pylos. Notice Neleus' son Pylaon above. Hades was called *pylartês*:
Il. 8.367 (in an allusion to Herakles' descent for Kerberos), 13.415; Mosch. 4.86; cf.
Th. 4F. Notice Orph. Hymn. Mag. 3.5, πύλας κλειτοῦ ἀδάμαντος ("Αιδου). Near Elean Pylos
H. fought and killed a brigand Sauros (Lizard), who molested wayfarers (Paus. 6.21.3);
the lizard-dragon recurs in Greek myth only in the exploit of Apollo Sauroktonos: Plin.
NH 34.8.70; cf. Mart. 14.172.

[15] On Antaios see Pind. *Isthm.* 3.70–73 with Schol. Vet.; Plato *Theait.* 169B; Apollod.
2.5.11; Diod. 4.17.4; Gabinius *ap.* Strab. 17.3.8, p. 829; Philostr. *Imag.* 2.21; Ovid *Met.*
9.183 f.; Lucan BC 4.589–655; Hyg. *Fab.* 31.1. On the skulls see Pind. *loc. cit.* Ant. was

The Antaios legend thus repeats the pattern encountered in the legends of Lityerses, Syleus, and Phorbas. Like Syleus, Antaios had a female partner, his wife Tingis, eponym of Tangier, or Iphinoe (Th. 1C). After Herakles killed Antaios he took her as his mistress (Th. 8D). Whether he took her forcefully or she had betrayed her husband for love of the hero is nowhere said. Now it is significant that Antaios is placed in the very land of the Gorgon, in farthest Libya, specifically in the regions between Tangier and the Lixos River (Th. 2A), but once also by Lake Tritonis, and once on the Bagrada River in Tunis. As Medusa was either a queen or marauder, so Antaios, usually called king of his Libyan land, is also a cave-dwelling brigand who brought death to both his Libyan neighbors and foreigners who ventured that way (Ths. 2B, 4A). As Medusa's abode was surrounded by the petrified images of men (p. 284), so Antaios' wrestling place was set in the midst of a graveyard: all about were gravestones and funeral mounds (Th. 3F). This, of course, is a variation upon his collection of skulls.[16]

Moreover, according to Apollodoros, Herakles was then on his way to get the apples of the Hesperides. On setting out from home he did not know how to reach their garden, so that he first went to nymphs, daughters of Zeus and Themis, who told him where to find Nereus. So Herakles, catching Nereus while he slept, had to wrestle with him while he went through the whole repertoire of changes of shape that sea gods have; and binding him, he did not release him until he had learned what he wanted to know. Then Herakles went to Libya, where he met Antaios. Now the nymphs born of Zeus and Themis are either the Hours or the Moirai. Herakles needed their help precisely as Perseus needed help from nymphs when he too had to go to the regions of Atlas and the

---

gigantic: in his tomb Sertorius discovered a skeleton sixty cubits long (Plut. *Sert.* 9); cp. Ketos' skeleton, p. 276 (Th. 3A); cf. Gabin. *loc. cit.* He looked like a *thêrion* (Th. 3B; Philostr.) and ate lions (Th. 4D; Lucan 4.602). As Philostr. describes him, he was almost as broad as tall; though he had a head, he otherwise recalls Kabandha of the *Râmâyaṇa* (p. 206). Notice too that he was identified with a hill, which was also called his tomb (Th. 10A): Mela 3.10.106.

[16] Antaios' wife: Pherek. 76, 1.81 J; Plut. *Sert.* 9; EM 679. Morocco: Gabin., Plut., Mela, *locc. cit.* (note 15). Tritonis: Pherek. 75, 1.80 J; Bagrada: Lucan BC 4.587–590; the Bagrada was the scene of combat between Regulus and a gigantic snake: Sil. Ital. 6.118–293; see Bassett (1955). Antaios' cave: Lucan BC 4.589 f., 601. Slaughter of Libyans, etc.: *ibid.* 605 f. His *hybris*: Philostr. *Imag.* 2.21.1 f. His graveyard: *ibid.*

western shores of Libya. Except for a few shifts, the episodes are much the same. Perseus forced the Graiai to show him the way to the Naiads, who willingly gave him the means of his success; whereas the nymphs willingly, it seems, showed Herakles the way to Nereus, whom he had to force to show him the way to his goal. It was Medusa whom Perseus found sleeping, not the person who would show him the way. The wrestle with Nereus is a doublet of the wrestle with Antaios. Both seem to be warders of the Hesperides' garden (Th. 2c). And as the warder of the golden apples, Antaios, who was actually identified with a hill (p. 331, note 15), would appear to be identical with Atlas; or perhaps it is better to say that he alternates with him. For Antaios reigned on the Barbary Coast, and was located by the ancients near either end of the Atlas Range, the very regions where Atlas still lived and ruled as king in the Hesperides legend. Both tried to keep heroes from reaching the Hesperides. Finally, it was sometimes said that Ge was Atlas' mother and that Poseidon was his father, though the two are not joined as parents in any one source.[17]

The Libyan Lamia, Poseidon's daughter, lived in this very region. She was half sister of Antaios; and there is more to this relationship than merely the coincidence of Poseidon's being considered father of both. For Lamia is a form of Hekate, who was called Antaia. In verses assigned to Sophocles an *antaios* and a *deima* are her creatures. When we learn from Hesychios that the *antaia* are *daimonia* sent by Hekate, we perceive that the word is a synonym of *Hekataia* (p. 117). Now an *antaios* or *antaion* (accoster) is an apparition, a ghost or revenant. The death spirit

---

[17] Herakles was on his way to Hesperides: Apollod. 2.5.11; on his way back: Philostr. *Imag.* 2.21.2; on his way to Geryon: Diod. 4.17.4; or he went to rid the land of Antaios: Pind. *Isthm.* 3.70–73; Lucan BC 4.609–611. Daughters of Zeus and Themis: Hes. *Theog.* 901–906; Pherek. 16a, 1.65 J (they lived in a cave like the Graiai). Atlas as king: Diod. 3.60.1; Ovid *Met.* 4.628, 633. Atlas Ge's son: Diod. 3.60.1; Hyg. *Fab.* praef. 3; Poseidon's son: Plato *Critias* 113D–114A; Schol. Vet. on Plato *Tim.* 24E. Notice that H's first adventure on his quest of the apples in Apollodoros' sequence is his meeting with Kyknos (= Lykaon, p. 30) on the Echedoros. Apollod. says that the Hesperides and Atlas were not in Libya, but among the Hyperboreans; but for confusions of the several paradises see p. 345. A bridge between the combats with Nereus and with Antaios can be seen in H's combat with *Gêras* (Old Age); for Nereus is a *Halios Gerôn*, and the combat with Old Age is a variant of the combat with Death; see vase paintings cited or reproduced in LM 3.2083–2085. *Senectus* appears beside *Metus* among the creatures of Hades in Virg. *Aen.* 6.275.

has received this term as a proper name when he is called Antaios;
and his sister-consort is Antaia. So Antaios' strange power of receiving strength from contact with the earth becomes comprehensible when one realises that he is a spectre (Th. 3F) whose
strength resides in the earth from which he rises and into which
he can disappear, and who perishes if he loses contact with the
ground. Here is another version of Herakles' bout with Death at
the gate, i.e., the Gates of Herakles (when Antaios resides at
Tangier), the passage to the River Ocean and to Geryon's realm.[18]

But there was a different story about Antaios. According to
Pindar, King Antaios of Irasa in Cyrenaica had a beautiful daughter who had many suitors both native and foreign. So he instituted
a foot race, placing his daughter at the finish line to become the
bride of the runner who should first put his hand upon her; and
she was won by Alexidamos. It has been disputed, even by ancient
commentators, that this is the same Antaios as he whom Herakles
fought. But as good an authority as Pherekydes of Athens says
that Herakles' opponent lived in Irasa. Moreover there is a link
in the theme of bride-wager, for the Cyrenaic Antaios has this
institution in common with Oinomaos, Euenos, and Atalanta's
father. Of all these kings it is said that they heaped up or hung
up the skulls of those suitors who lost the race; and the first two
are linked with Phorbas, Kyknos, and Antaios. So we can conjecture a story in which Antaios himself ran a race with all comers,
offering his daughter as prize to anyone who could outstrip him,
but who would die if Antaios won; and we may suppose that she
stood at the goal purposely to lure men into making the attempt
to win her. The substitution of contest for combat we have already encountered, particularly in the Kyknos legend.[19]

---

[18] Hekate Antaia, *antaioi, antaia*: Soph. frag. 311 Nauck²; Hesych. A5308. Antaios
as spectre: Nilsson (1932) 215; Radermacher (1938) 287–291. Herakles' Alkyoneus is a
double of Antaios; he could not die on his native soil of Pallene, so that H., acting again
on Athena's advice, dragged him beyond the borders to kill him: Apollod. 1.6.1. On vase
paintings Athena is seen backing H. against Antaios (Th. 7D), while Ge backs Antaios:
citations in Vian (1952) 43 f.; compare with figs. 4–11. Hermes backs H. (Th. 7E) on
vase *r* (Vian). Apollod. makes H's meeting with Alkyoneus part of the Gigantomachy;
but as Vian (*ibid.* 217–221) shows, it was actually one of the series of combats with cattle-
rustlers that H. fought on the way back from Erytheia; cf. Croon (1952) 53–57.

[19] Pind. *Pyth.* 9.105–125; Pherek. 75, 1.80 J. Oinomaos' skulls: Soph. *ap.* Schol. Vet.
in Pind. *Isthm.* 3.72 (92); Apollod.*Epit.* 2.5.; Tzetz. on Lyk. 160; Hyg. *Fab.* 185.2. Euenos'

In Busiris, the savage Egyptian king, who sacrificed all foreigners that came to his shores, and whom Herakles killed after having allowed himself to be dressed as a sacrificial victim, we have another form of Antaios. He too is a son of Poseidon. His name is a Greek version of an Egyptian compound that contains the name Osiris, who, though Set's victim, was also a ruler over the dead. Again the hero rescues the death god's victims. There is a trace of a story that Busiris demanded young women: for Diodoros says that he sent pirates to carry off the Hesperid nymphs for himself, but that Herakles came along at the right time to rescue them and to kill the pirates.[20]

GERYON AND CACUS

The encounters with Antaios and Busiris, forerunners of Herakles' meeting with the monstrous Geryon (Geryoneus, Geryones) in the narrative of Diodoros, are actually doublets of the same story. Geryon has already entered into this study a number of times, and his likeness in general to various representatives of the dragon enemy has been seen in his monstrous form: either he had the entire bodies of three men joined together, so that he had not only three heads and six arms, but six legs too (Th. 3c); or the three bodies came together at his waist, so that his lower body was single (fig. 26). He was, furthermore, the son of Chrysaor and the Oceanid Kallirrhoe, the grandson of Poseidon and Medusa and of Ocean and Tethys (Ths. 1A, 1B). It remains now to realise, as

skulls: Bacchyl. 20 and frag. 20A Snell; Tzetz. *loc. cit.* Both Oinomaos and Euenos were Ares' sons: Paus. 5.22.6; Apollod. 1.7.7. Euenos was identified with the Aetolian river Euenos (p. 354); as such his parents were Ocean and Tethys: Hes. *Theog.* 337–345. Atalanta was suckled by a she-bear and transformed into a lion: see Apollod. 3.9.2; Ovid *Met.* 10.560–704 (notice how Atalanta's beauty lures Hippomenes to try, 578–596). *Pyth.* 9.107 f. shows a link between one Antaios and the other: the explicit reference to *xenoi* who came, together with *syngonoi*, to Irasa to woo the daughter. The race suggests a connection with actual rituals; for rites and sacrifices in honor of Antaios (Th. 10D) see Plut. *Sert.* 9. Since Oinomaos set the race because he loved his own daughter, we may suppose that the same thing was said of Antaios; hence the daughter called Alkeis or Barke (Schol. Vet. on *Pyth.* 9.105 [183]) may be one with the wife Tingis-Iphinoe.

[20] Apollod. 2.5.11; Diod. 4.27.2–4; Hyg. *Fab.* 31.2 and 56. Phrasios, who instructed Busiris to make these sacrifices, has the name of a son of Neleus. Osiris as ruler of the dead: Frankfort (1948) 197–212; Černy (1952) 88 f. Antaios was located in Egypt too: he gave Antaios' Village ('Ανταίου Κώμη) its Greek name; it was said to be the scene of both Horos' killing of Typhon-Set and Herakles' combat with Antaios, evidence that the two combats were identified.

several scholars have already made clear, that he is the king of the dead, a form of Thanatos or Hades (Th. 3F).[21]

In summary, the following reasons are given for interpreting Geryon as Thanatos: (1) His island of Erytheia (Red Land) lay across the Ocean Stream (Th. 2E), according to Hesiod, in the darkness. Though later authors identified Erytheia with Gades or

FIGURE 26. HERAKLES AND GERYON

Tartessos, or said that it lay opposite Gades, they still placed it in the sunset regions at the western edge of the world. (2) Geryon had great herds of kine like Admetos or Hades himself. (3) Guarding the cattle were Eurytion, son of Ares and Erytheia, and the

[21] On Geryon see Hes. *Theog.* 287–294, 979–983; Stesich. frags. 5–10 Bergk; Hekat. 26, 1.14 J; Pind. frag. 152 Bowra; Aesch. frag. 74 Nauck[2] and *Agam.* 870; Eur. *Her.* 423 f.; Apollod. 2.5.10; Diod. 4.17 f.; epigr. *ap.* ps.-Aristot. *Mir. Ausc.* 133; Philostr. *Vit. Ap.* 5.4 f.; Ovid *Met.* 9.184 f.; Hyg. *Fab.* 30.11; Pedias. 10; Palaiph. 24; Col. Sal. *Lab. Herc.* 3.28; for a complete list of the ancient sources see Croon (1952) 89–92 (App. A); for a complete list of vase-paintings see *ibid.* 93–103 (App. B). In fig. 26 notice that G. in armor resembles a monstrous Kyknos; cp. figs. 8–11. Many vases show Athena, Hermes, and Iolaos as Herakles' helpers (Ths. 7D, 7E). On one Nike wreathes H. (Th. 10B): Croon 102, no. 53. The demonstration that G. is a death god is made by Radermacher (1903) 42–44; Schweitzer (1922) 87 f., 152; Croon 31 f.; and authorities cited by Schweitzer 87, note 4, and Croon 32, note 18. But see Rose (1954), who interprets G. to be an "upper chthonian" of the sort who control riches, and his realm to be a "World Below," distinct from Hades' realm, as seen in the Greek folktale of Dawkins (1953) 259 f. But that place is the earthly paradise, which cannot be clearly separated from the death realm (see p. 382). Notice the connection between G. and Hesperides (see note 24).

two-headed hound Orthos (Orthros) (Th. 3B), son of Typhon and Echidna, obviously a double of Kerberos. (4) Menoites, Hades' herdsman, was also pasturing Hades' kine in Erytheia when Herakles arrived, according to Apollodoros' narrative, and he reported Herakles' theft of the cattle to Geryon. Later, when Herakles descended to the underworld to get Kerberos, he encountered Menoites again. Wanting to offer blood to the ghosts, he seized one of Hades' cows; when Menoites challenged him to wrestle, Herakles threw his arms about his body, crushed his ribs, and would have destroyed him, had not Persephone begged him off. It is apparent that Menoites and Eurytion are the same herdsman of the dead, who is himself an offshoot of the warder, guide, and ruler of the dead: Thanatos, Hades, Geryon, Antaios.[22]

Hesiod had simply placed Geryon vaguely on the farther shore of Ocean; and there is evidence that the Greeks had assigned him to various places in Italy, Sicily, and Greece, among them the once Dryopian regions of Ambrakia and the Spercheios Valley, where there was a town called Erythrai. We have already seen that Geryon was also placed in Lydia (p. 108), where he had been identified with the native river god Hyllos. But quite early Gades was established as his home.[23]

---

[22] (1) Hes. *Theog.* 292–294; Stes. frag. 5 Bergk; Aesch. frag. 74 Nauck². While Apollod. identifies Erytheia with Gadeira (Gades), he says that Herakles got Helios' vessel to sail across Ocean to Erytheia and that, having taken the cattle and put them in the vessel, he sailed back to Tartessos, which is either identical with Gades or very near it: see Croon (1952) 18, note 25. Erytheia = Gades: Herod. 4.8.2; Strabo 3.2.11, p. 148; Pliny NH 4.22.120; Mela 3.6.46 f.; Diod. Philostr., Pedias., *locc. cit.* (see note 21). (2) Diod. *loc. cit.* (3) Hes., Apollod., Pedias., *locc. cit.* (see note 21); Schol. Vet. on Apollon. *Arg.* 4.1399; Serv.-Dan. *Aen.* 8.299. (4) Apollod. 2.5.10 f. Notice the similarity to the Theiodamas episode (p. 37) in H's killing of the beast against the swain's wish. The likeness is the more significant in that H's encounter with the Rhodian ploughman took place on his way to the Hesperides. The labor of the Augeian stables is but another variant of the Geryon legend: (*a*) Augeias was son of Helios or Poseidon or Phorbas (p. 50); it should be noticed that H. drew his bow against Helios, when the god oppressed him with heat, just as he did against Ocean on the same adventure, when the latter tossed his boat. (*b*) Augeias had large herds which H. took, (*c*) after killing Eurytos (p. 483) and Kteatos, sons of Poseidon or of Augeias' brother Aktor, Siamese twins (i.e., a two-headed Geryon): Apollod. 2.5.5, 2.7.2; Pind. *Ol.* 10.24–42. Notice that a severe sickness came upon H. when he first marched against the Eleans, and he had to make a truce with them (Th. 8A); but when the twins treacherously attacked his army, he regained his vigor. Also H's attack on Elis precedes his attack on Pylos and Neleus in the systematised legend cycle. The Thessalian Aktor was father of Eurytion and Menoitios: Apollod. 1.8.2, 1.9.16, 3.13.1. See Schweitzer (1922) 107–129.

[23] On Geryon's abode in Italy, Sicily, or Greece see Croon (1952) 30, 36–52, 61–66; Hekataios (26, 1.14 J) denied that G. had lived in Spain, and placed him in Ambrakia.

There was good reason, it would seem, why among all the Phoenician colonies of the west the Geryon myth should become especially attached to Gades. There Geryon had a tomb, on which grew two pine trees, whose leaves, it was said, dripped with blood. There too Melqart, with whom Herakles was identified, had an especially important cult. So Herakles of Gades is Baal, while Geryon, we may suppose, is either Yam or Mot, or a fusion of the two. For the city had an altar of *Gêras* (Old Age), and there alone, according to Philostratos, men sang hymns in honor of Thanatos (Mot). Not only is Geras an opponent of Herakles (see p. 332, note 17), but, not to mention the Halios Geron, he recalls the *Gerôn* Ophion or Ogygos, for whom in one tradition (p. 231) Tartessos was a stronghold for war against the gods. Ophion-Ogygos is Ocean, who also opposed Herakles during his far-western ventures (see note 22). The Greeks, of course, gave Greek names to Phoenician gods and demons. There in southwestern Spain, it seems, they came upon the place which Phoenician colonists imagined to be the scene of Baal's combats with Yam and Mot. This fitted well the tale of Herakles' combat by the western Ocean at the portals of darkness with a monstrous enemy, Thanatos or Ocean or Geryon, a tale that had already taken shape among the Greeks when they first sailed into western seas; it was, after all, a scion of the same stock.[24]

The dragoness of the combat myth is likely to become Hera in a Herakles legend. So we are told that Hera helped Geryon (Th. 1c) and that it was in this combat that Herakles wounded her upon her right breast. This wound she was also said to have received at Pylos, as we have seen. Now when Isocrates tells us that Herakles made war on Neleus and his sons, and killed all

---

[24] Herakles' worship at Gades: Polyb. *ap.* Strab. 3.5.7, p. 172; Diod. 4.18.3; Arr. *Anab.* 2.16.4; Philostr. *Vit. Ap.* 5.4 f. Arrian says that this was the Tyrian H. and that his temple and rites were Phoenician; cf. Philostr. (Th. 10D). Geryon's tomb and tree: Philostr.; Paus. 1.35.8 (tree only). Geras, Thanatos: Philostr., who mentions also an altar of Penia; cf. Virg. *Aen.* 6.276, where *Egestas* appears beside Senectus, Metus, Discordia, etc., among the demons at the mouth of Orcus. Perhaps G's name was popularly connected with *gêras, gerôn:* see p. 341, note 30. According to Philostr., the Islands of the Blest were not far from Gades, near the shores of Libya; they can be identified with the Hesperides' Garden and Atlantis. Notice that G., Atlas, Phorkys, and Medusa alike were said to rule over rich islands to the west of Libya (Th. 2A). In a so-called Euhemeristic version H. is said to have gone west with an army to fight G's forces (Th. 7G), as Perseus is said to have attacked the Gorgons' realm with an army (p. 295).

except Nestor, because they had robbed him of the Erytheian kine, we can see that the Geryon tale is but another form of the combat with Hades and his queen at the gate.[25]

Hera enters into Apollodoros' narrative in a different way: after Herakles had recovered his cattle from various robbers and was driving them beside the Ionian Sea, Hera sent a gadfly (*oistros*) to stampede the cattle, causing them to become scattered and some to be permanently lost. So Hera joins Skylla, Echidna, and Kelto as a woman who robbed him of these cattle; furthermore one is reminded of the gadfly that Hera sent to torment the heifer Io, who gave the Ionian Sea its name when she ran beside it in her frenzy; and this cow Hermes had stolen from Argos Panoptes, who is presented as the monstrous herdsman in that story. Since Io, identified with Isis, is said to have searched for and found her child whom the Kuretes had stolen at Hera's command, and since she seems to be a variant of Europa, mate of the bull Zeus (p. 314), she may have more to do with Geryon's herd than appears at first sight.[26]

In earlier chapters (especially chapter vi) I have had occasion to mention several bandits, robber barons, and monstrous women who attempted to take Geryon's kine from Herakles, and who were usually successful in getting possession of them, or at least some of them, for a time. I have found twenty-one of these cattle-lifters, and there may be more. The male robbers, such as Eryx, Lakinios, and Cacus, are plainly doubles of Geryon; and I have just pointed to those versions that place Geryon himself in Italy or Greece. Moreover, as Apollodoros tells the story, Geryon himself attacked Herakles when the hero was already driving the herd toward home after killing Eurytion and Orthos to get it. To these robbers and opponents that Herakles encountered on his way back should be added those who opposed him on his way west, whether to Erytheia or to the Hesperides: there are at least ten of them.[27]

---

[25] Ptol. Heph. 2 (Phot. *Bibl.* p. 147 Bekk.); Isocr. 6.19. In an Etruscan painting Geryon, three-headed and labelled Gerun, is plainly an armed attendant of Hades and Persephone: *Mon. Inst.* 9.15. See Bayet (1923) 72–76.

[26] For Io's story see Aesch. *Pr.* 640–886; Apollod. 2.1.3; Ovid *Met.* 1.568–750.

[27] On his *nostos* Herakles encountered Kelto, Alebion-Derkynos, Kerkopes, Cacus, Faunus, the Albani, Gigantes, Eryx, six Sicanian generals, Laestrygons, Charybdis, Skylla, Lakinios, Lokros, Kroton, Larinos (Kelts, Chaonians, and Thesprotians), Neleus

Best known of the rustlers of the Erytheian kine to the reader of classical literature is Cacus, monstrous fire-breathing giant, son of Vulcan, who lived on the Aventine Hill. That he is something more than merely another double of Geryon has been perceived by several scholars beginning with Bréal. For the story involves a pair of ancient Italian fire deities, Cacus and his sister Caca, who is a forerunner or by-form of Vesta; the hero's name in the native tradition was not Herakles but Garanus or Recaranus; the story was *aition* of the Ara Maxima and ancient rites of the old Roman religion in which the Salian brotherhood took part; and it is attested only by Latin authors save for Dionysios of Halikarnassos in his book on Roman antiquities. The form in which we know the story may very well have grown out of a Roman or Italian variant of the combat myth. But once Greek and Italian cultures had met and mingled, the Cacus myth became an episode of Herakles' *nostos* (home-return) from Erytheia, and was no doubt remodelled to a great extent upon the Greek Geryon myth, which was well known in southern Italy. Yet it must have been something like that myth to begin with. Much study has been spent upon the Cacus myth, and it would be profitless to review the arguments and conclusions that scholars have advanced. I shall therefore limit my treatment to a few significant observations.[28]

If there was an early Italian variant of the combat myth, as I believe there was, the combatants were certainly not called Cacus and Herakles. I have just pointed out that Herakles replaces a native hero; while Cacus seems to be a displaced god, once important in worship on the Palatine, but later identified with the enemy. As a fire god, and as such probably connected early with

---

and sons, Alkyoneus, Strymon, Echidna, Hera. On the way west he encountered Kyknos, Ares, Nereus, Antaios, Busiris, Emathion, Rhodian Theiodamas, Atlas, Helios, Ocean, and many wild beasts (also Pyrene, p. 49); in the western land he met Geryon, Eurytion, Orthos, Menoites, Ladon. On the closely related journey for Diomedes' horses he met Kyknos, Lykaon, Ares, Diomedes, the Bistones.

[28] Cacus myth: Virg. *Aen.* 8.185–275; Prop. 4.9.1–20; Ovid *Fasti* 1.543–586, 5.643–652, 6.79–82; Livy 1.7.3–7; Dionys. Hal. *Ant. Rom.* 1.39–42; Cassius Hemina and *Libri Pontificales ap. Orig. Gent. Rom.* 6 *sq.*; Serv. *Aen.* 8.190; Col. Sal. *Lab. Herc.* 3.30. Though the Greek Diodoros (4.21) mentions Herakles' visit to Rome, he says nothing about the combat. Caca: Serv. *loc. cit.*; Firm. Lact. *Div. Inst.* 1.20.5; Vat. Myth. II 153, III 13.1; Col. Sal. *loc. cit.* 6. Garanus: Cassius *loc. cit.*; Verrius Flaccus *ap.* Serv.-Dan. *Aen.* 8.203. For studies of the Cacus myth see Bréal (1863), Winter (1910), Bayet (1926), Sbordone (1941), LM 1.2270–2290, and works cited by them; see also Croon (1952) 22 f. with note 39.

underground powers, he easily fluctuated from benevolent to malevolent spirit. He was not the only native deity to be identified with Herakles' enemy; for according to Derkyllos, a comparatively early authority on Roman subjects, it was Faunus whom the hero killed: when he came by with Geryon's kine, he was received and entertained by Faunus, who as Hermes' son had the habit of sacrificing foreigners to his father (cp. Busiris, Antaios, Kyknos). But Faunus was also considered to be a son of Mars, or of Picus, who is a form of Mars. Since Fauns were identified with the Greek Pans, Satyrs, and Silenes, it is significant that the early Roman annalist, Gnaeus Gellius, says that Cacus was a lieutenant of the Phrygian Marsyas, who likewise was commonly identified with Pan or Silenos; and we should notice that Satyros, Echidna's ally, had troubled the Arcadians and robbed them of their herds before Argos Panoptes fought and killed him, just as Cacus harried Evander's Arcadians on the Tiber.[29]

Scholars have already shown satisfactorily that Evander must be identified with Faunus: he was likewise a son of Mercury-Hermes by an Italian nymph; his name seems to be a translation of Faunus (benefactor); he was Herakles' host on the Palatine; and Herakles begot Latinus upon his daughter, whereas Latinus' mother is called Faunus' daughter in another source. According to one version of the story, Cacus was Evander's villainous slave, who seized the cattle while Herakles (Garanus) was staying under his master's roof. Now in Propertius' treatment of the story Cacus himself was Herakles' host and wronged his guest by stealing his cattle. Quite the contrary, he appears as Herakles' benevolent host, a pillar of the community, in Diodoros' narrative (who calls him Kakios), and there is no robbery or combat at all. So Cacus appears to have the same variety of role as Faunus-Evander. Either is the name of the deadly host into whose house the hero entered at risk of his life and cattle, and also of the good host, who treated Herakles well and established his worship. The good host is developed from the bad, just as Admetos from Hades-Thanatos. So the host became split into the good entertainer,

---

[29] Derkyllos *ap.* ps.-Plut. *Mor.* 315c; Cn. Gellius *ap.* Solin. 1.7 *sq.* Faunus son of Mars-Picus: Dionys. Hal. *Ant. Rom.* 1.31.2; Virg. *Aen.* 7.48; see LM 1.1454 f., 3.2494–2496. Satyros: Apollod. 2.1.2. For assimilation of Herakles to Argos Panoptes see Bayet (1923) 30. On Faunus as H's friend and ally see Dionys. *op. cit.* 1.42.3–43.1.

upon whom the name Evander had become fixed by the Augustan period, and the evil slave, herdsman, or brigand, who became known as Cacus, and all the more easily in that his name (*Cācus*) was wrongly identified with Greek *kakos*. But since he was really an old god, once revered, his name was sometimes given to the good host: conversely Evander never lost all traces of the evil host.[30]

As guest on the Palatine, Herakles was wronged either by his host or by his host's servant. According to Livy, he was fast asleep, overcome by too much food and wine (Th. 8c), after his fashion, when Cacus stole his kine. In respect to this sleep the story is closer to his adventure with the Scythian Echidna (pp. 97 f.) than to his meeting with Geryon: Herakles was fatigued from much travelling when he reached the pastures of the Forum Boarium, and so he let the cattle graze while he lay down to sleep (Th. 8A); on awaking from his sleep, he found that some were gone. In fact, the themes of host, entertainment, and hibernation, which are prominent in the Cacus myth, but entirely absent from the sources of the Geryon myth, forbid our supposing that the former is no more than a Roman translation of the latter.[31]

As Antaios had his consort Tingis, who betrayed him to the

---

[30] Evander = Faunus: Bayet (1926) 173–182; LM 1.1395. Cacus Evander's slave: Cassius *ap. Orig.* 6.2; Serv. *Aen.* 8.190. C. as host: Prop. 4.9.7 f.; Diod. 4.21.2. The bridge between an evil and a good C. can be seen in his Praenestine form of Caeculus Vulcan's son, conceived from a spark and found exposed beside a fire; on growing up he led a band of robbers for a long time, but finally founded Praeneste, where he established a festival of games: Cato *ap.* Serv. *et* Schol. Veron. *in Aen.* 7.678. Notice that the hero Garanus is described as a herdsman (*pastor*) of huge body and great strength: Verr. Flacc., Cassius, *locc. cit.*: i.e., in the same terms as the *pastor* Cacus in Liv. 1.7.5; for C. is variously described as slave, herdsman, brigand, householder, and king (Dionys. *Ant. Rom.* 1.42.2). Now the name *Garanus* may be related to Geryon's, who is found as Gerun in Etruria (see p. 338, note 25), and as an oracular god at Padova (as Faunus gave oracles at Tibur: Virg. *Aen.* 7.81–91; Ovid *Fasti* 4.649–664), beside the hot springs of Aponus (Th. 2D): Suet. *Tib.* 14. Notice too that in Sicily Herakles established a *temenos* for the hero Geryon: Diod. 4.24.3. Perhaps a Venetic god of phonetically similar name was identified with Geryon, or perhaps the latter name has an Italic or Keltic origin. Its meaning is hardly recoverable; but it certainly did not mean *roarer*. Popular etymology may have associated it variously with the roots of (1) *karanos, cranium,* (2) *gêras, gerôn,* and (3) *gêryein,* perhaps more with reference to oracles than to shouting. I might also recall Gerana, the crane-woman who mated with Kyknos in Italy (p. 101); it may be that a false etymology brought cranes into the myth. See Bréal (1863) 55–57; Winter (1910) 204–206, 253–256; Bayet (1926) 145–149; Benoit (1950) 90, and works that they cite.

[31] Since the crime was committed during his sleep, it may be significant that Faunus, Cacus' counterpart, was considered a nightmare demon and called Incubus: LM 1.1456.

hero, so Cacus had his sister Caca, who betrayed her brother to him. That she did so out of love for Herakles is clear from the tradition that he begot Latinus upon her double Fauna, the sister and wife of Faunus (Th. 8D). Or Latinus' mother was a daughter of Faunus and therefore a variant of Lavinia, Evander's daughter, upon whom Herakles begot Pallas. Fauna was identified with Bona Dea; and as Faunus' wife she corresponds to Carmenta, mother or wife of Evander. Under these names she allows us a glimpse of an unfriendly hostess: Carmenta's refusal, according to Cassius, to attend the rites of Herakles hints at an hostility to the hero that is still more evident from the tiff between Herakles and Bona Dea's priestess, when she forbade him to slake his thirst from the sanctuary's springs. When Herakles breaks through the door and takes the water that he wants, one recalls that to satisfy hunger he seized Theiodamas' ox.[32]

Now there can be little doubt that Cacus' cave into which he drove the stolen cattle represents the darkness of the other world and that Cacus is the death demon. The cave was deep and dark, never penetrated by the sun's rays, exactly like the infernal abodes of the dead (*infernas sedes et regna pallida*), as Virgil says in what appears to be more than a simile (*non secus ac si*). At its entrance were hung the skulls (*ora*) of Cacus' victims, their bones were strewn all about, and the ground was soaked with blood (cp. Phorbas, Kyknos, Antaios). Then when the hero broke in and rushed on Cacus, the monster belched forth clouds of smoke, filling the cave with a dark fog that made a "smoke-laden night" (*fumiferam noctem*), yet shot through with jets of flame. It was truly chaos that the hero invaded, and the way was barred by huge barriers of stone that he had to overthrow.[33]

---

[32] Fauna: Dion Cass. *ap.* Tzetz. *in* Lyc. 1232; Dionys. Hal. *Ant. Rom.* 1.43.1, who says that Latinus' mother was an Hyperborean maid whom Herakles married to Faunus on leaving Italy; one recalls the Scythian Echidna. Daughter of Faunus: Pomp. Trog. (Just. *Epit.*) 43.1.9. Lavinia: Dionys. *loc. cit.* Carmenta *vs.* H.: Cassius *ap. Orig.* 6.7. Bona Dea *vs.* H.: Prop. 4.9.21–70; cf. LM 1.789–795 (where her identification with Proserpina and Hekate and her relation to Juno, Kybele, and Semele are discussed), 1453 f. On relations of Fauna, Caca, Carmenta, Bona Dea see Bayet (1926) 362–371. Another link with the Antaios story is seen in H's seizing of Cacus in his arms and strangling him: Virg. *Aen.* 8.259–261. The MS of Conon 3 shows *Latinos* as the name of the cattle-rustler at Locri; but I accept Hoefer's emendation to *Lakinos*.

[33] Virg. *Aen.* 8.190–199, 211, 228–259; Ovid *Fasti* 1.555–558, 571 f. According to Virgil (264–267; cf. 194), Cacus was *semifer*, his body covered with bristles: the description

Herakles' theft of Geryon's kine and his recovery of cattle from brigands are remarkably like Indra's seizure or recovery of the soma cows, as Bréal and von Schroeder observed long ago. These scholars have only failed to perceive the cosmic meanings of the Vritra myth, as W. Norman Brown has worked it out (p. 196), and have consequently interpreted both the Vritra and Geryon myths as only conflicts of atmospheric phenomena; though von Schroeder comes nearer to the whole truth when he sees that the combats represent more kinds of physical strife than merely that of light against darkness. But Geryon or Cacus, like Vritra, is the chaos demon who withholds the cows, i.e., the waters that mean life, light, cosmos. It is significant that Geryon's beasts are literally cows; i.e., they are almost always referred to in the feminine gender. Bulls appear among the herds in the stories of Eryx and Cacus, but otherwise are almost unmentioned. But Geryon as Chaos is perhaps more nearly identified with death than is Vritra: the cosmic combat has become the harrowing of Hell, the rescue of the dead from Thanatos' keep, and so the soma cows become the death god's herds.[34]

But something of the old cosmic meanings have clung to the myth. Notice in particular what Diodoros has to say about the pillars of Herakles: there were some who said that in placing these pillars at Gibraltar he wished to narrow the strait in order to keep the huge sea monsters (*kêtê*) from leaving Ocean to enter the Mediterranean (*thalatta*); but others said that on the contrary he had dug this strait through a barrier of land in order to let the

---

suggests a boarlike monster (cp. Phorbas, Set). Prop. 4.9.10, 15, says that he had three heads. He was gigantic: Virg. 199; Ovid 553 f.; *Origo* 7.2. The myth in all versions shows Ths. 1A, 1B, 1C, 2B, 2C, 2D, 3A, 3B, 3C, 3D, 3F, 4A, 4B, 4C, 4D, 6A, 7A, 7B (Virg. 249 f., Prop. 15 f., Ovid 575 f.), 7E (Evander or Faunus as ally), 7F (Virg. 222–224), 7G (Diod. 4.21.5–7; Dionys. 1.41 f., Cato, Gellius), 8A, 8C, 8D, 10B, 10C (Dionys. 1.39.4), 10D; 9 may be seen in the lowing of the unseized cattle that betrayed the whereabouts of the stolen; according to Dionys. 1.39.3, Herakles drove the cattle past C's cave purposely to detect the hiding place. For H's purification (10c) in the Sicilian version of the Geryon myth see Schol. Vet. on Pind. *Ol.* 12.17 (25); cf. Diod. 4.23.1.

[34] Bréal (1863), von Schroeder (1914). Notice that in the Bona-Dea story Herakles breaks through a barrier to seize actual water. Since in India the cows were also goddesses, we may recall our surmise that Io was a member of the herd. Croon (1952: 67–71) thinks that Geryon's herds are the dead, and I believe that he is right in part. But Rose (1954: 215 f.) argues against this idea on the ground that the *eidôla* that went off to Hades' realm were never represented as kine. I'm not sure, however, that his argument is relevant: the Homeric *eidôla* and G's cattle may belong to quite different strata of folklore. While metaphor, as he says, does not produce myth, myth may produce metaphor.

waters of Ocean into the sea. That is, just as in myths of Mesopotamia, India, and China, the conquest of Chaos means control of the waters, either by holding them back and with them those monsters of the outer chaos that constantly seek to invade, or by setting them free for the world's use. Then Diodoros goes on to say that Herakles had cut the gorge of Tempe to run off the waters that once covered the Thessalian plain, and contrariwise had dammed the Kephisos River, thus creating Lake Kopais. Here we see Herakles the creator, a high god.[35]

Again, Diodoros and others speak of the Heraclean Way near Baiae, a narrow neck of land that separates the Lucrine Lake from the Bay of Naples, which men said Herakles had built to drive Geryon's cows across: here damming the waters and freeing the cows are fused into a single action. Nearby is Lake Avernus, sacred to Persephone, the passage to the underworld that Aeneas and the Sibyl used, an oracle of the dead, and the Phlegraean Fields (Solfatara), where the Gigantes attacked Herakles as he came by with the cows, when all the gods came to help Herakles against them (Th. 7G), a Gigantomachy in which he appears to be leader of the heavenly forces. Without doubt an early form of the Geryon myth was localised here.[36]

So there can be little doubt that Herakles is another Indra; and it is interesting to see that the feature of cows representing water, seen heretofore only in India, emerges again half a world away. But we have also noticed that the Herakles-Geryon combat is closely related to the Baal-Mot combat. So we must reject the theories of those scholars who confine the origin and transmission of these legends and themes to the Indo-European peoples. It is evident that, wherever the combat myth was first told, it spread throughout Asia, Europe, and North Africa.[37]

It is probable that in the Italian myth of Cacus-Faunus too the feature of freeing cows was present from the first. It is possible

---

[35] Diod. 4.18.4–7. It is interesting that Diod. interprets the damming of Lake Kopais, which destroyed everything that the waters covered, as Herakles' punishment of the Minyans of Orchomenos who had enslaved Thebes: i.e., it is attached to the Herakles-Erginos combat and, seemingly, identified with the Ogygian flood.

[36] Diod. 4.22.1 f.; Strabo 5.4.6, p. 245; Prop. 1.11.2, 3.18.4. Likewise Herakles cut the passes of the Alps and checked the banditry of the mountain tribes: Diod. 4.19.3 f. He made a lake in Sicily near a shrine of Geryon: Diod. 4.24.3.

[37] Bréal (1863) and von Schroeder (1914) do not look beyond the Indo-Europeans.

that this feature was taken over from the Greek Geryon myth, but we should notice that it appears in the earliest sources: Cassius Hemina speaks of Cacus' cattle-seizure, while Cato and Cn. Gellius make Cacus a plunderer, whose main object would surely be cattle-lifting.

The eighth labor, the taking of Diomedes' horses, as already pointed out (p. 99), seems to be a doublet of the Geryon story. Then too Herakles had first to deal with the guardians of the stalls; and he drove the horses off before he met Diomedes in combat and killed him. But a fusion has taken place: the beasts that are to be won are maneaters, monstrous allies of their master, and killed along with him in one version (Hyginus). But in another (Diodoros) they joined in the punishment of Diomedes by eating him and were tractable thereafter, though hostile to Herakles' taskmaster Eurystheus. They are horses that belong to the herdsman of the dead; and the dead are both the herdsman's subjects and vengeful demons like himself.[38]

In the Hesperides myth the same labor is repeated in a different dress. There is a close relation between the Hesperid and Erytheian ventures, in that the Hesperidean garden and Erytheia were both usually localised near the straits of Gibraltar (in fact, it is said that Erytheia was named after the Hesperid nymph so named), and that the Antaios and Busiris episodes are a prelude to either; to which correspondences may be added that on both journeys Herakles got from Helios the vessel in which to cross Ocean's stream. The garden was a paradise, often confused with the northern paradise of the Hyperboreans and the southern paradise of the Ethiopians. Yet it lay at the western edge of the world beyond Ocean, either on the borders of Night or within the dark recesses of earth; for Hesiod says both (cf. p. 227). The Hesperid nymphs were daughters of Erebos and Night, or of Atlas and Hesperis, or of Phorkys and Keto. As daughters of Night they were sisters of black Ker, Thanatos, Hypnos, Geras, Eris, and the

---

[38] Eur. *Alk.* 481–506; Apollod. 2.5.8; Diod. 4.15.3 f.; Hyg. *Fab.* 30.9; Pedias. 8. Notice that the Scythian Echidna took Herakles' horses rather than the Erytheian kine (p. 97). In this connection the horse form of the nightmare demon should not be overlooked. According to Hyg., two of the horses of Diomedes were named Podargus, masculine form of the Harpy's name (p. 236, note 25), and Dinus, masculine form of Deino, one of the Graiai, and in meaning a variant of Deimos.

Moirai; as daughters of Phorkys and Keto they were sisters of the Gorgons (who lived in the same place, according to Hesiod), Graiai, and the Hesperidean snake Ladon, guardian of the golden-apple tree, who was also said to be son of Typhon and Echidna. So once more we notice the virtual equivalence of Erebos, Atlas, Phorkys, and Typhon, all of whom merge once more with Ocean, whose garden this paradise was said to be. Originally, as Hesiod's testimony makes clear, the garden was a land of darkness and death, outside the cosmos. The paradise, a bright region set amidst the darkness, is a conception of the time when men began to imagine a pleasant otherworld for favored mortals.[39]

Now there were already men in antiquity who, pointing to the homonymy of *mêlon* "apple" and *mêlon* "sheep," maintained that the golden apples were originally beautiful sheep of golden fleece. It is probably true that verbal play helped to transform the imprisoned cattle or death-herdsman's flocks into the golden apples, tokens of potency. The cows that Vritra kept, we may remember, were also cosmic water, potent soma, and imprisoned goddesses. So Herakles' theft of the Hesperidean *mêla* is another story of the release of the waters and the freeing of the dead. In one version he killed Ladon outright, but in another he tricked Atlas into fetching the apples for him. Ladon, like Geryon, was a many-headed monster whom Hera favored: the golden apples which he guarded were hers. So the tenth and twelfth labors, in spite of the great differences in their outward dress, appear to be fundamentally the same story.[40]

---

[39] Hes. *Theog.* 215 f., 274 f., 333–335, 517 f.; Pherek. 16, 1.65 J; Diod. 4.26 f.; Apollod. 2.5.11; Pedias. 11; Hyg. *Fab.* 30.12. Hesperides = Hyperboreans: Apollod.; = Ethiopians: Virg. *Aen.* 4.480–486; cf. p. 288. Daughters of Erebos and Night: Hes. *Theog.* 215 f.; Hyg. *Fab.* praef. 1; of Atlas: Diod. 4.27.2; Schol. Vet. on Apollon. *Arg.* 4.1399; of Phorkys: Schol. *ibid.* Hesperides and Gorgons: Hes. *Theog.* 274 f.; see Fulg. p. 755 Stav. and Vat. Myth. III 13.5, who name Medusa among the Hesperides (see p. 337, note 24). The latter are usually named Aigle (also an alternative name for Koronis, Phlegyas' daughter), Erytheia, Hesperia, and Arethusa (pursued by a river god, Ovid *Met.* 5.572–641): Apollod. 2.5.11. According to Akusilaos and Epimenides (*ap.* Philodem. *Piet.* 92.24–29) the guardians of the apples were Harpies, who were the same as the Hesperides. On Ladon see Hes. *Theog.* 333–335; Apollon. *Arg.* 4.1396–1407; Apollod. 2.5.11; Hyg. *Fab.* 30.12, 151.1, praef. 39; he was usually called *ophis* or *drakôn*, which terms link him to Ophion, Python, and Theban Drakon; see further p. 372. Peisander (*ap.* Schol. Vet. *in* Apollon. *Arg.* 4.1396) says that he was born from Ge. He had a hundred heads, according to Apollod., but vase paintings show one or three: LM 1.2598–2603. For Ocean's garden see Aristoph. *Nub.* 271. See von Schroeder (1914) 67–83.

[40] On apples = sheep see Diod. 4.26.2–27.1; Agroitas 3, 4.295 M. The Hesperides

LAOMEDON AND HESIONE

Herakles gave the apples to Athena after he had brought them
back to Argos, as Perseus gave her the Gorgon's head that he had
won in the same region; so that from beginning to end Herakles'
Erytheian-Hesperidean journeys show features parallel to Perseus'
quest of Medusa. And Herakles' killing of the Trojan sea monster
and rescue of Hesione is almost an exact replica of the Andromeda story. The several sources of the Hesione story agree un-
usually well with one another, each narrative complementing
rather than contradicting the others, so that a summary can be
made from all of them together.

Poseidon and Apollo helped Laomedon build the walls of
Troy, whether they did so of their own choice or Zeus placed
them in bondage to Laomedon as a punishment for their conspiracy against him. In any case they worked for a stipulated
wage; but at the end of the term Laomedon refused to pay them,
and sent them off humiliated after making dire threats against
them. So in anger Poseidon sent both a flood and a vast *kêtos*
against Troy, and Apollo sent a plague. The Trojans consulted an
oracle, some say Apollo's, and were told that they must sacrifice
noble maids to the beast. In due course the turn of Laomedon's
own daughter, Hesione, came round; Laomedon proclaimed that
he would reward the man who should kill the monster with the
immortal horses that Zeus had given him in payment for Ganymedes. Hesione was already bound to a rock on the shore when
Herakles came by, saw her, and undertook to fight the monster
for the promised reward. Athena helped him, making a high rampart of stone, to which he retreated when the ketos rushed upon
him, and from which he leaped into the creature's open maw. He
spent three days in the monster's belly, hacking away at his entrails until he killed him. He came forth to receive the cheers of
the Trojans. It is said by some writers that Herakles had also
asked for Hesione in marriage and was given her; and it may be
that her father had offered marriage with her to the dragon-slayer

themselves become the imprisoned goddesses in the story of Busiris' attempt upon them,
p. 334. Hera's apples: Pherek. 16, 1.65 J; Apollod. 2.5.11; Hyg. *Astr.* 2.3. Present are
Ths. 1A, 1B, 1C, 2A, 2B, 2C, 2E, 3A, 3B, 3C, 3F, 6A, 7A, 7D, 7E, 8A, 10A, 10D.

as an additional prize. In any case, Herakles, being then engaged upon either his labors or the Argonautic voyage, left both Hesione and the horses with Laomedon until he should return. When later he came to take them, Laomedon, mythology's greatest welsher, refused to give them up. So Herakles gathered a fleet and army, made war on Troy, took the city, killed Laomedon, and drove off the horses; but Hesione he gave as wife to his ally Telamon.[41]

As in the Andromeda tale, Poseidon in wrath raised a sea monster, also called *kêtos*, against an offending king and people; they received an oracle that bade them appease the monster's appetite with a fair maiden; then came the hero, just in time to rescue the king's daughter by fighting and killing the monster. The Trojan Ketos is more closely identified with the companion flood than is his Ethiopian counterpart: for it is said that he spewed the floodwaters forth from his mouth or caused the flood by his movement through the sea. The episode of the hero's descent into the monster's interior is also more prominent in this story than in the other. That this is a descent to the death realm is indicated by the hero's sojourn of three days and his loss of hair. Furthermore hair is the seat of potency in many stories—e.g., that of Herakles' Hebrew counterpart Samson—i.e., among the dead Herakles lacked his hair, as Zeus his sinews.[42]

But whereas the frame is a doublet of the Perseus-Ketos tale, several features that we have seen in other tales have been superimposed: (1) Whereas Apollo is more often said in later sources to have worked with Poseidon upon the walls, the Iliad says that he tended herds for Laomedon (compare Admetos' herds). (2) It was Apollo's oracle that ordered the sacrifice of Hesione, as in the tales of Sybaris, Poine-Ker, and Heros. (3) Apollo sent a plague upon the land (cp. Poine-Ker). (4) Though in most sources Hesione only is exposed, there is sufficient evidence that other

---

[41] Il. 5.638–642, 648–651, 7.452 f., 20.145–148, 21.441–457; Hellan. 26*b*, 1.114 J; Apollod. 2.5.9, 2.6.4; Diod. 4.32, 4.42; Lyk. 33–38 with Schol. Vet. on 37; Ovid *Met.* 11.199–217; Val. Flacc. *Arg.* 2.451–578; Hyg. *Fab.* 89 (cf. 31.4); Serv. or Serv.-Dan. *Aen.* 1.550, 5.30, 8.157; Schol. Vet. or Tzetz. on Lyk. 34, 472, 952; Vat. Myth. I 136, 137, II 193; Col. Sal. *Lab. Herc.* 3.16.

[42] Ketos causes flood: Tzetz. on Lyk. 34; Val. Flacc. 2.497–517. Herakles' descent into K's belly: Hellan., Lyk., Schol. Vet. or Tzetz. on Lyk. 34, 37. Lucian *DMort.* 10.9, 20.4, emphasises the hairlessness of skeletons (one form in which the spook is conceived).

maids had been sacrificed before her (cp. Sybaris, Heros). (5) Herakles fled at first before Ketos' onrush (cp. Kyknos). (6) Herakles drove off the herd of horses that Laomedon had withheld. It is notable that the divine horses are the great prize of victory, whereas the hero's marriage to the rescued princess has almost disappeared from the story as we have it. Only Diodoros and Hyginus (whom a Vatican Mythographer follows) say that Herakles was to take Hesione with him back to Greece, presumably as his wife. In fact, Hesione has almost reached the status of the victim in the St. George legend, where marriage to her savior is out of the question. Yet, as the discussion of the myths of Geryon, the Hesperides, and Vritra have made clear, the divine herd and Hesione must represent the same meed of victory: the cattle that are also goddesses whom the demon has confined. So this is very much a myth of the freeing of the soma cattle, here conceived as Zeus's horses of wondrous powers; and we notice that wherever Herakles is introduced, parallels to Indic myth become evident, whereas the Perseus myth finds its parallels almost exclusively in Near-Eastern myth (but there is the remarkable Japanese myth of Susanowo and the dragon, p. 500). (7) After Herakles took Troy, killed Laomedon, and recovered the princess that had been refused him, he married her to Telamon, as in taking Oichalia and killing Eurytos, he married Iole to Hyllos (p. 109, note 35). (8) As in the Cacus myth, an altar was founded in Herakles' honor.[43]

Since Laomedon corresponds to Kepheus, it is significant for the interpretation of the latter as a king of the dead and an enemy

---

[43] (1) Il. 21.448 f.; Paus. 7.20.4. (2) Diod., Hyg., Serv. *Aen.* 1.550, Vat. Myths. But according to Val. Flacc. and Serv.-Dan. (*Aen.* 5.30) Laomedon consulted Ammon's oracle; no doubt this is taken over from the Andromeda story. (3) Apollod., Diod., Val. Flacc., Vat. Myth. I 136. No doubt the classical myth is composite, made up of two versions, in which either Poseidon or Apollo is the offended god, one sending a flood demon, the other a plague demon. Notice that the blight, which, according to Diod., came as an additional punishment upon the country, was certainly closely identified with the dragon himself; for Hellan. says that he destroyed the crops. (4) Hyg., Val. Flacc., Schol. Vet. and Tzetz. on Lyk. 472, 952; Serv. or Serv.-Dan. *Aen.* 1.550, 5.30. (5) Il. 20.145–148 with Scholl. BT. (6) Cf. Hellan. especially; also Hyg. on the horses' powers. (7) E.g. Apollod., Diod., Ovid, Hyg. There had probably been a version in which Telamon was the hero. (8) Apollod., Hellan. 109, 1.134 J. The evidences of fusion are two offended gods, three kinds of affliction sent besides the dragon himself, two heroes, two rewards for victory, two refusals of Laomedon to pay a promised reward, two attacks on Troy to punish Laomedon. Augeias too, another herd-owner, refused Herakles the payment due him: Apollod. 2.5.5.

of Perseus (1) that Laomedon was an owner of herds; (2) that he opposed Herakles, even planned to kill him, and fought in battle against him; (3) that he held gods in servitude and humiliated them with threats that he would bind them, sell them in distant lands, and cut off their ears (cp. Echetos, the maimer of men, p. 482); (4) that he did sell the daughters of his Trojan opponents to traders to be transported to distant lands or to be exposed to wild beasts (cp. Nauplios, p. 481); (5) and that he ordered the Trojan nobles to sacrifice their daughters. All these deeds and characteristics point to the traits of the death demon that have been noticed in preceding chapters.[44]

ACHELOOS, NESSOS, AND AMALTHEIA

A like doubling of the prize of victory can be seen in the combat with Acheloos. Deianeira was destined to marry Acheloos, much against her will (at least in later sources): for though a bride contest had been set by her father Oineus, all suitors retired before Acheloos—save Herakles, who arrived just in time to challenge the river god and defeat him, thus winning Deianeira for himself. But he also won the horn of Amaltheia, which was identified with Acheloos' horn that Herakles had broken from his head (fig. 22); or, if the two horns are not identified, it is said that Acheloos recovered his own horn by trading Amaltheia's horn for it. This was the cornucopia, the wonder horn from which every kind of fruit, or anything that one wanted to eat or drink, could be magically drawn in abundance. Amaltheia was the goat that nursed the infant Zeus in the Dictaean Cave: her two horns it is sometimes said, yielded nectar and ambrosia. She is the Hellenic counterpart of Kamaduh, the Wonder-Cow of Hindu mythology, as her ambrosia and nectar are the Hellenic counterparts of soma.

---

[44] (2) See esp. Val. Flacc. (3) Il. 21.441–457. (4) and (5) Schol. Vet. or Tzetz. on Lyk. 472, 952; Serv.-Dan. *Aen.* 5.30. Laomedon wanted to spare Hesione, according to Vat. Myths. and Tzetz., but his subjects would not let him; cf. St. George's legend, p. 520. The discussion so far has revealed Ths. 1B, 2E, 3B, 3F, 3G, 4A, 4B, 4C, 4D, 4E, 6A, 7A, 7C, 7D, 7E, 7G, 8A, 8B, 8D, 10D. Others present are 3A: e.g., Val. Flacc. 2.478–480, the monster surpassed mountain or sea; 3C: Val. Flacc. 2.503 (cf. 514, 530), he had a thousand coils; 5A: when Herakles took Troy he disposed of the throne as he pleased (Apollod. 2.6.4, Hyg.); 7B: Val. Flacc. 2.521–530, H. used numerous arrows and boulders; 10B: Val. Flacc. 2.536–539; probably 1C also in that Hesione is the name of a daughter of Ocean and wife of Nauplios; the same is true of Klymene (p. 481): see Aesch. *Pr.* 558 f.; Akusilaos 34, 1.56 J; Kerkops *ap.* Apollod. 2.1.5.

So in the Acheloos myth the soma and the dragon's potency are fused in a single horn of the river god.[45]

It has already been pointed out (p. 232) that Acheloos was once identified with Ocean and, in fact, with all waters, which, it was said, were formerly called by his name; as a specific river god he was said to be born of Ocean and Tethys; and it was also said that his mother was Ge. Amaltheia was Ocean's daughter; and the name "Amaltheia's horn" was given to the fertile land of the Acheloos delta. It was said that Herakles recovered that land for men's use by diverting the course of the Acheloos. We need not see Euhemerism here any more than in the Vedas: the breaking of the horn and the turning of the river's course are one and the same to the mythical eye, just as the death of Vritra was the end of drought. Or if it be Euhemerism, it is like that of Chinese myth (p. 492), in which the outlines of the original myth remain. So here Herakles is once more the hero who defeats the chaos dragon and wrests from him the soma-waters that contain all the materials of world order.[46]

According to Hyginus, Herakles gave the horn to the Hesperides; while Hesychios says that Hermes gave it to Herakles when the hero was about to drive off Geryon's cows. Hence Amaltheia's horn appears to be closely associated with the prizes of Herakles' far-western ventures. On the other hand, the Geryon adventure was sometimes localised in Epiros, specifically in the Ambracian-Amphilochian country (e.g., by Hekataios; see p. 336, note 23), which lies between the Acheloos River and the Ambracic Gulf. Or for Geryon a certain Larinos is substituted, a rustler of the Erytheian kine; or Geryon-Larinos dissolves into Epirotic peoples: Chaonians, Thesprotians, and Kelts, who attacked Herakles when he came through Ambrakia with the cattle. This was an

---

[45] For the Acheloos-combat see Pind. *ap.* Scholl. AB *in Il.* 21.194; Soph. *Trach.* 6–27, 503–530; Diod. 4.35. 3 f.; Apollod. 1.8.1, 2.7.5; Ovid *Met.* 8.879–9.92; Hyg. *Fab.* 31.7; Serv.-Dan. *Georg.* 1.8, *Aen.* 8.299. Amaltheia as Zeus's nurse: Call. *Hymn* 1.48 f. with Schol. on 49; see ps.-Eratosth. 13; Ovid *Fasti* 5.112–114, 119–121; Scholl. AB on Il. 15.229; Hesych. A3412. For her horn see also Pind., Diod., *locc. cit.*: Pherek. 42, 1.74 J; Strabo 10.2.19, p. 458; Ovid *Met.* 9.87–92.

[46] Diod. 4.35.3 f.; Schol. T on Il. 21.194. Amaltheia Ocean's daughter: Pind. *loc. cit.* She is called Helios' daughter in ps.-Eratosth. 13, interesting in view of the alternation of Ocean and Helios as Herakles' opponents on his crossing to Erytheia (p. 336, note 22); remember too that Helios was a father of the northwestern Phorbas (p. 50), and that Phorbas was another name of the Acheloos River (p. 88).

area where Dryopians settled (p. 41); and the Thesprotian King Phylas, whom Herakles attacked and killed at Ephyra (at the mouth of the Acheron River), taking his daughter Astyoche captive, was also called king of Dryopes; and this attack Herakles made in company with the Calydonians—just after he had fought Acheloos, as Apollodoros and Diodoros present the sequence of events.[47]

In the defeat of Acheloos and the winning of the horn of plenty we see the old myth of cosmos against chaos preserved more clearly perhaps than in the Geryon combat. Not so much as the latter myth, yet to some extent, it has also taken on the special character of an attack on death. (1) It was in Hades' realm that Herakles got Meleager's consent to marry his sister Deianeira. (2) Acheloos is coupled with Antaios as Herakles' opponent in the wrestling bout that gave the hero the name Palaimon (wrestler). (3) The coupling with Antaios is made more significant by the tradition that the Acheloos River was once called Thoas: for Thoas was the name of that Tauric king who sacrificed foreigners in the manner of Busiris. (4) Another earlier name of the river was Thestios, so called from a son of Ares. Now Ares helped Acheloos against Herakles, exactly as he helped Kyknos against him, or stood in his own person against him at Pylos. (5) In this connection it is significant that Meleager was said to be a son of Ares rather than of Oineus, if we recall that Oineus set the bride contest and was willing to surrender his daughter to Acheloos. Among his other children, moreover, appear Klymenos and Gorge. (6) Acheloos was the father of the Sirens, the companions of Persephone, whose western island was strewn with the bones and putrefying flesh of their victims.[48]

The likeness of Sirens to Harpies as bird-women has long been noticed; the chief difference seems to be that the Sirens are seductive and the Harpies frightful. Both are death spirits, the Sirens behaving more in the manner of Lamias and Empusas, the Har-

---

[47] Hyg. *Fab.* 31.7; Hesych. A3412. On Geryon-Larinos in Epiros see Croon (1952) 49–52 and his citations in note 33, p. 21; cf. Nic. *ap.* Ant. Lib. 4.6.

[48] (1) Pind. *loc. cit.* (2) Pherek. 76, 1.80 f. J. (3) Strabo 10.2.1, p. 450; Tauric Thoas: Eur. IT 30–41. (4) Thestios: ps.-Plut. *Fluv.* 22.1. Ares' help: Paus. 6.19.12. (5) Apollod. 1.8.1 f. Gorge married Andraimon, whose wife was also called Dryope (p. 57). (6) Apollon. *Arg.* 4.893–896; Apollod. 1.3.4, 1.7.10; Ovid *Met.* 5.552–563; Hyg. *Fab.* praef. 30; Serv.-Dan. *Georg.* 1.8. Sirens' island: Od. 12.45 f.

pies in that of the Gorgons and Erinyes, with whom they are
sometimes identified. But the Harpies were also identified with
the Hesperid nymphs. It should be noticed too that their principal abode is the Strophades, an island group in the Ionian Sea,
not far (about seventy-five miles) from the Echinades, the transmuted Sirens, that lay opposite Acheloos' mouth, and which were
the outlying alluvial deposits of the river, destined to become
part of Amaltheia's horn, Herakles' gift to the Hesperides. Such
island groups were likely to become in folklore the abode of
nymphs, whether gracious or deadly, whether called Nereids or
Gorgons. All such sea spirits are called Gorgons in the folklore
of Greece today (p. 284); they are at once charming and dangerous. It should be noticed that the ancient Gorgons combine the
charm of the Sirens (e.g., Medusa's beauty; cp. Skylla's and
Sphinx's) with the frightfulness of the Harpies.[49]

Since Sirens are variants of Gorgons, Harpies, and Hesperides,
they are the nymphs who filled Amaltheia's horn with fruits.
Amaltheia was sister of Acheloos as Ocean's daughter, and either
he had her horn on his own head or she gave it to him when he
asked for it. In the former version he must either have worn it
with her consent or have taken it away from her. There is evidence that the story was told both ways. For as Zeus's nurse she
was a benevolent deity who one day lost a horn through mishap.
But she was also of such frightful appearance that the sight of her
terrified the Titans, so that Zeus on growing up used her hide,
the aegis, in his war against them. In one account the hide of her
back had a Gorgon's face upon it; but at first it must have been
her own countenance that inspired terror. This goat-nurse whose
hide became the aegis was called Aix Helios' daughter in the
writings ascribed to Musaios, which distinguished her from the

---

[49] Sirens like Harpies: Harrison (1922) 177, 199 f.; LM 1.1843 f. Harpies = Gorgons: see vase paintings in Woodward (1937) figs. 5a, 10, 11a; Harrison, figs. 19, 20. Harpies = Erinyes: Aesch. *Eum.* 50–52; Virg. *Aen.* 3.252; cf. Od. 20.77 f. Strophades: Virg. *Aen.* 3.209–218; Schol. Vet. on Apollon. *Arg.* 2.285. That the nymphs who became the Echinades were the Sirens is, I think, a reasonable deduction from Ovid *Met.* 5.552–563 taken to-gether with 8.580–610 and Lucian *Salt.* 50. The islands that were literally produced by Acheloos were likely to be called his daughters, Acheloides; but in another story they were nymphs that had offended him; yet one of them was his beloved Perimele. Now, according to ps.-Plut. *Fluv.* 22.1, Acheloos cohabited with his own daughter Kleitoria; and the Sirens were his daughters.

nymph Amaltheia, her owner. But the goat is usually called Amaltheia in the sources. So the face upon the aegis was either the Gorgon's or the goat Amaltheia's, and the material of the aegis was the hide of either the Gorgon Aigis (p. 244) or of Amaltheia who was called Aix, merely a variant of the same name (cp. Aix Python's son, p. 20). So the Amaltheia of Acheloos' horn represents the original dragoness of the myth; but she later merged with the Sirens and with Deianeira.[50]

Deianeira, daughter of Dionysos-Oineus, also has two different characters in the sources. She was on the one hand the prize of a bride contest that her father set, and she favored the hero who finally won her; and so she may be grouped with Hippodameia, Alkeis-Barke, and Atalanta (p. 334, note 19). Like Atalanta, she trained herself in men's pursuits: hunting, chariot-driving, and warfare. It has already been observed that she armed herself and helped Herakles fight the Dryopes (p. 37). On the other hand, she brought death upon the hero while he cohabited with her; the parallel to Delilah has often been noticed, and I have pointed out correspondences between Deianeira and Omphale (p. 109).[51]

Herakles' death was caused by the Hydra's poison which the Centaur Nessos had given to Deianeira. Now the Nessos story repeats the Acheloos story: for Nessos is the spirit of the River Euenos (which is much nearer to Calydon than is the Acheloos) conceived in horse form instead of bull form; a water deity may take the form of either horse or bull, e.g., Poseidon himself, who often takes the place of river-gods in myth. Either river-god, then, wants Deianeira and so comes into conflict with Herakles, who either maims or kills him.[52]

---

[50] Nymphs fill Amaltheia's horn: Ovid *Fasti* 5.123 f.; Hyg. *Fab.* 31.7. Amaltheia breaks her horn: *Fasti* 5.121 f. She becomes aegis: ps.-Mus. *ap.* ps.-Eratosth. 13; Scholl. AB on Il. 15.229. Notice that Hera's image at Koroneia carried Siren figures in its hand; Hera persuaded the Sirens to contest the Muses in song; but the Muses won and plucked their wings: Paus. 9.34.3. Notice that in nearby Daulis Pyreneus made his attempt upon the Muses (p. 44).

[51] Deianeira warrior maiden: Apollod. 1.8.1. Death of Herakles: Soph. *Trach;* Apollod. 2.7.7; Diod. 4.38; Ovid *Her.* 9, *Met.* 9.134–258; Sen. *HOe:* Hyg. *Fab.* 36.

[52] Archil. frag. 147 Bergk; Soph. *Trach.* 555–577; Apollod. 2.7.6; Diod. 4.36.3–5; Ovid *Met.* 9.101–133; Hyg. *Fab.* 34. There was a version in which Nessos lived on after being wounded by Herakles' poisoned arrow: Paus. 10.38.2. His tomb, like Antaios's, was a hill, at the foot of which issued a spring of bad-smelling water (Strabo 9.4.8, p. 427); or his corpse, like Python's, lay unburied in Lokris and made a terrible stench; in fact, ancient authorities differed on whether it was Nessos' body or Python's that the sea washed

The virtual identity of Acheloos and Nessos-Euenos as river-spirits who were opponents of Herakles vis-à-vis Deianeira is made certain by an intermediate story in which Herakles won Deianeira from the Centaur Eurytion. Dexamenos (whose name indicates that he too is a guest receiver), King of Olenos (in Aitolia or just across the strait in Achaia), was Deianeira's father; once when he was Herakles' host, the hero seduced his daughter and gave his word that he would return to marry her. But while Herakles was gone, the Centaur Eurytion demanded of Dexamenos that Deianeira be married to him; and in fear Dexamenos consented. Herakles came back on the wedding day just in time to kill Eurytion and his brother Centaurs and recover his bride. Here Eurytion, a Centaur and son of Ixion and Nephele, as was Nessos, takes the place of Acheloos as fearful suitor of Deianeira to whom her father deferred. Apollodoros calls the girl Mnesimache (battle minded), and Diodoros calls her Hippolyte. Both are names suitable to the warrior maid Deianeira. In Herakles' ninth labor, his quest of the Amazon-queen Hippolyta's girdle, he met and killed an Amazon named Deianeira. Eurytion is the namesake of Geryon's herdsman and of the Centaur who tried to take Peirithoos' bride from him in another legend of a brawl with Centaurs at a wedding feast. The Centaur's name has also the variant form Eurytos, which recurs among Herakles' enemies: e.g., the king of Oichalia (p. 43), and one of Aktor's twin sons (p. 336, note 22), who is said to have married Dexamenos' daughter Theraiphone (wild-beast slayer), also a name that suits the virago Deianeira. In this story she actually became the enemy's wife.[53]

So the Deianeira who married Herakles and who killed him

---

up to the Locrian shore: Plut. *Mor.* 294ғ; Paus. 10.38.2. There may be a hint of Nessos as the river spirit in Ovid *Met.* 9.117. Hesiod mentions a river god Nessos, son of Ocean and Tethys, whom he places beside Acheloos (*Theog.* 340 f.). Notice too Euenos, father of Marpessa (p. 333, note 19).

[53] Dexamenos and Eurytion: Bacchyl. frag. 44 Snell; Hermesianax *ap.* Paus. 7.18.1; Hyg. *Fab.* 31.11, 33; Apollod. 2.5.5; Diod. 4.33.1. Amazon Deianeira: Diod. 4.16.3. On Peirithoos' Centaur brawl see Fontenrose, RE 19.116–120. Eurytos-Theraiphone: Paus. 5.3.3, who says that Kteatos married her sister Theronike, a name that has the same meaning; Dexamenos' daughter has become twins to suit Aktor's sons. Since the name Eurypylos appears in the Argonautic legend as an alternative to Eurytos (p. 482), it is important to see that Dexamenos had a son named Eurypylos, who was identified with the hero of Paus. 7.19 (p. 483, note 10).

unwittingly appears to be descended from the wife, sister, or daughter of the enemy who lured the hero to destruction. Acheloos' consort became Amaltheia, the Sirens, or Deianeira in the various forms of the legend that took shape.[54]

<h3 style="text-align:center">HYDRA AND LION</h3>

Through Deianeira not only Nessos but also the Hydra of Lerna struck back at Herakles. The Hydra was the most formidable dragoness that Herakles encountered. She was daughter of Typhon and Echidna; and indeed she is herself sometimes called Echidna. She was huge of size and so poisonous that her very breath killed men. She lived in a cave under a plane tree beside the spring of Amymone in the Lernaean swamp, whence she attacked men and cattle on the Argive plain. She had many heads, usually said to be nine in number, of which the central head was immortal; but mortal or immortal, it seems, any head on being lopped off was at once replaced by two (cp. Ravana, p. 206). She was helped by a crab (*Karkinos*), who bit Herakles' foot; but the hero trampled him to death. Iolaos cauterised Hydra's necks as Herakles cut the heads off; Athena had so advised them. Herakles buried the immortal head beneath a huge rock. In the cycle of labors ordered by Eurystheus, this was the second; but Hesiod says that Hydra was raised by Hera against Herakles.[55]

Hera's hostility pursued Herakles throughout his adventures.

---

[54] Stoessl (1945) arrives at a similar judgement of the earliest Deianeira, but on the wrong grounds. E.g., he misinterprets Dion Chrys. 60.1 to mean that Deianeira intentionally kept Herakles at a distance through desire for Nessos' advances. No extant source of the Nessos story shows anything but D's aversion to N.; and her original character cannot be inferred from a study of the literary sources alone, but only in the manner indicated above.

The discussion of the Acheloos-Nessos-Eurytion complex shows Ths. 1A, 1B, 1C, 2A, 2D, 2E, 3B, 3E, 3F, 3G, 4E, 6A, 7A, 7C, 7G, 8A, 8D, 10A, 10B. Also present are 2B: Ovid *Met.* 8.562–564; 3A: *ibid.* 9.39 f.; 4F: Nessos held the Euenos ford; 7D, 7E: Paus. 6.19.12. For 4A cf. Eurytion's *vis* in Hyg. *Fab.* 33.1, and Axenos as another name of Acheloos, ps.-Plut. *Fluv.* 22.1; on the contrary notice A's hospitality in *Met.* 8.550–573. As we have noticed in such a figure as Lityerses the death-spirit's hospitality and inhospitality are two faces of one coin.

[55] Hes. *Theog.* 313–318; Eur. *Her.* 419–422; Peisander *ap.* Paus. 2.37.4; Panyasis *ap.* ps.-Eratosth. 11; Apollod. 2.5.2; Diod. 4.11.5 f.; Ovid *Met.* 9.69–74; Hyg. *Fab.* 30.3, 151.1; Palaiph. 38; Pedias. 2; Col. Sal. *Lab. Herc.* 3.9 f. Palaiph. says that the Hydra had fifty heads, and Diod. says one hundred. The story has Ths. 1A, 1B, 1C, 2B, 2D, 2E, 3A, 3B, 3C, 3D, 4A, 4D, 4F (cf. Palaiph.), 5B, 6A, 6B, 7A, 7B, 7D, 7E, 7G (cf. Palaiph.), 9, 10A. As Hydra guarded the spring Amymone, it is significant that the nymph Amymone was mistress of Poseidon, and that Nauplios was their son: Apollod. 2.1.4 f.

She sent two huge snakes against him when he was a babe in his cradle, but the precocious infant strangled them easily. She favored Eurystheus, Herakles' taskmaster, who resembles Susanowo as underworld lord (p. 502), in that he imposed difficult tasks upon the hero whom he held within his power. So we see Hera inciting dragons and demons against Herakles just as she did against Apollo.[56]

In talking about Herakles it is hard to know where to stop, so vast is the subject. Every exploit is worth study; but those selected for treatment in this chapter reveal best, I believe, the place that the Herakles legends occupy in the whole complex of the combat myth. Just about every theme of our list is represented somewhere; also all subplots of the basic type may be seen behind the shifting scenery of the legends: subtype IV most often, and subtype III most obscurely. But we have seen Herakles, like another Zeus or Indra, bringing order out of chaos. And in one way or another we have seen him descend to the dead and return in victory, a mighty god. It may be that a further study of Herakles will throw more light on the relation between god and hero. In this connection, the story of his first labor is significant. Before Herakles met the lion, as Apollodoros tells the story, he instructed King Molorchos to make sacrifice on the thirtieth day to Zeus Savior, should he return alive, but if he died, then to make offerings as to a hero. Herakles came back on the thirtieth day, just as Molorchos was beginning to make offerings to the dead Herakles, and sacrifices were then made to Zeus Savior. It seems to me, from the very way in which the alternative is expressed, that Zeus Savior is the victorious Herakles, risen from the dead to the gods. But during the thirty days of his absence, when he went deep within the lion's cave (the lion was a son of Typhon and Echidna), he received offerings as a hero. Molorchos was engaged upon these when Herakles returned; just as in the Easter rituals of today, the ceremonies of entombment and lamentation immediately precede the festival of resurrection, especially in the Eastern Church. This conclusion is supported by a Virgilian Scholiast, who may have taken the story from Callimachus: Herakles told Molorchos to make sacrifice of a goat to the victorious god (*victori deo*) if he

---

[56] See Apollod. 2.4.8; Il. 19.95–133.

returned, otherwise to the dead (*Manibus*). Hera, who didn't want Herakles to receive divine honors, sent a deep sleep upon him after he had killed the lion; so when he got back to Molorchos, the king had already killed the goat and was in the process of making sacrifice to the dead.[57]

Without question Herakles ranks with Zeus and Apollo as dragon fighter in the myth-making of the Greeks; any one of the three might be the champion in the great variety of tales that ring the changes on the combat theme. The other dragon fighters like Perseus and Kadmos tended to recede before these three, keeping one or two tales that had become securely attached to their names. Yet there is something distinctive about Herakles: he is specifically cast as the conqueror of death; it is Thanatos whom he meets again and again under many names and forms. And in saying this I mean something much more specific than the truism that a warrior faces death when engaged in mortal combat: I mean that the original and typical Herakles legend, reflected in every legend of the cycle, is the hero's combat with and victory over the death lord himself.

Tables 9 to 12 follow this chapter. Table 9 presents graphically the correspondences of themes, and table 10 the correspondences of plot components among thirteen myths or myth complexes, five of them being key myths of tables 3 and 4, and eight of them significant legends or legend groups of chapters xi and xii and appendices 4 and 5, so as to show the close agreement of one group to the other and of the several myths to one another.

Table 11 presents the correspondences of themes among twenty-one myths or legends, most of which belong to subtype IV (p. 265). These are the myths of Herakles discussed in chapters ii, vi, and xii, Apollo-Phorbas, Eurybatos-Sybaris, Euthymos-Heros, Koroibos-Poine, Perseus-Ketos, Beowulf-Grendel, Sigurd-Fafnir, St. George *vs.* dragon, and the oriental myths of Nergal-Ereshkigal, Gilgamesh-Humbaba, Rama-Ravana, and Susanowo's dragon.

Table 12 compares the myths of table 11, excepting *Geryon* and *Hydra,* according to the plot components of subtype IV.

---

[57] Apollod. 2.5.1; Prob. *Georg.* 3.19 (Call. frag. 54 Pf.); Pedias. 1; Col. Sal. *Lab. Herc.* 3.8. It seems that the champion's opponent of mixed lion and dragon shape, e.g., Labbu, has become two separate enemies of Herakles. Behind the story of the sacrifices lie such sacrifices as were made to H. at Sikyon: Paus. 2.10.1.

TABLE 9

Correspondences of Themes

Theme	Python	Typhon	Tiamat	Vritra	Ymir-FG	Yam-Mot	Ketos-Medusa	Drakon	Geryon-Cacus	Acheloos-Nessos	Grendel-Firedrake	Fafnir	St. George's dragon
1A	X	X	X	X	X	X	X	X	X	X	X		
1B	X	X	X	X	X	X	X	X	X	X	x	x	
1C	X	X	X	x	X	x	x	x	X	x	X	x	x
2A a	X	X						x					
2A b	X	X						X					
2A c	x							x	x	X			
2A d	x	X					x		x				
2A e		X					X		x				X
2A f		X				X	X		x				X
2A g							X		X				x
2B	X	X		X	x		X	X	X	X	X	X	
2C	X			x			x	X	x		x		
2D	X	X		X	x		X	X	X	X			X
2E	x	X	X	X	X	X	X		X	X	X		X
3A	X	X	X	X	X		X	X	X	X	X	X	X
3B	X	X	x	X	x	X	X	X	X	X	X	X	X
3C	x	X	X		x	X	x	x	X				x
3D	x	X			x	x	X	X	X		X	X	X
3E					x					X		X	
3F	x	x	X	X	X	X	X	X	X	x	X	X	X
3G		x		X	X		X	X		X			
4A	X	X	X	X	X	X	X	X	X	x	X	X	X
4B	x			X		X	X		x			x	X
4C	x						X	x	X		X	X	X
4D	X	X	x	X	X	X	X	X	X		X		X
4E	X	X				x	X			X		X	X
4F	X			X		x		x	x	X	x		X
4G	X	X		X				x					X

(*Continued*)

TABLE 9 (continued)

Theme	Python	Typhon	Tiamat	Vritra	Ymir-FG	Yam-Mot	Ketos-Medusa	Drakon	Geryon-Cacus	Acheloos-Nessos	Grendel-Firedrake	Fafnir	St. George's dragon
5A	X	X	X	X	X	X	X	X			x	X	x
5B	X	X	X				X	x				x	
6A	X	X	X	X	X	X	X	X	X	X	X	X	X
6B	X	X	X	X	X	X	X	X			X	X	X
7A	X	X	X	X	X	X	X	X	X	X	X	X	X
7B	X	X		X		x		x	x		X	X	
7C	x	X	X	X		X	X	X		x	X	x	X
7D	X	X	x			X	X	X	X	X	x		
7E	X	X	X	X	X	X	X		X	X	X	X	X
7F	X	X					x	X	X		X	X	
7G	x	x	X	X	X		x	x	x	x	x	x	x
8A	x	X	X	X	X	X	x	x	x	x	X	X	x
8C	x						X	X	X		x	X	
8D	x				x		X	x	X	X		X	x
8E	X		X	X		X	x				X		
9	x	X	X	X		x	X	x	x		x	X	
10A	X	X	X	X	X		X		x	X	X	X	X
10B	X	x	X	X		X	X	x	X	x	X	X	X
10C	X			X		x	X	X	X			X	
10D	X		X	X		X	X	X	X				X

NOTE: Subdivisions of 2A: (a) Delphi, Parnassos, (b) Boeotia, (c) Northwest Greece, (d) Lydia, Phrygia, (e) Cilicia, Cappadocia, (f) Syria, Palestine, (g) Atlantis; Atlas Range, Morocco, Tartessos-Gades, islands to the west. 6A indicates in this table the presence of a champion willing to face the enemy. 8B does not appear in any myth not included in previous tables, and so has been omitted from this. *Python* and *Vritra* are defined as in table 3. *Ymir-FG* means the myths of combat between Norse gods and Frost Giants from the beginning until Ragnarök. *Ketos-Medusa* includes Perseus' troubles with Akrisios, Polydektes, Proitos, Kepheus, Phineus. *Drakon* includes Kadmos' relations with the Sphinx. *Geryon-Cacus* means the whole complex of legends concerning Herakles' quests of Geryon's cattle and of the Hesperidean apples. *Fafnir* includes all Sigurd-Siegfried's conflicts in the Nibelung-Volsung legend.

TABLE 10

Correspondences of Plot Components

Component	Python	Typhon	Tiamat	Vritra	Ymir-FG	Yam-Mot	Ketos-Medusa	Drakon	Geryon-Cacus	Acheloos-Nessos	Grendel-Firedrake	Fafnir	St. George's dragon
A	X	X	X	X	x	x	X	x	X	X	X	X	x
B, 1			X	X	X	X	X	x	x	X	X	x	X
B, 2	x	X	X	X	X	X	X	x	X	X			
B, 3	X	X	X	X	X		X	X	X	X	X	X	X
B, 4	X	X	X	X	X	X	X	X	X	X	X	X	X
B, 5	X	X	X	X	X	X	X	X	X	X	X	X	X
C, 1a	X		X	X	X	X	X	X	x	x	x	x	X
C, 1b	x	X	X		X	X			x	x			
C, 2			X	X	X			x			x		
C, 3	x	x	X	X	X			x				x	
C, 4	x	x	X	X	X		x	x	x	x	x		x
D, 1	x	X	X	X		X	x	x		x	x		x
D, 2	x	X	X	X	X	X	X	X	X	X	X	X	X
E, 1a			X	X	X	X	X						
E, 1b	x	X		X	X		x	x			X	X	x
E, 1c	x				x	X	x	x	x	x		x	x
F, 1	X	X	X	X		X	X	X	X		X	X	X
F, 2	X	X		x		x	x			X			x
G, 1c						X	x						
G, 2b + H, 1b	x		X		X	x					X	x	
H, 1a	x	X	X	X		X	X	x	x	X	X	X	x
H, 2	X	X	X	X	X	X	X	X	X	X	X	X	X
H, 3	X	X		X		X		x	x		X	X	
H, 4	X	X	X	X	X	X	X	X	X		x	x	X
H, 5	x	X	X	X			x	X	x	x	X	x	x
I, 1	X	X	X	X	X	X	X	X	x	x	X	X	X

Note: Terms are defined as in table 9. Those components are omitted that do not enter into myths not included in previous tables.

TABLE 11

Correspondences of Themes, Subtype IV

Theme	Thanatos	Sybaris	Heros	Poine-Ker	Pylos enemy	Ketos	Trojan Ketos	St. George's dragon	Susanowo's dragon	Geryon	Cacus	Ereshkigal	Ravana	Grendel	Fafnir	Lityerses-Syleus	Kyknos	Antaios	Phorbas-Phlegyas	Humbaba	Hydra
1A	X			x	X					X	X	x		X			x	X	x		X
1B	X					X	X	X		X	X	x		x	x		X	X	x		X
1C	x	X			X	x	x	x		x	X		X	X	x	X		X			X
2A a		X																	X		
2A b	X																X		X		
2A c							X			x						X					
2A d						X		X													
2A e						X		X												x	
2A f			X							x	x						x				
2A g						X		x		X								X			
2B		X									X		x	X	X			X	X	X	X
2C											x			x			X	x		X	
2D		X				X		X		X	x										X
2E			x		X	X	X	X		X			X	X				x		X	X
3A		X				X	X	X	X		X		X	X	X		X	X	X	X	X
3B	x	X	X	X	X	X	X	X	X	x	X		X	X	X		x	x	x	X	X
3C							x	x	X	X	x		X								X
3D								X	X		X		x	X	X		x			X	X
3E					X								X		X						
3F	X	X	X	X	X	X	x	X	x	X	X	X	X	X	X	x	X	X	X	X	x
3G	x					X	X		X											X	
4A	x	X	X	X	x	X	X	X	X		X		X	X	X	X	X	X	X	X	X
4B		x	X			x	x	X	x		x		X		x				X		
4C	X	X	X	X		X	X	X	X		X			X	X						
4D		X		X		X	X	X	X		X		X	X		X		X			X
4E	X		X			X	X	X	X				X		X	X			x		
4F					X			X						x			X	X	X	x	x
5A						x	x	x					X	x	X				X	X	
5B				X	X								X		x					x	X
6A	X	X	X	X	X	X	X	X	X	X	X	X	X	X	X	X	X	X	X	X	X
6B	x	X	X	X		X		X				x	X	X	X					X	X

TABLE 11 (continued)

Theme	Thanatos	Sybaris	Heros	Poine-Ker	Pylos enemy	Ketos	Trojan Ketos	St. George's dragon	Susanowo's dragon	Geryon	Cacus	Ereshkigal	Ravana	Grendel	Fafnir	Lityerses-Syleus	Kyknos	Antaios	Phorbas-Phlegyas	Humbaba	Hydra
7A	X	X	X	X	X	X	X	X	X	X	X	X	X	X	X	X	X	X	X	X	X
7B						X					x			x	X		x	x			X
7C	x	X	X	X		X	X	X				X	x	X	x						
7D					X	x	X			X				x			X	x	X		X
7E					X	x	X	X	X	X	X	X	X	X	X		X	x	X	X	X
7F					X	x					X			X	X						
7G					x	x	x	x		x	x		X	x	x				x		x
8A	X	x	x	x	x	x	X	x	x	x	x	X	X	X	X	x	x	x	x	x	
8C	x					x					X	x		x	X	X					
8D		x		x		X	X	x			X	X	X		X	X		X			
8E				x									X	X							
9	X					X			X					x	X	X		X	X		X
10A						X		X	X					X	X	X	X	x	X	X	X
10B						X	X	X	x	x	X		X	X	X					x	
10C	x					X				x	X				X						
10D		x	X	X		X	X	X			X	X		X		X	x	X			

NOTE: Subdivisions of 2A: (a) Delphi, Parnassos, (b) Thessaly, (c) Lydia, Phrygia, (d) Cilicia, Cappadocia, (e) Syria, Palestine, (f) Southern Italy, (g) Atlantis (see note to table 9). 4G and 8B are omitted, since they occur only uncertainly in but one or two of these myths. *Thanatos* means the Alkestis story. *Pylos enemy* means Herakles' opponent at Pylos, whether called Hades, Poseidon, Ares, or Periklymenos. *Ketos* means the Andromeda story only. *Geryon, Cacus,* and *Antaios* mean Herakles' combats with these opponents only; the surrounding combats and Hesperides adventure are not included. *Grendel* does not include the Firedrake combat. *Fafnir* is defined as in table 9.

TABLE 12

CORRESPONDENCES OF PLOT COMPONENTS, SUBTYPE IV

Myth	1	2a	2b	2c	2d	3a	3b	3c	3d	4a	4b	5
Thanatos		X	x				X			X	X	X
Sybaris	X	X	X			X	X				X	X
Heros	X	X	X	X		X	X				X	X
Poine-Ker	X	X	X				X		X			X
Pylos enemy	X	x			x				X	X		X
Ketos	X	X	X			X	X			x	X	X
Trojan Ketos	X	X	X			x	X			x	X	X
St. George's dragon	X	X	X		x	x	X	x	x		X	X
Susanowo's dragon	X	X	X			X	X			x	X	X
Cacus	X	X		x	x		x			X		X
Ereshkigal	X	x	X					x	X	X		x
Ravana	X	x	x			X	X			x		X
Grendel	X	X			x				X	X	X	X
Fafnir	x	x				X	X	x		X	X	X
Lityerses-Syleus	X	x			X		X		X	x		X
Kyknos	X				X			X	X	x		X
Antaios	X				X				X	x		X
Phorbas-Phlegyas	X			X	X			x	X	x		X
Humbaba	x				X			X	X	X		X

XIII

EARLIER FORMS OF THE DELPHIC MYTH

Now it is time to go back to rocky Pytho. There our journey began, when our study of Apollo's combat with the dragon was limited to the surviving sources of the myth. But now that we have wandered over three continents, seen the combat myth in many guises among many peoples, and discerned a basic pattern that underlies these variant mythical expressions, and which has, moreover, in its several expressions, a fairly definite range of meanings, we can look once more at the Delphic dragon combat, bringing to it all the knowledge and insight that we have gained along the way.

I have already mentioned Gruppe's view of the early Apollo-dragon combat (p. 252), based on the Homeric Hymn: namely, that Apollo fought Typhon immediately after his birth, while Zeus lay helpless in the Corycian Cave, and after killing the monster, brought order back to a disrupted world. The earliest scene, he thinks, was Delos—thither Typhon had pursued the pregnant Leto, knowing that her son would kill him, if born— later Delphi adopted an altered form of the myth, in which the dragon eventually became known as Python. If Gruppe had realised that Apollo really had two opponents, both a male and a female dragon, and that the latter is not merely a variation on the former, he might, with a glance at cognate myths, have reconciled the Delian and Delphian scenes by supposing that after Apollo had killed Typhon on Delos, he set out at once for Pytho to settle accounts with the dragoness, the dragon's evil consort, who had incited him in the first place. Such a conjecture might account for Typhon's sudden disappearance from the Hymn (if, indeed, there is not a lacuna after 355), and also for the brief reminder of him in Apollo's speech of triumph over the dying dragoness, when he tells her that Typhoeus will not ward death from her. Even Typhon alive could not recall her from death, once she had her death wound; how much less could Typhon dead.[1]

TELPHUSA

Actually Apollo does settle an account in the Homeric Hymn, but after his victory over the dragoness. He had gone through Thessaly and Boeotia looking for the right place in which to build his temple that would be an oracle for men, and he had chosen Telphusa. But the spring nymph discouraged him from building there and told him that Krisa (meaning Pytho) was much more suitable. This she did, it seems, not only to keep her abode to herself, but also because she knew that there lived at Pytho an awful dragoness who would surely kill the young god. For after Apollo's victory over the dragoness he realised that Telphusa had spoken deceitfully; and he went back to her in wrath, charged her with her deceit, and buried her spring beneath a shower of stones, the mythical beginning of Mount Tilphossion. Then he established a shrine for himself in that place too.[2]

So Telphusa, spirit of a spring like Sybaris, or like Delphyne herself, beguiled Apollo and tried to send him to his death. In doing this she recalls the seductive dragoness of the Venusberg or Siren theme. So we must look more closely at the nymph Tel-

---

[1] Gruppe (1906) 236, 1255-1259; he points to the vase painting (see fig. 1) which shows two palm trees beside the place of combat (1257, note 4); it pictures a version, moreover, in which Leto carries the infant Apollo. See Dornseiff (1933) 29.

[2] Hom. Hymn 3.242-276, 375-387. Though the poet appears to say that Apollo destroyed Telphusa by burying her spring beneath stones, actually she continued to live and flow; the story is meant to explain why this spring gushes forth from beneath an overhanging rock: see AHS on Hymn 3.244, 383. Apollo's great wrath is inadequately motivated, if we suppose that Telphusa knew nothing about the dangerous dragoness and used her guile merely to keep her residence to herself; in fact, she tells the truth about the advantages of Pytho, and thereafter Apollo evidently considered it a superior site to his Telphusian shrine. See Dornseiff (1933) 13.

phusa and inquire whether she may not be a second representative of the dragoness in the Hymn.

We very soon strike pay dirt. Poseidon, we learn from the Cyclic poets, took the form of a horse and lay with Erinys beside the Boeotian spring Tilphusa, whereupon she conceived and bore the fleet horse Areion. It was this horse that Herakles used in his race with Kyknos (p. 30); or, as the *Shield* has it, in his combat with him. The mother Erinys was named Tilphossa, as is clear from the Scholiast who says that Ares and the Erinys Tilphossa were parents of Theban Drakon (p. 308). Since the name Areion seems to be more appropriate to Ares' son than to Poseidon's, we may see here an original identity of Drakon and Areion. The Greeks associated both snakes and horses with springs.[3]

The same name and myth are found in the Arcadian city Thelpusa. The city, it is said, got its name from the nymph Thelpusa or Telphusa, Ladon's daughter. She was called Erinys, as in Boeotia, and known as Demeter Erinys at her shrine in Thelpusian Onkeion. A Scholiast explicitly identifies the Erinys Tilphosaia, mentioned by Callimachus, with the Arcadian Erinys Demeter. According to the myth, Poseidon followed Demeter when the goddess wandered in search of her lost daughter. To avoid him she took the form of a mare and joined the herds of King Onkios; but Poseidon turned himself into a stallion to copulate with her, impregnating her with the horse Areion and a daughter whose name was known only to initiates of the local mysteries; Demeter's anger at being so used gave her the name Erinys, and Poseidon got himself the name Hippios. According to Apollodoros, Demeter took the form of an Erinys during her copulation with Poseidon.[4]

---

[3] Poseidon-Erinys: Cycl. *ap.* Scholl. ABT *in Il.* 23.346; Schol. T agrees with *Shield* 120 in saying that Herakles had Areion for his combat with Kyknos. The Scholl. also call Areion's mother a Harpy. Ares-Erinys: Schol. Vet. on Soph. *Ant.* 126. Telphusa's name appears in several forms: *Telphus(s)a, Tilphus(s)a, Tilphôs(s)a, Telphusia, Thelpusa* (Arcadian only), *Tilphôs(s)ia.* Apollo's epithet and the mountain show corresponding masculine and neuter forms.

[4] Arcadian nymph Thelpusa: Paus. 8.25.2; Herodian *Orth.* II 589 Lentz; Steph. Byz. 409 Holst. Erinys Tilphossia: Call. frag. 652 Pf.; Schol. Vet. on Lyk. 1038, 1040, 1225; see Lyk. 1040 f., who says that Ladon's Telphusa is a helper of *dikê*. Demeter Erinys: Antimachos *ap.* Paus. 8.25.4; Paus. 8.25.4–7, 11; Schol. Vet. on Lyk. 153 with Schol. Vet.; Apollod. 3.6.8. On coins of Thelpusa, Demeter is seen with the snaky locks of an Erinys: BMCC, Peloponnesus, p. 204, pl. 37.22. See Immerwahr (1891) 113–122.

The daughter born to Poseidon and Demeter was Despoina (Mistress), a goddess whom the Arcadians honored above all other deities, according to Pausanias, especially at her shrine near Lykosura, where she was the center of a mystery cult. For Despoina was also worshipped beside the Black Demeter (Melaina) of Phigalia, where exactly the same myth of Poseidon Hippios' union with Demeter was told as at Thelpusa, the only difference being that Despoina alone was born to them. It is apparent, therefore, that the Despoina who was daughter of Poseidon and Demeter at Lykosura and Phigalia, and whose name was known only to initiates, was identical with Demeter's daughter in Thelpusa. It is furthermore apparent that Poseidon takes Zeus's place as Demeter's mate in Arcadia, and that Despoina is the goddess who was known elsewhere as Kora-Persephone; though neither Kora nor Persephone could be her Arcadian mystic name, since Pausanias, who knew the mystic name, distinguishes Zeus's daughter from Poseidon's, giving these names to the former (Kora, moreover, is no more a personal name than is Despoina). For Zeus's daughter has little place in Arcadian cult and is obviously an importation; Despoina is her native counterpart.[5]

Despoina-Kora is, moreover, a double of her mother, the two being the young grain and ripe grain, according to H. J. Rose (note 5). This grain goddess, like most fertility deities, is also a goddess of the dead, a character that is prominent in Arcadia, visible in Demeter Erinys and the Black Demeter. Beside the seated Demeter and Despoina of Lykosura stood an image of

[5] Despoina of Lykosura: Paus. 8.37. Demeter Melaina and Despoina of Phigalia: Paus. 8.42. At first Zeus's daughter Kora was probably distinct from the dread Persephone, queen of the dead: see Rose (1928) 91, 99 note 56. They were most likely identified by way of the myth of Hades' rape of Kora: she whom Hades seized to become his wife must obviously be Persephone, his consort. The Kora of the well-known myth, we should notice, is the Death's bride of Th. 4E, the abducted or sacrificed maiden whom the hero must rescue; probably that hero was Hermes, whose role as dragon slayer is noticed several times in this study (e.g., pp. 252, 483); but the story was separated from the combat myth and given a different ending, somewhat analogous to that of the Nergal-Ereshkigal myth (p. 175), with sexes reversed. There is a conclusion in reconciliation; but even so, notice the cyclic character of the myth: Hades seizes the maiden, but must give her up; then periodically he receives and surrenders her again. It is like the alternation of Baal's death with Mot's: both myths were tied closely to the seasonal rituals. But Persephone is the eternal queen of the dead, a form of Hekate; her role as hero's enemy and seductive temptress may be seen behind the Adonis and Peirithoos myths, as we have them. So in the Hades-Persephone myth we see the dragoness identified with the rescued maiden (see p. 537). In Arcadia, Hades' rape of Kora is replaced by Poseidon's of Demeter.

Artemis, holding a torch in one hand (like the Demeter beside her), two snakes in the other; and beside the entrance to their sanctuary stood the temple of Artemis Hegemone, which sheltered a bronze image of Artemis holding two torches. The torches and snakes reveal the underworld Artemis, who is Hekate. Small figures of snakes and other creatures were attached to the mare's-head image of Black Demeter at Phigalia; whereas Demeter Erinys of Thelpusa was portrayed with snaky locks (note 4). Beside the altars of Demeter and Despoina in Lykosura stood a third for the Great Mother (*Megalê Mêtêr*), surely a third form of the same goddess. For here in Arcadia it is especially evident that Demeter is the mother goddess and earth goddess. She has the two natures of Ge, representing life and death, Eros and Thanatos. In fact, the poet Antimachos said that Thelpusian Areion was Ge's son, implying that he was born without a father (αὐτὴ Γαῖ' ἀνέδωκε), though elsewhere he recognised that Areion was Poseidon's son. Demeter, like Ge, was called Chthonia, as at Hermione, where she was associated with Klymenos (p. 479). So Demeter-Kora was paired with all three Olympian brothers: Zeus, Poseidon, Hades.[6]

It is generally recognised that the Boeotian Telphusa must be related to the Arcadian, though it is hard to determine in which district the name occurred first. There are several coincidences of name and circumstance other than those already mentioned. The Thelpusian sanctuary of Demeter Erinys was actually located in a suburb called Onkeion, whose eponym was Onk(i)os, son of Apollo Onkaios; Kadmos founded the cult of Athena Onga (or Onka) in Thebes after killing the dragon son of Ares

---

[6] Paus. 8.25, 37, 42; Antim. *ap.* Paus. 8.25.4, 9. Demeter Chthonia: Paus. 2.35.4 f. (Hermione), 3.14.5 (Sparta). The stoa wall of the Lycosuran Despoina's shrine showed reliefs of the Moirai, who are close to the Erinyes (p. 429), and Zeus Moiragetes (Paus. 8.37.1). It was the Moirai who persuaded Demeter to give up her wrath against Poseidon (Paus. 8.42.3). A hunting dog was seen crouching at the foot of Artemis in the sculpture group mentioned above; Lyk. 1040 f. calls the Erinys Telphusia *skylax* "that lives beside Ladon's stream." Paus. 8.37.6 cites Aeschylus for a so-called Egyptian story in which Artemis was Demeter's daughter. Phigalia also had a cult of Eurynome, locally identified with Artemis (Paus. 8.41.4–6; see p. 231); cf. Strabo 8.3.15, p. 344, and the Eleusinian mysteries. Notice Demeter Eleusinia at Arcadian Telphusa, in whose shrine were images of Demeter and Dionysos: Paus. 8.25.2 f. Notice that the Demeter Melaina of Phigalia had a sacred cave on Mount Olive, and that her snaky-locked mare-headed image carried a dolphin and a dove. On Demeter as death goddess see Farnell (1907) III 48–65; LM 2.1333–1337.

and Telphusa. Some scholars see the same name in Boeotian Onchestos, a town situated at the western base of Sphinx Mountain, only a few miles from the spring Telphusa; and they relate it to *Ôgygos* and *Ôkeanos*. Arcadian Ladon is called Ogygian by the geographical poet Dionysios. The springs of Ladon rise from under a mountain in the manner of the Boeotian spring Telphusa. Ladon was also a former name of the Theban Ismenos (p. 311) and the name of the Hesperidean dragon. It is probable that Ladon, like Acheloos and other rivers, was assimilated to the River Ocean. Moreover, Haliartos, at the foot of Telphusa's mountain (Tilphossion), had a cult of goddesses called Praxidikai, daughters of Ogygos. These Praxidikai, exactors of justice, seem to be Erinyes, and so must have been closely related to nearby Telphusa. Furthermore Persephone was called Praxidike. Though our scanty information about the cults on and around Mount Tilphossion in Boeotia includes no mention of Demeter, she was worshipped under the byname Europa in Lebadeia (Livadhia) at the northern foot of neighboring Laphystion. Her nearness becomes more significant when we learn that Demeter Europa was nurse of the oracular hero or chthonian deity of Lebadeia—Trophonios Erginos' son, who was builder of Apollo's temple at Delphi and robber of Hyrieus' treasury; and when we recall that Europa was mistress of Poseidon Hipparchos, daughter of Tityos, and mother of Euphemos (p. 482).[7]

Now it becomes evident that the myth of Poseidon's union with Telphusa Erinys, wherefrom the fleet horse Areion was born, is little different from that of Poseidon's union with Medusa, wherefrom the winged horse Pegasos was born. Pegasos' birth is associated with the spring Hippokrene on Mount Helikon, of which Tilphossion forms a spur; it is perhaps six miles from the spring

---

[7] On relation of the two Telphusai see Immerwahr (1891) 113, Farnell (1907) III 52–56; see also Wilamowitz (1931) 398–407, who points out some of the links that connect Thelpusa, Demeter Erinys, Demeter Melaina, etc. Onkeion, etc.: Paus. 8.25.4 f., 10 f.; Antim. *ap.* Paus. 8.25.9; on the name and its relations see Immerwahr 117; LM 3.911. Ogygian Ladon: Dionys. Per. 417. Sources of Ladon: Paus. 8.20.1. Ismenos = Ladon: Paus. 9.10.6. Praxidikai: Paus. 9.33.3; Dionys. Chalk. 3, 4.394 M. Persephone Praxidike: Orph. Hymn 29.5. Demeter Europa: Paus. 9.39.4 f. Trophonios: Hom. Hymn 3.295–297; Pind. frags. 2 f. Bowra; Paus. 9.37.5, 10.5.13. Europa Tityos' daughter bore Euphemos on the banks of Kephisos: Pind. *Pyth.* 4.46; here Poseidon and Kephisos are to be identified; concerning Melaina-Melantho, see p. 47. That Europa's father is the Tityos of Panopeus, which is near Lebadeia, is evident from Schol. Vet. on Apollon. *Arg.* 1.181.

Telphusa. The likeness of Gorgons to Erinyes has already been
pointed out, and also the nearness of both to Harpies. For in the
Boeotian tradition Areion's mother was known as either Harpy
or Erinys (p. 367, note 3). As the Erinys was a mare when
Poseidon begot Areion upon her, and her image at Phigalia had
a mare's head, so Medusa was pictured in the form of a horse by
archaic artists (p. 288, note 23). As Herakles used Areion to defeat Kyknos, so Bellerophon used Pegasos to defeat Chimaira and
other enemies. In fact, a scene engraved upon an Etruscan mirror
shows the name Areion (Ario) over Bellerophon's winged horse.[8]

So, since the nymph Telphusa turns out to be an underworld
goddess, Erinys or Harpy, a double of Medusa, mate of Poseidon
or Ares, mother of monsters, herself partly snake or horse (or
dog), there is no difficulty in identifying her with the dragoness
Delphyne as Apollo's enemy. But she is the alluring rather than
the frightful demoness. Apollo was attracted by her lovely and
pleasant surroundings (χῶρος ἐρατός, ἀπήμων); he found the spring,
i.e., the nymph herself, charming (καλλίρροον ὕδωρ), and he wanted
to stay there; but she sent him to dragon-haunted Pytho. Now
Apollo was an intruder at Telphusa as at Delphi. His predecessor
appears to have been Teiresias. For there is a story that Teiresias
fled with many Thebans from their city when the Epigonoi took
it; or the Epigonoi captured him and took him with others on
the road to Delphi to offer them to Apollo; but, whether as fugi-
tive or captive, Teiresias came to the spring Telphusa and drank
of it to slake his thirst; and so cold was the water that he could
not endure it and died; there he was buried with divine (iso-
theoi) honors, and his tomb could be seen in later times. Here, of
course, no more is said than that the spring caused an old seer's
death. But we should recall two other stories about Teiresias. (1)
One day while hunting he accidentally came upon Athena as she
bathed in the waters of the spring Hippokrene and saw her
naked; so she struck him blind for his unwitting error. Now
Athena seems out of character here as a goddess who bathes in
forest pools amidst a band of companion nymphs. She has usurped

---

[8] See Ovid Met. 6.118–120; Serv.-Dan. Georg. 3.122; both bring together Neptune-
Poseidon's affairs with Medusa and Ceres-Demeter. Notice Aesch. Eum. 48–51, where the
Pythia calls the Erinyes Gorgons and likens them to Harpies. Mirror: Mon. Inst. 6.29.1.
For Bellerophon on Pegasos see Apollod. 2.3.2.

Artemis' place, and this is the story of Artemis and Aktaion, which ends with Aktaion's death. (2) One day as Teiresias walked in the forest, he came upon two snakes copulating, and striking them with his staff, at once became a woman. In the first story the goddess of a spring either kills or blinds the hero; and blindness may be considered a death equivalent in this tale. In the other the hero's encounter with two snakes, who are mates, costs him his virility; after eight years, the story goes on to say, he encountered them again and regained his manhood. So, dimly it may be, but none the less with fair certainty, we can see Teiresias as the slayer of Telphusa and her mate, but only after he had suffered death from them himself, having been enticed to destruction by the nymph at her spring. Teiresias' tomb beside Telphusa's spring marks this as the scene of his heroic or chthonian worship; so that we may surmise that Teiresias originally belonged here, whence his legend spread out to other parts of Boeotia. One place was *Opheôs Kephalê*, Snake's Head, between Thebes and Glisas. There it was said that the snake (*Ophis*) put his head forth from his hole as Teiresias happened by, whereupon Teiresias cut his head off. The name Ophis and the locality relate this snake to the Theban Echion and Drakon.[9]

Now, though the initial T of Telphusa (and the variant spellings) is well established for both Boeotia and Arcadia, it is interesting that manuscripts of the Homeric Hymn read *Delphusa*, and that the form *Delphusia* for the Arcadian city is found in the text of Stephanos of Byzantion, who cites Androtion. Delphusa is the name of one of Delphi's three springs; and it is quite possible that this is the dragoness-guarded spring to which the Hymn refers (see Appendix 6). So the scribe's error that produced the reading *Delphusa* for *Telphusa* coincides with a genuine relationship between names. That is, *Telph-* or *Tilph-* appears to be a

---

[9] Telphusa's beauty: Hom. Hymn 3.244, 376, 380, 385. Teiresias and Telphusa: Paus. 9.33.1; Diod. 4.66.5, 4.67.1; Apollod. 3.7.3; Aristoph. (Gram. ?) *ap*. Ath. 2.41ᴇ; Strabo 9.2.27, 36, pp. 411, 413. (1) Apollod. 3.6.7, citing Pherek.; Call. *Hymn* 5.57–136; Nonn. *Dion.* 20.399–402. (2) Apollod. 3.6.7, citing Hesiod; Ovid *Met.* 3.324–331; Hyg. *Fab.* 75. Aktaion: Apollod. 3.4.4; Ovid *Met.* 3.138–252. Aktaion's pool was on Mount Kithairon; but the description of the spring which fed it, as Ovid has it (155–162), could easily fit Telphusa. Notice Schol. on Clem. Alex. *Protr.* 1, p. 3 P: the Delphians said that the dragon whom Apollo killed was father of tragedy on Kithairon and Helikon. For Teiresias and Ophis see Paus. 9.19.3.

cognate of *Delph-*, as several scholars have already conjectured. The meaning matters little, though the base has been connected with *delphys* "womb" and interpreted as *hollow, cavity;* the ancients, however, associated *Delph-* with *delphis* "dolphin," as the Hymn makes clear. But it is probably a pre-Hellenic name, whatever its meaning. In any case, I think that the names Telphusa and Delphusa are built on the same base; myth supports etymology in this instance.[10]

What the Hymn gives us, then, is a fusion of two local myths of Apollo's encounter with a dragon pair. There were sacred places, identically named, one on Parnassos, the other by Helikon, each of which Apollo took over from an indigenous deity. There was a time when the two shrines were of equal importance, each serving mainly its own neighborhood; but from the eighth century, as we shall see, the Parnassian shrine began to eclipse its Boeotian namesake. In fact, the Hymn is intended to emphasise Delphi's superiority over Telphusa; but it must explain why Apollo is also established at the inferior place. It is probable that Telphusa once had an oracular shrine too. The presence of Teiresias' tomb points that way, and so do Apollo's words in the Hymn: on his arrival he tells Telphusa that he intends to build there a lovely temple to be an oracle for men of all Hellas, where he will give them true responses, the very words that he speaks later on coming to Pytho.[11]

The Hymn's fusion of versions brings about an interesting change in the myth. Instead of a dragon pair, male and female, the champion encounters two dragonesses. The Delphian dragoness occupies the place that the male dragon should have: it is she to whose deadly home the god is enticed, and she is killed first, whereupon the god goes off to deal with her accomplice. Ordinarily the male dragon is met in the first encounter. But he is not absent either: the Delphian dragoness has reared Typhon to be a

---

[10] See AHS, critical apparatus on Hom. Hymn 3.244, 247. At 244 all MSS read δελφούσης, corrected only in Brussels 74. At 247 and 256 all except Leiden 22 have the form in initial delta. On the etymology see Gruppe (1906) 744, note 19, with authorities cited; Kern (1926) 79; Schachermeyr (1950) 40. (See also Addenda, following Indices.)

[11] Hom. Hymn 3.247–253, 287–293. It may be that the Hymn supposed Apollo to have abandoned his design of founding an oracle at Telphusa; but he did return there and establish his cult, where he was afterwards worshipped as Apollo Telphusios (*ibid.* 384–386).

bane to men, and Apollo has apparently disposed of him before killing her. But, unless there is a lacuna, the Apollo-Typhon combat has dropped out of the Hymn, because the entry of Telphusa into the narrative, due to the fusion of two local versions of the myth, has pushed the Apollo-Delphyne combat into the place that the Typhon combat had occupied.

DIONYSOS AT DELPHI

The Hymn's Typhon is the Python of later writers: that we have already established. Now we must ask just how important was this Python-Typhon to the Delphic sanctuary. What place did he have outside of the myth? And was the myth anything more than the expression of a desire to make a great champion out of the Pythian god or to give a supposedly historical reason for the foundation of certain festivals, in particular the Pythian and Septerion?

It is plain from the myth, as usually told in the fifth century and later, that Python (and Delphyne) either held the site of Pytho or guarded it for Ge. But Python's Delphic residence may be purely a device of the myth: if Apollo killed a dragon to win the place, then the dragon must have lived there. However, there are ancient writers who say that Python spoke oracles at Delphi before Apollo came, or even that his influence was still felt by the Pythia. Such statements, made as they are by late writers, could be dismissed as due to confusion or ignorance, were it not for pretty good evidence that Python actually had a place in Delphic cult. According to Clement of Alexandria, Python received worship there, and the Pythian games were first celebrated as funeral games in his honor, when an epitaphion was sung for him. Moreover it was said either that his bones and teeth were kept in the kettle that stood upon the mantic tripod, or that his hide was wrapped around the tripod. But most interesting of all is the evidence that the omphalos of Delphi was his tomb. This is said by as good an authority as Varro; and it is supported by Hesychios, who says the same thing, and by a Pompeian mural painting (fig. 27), which shows Python coiled around the omphalos. If all this evidence is put together, it appears that some bones kept in the tripod kettle were considered to be Python's, and that

FIGURE 28. OMPHALOS AT DELPHI

something wrapped around the omphalos was said to be his hide. Those writers who put his skin on the tripod seem to have confused the one fact with the other. In any case tripod and omphalos together have something to do with Python's remains.[12]

Now much the same statements were made about Dionysos at Delphi, as Leicester Holland has perceived: (1) Dionysos spoke

FIGURE 27. APOLLO, PYTHON, AND OMPHALOS

oracles at Delphi before Apollo did; (2) his bones were placed in a basin beside the tripod; (3) the omphalos was his tomb. It is well known, moreover, that Dionysos was second only to Apollo in Delphian and Parnassian worship; Plutarch, in fact, assigns to Dionysos an equal share with Apollo in Delphi.[13]

[12] Python spoke oracles: Hyg. *Fab.* 140.1; Oros. *Hist.* 6.15; Schol. Vet. on Lyk. 200; his enduring influence: ps.-Lucian *Astr.* 23; Suid. Π3140; he once ruled Delphi: Arg. 1 to Pind. *Pyth.*: and notice Eur. IT 1245–1248: Python took care of (ἄμφεπε) the Pythian shrine; worshipped at Delphi: Clem. Alex. *Protr.* 1.1, p. 2 P, 2.34, p. 29 P; on his funeral rites see Hyg. *Fab.* 140.5; ps.-Plut. *Mor.* 1136c; bones in tripod-kettle: Hyg. *Fab.* 140.5; Serv.-Dan. *Aen.* 3.360; hide on tripod: Serv. *Aen.* 3.92, 6.347; Schol. on Stat. *Theb.* 1.509; Vat. Myth. III 8.5; Eust. on Dionys. Per. 441; see also Dionys. Per. 441–444, who puts Delphyne's *holkos*, bristling with scales, beside the tripod; and Nonn. *Dion.* 9.257–260: the snake was coiled around the tripod; omphalos as Python's tomb: Varro LL 7.17; Hesych. T1134. (See also Addenda, following Indices.)

[13] L. B. Holland (1933), especially 201–207. Though I was once skeptical of Holland's identification of Delphic Dionysos with Python and called his article venturesome in OCD, s.v. *Omphalos*, I have been led irresistibly to much the same conclusion. His article is, however, vitiated by a number of mistakes, and his theory about the use of the omphalos in the mantic mechanism (207–214) has to be abandoned; for Bousquet (1951) has shown that the rounded piece of limestone that has what seemed to be ΓΑΣ in archaic letters on its side, and which the French excavators had identified with the genuine omphalos, is really the cupola of a wayside *proskynitarion*, and that the metal blade wedged in the hole drilled through it bears an inscription that can certainly be dated about 1860 A.D.

The worship of Dionysos at Delphi is well attested; see especially Aesch. *Eum.* 24–26; Plut. *Mor.* 365A, 388E; Philodamos' hymn, BCH LV (1931) 357–362.

1. A Pindaric Scholiast says that Python ruled the prophetic tripod on which Dionysos was the first to speak oracles; that then Apollo killed the snake and took over.[14]

2. In what has often been called an Orphic myth, but is probably an old myth of the Greek peoples, one of several theogonies that were current in preclassical times, the Titans seized the child Dionysos and cut him to pieces; then either Titans or Zeus gave the remains to Apollo that he might bury them, and he put them in a basin, took them to Delphi, and set them beside the tripod.[15]

3. The Christian writer Tatian says that the omphalos is Dionysos' tomb. If his information can be trusted, then both Dionysos and Python were given the same tomb at Delphi, and one would conclude that the two names were given to one original deity, however it may have happened that the two were thus brought together. In any case, Dionysos had a tomb at Delphi, whether or not it was identified with the omphalos, and most Hellenes eventually accepted the Delphian tradition that the god was buried there. And his grave was placed beside the golden image of Apollo that stood in the adyton, i.e., the inner room where the omphalos and tripod also stood. If the omphalos was not set directly over the grave, still it must have been remarkably close.[16]

Now most likely the Delphic omphalos stone was not meant at first to represent a navel, or to mark Delphi as earth's central

---

[14] Arg. 1 to Pind. *Pyth.*, . . . τὸ μαντεῖον ἐν ᾧ πρώτῃ Νὺξ ἐχρησμώδησεν, εἶτα Θέμις, Πυθῶνος δὲ τότε κυριεύσαντος τοῦ προφητικοῦ τρίποδος ἐν ᾧ πρῶτος Διόνυσος ἐθεμίστευσε, ... These words are taken to mean that Python served Themis, Dionysos served Nyx; see LM 1.1034; Mommsen (1878) 173, note. Actually πρώτῃ Νὺξ contradicts πρῶτος Διόνυσος, if the verbs are synonymous; and I don't see what distinction can be made in this context. See Paus. 10.5.6 on Ge's speaking her own oracles. The meaning may be that Nyx, Themis, and Python ruled the oracle in succession; Nyx and Themis spoke oracles themselves; Python established the tripod, from which Dionysos spoke as his prophet.

[15] Call. frag. 643 Pf.; Clem. Alex. *Protr.* 2.18, p. 15 P; EM 255. See Linforth (1941) 307–364 on this myth; he shows that though some *Orphikoi* made use of it, there is no evidence that it was an "Orphic" myth in the sense that "Orphics" had invented it or that it was their special property. They took it from the common stock of Hellenic myth, just as they also took and used the Hesiodic myth.

[16] Omphalos as Dionysos' tomb: Tatian *Adv. Gr.* 8; D's grave in Apollo's temple: Plut. *Mor.* 365A; Philochoros 7, 3B. 100 J; Deinarchos *ap.* Eus. *Chron. an.* 718 *et ap.* Malal. 2, p. 45 Dind.; Cedren. 1, p. 43 Bekk.; Call., Clem. Alex., EM, *locc. cit.* (see note 15). For the position of the golden Apollo see Paus. 10.24.5. Ps.-Clem. Rom. *Recogn.* 10.24 says that D. had a tomb in Thebes. It is reasonable to believe that he had a Theban tomb, but this is the only evidence.

point, but to represent a beehive tomb, as several scholars have thought, and as Varro seems to say when he describes the omphalos as like a treasury in appearance. That is, the tombstone, as it really was, had been fashioned in the image of a Mycenaean tomb. And this tomb held, so they said, for part of the year at least, the body of a god who was called either Dionysos or Python.[17]

It would seem then to be no casual juxtaposition of Dionysos and Python, when Euripides says that Parnassos' peak, participant in Dionysos' rites, was the place where Python served Earth's oracle, and when the Pindaric Scholiast says that Dionysos spoke oracles at Delphi from the tripod that Python ruled. Moreover the two are linked through the Delphic Herois. According to Plutarch, the Herois was one of three Delphic festivals that were held every eight years; all he says about it is that its secrets were known only to the Thyiads, and that its ritual seemed to enact the bringing up of Semele from the lower world. The Thyiads were Dionysos' servants and Semele was his mother, whom the god himself brought up from Hades. But from the festival's name one may gather that she who came up was called Herois, a title that meant Mistress (a better translation than *heroine*). According to John of Antioch, Delphyne of Delphi was an ancient *hêrôis:* he uses the very word that was the name of the Thyiads' festival. This deity can therefore be identified with either Delphyne, Typhon-Python's fostermother, or Semele, Dionysos' mother. Now since *Hêra* is but another form of the title *Hêrôis,*

---

[17] On the relation of omphalos to beehive tomb see Harrison (1927) 399–405; L. B. Holland (1933) 205 f.; see also Rohde (1925) 110, notes 31 f., who considers Tatian's identification of omphalos with Dionysos' tomb untrustworthy; but Rohde did not realise that Python and the Delphic Dionysos might be identified. Fig. 28 shows the stone that is now considered more likely to be the genuine omphalos; see Bousquet (1951) 223. Before the false pretender (see p. 375, note 13) was dethroned, this omphalos held third place among the three stones called omphaloi found in the excavations of Delphi. It lay neglected on the grass below the Athenian treasury, where it was still to be seen in March, 1952, the date of fig. 28. Before 1951 it was thought to be just another of perhaps many copies of the true omphalos, and it was outranked by the elaborate omphalos that once stood before the temple, now in the Delphi Museum, which Pausanias (10.16.3) thought to be the real omphalos, but which is certainly its chief representative, a show piece for visitors. On the treasury shape see Varro LL 7.17. The beehive tombs were called treasuries: Paus. 2.16.6. Harrison (400 f.) thinks that the treasury which Varro had in mind was a sort of household money bank; but she believes that the omphalos was meant to represent a tomb.

we can understand why Hera is Typhon's mother in the Homeric Hymn: she is not the goddess of Argos, but the Mistress, mother of the ancient Parnassian deity who was called Python or Dionysos. She was identified with the earth, and so was also called Ge by the Greeks.[18]

The association of Dionysos with Python may not appear so strange, once we realise that Dionysos took the form of snakes and several kinds of beasts or was associated with them. According to the myth of his dismemberment by the Titans, a myth that was associated with Delphi, he was born of Persephone, after Zeus, taking snake form, had impregnated her; and the child had the appearance of a bull. In telling this story Clement quotes a poet's verse "bull father of snake and snake father of bull." This may mean that sometimes Zeus mated as bull, producing a snake Dionysos. Moreover Zeus mated as bull with Europa; Europa was Demeter's name at Lebadeia; and Demeter was also called mother of Dionysos in the dismemberment myth. In this tale the divine child tried to elude the Titans by taking the forms of lion, horse, snake, tiger, and bull in succession; he had, therefore, the power that belonged generally to sea and underworld demons. The chorus of the *Bacchae* call on Dionysos to appear as bull, many-headed snake, or tawny lion. In poetry and art Dionysos is often accompanied by snakes; and his Maenads carry them or wear them in their hair (e.g., the Bacchant Ino; see note 18).[19]

Not only is Dionysos a bull, but also a goat. This is the form that he took in Egypt when he disguised himself to escape Typhon, when as a full-fledged Olympian he was numbered among the heavenly gods that fought monsters and giants. His goat nature is indicated by such epithets as Eriphios and Melanaigis. He was attended by goat spirits, the Panes and Tityroi. So once more Aix Python's son comes to mind (p. 20), a goat that was son of a

---

[18] Eur. IT 1243–1248; Arg. 1 to Pind. *Pyth.*; Plut. *Mor.* 293c; Joh. Ant. 1.20 (4.539 M). Another link may be seen in Nonn. *Dion.* 9.257–260: Ino, bringing Dionysos' rites to Delphi, took the snake that was coiled around the tripod and wrapped him around her head.

[19] Zeus-Persephone-Dionysos: Clem. Alex. *Protr.* 2.16, p. 14 P; Nonn. *Dion.* 5.565–571, 6.155–168. Demeter as Dionysos' mother: Diod. 3.62.6, 3.64.1; at Eleusis she was mother of Iakchos, a form of Dionysos: LM 2.2. Dionysos' transformations: Nonn. *Dion.* 6.175–205. On snakes in the myth and cult of Dionysos see Küster (1913) 118 f., Schauenburg (1953) 65 f., and their citations. Dionysos as bull: Lyk. 209; Nonn. *Dion.* 6.165, 197–205. See Eur. *Bacch.* 1017–1019.

snake. If Aix is Dionysos, then he spoke the oracles from the tripod that his father controlled: for the first *Argumentum* of Pindar's *Pythians* may be so interpreted (p. 376, note 14). By the time this story was formed, Python and Dionysos had been distinguished: the old Parnassian deity had become two persons. Now we can see a reason why the omphalos was called goaty (*Aigaios*).[20]

This Dionysos of Delphi was a god of death and winter. Nothing is more certainly known about him than that he was the center of Delphic worship for the three winter months, when Apollo was absent. It is Plutarch who tells us this, himself a priest of the Pythian Apollo, Amphictyonic official, and frequent visitor to Delphi. He says that for nine months the paean was sung in Apollo's honor at sacrifices, but at the beginning of winter the paeans suddenly ceased; then for three months men sang dithyrambs and addressed themselves to Dionysos rather than to Apollo. His testimony must be accepted, though the belief and rituals indicated have little or nothing to do with the consultation of the oracle, since there are indications that responses were given in winter, or with Dionysos' biennial festival on the slopes of the mountain, since they plainly point to an annual cycle, or with any cult of Dionysos outside of the great temple.[21]

But Plutarch's testimony leads to a startling conclusion: that Dionysos at Delphi was alive through the winter and dead through the rest of the year. Our impressions of Dionysos have

---

[20] Dionysos as goat: Ovid *Met.* 5.329; D. Eriphios: Hesych. E5924; D. Melanaigis: Paus. 2.35.1. See LM 1.1058 f. Omphalos Aigaios: Hesych. O846 (cf. A1749); for the entry MSS read ὀμφαλὸς Αἰγός, which was emended to Αἰγαῖος by Salmasius. But perhaps Αἰγός should stand, the adjective in the definition being an equivalent; either way it is "omphalos of Aix." Notice Steph. Byz. 25 Holst., who speaks of a plain called Aigaion next to Kirrha, Delphi's seaport; he says that a she-goat once came (φερομένην) from the mountain around the *Pythion;* she would be Aix's consort. According to Dionys. Skyt. *ap.* Diod. 3.68.1 *sq.*, D. was son of Ammon and Amaltheia, who were often pictured as ram and goat respectively.

[21] Plut. *Mor.* 389c. Plutarch as priest and *epimeletês;* SIG 829A, 843; Plut. *Mor.* 792F, 700E. According to Schol. Vet. on Pind. *Pyth.* 4.5(8), oracles received during the winter months were considered less trustworthy. This was probably folklore that attempted to combine the fact of wintertime oracular activity with the tradition of Apollo's winter absence; whereas the two things were in fact unrelated. While Dionysos' great festival was biennial, the Thyiads' awakening of Liknites, the infant Dionysos, in the temple, may have occurred every year at the beginning of winter to open the god's annual reign: Plut. *Mor.* 365A. On Dionysos at Delphi see Mommsen (1878) 112–118, 263–277; Jeanmaire (1951) 187–197.

been the opposite: he has seemed to be a god of springtime and
summer, of harvest and vintage, of the renewal of life and the
ripening of fruits; and so he often was. But he was also a god of
death, a ruler of the underworld, like Osiris, with whom he was
identified. For there is a good deal of evidence that links him
with Hades and the dead. Herakleitos said that Hades and
Dionysos are the same. Dionysos the fertility god and Hades the
death lord meet in the figure of Pluto. As Schauenburg has recently shown, referring to many vase paintings and other art
works, Pluto, even when presented as Hades, has Dionysiac attributes, and Dionysos is portrayed as a ruler of the dead. Pluto, a
god of the fertility and wealth that rises from underground, became identified with Hades. His principal attribute is the cornucopia, whereas Dionysos usually carries the drinking horn. But
Dionysos sometimes takes over Pluto's horn of plenty, and so does
Hades (so Acheloos' possession of Amaltheia's horn also links him
with the death god, p. 350).[22]

It is this chthonian Dionysos who ruled Delphi in winter. That
is, the name Dionysos was given to an old local deity, known also
as Python, a spirit of death and winter. He was also a fertility
spirit; and so, since he was very like Dionysos, he easily acquired
the name. It may be true that both alike are derived from an
ancient Mediterranean deity who assumed a different name and
complexion in every region, perhaps in every village, and that the
cult and name of Dionysos spread out from its native land and
absorbed many of the cults that had worshipped the ancient god
under other names. As Jeanmaire suggests, the chthonian Dionysos manifested himself especially at the winter festival when the
souls of the dead rose to walk briefly in the upper world again, the
festival that the Athenians called Anthesteria, whose Delphian
counterpart was perhaps the Theophania. These festivals occurred in February, when Mediterranean spring begins. The
Theophania marked the end of Dionysos' reign and Apollo's

---

[22] Schauenburg (1953); see pp. 41–46 for a list of 23 paintings and reliefs that show
Pluto-Hades with cornucopia, and his figs. 1, 4–6. Herakleitos, frag. 15 Diels. See Hesych.
1958, where *Isodaitês*, an epithet of Dionysos (Plut. *Mor.* 389A), is defined as Pluto or
Pluto's son. On Dionysos see further Plut. *Mor.* 714c; Farnell (1909) 127–129.

return; Dionysos and the ghosts descended once more to Hades' realm.[23]

While Dionysos lies in the tomb, Apollo reigns in Delphi; while Apollo is absent Dionysos reigns. If Dionysos' absence means Dionysos' death, so Apollo's absence must mean Apollo's death. And we have already found that there is some evidence for a tomb of a slain Apollo at Delphi (p. 86); though very little in contrast to the well-documented tomb of Dionysos; wherefore scholars have tended to discount it, attributing it to confusion or ignorance. But Porphyry's testimony receives some support from Euhemeros and Mnaseas (if Fulgentius, who cites him, can be trusted). Euhemeros mentioned a tomb of Apollo Delphicus among other tombs of gods. Minucius Felix, who cites him, is fairly trustworthy; but since Euhemeros' testimony runs the risk of being considered Euhemeristic, it is well to point out that he also mentioned a tomb of Dictaean Zeus, who certainly had one. Mnaseas, who wrote on Delphic history, probably referred to Delphic lore when he said (if he did) that Zeus killed Apollo with his thunderbolt, whereupon undertakers (*vespillones*) laid Apollo away in his tomb. We have seen that it was Zeus who imposed upon Apollo his servitude to Admetos for his killing of either the Cyclopes or Python (p. 326). And according to Pherekydes of Athens, Zeus killed Asklepios at Delphi. Asklepios as Apollo's son represents the healer Apollo; and Apollo's servitude was joined to the Asklepios myth. So the evidence for a death and tomb of Apollo at Delphi is not so weak as it may appear at first sight.[24]

So much for the direct evidence. Apollo's death can also be

---

[23] Jeanmaire (1951) 195. On Theophania see Mommsen (1878) 280–297. Rising of dead at Anthesteria: Hesych. Θ924, M1313; Phot. *Lex.* 1.286, 423 Nab.; notice that the ghosts were called Keres in the cry, Θύραζε Κῆρες (Κᾶρες), οὐκέτ' Ἀνθεστήρια; see Harrison (1922) 32–76; (1927) 275–277, 288–294; Jeanmaire 48–56. This was the very time of Roman Lupercalia and Feralia, when

> The graves stood tenantless and the sheeted dead
> Did squeak and gibber in the Roman streets.

See Ovid *Fasti* 2.266–302, 533–616.

[24] Euhemeros, T 4 *f*, 1.301 J, *ap.* Min. Fel. *Oct.* 21.1; Mnaseas 16, 3.152 M, *ap.* Fulg. p. 769 Stav. Rohde (1925) 110, note 32, rejects the evidence for a tomb of Apollo, but he failed to look beyond the direct testimony. Asklepios at Delphi: Pherek. 35, 1.71 f. J. Porphyry says that Apollo was buried "at the so-called Tripod," which means that his tomb was located quite close to that of Dionysos; if indeed it was not the same tomb, a true Box-and-Cox arrangement.

inferred from his annual absence, as I have suggested. For he spent his winters in the Hyperborean land; and that, we have seen (p. 345), is an otherworldly paradise on the farther bank of Ocean, very like the paradises of Ethiopians and Hesperides, with which it was sometimes confused. In general the ancients placed it in the far north, interpreting the name to mean "beyond the north wind." It was a pleasant land of eternal summer, where the inhabitants lived without sorrow or pain lives that might last as long as they wished; when weary of life they threw themselves into the sea from a rock.[25]

According to the poet Alkaios, immediately after Apollo's birth Zeus sent his son to Delphi on a chariot of swans; but Apollo directed his vehicle to the Hyperboreans instead. When the Delphians heard of this, they composed paeans and formed choruses about the tripod, calling upon the god to come to them from the Hyperborean land. After staying there a whole year he heeded the Delphians' plea and drove his swan chariot to Delphi. This is very different from any other story of Apollo's coming to Delphi: there is no dragon combat; Apollo did not go directly from Delos to Delphi; he went instead to the Hyperboreans of his own free will, apparently disobeying his father's instructions. We must turn to Apollonios to find a reason for this. The poet refers to what he calls a Keltic story: Apollo went to the Hyperborean land, leaving bright heaven in consequence of his father's rebuke (ἐκ πατρὸς ἐνιπῆς), grieving for his son Asklepios whom Zeus had killed. In speaking of a rebuke (*enipê*) the poet hints at the usual story of Zeus's punishment of Apollo for his vengeful killing of the Cyclopes. It is also likely that the word (*enipê*) implies a command of Zeus that banished Apollo to the Hyperboreans. For the

---

[25] Apollo's visits to the Hyperboreans: Alkaios, frags. 2 f. Bergk; Apollon. *Arg.* 2.674 f., 4.612–614; Diod. 2.47.6; Cic. ND 3.23.57; ps.-Erat. *Cat.* 29; Claud. 28.25–34. Alkaios and Claudian imply an annual visit. According to Virg. *Aen.* 4.143 f., Apollo spent his winters in Lykia, which seems to be another location of the Hyperboreans: see Suid. Ω71 and p. 281 above. Diodoros' Metonic year (19 years) has nothing to do with Delphic tradition or cult; it belongs to learned speculation. Hyperborean paradise: Pind. *Pyth.* 10.29–48; Diod. 2.47; Plin. NH 4.12.89; located in north: Herod. 4.13.32–36; Pind. *Ol.* 3.31; Call. *Hymn* 4.281 f.; Plin. *loc. cit.*; Mela 3.5.36; connected with Atlas and Hesperides: Apollod. 2.5.11; located in Asia: Plin. NH 4.12.90; cf. Ctes. *Ind.* 12, where the gold-guarding griffons (cf. Herod. 4.13.1) are located on the borders of India. See Fontenrose (1943). In Bacchyl. 3.58–61 Apollo transports Croesus from his funeral pyre to the Hyperboreans, i.e., Croesus in death went to Apollo's paradise.

pseudo-Eratosthenes says that Apollo, after killing the Cyclopes, hid the avenging arrow among the Hyperboreans, and brought it back only when Zeus absolved him of murder and released him from servitude to Admetos. This testimony brings together the Hyperborean land and Admetos' realm, to either of which Apollo went after killing the Cyclopes. We may recall now the story attributed to Mnaseas, that Apollo was laid away in his tomb after Zeus had killed him with his thunderbolt. So we may suppose that Alkaios modified the myth so as to remove from it all trace of hostility between Zeus and Apollo, and to reconcile it with the belief, which the Delphian priesthood had by that time adopted, that Apollo spoke oracles for Zeus.[26]

It is a fact of the Delphic religious calendar that every year Apollo returned from his three-months' absence on the seventh of Bysios (approximately February), on which day his return was celebrated and the oracular service was at one time renewed (though later the oracle does not seem to have been idle for the whole winter). But Alkaios says that his absence lasted one year, and that he returned to Delphi in midsummer. Such are the incongruities between myth and the facts of cult, of which we shall see more in chapter xv. But Alkaios' testimony is valuable for bringing out a connection between Apollo's return from the Hyperboreans and his octennial return from Tempe in the Septerion festival. Two different festivals have been brought under the canopy of a single myth.[27]

The paeans, lyrics, and choruses of youths that were instituted by the Delphians to call Apollo back from the Hyperboreans have a close parallel in the rites of Apollo's festival at Sikyon. I have already referred to the story (pp. 86 f.) that Apollo and Artemis came to Sikyon's Aigialeia after killing Python to seek purification, and that there a terror (deima, see p. 329) came upon them, causing them to flee. When the seers (manteis) told the people to propitiate Apollo and Artemis, they organised a chorus of seven young men and seven maidens to make supplication to the absent gods, the mythical precedent for a recurring ceremony

[26] Alkaios, frag. 2 Bergk; Apollon. Arg. 4.611–617; ps.-Erat. Cat. 29.
[27] Apollo's return on Bysios 7: Plut. Mor. 292ε, 389c; Prokop. Epist. p. 540 Hercher; Mommsen (1878) 280–291; Halliday (1928) 61 f.

in Apollo's festival at Sikyon. I have already pointed out that Pausanias, in telling this story, has preserved Sikyon's own version of the Python myth, localised in its own territory. It is to this version that the alternative story of Apollo's flight to Crete for purification belongs. It may be more correct to say that Sikyon remade an old local variant of the combat myth upon the model of the Delphic Apollo-Python myth, after that had become part of pan-Hellenic mythology. That is, the antagonists of the old local myth were not at first called Apollo and Python. For it seems that the Sicyonians had assimilated the local myth to two other pan-Hellenic myths. (1) They said that Meleager had dedicated the spear with which he had killed the Calydonian boar in the temple of Peitho (Persuasion), the foundation of which was referred to the supplications of the fourteen young people who persuaded the twins to return to Sikyon, and which, moreover, stood beside Boar River. (2) In the same temple of Peitho had been placed the pipes that Marsyas had used in his unsuccessful contest with Apollo. That is, the enemy in the original Sicyonian myth had a form and character that allowed him to be identified with a snake, a boar, a Silenos, and panic fear. He was the old enemy who could take many forms.

The Marsyas of the Sicyonian myth was Silenos, as Pausanias calls him once in his remarks on the temple of Peitho. The true Marsyas was a Phrygian nature spirit and river god, often identified by the Greeks with Silenos or Pan, as in the Midas legends. But the story of his musical contest with Apollo may be a Greek story that was transferred to Marsyas. We have already seen several instances wherein the combat became reduced to a contest, athletic or musical: Apollo or Herakles against Eurytos, Kadmos or Apollo against Linos, Herakles against Kyknos and Lityerses. We should now recall that the Apollo who was buried at Delphi was called son of Silenos in the elegy that Porphyry ascribed to Pythagoras (p. 86). This is not the only reference to an Apollo who was son of Silenos. Clement of Alexandria and Ampelius, obviously drawing upon a common source, which seems to be one of Aristotle's works, distinguish five Apollos, of whom one was the Arcadian Apollo Nomios, son of Silenos. Cicero draws upon the same source, mentioning the Arcadian Apollo without naming his father. Now the second Apollo mentioned by Aristotle, if he is the common source of Cicero and the others, is the Cretan Apollo, son of Korybas. Korybas stands to the Korybantes, commonly identified with the Cretan Kuretes, as Silenos to the Silenoi. The Korybantes and Kuretes differ from Silenoi in having wholly human form, but they were likewise demonic beings of field and forest, dancers and revellers in the train of the Great Mother and of Dionysos. Korybas as Apollo's father is a variant of Silenos. Now Cicero adds that Apollo Korybas' son fought with Zeus for the island of Crete. He says no more, but obviously Zeus was victor, and inevitably the loser Apollo was sent into banishment or death. In the next sentence Cicero mentions Apollo Zeus's son, saying that he came to Delphi from the Hyperboreans. Since Silenoi and Satyrs are but two names for the same creatures, men with tails, legs, and ears of horses, we should look once more at Satyros who plundered the Arcadians' flocks and whom the hero Argos Panoptes killed along with Echidna and a fierce bull. Here is Satyros as the great enemy himself, partner of the dragoness; it is a very ancient myth of the Peloponnesos.[28]

The foregoing evidence gives still stronger support to Porphyry's testimony about a Delphic tomb of Apollo Silenos' son. It is probable that Silenos is a form of the old Cretan or Aegean god who became identified with the Indo-European Zeus, but who was really much more like Dionysos, a dying god who had a tomb in Crete and who was attended by Kuretes. Silenos also had tombs in Pergamon and in Palestine; in the latter country he had been identified with some Semitic deity. Silenos was tutor or foster father of Dionysos, with whom he is constantly associated in myth and art. The foster father of classical myth is always likely to be the father of early myth. So we find that Silenos bears the same relation to Dionysos as to Apollo. But he is not entirely distinct from Dionysos-Python: mythical genealogy and system-mak-

---

[28] Marsyas' contest with Apollo: Paus. 2.7.9; Apollod. 1.4.2; Ovid *Met.* 6.383–400, 11.153–171. Apollo Silenos' son and Korybas' son: Aristot. *ap.* Clem. Alex. *Protr.* 2.28, p. 24 P; Cic. ND 3.23.57; Ampel. 9.6. On likeness of Korybantes-Kuretes to Silenoi-Satyroi see Strabo 10.3.12, 19, pp. 469, 471 f., who cites verses of Hesiod (frag. 198 Rz.) that associate Satyrs and Kuretes. Satyros: Apollod. 2.1.2. According to Serv.-Dan. *Aen.* 3.111, Korybas was the son of Persephone-Kora; he therefore had the same mother as the Delphic Dionysos.

ing paradoxically obscure the truth by making too sharp distinctions among mythical persons.[29]

What we discover is a form of the myth in which the champion's father, the king of gods, favors the dragon, who seems to be the champion's brother. When the champion kills the dragon, the father in anger kills him in turn; that is, he sends him off to the death realm, whence finally the champion returns in victory, either to overthrow his father or to force him into the background. This is the Ugaritic myth, if we can believe that Baal's sojourn in Mot's realm was a punishment that El put upon him for killing Yam, his brother; and the fragment on "The Harrowing of Baal" (p. 131) supports this conjecture: for El and Asherat raised up monsters to compass Baal's death. Now we can see why Apollo's death became identified with his purification, which occurred after his apparent triumph over Python. The punishment of one form of the myth became identified with the ritual purification of another. A closely parallel development occurs in Indic myth when Tvashtri excluded his son Indra from the soma after Indra had killed Viçvarupa, and when, after Indra had killed Vritra, he ran off to the end of earth and lay there as one dead: these are two statements of one mythical event (pp. 198, 201).

So Apollo's sojourn among the Hyperboreans is the death that his father dealt him. It is to this death or absence that Aeschylus refers in the *Suppliants,* speaking of Apollo as a god exiled from heaven. While his stay among Hyperboreans is usually described as if it were a visit to a sunny winter resort, yet there is evidence to show that their land was part of the death realm. It lay beyond Ocean surrounded by deep darkness and cold. The time of Apollo's residence there was not a time of joy, as one might expect

---

[29] Zeus's tomb: Call. *Hymn* 1.8 f.; Porph. *Vit. Pyth.* 17; Ptol. Heph. *Nov. Hist.* 2, pp. 147 f. Bekk. Silenos' tombs: Paus. 6.24.8; it is noteworthy that Yahweh was identified with Dionysos: Plut. *Mor.* 671c–672c. Dionysos' foster father: e.g., Ovid *Met.* 11.99. Marsyas' father is called Olympos by Apollod. 1.4.2.; and that Olympos is also said to be the pupil of Marsyas: Plato *Symp.* 215c; Ovid *Met.* 6.393; Hyg. *Fab.* 273.11. According to Diod. 3.73.4 and Ptol. Heph. *loc. cit.*, Olympos was fosterfather and guardian of Zeus, who received his epithet Olympios from him; Zeus killed him one day (cp. Herakles and Linos); and the tomb of Zeus in Crete is really the tomb of Olympos. This testimony goes far to show that Olympos is that old Aegean god with whom Zeus was identified.

from descriptions of the northern paradise, but of sorrow. Claudian says that Delphi is sorrowful and silent during Apollo's absence, but joy is renewed on his return. One is reminded of modern Delphi from Good Friday to Easter morning. But if anyone supposes that the sorrow was the Delphians' only, due to Apollo's absence from their shrine, he can learn from Apollonios that Apollo shed tears when he went to the Hyperborean land; thence flows the Eridanos, on whose banks the Heliades wail without cease; and extremely low spirits came over the Argonauts as they sailed that river of amber tears. Herodotos says that the Hyperborean land lay beyond the gold-guarding griffons, who lived beyond the one-eyed Arimaspians. His source was the *Arimaspea*, attributed to Aristeas, upon which Aeschylus also drew in verses that we have already noticed (p. 280), which place the Gorgons and Graiai near the eastern end of the world; beyond them are griffons and the one-eyed, horse-riding Arimaspian host, who live beside Pluto's stream, which runs with gold; still farther is the Ethiopian paradise. The Arimaspians are a fusion of Cyclopes with Silenoi or Centaurs. The Cyclopes, we have seen, are one version of that enemy whose death brought servitude and exile to Apollo. So the Hyperborean land is much like Utnapishtim's Far-Away, an island of light amidst darkness and monsters. It may have taken on this character simply because Apollo lived there for part of every year. For Apollo tended to become divorced from all association with death and the underworld; his annual death was generally forgotten; and so *pari passu* the Hyperborean land became his pleasant winter resort.[30]

It may readily be granted that Apollo's Hyperborean absence means his annual death, that he had a tomb at Delphi, and that Zeus caused his death. But there is still a gap in the argument. What evidence is there of hostility between Apollo and Dionysos? The evidence, indeed, points the other way: their mutual relations at Delphi seem to have been very cordial. Unless one is

---

[30] Apollo's exile: Aesch. *Suppl.* 214. Hyperborean land: Herod. 3.116, 4.13, 27, 32; Claud. 28.25–34; Apollon. *Arg.* 4.611–626; Aesch. *Pr.* 792–809. Herod. 4.25.1 speaks of a Scythian tradition of goat-legged men in the northern mountains. Two of the Greek shamans, Aristeas and Abaris, were associated with the Hyperborean land: Herod. 4.13–16, 36.

willing to accept the conclusion that Python and the Delphic Dionysos are virtually the same, then there is no direct evidence of strife between Apollo and Dionysos. But Dionysos fought Perseus: that combat is well attested and is associated with Delphi; for much the same statement is made as in the myth of Dionysos' death from the Titans: according to Deinarchos, Dionysos was killed by Perseus and buried at Delphi beside the golden Apollo. But a Scholiast says that Perseus cast Dionysos into the lake of Lerna, which we recognise as Hydra's lair; it is a more suitable burial place for a Dionysos killed by Perseus. Pausanias and Nonnos place the combat at Argos, but modify the story: Perseus killed the Maenad followers of Dionysos, and god and hero were finally reconciled. It is an Argive story about an Argive hero, told in the Argolid before Delphi had become prominent. In Deinarchos' version, Perseus the Argive champion is substituted for Apollo the Delphian champion, simply because the Perseus-Dionysos combat was still fairly well known; whereas Apollo's hostility to Dionysos was reduced in the Titan myth to receiving Dionysos' remains and burying them. But we learn from Callimachus and Euphorion (if Tzetzes can be trusted) that it was the Titans, not Zeus, who gave the fragments of Dionysos to Apollo.[31]

We also learn that Dionysos defeated Perseus and destroyed Argos. Euphorion said that Dionysos and his Bacchic women vanquished Argos in his war against Perseus; and Kephalion that Perseus fled from Dionysos and took refuge in Assyria, where Belimos was king (cp. his flight from Kepheus, p. 294). So we begin to see an alternation at Argos too: first Dionysos kills Perseus; then Perseus kills Dionysos. There too, probably, the year was divided between the two, in earlier times at any rate; for historical Argos appears to have turned its religious attention elsewhere, forgetting the old cycle. So from Argos and Delphi we have a record of an ancient myth in which a heavenly god and an underworld god, waging eternal combat, alternated in life and death; and we see traces of it in other cities too, e.g., Sikyon. Per-

---

[31] Deinarchos *ap.* Eus. *Chron. an.* 718 *et ap.* Sync. 307 *et ap.* Cyril. *Contra Jul.* 10.342; Aug. *Civ. Dei* 18.13; Schol. T on Il. 14.319; Tzetz. on Lyk. 207; Paus. 2.20.4, 2.22.1, 2.23.7; Nonn. *Dion.* 47.498–741, 25.105–112; Call. frag. 643 Pf. According to Malal. 2, p. 45 Dind., Dionysos died at Delphi in flight from Lykurgos. In the *Indus Athis*, whom Perseus killed during the wedding-feast brawl with Phineus, we may see a mutation of Dionysos: Ovid *Met.* 5.47–73.

haps the myth and its attendant rituals were once known in every part of the peninsula.[32]

It must now be evident that the Apollo-Dionysos cycle of Delphi is very like the Baal-Mot cycle of Ugarit. It is another example of Box and Cox. Though Apollo has the advantage and is adjudged victor and king, he never wins final victory; his opponent is ever renewed and sends him once more to death. His opponent is also a mighty god, worshipped and propitiated. Hence the final act of the myth is reconciliation as in the Ugaritic myth (p. 181) and the Argive myth of Perseus and Dionysos, in which, according to Pausanias, Dionysos, after making war on Perseus, finally made peace with Argos, and thereafter was greatly honored there. At Delphi this reconciliation was expressed in actual worship: the old myth was largely forgotten—though not entirely, remaining known, perhaps, only to priests and other cult-personnel, who were reluctant, though probably not forbidden, to disclose it. Apollo's death and tomb could not be entirely ignored; but Delphic policy was to keep them from general knowledge. Dionysos' tomb, however, could be shown to anyone; for he was recognised as a dying god everywhere. Probably it was due to the classical harmony of Delphic cults that Dionysos and Python became distinguished: then Apollo's opponent was Python, utterly destroyed, while Dionysos, a name borrowed from the widespread Dionysiac cult and given to the wintertime ruler, was Apollo's associate in temple and cult. But there remained records or traditions that did not allow men to forget entirely that the tomb of Dionysos had been called Python's tomb.[33]

---

[32] Kephalion 1, 2A.440 J; Euphorion *ap.* EM 687. Certainly Dionysiac combat was prominent in Argive tradition. Akrisios was hostile to Dionysos (Ovid *Met.* 4.607–610), and so were Perseus' cousins, the Proitides: Hes. frag. 27 Rz.; Apollod. 2.2.2. It was also said that the Proitides found relief from their madness on the site of that same temple of Peitho at Sikyon which had a place in the Apollo-Python, Apollo-Marsyas, and Calydonian-boar myths: it was Proitos who built it in thanksgiving: Paus. 2.7.8. So we may surmise that the Proitides helped Perseus against his enemy as Artemis helped Apollo: both correspond to Anat. Notice a temple of Artemis Peitho at Argos: Paus. 2.21.1. One of Dionysos' Bacchae whom Perseus killed was called Choreia and received special honor at her tomb in Argos (Paus. 2.20.4); not far from her tomb was the barrow which held Medusa's head (Paus. 2.21.5). The women who fought for Dionysos against Perseus were called Haliai, women of the sea (Paus. 2.22.1). The Argive Dionysos was called *Krêsios*, which indicates that he was very close to the Cretan Zeus (Paus. 2.23.7).

[33] Paus. 2.23.7. Cyril (*Contra Jul.* 10.342) first quotes Deinarchos on the burial of Dionysos at Delphi after Perseus had killed him; then immediately he quotes Porphyry

In chapter i five versions of the Python myth were outlined, all of which were referred to a Delphic scene. Later we found that Sikyon and Tegyra also had versions of the myth, which were apparently similar to version C or D, since Leto or Artemis was involved. The several so-called derivative legends, in which the opponent is not called Python, and the champion is not always Apollo, conform more or less closely to one or another of the five versions. These five are literary versions of the classical period, modified according to writers' preconceptions and purposes, reflecting contemporary attitudes to the divine participants, in particular the desire to remove everything that might reduce Apollo's dignity. Behind these five versions, preceding and underlying them, we can now perceive three variants of the combat myth, each of which reached Delphi at a different time.

1. Probably the earliest form of the myth to reach Delphi was descended, directly or indirectly, from the Canaanite myth of Baal and Mot, through the Perseus myth, which I have conjectured to be the oldest variant to reach Greece (p. 306), perhaps in the second millennium B.C., though Perseus may not have been the earliest Greek name of the hero. This myth, first established in the Argolid, moved thence to Delphi and to many other places. In this earliest Delphic combat myth the champion was not yet called Apollo, and his opponent was most probably not yet called Python. The dragon was allied with or favored by his father, a local counterpart of El, who was later identified with Zeus or Poseidon (see pp. 394–397 below). Later tradition tended to confuse the father and son, owing to like nature, possible original identity, and common opposition to the champion. The dragoness seems superficially ignored, as in the Baal poems. But she was present as wife of either father or son: she was later called Ge.

2. Also fairly early, perhaps, is the Telphusian myth. In this the dragoness has a prominent part; for the Venusberg episode is almost all of it that remains visible to the unaided eye. It is closely related to the Kadmos and Sphinx myths, i.e., to what we might call the Boeotian variant; it has also interesting connections with the Medusa myth. It was told in Boeotian Telphusa, where the

on Apollo's tomb at Delphi. The alternation of A. and D. in life and death at Delphi was perceived by Usener (1904) 333 f.; see p. 398. Notice the early Theban myth: Ismenos > Apollo killed his brother Kaanthos (p. 319).

hero was called Teiresias before Apollo took over; and it moved from there to Delphi, to a place and people of the same name. This variant too is derived ultimately from the Canaanite myth. One recalls the Aqhat myth, in which the hero was lured into the enemy's power.

3. The third variant probably came to Delphi with Apollo. This is the version that is outlined in the prologue to this chapter and which, with the exception of the double-dragon feature, was first perceived by Otto Gruppe. Since it belongs to subtype II, it closely resembles the Egyptian myth of Osiris, Horos, and Set, and no doubt the Egyptian myth had an influence upon it. We have seen that Horos was identified with Apollo, probably in the seventh or sixth century. But I am inclined to derive this variant primarily from Anatolia, since there are several connections between Delphi and Anatolia, which will appear as we proceed. In discussing Hittite myths we noticed the roles of the hero Hupasiyas and the Weather God's son, who opposed or tricked the dragon while the Weather God was *hors de combat*. The son tends to take the father's place: subtype II is built on subtype I, which is nearest to the archetype. So in the Delphic myth the son displaced the father: that is, Apollo displaced Zeus and reigned as king of the gods. Zeus was revived, but thereafter had a secondary, though respected, position. So this version ends much as the first does, with Apollo's supremacy over Zeus. It follows, therefore, that there was a time when the Delphians looked upon Apollo as king of the gods. They did so because he had stepped into the shoes of the old local champion-god, who was probably a deity of sky and weather. At this time Zeus, i.e., the Hellenic sky god who bore that name, was either not yet worshipped there or had a subordinate cult. His name may have been carried with the Anatolian myth to Delphi as the name of the dragon-slain father, and then transferred in due course, as in Crete, to the old fertility god in his role of father in the earliest Delphic myth. But the name never became firmly attached to the latter figure. For the Delphians also called him Kronos and Poseidon. According to one of the varying legends of Apollo's predecessors at Delphi, Kronos once spoke oracles there. Though reported by a Scholiast, it seems to be a scrap of ancient myth: a later version would have said

Poseidon or Dionysos. There is other evidence that Kronos had a place at Delphi: there was a revered stone above the temple which men said was that stone which Rhea had given to Kronos to swallow instead of the infant Zeus, and which later Kronos had vomited along with his progeny. The stone was probably an ancient symbol of the Delphic god who became known as either Kronos or Zeus: in the myth the stone that Kronos had incorporated also represented Zeus.[34]

The cult of Zeus as Apollo's superior entered Delphic worship rather late; for the earlier state of affairs is still reflected in the Hymn (about 600 B.C.), especially if one considers the Hymn a unity and refrains from dividing it into Delian and Delphian parts. Once Zeus had become the pan-Hellenic king of gods and men, and his cult was accepted everywhere, thanks to the Homeric and Hesiodic poems and to the growing importance of Olympia, it was inevitable that his supremacy be reconciled to Apollo's rulership at Delphi.

Before Hesiod's time a myth of weather god against dragon came to Greece from Cilicia and became widely known. This was not the first time that a Cilician form of the myth had reached Greece (p. 279). But since Zeus was now supreme Hellenic god, he was identified with the champion, a Cilician Baal, whereas the opponent's name Typhon remained unchanged. It was but a local variant of the Anatolian myth that had come to Delphi with Apollo as champion (variant 3 above), so that at Delphi it could be easily fitted to the local myth, and the name Zeus be given, perhaps for the first time, to that father-god whom Typhon killed and mutilated and whose cause Apollo assumed. But the Corycian variant, as we may call it, was a pure example of subtype I: Baal-Zeus, though helped by a son, was his own avenger and preserved his full sovereignty. It was more like Puruli II, whereas the Apollo variant was more like a form of Puruli I (pp. 121 f.) in which the younger god's role had been magnified. Outside of

---

[34] Schol. Vet. on Lyk. 200, οἱ δὲ . . . φασιν ὅτι τὸ ἐν Δελφοῖς μαντεῖον πρότερον τοῦ Κρόνου ἦν. But Mommsen (1878: 284, note 3) denies that Kronos was ever supposed to have spoken oracles at Delphi; he thinks that the *promantis Kronos* of Lyk. 202 refers to the snake of Aulis. But that too, if true, has some relevance to our discussion. Kronos' stone at Delphi: Hes. *Theog.* 498–500; Paus. 10.24.6. The stone was anointed with oil and wrapped with white woolen fillets. This suggests a relation to the omphalos, which was similarly treated. See Mommsen 27–31.

Delphi (and there too in later times) the Hellenes saw two distinct myths, Zeus against Typhon and Apollo against Typhon or Python, the latter name finally ousting the other, which was reserved for Zeus's combat.

Here we may notice the varying fortunes of the mythical *interrex* or temporary king, the god who attempts to rule during the champion-god's death but proves inadequate, e.g., Ashtar of Ugarit. He may, on the one hand, become the victorious younger god of subtype II, Apollo or Horos; that is, he is no longer a failure, but literally takes his father's place; the next step is hostility between father and son. On the other hand, his attempt to take the throne may be considered rivalry with or opposition to the champion; hence he may be allied with or identified with the enemy, e.g., Nahusha or Dionysos.[35]

For in the Titan myth Dionysos as a child sat himself on Zeus's throne during his father's absence, wore his crown, and wielded his sceptre and thunderbolt. Then the Titans, incited by Hera, lured him with toys to his destruction. Zeus on his return punished the Titans. In this story Dionysos is the original temporary king who fails to hold the throne; but differently from Ashtar's his failure coincides with his death: for, as often, *interrex* and dying god are combined. Now in the several versions of Dionysiac myth Dionysos experienced both fortunes of the *interrex* role that we have just noticed. On the one hand he became a champion: in a so-called Libyan version of the Titan myth his father Zeus-Ammon fled to Crete, but Dionysos stayed to fight and defeat Kronos and his hosts. Similar is the valiant part that Dionysos played in the Gigantomachy. Here Dionysos has Apollo's role or Zeus's own. On the other hand, it was the hero Perseus that killed Dionysos, who was buried at Delphi in the same tomb that was said to be Python's. There the name Dionysos was given to the champion-god's old enemy. His character in general suggested that identification, and so did his role as temporary king in the Titan myth, which, as we see, was specifically connected with Delphi. For Delphi's wintertime king really was an *interrex*.[36]

---

[35] On *interrex* see Gaster (1950) 34, 196 f., note; see p. 205 above.

[36] Dionysos as *interrex*: Firm. Mat. *Err.* 6; Nonn. *Dion.* 6.165–205. Arnobius (*Adv. Gent.* 5.19) tells a crude story: the Titans, after cutting Dionysos up, began to cook the

It is plain that, both early and late, the Delphic combat myth was told in several versions, which mingled one with another and with the combat myths of other cities, each told much as it suited the teller's pleasure to tell it, hence constantly changing and shifting. But the main strands can be detected, the principal variations on the theme. All that I have said concerning divine names —when they were used or when not used at Delphi and elsewhere —is of course speculative. But the names are not so important as the myth components. About these we have enough good information to support the reconstruction of Delphic myth that has been made.

With this reconstruction it can be said that we have reached the climax of our argument. But there are a few more problems that must be dealt with.

POSEIDON AND PYRRHOS

Poseidon too was prominent in worship at Delphi. He had an altar within the very temple of Apollo, an unusual location even for the temple god's own altar, which was almost invariably outdoors. According to Pausanias, who cites pseudo-Musaios' *Eumolpia*, quoting two verses, Ge (Chthonia) and Poseidon once held the oracle in partnership; moreover Poseidon delivered oracles through his prophet Pyrkon. He was father of Parnassos and Delphos, eponyms of mountain and city; though some writers said that Delphos' father was Apollo (p. 47). His mate was Melantho or Melaina, probably a form of Ge.[37]

It was said that when Apollo came to Delphi he made an exchange with Poseidon, giving his uncle the island of Kalaureia in return. Though several writers mention no conflict between the two before they made this bargain, others say that there was a contest between Apollo and Poseidon for Delphi, as between other deities and Poseidon for Athens, Argos, Corinth, Aegina, and

---

pieces; Zeus was lured by the savor and ran to the spot, where he discovered the crime. Here the dying god's own flesh is the food that entices the champion-god: Theme 4D is merged with 8c. Dionysos in Gigantomachy: Apollod. 1.6.2: he killed a giant named Eurytos. Dionysos victor over Titans: Diod. 3.71 f.

[37] Poseidon at Delphi: Paus. 10.5.6, 6.1, 24.4.; Aesch. *Eum.* 27; FD 3.2.191.26 f.; Men. Rhet. p.362 Sp. See p. 47, note 5. According to Hesych. Π4433, priests at Delphi who divined from burnt offerings were called *pyrkooi*. Nauplios (p. 481) was called *Pyrkaeus* (Poll. 9.156); hence Pyrkon may be considered a double of Poseidon.

Naxos; and that Poseidon was defeated in that contest as in the others.[38]

Hence the role of Poseidon at Delphi is very similar to Dionysos' role, the chief difference being altar instead of tomb in Apollo's temple. Furthermore the Delphic-Poseidon lore supplies what we found missing in the evidence for the Apollo-Dionysos combat, viz., the enemy's consort (but see p. 377). For Poseidon's consort was Ge, whom Apollo ousted; and Menander Rhetor says that Apollo had to contest Delphi with Poseidon, Themis, and Nyx. It is tempting to see an exact correspondence to Ugaritic myth: Poseidon as Yam, Dionysos as Mot, Zeus or Kronos as El, Apollo as Baal, and Ge as Asherat; for the Ugaritic texts several times call her Asherat Yam, i.e., Asherat of Sea. But the evidence points rather to Poseidon as an alternative to Zeus in the El role, and to the son Python-Dionysos as Yam and Mot together (but if they are distinguished Python is Yam and Dionysos is Mot). For not only does it appear that Poseidon and Ge were supreme rulers of Delphi, but the relation of Poseidon the father-ruler to the prophet Pyrkon looks very much like that of Python as ruler to the prophet Dionysos. Poseidon, then, is another name given (in later times) to that early Delphian father-god who was also identified with Zeus and Kronos; and so, like Zeus, he was often confounded with the son, Python-Dionysos.[39]

Long before the ancient Delphian god had received the name of Poseidon he had been identified with the rivers Pleistos and Kephisos. In Aeschylus' *Eumenides* (27) the Pythia couples Pleistos and Poseidon in her prayer. The pair Kephisos and Melantho is repeated in Poseidon and Melaina-Melantho, Kephisos' daughter. These rivers, we have seen, were associated with Python (p. 144).

Poseidon's part in the Telphusian version of the myth has already been made plain: how he mated with Telphusa and pro-

---

[38] Exchange for Kalaureia: Philostephanos 18, 3.31 M; Paus. 2.33.2, 10.5.6; Schol. Vet. on Lyk. 617. Strabo (8.6.14, pp. 373 f.) says that Poseidon exchanged Delos for Kalaureia with Leto, Delphi for Tainaron with Apollo. Contest for Delphi: Plut. *Mor.* 741A; Men. Rhet. p. 362 Sp. Apollo and Poseidon were rival wooers of Hestia, according to Hom. Hymn 5.24.

[39] Asherat Yam: e.g. Ugaritic text 51.1.15, 22 (Gordon 1947: 139 f.); cf. Gaster (1950) 123, note 16.

duced Areion; and we have seen that the myth of Poseidon-Telphusa-Areion repeats the neighboring myth of Poseidon-Medusa-Pegasos. Telphusa was identified with Demeter in Arcadia; and Demeter or Persephone was Dionysos' mother in an important version of the Dionysiac legend. Demeter and Dionysos were often associated in Boeotian worship. So whereas the myths told in Poseidon's name supply the dragoness to the earliest Delphic myth, they supply the dragon to the Telphusian myth: more accurately a figure who may be taken as either dragon or overthrown father-god.[40]

Whereas Apollo's rival has the form of snake, bull, or goat when called Dionysos, he is horse or dolphin when called Poseidon. Poseidon was Hippios as mate of Telphusa; and he took dolphin form to mate with Melantho, Delphos' mother. It may be that Apollo, who took dolphin form in the Hymn when he guided Cretan sailors to Delphi, acquired that guise from his Delphic predecessor; or it may be that an old Aegean sea deity became the Hellenic Poseidon in some places, Apollo Delphinios in others. It appears that Poseidon was called Amoibeus at Delphi, perhaps because of his numerous changes of shape.[41]

So we may conclude that in pre-Apolline Delphi there were worshipped a god who was later identified with Poseidon, Zeus, or Kronos; his son who was later called Python (Typhon), Pyrkon, Delphos, or Dionysos, and who stood in about the same relation to his father as Persephone to Demeter, merely his reflection in nature and functions; and his consort who was later called Ge, Themis, Nyx, Delphyne, or Telphusa. Our sources differ about the succession of deities who ruled Delphi before Apollo came. Aeschylus says Gaia, Themis, Phoibe; Euripides omits Phoibe; so does Pausanias, but adds that Poseidon was Ge's consort; the Pindaric Scholiast says Night, Themis, and then Python as either successor or consort of Themis (see p. 376, note 14). Not very different is Menander Rhetor, who says that Apollo contested Delphi with Poseidon, Themis, and Night. Now those scholars

---

[40] In Boeotia shrines of Demeter and Dionysos were neighbors at Potniai, Thebes, Anthedon, Kopai: Paus. 9.8.1 f., 16.5 f., 22.5 f., 24.1.

[41] Poseidon as dolphin: Ovid *Met.* 6.120. Apollo as dolphin: Hom. Hymn 3.400–496: in the πῦρ ἐπικαλοῦντες of Hymn 3.491, 509, we may see an allusion to Pyrkon. Poseidon Amoibeus: Schol. Vet. on Lyk. 617.

who maintain that the myth of Apollo's predecessors at Delphi, especially as Aeschylus tells it, was framed with the purpose of fitting Delphic origins to the Hesiodic theogony, are undoubtedly right. But it cannot be dismissed entirely: there was something to build upon, an ancient king and queen of gods, known later as Poseidon and Ge, Poseidon and Nyx, Zeus and Themis, Zeus and Hera, Kronos and Rhea (?), and by other names too. There is evidence for a single goddess in those sources in which Ge is the only predecessor mentioned, still ruling at Delphi when Apollo came. Though Euripides has Apollo drive Themis from the oracular seat after killing Python, it is Ge who tries to disrupt Apollo's oracle by sending dream phantoms to men.[42]

In the classical period an effort was made to remove tales of conflict from the sacred history of Delphi. Aeschylus makes no mention of combat or contest in the opening lines of the *Eumenides:* Phoibe Ge's daughter gave the oracle to Apollo as a gift; there was nothing but harmony and good will among the Delphian gods. So the Olympian Poseidon, he who fought Titans and Gigantes, helped Leto to escape Python by giving her refuge on Delos; and he blasted the island of the wicked Phlegyans.[43]

Beside the altar (*bômos*) of Poseidon in Apollo's temple stood a different kind of altar, the hearth altar that is called *eschara* or *hestia*, and which is usually associated with the worship of heroes and chthonian powers. There it was said that Achilles' son, Pyrrhos or Neoptolemos, was killed, when he came to Delphi to ask satisfaction from Apollo for the god's murder of his father, or to consult the god because his wife had given him no children, or to plunder the shrine; or, some say, he turned to plunder and destruction when the god refused him either satisfaction or a response. He was killed either by a Delphian priest, Machaireus,

---

[42] Aesch. *Eum.* 1–8; Eur. IT 1259–1269; Paus. 10.5.5 f.; Aristonoos, paean *ap.* FD 3.2.191.18–20; Arg. 1 to Pind. *Pyth.;* Men. Rhet. p. 362 Sp. Though the Scholiast (Arg. 1) does not put Ge in his sequence, he later says that the oracle was Ge's. Ge held Delphi when Apollo came: Ael. VH 3.1; cf. Pind. frag. 261 Bowra. See Amandry (1950) 201–214 on the fitting together of Delphic and Hesiodic myth: Phoibe was meant to fill the gap between the overthrow of the Titans and Apollo's arrival.

[43] Poseidon and Leto: Lucian *DMar.* 10; Hyg. 53.2, 140.3 f. According to Lucian and Hyginus, Delos lay beneath the waters when Apollo was born: here we have a glimpse of the old watery chaos in which the elements of cosmos still lay hidden. Poseidon and Phlegyans: Nonn. *Dion.* 18.36–38; Vat. Myth. I 205, II 109.

seemingly a personification of the Delphic knife, or by Orestes in rivalry over Hermione; the Delphians were guilty in either case, since Orestes was assisted by Delphian priests and attendants. Or it may have been Apollo himself who struck Pyrrhos down. Yet Pyrrhos was buried beneath the temple's threshold; later his body was removed to a tomb that was made within Apollo's temenos on the terrace just above the temple, a little to the northeast of the latter building; the tomb was enclosed by a wall (*peribolos*), so as to make a shrine within a shrine.[44]

It is significant that Kronos' stone was placed just above Pyrrhos' shrine, and that just to the west stood a small temple of Poseidon. In Pyrrhos' enclosure, beneath the layers of the classical period, have been found Mycenaean remains, which may be those of a cult site. The evidence, both literary and archaeological, points to a very ancient cult, whose deity became identified with Achilles' son. Usener sees in Pyrrhos and Orestes the forerunners of Apollo and Dionysos respectively, one succeeding the other in the annual cycle. Radermacher, on the contrary, sees Orestes as Apollo, Pyrrhos as Dionysos.[45]

It is easy to see an enemy of Apollo in Pyrrhos. For Pausanias, his attack was the third of a legendary series: earlier were the assaults of the Euboean brigand Krios' son and of Phlegyas. In fact, Pyrrhos could be looked upon as a variant of Phlegyas. His name has much the same meaning: he is the flame colored, whereas Phlegyas is the flaming. Both Phlegyas and Pyrrhos set fire to Apollo's temple at Delphi, and Pyrrhos burned down a temple of Apollo that stood by the road from Corinth to Sikyon —we have seen that Sikyon had the Apollo-Python myth in com-

---

[44] Pyrrhos' death at Delphi: Eur. *Andr.* 50–55, 1063–1165; Pind. *Paean* 6.111–120, *Nem.* 7.33–48; Pherek. 64, 1.78 J; Asklepiades 15, 1.171 J; Strabo 9.3.9, p. 421; Paus. 10.7.1, 24.4; Apollod. *Epit.* 6.14. According to *Andr.* 50–55, Pyrrhos made two trips to Delphi, the first to ask satisfaction, the second to give the god recompense for the destruction that he had wrought after being refused. The place of murder is called *hestia* by Paus. 10.24.4; and the *eschara* of *Andr.* 1240 is probably the same place. For burial beneath the temple threshold see Pherek., Asklep., *locc. cit.* For the tomb see Strabo *loc. cit.*, Paus. 10.24.6.

[45] For location see Paus. 10.24.6; Daux (1936) 168 and pl. VIII. On Pyrrhos *vs.* Orestes see Usener (1904) 329–339, Radermacher (1903) 51–54. See also Defradas (1954) 146–156, who sees an ancient hero cult, whose hero became identified with Achilles' son; but he does not mention an Orestes-Pyrrhos cycle.

mon with Delphi. The legendary Pyrrhos was a Myrmidon of Thessalian Phthiotis; and the hero Pyrrhos who had a tomb at Delphi was especially worshipped by the Ainianes, who sent a representative band of worshippers (*theória*) every four years to his Delphic shrine at the time of the Pythian festival. The Ainianes lived in the Spercheios Valley, next to the Dryopes, just across the Othrys range from Phthiotis; still earlier they had lived in Thessaly, Epiros, and Kirrha (in Delphic territory), neighbors to Lapiths and Dryopes, with whom they had intermittent wars, and it seems that sections of the Ainianes remained in those areas. They were probably closely related to their neighbors, one of the early proto-Achaean peoples. So Pyrrhos the Myrmidon, hero of Ainianes, has an ethnic origin which is very close to that of Phlegyas the Lapith.[46]

It was said that Pyrrhos invented the pyrrhic dance, and that the town of Pyrrhichos in Laconia took its name from him. But both dance and town were also connected with the god Pyrrhichos, one of the Kuretes. Now the people of Malea identified Pyrrhichos with Silenos, saying that Silenos, after being reared at Malea, had moved to Pyrrhichos, where he opened a well for the inhabitants, their main source of water (cp. St. George's dragon). According to Nonnos, it was Pyrrhichos, an Idaean Dactyl, who gathered an army of Satyrs, Silenoi, Centaurs, and Korybantes for Dionysos. In view of Silenos' place in Delphic lore, his relation to Dionysos, and Pyrrhos' role as dancer, which likens him to dancing sprites like the Silenoi and Kuretes, we have some grounds for identifying the original Pyrrhos of Delphi with Pyrrhichos-Silenos.[47]

Yet there is reason to agree with Usener that Pyrrhos is an earlier Apollo. He came with two Hyperborean heroes to help the Delphians meet the Gauls' attack: so said the legend that sprang

---

[46] Paus. 10.7.1; see 2.5.5 and Apollod. *Epit.* 6.14 on the burning of Apollo's temples. The Ainianes' worship of Pyrrhos at Delphi is described in detail by Heliod. *Aith.* 2.34 f., 3.1–6. On Ainianes and their migrations see Béquignon (1937) 148–158 and passages there cited.

[47] Paus. 3.25.1–3; Nonn. *Dion.* 13.35–46, 14.33–35. On the Pyrrhic dance see Lucian *Salt.* 9; Plin. NH 7.56.204, who says that the Kuretes taught the armed dance and Pyrrhos the pyrrhic, both in Crete.

up soon after 279 B.C. The Ainianes' quadrennial ritual coincided with Apollo's great festival. One may conjecture, therefore, that Pyrrhos was present in summer, but absent among Hyperboreans in winter. Moreover, since Achilles' son was taker of the enemy stronghold Troy and slayer of the enemy king Priam, one may expect the Pyrrhos of Delphi to have a corresponding role, since the two were identified. In fact, Usener holds that the ritual of the Septerion (p. 453), which was interpreted to represent Apollo's combat with Python, had once been explained as the fall of Ilion and the burning of Priam's palace. This is speculative indeed; but there was a month called Ilaios at Delphi. More significant still is the tradition that Pyrrhos was killed when he quarreled with the Delphians over their malpractices in the conduct of sacrifices: like Eli's sons, they took the meat of victims for themselves, and when Pyrrhos tried to recover the meat, Machaireus killed him. Here is a righteous Pyrrhos against wicked keepers of the Delphic shrine. Besides, there was a story that Pyrrhos' corpse was first taken home to Thessalian Phthia, but later was sent back to Delphi: just as Apollo spent his time of expiation or exile—his death—in Thessalian Pherai or Tempe, and later returned to Delphi.[48]

It is likely, therefore, that the Delphic Pyrrhos represents the pre-Apolline deity who fought the dragon of death and chaos, but was ousted by Apollo from his prominent position; i.e., his cult was subordinated to Apollo's, and Apollo took over the champion role. The supersession of his cult by Apollo's was reflected in myth as hostility between Apollo and Pyrrhos, so that Pyrrhos became confused with the old enemy Python-Dionysos. Of this I have more to say later. Orestes, Pyrrhos' opponent in later myth, has no doubt taken over the role of either champion or enemy, according to the role assigned to Pyrrhos. But though Orestes' legend is connected with Phokis, he seems to have had no place in Delphic cult, and his place in Delphic myth appears to be

---

[48] Pyrrhos *vs.* Gauls: Paus. 1.4.4, 10.23.2. Pausanias is certainly mistaken in saying that before 279 the Delphians had not worshipped Pyrrhos, though Ziegler (RE 16.2454–2456) agrees with him. One cannot even say that the hero of the tomb was then first called Pyrrhos or Neoptolemos. For Pindar and Euripides mention Pyrrhos' tomb and honors at Delphi (see p. 398, note 44). See Usener (1904) 313–339. Pyrrhos vs. Delphian abuses: Pherek. 64, 1.78 J; see 64*b* and Eur. *Andr.* 1159 for the taking of the dead Pyrrhos to Phthia.

entirely due to the Delphians' efforts to relate all the great Hellenic legends to their shrine.[49]

HERAKLES AND THE TRIPOD

The Pythian Apollo came into conflict with another hero too, the very hero who fought for the Delphic shrine against Kyknos and the Dryopes. The story goes that Herakles came to Delphi one day to consult the oracle, some say after the frenzy in which he killed Megara and her children, others say after his murder of Iphitos. But Apollo (or the Pythia) refused to give him a response, considering his crime too terrible for dealings with him (or it is said that the Pythia told him that the god was not then present for the speaking of oracles). Then Herakles seized the prophetic tripod and started to carry it off in anger at being refused, or to set up an oracle of his own; but Apollo came quickly to prevent him; and a struggle began between them. There is more than one conclusion. (1) The two sons of Zeus were soon reconciled, apparently through the efforts of Leto, Artemis, and Athena. Herakles surrendered the tripod to Apollo; and, according to the people of Laconian Gytheion, the two thereupon joined together to found their city in perfect amity. (2) Zeus separated his sons by casting a thunderbolt between them; he made Herakles restore the tripod, and, either by direct command or through Apollo's oracle, imposed a term of servitude upon him, either under Eurystheus, if his killing of Megara's children had brought him to Delphi, or under Omphale, if his murder of Iphitos had preceded. (3) Herakles carried the tripod to Arcadian Pheneos and left it there; a thousand years later Apollo flooded this city to punish its people for receiving the tripod.[50]

---

[49] As Defradas sees it (1954: 160–204) the Orestes of the *Oresteia* is a creation of Delphic propaganda. I would add that once Orestes had been adopted by the Delphians they opposed him as the avenger of his father's murder, who had also piously sought purification from the stain of matricide, to the impious Pyrrhos, who, after pitilessly slaughtering old Priam at Zeus's altar, had never sought atonement. The legend of Pyrrhos' quarrel with corrupt Delphian priests may have irked the priesthood and given them a bias against Pyrrhos in later times.

[50] (1) Paus. 3.21.8, 10.13.7 f. (2) Apollod. 2.6.2; Hyg. *Fab.* 32.3 f.; Serv.-Dan. *Aen.* 8.300. (3) Plut. *Mor.* 557c, 560d. Other references to the incident: Cic. ND 3.16.42; Plut. *Mor.* 387d, 413a; Paus. 8.37.1; ps.-Callisth. 1.45(125); Schol. Vet. on Pind. *Ol.* 9.29(43). The subject was often represented in art from the seventh century down; see Overbeck, *Kunstmythologie* III 391–415; Defradas (1954) 124–126.

Though at first glance this story may appear to have nothing to do with the kind of combat that we have been studying, several features should be noticed.

1. It appears that for Apollo loss of the tripod meant loss of his prophetic powers, and that Herakles gained prophetic powers from possession of the tripod. It is like the story of Enlil, Zu, and the tablet of destinies (pp. 147 f.).[51]

2. According to Klearchos of Soloi, Herakles, whom he calls son of Briareos, took one of the Delphic treasures, as was then the custom, set out for the pillars of Herakles, and conquered the folk of that region (a rationalising allusion to Geryon, Antaios, Ladon). Klearchos does not say that the hero took a tripod; but gold, silver, and bronze tripods were a common form of dedication. In any case, this valuable object seems to have given Herakles the power that he needed to conquer demons at the ends of earth. It is an instrument of potency; so that Herakles, on the one hand, resembles Zu in his seizure of it, and, on the other, resembles Perseus, who overcame an enemy in the same western world with potent objects that the Olympian gods gave him.[52]

3. It appears that Herakles Briareos' son set up the victory-bringing tripod or treasure at Gibraltar to become what later generations knew as the pillars of Herakles. For, according to Aristotle, they were also called the pillars of Briareos. We have already noticed that Herakles' work at the straits meant control of the waters (pp. 343 f.).[53]

4. According to a story that Euripides knew, Herakles took a tripod from Troy, when he captured that city, and gave it to

---

[51] The tripod cauldron, as we have seen, contained the bones of Python-Dionysos, from which the Pythia received her inspiration. This is perhaps a later way of describing the potency inherent in the tripod. But its containing parts of a body recalls that Briareos, father of the tripod-seizer (see 2 below), was about to take the potent entrails of the serpent-bull, when he was anticipated by Zeus's hawk (p. 245).

[52] Klearchos 56, 2.320 M; I believe that κατά τι παλαιὸν ἔθος must be taken with λαβόντα τι; but Defradas (1954: 126, note 4) thinks that it may depend upon the verbal sense of κειμηλίων; that, I think, would be rather forced. For treasures in tripod form see Defradas 143 f. We may now recall that the hero Koroibos, after reconciliation with Apollo, carried off a Delphic tripod with the god's consent (p. 105).

[53] Aristot. frag. 678 Rose. Briareos as Herakles' father may be likened to Silenos as Apollo's. Like his brothers the Cyclopes he has an ambiguous role, sometimes on the right side, sometimes not. His form resembles Typhon's, and he was Kronos' chief aid in the attempt to recover heaven's throne: Ovid Fasti 3.796–806. According to Pherek. Syr. (p. 234), Herakles was called Chronos, which name is surely a play upon Kronos.

Theseus to set up beside the Pythian altar in Athens. There the tripod is wrested from an enemy's stronghold in a war that follows upon Herakles' victory over a flood monster.[54]

5. Zeus separated Herakles and Apollo, exactly as he separated Herakles and Ares after the Kyknos combat.

6. Zeus punished Herakles for his seizure of the tripod and sent him into servitude for a period, just as he punished Apollo with servitude for killing the Cyclopes.

7. As Apollo helped Poseidon send a flood upon Troy after being cheated of his wages, so he sent a flood upon Pheneos after being deprived of his tripod. This may be the god's righteous punishment of robbers; it may also be the enemy's devastation.

8. Herakles returned from servitude to seize Oichalia and kill Eurytos, Iphitos' father. The story of Herakles, Eurytos, and Iphitos repeats that of Apollo, Zeus, and Python-Dionysos (or the Cyclopes). In the son Iphitos (the mighty) we see a death god: he was a lord of herds, horses and oxen; his name, or its variant Iphis, is also borne by the brother of Herakles' taskmaster Eurystheus (and its variant Iphikles is the name of Herakles' twin brother, Automedusa's husband, who shows signs of having been the forerunner of Eurystheus as Herakles' rival); his father Eurytos, son of the Black One (Melaneus), has a name that recurs among brigands and demons, as we have seen. For killing Iphitos, Zeus (or Apollo) imposed an expiatory servitude upon Herakles, so that Zeus steps into Eurytos' place as avenger. Though from the Odyssey down Herakles is pictured as a violent and ruthless criminal for murdering his guest and taking his horses, he is also said to have been wronged by Eurytos and Eurytos' sons, who cheated him and treated him despitefully in their house and at their table (Th. 8c). In the background can be discerned another version of the cattle of cosmos, soma, water, life, that Herakles wrests from the demon king after killing him.[55]

9. Herakles and Apollo also had a dispute over the Cerynitian hind. Herakles finally caught her after chasing her for a year; then slinging her over his shoulders he started to carry her off to

---

[54] Eur. *Suppl.* 1197–1200.

[55] Od. 21.22–30 and Schol. on 22; Soph. *Trach.* 262–280; Diod. 4.31.3; Apollod. 2.6.2; see pp. 43, 355. For Iphitos' herds see also Plut. *Mor.* 553c. Eurystheus' brother: Diod. 4.48.4. Automedusa: Apollod. 2.4.11.

Mycenae. But since the hind was sacred to Artemis, she and Apollo ran after Herakles and tried to take the hind from him. There was a tussle as over the tripod; and the story ends with reconciliation. The hind, whose name was Kerynia or Taygete, and who roamed Mount Artemision, is really Artemis herself, who often took that form. The year-long pursuit recalls Minos' nine-months' pursuit of Britomartis-Diktynna, the Cretan Artemis. It was also said that Herakles pursued the hind to all quarters of the earth, and in particular to Scythia; there horse-driving (*hipposoa*) Artemis received him. No more is said; but in this Artemis we may see the Echidna who received Herakles after driving off his horses. Artemis and Echidna meet in Hekate. In the Scythian tale Herakles deals with the death queen. But the hind that he carries off is a tripod equivalent too. She can be looked at as captive goddess, soma cow, and demoness in one body, not the first time that such a combination has appeared to us (cf. p. 353). Tripod dispute and hind dispute are essentially the same story. One is Delphian, the other Achaean.[56]

As in the conflicts of Gilgamesh and Enkidu, Bata and Pharaoh, Indra and Garuda, it is hard to tell which is hero, which villain. But after reviewing the nine features above and noticing whither each points, it becomes evident that Herakles is still the champion who invades the enemy's own lair to achieve his object. It must be with him as with Pyrrhos: the conflict between him and Apollo is a mythical reflection of cult history. But it is not a reflection of the same events. Rather, it seems to point back to a time when the Herakles cult competed with the Apollo cult for supremacy at Delphi. It may be that the Delphic champion narrowly escaped acquiring the name of Herakles. It is plain that elsewhere in that region, within fifty miles of Delphi, it was Herakles who became the great dragon fighter: witness the myths of Kyknos, Laogoras, Erginos, Nessos. Since the Herakles cult lost at Delphi itself, a deliberate attempt, it would seem, was made to put Herakles in

---

[56] Cerynitian hind: Pind. *Ol.* 3.25–32 with Scholl. Vett. on 28 f. (50, 53); Eur. *Her.* 375–379; Apollod. 2.5.3; Diod. 4.13.1; Pedias. 3. According to Eur. the hind was destructive. Taygete was a daughter of Atlas. The hind was caught by Herakles while crossing the Ladon River. Minos and Britomartis: Call. *Hymn* 3.189–205; Diod. 5.76.3 f.; Paus. 2.30.3; Ant. Lib. 40. Notice that, according to Diod., H. caught the hind with nets; notice that Britomartis fell into nets in her flight; or H. caught the hind sleeping (Diod.), as Perseus caught Medusa.

the wrong, to give him for once a villainous role. But the attempt had little success: Herakles was too well known as a hero.[57]

But what failed with the pan-Hellenic Herakles may have been successful with a less widely known hero. We have already noticed (p. 25) that the Lapith Phorbas, a brigand opponent of Apollo at Panopeus and Daulis, was a great dragon slayer on the island of Rhodes; and that Argos, monstrous guardian of captive Io, was victor over the monsters Satyros, Echidna, and the destroying bull (bull of heaven?), to whom may be added the murderers of Apis. Argos clothed himself in the bull's hide, as Herakles in the lion's skin. It is probable that Phorbas was succeeded by Apollo, Argos by Herakles, and that the former in each case then became transformed into the enemy. It may be that Phorbas was the name of the god whom Apollo succeeded at Delphi, though I doubt it. The name is more likely to have been Pyrrhos, Deukalion, or Lykos, as we shall see in the next chapter.[58]

---

[57] On the tripod dispute and its place in Delphic propaganda see Defràdas (1954) 123–146. But I doubt that the event reflected is anything so late as the entry of the Amphictyony into Delphic affairs about 600 B.C. Old myths were given a new life on suitable occasions. For Herakles' worship at Delphi see Michel *Rec. Inscr.* 995, pt. IV 11; BCH XXIII (1899) 571; *Berl. Philol. Woch.* XXXII (1912) 61; there was an *Herakleia* festival and a month *Herakleios;* see Mommsen (1878) 119, 122, 313-322.

[58] Apollod. 2.1.1–3; Apis was killed by Thelxion and Telchines; Argos Panoptes avenged him. Apis seems to be the counterpart of Anu-Uranos, Argos of Teshub-Baal-Zeus. Telchines' name indicates his nearness to Silenos-Satyros.

XIV

THE CORYCIAN CAVE

It is evident that the Delphic myth of Apollo's combat with Python was made up of several variants of the combat myth, and that it took several forms in the course of Delphic history, all of which are reflected in the several versions of the classical period. I have expressed my belief that one variant came with Apollo's cult to Delphi, and that it came out of Asia Minor. I would add, for reasons that I shall soon make clear, that this variant came from Cappadocia, which lies just north of Cilicia and includes a region that also bore the name Cilicia. In history and ethnic character Cappadocia and Cilicia have always been closely related, both being parts of the old Hittite kingdom. In the documents of the Hittites are found the divine names Apuluna(s) and Appaliuna(s), from one or the other of which, if they are not two forms of the same name, the Greek Apollo may have received his name. Apulunas, it may be, was a god of entrances and doorways, a function that would very probably connect him with the seasons. He may very well have been the weather god in some localities and have taken over the role of dragon fighter from the Weather God of the Puruli myth; and it may have been this local variant that moved westward into Greece and merged at Delphi and elsewhere with those variants of Canaanite origin (as we have inferred) that were already on the ground.[1]

---

[1] See Hrozný (1936), Laroche (1947) 80. For Apollo as storm god see Herod. 1.87.1 f.

THE CILICIAN CAVE

It was from Korykos in Cilicia that the principal version of the Zeus-Typhon myth came to Greece, though it has also been evident that Syrian, Canaanite, and Egyptian variants played their part in shaping the Greek myth. In contrast to the Apollo-Python myth, whose Anatolian component became thoroughly imbedded in Greek cult, the Greek myth of Zeus against Typhon, as told by Apollodoros, is a direct translation of a Cilician original and attached itself to no Greek cults or rituals as *aition*. For Greeks it was purely a story of a great combat that Zeus once had with a monster. But it was attached to a Cilician cult, that of the god of Korykos, whose temple stood near the Corycian Cave. In Hellenised Korykos this god became Zeus Korykios, the ruins of whose temple can still be seen. The Semitic population of Cilicia called him Baal; and the Hittites called him by whatever name they gave the Weather God (perhaps the Hurrian name Teshub). It is important to realise that in Cilicia Semite mingled with Anatolian.[2]

It is probable that Typhon or Typhoeus is a Hellenised form of the name that Cilicians gave to the dragon, whatever its meaning. For we have seen that from very early Typhon was placed in Cilicia, and that sources as early as the fifth century B.C. place him specifically in the Corycian Cave. Since Apollo's opponent is also called Typhon in the earliest source of the Apolline dragon myth, and occasionally afterwards, and as the name Python may be a variant of the same name, it seems likely that the Apollo-Python myth came to Greece from approximately the same region as the Zeus-Typhon myth. When in this chapter I speak of the Apollo-Python myth I shall mean that particular myth which, as I have conjectured, moved from Anatolia to Delphi and other Greek cities, carrying the names Apollo and Typhon (whatever their exact form at any stage) with it; and which became the third form of the early Delphic myth described in the last chapter.

It may be that the myth carried other names from Anatolia to Phokis. Striking is the presence of a *Korykion antron* both near

---

[2] See Bent (1891) 214–216, Hicks (1891) 240 (no. 24), 242 (no. 26), 258 (no. 30). Sandon (Šantaš) must be taken into account too, since the Hittites identified him with Marduk: Laroche (1947) 88.

Cilician Korykos and on Mount Parnassos in Phokis, both connected with the local combat myth. In Cilicia the name merely relates the cave to the city of Korykos nearby; on Parnassos it has no obvious explanation. To say that the Parnassian cave was so named because it looks like a wallet (*korykos*) does not carry conviction; it sounds more like a folk etymology. It is simpler to suppose that the Parnassian cave was named after the Corycian Cave of Cilicia, precisely because the same myth became attached to it. So, it seems to me, the occurrence of the names Typhon and Corycian in both myths relates them especially closely to each other. But the dragon myth was told throughout Anatolia and Syria, being attached to rites in perhaps every town and village. So the Apollo-Python myth did not necessarily come from Korykos itself. I have suggested Cappadocia, since there, in the very heart of the Hittite kingdom, in mountainous country by the Halys River, a city called Parnassos once stood. The name Korykos recurs in Asia Minor, e.g., in Lykia and near Erythrai; so there may have been a cave called Corycian in the mountains near Cappadocian Parnassos. But it is perhaps more probable that the Corycian Cave of Korykos was known as Typhon's home in many, perhaps all, Anatolian versions of the myth.[3]

For there can be no doubt that the Corycian Cave was preëminently the home of Typhon and Echidna. It is located a few miles west of ancient Korykos, and a little over a mile inland from the sea. The name is given to both an open chasm that is approximately 900 feet long, 65 feet wide, and 100 to 200 feet deep, and to a cavern, 200 feet deep, at its southern end. The cavern has a spring within it; a roar of water flowing deep underground can be heard; stalactites hang from the ceiling. There is also a shallow grotto on the east side of the chasm. On the plateau at the western edge of the chasm is the temple of Zeus Korykios. Inscriptions

---

[3] Cappadocian Parnassos: Ramsay (1890) 255, 298–300. Lycian Korykos: Sundwall (1913) 124; Erythraean Korykon: Paus. 10.12.7. It is interesting to observe that 24 miles from Cappadocian Parnassos was the city of Nysa, a name that is important in the myths of Dionysos: Ramsay 287 f. There, it was said, the contest between Apollo and Marsyas took place: Dionys. Skyt. *ap.* Diod. 3.59.2–5; and there the Moirai deceived Typhon during his flight from Zeus. Another coincidence of name lies between the village Anemoreia on the slopes of Parnassos near Delphi (modern Arachova), which is actually associated with the killing of Python, and a city and two promontories called Anemurion in Cilicia, one close to Korykos: Strabo 9.3.15, p. 423; 14.5.3, 5, pp. 669 f. See p. 280 on coins of Anemurion.

show that Pan and Hermes were worshipped at the cave itself, probably in an old temple at its mouth. Only a hundred yards to the east of the Corycian chasm is another, about a quarter-mile in circumference, which was specifically called Typhon's cave (*specus Typhoneus*), the bottom of which is nearly inaccessible because of its steep sides. It may be connected by an underground passage with the Corycian Cave (but I cannot verify this). Its name would indicate that it was really Typhon's home. But Apollodoros and others make it fairly certain that Typhon and Echidna lived in the other cave and that there Zeus was laid away. The evidence allows us to frame the following hypothesis about Cilician beliefs concerning the caves. The name Corycian Cave was often used to mean both chasms taken together and considered to be essentially a unit with subdivisions. Echidna, before defeat, possessed the larger chamber: there Hesiod places her, and Typhon, putting Zeus and his sinews away in the Corycian Cave, placed them in the keeping of Delphyne, who is Echidna. Typhon, at first the lesser male partner, occupied the smaller chasm. Then when Zeus, i.e., the Weather God, defeated Typhon and Echidna he took the larger cave for himself and his sons; but the other chasm, not allowing descent, was considered an approach to the underworld, Typhon's nether realm; hence its name. According to J. T. Bent, the natives call it Purgatory, whereas the bigger chasm is Paradise. A third chasm of the same kind should be mentioned, about five miles northeast of the other two, known as the Olban Cave, since near it is the site of ancient Olba. It is certain that Zeus Olbios (Baal of Olba) was worshipped there, and quite likely that Typhon was associated with it too.[4]

THE PARNASSIAN CAVE

The Corycian Cave of Mount Parnassos in Phokis is situated on a steep slope about 500 feet above the Parnassian plateau, 4,460 feet above sea level, and so about 2,600 feet above Delphi, 3,600 feet below the highest summit of Parnassos. It is a limestone

---

[4] On the Corycian Cave of Cilicia see Strabo 14.5.5, pp. 670 f.; Mela 1.72–75; Solin. 38.7 f.; Bent (1891) 212–215; Frazer (1914) I 152–155. Typhon's cave: see Mela 1.76; Bent 214; Frazer 155 f. Olban cave: Bent 208–210, Frazer 158. The underground stream was called *Áôos*, which was also a name of Adonis, according to EM 117; see epigram, Hicks (1891) 240, no. 24.

cavern, impressive to the natives in every era, even if small compared to Mercer's Cave, for example, to say nothing of Carlsbad Caverns. It has two chambers and a gallery. The front chamber is 200 feet long, about the same as the underground part of the Cilician cave; the rear chamber is smaller and extremely dark. In both, water drips from the ceiling, forming stalagmites, and stalactites hang down. Inscriptions confirm the testimony of ancient authors that the cave was sacred to Pan and the Nymphs.[5]

But while the Corycian Cave of Cilicia was certainly the lair of Typhon and Echidna-Delphyne, and certainly the scene of at least part of the combat, the Corycian Cave of Parnassos lies considerably above Pytho (as I shall call Delphi's historical site), the traditional scene of Apollo's combat, whence it can be reached only by a stiff climb for seven miles over mountain trails. I have, however, already cited evidence (p. 78) from Apollonios and others that points to a combat by the Corycian Cave: for the Corycian nymphs cheered Apollo with cries of *Hie Paian* as he fought the dragon. A Scholiast adds that the Parnassian nymphs brought gifts to Apollo after his victory. That Apollonios, or his source, had the Corycian Cave in mind is made still more likely by his placing Apollo's victory beneath a rocky ridge of Parnassos. For men actually pointed out the place where Apollo stood to shoot his arrows at the dragon. It was called the Lookout Place (*Katopteutêrios Topos, Katoptêrion Chôrion*) or Archer's Hill (*Toxiu Bunos*); and, according to Strabo, it overhung Anemoreia; that is, it is the ridge above Arachova. From that point the god could look directly across the Arachovite meadows (*livadhia*) of the Parnassian plateau to the Corycian Cave. But it does not at all suit a combat scene at Pytho.[6]

It is significant that the same deities were worshipped at both

---

[5] Paus. 10.32; see Frazer on 10.32.2. See SGDI 1536 for inscriptions. See note 7.

[6] Citations on p. 78, note 5; the gifts are mentioned in Arg. 3 to Pind. *Pyth.* Lookout Place: Schol. Vet. on Eur. *Phoen.* 233; Strabo 9.3.15, p. 423; Anth. Pal. 3.6; Steph. Byz. 61 Holst. (who mentions Apollo Lykoreus). Archer's Hill: Hesych. T1134, who mentions one at Sikyon too, thus indicating another coincidence between the myths of Delphi and Sikyon; he also says that the Delphian place was called *Napê*, i.e., vale or glen. This must be the *Parnassia napê* of Paus. 10.6.1, which seems to mean the Parnassian plateau as a hollow surrounded by hills; for Anonn. *ap.* Schol. Vet. *in* Pind. *Pyth.* 6.5 say that Delphi was divided into three parts: high, middle, [and low], and that the so-called Nape was in the middle part, i.e., halfway up the mountain.

Corycian Caves: Pan, the Nymphs, and Zeus; Hermes too, who was worshipped at the Cilician cave, has something to do with the Parnassian cave, as we shall soon see. Moreover the Dionysos of the Parnassian cave corresponds to the Adonis of the Cilician (p. 409, note 4). Pan, who helped Zeus against Typhon, taught Apollo the mantic art, just before Apollo went to Delphi; it is also said that Apollo learned it from Parnassian nymphs; and nymphs, we see, were associated with Pan at the cave.[7]

So if the correspondence between the two Corycian Caves is to be complete, the Parnassian cave must have once been considered the lair of Python and Delphyne. This conclusion seems all the more convincing, once we realise that there is nothing at Pytho that can be properly called a cave. Yet the sources constantly speak of an *antron* that the dragon inhabited. At Pytho men could either suppose that Python lived in the oracular chasm, which didn't exist, or in the narrow, but open, chasm of the Castalian gorge, a suitable lair in default of a better, yet rather like the Cilician chasm without a cave. But the Corycian Cave is exactly what is wanted for a dragon's lair.

This conclusion becomes all the more probable when we realise that Dionysos was worshipped at the Corycian Cave. Many ancient writers allude to the biennial celebration of Dionysos' rites on the heights of Parnassos, when the god's Maenads, there called Thyiads, roamed the plateau and slopes with blazing torches. Thyiads are mentioned along with Pan and Nymphs in one of the cave's inscriptions (note 5). For the name was given not only to the human Maenads, but also to the mythical nymphs that attended Dionysos. Sophocles speaks of the Bacchic Corycian nymphs (*Kôrykiai nymphai Bakchides*); Nonnos of Corycian Bacchants (*Kôrykides Bakchai*). Aeschylus' Pythia at the beginning of the *Eumenides* invokes Dionysos, leader of Bacchants, immediately after invoking the Corycian nymphs. Delphi had a suburb called Thuia, named for the eponymous heroine of Thyiads (*Thuiades;* it was on the hill just west of Pytho); she

---

[7] Deities of Cilician cave: Hicks (1891) 240, no. 24 (Pan, Hermes); Steph. Byz. 266 Holst. (Nymphs); for Zeus see citations in notes 2 and 4 of this chapter. Of Parnassian cave: SGDI 1536, Paus. 10.32.7 (Pan, Nymphs); Strabo 9.3.1, p. 417 (Nymphs); Steph. Byz. 279 Holst. (Zeus Lykoreus). Pan, Apollo's teacher: Apollod. 1.4.1; Parnassian nymphs taught him: Hom. Hymn 4.556 f. The present-day Parnassians still consider this cave to be a haunt of nymphs: Lawson (1910) 161 f.

was a daughter of Kephisos or Kastalios and introduced the worship of Dionysos, whereas the Corycian nymphs were daughters of Pleistos. Both rivers and the spring were associated, perhaps identified, with Python (p. 144).[8]

Apollo too was worshipped in or near the Corycian Cave, so that the central worship and myth of Delphi seems to have been established at both Pytho and the Corycian Cave. For in Pan we may see Silenos, and in the Corycian nymphs the daughters of Triopas whom Porphyry mentions. Now the Corycian Cave's very name and its character suggest that it was the earliest scene of both myth and ritual of combat. The very state of the evidence supports this suggestion: the earlier and less accessible scene, relatively unfrequented in later times, was still remembered, but only to the inhabitants of the neighborhood and to those few others whose duty or pleasure it was to conserve the ancient religious traditions; consequently it is seldom mentioned in the surviving literature.[9]

LYKOREIA

But we do not have to rely on reckoning the more or less probable course of events; we have positive evidence that the Corycian Cave was the original seat of Delphic worship. Strabo tells us that before the Delphians occupied the site of Pytho they lived higher up the mountain at Lykoreia. He is supported by the Scholiast on Apollonios' *Argonautica,* who says that the Delphians were formerly called *Lykōreis* from the village of Lykoreia. Lykoreia was once a city, situated on the Parnassian plateau; or, if Ulrichs is right, on a hill at the edge of it, southwest of the Corycian Cave. Its territory included the cave and the plateau, or most of it. Strabo's evidence means that Lykoreia was the original

---

[8] Dionysos' rites on Parnassos: e.g., Eur. *Bacch.* 557–559; Soph. *Ant.* 1126–1130; Paus. 10.32.7; Macrob. *Sat.* 1.18.3–5, who, speaking of Bacchic caverns on Parnassos, appears to be alluding to the Corycian Cave. Bacchant Corycian nymphs: Soph. *loc. cit.;* Nonn. *Dion.* 9.287; cf. Aesch. *Eum.* 22–25. Thuia: Herod. 7.178.2; Paus. 10.6.4. Daughters of Pleistos: Apollon. *Arg.* 2.711. Ulrichs (1840) 120 mentions a May festival that the villagers of Delphi and Arachova celebrate with dance and song on the Parnassian plateau; it is still celebrated.

[9] The Thyiads honored Apollo on Parnassos: Paus. 10.32.7. Apollo Lykoreus or Lykoreios was worshipped in the nearby town: Apollon. *Arg.* 4.1490 with Schol. Vet.; Call. *Hymn* 2.19; Steph. Byz. 61 Holst.; Anth. Pal. 6.54.1; EM 571; Orph. Hymn 34.1.

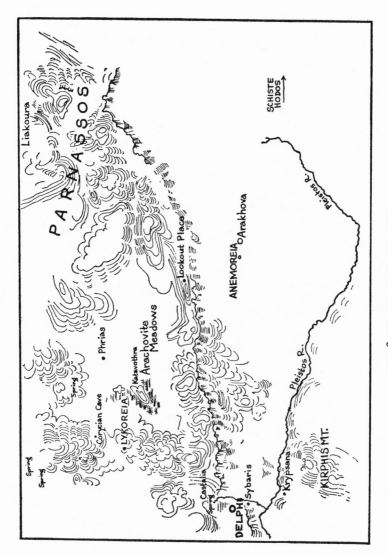

MAP 3. DELPHI AND NEIGHBORHOOD

Delphi, the city of the tribe *Delphoi,* and that at some time, which must be earlier than 800 B.C., they moved down the mountain to the site of Pytho.[10]

Strabo's testimony is confirmed by the most widespread version of the myth of Deukalion's flood, that which places the landing of his ark on Mount Parnassos. For it was said that the ark landed at Lykoreia, that flood survivors founded the city of Lykoreia, or that Deukalion was ruling as king in Lykoreia when the flood came. When Menander Rhetor says that Delphi was founded immediately after the flood, he refers to the same legend: it was the ancient seat of the Delphoi, Lykoreia, that was built then.[11]

It is very likely that ancient Lykoreia with its Corycian Cave was not only the first city of the Delphians, but also the first site of the Delphic oracle. It has puzzled scholars that the oracular chasm or cave of which several ancient authorities speak has not been discovered in the excavations of Delphi. Geologists have found not the slightest trace of a fissure in the rock beneath the sanctuary. In particular, the region is not the kind to have a chasm or crevice that exhales toxic vapors, such as some ancient writers mention. The sanctuary stands on a compact bed of clay and schist, which is overlaid by calcareous rock and soil. There is no trace even of a limestone sink, not to mention the gaseous fissures of igneous country. So scholars have had recourse to supposing that the chasm and vapors were misinterpretations of a room beneath the temple's adyton and man-produced fumigations. But if in the allusions to an oracular chasm we see mem-

---

[10] Strabo 9.3.3, p. 418; Schol. Vet. on Apollon. *Arg.* 2.711, 4.1490; Ulrichs (1840) 120. The ancient association of Delphi with the Corycian Cave was commemorated on a coin type of Delphi: JHS VIII (1887) 19, Hadrianic period. Plut. *Mor.* 394F leaves little doubt that the Corycian Cave was close to Lykoreia. Further evidence that Lykoreia was the first Delphi is the Pindaric Scholiast's statement (on *Pyth.* 1 *inscr.*) that Delphi was first called *Napê* (see p. 410, note 6). The name was poetically transferred to Pytho or Krisa: Pind. *Pyth.* 6.9. See Map 3.

[11] Marmor Parium 4–7; Paus. 10.6.2; Lucian *Tim.* 3; Men. Rhet. p. 354 Sp.; cf. Pind. *Ol.* 9.41–44 with Schol. Vet.; Apollod. 1.7.2.; Andron 8, 1.162 J; Ovid *Met.* 1.313–319. Delphos, Deukalion's grandson: Call. frag. 52 Pf.; Schol. Vet. on Eur. *Or.* 1094. See Fontenrose (1945) 101, 110 f. Since Kadmos found the source of Ismenos in a cave called Corycian (p. 311, note 67), and since his opponent was called Delphynes (Schol. Vet. on Eur. *Phoen.* 238), it is interesting to find that Kadmeia (Thebes) too was said to have been founded after Deukalion's flood: Diod. 19.53.4. Probably Deukalion ruled in the city that the hero Parnassos founded and which was destroyed in the flood; but, according to Pausanias, the name Lykoreia was entirely postdiluvian. A peak of Parnassos was also called Lykoreia: Fontenrose 101, note 31.

ories of the Corycian Cave, then everything is accounted for except the toxic vapors; and they seem to be no more than late fantasies, due perhaps to an old tradition that the harmless vapors or cold currents of air which were seen or felt as they issued from the cave, perhaps on a chill morning, had the power to inspire men with prophecy. For there are different accounts of the vapors: they are not always said to be gaseous or toxic. We should notice Pompeius Trogus' testimony in particular:

in hoc rupis anfractu media ferme montis altitudine planities exigua est atque in ea profundum terrae foramen quod in oracula patet, ex quo frigidus spiritus vi quadam velut vento in sublime expulsus mentes vatum in vecordiam vertit impletasque deo responsa consulentibus dare cogit.

A small plain among the rocks, halfway up the mountain, a hole in the earth—these words describe the site of the Corycian Cave; they do not describe Pytho. Though Trogus and his Greek sources had Pytho in mind, they had picked up a tradition which had clung to Delphic lore from the days when the Delphoi lived in Lykoreia.[12]

Since the Greeks considered limestone caverns in general to be passages to the lower world and the dead, the Corycian Cave can hardly be an exception. Since it was the lair of the death lord himself, who was later called Python or Dionysos, and of his consort, it is very probable that at first it housed an oracle of the dead. For this is exactly what Delphic mythology tells us, if we but transfer the scene from Pytho to Lykoreia. We have seen that Euripides says that Ge sent dream phantoms by night to men, after Apollo had taken over Pytho (p. 397), and that the Pindaric Scholiast says Night first spoke oracles at the Delphic shrine, and Python once ruled over the tripod from which Dionysos first spoke oracles (p. 376). Since Ge and Night are but two names for the old pre-Apolline goddess, we can gather from this evidence that

---

[12] Amandry (1950) 215–230 with citations in notes on p. 220. Room under adyton: L. B. Holland (1933) 207–214. Strabo (9.3.5, p. 419) speaks of *antron koilon* whence rises *pneuma enthusiastikon*; see also Lucan BC 5.82–84; ps.-Lucian *Nero* 10; Iambl. *Myst.* 3.11. Notice that Plutarch (*Mor.* 433cd), who has Pytho in mind, though speaking of a mantic *pneuma* from earth, does not speak of a chasm or cave. See Pomp. Trog. (Just. *Epit.*) 24.6.9.

after the founding of Apollo's shrine at Pytho the dream oracle
at Lykoreia continued to function.[13]

The Sibyl of Delphic legend, who should not be confused with
the historical Pythia of Apollo's temple, seems to be another
version of the ancient goddess. The Delphic Sibyl was called
Herophile, a name that suggests the Hera and Herois of Delphic
legend and cult. She was the daughter of Zeus and Lamia Poseidon's daughter. Parnassos had the Lamia Sybaris, a form of the
dragoness; her consort must be Zeus's predecessor, who was called
Silenos or Pan. The people of Erythrai, Ionian city on the Lydian
coast, also claimed Herophile. Their country had a Mount Korykon, in whose side was the cave in which Herophile was born.
The cave in a mountain so named would certainly be called
Corycian. The Erythraeans said that her mother was the nymph
Idaia, which is a name of the Great Mother. According to
Pausanias, Herophile called herself Artemis and Apollo's wife. So
she may be identified with Korykia, first of Corycian nymphs,
whom Apollo loved, begetting Lykoros upon her.[14]

---

[13] On Ge's dream oracle see Wilamowitz (1932) 28. For Hades entrances see LM
6.48–63; RE 10.2383–2387; Croon (1952) 75–83. Into such limestone caves as Moaning
Cave and Mercer's Cave in Calaveras County, California, the "Middle Horizon" people
threw their dead. They probably thought that they were delivering them directly to the
land of death; at Moaning Cave they could not see or descend into the depths. The moan
that used to issue from the cave must have contributed to the illusion. There are other
such mortuary caves in Calaveras County and elsewhere in California; 1 mention those
that I have visited. It was this conception of the caves that caused the later Miwok to
avoid them. They enter into Miwok mythology as the homes of a cannibal giant of stone,
Chehalumche, who carried his victims there to eat them; hence the bones. Typhon,
Ullikummi, Polyphemos, come to mind at once. On these caves see Wallace (1951), Heizer
(1952).

The question may be asked whether the Corycian Cave of Cilicia was an oracular
place; Bent (1891: 213) thinks that oracles were spoken at both Corycian and Olban Caves.

[14] Most of this information comes from Paus. 10.12. Apollo and Korykia: Paus.
10.6.3; EM 571; Schol. Vet. on Apollon. *Arg.* 2.711. Thuia is the same nymph, mistress
of Apollo and mother of Delphos: Paus. 10.6.4. Or Delphos' mother was Melaina or
Melantho who is Ge, and his father was Poseidon (p. 47); notice Parnassos, son of
Poseidon and the nymph Kleodora: Paus. 10.6.1. The Sibyl was also called Daphne,
according to Diod. 4.66.5 f.; she was that daughter of Teiresias who is usually called Manto;
when her father died at Telphusa's spring, she was taken by the Epigonoi to Delphi,
where she was much favored by Apollo. According to Paus. 10.5.5, a Parnassian nymph
called Daphnis was the first promantis of Ge's oracle. While this Daphnis has something
to do with Boeotian Telphusa, the Arcadian Daphne, Apollo's beloved, was daughter of
Ladon, the river that flowed past Arcadian Thelpusa, and whose springs are about six
miles from Arcadian Lykuria, near which Herakles made a channel for the River Aroanios:
Paus. 8.19.4–20.4 (see p. 425, note 28). The nymph Kastalia, who leaped into the spring
when Apollo pursued her, is a variant of Daphne: Lact. Plac. *Theb.* 1.698. She was a

Ovid's version of the flood myth, which is probably derived from Nicander's version, supports the conclusions that I have drawn, and illustrates very well how the older site left its mark upon Delphic lore. After Deukalion and Pyrrha had landed on Parnassos, they worshipped the Corycian nymphs, the mountain spirits (*numina montis*), and Themis, who then spoke oracles there. Wishing to receive an oracle, they first cleansed themselves in the waters of Kephisos and then went to Themis' shrine. Now the springs of Kephisos lie on the north slopes of Parnassos, much nearer to the Corycian Cave than to Pytho; in fact, it is a fairly short distance from the cave to the nearest part of Kephisos' watershed. In any case, it is significant that the goddess of the oracle was honored with the Corycian nymphs immediately after Deukalion's landing, which was placed at Lykoreia.[15]

Both a god and a goddess spoke oracles there, they whom Pausanias calls Ge and Poseidon; the Pindaric Scholiast calls them Nyx-Themis and Python-Dionysos. It is evident, therefore, that oracular chasm and dragon's lair were one and the same. This can be inferred from Strabo's calling the oracular chasm a cave and from Apollodoros' statement that Python as Ge's warder tried to keep Apollo away from the oracular chasm. Moreover the mantic tripod which men thought to be set up over a chasm was actually placed over the supposed tomb of Python, whose breath, it was said, inspired the prophetess (p. 374). Probably this belief had as much as actual vapors or air currents to do with forming the tradition of exhalations from a chasm. To belief and tradition add the tale that Pytho got its name from the dragon's putrefying corpse, and the mixture will yield the mephitic gasses.[16]

The ancient myth is rationalised in a story told by Diodoros and known also to Plutarch, Pausanias, and a Euripidean Scholiast. It was said that goats discovered the oracular chasm. The herdsman noticed that some of his goats, on going up to the edge of a certain cleft, began to leap about strangely and to utter

daughter of Acheloos, according to Panyasis (*ap.* Paus. 10.8.9), who says that Herakles crossing Parnassos came to her spring. She was wife of Delphos, according to Schol. Vet. on Eur. *Or.* 1094.

[15] Ovid *Met.* 1.313–321, 367–373; see Map 3 and Frazer and Van Buren (1930) Map x.

[16] Strabo 9.3.5, p. 419; Apollod. 1.4.1.

strange voices. So he went to the edge and was affected in the same manner. First of all, it is plain that this story suits the Corycian Cave better than it does Pytho. Then, the mantically inspired goats at once recall Aix, Python's son, Pan of the Corycian Cave, and the goat Dionysos. And the herdsman's name was Koretas, according to Plutarch. That is, he was the eponym of Kuretes, of whose name *Korêtas* appears to be a first-declension variant in the singular number; and so he is fellow of Korybas, Silenos, Pan, Marsyas. Now in the Scholiast's version the chasm is called *chaos,* and the herdsman tells men that he learned his mantic speech from a certain *chaos* (ἀπὸ χάους τινός). There it is clear that the chasm is a passage into the underworld darkness, whence rise the prophetic influences.[17]

The conclusion that the first Delphic oracle was established at the Corycian Cave of Lykoreia and later was moved to the site of Pytho is also borne out by the results of the French School's excavations at Delphi. It is certain that there was no important sanctuary on or near the site of Apollo's temple at Delphi before the eighth century B.C. Pottery and bronzes indicate a foundation towards the end of that century. There are remains of Mycenaean and geometric structures beneath; but most seem more likely to be residences than temples. A number of cult objects have been found in the early layers, as might be expected, and there was probably a shrine on the site of Pyrrhos' temple; but there is nothing to indicate more than a minor cult of the village. For the centuries before 800 much more has been found in the sanctuary of Athena Pronaia and its terrace, including the gymnasium area, enough to indicate that it was a cult site in Mycenaean times, where presumably a goddess had the principal worship, she who became the Delphic Athena. But it is plain from the finds, religious and domestic, that Pytho was then only a poor village, quite without the fame and riches that Apollo's oracle was destined to bring to it.[18]

A great change began in the eighth century with the foundation

---

[17] Diod. 16.26.1–4; Plut. *Mor.* 433CD, 435D; Paus. 10.5.7; Schol. Vet. on Eur. *Or.* 165. Notice that the Erythraean Sibyl's father was a shepherd: Paus. 10.12.7.

[18] See Amandry (1950) 207–209, 231 f.; Defradas (1954) 22–27. It is significant that Pytho quite early had close relations with Sikyon, where the Python myth was also at home.

of Apollo's sanctuary, which within two centuries became a pan-Hellenic shrine. It is reasonable to suppose that Apollo was then introduced to Pytho. But was his coming to Pytho coincident with the movement of the Delphoi down the mountain to Pytho? If the Delphian's migration could be dated, an answer might be given. Since the Delphians as Phocians were northwestern Greeks and presumably participated in the Dorian movement southward, and since they lived for a time in Lykoreia, the eighth century may seem about right. But this is largely speculation.

Was Apollo's cult new, or did he replace an older god? We have seen reason to believe that though he came provided with a myth, he encountered native variants of the same myth type that were already on the spot and attached to an earlier god of sky and summer, who was remembered as Pyrrhos-Neoptolemos in later times. Since Pyrrhos was worshipped at Pytho, and was said to have been buried beneath the floor of Apollo's temple before he was given a separate shrine, we might suppose that it was his cult that the Delphians brought to Delphi, and that later his cult declined as Apollo's increased. But the cave by Lykoreia is called Corycian, a name that probably came with Apollo's cult and myth from Anatolia, and which was given to the cave because it was considered to be the dragon's lair. Could it have been so named if Apollo with his Anatolian myth came first to Pytho and stopped there? There is also a question about Lykoreia. Did the Delphians found it? Or did they take over an already established city? And were they Apollo worshippers when they came? The fact is that the historical sequence of events is still beyond our reach. It is probable that Parnassos was settled before the Phocians came; that is about all that we should venture to say now.[19]

PYRRHOS, DEUKALION, LYKOROS

But the evidence concerning Lykoreia does enable us to say something about Apollo's predecessor. It is probable that the early Greek settlers knew him as Pyrrhos, among other names. For the name indicates that he was the partner of Pyrrha. So another name for him was Deukalion, who was king and founder

---

[19] It is possible that the name Corycian was carried from Cilicia to Parnassos with the Perseus legend and its offshoots.

of Lykoreia. Deukalion was the Greek Noah, and Pyrrha was his sister (represented usually as a first cousin) and wife. In the legends of Perseus and Herakles we noticed that the dragon was identified with flood; earlier we saw that the aboriginal chaos of waters, which returned to overwhelm earth in the deluge, was a living creature who became the enemy of the heavenly gods. But in the well-known Near-Eastern flood myth the flood has lost its anthropomorphic or theriomorphic attributes and become simply a deluge of waters; and a different type of story has been formed. Of the Greek variant Deukalion became the hero, and precisely in this region, probably because he was already known as victor over the great chaos dragon. Support for this conclusion comes from Diodoros, who says that Dionysos perished in Deukalion's flood, but that after the flood rains he rose from death. Here can be seen the old Baal-Mot cycle, the earliest form of the combat myth on Parnassos.[20]

The importance of Deukalion in Delphic worship may be seen in the sacrifice called Aigle, which commemorated the great flood. Since the corresponding Athenian rituals took place in the month Anthesterion, it is likely that Mommsen was right in placing Aigle in the Delphic month Bysios, roughly corresponding to our February. This, moreover, was the month in which Apollo returned to Delphi from the Hyperboreans. So Deukalion's return from the deep occurred at the same time as Apollo's return from the dead. Deukalion's place at Delphi is also manifest in his legendary relation to the Hosioi, important officials who assisted the priests in performing the rites. According to the local lore, as Plutarch reports it, the Hosioi were descendants of Deukalion.[21]

---

[20] See Fontenrose (1945) 94 f., 110–113, 115–117. On Pyrrha's relation to Deukalion notice Ovid *Met.* 1.351 f., where Deukalion says to her, O soror o conjunx, . . . quam commune mihi genus et patruelis origo, ... Dionysos' death: Diod. 3.62.10, who says that Dionysos' fruits died with him; then Dionysos as the vine was revived by the flood rains and grew again (and the rainy season begins about November); cp. Genesis 9.20 f.: Noah plants the vine and makes wine after the flood. Pyrrhos and Pyrrha are the red pair; it is interesting to notice that the name Adam has in Hebrew the consonants of the root which means *red*. For dragon as flood notice Labbu, whose blood flowed forth in floods (p. 147); cf. Ymir, p. 524, note 6.

[21] Aigle: Bekk. Anecd. 354; see Mommsen (1878) 291–293. Hosioi: Plut. *Mor.* 292D. On the other hand, as Ogygos, the primeval flood, might become the flood hero, so Deukalion as hero might become identified with the flood; hence he is the father of Melaina, the dark earth, who becomes the consort of Poseidon or Kephisos.

But the early hero-god had a third name too, Lykoros (Lyko-reus) or Lykos. In Delphian legend of later times Lykoros was son of Apollo and Korykia. He was eponym, founder, and king of Lykoreia. He was grandfather of the hero Delphos through his daughter Kelaino, whose name means the same thing as Melaina or Melantho (p. 47). Now Deukalion was also founder and king of Lykoreia and grandfather of Delphos through his daughter or granddaughter Melaina-Melantho. So the two heroes can be identified, a conclusion which is supported by Pausanias, who says that the inhabitants of the hero Parnassos' city were saved from the floodwaters by the howling of wolves (lykoi), who guided them to the heights; so that when they built their new city they called it Lykoreia (Wolf City). This is plainly the old myth rationalised: it was Deukalion who founded the city after the flood, and the wolves are derived from the name and attributes of Lykoros. Hence we may infer that either Deukalion or Lykoros (Lykos) was the name of the hero who founded Lykoreia after the flood.[22]

Lykôros seems to mean Wolf-Warder, a good name for a hero, since the enemy may take wolf form. But he was apparently known as Lykos too. Hence he is represented as a wolf-savior, and not only in the flood myth. There was an image of a wolf in bronze at Delphi to commemorate a wolf that had discovered a temple robber and the place among the forests of Parnassos where he had buried his stolen treasures. According to Pausanias, he attacked the robber in his sleep and killed him; then he went every day to Delphi and howled until men followed him and found the stolen gold. The attack on a sleeping enemy is a theme already familiar to us; and we have just noticed the delivering cries of wolves in the flood myth. In another story it is a hawk that attacked a temple robber at Delphi and betrayed him. The wolf or hawk is the divine champion himself. Apollo could be wolf or hawk; his wolf form becomes separated from him in the story that after he killed Python a wolf brought him laurel from Tempe. But the legend of Lykoreia's founding shows

---

[22] Paus. 10.6.2 f.; Steph. Byz. 279 Holst.; EM 571; see p. 416, note 14. Prometheus, Deukalion's father, had a son named Lykos: Schol. Vet. on Lyk. 132.

that before the Apollo cult came to Parnassos, Lykoros was a hero who could take wolf form.[23]

Whereas in these tales a wolf helped Apollo and the Delphians, in another a certain Lykos entered the adyton and tried to carry off Apollo's tripod, whereupon he was stoned to death. This happened, it was said, during the Crisaean War (First Sacred War) of the early sixth century, about which legends began to cluster soon after the event: incidents of the Phlegyan War and other legendary attacks on Delphi were no doubt transferred to it. But this fragment of pseudohistory contains the name of the original tripod seizer of Delphi: he was called Lykos before Herakles. The indigenous hero Lykos(Lykoros)-Pyrrhos-Deukalion, when replaced by Apollo as champion, was pushed into the role of enemy and desecrator of Apollo's shrine. Later when he was identified with Herakles and Neoptolemos, his evil deeds were attributed to them, and Herakles became the tripod seizer.[24]

If Lykoros is the same as Delphos (p. 416, note 14), my argument that he was Apollo's predecessor in Delphic cult and myth is confirmed by Aeschylus, who says that Delphos was ruler of the land when Apollo came. Anxious to remove all trace of strife from Delphic myth, Aeschylus says that Delphos and his people welcomed and honored Apollo.[25]

---

[23] *Lykôreia* may mean Wolf Mountain City, and *Lykôreus* Wolf Mountain dweller. Perhaps in these names we can detect an earlier name of Parnassos, whose peak is still called Liakura or Lykeri; for the name Parnassos, as I have said, may have come from Anatolia with the Apollo-cult. Wolf and robber: Paus. 10.14.7; Ael. NA 10.26, 12.40. Hawk: Ael. NA 2.43. On the wolf from Tempe see Serv.-Dan. *Aen.* 4.377, where one also learns that Apollo took wolf form to lie with Kyrene and to kill Telchines; also that he fought and killed a certain Lykos, and that as a pastoral god he killed wolves. According to Curt. 3.1.5, the Marsyas River was also called Lykos. Notice that Deukalion-Lykoros' character is closely parallel to that of the Arcadian flood-hero *Lykaon*. Lykaon took wolf form, and after the flood he founded Lykosura, another wolf city: see Fontenrose (1945) 97–109. Notice that Kyknos killed a man named Lykos, said to be a Thracian, which may mean Daulian (pp. 51, 60).

[24] Hipp. Corp. 9.412 Littré. Lykos-Deukalion as enemy would become assimilated to Dionysos. Notice the image at Hierapolis that the Syrians called Dionysos or Deukalion or Semiramis, according to Lucian *Syr. Dea* 33. Lucian calls it *sêmeion*, intending the Greek word that means "sign," but has perhaps seized upon a native name of the deity represented, Eshmun, also present in the first part of *Semiramis*. Eshmun is a Dionysos-like god. See Fontenrose (1951) 141, note 70.

[25] Aesch. *Eum.* 15 f. Of the names of the pre-Apolline hero Deukalion only may be pre-Hellenic, and so may antedate the others.

MEN OF OAK AND STONE

It is probable, though not certain, that the mythical strife between Apollo and Pyrrhos-Lykos reflects strife between peoples. The Dryopes at one time lived near Lykoreia, according to Pausanias. We have discussed the legend in which they were a violent people who committed crimes against the Delphic shrine until Herakles went forth and defeated them, killing their king. The Phlegyans too once lived next to Delphi and molested the shrine and its visitors, according to the accepted legend. Yet it is said that the Delphians had a Phlegyan shrine of Apollo. Moreover the three maids who wept for Apollo at his tomb were daughters of Triopas, a name that belongs to Lapith-Phlegyan genealogy, e.g., as father or son of Phorbas. The sources indicate that these peoples once held the whole region; and it is probable that they belonged to the earliest Greek inhabitants of the peninsula, closely related to the Minyans. So it is also probable that they were either the founders of Lykoreia or the first Hellenic possessors. It is interesting to observe that the Lapiths and Dryopes have names that can be interpreted as "stone people" and "oak people," whether these be true or folk etymologies. Now the conclusion of the Greek flood myth is well known: how Deukalion and Pyrrha cast stones behind them, which at once became transformed into men and women. There were also myths current that the first men were born from trees. These considerations add meaning to the Homeric saying, οὐ γὰρ ἀπὸ δρυός ἐσσι παλαιφάτου οὐδ' ἀπὸ πέτρης (for you were not born of ancient oak or stone). It means not only "you had human parents," but also "you are not the first man, Dryops or Lapith, sprung from oak or stone." So the Lapiths and Dryopes were the people who grew from Deukalion's stones, as the Thebans were the men who grew up from the dragon's teeth that Kadmos sowed. Theocritus links Lapiths with Deukaliones in speaking of the earliest Greek peoples.[26]

---

[26] Schol. on Nic. *Ther.* 685, . . . οἱ Δελφοὶ Ἀπόλλωνος ἱερὸν Φλεγυῆιον ἱδρύσαντο. On first men from stone and tree see Fontenrose (1945) 113–116 and citations. See Il. 22.126; Od. 19.163; Hes. *Theog.* 35. A known Greek cognate of Latin *lapid-* is *lepas* "rock," and an early dialect may have had a form exactly or nearly like Latin *lapis*. The actual derivation of *Lapithês* is of course unknown. See Theocr. 15.141, Lapithai kai Deukaliônes; in the preceding line he mentions Pyrrhos.

Something of the sequence of Hellenic peoples at Lykoreia and Pytho and of the principal gods worshipped may now be conjectured. The Lapiths and Dryopes were the first Hellenes to possess the shrine and oracle at the Corycian Cave of Lykoreia; it may or may not have been a pre-Hellenic cult site. There they had a cult and myth of Lykos-Deukalion-Pyrrhos and of his counterpart, the later Python-Dionysos. Then came the Dorian invasion; and perhaps it was then that Herakles was substituted for Lykos as champion and chief object of cult, or that an attempt was made to do so. For though it is true that Herakles' cult was old and nearly pan-Hellenic, and was not limited to Dorians, it is also true that in the legends he was consistently the friend of Dorians and enemy of the oldest Greek peoples: Lapiths, Dryopes, Minyans. Little of his cult is found in the places where Lapiths and Dryopes made their final settlements, e.g., Asine and Hermione. The southward moving Dorians left the Phocians behind, among whom were the Delphoi. At some time the Delphoi adopted the cult and myth of Apollo, placing him in the forefront of their worship and considering him to be the great dragon slayer.[27]

The hero-gods of the displaced peoples tended to become cast in the role of dragon or brigand. Herakles acquired enemies that had been heroes of the earliest Hellenes: the Lapiths Koronos, Augeias, and Aktor's sons; the Dryopes Laogoras, Phylas, Amyntor, Eurytos, Kyknos; the Minyans Erginos and Neleus. He had an enemy named Lykos, though the scene is Thebes, not Lykoreia or Pytho. Then Apollo on succeeding Herakles not only took over Lapith-Dryopian enemies, e.g., Lykos, Phorbas, Phlegyas, Eurytos, but also the superseded Herakles. Phorbas and Kyknos seem to be the same hero-god as Lykos-Pyrrhos-Deukalion, though probably their names were not used for him in Lykoreia, but in the Lapith settlements of the Kephisos Valley and in Dryopis. For Lykoreia was but one town among many; there was nothing unique about its cults and myths, not even the possession of an oracle. This ancient hero was not superseded everywhere: there

---

[27] See Farnell (1921) 103–135, Defradas (1954) 135 f., against regarding Herakles as primarily a Dorian hero. The names Pyrrhos and Pyrrha may have been given to the Parnassian hero and his consort by the Ainianes, who for a time occupied Kirrha: Plut. *Mor.* 294A, 297BC. For war between Phocians and Phlegyans see Paus. 8.4.4, 10.34.2.

were places where the divine champion kept the name of Phorbas, Kyknos, Lykos, or Pyrrhos. Likewise Herakles did not give
way to Apollo everywhere even in the neighborhood of Parnassos.
In Boeotia and the Oita region Herakles remained the demon
slayer in legends that were obviously influenced by or closely
related to the Delphic dragon myth, but in which Apollo did
not displace him. Apollo, it seems, was so much disliked in some
localities that as Herakles' opponent it was he rather than Herakles who became the villain: his darker side shows through some
versions of the tripod myth.[28]

In saying that Apollo superseded or displaced an earlier god I
mean that he became the principal god of Delphic worship in
the other's stead and that he took the other's place in mythology.
It is obvious that the older deity and his cult were not effaced,
but reduced. The cults of Pyrrhos and Herakles were maintained
at Pytho; at Lykoreia Pyrrhos' worship continued, no doubt,
under the name of Lykoros. It did not matter that local mythology put them in a rather bad light. We must remember that the
enemy, although and precisely because he is fearful, always receives cult: there can be no doubt about the worship of most
dragons and demons that have been mentioned in these pages.
Pyrrhos, it was said (p. 398), was first buried under the threshold
of the temple; then he was given his own shrine. This may mean
that the first temple at Pytho was dedicated to him and that
Apollo had not yet come to Pytho when it was built; or that
Pyrrhos was worshipped in pre-Delphian Pytho; or that he and
Apollo came down the mountain together. In the late legend that

---

[28] Herakles vs. Lykos: Eur. Her. passim; Hyg. Fab. 32; there is also Lykaon Kyknos'
brother (pp. 30 f.). For Lykos as a hero at Athens see LM 2.2187 f. A Lykos was slayer
of Phlegyas (p. 53). Asklepios as Phlegyas' grandson, worshipped in the Epidauros-
Troizen region, is also an old Lapith hero. His name, however, was probably not used
in the Parnassos region until late. We have noticed that the myth of Apollo, Koronis,
and Asklepios was at several points connected with Delphi. Several correspondences
suggest themselves: Phlegyas = Silenos; Ischys = Python-Dionysos; Koronis = Delphyne
(when killed by Apollo) or = Korykia or Thuia (when loved by Apollo); Asklepios =
Lykoros or Delphos, who is simply a double of the father; Zeus repeats Phlegyas and the
Cyclopes repeat Ischys; for Ischys as helper of the Cyclopes see LM 2.360, where Hes.
Theog. 146 is cited. Koronis was also called Aigle, which is the name of the sacrifice at
Delphi connected with Deukalion's flood (note 21): Isyllos, hymn, IG 4²128 IV (Edelstein
1945: T 594; see ibid. II 90, note 54). On the myth of Asklepios see Edelstein II 1–64.
It is repeated in the myth of Apollo and Daphne, who = Koronis; Leukippos = Ischys;
Ladon = Phlegyas: Paus. 8.20; Parth. 15 (see p. 416, note 14).

Pyrrhos helped the Delphians check the Gauls under Brennos, we can see a Delphic decision to give more honor to Pyrrhos. Hence Pausanias says that the Delphians began to give Pyrrhos heroic honors then, though it is clear from Pindar that he was worshipped at Delphi long before.[29]

THE THREE SISTERS ON PARNASSOS

But was Lykoros-Pyrrhos a speaker of oracles at the Corycian Cave? Delphic myth mentions only the chthonian goddess Ge-Themis-Nyx and the chthonian god who is called Poseidon, Python, and Dionysos, as speakers or senders of oracles before Apollo came. The cave had a dream oracle, and the dream visions were ghosts of the dead. Since Pyrrhos was probably not a chthonian god and not likely to send that kind of oracle, either he was not an oracular god or his oracles were of a different sort. It is plain that with Apollo, who took over the speaking of oracles entirely, perhaps because he came to Delphi as an oracle-speaking god, a different kind of divination was instituted, though it may have been influenced by the methods of the old Corycian shrine. It is possible that Lykoros-Pyrrhos gave oracles after his fashion, perhaps through lots, during his part of the year; but the dream oracle of the chthonian powers was probably available at all times; if the messages came from the dead, it made little difference whether the god was on earth or below.

Strabo and Plutarch speak of Lykoreia as if it were still inhabited in their times; at least the site was still known by that name, and it is reasonable to suppose that the town endured after the Delphoi abandoned it. A remnant of the Delphoi or survivors of the pre-Phocian population may have stayed there; or other Phocians may have occupied the town which the Delphoi abandoned. It may be that the Delphoi were forced out, though it is reasonable to suppose that they moved in order to have a better and more accessible oracle. But was the oracle at the Corycian Cave abandoned? To judge from the phenomenon of religious conservatism alone, one would answer that it was probably maintained, at least for a time.

But we need not rely solely on probability: there is positive

---

[29] See Paus. 1.4.4, and pp. 398, note 44, 400, note 48.

evidence in the Homeric Hymn to Hermes that the Corycian
Cave was still a going concern in the sixth century B.C. Towards
the Hymn's close, Apollo, becoming reconciled to Hermes, tells
him that he must not aspire to be an oracle-speaking god; for to
speak Zeus's will belongs to himself alone. Yet he grants Hermes
a consolation prize. There are, he says, three maiden sisters who
live under a fold of Parnassos (ὑπὸ πτυχὶ Παρνησοῖο), teachers of
divination, from whom Apollo himself learned while he was still
a boy tending cattle. They "eat honeycomb and bring everything
to pass"; when they get yellow honey to eat, they speak truth;
when they are deprived of the god's sweet food, they speak un-
truthful responses. They flit about on wings and sprinkle their
hair with white meal. Hermes can have these sisters and amuse
himself as much as he pleases with their kind of divination. Apparently Hermes is to control their oracle, and the sisters will
speak his messages.[30]

The sisters' oracle was located on Parnassos, but not at Delphi:
Apollo says that it was apart (ἀπάνευθε) under a fold of the mountain, which means the same thing as Apollonios' "under a rocky
ridge of Parnassos," the place where Apollo was cheered by the
Corycian nymphs as he fought the dragon. From these sisters
Apollo learned divination. According to Apollodoros, it was Pan
who taught him this art. Pan and the Corycian nymphs were
worshipped together at the Corycian Cave. Again, when the poet
says that they become inspired from eating honey, he uses the
verb (θυίωσιν 560) that is cognate to the name *Thuiades,* whose
relation to the Corycian nymphs has been observed. So we can be
fairly sure that the three sisters were the Corycian nymphs.

The sisters have been identified with the Thriai of later writers.
Pherekydes made the first known use of this name, saying that
the Thriai were daughters of Zeus. Philochoros (*ca.* 300 B.C.) says
that they were three nymphs, nurses of Apollo, who lived on
Parnassos, a statement that accords very well with the Hymn. But
he adds that the mantic pebbles or lots (*psêphoi*) are called
thriai after them, words which imply that this was their mode of
divination. Late lexicographers also connect the Thriai with

---

[30] Hom. Hymn 4.533–567. Glaukos was also said to have taught Apollo divination;
he is a maritime equivalent of Pan. See p. 484.

mantic pebbles; and a Scholiast says that three nymphs invented the *thriai*. Hesychios adds that they were the first *manteis* and were nymphs.[31]

But there is nothing in the Hymn to show that the three sisters used lots. They get inspiration from honey and they answer questions; but nothing else is said about their method. These words do not exclude a lot oracle, but they seem to indicate mantic inspiration of a higher sort. Divination by lots was a very common practice, lacking prestige and authority: the lexicographers and proverb collectors quote the proverb "There are many pebble-tossers, but few seers." It is true that Apollo turns the sisters' divination over to Hermes as something trivial, about which Zeus cares nothing, since it cannot disclose his will. Yet the sisters speak truth when they get honey and bring their responses to fulfilment.[32]

The reference to honey-eating is significant. Pindar called the Pythia Delphic bee. Pausanias says that the second temple at Delphi was made by bees of honeycomb and feathers, and that Apollo sent it to the Hyperborean land. In these traditions we may see memories of the old oracle at the Corycian Cave. The equation of the nymphs with bees suits an oracle of dream visions sent up from the dead; for the souls of the dead were often identified with bees in antiquity. The tiny winged Keres or ghosts seen in vase paintings resemble bees.[33]

---

[31] Pherek. 49, 1.75 J; Philoch. 195, 3в.153 J; Hesych. Θ743; Steph. Byz. 209 Holst.; Schol. on Call. *Hymn* 2.45. Callimachus (*ibid.*) says that *thriai* and *manties* belong to Apollo.

[32] Zenob. 5.75; Hesych., Steph. Byz., *locc. cit.* In the Hymn (557) Apollo, saying that he had learned the sisters' divination, adds πατὴρ δ' ἐμὸς οὐκ ἀλέγιζεν, referring back to his remarks about true prophecy, where he says (535) τὸ γὰρ οἶδε Διὸς νόος. There is nothing to indicate that the three sisters were old women, as some scholars have assumed them to be from their powdering their hair with flour. But certainly that is no way to say that they were aged. Rather a ritual practice is referred to; cf. Aristoph. *Eccl.* 732 (Kanephoroi). They are in fact called *parthenoi* (Hymn 553), which usually implies young women; *parthenos* does not necessarily mean *virgin*, especially in earlier literature. At first, I believe, it meant much the same as *nymphê* (see Il. 9.560), a young marriageable woman. Notice in Il. 16.179 f. that Eudoros is called *parthenios*, because his mother Polydora was a *parthenos*, an unwedded woman; but Hermes had impregnated her. As for their powdered hair, notice the white maidens (*leukai korai*) who Apollo said would help him against the Gauls; in that battle Pyrrhos also helped him.

[33] Pind. *Pyth.* 4.60; Paus. 10.5.9 f.; cf. Strabo 9.3.9, p. 421; the first temple was made of laurel (*daphnê*). Souls of dead as bees: Porph. *Antr.* 18 f.; LM 2.2640 f. Bees nourished the infant Zeus in his Cretan cave: Boio *ap.* Ant. Lib. 19; cf. Diod. 5.70.3, where the nymphs feed him honey; whence Amaltheia is given a sister Melissa; see LM 2.2638 f.

The old oracle of the god and goddess at the Corycian Cave was a dream oracle. The three nymphs seem to be forms of the goddess, separated off from her, perhaps as daughters—mantic spirits that mediated between her and mortal men. Their names, perhaps, were Korykia, Daphne (Daphnis), and Thuia; but probably other names (as Melantho) were also given to them. Since all three were beloved of Apollo, they seem to have taken on the part of the enemy's daughter who falls in love with the hero. That is true of Korykia and Thuia at least; but the Daphne myth indicates the nymph's hostility to the hero. As we have noticed, the Corycian nymphs cheered Apollo and taught him the mantic art (it may be that, as elsewhere, the enemy's friendly daughter or wife became a captive maiden; and two or three captive maidens, of whom the hero marries one, are frequently found in folktales: p. 533). It need not surprise us if the myth was told in several different forms among the same people in the same period; and certainly its details changed from generation to generation, in keeping with the Greeks' active and prolific myth-making imagination. So, once the nymphs became friendly to the hero in the myth, they may have become attached to divination that was done in his name. If the hero, whatever his name originally, had a lot oracle in Lykoreia, then the association of the nymphs with lots is accounted for.

It is also noteworthy that Apollo in the Hymn (552) calls the three sisters either *semnai* or *moirai*. The best manuscript has the former, all others the latter reading. The Erinyes were euphemistically called Semnai: so we know from Aeschylus' *Eumenides,* and there is abundant evidence besides. The association of Erinyes with Moirai has been pointed out. In Apollo's temple at Delphi the images of the two Moirai stood beside Poseidon's altar and the hearth where Pyrrhos was killed. If anyone should object that these were two, not three, Moirai, then he should notice that Pausanias expressly says that the third Moira was replaced by Zeus and Apollo Moiragetai. At the rival cult site of Telphusa in Haliartos we find the Erinyes under the name of Praxidikai; their shrine, in which men took oaths, was

---

Priestesses of Demeter were called bees: Porph. *Antr.* 18; LM 2.2640 f. For vase paintings of Keres see Harrison (1922) figs. 7, 25, 166, and pp. 182 f.; (1927) figs. 77, 78.

located at the foot of Mount Tilphossion. They were daughters of Ogygos, the Boeotian king and flood hero, as the Parnassian nymph Melantho was daughter of Deukalion.[34]

Sister groups, usually three in number, are frequent in Greek mythology. We have noticed Gorgons, Graiai, Harpies, Sirens, Erinyes, as enemies of the hero; the three daughters of Triopas as mourners for Apollo; the Proitides as enemies of Dionysos; the Hesperides as either friends or enemies of Herakles. The Moirai helped Zeus to vanquish Typhon, just as the Corycian nymphs supported Apollo. The Muses should be noticed too, though they are not usually three in number. They were worshipped beside Ge at Delphi, were neighbors of Telphusa on Helikon, and were attacked by Pyreneus (p. 44). Undoubtedly the Delphic Muses are the Parnassian sisters after their descent from Lykoreia to Pytho. In Ugaritic mythology we find the three daughters of Baal (p. 134, note 25), in Hittite myth the three Gulses or Fates (p. 125). Since we have conjectured both Canaanite and Hittite influence upon the earliest Parnassian cults, it may be that the Corycian nymphs have an Asiatic origin. These sister groups, we notice, range from implacable hostility to the hero to complete support of him. Keres are both good and bad.[35]

The honey that the nymphs eat to get mantic inspiration is nectar or soma. Either the sisters give it to the hero, if they are friendly to him, or he takes it from them and their lord, if they

---

[34] *Semnai theai;* Aesch. *Eum.* 1041; see LM 4.703–707; Harrison (1922) 239–253, who makes a distinction between Semnai and Erinyes. Moirai of Delphi: Paus. 10.24.4. Praxidikai: Paus. 9.33.3; Dionys. Chalk. 3, 4.394 M. The Praxidikai were associated with Hermes in *defixiones:* LM 3.2916. The name of one was Thelxinia, a variant of Telchinia: Dionys. Chalk. *loc. cit.;* and see p. 405, note 58; for association of Erinyes and Telchines see LM 3.2920 f. In historical Delphi lots were used in minor ways; and it was also said that the tripod basin contained lots (*psēphoi*); they were apparently identified with Python's bones. See Amandry (1950) 25–36.

[35] Compare the grayness of the Graiai with the Parnassian nymphs' powdered hair. The swan form that Aesch. *Pr.* 795 attributes to the Graiai may not only recall Kyknos, but Apollo's swan chariot that carries him to and from the Hyperboreans. But, according to Claud. 28.30, Apollo's Hyperborean chariot was drawn by griffons. It may have seemed a bit forced in chapter iii to connect Kyknos' swan nature with winged dragons, especially if they are wicked, for our feeling about swans is colored by English poetry. But in the evidence cited here and elsewhere (e.g., the myth of Gerana, p. 101) the connection has been confirmed. Moreover the swan's long thin neck, its small head with beady eyes, and its hiss, would hardly escape the ancients' notice: it is a very snakelike bird and not good-tempered. Notice the black-figured vase painting, Harrison (1922) fig. 25: the bird that Miss Harrison calls vulturelike looks rather more like a swan; Parke (1956) 18–19.

are hostile. The potent substance may become a treasure that nymphs or dragons guard (p. 527). So we are not surprised to learn from Philoxenos (400 B.C.) that either the chambers of the Corycian Cave held gold, or the Corycian nymphs were clothed in gold. According to the ancient Delphians there were times when the cave looked golden (it is true that varying light and shadow produce colorful effects in limestone caves). The cave is a passage to the other world where live the Hyperboreans, in whose land stands the treasury of golden honey, the ancient temple of honeycomb; whence, we may believe, their joyous banquets were supplied with endless nectar and ambrosia. There is the Grail Paradise in embryo (pp. 540 f.). The actual and local is constantly merged with the mythical and otherworldly, the nearby cave with the distant Hyperborean land. And so the Delphians were called Hyperboreans, as Mnaseas says.[36]

There is evidence not only that the Corycian Cave's oracle remained in operation, but that for a time there was keen competition between Lykoreia and Pytho. In Euripides' often-cited verses on the mythical history of Delphi, it is said that Ge took honor away from Apollo's new oracle by sending dream visions to reveal the future to men; then Apollo went to Olympos and complained to Zeus, who put an end to the dream oracle and restored honor to Apollo. Or the goddess who thwarted Apollo is called Athena. It was said that she discovered divination with pebbles, i.e., *thriai* or *psêphoi*, which soon surpassed the Delphic oracles in fame; whereupon Zeus favored Apollo by making the pebble oracles false. It looks as if at first the old oracle had the incumbent's advantage, so that the new Pythian oracle had little custom for a time. In this situation we may see the beginnings of Delphic propaganda, when the Pythian priests, determined on success, devised ways and means of enhancing their shrine's repute. Either through their success or perhaps through violence the Corycian oracle came to an end or ceased to be a serious threat to Pytho. Certainly from 500 B.C. at the latest, the Delphic city-state's territory included the old site of Lykoreia.[37]

---

[36] Philoxenos, frag. 14 Bergk; Antig. *Hist. Mir.* 127; Mnaseas 24, 3.153 M.

[37] Eur. IT 1262–1281; Zenob. 5.75; Steph. Byz. 209 Holst. That the story is told in terms of both dream oracle and of *thriai* is further proof that the three sisters called Thriai

Finally we observe that Apollo let Hermes become the god of
the sisters' oracle; and the story must reflect some reality of cult.
Hermes was father of Pan, god of the Corycian Cave and patron
of flocks and herds. He was also father of Autolykos, master thief,
both lord and lifter of cattle, who lived on Parnassos, as we learn
from the Odyssey. In fact Autolykos has all the traits of Hermes
the thief and may be identified with him; while Pan comes close
to Hermes as pastoral god. Autolykos Hermes' son was an Argonaut, according to Apollodoros; and as such he can be identified
with that Autolykos who had an oracle at Sinope. For the latter
joined the Argonauts when they put in at Sinope; and he was
Herakles' companion on the Amazon adventure; whereas Hermes'
son instructed Herakles in wrestling. Above all, we should not
fail to notice the second element in Autolykos' name: he is that
Lykos who was worshipped at Lykoreia. In the classical Autolykos
of Parnassos, Lykos and his opponent have come together. It
should be noticed that Hermes' theft of Apollo's cattle, the subject of the Hymn, is very much like Herakles' theft of the tripod,
a sequence of robbery, quarrel, and reconciliation. In that story
the principal roles are again ambiguous. Hermes is the brigand
Autolykos, cattle rustler, or he is the heroic savior of the cattle
for mankind. Apollo is the champion who recovers the stolen
cattle, or he is the grim cattle lord who withholds them.[38]

---

belonged to the pre-Apolline oracle at the Corycian Cave. The introduction of Athena
has been attributed to the folk etymology which connects *thriai* with the Thriasian Plain
of Attica: LM 5.870 f., Amandry (1950) 28. But we should not forget that the cult of
Athena Pronaia was very important at Delphi, second only to Apollo's and certainly older.

[38] Hermes Pan's father: Hom. Hymn 19. Father of Autolykos: Apollod. 1.9.16; Paus.
8.4.6; Ovid *Met.* 11.303–315. Autolykos on Parnassos: Od. 19.392–466; Paus. 8.4.6,
10.8.8; cattle-lifter: Hyg. *Fab.* 201; and see p. 43; Argonaut: Apollod. 1.9.16; Apollon.
Arg. 2.955–961; Hyg. *Fab.* 14.30; oracle at Sinope: Strabo 12.3.11, p. 546; companion of
Herakles: Apollon., Hyg., *loc. cit.*; teacher of H.: Apollod. 2.4.9; Theocr. 24.111–118. He
could change his own shape and the shape of his cattle: Hyg. *Fab.* 201; Serv. *Aen.* 2.79.
Autolykos was grandfather of Odysseus, who visited him on Parnassos and joined him
and his sons in a boarhunt. First Odysseus was wounded by the boar, but then killed
him: another variant of the combat between hero and the enemy as boar; note the dark
copse in which the boar lived and how his eyes flashed fire. The Odyssey's description of
the Parnassian region where they hunted the boar suits the neighborhood of Lykoreia
very well; but inevitably the scene was placed at Pytho in later times; see Od. 19.428–454;
Paus. 10.8.8. Theocr. (*loc. cit.*) calls Autolykos Harpalykos of Panopeus (Phanoteus),
whose awful countenance frightened men even at a distance, so that they dreaded entering
into a boxing or wrestling match with him; that is, he is the great boxer of Panopeus,
Phorbas.
  For a less heroic Apollo we should recall the god who was willing to appease Sybaris
and Heros, and who sent Poine against Argos. It may be that in some regions Apollo was

Manifold are the ways of Delphic myth as of all Hellenic myth. But behind all shifts and changes, contradictions and inconsistencies, we can discern a combat between a heavenly power and a chthonian power, each of whom was variously named. In myth it finally became the combat of Apollo against Python. The myth in all its versions was built upon the pattern of the widespread combat myth of the old world. But it was adapted as everywhere to local conditions and events. Knowledge of the myth has served to clarify Delphic cults and early history. We see dimly, but we do see, momentous happenings in early times on Parnassos. It is dangerous to deduce history from myth; but in this instance there are nonmythical sources, literary and archaeological, to support the reconstruction.[39]

---

on his way to becoming an older, displaced god vis-à-vis Herakles, Koroibos, or Hermes; that is, he was settling into the role of Kronos. But the building-up of the pan-Hellenic Olympian pantheon probably checked this process. We should also recall the earliest Apollo of Greek literature, the destroying, plague-sending god of the Iliad; he had not yet become the pleasant, soothsaying god of the classical period.

[39] Now that the study of the last two chapters has been made, we can see that no theme of the combat myth is missing from the Delphic variant. In table 3, Themes 3E, 3G, and 8B are unchecked. But now we see the dragon identified with flood (3G); that Apollo was robbed of a potent object (8B); and that Dionysos and Autolykos could assume various shapes (3E). Also in table 5 certain plot components can be added: B,1—Python-Dionysos as death spirit, and the Corycian Cave as the mouth of darkness and chaos; E, 2 = Th. 3G; G, 2a follows from the combination of E, 2 and G, 2b. So the pattern is complete, and nearly every possible variation of it was known at Delphi.

XV

THE RITUALS

Through the previous fourteen chapters I have given most of my attention to mythical narratives alone. Hence some readers may have gathered the impression that I underestimate the importance of rituals in a study of myth. But I hasten to assure them that I do not. This is, however, primarily a study of folk narratives; and it seemed to me the better course not to mingle cult with myth all the way through, but to study the myth first as a narrative, to deal with it as one would deal with a folktale, finding and analysing variants, and then to draw all the conclusions possible from such a concentrated study. So, though it has been impossible to ignore cult and ritual, still they have presented themselves almost entirely as features of the myth variants, the final episodes, in which the victorious god ordains cult or ritual. Thus an aetiological crown caps the preceding narrative. Yet in the last two chapters we found excursions into cult history necessary. Now it is time that we looked more closely at some rituals.

It is undeniable that myths are closely attached to rituals. In fact, if a story has not been associated with cult or ritual, explicitly or implicitly, it is better not to call it myth, but legend or folktale. Yet the question remains: just what is the relation of the myth to the ritual? Which is first? Does the ritual enact the myth or represent it symbolically? Or is the myth suggested by the

434

ritual? Does every episode of the myth correspond to a ritual act, or is the relation of myth to ritual rather loose and adventitious? Scholars from Robertson Smith and J. M. Robertson to Raglan and Gaster have seen a very close connection between ritual and myth, though they have disagreed about the precise nature of the relation. Robertson Smith saw in myth an interpretation of ritual that was imposed upon it later. Jane Harrison spoke of myth as "the spoken correlative of things done." Gaster sees myth and ritual as two parts of an organic whole: "Ritual and myth are . . . correlatives in a single whole, and it is their organic combination that, in fact, produces Drama. It follows that . . . the 'plot' of the Seasonal Myth will be basically identical with the pattern of the Seasonal Ritual." In myth he sees the ideal, enduring, transcendental counterpart of the ritual acts that are performed at certain times in certain places by human beings for their community's good; that is, the cosmic events of myth are reënacted in the rites.[1]

In his analysis of Near-Eastern seasonal rituals, i.e., those attached to the festivals of solstice or equinox, of the new year, which mark the change from winter to summer or of dry to rainy season, Gaster finds a consistent pattern of mortification, purgation, invigoration, jubilation; the first two stages belong to a period of "emptying" and "suspended animation," which he calls *kenôsis;* the latter two to a period of renewal and replenishment (*plêrôsis*). With this analysis we can agree: the rites adduced certainly reveal this pattern. Then Gaster goes on to analyse the accompanying myths and believes that he finds the same pattern; and most of the myths which he adduces are representatives of the combat myth which we have been discussing. Out of our own analysis we can agree that in a general way the god's death and resurrection correspond to the waning and waxing of life that are symbolised in the rites. Obviously there must be a measure of agreement or similarity if one is to be associated with the other. But are the myths so plainly divided into four parts that correspond to the four stages of the rituals? Furthermore, do the myths correspond with the rites feature for feature? It is not obvious at

---

[1] Gaster (1950) 3–6, 49–72 (quotation from page 49); see also Hocart (1952) 9–27, Raglan (1936). For earlier views see Gaster 5, Fontenrose (1948) 166 f.

first glance, or from Gaster's argument, that the fit is nearly so close as that. Hence we must briefly study some chosen rituals and festivals, concluding with Delphic rituals, since Delphic myth is our main concern.[2]

We are fortunate in having both *Enuma elish* and part of the temple program of the Babylonian New-Year festival called Akitu, on two days of which *Enuma elish* was recited. Much the same festival was celebrated in every city of Mesopotamia, either near the spring equinox after the stormy Mesopotamian winter, or near the autumn equinox, after the drought and heat of summer. In Babylon it was a spring festival, held in the month Nisan. On every day of the festival (1) the high priest rose before sunrise and washed with river water, making himself ceremonially pure; (2) then he went to the temple and prayed to Bel-Marduk and to Beltiya (Beltis, Belit), his consort, making offerings. The prayers abound with fulsome praises of Marduk; but there is nothing said that can be considered a direct allusion to the combat myth. "O Bel, who fells the mighty with his glance" is about the closest that one can come. (3) The other priests and the cantors performed certain rites in the traditional manner. (4) On the second day the high priest thrice spoke an incantation, of which the text is mutilated, but in which are references to evil enemies who are strong, to the enemy and brigand, to an exorcism, and to Marduk's unalterable curse and decree. Here *à la rigueur* we may see an allusion to the combat; but there follow remarks on the purifying of the temple. (5) On the third day the high priest summoned three artisans and gave them gold and precious stones for the making of two images to be used on the sixth day; and portions of the sacrificial victims were given to these artisans on four successive days (third to sixth). (6) The images received food offerings on these same days; one held a snake in its left hand, the other a scorpion, and both raised their right hands to Marduk's son Nabu. (7) On the fourth day the high priest blessed the temple Esagil. (8) On the evening of the fourth day he recited *Enuma*

---

[2] Gaster (1950) 6–72. Gaster finds the ritual pattern to be worldwide; but his subject is Near-Eastern ritual and myth; see especially 34–43.

elish. (9) On the fifth day the temples of Marduk and Nabu were purified. (10) A ram was killed and a subordinate priest used its body in the purifying rituals; then this priest threw the ram's body, and the butcher threw its head, into the river. (11) The subordinate priest and the butcher went out into the country and stayed there until the twelfth day. (12) The three artisans carried a golden canopy from Marduk's treasury and covered Nabu's chapel with it. (13) The high priest and artisans recited a sort of incantation to assist the purifying rites; they called upon all evil to leave the temple, saying "May the god Bel kill you, evil demon! Wherever you are, be suppressed!" (14) After offerings of food, incense, and wine, with prayer to Marduk and Nabu in their temples, they took water to the king for the cleansing of his hands; (15) then they escorted him to Esagil. (16) Before Bel's image the high priest took from the king his sceptre, crown, and sword, placing them on a chair before Bel's image. (17) The priest struck the king on his cheek and pulled him by his ears to the ground, making him bow before Bel. (18) The king then protested his innocence of all wrong-doing during the previous year. (19) The high priest announced Bel's blessings and instructions. (20) The royal insignia were then given back to the king. (21) The high priest again struck the king's cheek; if he made the tears flow, then Bel was favorable; if not, then Bel was angry: the enemy would rise up and cause the king's downfall. (22) At sunset (fifth day) the high priest tied forty reeds together in a palm branch and placed the bundle in a hole that had been dug in the Exalted Courtyard, along with honey, cream, and oil. (23) He set all this on fire after placing a white bull before the hole. (24) To the bull he addressed a recitation, most of which is lost. (25) On the sixth day the image of Nabu was carried from Nabu's temple to the river, ferried across, and then carried to Marduk's temple Esagil. (26) When Nabu reached the temple, victims were slaughtered and cast into a fire that had been built before him.[3]

This is all that the document which contains the "Temple Pro-

---

[3] The text of the New Year's Program has been translated into English by A. Sachs (from whom I quote) *ap*. Pritchard (1950) 331–334, Mendelsohn (1955) 129–139, and by Hooke (1953) 103–110; translated into German by Zimmern (1926) 4–13. For accounts of the festival see Pallis (1926) 120–248, Frankfort (1948) 313–333, Gaster (1950) 35–37, Levy (1953) 35–43.

gram" tells us; for it breaks off during the description of the events of the fifth day (but it has already said something about the sixth day). It is at once apparent that in these proceedings we do not have an enactment of the myth or anything like it. It is true that the king is ritually deposed and humiliated (17), his badges of office taken away (16), and that these events were referred to the god's death in the myth. But if the king represents Marduk, the priest who humiliates him certainly does not represent Tiamat or Kingu. Furthermore the second striking of the king's cheek (21) occurs after his restoration and expressly for the sake of an omen. Bel himself is also present in his image as a participant distinct from the king. The taking of the royal insignia recalls Zu's taking of the tablet of destinies. But the Zu combat is another story; and the priest who removes the insignia returns them. Again there are rituals of exorcism, the casting out of evil demons from the temples (4, 13); a scapegoat ram is killed and thrown into the river; and it appears that the demons were identified with Tiamat's hosts: for Marduk is invoked against them. But the connection is remote; the rites mentioned are essentially meant to cleanse from pollution. Also Nabu's coming from Borsippa to Babylon was interpreted as his search for his lost father Marduk, as we shall presently see; but it was really a procession rather than the enactment of a search. Finally, there is the recital of *Enuma elish,* which means only that the myth was associated with the festival. The recital was a meaningful event; but we should notice that it was one event among others, which do not purport to enact it. For the rest, the program contains directions for prayers, offerings, sacrifices, purifying rituals.

Yet it may be objected that the program fragment covers only the first five days, days of purification and preparation for the more important seven days (Nisan 6–12) that followed. Days 5–8, according to Pallis, were concerned with Marduk's disappearance, the search for him, and his rescue or resurrection. This part of the festival is known from a document already referred to (p. 161), that which tells of Bel's confinement in the mountain. It is the dilapidated text of a ritual commentary, which expressly interprets festival events in terms of myth. Where it first becomes intelligible we learn that (1) Bel is confined within the mountain (probably represented by the great tower). (2) A messenger whom the gods send forth searches for Bel and finds the place of confinement, where the guards question him, and carries the news back to Belit; he is represented by a priest. (3) People run through the streets looking for Bel, asking where he is held captive. (4) Belit finds his tomb, watches by him, weeps for him, bathes his wounds with black wool, calls on Sin and Shamash (moon and sun) to give him life. (5) Certain gods had confined Baal, cutting him off from sun, light, and life (commentary only). (6) A son of Ashur, who is guard of the "fortress," protests his rectitude; his role is by no means clear. (7) On Nisan 8 a pig is killed; this animal appears to represent the transgressor who is referred to three times in the text, and who seems to be interpreted as Bel's slayer. His head is severed and hung on the canopy of Belit's shrine. Someone, perhaps Belit, asks, "Who is the culprit?" (8) There is tumult and fighting in the city. (9) Nabu comes to the city (Nisan 6); his image is carried in procession from Borsippa to Esagil. (10) There are ritual laments, exorcising spells, wailing of the people. (11) Apparently before Belit goes to Bel's prison or tomb, his garments and adornments have been brought to her. (12) *Enuma elish* and "Ashur's good deeds" are recited to give Bel strength or life. (13) Water is brought that has power to banish plague; it seems to be expressly associated with the primeval waters of the myth, though the text is not clear. (14) There are footraces, which are referred, however, to Ninurta's victory over Zu. (15) A chariot without its master (Bel?) goes speeding along the processional way to the Akitu house. (16) The gods bore holes in the door of Bel's prison and fight a battle inside; Bel is delivered; a "window-door" is shown.[4]

It is evident from this text that the interpreters of the ritual acts believed that the series reënacted events of myth. And a tolerably consistent myth emerges from their commentary: Bel's enemies have confined (killed) him; men and gods, including his wife Belit and son Nabu, search for him; they find that he is dead and wail for him; the murderer is found and killed; the gods attack the prison and rescue Bel. But it is equally evident that this is not the myth of *Enuma elish* as we know it. However, if one

[4] For the text see p. 161, note 33; see Frankfort (1948) 321–325.

supposes with Pallis that the title *Enuma elish* does not necessarily refer to the creation epic that has come down to us under
that name, but may mean any version of the creation myth, then
it may be better to say that there is nothing here of Marduk's
combat with and victory over Tiamat and Kingu. On the contrary, Bel has no part in the combat. He does not kill the transgressor; the latter's death does not free him; the gods in general
fight the battle that delivers him.[5]

This myth can be expressed in two ways. (*a*) A god has disappeared; the other gods search for him, above all his wife-sister,
and make every effort to recover him; and after much searching
and weeping and wailing the god is found and brought back.
This, with some differences of detail, is the myth of Tammuz.
(*b*) A transgressor has bound the god and deprived him of his
power; somebody kills the transgressor and beheads him; the god
is thereafter released and recovers his power. This is nearly the
myth of Enlil, Ninurta, and Zu; and, in fact, the text all but says
so. The reference to Zu's defeat answers the question that was
asked a few lines earlier, "Who is the culprit?" In the intervening
lines the culprit is mentioned again. One notices that the bound
god is always called Bel in this text, never Marduk. For the myth
antedates the supremacy of Babylon and Marduk. It is the ancient
myth of Nippur. Bel is Enlil; Zu has robbed him of his power,
which is his life; Ninurta goes out on Ashur's order (for the text
is an Assyrian copy, and Ashur takes Anu's place) and kills Zu. It
is plain, therefore, that Tammuz and Enlil were brought together
in the suffering Bel of Babylon. We know that this fusion was
actually made in Marduk, Bel of Babylon (p. 164). It was in just
such a way as this, perhaps, that the combat myth acquired its
episode of the champion's initial defeat and death.[6]

---

[5] The difficulties of fitting the myth to the festival are perceived by Pallis (1926)
213 f., 218–220, 234–238; Frankfort (1948) 327–329; Levy (1953) 36. But Pallis thinks
that the events of Nisan 5–8 (see Pallis 245) reënact closely the myth of Bel's death and
resurrection (Pallis 249–253). To judge from Semitic practice, I do not think that any
version of the creation myth could be called *Enuma elish* unless it began with those words.

[6] The mingling of traditions creates some confusion: e.g., both Nabu and Ninurta
as helpers of the vanished Bel. It is doubtful whether Nabu leads the gods who storm Bel's
prison. He may be an *interrex*. It is said that he comes for his father's welfare; it is not
definitely said that he has come to search for his father. Of course, if Marduk instead of
Enlil becomes Bel, then Nabu as Marduk's son may become assimilated to Ninurta as
Enlil's. In the next commentary referred to (see note 8) Bel certainly means Enlil.

Now even though this series of ritual acts is interpreted in terms of the myth of Bel's death, does it really correspond very closely to it? Certain features of the ritual seem to have the dying god in mind, as in Mediterranean Easter celebrations, and so may have been originally instituted to suit his myth: the priest who goes as messenger to the tower and returns with tidings (2); the priestess who goes as Belit to the tower (4); the questions and prayers of the priestly participants and crowd, "Where is Bel?" "Who will deliver him?" "Who is the culprit?" "Let Bel live" (2–4, 7). But the lamentations and exorcisms did not necessarily act out a myth; it is conceivable that they were once purely ritual acts, not yet interpreted as commemorating mythic events. So it may be with the carrying of Nabu's image across the river (9); for the gods of many cities came to Babylon in this way for the festival as guests of Bel; it was a traditional feature of an ancient ceremony. But Nabu lived just across the river; he became Marduk's son; hence we may suppose that the myth would give his arrival and presence a special interpretation.[7]

Now what about the ritual enactment of combat? (*a*) There were tumult and fighting in the streets (8). This commotion could easily be a premythical concomitant of a festival, part of the expected celebration and carnival spirit. Mythically interpreted, it could as easily be referred to the return to chaos during the god's death as to combat or gigantomachy. (*b*) A pig was slaughtered, representing the transgressor Zu (7). The mythical interpretation was obviously imposed later. Still one may conjecture an earlier myth: Tammuz killed by a boar. But Tammuz is not Adonis, and his slayer seems to be either lion or brigand (p. 164). In any case the killing of a pig in piacular rites is so common that we can consider it an ancient premythical part of the program. (*c*) According to the commentary, the gods broke through a door and fought inside to free Bel (16). But the only ritual act seems to be the showing of an object called "window-door." Again we can suppose an old rite that was reinterpreted in terms of a combat myth. Yet the mythical interpretation itself conforms to neither the Zu myth nor the Tiamat myth. (*d*) We can hardly sup-

---

[7] Assembly of gods: Pallis (1926) 133–136; Frankfort (1948) 318, 325 f., 331–333.

pose that footraces (14) were originally instituted to reënact or commemorate Ninurta's victory over Zu.

This ritual commentary, then, shows no correspondence of ritual with myth. Rather it tends to show the true relation between them: that exegetes had recourse to the events of myth in order to interpret the rites. This relation becomes even clearer in two other ritual commentaries. In one, which apparently refers to the New-Year Festival, we find such entries as "The fire which is kindled, that is Marduk . . . in his childhood ——— (those) who throw high the burning arrows, those are the gods . . . when they heard ———." These burning arrows are said to be Bel's arrows which slew his mighty enemies. But Bel makes no use of burning arrows in *Enuma elish*. The sheep that is burned in the fire is Kingu, when the gods burned him with fire, says the commentary. But Kingu was not killed in this way in *Enuma elish*. Moreover Zu and Asag are called hostile gods, whom the father and brothers of Bel overthrew; here it is evident that events of the Akitu festival are referred to all three combat myths of pp. 147–150, and that Zu and Asag-Labbu were numbered among Tiamat's hosts. But it is Bel's father and brothers who killed them, according to the interpretation; and the only ritual act appears to be the aforementioned throwing of burning arrows into the air. Then it is said that the king, holding a weapon, represents Marduk (likely enough); the king burns a kid in the fire: his act is the burning of the sons of Bel (Enlil) and Ea, i.e., the rebel gods. Then the king breaks a pot with a hammer, representing Marduk when he smashed some enemy. So it goes with other ceremonies. Throughout, old rites, in many of which fire was employed and victims were burnt, are referred to the gods' combats with their enemies. Yet it is doubtful whether the uninterpreted acts would compel an observer to think of any combat, not to mention the specific combats of the myths, or conversely that the myth would ever remind anyone of the rites.[8]

Still another commentary on the New-Year Festival reinforces the impression already received of a rather loose fit between myth and ritual. This text appears to refer to the carriages of a procession and their contents. The king rode in an "Elamitic wagon

---

[8] Pallis (1926) 213–218, Hooke (1953) 113 f., whose translation I quote.

without seat," drawn by horses. The king is interpreted as Ninurta; the man beside him holds Zu's severed tongues in his
hand; the carriage carries Enmesharra's (Kingu's) body; the
horses are Zu's ghost (*eṭimmu, Totendämon*); on some wall is
fastened the threshold of Enmesharra's house; the fat of a fleece,
perhaps carried on the wagon, is called an abomination to Enmesharra. Again it is noteworthy that the commentary refers to both
Zu and Kingu. Since the king is called Ninurta, and since Asag as
well as Kingu was called Enmesharra, the interpretation seems to
be based on the Enlil-Ninurta cycle of Nippur rather than on the
Marduk-Tiamat myth. Though it is possible that the carriage was
made up to represent Ninurta's victory over two enemies, it is
more likely that the mythical interpretation is later than the carriage. It puts the king in Enmesharra's funeral wagon, drawn by
the ghost of Zu. This is understandable in terms of cult, for
Enmesharra was a worshipped and propitiated deity; we have
seen several times that the mythical monsters were really gods.
But it is not comprehensible in terms of the myth and an hypothetical representation of it, in which the champion despatches
the fearful enemy, mutilates his body, and casts him into the
depths—funeral honors are out of the question and certainly are
not mentioned in the mythical texts.[9]

Further on, interpretations are clearly made from *Enuma elish*,
though Zu is not forgotten. A steer and seven sheep are thrown
alive into a pit: they are Kingu and his seven sons. Somebody
throws a dove into the air and cuts it in two with his sword: the
dove is Tiamat, who was cut in two by Marduk. That a dove
should be chosen to represent the horrible Tiamat, and that this
easy slaughter of an inoffensive bird should intentionally be
either a dramatic or a symbolic representation of the great combat
is incredible. The most one can concede is that the myth suggested the cutting of the bird into two approximately equal parts
(*zwei Hälften*). The text returns to the king, who is still Ninurta,
his father's avenger. He receives his sceptre and throne and is
dressed in his royal garb; the commentary apparently does not
refer here to the events of the fifth day, but to rites that followed

---

[9] Ebeling (1931) 28–37, upon whose translation I rely; see 33 for the passage discussed,
and 29 for Asag = Enmesharra.

the procession on the ninth. Then cedar wood burnt before the king represents the melting of the evil god's flesh; again we see a fire ritual interpreted from the punishment of enemies that was effected by quite other means in the myth. Finally the commentary closes with words that reveal the adventitious nature of the mythical interpretation: as I understand them, the man who knows may reveal the interpretation to anyone who knows; but he should not reveal it to anybody who has not been instructed: that is, only initiates may know the meaning of the rites.[10]

From scattered sources we learn of other rites on the last four or five days of the festival: the ceremonies of determining the destinies, for which the images of the gods were gathered in a special chamber; a banquet at the Akitu house after the procession thither, when, it seems, the king and priests were the gods' table companions, a ceremony that resembled the Roman *lectisternium;* the sacred marriage, the wedding of Bel and Belit. The determination of destinies and the banquet correspond exactly with the myth, as it is told in *Enuma elish.* But we should notice that the climax of the festival corresponds to the postclimactic conclusion of the myth; the whole of the rites of renewal and jubilation corresponds to the myth's epilogue, which can be amputated without affecting the essential story: it is the closing formula, "and so the god recovered his throne and ruled justly; the gods rejoiced and celebrated his victory with a great feast." The sacred marriage, however, which is the supreme ceremony of the festival, corresponds to nothing that is made explicit in *Enuma elish* or in the Zu and Asag-Labbu myths. Of course, the champion recovered his wife, if he had one; and we know that Marduk and Ninurta had consorts, though the texts of the aforesaid myths make nothing of them. In many cognate myths we have seen the hero rescue a goddess or heroine and marry her. But in Mesopotamian mythology, so far as we know it, we find no such episode; we find only Inanna or Belit trying to recover Tammuz or Bel. That, as I have pointed out, is the earliest myth to be associated with the Akitu Festival. The sacred marriage corre-

---

[10] See Ebeling (1931) 36 f. The commentary is loaded with interpretation, much of which can be called theological, not referring to ritual acts. The closing formula in Ebeling's translation is: Geheimnis der grossen Götter. Der Wissende soll es dem Wissenden zeigen, der nicht Wissende soll es nicht sehen. . . .

sponds to the union or reunion of husband and wife. But the rite is very ancient and very primitive; and it would be dangerous to say that it was instituted solely to represent Bel's marriage with Belit.[11]

There remains the question whether a myth was enacted or mimed during the festival. Pallis believes that a ritual drama, enacting Marduk's victory over Tiamat, took place in the Akitu house, probably on the tenth day. But, as Frankfort points out, there is no evidence to show "that the battle against Tiamat was mimed." In any case, such a drama would mean the same as the reading of *Enuma elish:* it would be one rite among others, inserted in the series for the purpose of relating the myth to the festival.[12]

The Akitu rituals as a whole cannot be said either to enact or to symbolise the combat myth; nor can it be said that the myth was invented to interpret the rituals; for the ritual sequence varies greatly from the myth sequence, nor do specific rites very often resemble mythical events. We know only that *Enuma elish* was recited at the festival, that festival events were interpreted in terms of the combats of Marduk and Ninurta with Tiamat, Zu, and Asag-Labbu, and of Bel's death and resurrection. Obviously the myth and ritual affected each other; but aside from certain superficial details the only part of the myth that appears to be formed from the rituals is the conclusion. It seems, therefore, that the myth's epilogue is the principal bond between myth and ritual.

For the rest, the rituals show the sequence that Gaster points out: rites of purification and expiation are followed by rites of renewal and jubilation. They are ancient magical rites, designed to expel the old year and bring in the new, to banish winter or drought and summon the season of growth and rain, to renew the king's power for another year or to inaugurate his successor; for the king embodied his community and represented the god, summing up in his own potency all the potency of his realm, which included town, field, and sky, and all the forces within them. In

---

[11] See Pallis (1926) 183–200, 246–248; Frankfort (1948) 325–333; Gaster (1950) 35–37. Gaster speaks also of the appointment of an *interrex* and the killing of a human scapegoat; but both are questionable, and in any case would hardly be enactments of the myth.

[12] Pallis (1926) 247, 255–269; Frankfort (1948) 327.

the earliest celebrations of these rites no gods were necessary; or, if you will, the gods were the powers themselves, winter and storm and year and growth, all equally alive and concrete. But at first the powers or gods were coerced by the rites. Only gradually were they viewed as free actors who could decide the year's destiny; then it was that prayer began. But in the Akitu Festival magic remained dominant to the end. If the rites were not performed, the year, the land, and the king could not be renewed. It is plain that these rituals would suit, perhaps suggest, the myth of a vanished god, whom the efforts of other gods recalled to life, though it is doubtful whether they could provide all the details of actual dying-god myths. Later still the seasonal changes would be seen as a battle of cosmic forces in which the god was first defeated, then victorious. But the myth that was adopted to clothe the conception had no appreciable effect upon the rituals.[13]

OTHER ORIENTAL RITUALS

Since Mesopotamia has yielded the most ancient records of the combat myth and may be the country of the archetype, I have discussed the correspondence of Babylonian rituals with the associated rituals in some detail. Now that we have seen just how much, or how little, correspondence there was, and have had a clearer view of the relation between the myth and the rituals, no great effort will be needed to show that the same relation obtained between the combat myth and associated rituals in other oriental lands.

We are fortunate in having from ancient Egypt the Ramesseum Dramatic Papyrus, whose mythical data have already been summarised (p. 181). Here, if anywhere, we can discover how close is the fit between things done, words spoken, and the myth. For the document is divided into forty-six parts or scenes, and each part contains (1) a statement of a ritual act performed, (2) the mythical interpretation of the act, (3) words spoken by participants who represent gods. There are also certain annotations or stage

---

[13] Frankfort (1948) 277–281, (1949) 215 f.; Gaster (1950) 32 f. Of course, some would say that myth is already present in the animistic views of the first performers of the ritual. But it seems to me that the term *myth* becomes too loosely employed if it is to include the sum of man's ideas and feelings about gods. The term is more usefully restricted to narrative sequences of a certain kind. If *myth* is to have the larger meaning, then we need another term for the narratives. See p. 3 f.

directions, which give information that can be included under 1 or 2 above. Hence the papyrus text has been called a drama or mystery play, which was performed at the time of a new king's succession.[14]

For instance, in the first scene (1) the king's ceremonial boat is made ready on the river; (2) Horos speaks about his eye to his children; (3) Horos says, "Bring me my eye, that it may open upon the river." That is, the boat is Horos' eye. But in the second scene (1) the king's sons place eight jars in the boat's bow; (2) Thoth puts Osiris on Set's back to be carried aloft; Set mounts to heaven; (3) Thoth says to Set, "You cannot tarry long under him who is greater than you," and to Osiris, "His heart ought not to become cold under its burden." The boat is now Set, the jars are the dead Osiris, the princes are Thoth, and the river is heaven.

So it goes, scene after scene. There are sacrifices, offerings, laments, dances, songs. When the boat is ready the princes bring the royal insignia to the king, among which are two sceptres and a club. The insignia are Horos' eye, which Thoth presents to him. Later at Letopolis the princes hand the king a jar of wine, which means that Horos recovers the eye which Set took from him. In the next scene someone hands the king a string of beads: Horos again recovers his eye. Horos' eye, either that which Set took or that which he did not, is identified also with wood, bread, beer, cakes, milk, oil, wine, earthenware, a gold ring or circlet, tables, plumes, and still other objects. The climax of the ritual sequence is the coronation ceremony. The king receives two plumes and a circlet: as Horos he now has both his eyes. Finally the king girds himself in a stomacher, which is Osiris: the ceremony signifies the transfer of power from old to new king, from Osiris to Horos, and the mystical identity of one with the other. Finally there is a banquet, at which all the nobles of Upper and Lower Egypt are present.

All this is interpreted as Horos' triumph over Set, his recovery of his eye, his punishment of Set, who is several times charged with Osiris' corpse to carry it to heaven, and his final confirmation as sovereign of a united Egypt. The persons of the myth, Horos,

[14] Sethe (1928), Frankfort (1948) 125–139, Gaster (1950) 384–403. I have made the renderings below from Sethe's German translation of the text.

Set, Osiris, Isis, Thoth, are each identified with various persons, animals, and objects; there is no actor who carries a role. But the gods' speeches were certainly recited at the ceremonies, probably by king and priests. They form the link between myth and ritual, making explicit the interpretation of the rites in terms of the Horos-Set-Osiris myth. But the scenes and speeches show almost no dramatic or narrative sequence. The recovery of the eye, the defeat and punishment of Set, happen again and again.

But is the combat enacted? That is the center of the myth and should form the focal point of a drama. In scene five, barley grains are strewn upon a threshing floor: they seem to represent Horos' inviolate eye. In scene nine, oxen trample the strewn barley: Set and his henchmen are beating and killing Osiris. Horos, represented probably by the king, tells them to stop beating his father. Then Horos beats the oxen: he has defeated Set's host. Then the threshed barley is loaded on the backs of donkeys and carried off: Osiris' body is once more loaded on Set's back and carried to heaven. Obviously this is an ancient agricultural ritual that has been attached to the succession ceremonies. It has magical import for both the annual yield and the prosperity of the king's reign. The oxen and donkeys perform a useful service: as Frankfort says, "after all, the grain must be threshed." The beating of the oxen may be in origin no more than the rough means employed to keep beasts at their task. Yet in the mythical interpretation the oxen and donkeys become the wicked enemies of Osiris; the threshing becomes a murderous deed. Upon the threshing, represented here by a ritual enacting of the process, has been superimposed the same myth of the dying god as was told in Mesopotamia and elsewhere. Though from primitive times, no doubt, the Egyptians endowed the barley with life, neither the mowing nor the threshing would inevitably produce such a myth. It is more likely that a myth, invented in one place, was diffused over a wide area; having been attached at some point to fertility and agricultural rituals, it became the interpreting myth of such rituals wherever it was adopted. But, however that may be, a threshing scene can hardly be said to enact Osiris' death or even to suggest the myth. For it can be interpreted in several ways: in the Ugaritic myth the winnowing of the grain was interpreted to be

Anat's cutting up of Mot, the enemy (p. 253). But the dying-god myth is not the combat myth, though often joined to it. To the combat, to gigantomachy in fact, corresponds a banal beating of livestock, which is, furthermore, not the central point of the ritual sequence, but merely a preliminary act.

In scene twelve, goats represent Set's followers, whose heads must be bowed in submission to Horos. A goat and goose are beheaded and sacrificed: both represent Set. The identifying of a sacrificial victim with the enemy was also noticed in the Akitu Festival. But we can hardly suppose that this sacrifice, embedded among agricultural and coronation rituals, was instituted to represent Horos' victory over Set.

In scene fifteen, a pillar (Set) is bound with a rope, struck by Horos' sons, and made to bow in submission. Why a pillar for Set, if this is a dramatic representation? Why bound with a rope and struck, and not by Horos, but his sons? It looks like a rite whose original meaning has been forgotten.

In scene eighteen, there is a match between boxers, who are of course Horos and Set; there are also fights between the followers of each. Geb stops the fighting (the mythical reconciliation, p. 181). It may be that these contests were instituted to represent the mythical combat. But contests were a common feature of festivals; and in most instances it is very unlikely that they were meant to enact combats of gods with their enemies. Furthermore, if the bout or race of a festival program was a genuine contest, the outcome could not be foreseen. Then how could the roles of hero and enemy be assigned to contestants beforehand? Until the contest was over, nobody could know who represented the victorious god. This question must be faced by anyone who would maintain that a festival contest was really instituted to dramatise the combat of myth.

All the ritual acts mentioned belong to the third of the six parts into which Frankfort divides the coronation ritual. As in the Babylonian Akitu Festival, the rites of coronation, jubilation, and feasting take up a disproportionate amount of the rituals, if they are looked upon as a dramatic reproduction of the myth; in this case the whole latter half of the ritual sequence corresponds to the myth's epilogue. Again, as in Babylon, the correspondence in content, aside from the proportions, between the rituals and the myth is closest at the conclusion. But coronation, festivity, banquet, may form the conclusion of any myth which ends happily.

While undeniably the rudiments of ritual drama can be seen in the speeches of the coronation ritual, to speak of drama or mystery play is to exaggerate these rudiments. There is as much and as little drama as can be seen in the British coronation ritual or in the celebration of the mass. Yet while it is probable that the myth contributed nothing but the speeches to the rites, we can see that the rites had a considerable effect upon the details of the myth. In the first place they, or similar rites, gave the myth its proper names: the divine combatants are called Horos and Set simply because the combat myth was adopted by Egyptians and associated with their rituals. Possibly Set's donkey form, certainly Horos' eye as the severed member, entered the myth from these rites. The association of the myth with such rituals probably explains the formlessness and repetitions of such a mythical document as "The Contest of Horos and Set" (p. 179).[15]

It is important to understand that the combat myths were not employed for seasonal and succession rituals only. Since the enemy was identified with all violent and destructive forces, the myth was associated with rituals that were employed only when occasion required. For instance, the texts of the Metternich stele are actually incantations to be used against the poisonous bites of reptiles and scorpions. The first incantation drives the poison out by asserting Horos' victory over Apep. Another recounts the story of how Isis' spells revived Usert's child, and how Thoth's spells revived the child Horos, after each had been killed by a scorpion. No doubt there were acts or rituals that accompanied these spells. Here we see that the myth accompanies a purely magical rite of healing or prophylaxis. The practice of this kind of magic is surely older than the combat myth. Once men knew the myth, they used it to inform the spells that were recited

---

[15] An annual festival was celebrated at the season of the flood's end; and it may be that in coronation years the appropriate ceremonies were added. The renewal of the king's own potency took place at the Sed Festival, which was held about the same time of year, but did not include the above rituals. See Frankfort (1948) 79–88. It is likely that the so-called Memphite Creation Drama accompanied rituals too, though Frankfort does well to call it simply the Memphite Theology; see Sethe (1928) 1–80, Frankfort 24–32, Gaster (1950) 407–411.

against reptiles and their poisons. It is as unlikely that the myth
sprang from these rites and spells as that the latter were meant to
act out the myth.[16]

This magical text shows plainly that men endowed the very
recitation of mythical events with magical power. The magical
efficacy of reciting mythical texts is explicitly stated in the Babylonian ritual commentary on Bel's death: *Enuma elish* and
Ashur's deeds are recited to give Bel life and strength. As Hocart
and others have shown, and indeed as the texts with their commentaries make clear enough, the Vedas with their manifold
mythical episodes and allusions were recited or chanted along
with the performance of particular rituals in order to accomplish
the very end desired, the renewal of the world at the new year,
the banishing of drought, the winning of good things, the warding
off of evil. The god's success in the myth ensures a successful
outcome to the ritual acts. Hymns that extolled Indra's victory
over Vritra or Viçvarupa were sung in accompaniment to the
soma sacrifices and many other rituals. But this does not mean
that the myth was born with the ritual. One need not read very
far in the *Brahmanas* to realise how casual sometimes is the association of the myth with the rites described: it differs no whit
from that which has been observed in Babylon and Egypt. Notice the manner in which the *Sanhita* employs the myth to state
the primeval antecedent of a rite. The *tridhātu* sacrifice has three
constituents. There are three cakes, made each of different in-
gredients, placed on a set of four potsherds. The myth is then
introduced solely to explain the threefold nature of the offering.
When Tvashtri cast the remains of the soma on the fire, Vritra
grew out of them and enveloped the three worlds. When Indra
called on Vishnu to help him, Vishnu divided himself into three
parts, thus putting himself into each of the three worlds. By using
each third in turn to give power to his thunderbolt, Indra forced
Vritra's submission. Here we see how the rite has introduced
"three" into the myth; furthermore Vishnu's participation may be
wholly due to the fact that the offering was made to Indra and
Vishnu. But it seems obvious that the whole ceremony, as described, was not framed to represent the myth described, much

---

[16] Budge (1912) lxviii–lxxix, 143–145, 157–197.

less the Indra-Vritra myth as usually told. Nor is this the only
myth adduced: it is said that Prajapati created cattle with the
threefold offering; hence the man who knows this, i.e., who re-
cites the proper formula while he makes this sacrifice for the
purpose of acquiring cattle, will get them from the source whence
Prajapati created them. The commentary thus demonstrates that
magical power was believed to reside in knowledge of the myth;
it does not prove that the myth and rite are two faces of one coin.
If they are, why two myths? [17]

Is the myth necessary to give the ritual its intention, as Hocart
says? Do not the performers intend to acquire certain goods and
avert certain evils? When rituals were first devised, men thought
that objects and unseen forces were living beings like themselves.
The rituals were intended to coerce these beings for specific purposes. This primary meaning can still be seen in the rituals that
we have looked at, even after myths have been associated with
them.

The text of the Hittite Puruli myth also contains ritual directions and interpretations which plainly show the original magical
meaning of the acts performed. The document is introduced with
the statements that when the Weather God sends rain, the Puruli
prayer is no longer said, and that the festival is celebrated in the
drought season. Following the first version of the myth comes a
bit of interpretation, and then directions for prayer and for thank
offerings, if rain fall in Nerik. There the text breaks off. After
the second version follow directions for a procession of priests
and their assistants with images of gods in the van; for an offering
of grain to a god and to a goddess who is said to take precedence
over the Weather God; and for a bit of dialogue in which the gods
say that they are going to Nerik to be installed, and the marshal
assures them that they will be installed on their thrones in the
several cities with proper etiquette, and that the king will allot
each deity a house, barn, servant's quarters, and so much meadow
and orchard for his residence. There is nothing in this ritual that
shows resemblance to the myth. Upon ancient rites of magical
meaning has been imposed a myth of combat between rain god

---

[17] TS 2.4.11 f.; Hocart (1952) 9–27.

and drought demon, which suits the intention of the festival, but has had no effect upon the ritual acts.[18]

Since for Delphians and Hellenes in general the myth of Apollo's combat with Python was the mythical precedent of two Delphic festivals, we may now inquire whether at Delphi myth and ritual were any more closely associated than we have found them to be farther east. Do we have evidence there that they formed an inseparable whole?

Every eight years the Delphians celebrated three "nine-year" festivals. One of these was called Septerion, which, according to the sources, was considered by the Delphians to represent Apollo's combat with Python. Plutarch and Aelian tell us a good deal about what was done. In Apollo's temenos, on the south side of the second lap of the Sacred Way (as it is known to the excavators), opposite the Athenian Portico, is a level space that was called halós (threshing floor), which can also be reached by a flight of steps called Dolonia that ascends from the terrace to the south. Here a temporary structure, called either hut (kalias) or tent (skênê) was set up; in it or beside it a table was placed. Up the Dolonia steps came a band of youths in silence, carrying lighted torches, escorting a boy, of whom it was required that both his parents be living. They ran up to the hut, set it on fire with their torches, overturned the table, and then turned about, ran from the sanctuary, and went clear to the Vale of Tempe in Thessaly. There the boy and his companions, after being purified, made elaborate sacrifices and gathered boughs of laurel from a special tree. Then after breaking their fast at Deipnias, just outside of Tempe, they walked back in triumph to Delphi, led by the boy as architheóros, accompanied by the music of flutes, wearing laurel crowns and carrying boughs from which the crowns of Pythian victors would be made, and attended over portions of their way by the peoples through whose lands they passed. They went and came back on the Pythian Way, which from Delphi ran through Ozolian Lokris and Doris, across Oita into Malis and

---

[18] Puruli Text I, III, VI: Gaster (1950) 325, 329–332, 334–336.

Ainis, then across Othrys and through the Thessalian plain to Tempe.[19]

Certain correspondences between myth and rites are explicitly shown in the sources. The Delphians said that the hut represented Python's lair; that the flight to Tempe and cleansing rites represented Apollo's wanderings, servitude, and purification; that the tree from which boughs were taken was that from whose boughs Apollo had crowned himself. The boy obviously represented Apollo; his companions may have represented the Delphians of version E1 (pp. 19–21), who informed Apollo of Python's whereabouts and set fire to his tent. The sacrifices in Tempe may represent the funeral honors that Python's son Aix undertook. To this extent it is possible to see imitation of the myth.

But even in antiquity men noticed discrepancies between the myth and the Septerion ritual. Plutarch's Kleombrotos pointed out that the temporary structure was made up to represent a king's dwelling rather than a dragon's cave; that the flight, servitude, and cleansing rites presupposed a curse or crime. We may add that there appears to be no combat in the rites, nor anybody or anything to represent Python. There are only the burning of the hut and overturning of a table, which are not done by the boy who represents Apollo, but by his companions. The Delphians' burning of Python's residence as an incident of the myth is mentioned only by Strabo, citing Ephoros (version E1), who connects it with the rite as the mythical precedent which the Delphians recognised. But even in this version of the myth the firing of the hut follows upon Apollo's combat and victory, which have no counterpart in the ritual. Again, the journey to Tempe is not so close to the local myth's final episode as may appear at first sight. Notice that Apollo's representative and his companions fly from the scene and go to Tempe; but in a local version of the very myth that was associated with the Septerion, as Plutarch knew it, it was Python

---

[19] Plut. *Mor.* 293c, 418AB, 1136A; Ael. VH 3.1; Strabo 9.3.12, p. 422; Steph. Byz. 149 Holst.; Arg. 3 to Pind. *Pyth.* See Mommsen (1878) 206–213, Schreiber (1879) 9–38, Usener (1904) 313–339, Harrison (1927) 425–429, Halliday (1928) 66–71, Jeanmaire (1939) 387–411, Defradas (1954) 97–101; further citations in Defradas 97, note 1. The name is found only at Plut. *Mor.* 293c; there is no need to emend to *Stepterion*, as some scholars have done. Scholars usually say that the attack on the hut took place at night. But nothing is said other than that the band carried lighted torches, which were used to ignite the hut.

who fled wounded to Tempe, pursued by Apollo. Also, according to Plutarch's version, Python's funeral rites took place at Tempe. No such rites are explicitly mentioned in the description of the festival; and Python's tomb, at any rate, was located in Delphi. It should also be recalled that some accounts of the Python myth send Apollo to Crete or Argos for purification.

Since even in antiquity the Plutarchian Kleombrotos expressed an enlightened man's doubt that the Septerion rites imitated Apollo's combat with Python, modern scholars in general have agreed that the rites long preceded the interpretation in terms of the Python myth. There has been no talk about organic unity of myth and ritual in this instance. Even so, Jane Harrison at one time assumed that the hut contained a snake, and Mommsen supposed that an arrow was shot into the hut. So willing, however, are scholars to heed Plutarch and to separate the myth from the ritual that Halliday believes they were not associated until the fourth century, Ephoros' time, "when the rationalistic version was applied for the purposes of explanation." Yet Kleombrotos plainly tells us, and Halliday admits, that the hut was supposed to represent Python's cave in the Delphians' interpretation. For we must realise that Kleombrotos opposes mythical cave to actual hut as he opposes Apollo's mythical flight to the actual rites in Tempe, i.e., the official interpretation to the things done. Whether version E is or is not "rationalistic" (see pp. 19 f.), it was not the official Delphian version of the myth. Finally, it can be said, I believe, that the variance between Septerion ritual and Python myth is no greater than that between Akitu ritual and Tiamat myth, or that between the Egyptian succession ritual and the Horos-Set myth. Only Kleombrotos' words have made a difference in modern estimates.[20]

---

[20] Plut. *Mor.* 418AB, . . . ἥ τε γὰρ ἱσταμένη καλιὰς ἐνταῦθα περὶ τὴν ἅλω δι' ἐννέα ἐτῶν οὐ φωλεώδης τοῦ δράκοντος χειὰ ἀλλὰ μίμημα τυραννικῆς ἢ βασιλικῆς ἐστιν οἰκήσεως . . . καὶ τελευταῖον αἵ τε πλάναι καὶ ἡ λατρεία τοῦ παιδὸς οἵ τε γιγνόμενοι περὶ τὰ Τέμπη καθαρμοὶ μεγάλου τινὸς ἄγους καὶ τολμήματος ὑποψίαν ἔχουσι. παγγέλοιον γάρ ἐστιν . . . τὸν Ἀπόλλωνα κτείναντα θηρίον φεύγειν ἐπὶ πέρατα τῆς Ἑλλάδος ἁγνισμοῦ δεόμενον, ... The upsetting of the table has no counterpart in the Apollo-Python myth. But it has one in the flood myth of Arcadia. Since that is a variant of the Near-Eastern flood-myth, and since Deukalion, hero of the best-known Greek variant, had a place at Delphi (p. 420), it may be that the Deukalion myth was once associated with the Septerion rites. See Fontenrose (1945) 106.

As several scholars have seen, the Septerion festival was a sequence of cleansing and expiatory rites. Certainly the eight-year
interval indicates a periodic purging and renewal of the community, once represented by its king; for Delphi was once a
monarchy. Hence the regal adornment of the *halôs* hut, the burning of which, I suggest, has the same meaning as the king's humiliation in Babylon. The boy who fled to Tempe was a scapegoat, as Halliday points out; thither he carried all the community's guilt, of which he then ridded himself, coming back
cleansed and transformed. The eight-year interval resembles the
seven-year period of the Baal-Mot cycle of the Ugaritic texts (p.
131).

The Pythian festival was also celebrated every eight years until
590 B.C. Then the only contests were musical: citharodes vied
with one another in singing hymns in honor of the god, and the
winner received a prize. In 586 the festival was celebrated after a
four-year interval; then athletic contests were introduced. It may
be that the Amphictyony seized control of the festival in that
year. In 582 the Amphictyons definitely made it a quadrennial,
pan-Hellenic, agonistic festival, in which all victors, whether in
athletic or musical contests, would receive a crown of laurel. The
new festival was modelled upon the festival of Olympian Zeus in
Elis.[21]

The Amphictyons instituted the quadrennial festival to celebrate their victory over Krisa in the First Sacred War. But the
mythical occasion was said to be Apollo's victory over Python: for
the myth of the local octennial festival was carried over to the
pan-Hellenic quadrennial games. The ancient Pythian festival
had been closely attached to the Septerion; for in the latter festival, as we have seen, the participants brought laurel boughs from
Tempe for Pythian victors' crowns. Though that could not have
been the purpose of the laurel before 582 B.C., the custom estab-
lishes both a temporal and a meaningful relation between the two
festivals. It is probable that at one time the Python combat was

---

[21] Institution of the festival: Strabo 9.3.10, p. 421; Paus. 10.7. Octennial: Arg. 3 to
Pind. *Pyth.*; Schol. on Od. 3.267; Cens. *De Die Nat.* 18.6. See Mommsen (1878) 149–206,
213 f.; Schreiber (1879) 16–38.

considered to be the single precedent for the whole festival sequence.[22]

So the circumstances of the foundation of the pan-Hellenic festival are known, and it is clear from them that the athletic contests were not instituted to imitate or commemorate or symbolise Apollo's combat with Python, and that the earlier musical contests were designed solely to honor the god. For the rest, the festival had sacrifices, processions, and a banquet, as one would expect. There remains consideration of the Pythian nome (*Pythikos nomos*) as part of the musical program. This was played by a flutist, who was sometimes accompanied by *kithara* or *salpinx*. It was intended to represent Apollo's combat with Python, as our sources tell us. It had five parts, the names and meaning of which changed from time to time. Pollux gives us the clearest description: (1) *peira*, representing Apollo's inspection of the combat site; (2) *katakeleusmos*, Apollo's challenge to the dragon; (3) *iambikon*, the combat, during which were heard trumpet notes and the dragon's gnashing of teeth as Apollo's arrow struck home; (4) *spondeion*, the god's victory; (5) *katachoreusis*, the god's dance to celebrate his victory. According to the first *Argumentum* of Pindar's *Pythians*, the parts were (1) *peira*, Apollo's first attempt at combat with the dragon; (2) *iambos*, abusive language; (3) and (4) (the *Argumentum* names three parts, which seem to belong together, and does not mention a part for the combat itself) *daktylos*, *mêtrôon*, and *Krêtikon*, for Dionysos, Mother Ge, and Zeus respectively; (5) *syrigma*, the snake's hissing. Finally, Strabo describes a late form, composed by Timosthenes, who lived under the second Ptolemy: (1) *ankrusis*, a proem; (2) *ampeira*, first attempt at battle; (3) *katakeleusmos*, the combat; (4) *iambos* and *daktylos*, the paeans of victory, representing respectively abuse of the dragon and hymns; (5) *syringes*, the dragon's death, during which his last hissings are heard.[23]

---

[22] We do not know about the provision of laurel for the alternate celebrations of the Pythian games, when the Septerion was not celebrated. According to Paus. 10.5.9, the first temple of legend was made of laurel that had been brought from Tempe. For the Python combat as *aition* of the games see Ovid *Met.* 1.445–451; Lact. Plac. *Theb.* 6.8, 7.96; Argg. 1, 3, to Pind. *Pyth.*; Joh. Ant. 1.20, 4.539 M.

[23] Poll. *Onom.* 4.84; Arg. 1 to Pind. *Pyth.*; Strabo 9.3.10, pp. 421 f. See Mommsen (1878) 193 f., Schreiber (1879) 19–32.

There can be no doubt that the Pythian nome was a musical imitation of Apollo's combat with Python. The musicians, who were engaged in a contest with one another for the honor of being awarded the laurel crown, composed their versions with that combat in mind; and perhaps the flutist and his accompanists danced a mimic representation of the combat in time to the music. But the Pythian nome was born with the Amphictyonic festival: its inventor was Sakadas, who was crowned victor in 586, 582, and 578.[24]

Special notice must be given to the parts that the *Argumentum* indicates for Dionysos, Ge, and Zeus, in view of the conclusions reached in chapter xiii that all three names were given to ancient enemies of the champion. So it may be that the *Argumentum* has preserved the oldest pattern of the nome, that which Sakadas devised. For the first nome may have echoed older hymns of the octennial festival, which still carried versions of the combat that were nearer to the oldest Delphic combat myth, and in which the enemy may have been called either Python or Dionysos. This surmise is supported by what we know of the ancient festival. Among the songs sung was a dirge for Python. At any rate, it is said that the poet Olympos, who is assigned to the eighth century, played a dirge (*epikêdeion*) for Python on the flute in the Lydian nome. It is also said that Apollo sang an *epitaphion* over Python after his victory (see fig. 27); and that, in fact, the whole festival was intended to celebrate Python's funeral rites.[25]

The original nature of the Septerion and Pythian festivals may also be surmised from their association with the other two octennial festivals that Plutarch mentions. There were three such festivals in order, he says: Septerion, Herois, Charila. We can add the Pythian as a fourth in the period before 590. The Herois, we have seen, had something to do with Semele's resurrection and the Thyiads (p. 377). The Thyiads also took part in the Charila. The rituals of this festival were a purificatory sacrifice addressed to the heroine Charila and a ritual act: the king (a purely religious office in republican Delphi) sat before the people and dis-

---

[24] Paus. 2.22.8, 10.7.4; Poll. *Onom.* 4.78.
[25] Aristoxenos *ap.* ps.-Plut. *Mor.* 1136c; Ptol. Heph. *Nov. Hist.* 7, p. 153 Bekk.; Clem. Alex. *Protr.* 1, p. 2 P, 2, p. 29 P.

tributed barley and pulse to citizens and strangers alike; and as he sat there, a doll called Charila was brought before him; when everyone had received his share, the king struck the doll with his shoe; then the leader of the Thyiads took the doll to a ravine, where she put a rope around its neck and buried it at the site of Charila's grave.[26]

The myth told to explain these rites was this: Once a drought brought famine to the Delphians, so that they went to the king's doors. He handed out barley and pulse to the noblest suppliants only, since there wasn't enough for everybody. Then a little orphan girl came and importuned him so much that, becoming angry, he first struck her with his shoe and then threw it in her face. The girl, proud though poor, went off and hanged herself. The famine went on, and plague struck too. So the Delphians consulted their oracle and learned that they must propitiate the "maiden suicide" Charila. That was the name of the orphan girl; so she was propitiated and the octennial festival began.

At first sight this myth may look altogether unlike any myth that we have been dealing with. But notice (1) that Charila's coming coincides with famine and that her death brings plague and more famine: likewise in the Koroibos myth (p. 105) Psamathe's death brought plague to Argos; and when her avenging spirit was killed, the plague continued. (2) Charila went forth and hung herself in a ravine, where she was buried: the most likely ravine is that through which the creek Papadhia flows and in which the spring Sybaris is located, the spot where the Delphian counterpart of Psamathe's Ker fell when she was hurled over a precipice. (3) The Delphic Apollo told the Delphians to propitiate Charila: likewise he advised Delphians and Argives to propitiate Sybaris and Psamathe's Ker respectively. (4) The king drove her away as he gave food to his famished subjects: just as Herakles routed spirits of plague, famine, and flood, restoring the means of life to men. So we may say that in Plutarch's myth Charila has been transformed. She was at first the very spirit of drought and famine whom the king destroyed, winning food for his people. That is, she was the double of Sybaris across the Pleistos gorge, the dragoness, mother or wife of the enemy. So her

---

[26] Plut. *Mor.* 293b–f.

festival properly follows the Herois, when she rose from the lower depths in the drought season; then at the Charila she returned beneath the earth. It is possible that political changes in the Delphic state brought with them corresponding changes in the slant of the Charila myth, so that the heroine was transformed from demoness to a humble girl of the people.

Even though there are some correspondences between myth and rites of the Charila, it is obvious that there are also incongruities. The hanging and burying of a puppet is an ancient and well-known feature of seasonal rituals. The puppet is a scapegoat (*pharmakos*), as Halliday points out. The whole ritual of the Charila is piacular, just as is the Septerion ritual. The whole sequence of four festivals was meant to purge and renew the city and the land every eight years.[27]

Only the date of the Pythian festival is certainly known, Bukatios, probably from the sixth to the fourteenth, which means sometime in August. Plutarch's Kleombrotos speaks of the Septerion as recent in a dialogue that took place a few days before the Pythian festival. If the Septerion was celebrated at the summer solstice, then ample time would be allowed for the trip to Tempe and the return with boughs of laurel that would still be fresh enough for the games. The Herois and Charila followed the Septerion in that order, according to Plutarch (it is impossible, I think, to understand him in any other way). They may have fallen in the interval between Septerion and Pythian games; but more likely they were later. For the Charila, at least, the end of the drought season seems indicated.

Now the contention that these festivals and their rituals are older than any myth that was ever attached to them may be supported from inconsistencies of dates. The same complex of myth was applied to the annual alternation of Apollo and Dionysos in November and February, to the sequence of octennial festivals celebrated over the summer, and to the Pythian festival held in August every four years. Apollo returned from the Hyperboreans every year on Bysios 7 (February); yet every eight years in midsummer he returned triumphantly from Tempe; or, according to Alkaios (p. 382), he returned then from the Hyper-

---

[27] Halliday (1928) 72 f.

boreans. He killed Python in both June and August after 590; but he had already killed the winter king in February. Dionysos lay in the tomb from February to November every year; but he raised his mother from the dead in the summer, and his resurrection was celebrated every two years in the great Dionysiac festival on the mountain; though as Liknites he may have been awakened in Apollo's temple every year. It is apparent that different rituals of different import were eventually explained by variations upon a single myth of combat. It was the great Delphic myth, and it was fitted to all rituals and cults in one form or another.[28]

CONCLUDING REMARKS ON MYTH AND RITUAL

So at Delphi as in Asia there is no evidence that the combat myth grew out of the rituals to which it was joined as *aition* or that it had any appreciable effect upon them. The rituals did not enact the myth; the myth did not receive its plot from the rituals. This conclusion, after all, is what we should expect when we find that festivals and rites of widely different places, seasons, and meanings became associated with the same myth pattern. It is simpler to suppose that a well-known type of story was introduced in many places to serve as the primeval precedent of the rituals than to believe that in so many places the rituals spontaneously generated a uniform pattern of myth.

Yet the rituals had a profound effect upon the myth, with which they had become associated very early in Mesopotamia, Egypt, and India, lending it special features and themes which thereafter clung to it. The very association with cult, being early, made it truly a cult myth, so that as it spread it tended to become attached to new rituals. Sometimes, perhaps, it was carried with rituals from one land to another. The last episode of the story, after all, was that a cult or rite of commemoration had been established.

There must have been something in the rituals that drew this particular myth to them. If we review them we see that their

---

[28] Relevant to Delphic festivals are the Hyperborean offerings that were annually carried to Delos over a route that may have coincided in part with the Pythian Way from Tempe. Perhaps they came regularly to Delphi too. Aelian associates the Hyperborean offerings with the procession from Tempe (VH 3.1), and so does Farnell (1907) IV 101–111. See Herod. 4.32–36.

intention was to banish a hostile or at least unpleasant spirit and to win the help of a powerful spirit who was pleasant and beneficent, or at least capable of becoming so to those whom he favored. There were simple magical rites and spells meant to banish sickness, poison, famine, or to subdue the spirit of volcano, earthquake, and hurricane. There were rites that recurred annually, meant to banish the demons of winter or drought and call back the spirits of spring or rain—in short, to banish the old year and bring in the new. The annual rites often involved the renewal of the community's vigor in the person of the king, who might then represent or become identified with the good spirit. But sometimes the king's and community's renewal took place at longer intervals, anywhere from two to eight years, sometimes more. In all the rites mentioned, the opposition of good and bad spirit might be looked upon as a conflict. Hence the special suitability of the combat myth as *aition* of these festivals. It is not impossible that the entire interpretation of the combatants as chaos and cosmos, death and life, arose through the myth's connection with rituals of community renewal.[29]

We noticed that street fighting occurred in the Akitu festival and fistic contests in most of the festivals discussed. The contests were probably a disciplined development of irregular scrimmage. But it is doubtful whether these fights and contests were instituted to commemorate a mythical combat. More likely they had a purely magical purpose at first, to drive out evils and to promote fertility. For such festival phenomena are found in many lands and are variously explained in folklore. The familiar sham fights of rural festivals in Europe and Latin America do not necessarily invoke the combat myth of our study, even though variants of that myth are known in the regions concerned. Sometimes the celebrants assert that they are commemorating an historical conflict, such as that of Crusaders against Saracens or of Spaniards against Moors. A good example may be seen in John Steinbeck's *The Forgotten Village*. In the Mexican village of Santiago the people celebrate their fiesta:

---

[29] Initiation rites and puberty rites have not come to our attention in this study; but as Jeanmaire (1939) shows, they availed themselves often of this sort of myth.

Then, in front of the church, the people celebrated in dance the ancient war of Castilians and Moors.

They acted out a battle between peoples they did not know in a land they had never heard of in a time that was forgotten. And the people enjoyed the death of the king of the Moors, as they did every year.

Here history is being shaped into myth. In some places it was shaped to the combat myth, to the St. George variant, for instance. Long ago the war between Delphians and Phlegyans became a legend that was modelled upon the Apollo-Python combat.[30]

Certainly we must grant that historicised myths are later than the rituals with which they are associated. The *Jeu de Russon* near Tongres in Belgium, studied by Henri Grégoire, illustrates very well the manner in which an historical or pseudohistorical narrative, in this instance a saint's legend, may attach itself to rituals that are centuries older. Grégoire shows that the *Jeu* is nothing more nor less than the Whitsuntide ceremony in which the Wild Man is pursued, caught, and in make-believe beheaded or otherwise executed. But the act has become the martyrdom of St. Evermar. The Wild Man, called either Whitsun King or Whitsun Fool, has become both a Christian saint and the youngest pilgrim in his band; for the latter is the man who is chased and beheaded after St. Evermar, who is stabbed in the final scene, has been arrested. The persecutor, an odious tyrant and robber knight, is called Hako, who, as Grégoire shows, is none other than Hagen of Trony (Tronegen, Tongres), the Nibelung prince. So the saint's legend has replaced an older myth, which may have been a form of the combat myth. But even that myth was younger than these rites.[31]

My conclusion that the combat myth did not grow out of rituals, but had an independent origin and was later imposed upon them, does not hold for every myth in its relation to rituals.

---

[30] Steinbeck (1941) 77 f. On the meanings of festival combats see Grégoire (1934) 18; Gaster (1950) 21–24, 50, 56; and their citations.

[31] Grégoire (1934) 16–22. The Russon festival is a May-Day rather than a Whitsuntide festival. Hako, it should be noticed, suffers no death or defeat. He has the victor role of an ordinary Whitsuntide chase. Yet at Russon he is entwined with ivy in the manner of the pursued Wild Man elsewhere. Sometimes the Wild Man is called *Pfingsthagen*. So a reversal of roles has taken place.

Certainly some myths have received their whole frame and content from rites. But usually, I think, the myth has been taken out of the people's folklore to serve as *aition*. Yet from the moment that myth and rite have been joined they interpenetrate each other. The ritual gives to the myth the very names of its characters, much of its detail, and an aetiological character. The myth acts more slowly upon ritual, which is conservative. At first it may be limited to interpretation of ritual features. Gradually it may impose features upon the ritual, so that a rudimentary ritual drama may come into being. Then men may think of including in the festival program a mimetic representation of the mythical narrative through dance, song, gesture, action; then true ritual drama is born. So when ritual acts are deliberately devised to reproduce the myth, i.e., whenever myth precedes ritual, then drama is produced: ritual drama at first, a recurring performance of the cult's own myth; but afterwards freer, when the poet may dramatise any myth that he wishes.[32]

It follows from what I have said that I do not consider myths to be the oldest kind of story to appear among mankind. For if we restrict the term myth to stories that are associated with cults as *aitia*, and if most of the myth plots are drawn from a people's folktales or legends, then we must suppose that folktales and legends are older kinds of narrative. In any case it is hard to believe that no man ever thought of telling a story until somebody felt the need of providing a precedent for rituals, or until rituals had suggested a narrative sequence. To conjecture what happened in the prehistoric past on reasonable probabilities alone is dangerous, but I would suggest that man's first narratives were accounts of striking events of the immediate past: extraordinary perils and adventures during hunts, migrations, explorations, encounters with strangers. Such elementary narratives would soon turn to legend, which, if I am right, was the first kind of traditional tale to appear. Legends offered patterns for the framing of purely fictitious stories, and so folktales were the next to appear. Origins became a subject of both legends and folktales. When a story of the origins of a cult or rite was told, then myth was born.

---

[32] See Fontenrose (1948) 166 f.

CONCLUSION

Our study of the Python myth is complete, and the study outlined in the Introduction has been completed. We have found
that the Apollo-Python myth and the Zeus-Typhon myth are two
closely related expressions of a single antecedent myth, itself a
member of a myth family that ranged over most of Europe and
Asia. If the members of this family did not descend from a common original, as my use of the term family would indicate, then
the resemblance that they show one to another in pattern and
range of themes, which extends even to variations of pattern and
theme, is itself significant for students of mythology, folklore, and
culture. At any rate, in comparing the myths of this family,
and in establishing the common pattern that underlies it, we
made several important observations and discoveries.

1. The champion fought not a single enemy, as we assumed
at the outset, but two great enemies, male and female, of whom
the latter was even more terrible.

2. The enemy, whom we first saw in dragon shape as Python,
and then as a giant-brigand in Tityos and Phorbas, was a power
of the death realm and of the sea; and so was his consort.

3. Underworld and sea are virtually equivalent in this set of
myths.

4. The combat-myth is a myth of beginnings, a tale of conflict
between order and disorder, chaos and cosmos.

5. Chaos was dark and watery, the habitation of monsters and

demons, the land of the dead; it preceded the cosmos and still surrounds it.

6. Chaos was alive, an hermaphroditic creature, or two creatures, male and female, who are the dragon pair of the combat myth; hence their power among the dead and on the sea.

7. The dragon withheld the waters, which contained the materials of the ordered world; the hero had to kill him to release them.

8. The combat myth is also a myth of the recurring attacks of the forces of chaos upon the forces of order.

9. The gigantomachies and theomachies of Greek and oriental mythologies belong to the combat myth.

10. The divine champion was often identified with the dying fertility god.

11. On the other hand the dying fertility god was often identified with the enemy.

12. When the champion and his enemy are both dying gods who embody opposing seasons, a cycle of victory and defeat becomes established: e.g., the Baal-Mot cycle of Ugarit.

13. She who appears as Chaos-Hag and first mother is closely related to or identical with the great goddess of love and fertility, who often appears as the champion's sister or wife.

14. Hence the Venusberg theme has several expressions and outcomes. It leads to the Judith theme, the Medea theme, and the rescued-princess episode.

15. The champion's death takes a variety of forms, becoming transformed sometimes into a harrowing of Hell.

16. Many hero tales of combat between hero and dragon belong to a subtype of the combat myth, from which cosmic meanings have tended to disappear, though sometimes they cling to it in a disguised or obscure form.

With this part of the study behind us, we could go back to Greece and study the dragon combats of Perseus, Kadmos, and Herakles, aided by the results achieved and the knowledge gained from our survey of oriental myths. We could conclude that these legends were not heroised offshoots of the Apollo-Python and Zeus-Typhon myths, but that they descended from old myths of divine combat that had reached Greece even earlier. The Perseus

and Kadmos legends showed remarkable affinities to the Canaanite myths of Baal, Yam, and Mot; and we observed that Greek
traditions connected both with the Phoenician coast. We could
conclude that a Canaanite variant came to Greece before any
other, becoming the Perseus-Andromeda legend, followed later
by another from Phoenicia, which became the Kadmos legend.
It was also evident that Cilician and other Anatolian influences
had entered into the Perseus and Herakles legends; and it seemed
likely that Cilicia sent a combat myth to Greece before it sent the
Zeus-Typhon variant. All three heroes, as we call them, were
plainly old gods, who had receded before new gods. Perseus
showed clear traces of godhood in classical times. Herakles was
certainly worshipped as a god throughout antiquity, though as
a hero too; but his hero status belongs mostly to legend, and
even there his divinity shows through.

Now the Herakles legends not only have Near-Eastern connections, but several also show a surprising resemblance to the Indra-
Vritra myth of Vedic India. In the Geryon and Acheloos legends
Herakles is another Indra, fighting and killing the chaos dragon
to free or to control the waters and bring the cosmos into being.
Clearly a mixture of variants took place in the formation of several of the classical myths and legends of combat. In the Herakles
legends, we observed, the chaos demon is likely to take the particular form of the death lord. Every Herakles legend rings the
changes upon his victory over Thanatos, whom he meets under
various names and shapes.[1]

All three hero-gods had something to do with Delphi: Herakles
as tripod-robber and fighter of brigands who molested the shrine;
Kadmos as slayer of Delphyne's son, consulter of the oracle, and
follower of Pelagon's cow; Perseus as slayer of the Dionysos who
was buried at Delphi. The study of their legends, after the pre-

---

[1] The theme of a mortal man's defeat of Death in combat continues to capture the
creative imagination. Most recently Robinson Jeffers has treated the theme in *Hungerfield*
(*Hungerfield and Other Poems*, New York: Random House, 1954). Hungerfield waits at
his dying mother's bedside, ready to fight Death when he comes to fetch her. Her name
is Alcmena. "Death walked in human form, handsome and arrogant . . . a long, dark
and contemptuous face, emperor of all men, choosing the souls / That he would take"
(p. 7). Hungerfield wrestles with him and drives him away. Later Death comes back:
"Hungerfield turned and said, 'Is it you, Horse-face?' " (p. 22), whereupon one form of
the enemy comes to mind. See Benoit (1950).

ceding study of Greek and oriental combat myths, armed us to renew our attack upon Delphic myth. Then we found that not only could more information be wrung from the sources of the Python myth, but that more sources were available than had been apparent in the first chapter.

We can be fairly certain of the following statements: (1) Apollo fought both a dragon and a dragoness. (2) The Telphusa of the Homeric Hymn to Apollo is a double of the dragoness. (3) The dying-and-rising Dionysos of Delphi is a double of Python as the Delphic god's enemy, both being originally identical. (4) The Delphic Dionysos' alternation with Apollo in life and death reflects the earliest form of the Delphic combat myth, which was nearly identical with the Perseus-Dionysos myth of Argos. (5) The earliest Delphic myth was very like and closely related to the Canaanite myth of Baal and Mot. (6) The early fertility-and-death god, later called Dionysos or Python, was divided into a father and son. (7) The father became known as Silenos, Pan, Koretas, Kronos, Poseidon, Zeus (or sometimes Python). The son became known as Dionysos, Python, Delphynes, Pyrkon. (7) The consort became known as Ge, Themis, Nyx (or Styx, p. 548, note 7), Hera, Delphyne, Delphusa, Herois, Sibyl. (8) Apollo was not the name of the earliest champion, who was called Deukalion, Lykos, Lykoros, or Pyrrhos. (9) Later Apollo's predecessor in the champion role was transformed into Apollo's enemy, identified with Achilles' son Pyrrhos-Neoptolemos. (10) Herakles apparently once held the role of champion in Delphic myth, and likewise became an opponent of Apollo, as seen in the myth of the tripod-robbery. (11) The final stage of the Delphic combat myth was the classical myth of chapter i, in which the names Apollo and Python were used; in its main outlines it was the myth that Apollo brought with him from Anatolia, a local version of the Cilician myth of Zeus-Typhon, but it was merged at Delphi with the variants already on the ground.

Once these conclusions were reached, it became possible to say something about the early cult history of Delphi. In brief, we concluded that the Corycian Cave on Parnassos was so named because it was once considered to be the lair of Python-Typhon and Delphyne, the counterpart of the Corycian Cave of Cilicia which housed Typhon and Echidna-Delphyne. From this conclusion it followed that the scene of combat had once been placed in the neighborhood of the Corycian Cave, namely on the Parnassian plateau in or near the city of Lykoreia. When we discovered from good evidence that the Delphians had lived in Lykoreia before occupying the site of Pytho, it became apparent that Lykoreia was the first Delphi, and the Corycian Cave the first seat of the Delphic oracle. That the Corycian Cave was once an oracular shrine is clear from the conclusion of the Homeric Hymn to Hermes.

In the myths of Ge's and Poseidon's reign at Delphi, and in the myth of Deukalion's flood, which was associated with Parnassos and Lykoreia, and in the annual alternation of Apollo and Dionysos, we caught sight of the cosmic meanings of the combat myth: the primeval watery chaos, the primordial mother who with her progeny warred upon the gods, the conflict of order with disorder.

Finally, since along the way we often noticed that several forms of the combat myth were expressly designated in their own content as *aitia* of cults, rites, and festivals, we examined the hypothesis that they were enacted or symbolised in the rituals to which they were attached, or conversely that the plot of the combat myth was suggested by the rituals. We found that there was little correspondence between important variants of the combat myth and the rituals with which they were associated, and that, in these instances at least, the rites precede the myth, which was initially an independent legend or folktale that was brought into the service of the rites and fitted with an appropriate aetiological conclusion. This kind of myth seemed especially suitable to rites that were meant to check or banish harmful and undesirable phenomena or the powers resident in them.

In myth, if anywhere, we might suppose that we should find black and white, good and evil, clearly distinguished, especially if a myth's central theme is going to be the conflict of a good god against an evil demon. Yet, as in life itself, we find various shades of gray. We have seen myths in which it was hard to distinguish hero from villain; and we have seen the hero of one myth become the villain of another. The enemy is a spirit of both death and fertility; the champion sends both blessings and death upon men. In fact the role appears to be determined by the nature of the god rather than by his good or bad character. It is a heavenly god, in particular a sky god and ruler god, who becomes the champion. It is possible to run through the whole list of themes and show that the champion is the duplicate of his opponent. I shall confine myself mainly to the Greek combat myths in doing so.

1A and 1B: Zeus was son of Kronos and Rhea, grandson of Ge and Uranos. Apollo and Herakles were his sons. 1C: Zeus's mate was Hera, Typhon's mother, or Ge, also his mother, or Lamia, the dragoness herself. Herakles mated with several ogre's daughters or wives. Notice Apollo's affairs with Koronis and Sibyl.

2B: Zeus occupied the Corycian Cave of Cilicia. Apollo was probably worshipped at the Corycian Cave of Parnassos. Herakles passed a winter in a Scythian cave. 2D: Apollo controlled the three springs of Delphi, Zeus that of the Cilician cave and the heavenly springs of rain. Herakles was frequently worshipped at springs. 2E: Zeus is the supreme ruler of the sea; and in fact Poseidon may be considered to be Zeus as lord of the sea: for just as we find a Zeus Chthonios who is Hades, so we hear of Zeus Enalios and Zeus Thalassios. For Apollo as a maritime deity see the Homeric Hymn to Apollo.[2]

3B: We have seen Zeus as bull or snake; Apollo as snake or hawk or wolf. Herakles' lion nature may be seen in the lionskin that covered him and the lion's head which served as a hood for his own. 3C: Here we must turn to Indra, who had four arms, and to Marduk, who had two faces. The Greeks, who rejected heavenly monstrosities, assigned extra limbs to Zeus's helpers, the hundred-handed giants. 3D: Zeus's lightning was quite as effective as any fire that a dragon breathed. Also the very sight of him

---

[2] 2B: Notice that Apollo had a cave on the side of the Athenian acropolis: Paus. 1.28.4; see also Agora Inv. I 5517, a copy of which B. D. Meritt very kindly sent me. 2D: See Croon (1952). 2E: Zeus Enalios, etc.: Aesch. *ap*. Paus. 2.24.4; LM 6.624; Apollo: Hom. Hymn 3.391–441. Since the evidence for most points that follow has often been referred to in this work, few citations and cross-references are needed. Also I adduce only enough evidence to make the point; for most of the topics much more could be invoked.

brought death to Semele, and could kill anyone. 3E: Notice Zeus's numerous changes of shape in the pursuit of his amours. Apollo had the same habit (p. 57). 3F: I have mentioned Zeus Chthonios. Herakles received worship as a hero, i.e., as a chthonian power. 3G: The first Apollo to meet us in Greek literature is the Apollo of the Iliad, and his first action is to send his plague-bearing arrows through the Achaean camp. This is his principal character throughout the epic: he is Apollo the destroyer, a veritable plague demon. We should notice too that while the Delphic Apollo corresponds to Baal as champion and heavenly god, he rules over Mot's season, the time of summer drought. The reversal is no doubt due to the difference in physical conditions between Canaan and Delphi; yet the destroying Apollo should not be forgotten. Zeus was the sender of the flood, which could be personified as a dragon (p. 348). See 6A below.[3]

4A: An omnipotent god is ultimately responsible for sending death to everyone: it is Zeus's will that is done. Apart from that consideration Greek mythology has many instances of Zeus's and Apollo's injustice to mortal men. I have mentioned the violent and savage Herakles who killed Iphitos, Eunomos, and Megara's children, who robbed men of their cattle, and who carried off Apollo's tripod and Artemis' hind. 4B: Zeus's tyranny is manifest in his treatment of Prometheus. Apollo and Zeus-Ammon directed men to offer human tribute to monsters. 4C: Zeus (in eagle form too) carried off Ganymedes. See 4A above and 4E below. 4D: I need mention only Herakles' appetite. 4E: Zeus's lechery is the scandal of Greek mythology. 4F: We see Apollo as the guardian of his shrine, fighting and destroying the enemies and robbers who came his way: Krios' son, Phlegyans, Lykos, Persians, Gauls. Python did no differently as Ge's warder. Phorbas may have guarded the way to the Parnassian shrine from Panopeus in the days when Lapiths and Dryopians held the region; when the latter were driven out he became the brigand blockader of the road. 4G: Herakles dammed rivers and drained swamps (p. 343), but his work was looked upon as benevolent rather than as a with-

---

[3] 3C: Hackin AM 109, fig. 5; *Enuma elish* I 95–98. Animal forms are frequent among oriental gods: for Horos see p. 179. 3D: Apollod. 3.4.3; Ovid *Met.* 3.308 f.

holding of the waters. The meaning of this work depends upon the role in which the doer is cast.[4]

5A: Zeus was as much a usurper as Typhon wanted to be, and more successful. Apollo took Delphi from its former owners. 5B: Rhea preserved Zeus from being swallowed by Kronos; then Ge took the infant god and carried him to safety; later she advised him how to overthrow Kronos and defeat the Titans. So Ge reared Zeus against Kronos, as Typhon against Zeus.[5]

6A: Zeus and Typhon are equally the senders of storms. In general destructive and violent storms, hurricanes, and the like were attributed to the enemy, the beneficent rains and winds to the champion. Yet Zeus sent bad storms, when he wished, as well as good. Above all, he sent the storm that caused the flood. 6B: Typhon started his war on heaven soon after his birth.

7B: Nonnos tells of the numerous missiles that Typhon hurled against Zeus.[6]

8A is the reverse of 7A. 8B: Python lost his teeth of oracular power, which were placed in the tripod basin. Notice too his hide upon the omphalos (fig. 27). Acheloos lost his wonderful horn to Herakles. The Gorgon lost her deadly head to Perseus and Zeus. 8c and 8d are counterparts of 9, and the Venusberg theme is the counterpart of the Judith theme. 8E: The Gorgon sisters lamented Medusa (p. 303); and notice that dirge called the Lityerses song.

10A and 10B are counterparts of what the dragon did in his time of victory. 10D: Funeral rites were established for Python, heroic honors for Tityos. But I can recall no instance of the dragon's undergoing purification (10c); yet his crimes are expiated in his punishment (10A).

All themes not mentioned above are exactly the same for the champion and his partisans as for the enemy and his.

We might say that all gods are alike: they can work both good and harm; they can suffer and die. So it is easy to see how a reversal of roles might occur. A god's rank and province may

---

[4] 4A: Eunomos: Apollod. 2.7.6. 4c: *ibid.* 2.5.9, 3.12.2.

[5] Ge and Zeus: Hes. *Theog.* 477–484, 624–626; Apollod. 1.2.1.

[6] Nonn. *Dion.* 2.403–411, 439–474.

change: if the heavenly ruler-god becomes associated with the earth and fertility, if he becomes a dying god, or if he becomes demoted, so to speak, before some new god of invaders, then he may cross over to the divine opposition. But there need be no corresponding change in his behavior: there is only a shift of emphasis to his evil deeds. In any case, it becomes apparent that both creative and destructive forces are mingled on both sides of the divine combat. So myth is nearer to reality in this respect than that sort of partisanship in life or that sort of melodrama in literature which pits pure good on one side against pure evil on the other.

In general the hero-god champions the forces of creation, life, activity, and order. For creation is an active, life-asserting process that gives shape and form to unordered material. Life requires order, which means putting a limit upon action in certain directions. But an order that resists all change and further creative activity denies life and turns into its opposite: it becomes a state of inactivity and death. The dragon enemy champions the forces of chaos, destruction, inaction, and death. For the kind of activity that turns solely to disorder and destruction destroys life along with order, and so returns to chaos and death. This is only to say that both life forces and death forces are necessary in a properly balanced individual and world.

Zeus had another helper against Typhon: Eros, whose arrow put Typhon into the mood to be charmed by Kadmos' music. So says Nonnos, and we need not think that the episode is entirely his own fantasy. For in saying that Eros entered into and changed the savage heart of the chaos demon, Nonnos is saying once more what Hesiod had said in other words, that first of all Chaos was born, and then appeared Earth and Eros. Eros fertilised the lifeless mass of Chaos and infused it with love and life. He personifies the principle that the divine champion upholds. He does not appear as champion in his own person, though now and again we have caught sight of him: Typhon pursued him and his mother to destroy him, but they saved themselves in the waters of river or sea (p. 190). There he corresponds nearly to Apollo, when Python chased his mother, and mother and son were saved in the waters of the Aegean Sea. Again we noticed Eros hovering about

Perseus and Andromeda, when Ketos was fought and killed (fig. 25).[7]

So we may look upon the whole combat in all its forms as the conflict between Eros and Thanatos. It is that opposition between life instincts and death instincts that Freud was the first to formulate, albeit tentatively, as the central principle of all living organisms from the beginning; though it was seen dimly and expressed in dramatic or metaphysical terms by poets and philosophers before him. But in life the two kinds of instincts, though opposed, are always mingled. Thus do the fantasies of myth disguise the fundamental truths of the human spirit.[8]

---

[7] Nonn. *Dion.* 1.398–407. Notice the mating of Eros with Chaos mentioned by Aristophanes (p. 222).

[8] Freud BPP 54–79.

APPENDICES

APPENDIX 1

CHARON AND THE STEERSMAN OF ARGO

We have noticed Phorbas' skull-adorned dwelling place and his hideous visage, and can scarcely doubt that he is an underworld demon, a form of Thanatos. So it is especially noteworthy, in view of the identity of Phorbas with Phlegyas (p. 26), that Phlegyas appears in Dante's *Inferno* as ferryman of the dead over Styx into the fifth circle:

> Com' io vidi una nave piccioletta
> Venir per l'acqua verso noi in quella,
>   Sotto il governo d'un sol galeoto,
>   Che gridava: "Or se' giunta, anima fella?"
> "Flegiàs, Flegiàs, tu gridi a voto,"
>   Disse lo mio signore, "a questa volta.
>   Più non ci avrai che sol passando il loto." (8.15–21)

Havet thinks that Dante mistook the Phlegyas of *Aeneid* 6.618–620, companion in punishment of Ixion, Peirithoos, and Theseus, for a demon. But Dante, who knew the *Aeneid* thoroughly, surely realised that Virgil meant Phlegyas to be a condemned sinner. Furthermore Dante knew Statius' *Thebaid* well, where in a passage (1.712–715), which is certainly based on Virgil's text, Phlegyas is unmistakably a sinner undergoing punishment. So Dante either invented a role for Phlegyas or drew his character as infernal boatman from another source than Virgil's *Aeneid*. If he was inventing, why did he choose Phlegyas for his Stygian boatman? He had already used Charon for ferryman on Acheron, the first river, and since he needed another boatman for Styx he must have thought that Phlegyas suited the post. We have seen that Phlegyas did: after an intensive study of the ancient sources and cognate figures Phlegyas' demonic nature has been revealed. But could Dante have been so well acquainted with these sources, particularly with those written in Greek? If he did not invent this role for Phlegyas, then he must have had access to a source in which Phlegyas was plainly said to be a Stygian boatman. Living when he did, Dante may have known some ancient work that disappeared in the course of the next two centuries.[1]

Havet's argument implies that Phlegyas could not be both a punished sinner and an infernal demon. We need look no further than Christian folklore (whatever doctrine might say) to realise that dead sinners may be devils. Not only Phlegyas but the other stock sinners— Ixion, Sisyphos, Tantalos, Tityos—have both characters at once; the *daimôn* is not easily distinguished from the *hérôs*, the powerful, often malignant, ghost of a supposedly once mortal man. But whereas Christian folklore transforms sinners into devils, Tityos and Phlegyas show that in Greek folklore the sinners were demons to begin with, at home in Hades' realm, whence they ascended to invade man's domain and do evil; then after a champion had defeated and "killed" them, they returned to their place of origin. Heroic legend transformed the defeated demon who returned into a bad man who was killed, and his infernal abode into a place of punishment. Tityos lies outstretched over nine acres on Hades' floor, his body torn by vultures: originally the nine acres were his couch and the vultures were his servants. Phlegyas lies in an underworld cave, reclining at a feast which he cannot touch: originally the cave was his habitation, in which he enjoyed the feast (see p. 65, note 69).

The infernal boatman is a powerful demon who may in folklore become the lord of death himself. In modern Greece Charon, as Charos or Charondas, has subsumed the characters and functions of Thanatos, Hades, and Hermes Psychopompos. The name of Typhon too appears to have been attached to the ferryman of the dead. I refer to Tiphys, whom we meet in Greek legend as steersman of the *Argo*. His name obviously resembles Typhon's; and though similarity of name alone would hardly justify my linking them together, Hyginus in two places calls him son of Phorbas. Since elsewhere he is called son of Hagnias or Hagnios, it has been argued that an error has en-

---

[1] Havet (1888) 171 f. See p. 65, note 69, on Havet's position concerning *Aen.* 6.616–620.

tered Hyginus' text. Yet Tiphys is also the name of the nightmare demon who is often called Ephialtes, a vampirelike creature, male counterpart of Lamia and Empusa. Usener's identification of demon with steersman can be supported by a study of other steersmen of *Argo*.[2]

One of them was Erginos, who is usually called son of Poseidon and said to come from Miletos; but in the earliest extant allusion to him the poet Pindar calls him son of Klymenos. The Apollonian Scholiast agrees with Pindar and adds Buzyge as his mother, and Hyginus refers to anonymous authorities who called him son of Periklymenos from Orchomenos. They therefore identify him with Erginos, king of Orchomenos and enemy of Herakles (p. 42). Klymenos and Periklymenos are epithets of Hades. Significant is Erginos' white hair: he was a man strong and valiant, but with the appearance of old age upon him. Hades is often portrayed with white hair, and his might is great. Charon is an old man. According to Apollonios, though Erginos volunteered to take the helm after Tiphys' death, the Argonauts chose Ankaios. Herodoros, however, said that it was Erginos who steered after Tiphys' death, and Valerius Flaccus agrees with him, introducing a competition for the post among Ankaios, Erginos, and Nauplios, just as Apollonios does; in Valerius' version the Argonauts chose Erginos, a skilled helmsman.[3]

When Ankaios took the helm, according to Apollonios, he sailed down the Acheron River to the sea. He was, like Erginos, a son of Poseidon; his brothers, sons of Astypalaia, were named Eurypylos and Periklymenos; both names may be epithets of Hades. Besides

---

[2] On Charos see Waser (1898), Lawson (1910) 98–117, Heinemann (1913) 48 f., and the folk poem in Legrand (1899) 7. Tiphys Phorbas' son: Hyg. *Fab.* 14.9´ and 18. Hagnias' son: Apollon. *Arg.* 1.105, 560, 1296; Apollod. 1.9.16. Hagnias, i.e., sacred (tabooed) man, might well be the name of an underworld spirit. Hades is called Zeus Chthonios Hagnos, Orph. Hymn 41.7; ἱερώτατος, *ibid.* 18.17; and see Aesch. *Pers.* 628, χθόνιοι δαίμονες ἀγνοί. On possible error in Hyginus' text and against identification of demon with steersman see LM 5.974, 978 f., 981. For the identification see Usener (1899) 258. Tiphys as demon: Didymos *ap.* Schol. Vet. *in* Aristoph. *Vesp.* 1038; Hesych. T1007; Phot. *Lex.* 2.217 Nab. On Ephialtes see p. 329, note 12. See Laistner (1889), Roscher (1900), and Jones (1931) on the relation of nightmare phenomena to underworld demons in folklore. For the death spirit as herdsman see Croon (1952).

[3] Erginos: Pind. *Ol.* 4.23–31; Apollon. *Arg.* 1.185–187 with Schol. Vet. on 1.185; Val Flacc. *Arg.* 1.414–419; Hyg. *Fab.* 14.16. Successor to Tiphys: Apollon. *Arg.* 2.896–898; Herodoros 55, 1.226 J; Val. Flacc. *Arg.* 5.63–72. Klymenos: Paus. 2.35.9 f.; Lasos *ap.* Ath. 14.624E; Hesych. Π1736; other citations in LM 2.1228. For Hades with white hair see Schauenburg (1953) 51, 60, and his figs. 1, 6. Associated with Klymenos in Hermione was his sister Chthonia, a goddess behind whose temple there were three places called Klymenos' (place), Pluto's, and the Acherusian mere. In Klymenos' place was a chasm through which Herakles brought Kerberos up from the world below: Paus. *loc. cit.*

Erginos' father and Ankaios' brother there was also an Argonaut
Periklymenos, Neleus' son and Poseidon's grandson, the opponent of
Herakles at Pylos; his original identity with Hades or Thanatos is
discussed in chapter xii.[4]

Finally, it is noteworthy that Ankaios was killed by a boar, as was
Idmon, seer of the Argonauts. Idmon died among the Mariandynoi,
where at the same time Tiphys fell a victim to sickness. It is a striking
coincidence that steersman and seer of *Argo* died at the same place
and time. Moreover Valerius Flaccus says that Idmon too died from
sickness. It is probable that two or more names were given to the
same Bithynian deity, who was identified with an Argonaut. We know
that this deity had more than one name; for in later times the people
of Herakleia called him Agamestor. And we know that he was a deity
who died each year, was lamented, and then returned from the dead.[5]

Further evidence of a link between Tiphys and Idmon may be seen
in the Dactyl Titias or Titios, son of Zeus and Anchiale. He was worshipped in Herakleia beside Kybele as an indigenous hero (ἥρως
ἐγχώριος). He and his brother Dactyl Kyllenos were called *moirêgetai*,
i.e., guides of *moira*, destiny or doom. His son Priolas (also called
Iollas), killed by the Mysians, or by Amykos in a war with the Bebrykes, was lamented thereafter by the Mariandynoi; and so was another son, Bormos, who either died while hunting, like Idmon, or
disappeared into a spring while drawing water, like Hylas, and was
thereafter lamented at harvesttime by his countrymen. Especially
significant is the story that Titias boxed with Herakles at the funeral
games of Priolas and was killed by him. He was another Amykos or
Phorbas, whose role was reduced to contestant in funeral games, just
as happened with Kyknos (p. 30).[6]

---

[4] Ankaios the steersman: Apollon. *Arg.* 2.865–903; Hyg. *Fab.* 14.16, 26, 32, and 18.
Periklymenos: Hes. frag. 14 Rz.; Apollon. *Arg.* 1.156–160; Apollod. 1.9.9; Ovid *Met.*
12.556–572; Hyg. *Fab.* 10.2. On the combat at Pylos see pp. 327–330.

[5] Ankaios killed by boar: Aristot. frag. 571 Rose; Pherek. 36, 1.72 J. The other
Argonaut Ankaios was likewise killed by a boar, the Calydonian: Apollod. 1.8.2; Paus.
8.4.10; Ovid *Met.* 8.391–402; Hyg. *Fab.* 248. According to Pherekydes, it was the Calydonian boar that killed the former. The helmsman was Samian, the other Arcadian. They
were sometimes identified in antiquity: e.g. Apollod. 1.9.16, 23; see LM 1.355, RE 1.2219.
Death of Idmon and Tiphys: Herodoros, *loc. cit.*; Apollon. *Arg.* 2.815–863; Apollod. 1.9.23;
Hyg. *Fab.* 18, 248; Val. Flacc. *Arg.* 5.2 f. Another link between Idmon and other figures
studied may be seen in one of his mother's names, Kyrene: Hyg. *Fab.* 14.11. His father
was Apollo, though Herodoros (44, 1.224 J) says Abas, who was sometimes called son of
Poseidon (Hyg. *Fab.* 157.1). It may be significant that the two deaths occurred in the
kingdom of *Lykos* (Wolf); see pp. 421 f.

[6] Titias: Apollon. *Arg.* 1.1125–1131 with Schol. Vet. on 1.1126, who cites Maiandrios,
Kallistratos (also *ap.* Schol. Vet. *in* Aesch. *Pers.* 938), and Promathidas, and Theophanes;
Schol. Vet. on *Arg.* 2.780; Nymphis 5,3ʙ.330 J. Fight with Herakles: Apollon. *Arg.*

As son of Zeus, as opponent of the divine champion, and as a hero-ised figure who received worship at his tomb, Titias appears to be a variant of Tityos in character as well as in name. His mother Anchiale seems to be a form of Rhea-Kybele, and therefore of the earth goddess; for the mother of the Dactyls, being also called Ide, was therefore the goddess of Mount Ida, i.e., Kybele, often called Idaia or Idaean Mother. The Dactyls were born in the Dictaean Cave where Rhea bore Zeus, and were constant attendants of the Mother Goddess. So, if we may suppose that *Typhôn, Tityos,* and *Tiphys* are forms of the same name (p. 92, note 48), it follows that *Tiphys* and *Titias* are two forms of one name of the Mariandynian hero-demon who died and was lamented. He was also called Idmon, Agamestor, Priolas, and Bormos, and, in neighboring regions of Bithynia and Phrygia, Hylas, Amykos, and Lityerses: an ambiguous figure in folklore, now a lamented vegetation spirit, now a terrible death-dealing demon from the lower world. Each town or region, it seems, had its own name for him; hence the variety that we encounter. Now the steersman Ankaios, killed by a boar, was certainly a similar figure; for the Arcadian Ankaios, his fellow Argonaut, with whom the Samian steersman is originally identical (see note 4), received worship in his homeland.[7]

The third candidate for Tiphys' successor, Nauplios, never actually steered the *Argo,* according to extant sources, but he has legendary fame otherwise as a skilled navigator, and his very name reveals his marine character. He too was a son of Poseidon, or, in some sources, a descendant of Poseidon's son Nauplios. That he too was a spirit of death is shown in his legends. When Katreus, Minos' son, wanted to put his daughters Aërope and Klymene to death, because he feared death from them, or because they had acted wantonly, and when Aleos wanted to kill Auge because he feared death from her unborn son, they delivered their daughters to Nauplios, instructing him to drown them in the sea. He therefore resembles a male Poine or Ker

---

2.780–785 with Schol. Vet. on 2.780. Priolas: Apollon. and Schol. *ibid.;* also Schol. Vet. on 2.758; Poll. 4.55. Bormos: Schol. on Apollon., Nymphis, *locc. cit.;* Poll. 4.54 f. Bormos was also the name of the lament, and so is exactly parallel to Linos and Lityerses. Another brother, Mariandynos (who is sometimes father of Titias), instituted and taught the lament for Priolas (Kallistratos). His name suggests that he is the same dying hero, merely called the *Mariandynian* by neighboring peoples.

Since Herakles fought the Bebrykes under Amykos it is likely that there was once a story of contest between him and Amykos.

[7] Anchiale and Ide: Apollon. *Arg.* 1.1129–1131 with Schol. Vet. on 1.1126, citing Pherek., Hellanikos, Stesimbrotos, Mnaseas, and the *Phoronis.* The name *Iollas (Priolas)* is very like *Iolaos* and probably is the same as *Hylas;* see p. 109 and LM 3.2993. On the worship of Arcadian Ankaios see Schol. Vet. on Apollon. *Arg.* 1.164. Amykos had an *hérôon* in Bithynia: Apollod. *ap.* Schol. Vet. *in* Apollon. *Arg.* 2.159.

who brings death to those who have sinned against their father or who, wittingly or unwittingly, threaten his life; or an Echetos, maimer of men, to whom the undesirable are sent. Again, in revenge for his son Palamedes' death he brought shipwreck and death to many Achaeans as they sailed back from Troy, when he lighted a fire on Mount Kaphereus that lured them to disaster on the rocks of Euboea. This is consistent with Apollodoros' statement that he sailed the sea bringing death to whatever mariners he encountered by firing their ships, a marine counterpart of Phorbas or Kyknos (Th. 4F).[8]

A fourth candidate for steersman, who, according to Theotimos, actually held that post on the *Argo,* though he is more often called *prôreus* (lookout), was Euphemos. He too was a son of Poseidon, who gave him the power to walk upon the water. His mother was Europa, Tityos' daughter. He came from Tainaron, well known for its passage to the lower world. It was he who received a clod of earth from Triton in Libya; and this clod he either cast into the sea or into Hades' entrance at Tainaron, in which variation we again perceive sea and underworld as equivalents. His name, as the original euphemism, may be a designation of Hades or Thanatos, as Eumenides or Semnai Theai of the Erinyes.[9]

Triton, himself son of Poseidon, took the form of Eurypylos, king of Cyrene, also son of Poseidon, when he appeared to Euphemos and guided the *Argo* through the shoals. Or, as Apollonios has it, Triton and Eurypylos are the same. This Eurypylos is also called Eurytos. Eurypylos recurs as name of a brother of Ankaios, son of Poseidon and Astypalaia, who like Ormenos-Amyntor tried to refuse Herakles entrance to his land (Cos) and consequently was killed by him; also as name of a Dryopian prince of Ormenion who was grandson or father of Ormenos, nephew or grandfather of Amyntor. His name, which means

---

[8] Nauplios as son of Poseidon and sea rover: Apollon. *Arg.* 1.133–138; Apollod. 2.1.5; Paus. 2.38.2; Hyg. *Fab.* 14.11, 169.1, 169A.2. Katreus and daughters: Soph. *Aj.* 1295–1297; Eur. *ap.* Schol. Vet. *in* Soph. *Aj.* 1297; Apollod. 3.2. Auge: ps.-Alcid. *Od. in Pal.,* p. 185 St.; Apollod. 2.7.4, 3.9.1; Paus. 8.48.7. Achaeans' shipwreck: Eur. *Hel.* 767, 1126–1131; Apollod. *Epit.* 6.7–11; Hyg. *Fab.* 116, 249. Especially interesting is Nauplios' epithet at Eur. *Hel.* 1128, μονόχκωπος, usually explained as meaning that he went alone to Kaphereus. Charon appears on vase paintings with one oar or pole; see three lekythoi in *Ant. Denk.* 1.23; also LM 1.885: a different tradition from Eur. *Alk.* 252, where Charon's boat has two oars. Also Nauplios is called μακρόβιος at Apollod. 2.1.5: Charon is portrayed as an aged man; furthermore he shares the epithet with Rhodian nymphs (Hesych. M134) and the Ichthyophagoi of Ethiopia (Herod. 3.23), i.e. people who live at the ends of the earth. Echetos: Od. 18.84–87, 115 f.; 21.307–309.

[9] Pind. *Pyth.* 4.20–46 with Scholl. Vett.; Theotimos 2, 3B.426 J; Apollon. *Arg.* 1.179–184, 2.896 f., 4.1562 f., 1731–1758; Hyg. *Fab.* 14.15, 157.3. For euphemistic epithets of Hades cf. Eubuleus (Nic. *Alex.* 14; Hesych. E6736), πρηΰς (Anth. Pal. 7.733.8).

"he whose gates are wide," may well be an epithet of Hades. Eurytos recurs as the name not only of the great enemy of Herakles discussed in chapter ii, but also of two other enemies of Herakles: the son of Aktor or of Poseidon, twin brother of Kteatos, and a son of Hippokoon, killed by Herakles at Sparta; also as the name of a Giant whom Dionysos killed in the Gigantomachy and of the Centaur who provoked the brawl at the wedding feast of Peirithoos. Another Eurytos or Erytos was an Argonaut, son of Hermes, brother of Echion the snake-man.[10]

Argos, builder of the *Argo,* seems to be a mutation of that Argos who appears in legend both as a great Argive hero, a forerunner of Herakles, ridding the land of the cattle-robber Satyros, of Echidna, and of a destructive bull, and as the many-eyed giant, Argos Panoptes, whom Hermes killed. Both were distinguished by a garment of bull's hide, originally from the bull that the hero killed. Argos Panoptes was sometimes called son of Ge; and the shipbuilder's mother Argeia,

---

[10] On Eurypylos-Eurytos of Cyrene see Pind. *Pyth.* 4.20–46 with Scholl. Vett.; Apollon. *Arg.* 4.1551–1622 with Schol. Vet. on 1561, citing Phylarchos. His mother's name was Kelaino (p. 47); his son or brother was Lykaon (p. 30); see Akesandros 1, 3B.423 f. J; Schol. on *Arg., loc. cit.;* p. 43, note 27. Eurypylos of Cos: Apollod. 2.7.1. Eurypylos of Ormenion: Il. 2.734–736; Hyg. *Fab.* 97.6; Achaios, 4.286 M. Epithets of Hades: *eurythemilos* (of wide threshold), Soph. *ap.* PLG II, p. 245; CIG 5973*c; pylartês* (gate-keeper), Il. 8.367, 13.415; cf. epithets that mean "host of many": *polydegmôn,* Hom. Hymn 2.31: 404, 430; *polydektês, ibid.* 2.9; *polyxenos,* Aesch. frag. 228 Nauck². Eurytos-Kteatos, Apollod. 2.7.2. Hippokoon's son: *ibid.* 3.10.5. Giant Eurytos: *ibid.* 1.6.2. Centaur Eurytos: Ovid *Met.* 12.219–240. Argonaut: Pind. *Pyth.* 4.178 f.; Apollon. *Arg.* 1.52; Apollod. 1.9.16; Hyg. *Fab.* 14.3. The Centaur's name also appears in the form *Eurytion* (Od. 21.295–304; Paus. 5.10.8); another Centaur called Eurytion takes the place of Acheloos or Nessos as Herakles' rival for Deianeira: see p. 355. The name recurs in Geryon's herdsman, also killed by Herakles: Apollod. 2.5.10; see pp. 335 f.

Notice Eurypylos of Ormenion as hero in the cult myth of Artemis Triklaria of Patrai (Paus. 7.19). Because the lovers Melanippos and Komaitho, maiden priestess of Artemis, had desecrated Artemis' temple, plague and famine came upon the land. The city appealed to Delphi, whence the Pythia ordered the sacrifice of the lovers to the goddess, and thereafter every year of the most beautiful youth and maiden. The annual sacrifice ended when a foreign king came, carrying with him a foreign *daimon* (as the oracle had predicted): i.e., Eurypylos with a chest containing an image of Dionysos. Here is a faded version of the Sybaris and Alybas-Heros stories: notice the plague upon the land, the Delphic oracle's bidding to sacrifice the loveliest youth and maiden, and the fortunate intervention of a hero from abroad. Notice too the lover's name *Melanippos* "he of the black horse"; also that he had intercourse in a temple with Komaitho. He is a humanised and romanticised version of a death *daimon* like Heros of Temesa, whose victim became his mistress, a bride of Death, within his tomb or temple (p. 103, note 22). The legendary founder of nearby Triteia was called Melanippos, son of Ares and Triteia, Triton's daughter, who was priestess of Athena. The savage Artemis Triklaria, by whose temple ran the Pitiless (Ameilichos) River, must be much the same as Hekate. See Herbillon (1929) 38, 54, on Triklaria as an old, indigenous goddess of waters and fertility. In Eurypylos as hero rather than demon we see the shifting of role that we have noticed elsewhere. Notice that the analogous Eurybatos of the Sybaris myth is son of Euphemos.

as daughter of Ocean and Tethys, wife of Inachos, mother of Pelasgos, and bearing the name of the Argive land, a name that is also an epithet of the great Argive Hera, seems to be a form of Ge (or Hera). Her husband Inachos appears among the several fathers assigned to Argos Panoptes. Argos Panoptes was Hera's servant, and Argos the shipbuilder made an image of Hera (and also an image of the Great Mother). The *Argo* builder therefore seems to be a derivative of the hero-monster. The latter's relation to unworldly powers may be seen in his form of many-eyed dog, as Hipponax represents him. Again, Io called the gadfly (*oistros*) that pursued her, "phantom of earth-born Argos," who had risen from the shades to haunt her.[11]

There is a variant tradition that the builder, and also the helms-man, of the *Argo* was Glaukos, he who became a sea deity, sometimes called Old Man of the Sea (*Halios Gerôn*) along with Proteus and Nereus. According to Porris (Possis) Magnes, he was steering the *Argo* when Jason fought the Tyrrhenians, and he alone remained unwounded in the battle. Then he vanished into the sea, becoming a sea-*daimôn*. His impunity points to invulnerability, a characteristic of *daimones* (who may nevertheless be killed by a god or hero) which suits the immortality that Glaukos acquired in the usual myth either from an herb or from a spring. As a sea deity Glaukos has a fishtail and is accompanied by whales, dolphins, and big fish. He is given a number of fathers, among them Poseidon (Euanthes) and Polybos (Promathidas), who is also a father of Argos the shipbuilder. He loved Skylla and was himself loved by Circe. He is a soothsayer, like *daimones* of both sea and the dead, and especially a prophet of evils: destruction of cattle and crops and the like. He goes about all shores and islands once a year, and often on the shore he laments his immor-tality in Aeolic speech. He thus resembles a wandering spectre (aside from his dialect). He causes storms that wreck ships upon the sea (compare Nauplios above). Especially interesting is the story that

---

[11] Argos the builder: Apollon. *Arg.* 1.18 f., 111 f., 321–325; Hyg. *Fab.* 14.10, 32. Argos Panoptes: Aesch. *Pr.* 677–681; Apollod. 2.1.2 f., citing Pherek., Asklepiades, Kerkops, Akusilaos; Ovid *Met.* 1.622–667; Hyg. *Fab.* 145; Schol. Vet. on Eur. *Phoen.* 1116, citing Pherek., Dionysos, *Cycl.*, and *Aigimios.* Argos Zeus's son: Apollod. 2.1.1; Paus. 2.22.5; Hyg. *Fab.* 124, 145.1 f., 155.1. Arestor's son: (the builder) Apollon. *Arg.* 1.112, 325; (Argos Panoptes) Cycl. *ap.* Schol. *in Od.* 2.120; Pherek. *locc. cit.*; Ovid *Met.* 1.624; Hyg. *Fab.* 145.2. Hera Argeia: Il. 5.908; Hes. *Theog.* 11 f.; Aesch. *Suppl.* 299; Paus. 3.13.8. Mykene as mother of Argos Panoptes must likewise mean Hera, since the great sanctuary of Argive Hera was formerly in the territory of Mycenae. Image of Hera: Demetrios 1, 3в.7 J. Argos as dog: Tzetz. *Exeg. Il.* p. 153 Herm., who cites Hipponax for κυνάγχης as epithet of Hermes. With Argos' bullhide compare Arcadian Ankaios' bearskin: Apollon. *Arg.* 1.168, 2.118–120. Io's *oistros*; Aesch. *Pr.* 566–573.

when he wooed Ariadne, Dionysos fought and overpowered him, and bound him with grapevines (Theolytos), a story that brings him near to Lityerses and Syleus.[12]

Hence every steersman, lookout, builder, seer, and guide of the *Argo* proves to have manifold connections with demonic powers of sea, land, and underworld. It is likely that every one is a form of the boatman of the dead, Charon, who, as I have pointed out, has also a more general character as a spirit of death. So Tiphys the helmsman of the *Argo* springs from Tiphys the nightmare demon, a minion of Hades, and his name is very probably a variant of Typhon. The intimate relation of dragon and ogre to spectres and underworld demons is made evident in chapter vi.[13]

If the *Argo's* pilot is drawn ultimately from the Stygian boatman, then we are justified in agreeing with those scholars who have held that the Argonautic voyage has its roots in tales of voyages to the other world. It belongs to the story type wherein a band of heroes, each possessed of remarkable powers, sails over the sea to the land of the dead, where they meet a demonic being, overcome obstacles, perform difficult tasks, finally defeat the forces of death, and achieve

---

[12] Glaukos: Plat. *Rep.* 611D with Schol. Vet.; Ath. 7.296A–297c, citing Theolytos, Promathidas, Mnaseas, Euanthes, Aristotle, Possis, Nikanor, Alexandros Aitolos, Aischrion, Nicander, Hedylos, and Hedyle; Ovid *Met.* 13.900–14.74; Hyg. *Fab.* 199; Schol. Vet. on Apollon. *Arg.* 1.1310 (Polybos as father); Sid. Ap. *Carm.* 15.132–134; see LM 1.1678–1686. Euboia is mother of Glaukos and wife of Polybos: the name is probably an epithet of Hera; see Euboia, nurse of Hera, and the hill Euboia on whose slopes stood the temple of Argive Hera: see Paus. 2.17.1 f.; Plut. *Mor.* 657E; also Euboia as Phorbas' wife (p. 52). His mother is also named Alkyone (p. 107) as wife of Anthedon (Mnaseas), eponym of Glaukos' birthplace; she was a water nymph as mistress of Poseidon (Euanthes). According to the Platonic Scholiast, his parents were Sisyphos (p. 478) and Merope. But his father was Kopeus (Oarsman) of Anthedon, according to Theolytos. Glaukos taught Apollo the mantic art (Nicander, cf. p. 427); and he had an oracle on Delos in company with the Nereids (Aristotle). For his tour of all shores, laments, and prophecies of misfortune see Platonic Schol.; as sender of storms, Sid. Ap. He is fundamentally the same as Glaukos, Minos' son, who was restored to life by an herb: Apollod. 3.3.1 f. In Nicander's story Glaukos was a hunter and restored a hare to life with an herb before he became a sea deity. In Apollon. *Arg.* 1.1310–1328 his role is limited to giving prophecy to the Argonauts; therein he resembles Idmon and Eurypylos. He threw himself into the sea for love of Melikertes (Hedylos); or he loved Nereus (Nicander). As lover of Skylla he went into her cave (Hedyle). Polybos, Argos' father: Hyg. *Fab.* 14.10.

[13] Among the Argonauts the following should also be noticed: Admetos (p. 325), Atalanta (p. 354), Areios, Argos Phrixos' son, Askalaphos Ares' son, Asterion (p. 314), Augeias (p. 50), Autolykos (p. 432), Echion (p. 311), Eurytion Iros' son, Hylas, Ialmenos Ares' son, Iolaos, Iphitos Eurytos' son (p. 403), Iphitos Naubolos' son, Kepheus (p. 294), Klymenos, Klytios Eurytos' son, Koronos (p. 35), Menoitios (p. 328), Neleus (p. 336), Mopsos, Orpheus, Peirithoos, Periklymenos, Phokos (p. 106), Polyphemos (p. 533). See the lists in Apollon. *Arg.* 1.15–233; Apollod. 1.9.16; Hyg. *Fab.* 14; Val. Flacc. *Arg.* 1.353–483. Mopsos and Orpheus were also seers, whose connection with the realm of death is not far to seek. On the relation of Argonauts to animal helpers see Meuli (1921) 7–15.

their object. And this is but a maritime variant of the story in which the heroes go underground or to the edges of the world on foot.[14] For the *Argo* sails off to the ends of the earth, to a region called simply Land (*Aia*), later identified with Kolchis. Its dread king Aietes (Landman)—son of Perseis, who is Hekate; husband of Hekate herself; brother or father of Circe, whom the Argonauts also visited; father of the witch Medea; keeper of a grove and snake sacred to Ares—is plainly the infernal ruler. And many of the adventures along the way closely resemble stories that have appeared in this study. First of all, notice the Lemnian women who, as women who had killed their husbands, recall Omphale, Empusa (especially in the latter's role as Bride of Corinth [p. 116]), and the Danaides, who killed their bridegrooms and became stock figures of the underworld. The heroes couched with them, like Herakles with Echidna or Pyrene or Kelto (pp. 48 f., 97 f.). This is the Venusberg episode that enters into the myth complex (Th. 8D, p. 257). The Sirens, whom the Argonauts also met, come to much the same thing as the death-dealing mistress. Amykos, king of Bebrykes, has already appeared before us as another Phorbas whom Polydeukes vanquished. He was a son of Poseidon and a nymph. In the grove that surrounds him in Theocritus' idyll are poplars and cypresses, trees which the Greeks associated with the dead. He was fearfully ugly to look upon and voracious (ἀδηφάγος, Theocr. 22.115). In the Phineus episode Meuli sees the *Waldhaus* episode of the Bearson story and of the aforesaid story type. There too the heroes encountered Harpies, who are repeated in the Stymphalian birds of the Island of Ares, i.e., Keres of the island of Death. In fact, just about every episode of the tale can be related to the realm of death and to the underworld adventures of living heroes. The infernal king and queen appear in many guises. To demonstrate this in detail would require another book.[15]

---

[14] Aarne-Thompson (1928) Type 513B; Radermacher (1903) 60–72, (1938) 199–202, 348; Meuli (1921) 1–24, 82–118. See the Bearson story, p. 533 (Aarne-Thompson, Type 301).

[15] For the Argonautic story see Pind. *Pyth.* 4; Apollon. *Arg.*; Diod. 4.40–54; Apollod. 1.9.16–28; Ovid *Met.* 7.1–158; Val. Flacc. *Arg.*; Hyg. *Fab.* 12–25; Orphic *Arg.*; Bacon (1925). Perseis Aietes' mother: Hes. *Theog.* 956 f.; Apollod. 1.9.1. Perseis = Hekate: Apollon. *Arg.* 3.467, 478, 1035; 4.1020. Hekate as Aietes' wife: Dionys. 1, 1.229 J; Diod. 4.45.2 f. Bebrykes have already been met as the people of Pyrene in Spain (p. 48). Amykos: Theocr. 22; Apollon. *Arg.* 2.1–97; Apollod. 1.9.20; Hyg. *Fab.* 17; Val. Flacc. *Arg.* 4.99–343. He was gigantic in size (ὑπέροπλος), fearful to look upon (δεινὸς ἰδεῖν), and inhospitable (Theocr. 22.44–63). The lord of death is from one point of view very hospitable as the final host of all men; from another inhospitable as the challenger of all comers and bringer of suffering and death. Theocritus (22.94) compares Amykos to Tityos; Apollonios compares him to a monstrous son (πέλωρ τέκος) of Typhon or Ge, i.e., a Giant (2.38–40).

The boat of the heroes crosses the waters to the land of death. It may therefore be assimilated to or confused with the infernal boatman's craft which carries the dead across. In fact, since Herakles, Theseus, Peirithoos, and Aeneas (Virg. *Aen.* 6.388–397) crossed alive in Charon's boat, it is evident that heroes may cross to Hades' realm in the public carrier rather than in their own vessel. It is significant that in an Icelandic tale a queen was sent off in a stone boat over the sea by a giantess to a place of darkness where a three-headed giant lived. The giant, who recalls Geryon, and the giantess were the king and queen of the dead, and the boat was the carrier of the dead. In some tales the heroes' purpose is to rescue a maiden whom a demon of death has carried off untimely. The *Totenreich* may lie across the sea, or be an island in the sea, or be the sea itself.[16]

He was invincible until defeated by the divine champion; i.e., he is Thanatos. *Waldhaus:* Meuli (1921) 100–106; see p. 533. Aia: in Akkadian *erṣetu* means both *land* and *underworld* (see Theo Bauer's glossary). In ancient India Yama, god of death, was called lord of earth (see Apte's lexicon under *pṛthivî*). With Aietes compare the Landmaster of Japanese myth, pp. 501–503.

[16] Icelandic tale: Poestion (1884) XXXV, 289–297. The giant's sexual appetite should be noticed (Th. 4ᴇ). On sea as realm of death see Radermacher (1903) 73–75 and (1949), Kroll (1932) 225, Fontenrose (1951) 145; as the road to other world see Waser (1898) 154–157; cf. Böcklin's painting *Die Toteninsel.* Radermacher (1949) 307: Das Meer ist dem Griechen ein dämonisches Element.

APPENDIX 2

JUDITH AND HOLOFERNES

Several times I refer to the Judith theme, a combination of themes 4E, 8D, and 9, in which the heroine lures the enemy to his destruction by dressing herself seductively and leading him to suppose that he will enjoy her favors. It appears most plainly in Paghat's seduction of Yatpan in the Aqhat poem; it recurs in the myths of Ishtar and Hedammu, courtesan and Enkidu, Isis and Set, Astarte and Sea, Çaci and Nahusha (cp. Inanna and Bilulu-Girgire, Ishtar and Ullikummi, Apsarasas and Viçvarupa); it may be seen, though not so plainly, in the Hittite myth of Inaras' banquet for Illuyankas (p. 121); and something like it is seen in Anat's killing of Mot (p. 131). Hence the story of Judith and Holofernes deserves some discussion.

1. It is especially significant that Judith is a widow, mourning for her lost husband, and especially noteworthy that he died in the days of the barley harvest: the sun's heat struck him as he stood by the sheaf binders and he fell on his couch and died (Judith 8.2–6; Ths. 8A, 8E). Furthermore he belonged to the same tribe and clan as Judith; and he bore the name (Manasses, 8.2) of that king of Judah who was taken in chains to Babylon, and whom the Lord delivered after a term of captivity (II Chron. 33.11–13; apocalyptic Prayer of Manasses). He is Tammuz, the dying god, and Judith is his sister-wife Inanna-Ishtar. Notice too that in the time of thirst and famine the Bethulians felt that their god had deserted them (Judith 7.30 f., 8.11).

2. Judith was beautiful to look upon (8.7). She dressed herself in

488

all her finery, cosmetics, and jewels, went to Holofernes' tent, and easily charmed him with her voluptuous appearance (10.3 f., 11.22 f., 12.15 f.); exactly as Paghat or Ishtar arrayed themselves to charm Yatpan or Hedammu (Ths. 4E, 8D).

3. Judith sat at Holofernes' table; like Yatpan he drank far too much wine (12.10–13.2). In most of the stories mentioned above a feast accompanies the heroine's attempt at seduction (Th. 9, *a*, *b*).

4. Holofernes invaded the land with his army and destroyed cities, men, crops, flocks and herds, shrines (2.27, 4.1, 6.4; Ths. 4A, 4D). His hosts attacked the youth especially, destroyed babes, and ravished maidens (2.27, 16.4; Ths. 4C, 4E). They brought fire upon the land (16.4; Th. 3D).

5. Holofernes seized the spring which was Bethulia's only water-supply, and so brought thirst as well as famine upon the people (7, 8.9, 11.12 f.; Ths. 2D, 4G). As withholder of the waters he is like Vritra (Th. 2E); as holder of a spring, like Python and St. George's dragon (p. 517). The Assyrian host were so numerous that they stopped up rivers (Th. 4G) and covered the hills with their horse (compare Python covering Parnassos, p. 80; Th. 3A).

6. He wanted to destroy all the gods of conquered peoples, who must worship Nebuchadnezzar only (3.8, 4.1, 6.2): an historicised variant of the enemy's wish to overthrow the gods and rule the world (Ths. 5A, 4B). In his sovereign one can recognise the enemy's father (Th. 1B).

7. Judith hoodwinked him much as Paghat deceived Yatpan. She pretended that she had deserted the Hebrews and would betray them to him (11.11–19, 22 f.), as Paghat pretended that she had enemies against whom Yatpan could serve her (Th. 9, *c*). When Holofernes was drunk and off guard, and she was alone with him, she killed him with a sword (13.6–9), the probable conclusion of the Paghat-Yatpan episode (Ths. 7A, 7D).

Hence the Judith story appears to be especially close to the Aqhat myth of a nearby Canaanite people (Th. 2A; notice also proximity to the locale of myths of pp. 209–216 and to Joppa [p. 276] and Lydda [p. 516]). The following similarities to combat myths in general should also be noticed. (*a*) The appeasement theme can be seen in the coastal cities' submission to Holofernes (3.1–7; Th. 7C). (*b*) Achior, like Zeus, was bound and placed under a mountain (6.13; Th. 8A). (*c*) Holofernes' tent (Th. 2B) was located in a deep valley or ravine (*aulón*, 10.10 f.), and it was night when Judith went there and when she killed him (8.33; 10.22; 11.3, 5; 13.1, 13 f., so that behind the story we may see a descent to the death-realm (Th. 3F). In that ravine at the foot of the mountain rose the spring that brought water to the Bethulians above (compare p. 228). (d) Holofernes' head, which Judith cut off (Th. 10A), is a potent object like Medusa's; the enemy host's power resided in it. After the Hebrews set it upon their battlements, they won victory and power, which vanished utterly from the Assyrians (14.1–6, 11.15–19, 15.1). (e) Gigantomachy is reflected in the battles between Hebrews and Holofernes' host (Th. 7G). The enemy was completely routed (15.1–7; Th. 7A). (f) The Hebrews rejoiced greatly and celebrated their victory; they praised Judith, who also sang a victory song (13.14, 17–20; 14.7, 9; 15.8–10, 12–14; 16.1–17; Th. 10B). (g) Judith and the people purified themselves (12.7, 16.18; Th. 10c). Altogether 26 themes of the combat myth can be seen, many of them humanised, in the tale of Judith and Holofernes.

APPENDIX 3

COMBAT MYTHS OF CHINA, JAPAN, AND AMERICA

I have traced the combat myth in its several forms over an area that extends from India in the east to Italy and Sicily in the west. In Appendix 5 I show that it also travelled northwestwards through Europe to Britain, Scandinavia, and Iceland. That is, it is found throughout the Indo-European and Semitic areas. It would be well to glance briefly at quite different parts of the world, at the Far East and America, to see whether the same pattern of combat myth is also found there. I have neither the space nor the knowledge to go deeply into the myths of these distant lands but I feel that we should give some attention to them, if only to forestall the possible objection that we haven't looked beyond the borders of a circumscribed area.

China.—Everyone has seen pictures of Chinese dragons, lizardlike creatures, often winged, with vaguely bovine heads. It would be irrelevant for me to speculate upon the question whether they were imagined by the Chinese mind on Chinese soil or transmitted in oral tradition from west or south (that was perhaps carried by the original settlers themselves). We are interested here in patterns and themes of myth, and are aware that an imported tale type can attach itself to suitable figures of the native imagination.

The Chinese dragons can be divided into two classes: the native Chinese (i.e., pre-Buddhistic) dragons and the Nagas (p. 208), imported with Buddhism from India. The Chinese dragons are in general benevolent and beneficent deities, who send rain and bring good crops. They also bring thunderstorms, tempests, whirlwinds, and floods. Like Zeus or Baal, they bring both good and bad weather; for the god, we should not forget, can send both good and evil upon mortal men. And at this point we should also realise that dragons and snakes did not have a uniformly bad reputation in Greece and the Near East. Greece too had its benevolent reptilian deities: snakes that were spirits of springs, *genii loci,* embodiments or attributes of heroes or gods, e.g., Asklepios, Athena, Apollo (cf. p. 57), Zeus himself (p. 378).[1]

In the folklore of China, tempests, floods, and the like are caused by battles between dragon hosts, or sometimes by single combats between dragons. In some stories Heaven sends lightning to stop the dragons' battles and thereby causes destruction far and wide on earth. Such, it would seem, are most native Chinese stories of dragon combat, quite different from the combats that we have been studying. When we find a combat between dragon and man, it is quite likely to be the man who is at fault: the first emperor, when sailing over the sea, ordered his men to beat drums so as to frighten the Dragon King, who was, however, attracted by the noise; then on the emperor's orders his men riddled the dragon's body with arrows, and the ocean became red with his blood; that night the emperor dreamed that he wrestled with the Dragon King and lost; a few days later he died.[2]

At first sight there appears to be in Chinese mythology no native pre-Buddhistic tale of combat between divine champion and monster, whether or not attached to cosmogony. But the learning and insight of Henri Maspero have penetrated the thick layers of Euhemerism in the *Shu Ching* and brought to light ancient Chinese myths of the world's beginnings, among them a myth of watery chaos and combat. He found essentially the same story still told among the White Tai of northern Annam, a backward Chinese people, among whom, he believed, folklore of the ancient Chinese culture still survives.[3]

He reconstructs the *Shu Ching's* deluge myth as follows: The earth was covered with water. The Lord of Heaven sent one of his ministers to clear the earth and put it in order. But the minister met such

---

[1] On Chinese dragons see especially Visser (1913) 1–134, Combaz (1945) 172–205; also Harlez (1893) 155–176, E. Smith (1919) 95–101, Werner (1922) 208–224, Granet (1951) 28 f., Hackin AM 276–278. On the snake in Greek religion see Küster (1913).

[2] On the dragon fights see Visser (1913) 45–49, Combaz (1945) 175. Emperor and Dragon King: Hackin AM 277. I might also mention a gigantomachy between the Taoist immortals and the dragons that ended without victory for either side when the combatants were sprinkled with lustral water and lost their magic powers: see Doré (1915) 767–769, Werner (1922) 214–216. This story too contains a Dragon King, who seems to be a Buddhist conception: see Visser 128, Harlez (1893) 158 f.; but this does not mean that a native Chinese story could not be attached to him.

[3] Maspero (1924), especially 47–94.

obstacles that he failed. The Lord then sent another minister down, who succeeded in clearing the earth and making it fit for mankind to live in. This hero-god became the ancestor of the lords of earth and taught men the cultivation of the soil.[4]

Now the obstacles to success were mainly the dragons and other monsters that lived on earth. In the early Chinese myth they had a chief, Kung Kung (whose name resembles that of a cinema monster of the 1930's), who had the body of a snake, the face of a man, red hair, and horns (Ths. 3A, 3B). In the *Shu Ching* he has been transformed into an incompetent Minister of Works, who could not or did not prevent the floods. The Lord sent Kun to do the work; but he failed after nine years of effort. Then the Lord sent Yü, who is sometimes considered to be Kun's son. Yü was successful, and then he punished not only the unfortunate Minister of Works, but also Huan Tau, who had recommended him, and the unsuccessful Kun. The latter two were both confined upon a mountain, while Kung Kung was banished to an island (Th. 10A).[5]

Later Chinese sources of the so-called deluge legend (really, as Maspero shows, a myth of the primeval waters) complement the testimony of the *Shu Ching*. Though the ancient myth has been transformed in all of them, and occasionally Buddhistic details can be seen, some are less euhemerised and show more clearly the early form of the myth.

1. A tortoise and hawk taught Kun to make dikes to hold back the waters. But in doing so he used "living earth" and so brought on himself the Celestial Lord's wrath, who sent Chu Yung, his Minister of Justice, to kill him. Chu Yung killed Kun on Mount Yü and let the corpse lie there uncorrupted for three years. Then he cleft it open and Yü came forth. Kun, taking fish form, leaped into the Yellow River. Then the Lord told Yü to set the world in order. Yü vanquished clouds and rain on Rain-Cloud Mountain (Th. 3G). It is important to notice that thereupon he did not try to dam the waters, but worked hard at breaking through mountains and making canals to run them off.[6]

2. The monstrous Kung Kung ruled the earth (Th. 5A). Chu Yung was sent to fight him, but failed (Th. 8A). Then Chuan Hsü, sometimes called Chu Yung's son (Th. 7E), fought and defeated Kung Kung, who fled (Th. 7F). In his flight the monster broke the north-

---

[4] *Ibid.* 65.

[5] *Shu Ching* 1.3, 2.1.3 (Legge 1879: 34–36, 41). See Maspero (1924) 54, 59, 85–94. On Yü as Kun's son see Legge 35, note 2, and paragraph 1 below.

[6] Maspero (1924) 48–51. See *Shu Ching* 2.4.1 (Legge 1879: 57).

west column of heaven with his horns, displacing sun, moon, and stars (Th. 4A), and causing a flood on earth.[7]

3. To the preceding story is often joined the myth of Nü Kua, creatress of mankind, a goddess (but occasionally called a god), who is sometimes described as a snake with human or bovine head. She put the world in order at a time when the four columns of heaven were broken, fire burned and water flowed everywhere without cease, and wild beasts and birds preyed upon the people (Th. 4D; in the Tai myth it is rats and birds that cause trouble); in particular birds of prey carried off infants (Th. 4C) and the aged. Besides propping up the cardinal points she killed a black dragon and checked the floods (Th. 7D).[8]

4. Ch'ih Yu was a monster that had eight fingers, eight toes, and a bristly head—apparently a river god, since he came forth from the Siang River (Th. 2E). He pursued the Yellow Emperor, who finally made a stand against him with an army of bears, tigers, panthers, and other beasts. Finally the emperor sent a winged dragon, Ying Lung, against him. Ying Lung gathered the waters againgst Ch'ih Yu, who in turn got wind and rain from Fung Po, a Chinese Aiolos, and so the earth was flooded. Then the Yellow Emperor sent his daughter to stop the rain. After she had done so, Ying Lung pursued (Th. 7F) and killed Ch'ih Yu.[9]

This Chinese myth has obvious resemblances to Indian and Babylonian myths. We see the world in disorder and the earth covered with water; a fearful monster presides over the water and disorder; he is vanquished by a god who proceeds to put the earth in order. A difference can be seen in the preëxistent Lord of Heaven, to whose world the dragon enemy and floods come as an interruption. But the myth is thus told in western variants too (e.g., Labbu, Zu, Typhon); and the emperor plays the role of his Mesopotamian counterpart An or Anu in that he takes measures against the water demon and finds a champion to fight him. Probably the Chinese, like the Hebrews, shaped the myth in accordance with newer religious ideas. It was Confucianism that euhemerised Chinese mythology, as in the *Shu Ching*, and raised the Lord of Heaven to a position in which he could not be considered a grandson of the chaos dragon. As a corollary the world no longer begins in a watery chaos: the waters cover the earth only.

---

[7] Maspero (1924) 54 f., Werner (1922) 81 f.; see Eberhard (1937) p. 111.

[8] Maspero (1924) 52–54, Werner *loc. cit.*; see Eberhard (1937) pp. 111, 115.

[9] Maspero (1924) 55–58. On Fung Po see Doré (1915) 699.

But the hero is sent to free the earth from them, i.e., to separate the earth from the waters, and to make of earth a habitation for mankind. The dragon and the dragon's hosts resist his efforts. From one point of view he sets a barrier to the waters; from another he makes the confined waters flow; so that Yü in running the waters off from the earth looks very much like Indra freeing the waters. Exactly the same two aspects of controlling the waters appear to be present in the myth of Ninurta against Asag (p. 220).

The myth combines dragon and displaced god, much as in the Mesopotamian, Egyptian, Hurrian, and Greek myths. Yü succeeds Kun and kills him. Huan Tau is Kung Kung's backer. The displaced god is confused with the dragon, as elsewhere (p. 240): Kun becomes a fish-bodied spirit of the Yellow River, while the monstrous Ch'ih Yu, river god of the Siang, is sometimes a rebel against the emperor-god Huang Ti.

There is gigantomachy (Th. 7G): the enemy hosts are either beasts, birds, and reptiles, or rainstorms, clouds, and winds. But the champion's army in the Ying-Lung variant is made up of bears, panthers, and other beasts. In this perhaps we have an echo of Hanumat and his army of bears and monkeys (p. 207). But Yü took the form of a bear while he labored to clear the earth of water (see p. 493, note 6). And in the last two legends listed above (3 and 4), the hero and heroine are themselves dragons, a feature that seems to link this cosmogonic myth to the Chinese tales of combats between dragons that were mentioned earlier.[10]

The same two legends also show the goddess-helper. Nü Kua as creatress of mankind seems to be an old mother goddess; and like Anat she killed the enemy herself. The Princess Pa, the Yellow Emperor's daughter, on the other hand, is a goddess of aridity. But the early myth has no Tiamat and no dragoness, so far as one can judge from the sources. Her absence, however, may be due to the Confucian alterations noticed above. For when the Lord of Heaven was put first in the cosmogony, the conception of chaos and the chaos demons was bound to change. Yet in the *yang*, the active male principle, and the *yin*, the passive female principle, the origin of all creatures, we can see a philosophic reflection of the primeval couple who were at once

---

[10] A narrow line divides hero and dragon in Chinese myths as in some others (p. 174). According to one story, Ying Lung could not go back to heaven after killing Ch'ih Yu, but had to live underground. So he drew the waters after him and caused drought on earth; see Harlez (1893) 162. That is, the dragon killer, himself a good dragon, becomes Vritra, the evil dragon, who withholds the waters.

spirits of death and of fertility. And we find the dragoness in a later variant of the tale, the legend of Yi.[11]

In the failure of the first god who went out against the enemy we see a striking similarity to Mesopotamian myths: Kun has the same relation to Yü as Ea and Enlil to Marduk and Ninurta. We also find that the enemy's corpse is exposed upon a mountain, a feature that not only recalls the placing of Typhon under a mountain, but more exactly the exposure of Python's corpse on the slope of Parnassos (p. 64).

If we ask now whether this myth is a variant of the Python-Typhon type, I would answer that it is. There is no serious obstacle to believing that the myth travelled quite early from Mesopotamia or India to China. But if the Chinese myth is a spontaneous growth, the coincidence is remarkable.[12]

The legend of the divine archer Shên Yi is a later and elaborated form of the early Chinese myth, influenced perhaps by Indic variants that had come to China with Buddhism. In it can be seen themes that are lacking in the early myth. Yi takes the place of Yü or Chuan Hsü (in fact, Yi is made a helper of Yü in some versions of the Yü legend). In a time when floods covered the land, terrible storms destroyed houses and trees everywhere, and the heat of ten suns oppressed the world, a snake that was a thousand feet long had his lair beside Tung-T'ing Lake, where he caught and ate men; and gigantic wild boars devastated the land. Then Yao, emperor-god, sent Yi forth with three hundred men to rid the land of these monsters. In the combats that followed, Yi not only defeated and killed the snake and boars, but also overcame the lord of the winds Fung Po. The latter, often represented as an old man with a sack, takes the form of a winged dragon, sometimes described as having a stag's body, bird's head with horns,

---

[11] *Yang* and *yin;* Harlez (1893) 25, Werner (1922) 76, Hackin AM 271, Granet (1951) 29. According to Granet, *yang* encounters *yin* in the combats and matings of dragons that folklore attaches to the rain-making rituals. Shui Mu Niang-Niang, the Old Mother of the Waters of later Chinese mythology, is very like Tiamat; but she appears to be of Buddhist origin, and her opponents are Sun Hou Tzŭ and Kuan Yin P'u Sa, Chinese forms of Hanumat and Avalokiteçvara. The story uses the theme of tricking the enemy with subversive food (Th. 9, *a*): Kuan Yin, taking the form of a huckster woman, sold Shui Mu vermicelli that became chains within her. See Doré (1915) 796–798, Werner (1922) 220–222 (who translates Doré); Harlez (1893) 193–206; Hackin AM 352–358. Notice also the Mother of the Winds who fought the archer Yi (see note 13), and Shih Chi Niang-Niang, who opposed No Cha and Tai Yi (see p. 498, note 16).

[12] It contains more or less clearly Ths. 2B (see the Tai variant, Maspero 1924: 60 f.), 2E, 3A, 3B, 3C, 3D (see Nü-Kua variant), 3E, 3G, 4A, 4C, 4D, 5A, 6A (the Celestial Emperor), 6B, 7A, 7D, 7E, 7F, 7G, 8A (first opponent's defeat), 10A; perhaps others might be seen by someone who has command of all the sources.

and a snake's tail. He supported the rebel Ch'ih Yu: this is the alliance of the Ying Lung legend (see 4 above). In a euhemerised dress he is a wicked minister of the Shang tyrant Chou Wang, whom the founder of the Chou dynasty overthrew. But in his encounter with Yi he called himself Mother of the Winds, an epithet which suggests that the Chinese chaos demon once had his mate. Still another opponent of Yi was the river-god Ho Po. That he is another form of a single dragon enemy is indicated by Yi's striking both Ho Po and the Tung-T'ing snake in the left eye with his arrows. It is just here that the dragoness enters the tale along with the instrument of potency. Yi spared Hêng Ô, sister of Ho Po (Th. 1c), and made her his wife (Th. 8D). After this he got a magic pill, which could give him immortality and the power of flight, from the mother goddess Hsi Wang Mu (or Chin Mu), queen of the West and of the Immortals, to whose mountain Yi made a journey, whose attendant monsters and giant birds attacked him unsuccessfully, who entertained him, and for whom he built a luxurious palace (Ths. 1A, 8D). Hêng Ô stole Yi's pill from him (Th. 8B) and flew away to the moon. She became the moon goddess and Yi the sun god. Hsi Wang Mu and Hêng Ô are both identified with the *yin* principle.[13]

In Fung Po or Fei Lien, as he is also called, we see a Chinese version of the stormbird Zu-Garuda. Lei Kung, god of thunder, is another: he has the wings of a bat; head of a monkey; horns, beak, and talons of an eagle or owl; and a blue-black body. Like Zu-Garuda he has both good and bad traits.[14]

Li Ping, like Yü, broke through mountains to give a passage to the waters. He (or his son Erh Lang or another) is the hero of a widespread folktale that appears to be a variant of subtype IV (p. 265). A river-god demanded one or two maidens every year (Ths. 4B, 4c) and sent floods if they were not delivered to him. When Li Ping's daughter was to be sacrificed to him, Li went down into the river himself and fought the river-god, who had the shape either of a bull or of a snake. The hero took the enemy's form to fight him, as in the combat of Horos with Set (p. 179), and succeeded in defeating him, thus putting an end to the forced marriages and the floods. As in versions of the Euthymos-Heros tale (p. 103), the maiden sacrifice is

[13] Doré (1915) 489–491; Werner (1922) 136 f., 180–188, 204 f.; Harlez (1893) 78; Maspero (1924) 16, 82 f.; Hackin AM 272, 381–384. Shi Wang Mu was sometimes represented with tiger's teeth, leopard's tail, and plumes upon her head. The Yi legend shows, in addition to the themes of the Kung-Kung myth (see note 12),Ths. 1A, 1c, 3F, 4B, 8B, 8D.

[14] Doré (1915) 685–695, Werner (1922) 199–202, Hackin AM 274 f.

omitted in some accounts, and the demon sends floods or other misfortunes out of pure ill will.[15]

Once the Buddhists and Buddhist texts had come to China, bringing the Nagas with them, so to speak, the Indic dragon myths became current in Chinese mythology, either being naturalised under Chinese names of participants or influencing native myths. It would be pleasant to recount and study the story of No Cha and his conflict with Lung Wang (Dragon King), with Shih Chi Niang-Niang, the goddess of Skeleton Hill (Th. 3F), and with his father Li Ching; or the story of the Fire-Dragon's encounter with Li Ching and the Princess Lung Chi. But nothing would be gained by lingering over what are really late variants of an imported tale. Both Li Ching and No Cha seem to be forms of Indra. No Cha is a precocious boy, who fought the Dragon King at the age of seven (Th. 6B). Like Indra he is the relentless enemy of all evil demons; and his voice makes the thunder that shakes heaven and earth: he sends forth clouds from his mouth. He died for three years (Th. 8A), and his soul lay upon lotus flowers just before his resurrection (cf. p. 198). His magic bracelet is the "Horizon of Heaven and Earth," and he loses it (Th. 8B) along with his magic red garment to the goddess-enemy. His bracelet and Li Ching's pagoda are both thunderweapons; it is characteristic of Chinese stories that a hero throws something into the air which falls upon the enemy's head and destroys him.[16]

---

[15] Doré (1915) 587–590; Eberhard (1937) type 93 (pp. 135–139). The story of Hsi Mên Pao is a rationalised form of the Li Ping tale, standing to it in somewhat the same relation as the Apocryphal Bel and the Dragon stands to the Mesopotamian Labbu myth: that is, priests, witches, or despots deceive the people into making sacrifices to a demon who is either unreal or who doesn't really demand it. See Harlez (1893) 78–80, Werner (1922) 225–227, and especially Eberhard, type 95 (pp. 140–142). On these tales India, through Buddhism, has exerted its influence. See also Eberhard, type 96 (pp. 142 f.), which he calls *Fischgeist;* one variant is the story of Hsü and the alligator-dragon who took human form and married a high official's daughter; see Werner 273 f. It is noteworthy that the demon may be fish, reptile, or boar. See also Eberhard, types 98 (pp. 144–146), the hero who kills a man-eating dragon that demands one or two victims yearly, and 113 (pp. 171 f.), in which a ghost or walking corpse that hunts men at night is killed. In a variant of type 93 it is a jealous woman who becomes a river spirit and drowns those who cross her stream: she is certainly a Chinese Lamia. This class of tales shows Ths. 3E, 3F, 4A, 4B, 4C, 4D, 4E, 4F, 7C, and 10D (for most variants are origin tales of the founding of some temple or ritual), along with most of the themes listed in notes 12 and 13.

[16] Story of No Cha: *Fêng-shên-yên-i* 12–14 (Grube 1912: 156–195); summary in Werner (1922) 305–319; cf. Harlez (1893) 170 f. Li Ching and Fire-Dragon: *Fêng-shên-yên-i* 64 f. (Grube 603 f.); see Doré (1915) 800, Werner 236 f. Li Ching is identified with two Buddhist deities: *Vaiçramana*, carrier of a banner and stupa, who has become one of the Four Celestial Kings; and *Vajrapâṇi*, the thunderbolt-wielder, whose name is also an epithet of Indra's. It seems that the powers of the thunderbolt that one carries have passed over to the tower that the other carries; see Hackin AM 307–309, Grube 641.

Early and late, therefore, the cosmic combat myth was told in China and took a number of forms, as in other countries.

Japan.—In Japan as in China the earliest records show that dragons were deities of the waters: of fertilising rains, of streams, and also of storms. They have been identified with typhoons, and by extension of ideas have been thought to cause earthquakes. As in China and India dragons from the first have been both beneficent and destructive. Hence when quite early Japan felt the influence of China and later that of India, the native conceptions of dragons merged easily with the imported.[17]

The presence of dragons in a nation's folklore does not necessarily mean that the combat myth is found there too, especially since the latter, if found, need not cast the villain as a dragon, but can present him as giant, ogre, or evil demon. Yet considering the influence that Chinese and Indic cultures had upon Japan in folklore as in other respects, we would expect to find myths and folktales of one or another of the four subtypes defined in chapter x; and in fact we find some very interesting variants in the *Kojiki* and *Nihongi*, the best native treasuries of Japanese myth and legend.

But though the pattern is introduced early into the mythical history of the world, we do not find the sort of creation myth that has appeared elsewhere. Chaos was not watery, as the written sources describe it, but a formless mass in which sky and earth, male and female principles (*Yo* and *In*, i.e., *yang* and *yin*), were mixed together. It was very much like Ovid's chaos, and it behaved in the same way: the lighter elements rose up to form the sky, and the heavier sank down to become earth. Thereafter the first gods appeared, sprung from a white cloud, and the generations of the gods began. Chaos is not a person, and no combat of gods against chaotic forms is needed to bring order out of disorder and start the work of creation going. Has an older cosmogony been reworked and rationalised, as the Ovidian parallel might suggest? The *Kojiki* seems primitive and apparently was transmitted orally for a long time before it was written down (early eighth century A.D.). Yet the earth's soil floated about upon the sea at first and had to be consolidated by the creative pair Izanagi and Izanami. Here perhaps is a hint of a watery chaos in a still earlier myth. But there is no hint of combat at this early stage of the world's beginnings.[18]

---

[17] See Visser (1913) 135–230, especially 135–145, 152–178; Combaz (1945) 205–207.

[18] *Kojiki* 1.1–3, *Nihongi* 1.1 f., translated by Florenz (1919) 10–13, 123–126, and Wheeler (1952) 3–6; see also F. H. Davis MLJ 21 f. A possible hint of combat may be

But in the next generation, after the world has been formed, the god Susanowo fought an eight-headed, eight-tailed snake on earth (Ths. 3B, 3C). It is a story very like the legend of Perseus and Andromeda, with features that closely resemble those of other myths that we have seen. This snake was long enough to cover eight hills and valleys (Th. 3A); he bore two mountains on his back; and on his back and heads grew firs and pines. In this description we can see a chaos serpent like Vritra, who was identified with mountains (p. 196). He came every year to take and devour one of the maiden daughters of two old earth deities (Ths. 4B, 4C, 4D), when Susanowo, accompanied by his son, passed that way and saw the parents weeping. On discovering the reason for their tears, he offered to kill the snake on condition that the maid, whose beauty had stirred him, become his wife. The parents readily agreed, and at once Susanowo turned the girl into a comb, which he put in his hair. Then he filled eight tubs with sake, which the snake of course drained on his arrival, and so fell into a drunken sleep (Th. 9, *a*), giving Susanowo the chance to cut his heads off. Cutting open one tail, he found a marvelous sword. According to one source, the snake had stolen this sword from Amaterasu, the sun goddess, Susanowo's sister.[19]

That the snake is a death demon (Th. 3F) is indicated by his demanding the annual sacrifice to him of a beautiful maiden. Also when Susanowo cut his belly in eight pieces, each became a thunder spirit (Th. 3G). Now the thunder spirits lived among the dead, as is clear from the Orpheuslike tale of Izanagi and Izanami. Here is a good example of association of storm with death and darkness.[20]

Moreover it is interesting to see that the hero Susanowo is also a death god. He is an old Shinto ruler of the underworld, identified later with Emma-O, the Buddhist judge of the dead, and with Gozu-Tenwo, warden of the Buddhist sinners' Hell. He is at the same time

---

seen in the spear that the creative pair cast down into the sea and with which they brought up an island to live upon. But this looks more like an Earth-Diver myth. Date of *Kojiki*: Florenz vi, Wheeler xi, Hackin AM 385 (Eliséev). Cf. Ovid *Met.* 1.5–31.

[19] *Kojiki* 1.18, *Nihongi* 1.7 (Florenz 1919: 42–44, 164–170; Wheeler 1952: 33–36); Challaye (1950) 34–40, F. H. Davis MLJ 28–30, Hackin AM 392 f. Present are Ths. 3A, 3B, 3C, 3D, 3F, 4A, 4B, 4C, 4D, 4E, 6A, 7A, 7E, 8B (the sword taken from Amaterasu), 9, 10A, 10B. According to one version the snake took the old earth gods' children as soon as they were born; he was coming to take the most recent arrival, when Susanowo came by. The girl born then grew up to become Susanowo's wife. See *Nihongi* 1.7.2 (Florenz 167 f., Wheeler 35).

[20] *Kojiki* 1.7–9, *Nihongi* 1.3.3–1.4.10 (Florenz 1919: 19–25, 133–144; Wheeler 1952: 11–17); Challaye (1950) 17–25, F. H. Davis MLJ 23 f., Hackin AM 390. Notice the Lamia-like demoness of the underworld, and Izanami herself, who becomes a Japanese Hekate, the great goddess of the underworld; in revenge she strangles a thousand men every day in the land (a rough estimate of the death rate); see Florenz 25, Wheeler 15 f.

a god of the sea, fire, rain, and wind; and on his most pleasant side a god of love and marriage. It is evident, therefore, that he has about the same range as the dragon gods. In the mythology he is more often a violent, destructive, and malignant god than a knightly rescuer of maidens in distress. He illustrates very well the equivocal character that so many principals of the combat myth have shown, whether champions or enemies. It is just such a figure as Susanowo that lies behind the Greek Phorbas.[21]

Susanowo, when appointed to rule the sea (Th. 2E) by his father Izanagi, displayed a fierce temper and malignant disposition. He ruled badly and loved destruction (Ths. 4A, 4B); he brought death upon the young (Th. 4C); and his storming and raging were such as to wither mountain forests and meadows and to dry up rivers and seas (Ths. 3G, 4G). Evil demons gathered about him like buzzing flies. He gave his sister Amaterasu a very bad time, destroying her rice fields and behaving most disgustingly in her palace, so that she was forced to go away and seclude herself in a cave. The world became dark, now that the sun had gone from it. Through incantations and a ruse the gods finally brought her back. Then Susanowo was sent off to rule the lower world (Th. 3F).[22]

As ruler of the dead Susanowo becomes the ogre in a story that can be classed under subtype IV. The hero is Ohokuninushi (Great Land-Master). In the first part of the story he is a Joseph whose eighty brothers plot against him and try to compass his death. On a hunt they heated a stone which they had fashioned into the shape of a boar and rolled down a mountainside for Ohokuninushi to catch. He burned himself severely in doing so and died (Th. 8A), but was revived by two goddesses. In this episode we can see a faded dragon combat: the enemy as boar (Th. 3B), made of stone, fiery (Th. 3D), allied to dissident gods (Th. 7G), kills the hero-god. Again the brothers killed Ohokuninushi by putting him in a cleft tree and taking the wedge out (this is something like Set and the seventy-two getting Osiris into a coffin). But his goddess mother brought him back to life (Th. 7D). His brothers still pursued him, and a great god sent him off to the underworld to get advice from Susanowo. One can conjecture that in an earlier story Ohokuninushi, when killed by his enemies,

---

[21] On Susanowo see Florenz (1919) 29, note 31; Wheeler (1952) 456, note 15. As a fire god and trickster, who falls out with the deities of heaven, he recalls Prometheus and Loki. The relation of the fire-god myth to the dragon myth is a subject that demands study.

[22] *Kojiki* 1.12–17, *Nihongi* 1.5 f. (Florenz 1919: 30–42, 147–164; Wheeler 1952: 21–32); Challaye (1950) 26–33, F. H. Davis MLJ 25–28, Hackin AM 390–392.

went at once to the land of the dead, the house of his greatest enemy
(Th. 8A). When he reached his destination, and Susanowo's daughter
Suseribime, having come out of the house, saw him before the door,
they fell in love and were married at once (Th. 8D). Thereafter she
helped him through the trials that Susanowo put upon him. She gave
him a magic scarf that enabled him to sleep safely in the snake house,
and another for sleeping in the house of centipedes and wasps. Another time she thought that he had been burnt to death and wept for
him (Th. 8E). Finally Susanowo fell asleep as the two were lousing
his hair (the lice were centipedes); then Ohokuninushi quickly tied
his hair to a rafter, blocked the door with a huge rock, and escaped
with his wife, taking along Susanowo's marvelous sword, bow and
arrows, and a magic lute (Th. 9). The lute, striking against a tree,
awakened Susanowo, who pulled the palace down as he started from
his sleep. But Ohokuninushi escaped, receiving Susanowo's blessing in
the end, and returned to destroy his wicked brothers and rule the land
(Th. 5A).[23]

Ohokuninushi, like Susanowo, has the contrary character. Under his
rule the land became disorderly and full of troublesome demons
(Th. 3F). Here perhaps is a reflection of the Chinese Kung-Kung
myth. Amaterasu decided to send a heavenly god to subdue the land
that her son might rule over it. Four gods were sent in turn, who
either shrank before the task or failed to carry it out. One of them,
Amewakahiko, was loved by Land-Master's daughter and tarried on
earth with her, entirely forgetful of his mission, and, like his predecessor, got on well with his earthly host. He even killed the pheasant sent
after him with an arrow from the heavenly bow that his goddess
mother had given him. The arrow, cursed and flung back by the great
sky god, struck the errant god and killed him. Then his wife wept for
him, and his body was carried up to a tomb in the sky. Finally Takemikazuchi went to earth and persuaded Ohokuninushi to abdicate in
favor of Amaterasu's son. Combat is reduced to a test of strength
between Takemikazuchi and a son of the Land-Master and the conquest of the demons that infested the land.[24]

---

[23] *Kojiki* 1.21–23 (see Florenz 1919: 46–51, Wheeler 1952: 41–45). This is plainly a
Giant Killer myth; see Aarne-Thompson (1928) type 300. The myths of Susanowo's
relations with Amaterasu and Ohokuninushi show Ths. 1A, 1B, 1C, 2B, 2C, 2E, 3A, 3B, 3C,
3D, 3F, 3G, 4A, 4B, 4C, 4D, 4E, 4G, 5A, 6B, 7A, 7C, 7D, 7E, 7G, 8A, 8D, 8E, 9, 10A, 10D. In
fact, the three Susanowo tales taken together show a remarkable degree of correspondence
to all the myths of tables 3 to 6.

[24] *Kojiki* 1.30–32, *Nihongi* 2.1 f. (Florenz 1919: 60–69, 176–182; Wheeler 1952: 57–64);
F. H. Davis MLJ 30–32; Hackin AM 394 f.

It is said that Ohokuninushi went to rule over evil spirits and keep them from harm. His realm in the above story could as easily be the underworld as the earth's surface. The relations among Ohokuninushi, his daughter, and Amewakahiko, are the same as those among Susanowo, his daughter, and Ohokuninushi. The younger god steps into the place of the elder. And the *land* is often a euphemism for the realm of the dead (p. 486).

The sending forth of several gods who fail before one succeeds recalls the Mesopotamian myths of Tiamat, Labbu, and Zu. The disappearance of three of these gods in succession after they have gone forth recalls the Hahhimas myth (p. 125). And Amewakahiko, who is very much a Tannhäuser in the Venusberg, is also a Telipinu, in that he leaves the gods for a distant land and refuses to return, and in that birds are sent to summon him. Like Telipinu he is the sort of dying god who combines in himself opposite characters: he is at once the desired lost-god and a malignant deity whose heart has turned against the heavenly gods. But he received a celestial tomb, like Baal's, on the mountain of the gods (p. 130).[25]

So much for the combat as it enters into Japanese myths of the world's earliest days. It is also found several times in legend, as one might expect. Most of these variants are Buddhist creations, or at least strongly influenced by the Buddhist lore that came from India through China or Korea. The Shinto *Nihongi*, however, has a short legend that shows most of the characteristic features of subtype IV (Lityerses): a watersnake held the forks of a river and preyed upon the travellers who passed that way; the hero Agatamori gave the dragon a test to determine whether or not he should spare the dragon's life; the dragon failed and Agatamori killed him and his companions, whom he sought out in a cave at the river bottom.[26]

The familiar themes recur in Buddhist tales. The hero Raiko killed a goblin king, who used to carry off boys and girls to his mountain stronghold, where he and his minions first amused themselves with them and then made a feast on their flesh. Raiko and five companions went to the goblin's palace, got him drunk on sake, and cut off his

---

[25] Among the evil demons in the Land-Master's country were hordes of talking plants, trees, and stones: compare Asag's army (p. 147). To the themes noticed in notes 19 and 23, 7F may be added: the Land-Master's son fled from the hero.

[26] *Nihongi* 11.67 (Florenz 1919: 290 f.; Wheeler 1952: 247); Visser (1913) 138. A rationalised variant, in which the river-spirit is shown by the same test to have no power (see p. 498, note 15) is told in *Nihongi* 11.11 (Florenz 289, Wheeler 233), Visser 138 f. The two stories show Ths. 2B, 2E, 3A, 3B, 3E, 3F, 3G, 4A, 4F, 7A, 9 (and 8A, perhaps, in the hero's going down into the river to meet the dragon).

head, whence fire and smoke poured forth. This goblin's red skin and mop of white hair indicate that he was the Mountain Spider, the form that Raiko's enemy takes in two other stories. In one the spider appears both as an ugly hag and as a beautiful seductress who nearly destroys the hero. Interesting too is the story of the goddess Benten, who offered herself in marriage to a sea dragon in order to keep him from seizing and eating babies. It is very like the tale of Ishtar and Hedammu (p. 175) or of Astarte and Sea (p. 191). The only essential difference is that Benten did not intend to lure the dragon to destruction: she really wanted to marry him, and they lived happily ever after. But we do not know the outcome of the Astarte-Sea myth.[27]

So Japan received several forms of the combat myth, both early and late, most likely by way of China or Korea. It seems to have been superimposed upon a native cosmogony.

America.—However widespread the combat myth pattern in the Old World, one would hardly expect to find it among American aborigines before 1500. Perhaps the best place to look, in order to be pretty sure that the evidence is pre-Columbian, is in the *Popol Vuh,* the sacred book of the Quiché Maya of Guatemala.

According to its account of beginnings there was at first nothing but a calm sea and the sky. Here is a watery chaos, and it was dark too; but we should notice an important difference in that sky is separate from sea from the very first: it never was part of it. The sea contained the creator gods, the ancestors, and the light; and it is interesting to observe that the creator Gucumatz was conceived as a green-feathered serpent that swam in the waters, a form that recalls the chaos serpent of Eurasia and also Zu-Garuda. But we must observe that Gucumatz (or Kukulcan), while sometimes terrible in his wrath, is not a demon of disorder, satisfied with chaos: he is the creator of the world. He is in fact identical with the Mexican Quetzalcoatl. The myth has no conflict of cosmos against chaos: in general the work of creation proceeds peacefully.[28]

But in the sequel there appears a certain Vucub-Caquix, the great Macaw, who can be likened to Zu (Ths. 3A, 3B). As yet there was no sun or moon, though earth with its mountains, valleys, forests, rivers,

[27] Raiko: F. H. Davis MLJ 45–51. Benten: Challaye (1950) 53–55, Davis 207. Notice the spider woman's heap of skulls: Davis 51. Raiko shows many similarities to Beowulf (see pp. 529–531).
[28] *Popol Vuh* 1.1–3 (Goetz-Morley 1950: 81–93); cf. Spence (1913) 209 f. On Gucumatz see Goetz-Morley 81 f., notes 2, 3; Ortiz (1947) 100 f., 450–453. As in East Asia, so in America, rain deities are likely to have snake form: see E. Smith (1919) 83–92, Combaz (1945) 267 f.

and animals had already been formed. Vucub-Caquix pretended to be the sun and moon, because his eyes, nose, teeth, and throne shone like precious stones (Th. 3D). This is something like a claim to sovereignty (Th. 5A), though in an entirely different dress from anything that we have seen. The emphasis is placed upon the theme of false sun against true sun. With the blessing of the Creator, two young gods (Th. 6B), Hunahpu and Xbalanque, who were distressed at Macaw's vainglory and harmful behavior (Th. 4A) set out to shoot him with their blowguns while he ate (Th. 7E). They came to where he lived with his wife (Th. 1C) and two sons, and lay in ambush at the foot of a tree. When he climbed the tree to eat of its fruit, they struck him in the jaw with a shot from a blowgun. He fell to the ground; but when Hunahpu ran up to overpower him, he seized the young god's arm, wrenched it from his shoulder, and made for home (Ths. 8A, 8B). Later the brothers went in disguise to Macaw's house, and since his teeth pained him terribly from the blow that his jaw had received, they pretended to be dentists. So they pulled his teeth out, pierced his eyes, and thus killed him (Th. 9, c). Hunahpu then recovered his arm.[29]

This tale has surprising correspondences to the Zeus-Typhon myth. Hunahpu, like Zeus, grapples with the wounded enemy and loses part of his body in doing so. He does not, however, lose his life or become the enemy's prisoner. It is true that the Hittite Weather God remained at large after losing heart and eyes; but he seemed feeble without them, while Hunahpu apparently keeps his strength. Again, Vucub-Caquix is finally overcome by trickery when the young gods disguise themselves. He is ambushed at his dinner too, another instance of Theme 9; but this incident belongs to the earlier engagement before the god's discomfiture: the hero's stratagem fails, as it never does in the Old World myths. Also in the latter myths when two gods face the enemy, one is the other's superior, whereas Macaw's two opponents seem to be equals. Yet it is only one who loses an arm. Certain details have no parallel in the Eurasian combat myths: the old couple that help the boys trick Macaw, the dental scene, and roasting of the severed arm over a fire, another indication that Hunahpu's potency did not reside in it.

After the father was thus disposed of, the boys had trouble with his sons Zipacna and Cabracan. Both were gigantic demons of earthquake, volcanoes, and hurricane, who shook the mountains or carried them on their backs (Ths. 3A, 3G). In this respect they are much like

---

[29] *Popol Vuh* 1.4–6 (Goetz-Morley 1950: 93–99); Spence (1913) 210–213.

Typhon. Zipacna killed four hundred boys when they lay in drunken stupor. This is something like Theme 4c; but the boys had plotted Zipacna's death after he had helped them in a very friendly way: he outwitted them when they tried to trap him. But the brothers Hunahpu and Xbalanque avenged the boys. Since the giant ate only fish and crabs, they constructed a large figure that looked like a crab and put it deep down in a cave (Th. 9, c). When Zipacna went in to get it the hill slid and pinned him down (Th. 10A); thereafter he turned to stone. Here again are reminders of the Typhon myth: the demon baited with sea food and confined under a mountain. In fact trickery through food and trickery through disguise are neatly combined.[30]

The boys disposed of Cabracan in like manner. Pretending to be poor hunters, they told him of a huge mountain to the east and wondered whether he could demolish it; he set out with them, and on the way they killed and roasted birds. On one they rubbed white earth, speaking a magic formula as they did so. Cabracan's appetite was whetted by the savor of roasting birds, and he asked for one. They gave him the tainted bird, the eating of which took the strength from his limbs (Th. 9, a, d), much as though Pan's fried fish had had the effect of the Moirai's ephemeral fruits. Then the boys tied him up and buried him underground.[31]

But though the tricks played on the giant brothers resemble those of the Typhon myth, it should be observed that they suffice to overcome the pair, and that there is no combat. Yet it might be said that the three myths are variants of an original in which there was a combat, and that emphasis upon the trickery has blotted out the combat in two of them. But the Vucub-Caquix myth has very little combat either: none at all after the initial defeat of the heroes. This observation may support the hypothesis just mentioned; on the other hand it can support an argument that these are not combat myths at all, but indigenous myths whose interesting correspondences with the Typhon myth are merely coincidental.[32]

[30] *Popol Vuh* 1.7 f. (Goetz-Morley 1950: 99–104); Spence (1913) 213–216. On the nature of Macaw's giant sons see *PV* 1.5 (Goetz-Morley 95 with note 3); Ortiz (1947) 506–508.

[31] *Popol Vuh* 1.9 (Goetz-Morley 1950: 104–106); Spence (1913) 216–219.

[32] It is also noteworthy that Macaw and his sons are not very wicked as they are presented: they are merely considered too big and strong and too boastful. It is said just once vaguely that Macaw had done harm: see *Popol Vuh* 1.5 (Goetz-Morley 1950: 94); and there is the episode of the four hundred boys. Yet nothing is said in the Puruli myth either about Illuyankas' wicked behavior; but that lack may be due to the scantiness of the sources. In addition to the themes indicated in the text, two others may be dimly

But in another myth Hunahpu is definitely a dying god; so that it might be maintained that in an hypothetical breaking up of the myth into several stories among the Maya, each having a different emphasis, the descent to the dead became the subject of one of them, while disappearing from the others. In that story the brothers Hun-Hunahpu and Vucub-Hunahpu annoyed the lords of Xibalba, the Maya Hades, with the noise that they made while playing ball (cf. p. 149). So the lords challenged them to a ball game, thus luring them down to the land of the dead and keeping them there, somewhat as Mot lured Baal. There they were humiliated, an episode that recalls the story of Thor's visit to Jötunheim. Then the lords killed them and hung Hun-Hunahpu's head on a calabash tree; here we have a reminder of Phorbas (p. 25), for it is said that all the calabashes on the tree were skulls. One day a lord's daughter came to the tree; Hun-Hunahpu's head spit into her hand and so impregnated her (see the story of Bata, p. 192). He then sent her to his mother's house on earth. There she gave birth to Hunahpu and Xbalanque, whom we have already met. Their infant wails annoyed their grandmother and half-brothers, who in this respect resemble Tiamat and the rebel gods. The half-brothers planned to get rid of them on a hunting trip; but the two younger boys tricked them instead and turned them into monkeys. They too were fond of playing ball and inevitably received a challenge from the lords of Xibalba. They passed every test in the world below, using guile to do so, and were not humiliated as their father and uncle had been. Afterwards they were sent, like Ohokuninushi, to pass the nights in houses of ordeals, six of them altogether; but through their own cleverness and animal helpers they survived. Only when Hunahpu put his head forth from the House of Bats to see whether day had begun to dawn, did he suffer harm: his head was cut off and hung in the ball court. But a turtle was transformed into a makeshift head for Hunahpu, and he was soon none the worse for

---

seen: 2B in the nantze tree from which Macaw took his meal or in the cave which *Zipacná* entered to get his; 2E in *Zipacná*'s diet. Tables 3 and 4 show that the whole series on Macaw and sons clearly have only nine themes of the combat myth, and eight others more obscurely. Table 4 indicates no remarkable correspondence with any variant, except with the Japanese Susanowo myth. But a comparison of the Japanese and Maya myths with each other, with attention to all themes present in either, shows much less similarity than the table indicates. Likewise of the thirty-two plot components of tables 5 and 6 the Maya myth can be said to have only six, though seven others might be considered present in an altered form. It is not surprising that the Set myth contains all these components, since it has twenty-eight of the thirty-two, and all but one clearly. Hence an apparently perfect correspondence of *Vucub-Caquix* to *Set*, if only the former's share is looked at. But looking at Set's twenty-eight we see that the Maya story has least resemblance to it in a field of thirteen.

his experience; and not long thereafter by a trick he recovered his proper head. Afterwards the brothers voluntarily leaped into a fire and died; but five days later they reappeared. Finally they played upon the lords of Xibalba the trick that Medea played upon Pelias: after demonstrating how they could cut men and animals to pieces and bring them back to life, they allowed the lords of Xibalba to persuade them to perform the same operation on them, and they did the first part only. The underlords of Xibalba were then reduced in rank, being made into ugly demons who did menial work and consorted only with the wicked and unfortunate.[33]

As Spence says, this is a story of the Harrowing of Hell, and in the combat myth the champion's descent to the dead sometimes takes that form, as in the legends of Herakles and Gilgamesh. But in spite of the several interesting resemblances that I have pointed out, it would be hazardous to say that it is a variant of the combat type. Again it is trickery that is emphasised, especially the theme of the tricking of the trickster, already observed in the Zipacna myth, but not found in the Old-World myths that we have studied. And there is properly speaking no combat: aside from hateful feelings between deities, there are only the ball games, of which the boys win only the first of a series and play to a tie thereafter—their outcome, that is, does not involve final victory for the heroes and defeat for the enemies. Finally, my summary brings out only the resemblances; but from beginning to end there are episodes, themes, and details that have not been seen in variants of the combat myth. I can mention but a few: (1) the men charged with killing the girl whom Hun-Hunahpu's spittle impregnated spare her and bring back a false heart: a motive that is found in Snow White, but not in the combat myth. (2) The boys' grandmother does not believe that this girl is her daughter-in-law until she has miraculously performed a seemingly impossible task. (3) The boys clear the soil with self-working picks, but have trouble with the animals, who cause the brush and briers to spring up again overnight. (4) By a ruse they recover their parents' ball-game equipment from their grandmother. (5) There is a relay of animal messengers, each of whom swallows his predecessor to gain speed. (6) A mosquito helps them to distinguish between the lords of Xibalba and wooden images, all seated together in a row, by biting the sitters, and at the same time to learn the lords' names; so that they enter with initial success upon

---

[33] *Popol Vuh* 2 (Goetz-Morley 1950: 107–164); Spence (1913) 220–227. Thor in Jötunheim: Prose Edda, *Gylfaginning* 46. Medea and Pelias: Ovid *Met.* 7.297–356; Apollod. 1.9.27.

their sojourn in Xibalba. Notice that in all these episodes some sort of trick or device is employed. In their tales the Maya seem to have valued skilful deception and resourcefulness above prowess in battle.[34]

On the other hand, important themes of the combat myth are entirely lacking or nearly so in the whole series of Maya myths under study. So far as one can learn, the enemy does not have several heads or legs (Th. 3c), nor does he change his shape at will (Th. 3e). I have already pointed out how seldom he is charged with atrocious misdeeds: he does not appear to be cannibalistic (Th. 4d) or lecherous (Th. 4e). He does not block roads (Th. 4f) or rivers (Th. 4g). Little is done with the female companion (Ths. 1c, 5b). The wife of Vucub-Caquix plays only a minor part; the princess of Xibalba, while important otherwise, offers only a hint of the Venusberg theme (Th. 8d). The heroes do not seem to be weather gods, though they have the backing of Gucumatz-Huracan. The mothers and wives of the heroes, while taking part in other episodes, have nothing to do with helping them against their enemies (Th. 7d). There is nothing like the terror-appeasement theme (Th. 7c) or a gigantomachy (Th. 7g). Finally, nothing is said about the foundation of rituals or cults to commemorate these events (Th. 10d), though we may suppose that the myths actually have some connection with cult practices.[35]

What then are we to say about these Maya myths which show on the one hand such striking correspondences to the combat myth, but on the other such significant differences? Are they variants of the combat myth or quite independent growths? Do they support diffusionist theory or evolutionary? Elliot Smith would see in the correspondences sure evidence of diffusion from the Old World, probably across Indonesia and Polynesia; and he would say that the strange features and numerous differences are to be expected after the tale has travelled such a great distance and gone its own way on the American continent for so many centuries. Frazer and Combaz on the other hand would surely say that the human mind works in much the same way everywhere, that different peoples are likely to arrive at identical mythical conceptions, so that even if the tales were much more alike than they are, we need not conclude that they are scions of a single

---

[34] Ths. 3f, 3g, 4a, 6b, 7e, 8a, 8c, 8e, 9, 10a, only can be seen fairly clearly in this story; more obscurely or doubtfully present are 1c, 3b, 3d, 4c, 7a, 8d. In connection with distinctive episode (5) there is an *aition* for hawks' swallowing snakes; but notice that the story does not assert hostility as the reason, as in the Mesopotamian and Indian stories of enmity between bird of prey and snake (p. 204), but a friendly act.

[35] Absent too are Ths. 1a, 1b, 2a, 2c, 2d, 4b, 7b, 7f, 10b, 10c. Th. 3d is dimly suggested in Vucub-Caquix's resplendent face and in the House of Fire in Xibalba, which is closely analogous to the field of fire in the Ohokuninushi-Susanowo story.

stock. But before making a final statement on this subject, let us look briefly at a few native American myths from the Pacific Coast and neighboring regions of North America.[36]

The Washoe Indians about Lake Tahoe tell the story of a Zu-like bird called Ong. He was huge, with wings longer than the tallest pines (Ths. 3A, 3B). He had a human face covered with hard scales, and webbed feet. He made his nest at the bottom of the lake (Ths. 2B, 2D, 2E), whence flowed all the lake's waters, and to which they returned in great currents that often swept plants, animals, and men into the nest to become the greedy bird's food (Th. 4D). Often he flew about the shores looking for women, children, and hunters; and he dropped his catch into a current to be carried to his nest (Ths. 4C, 4E, 4A). But no arrow or spear could pierce his feathers or the scales on his face and legs: he had the invulnerable hide of Python and Tiamat. Now the chief's daughter was to be married to that hero who could claim the greatest exploit when the tribe gathered about the council fire to choose her husband. Tahoe, the young man whom she loved, decided to kill Ong. So he allowed Ong to seize him; but with a thong he tied himself to the bird's leg and couldn't be dropped (Th. 9). Ong tried without success to bite Tahoe, who sheltered himself under the webs of the bird's feet. And every time Ong opened his mouth to bite him, Tahoe threw in a handful of poisoned arrow-heads (Th. 7B). So Ong died, and Tahoe married the chief's daughter (Th. 10B).[37]

With good will twelve or thirteen themes of the combat myth can be discerned in this tale. Moreover the hero wins his bride by killing the monster, as in the legend of Perseus and Andromeda and some related tales, with the difference that she is not Ong's intended victim: there is nothing of the theme of offering a maiden to appease the monster. The hero's allowing himself to be carried aloft in Ong's talons, though different from anything seen in the combat myth so far, could nevertheless be a variation upon the hero's voluntary entry into the monster's belly, as it appears in some Old-World tales (pp. 207, 347) and in the American story of Coyote and Wishpoosh the giant beaver.

---

[36] E. Smith (1919) 83–95, 104, 233; Combaz (1945) 270 f., also 245, 248; Frazer's views on spontaneous indigenous origin are expressed in many places in his works.

[37] James (1915) 51–55: a story told by a Washoe squaw to Nonette McGlashan. The currents flowing out and returning recall the streams of the River Ocean in the underworld (p. 229). In Jackson County, Illinois, there used to be a rock carving that showed a winged dragon, which, to judge from a drawing that was made of it, looked something like Zu: E. Smith (1919) 92–94 and fig. 3.

Coyote is a culture hero of western America; he had also the power
of sending rain and hail (Th. 6A). In a myth told by several Columbia
River tribes he fought a gigantic and monstrous beaver (Ths. 3A, 3B)
called Wishpoosh, who lived in Lake Cle Elum (Th. 2E). This was a
terrible creature of fiery eyes (Th. 3D) and huge claws, with which he
seized all creatures that came near him: he swallowed shoals of
salmon, caught and ate whales (when later he was in the ocean), and
seized everybody who came to the lake, either eating or drowning him
(Ths. 4D, 4F, 4A). So Coyote decided to kill him. First he consulted his
three sisters (Th. 7D), who lived as huckleberries in his stomach. After
their usual initial reluctance and his threat to bring down hail upon
them unless they advised him, he made a long spear, which he fastened to his wrist with a stout cord. Then he went to the lake, where
the monster tried to seize him. He drove his spear into the enemy's
side, and so, when the latter plunged into the lake, he dragged Coyote
down with him (Th. 8A), according to the hero's plan (Th. 9),
which resembles Tahoe's. Then at the bottom of the lake they fought
for a long time with all their might and shook the neighboring mountains. Finally, as the waters poured out through a gap made in the
mountains, Wishpoosh went along with them, dragging Coyote behind
him (Th. 7F), and cutting the channels of the Yakima and Columbia
Rivers as he went, much as Typhon cut the channel of the Orontes in
his flight (p. 277). When he reached the ocean, Coyote, being exhausted, was nearly drowned and so gave up the fight for the time
(Th. 8A). After recovering his strength he once more consulted his
three huckleberry sisters, who advised him to change himself into a
fir bough. This Wishpoosh swallowed when it floated out upon the
lake (Th. 8A). Once in the monster's belly, Coyote resumed his own
shape, took a sharp knife, and began hacking at Wishpoosh's heart,
so that the monster died. Then Coyote came out and with Muskrat's
help created all the Indian tribes out of the carcass, which he cut to
pieces (Th. 10A). This feature recalls the treatment not only of Tiamat's dead body but even more closely that of Kingu's, from which
mankind was fashioned (p. 150).[38]

Of all American Indian myths noticed here this seems to have the
nearest resemblance to the Old World combat myth. Fourteen themes
are clearly present, among them a real combat, hard fought and
described in some detail. But one cannot be sure that the story is
entirely free of European influences brought by white settlers or
traders. Furthermore the Klickitat tale of Coyote and Nashlah, which

---

[38] Clark (1953) 172–175.

is very like the second half of the Wishpoosh myth, has no combat to speak of, and entirely lacks the combat of the first part. Nashlah was a monster who held rapids on the Columbia River and swallowed the people who passed in canoes. In one version Nashlah is female (Th. 1c). When Coyote, acting on his huckleberry sisters' advice, allowed himself to be swallowed by Nashlah, he carried dry wood and pitch with him and built a fire under the monster's heart. Then, after breaking four knives (Th. 7b), he cut the cords that held the heart. Within the body and released by the monster's death were all the people who had been swallowed, so that Nashlah's belly, like Tiamat's, seems to be the realm of death itself (Th. 3f). After he died Nashlah nevertheless continued to live in the rapids and received offerings (Th. 10d).[39]

In spite of striking parallels in theme, it is very unsafe to say that the myths of Wishpoosh and Nashlah are really variants of the combat myth. One notices the absence of important themes. The dragon has no wife or sister or mother, though Nashlah may be female without a partner. There is no hint of lechery or seduction, so that Themes 4e and 8d are entirely absent. There is no struggle for sovereignty, no submission or panic of gods before the monster, no god-helper in combat. Though the hero suffers a sort of death, he does so voluntarily and is in no way beguiled to his doom. Though the monster is a denizen of lake or river and has something to do with beginnings, he does not seem to be a chaos spirit. Conversely, the myth has strange and fantastic features such as the huckleberry sisters, whose shape and habitat is unlike anything that we have yet encountered in the combat myth, though they can no doubt be matched elsewhere. But their reluctance to advise Coyote until he threatens them likens them a bit to the Gray Sisters of the Perseus legend (p. 301).[40]

---

[39] *Ibid.* 89–91.

[40] The Chelan Indians of Washington tell the story (*ibid.* 70–72) of a monster that ate the elk, deer, and bears in great numbers (Th. 4d), so that he reduced the Indians to famine. They appealed to the Great Spirit (Th. 6a), who came down and killed the monster. But the enemy came back to life after a time, and again the Great Spirit came down to kill him; this time he cut him to pieces. Even so the monster came to life once again. This time the Great Spirit, after killing him, threw his corpse into a deep gorge and filled the gorge with water (Ths. 10a, 2e); thus was Lake Chelan formed. In another story the monster, a gigantic dragon (Ths. 3a, 3b), was still living in the lake. He seized a fisherman one day, carried him down into the lake (Th. 7a), and then came to the surface to tell the fisherman's wife that he was the spirit of the lake and that nobody must venture upon it. When two canoes full of warriors went forth to give battle, a storm came up (Th. 3g), and the dragon, rising up, seized one canoe and took it with its crew beneath the lake. The other warriors fled (Th. 7c). The first story is nothing more than the simple narrative that precedes the developed combat myth and forms its core (p. 217). The

The story type concerning monsters that is most widespread in North America is the tale of the theft of fire or light: (*a*) The earth is completely dark. (*b*) A monster has possession of fire or light, either possessing it from the first, or having stolen it from the earth. (*c*) The culture hero (often Coyote in the Far West), accompanied by helpers, steals the fire or light, outwitting the monster in one way or another. In some variants occurs the motive of the hero's turning himself into something that the monster's daughter swallows, so that she becomes impregnated and gives birth to a child, who, being the culture hero himself, grows up in the house and so finally runs off with the fire or light. Here is a reminder of the Bata story (p. 192), as well as of Hun-Hunahpu and the princess of Xibalba. But there is not much true combat in these tales. In the Maidu variant Thunder and his daughter, armed with wind, rain, and hail, chased the thieves; and Skunk (the people of the tales are often animals) shot Thunder as he caught up and killed him. This is about as much combat as one will find. As in the Maya myths, trickery is emphasised.[41]

Now, in the Tsimshian variant, the thief of light is Giant, who can fly when he puts on a raven skin; and he steals it from the Chief of Heaven. He is not only a Garuda who steals the soma, but a Prometheus who steals light from the supreme god for mankind's benefit. If this is a variant of an Old-World type, it belongs to the Prometheus type rather than to the combat myth. Yet it serves to make us more aware that the Prometheus figure is closely related to Typhon-Python and his cognates.[42]

---

second leaves victory to the dragon. Notice also the Quillayute tale of Kwatee and the Monster of Lake Quinault: *ibid*. 65. Kwatee's brother was swallowed by the monster, who was then killed by Kwatee's boiling the waters of the lake. His brother became a hermit crab in the monster's belly. The only themes present are 3A, 3B, 4D, 8A, 7E. Similar is the Kalapuya tale of Coyote and the Cave Monster of the Willamette Valley: *ibid*. 101 f. Coyote tricks the monster by hiding the sun and leading him to think that night has come. Then at the right time, by bringing the sun out, he blinds him and kills him (Ths. 2B, 3B, 4A, 4D, 6A, 7A, 9). This myth has a characteristic American theme: the making of a rope of arrows for going from earth to heaven. For a southern Paiute tale of an infant who, like Apollo or Indra as babes, killed a cannibalistic giant, see Steward (1936) 424 f.; cf. 428 f.

[41] S. Thompson (1929) 22–24 (Tsimshian tale, British Columbia); 40–42 (Maidu, Central California); 281, note 42; 289, note 63. Clark (1953) 38 f. (Snoqualmie, Washington), 118–120 (Nez Percé, Idaho), 150–152 (Puget Sound), 187–192 (northwest in general). Clearly present are Ths. 1c, 3A, 3B, 3G, 4A, 6A, 7c, 7E, 9; obscurely or occasionally 3D, 5A, 7A, 8A. Theme 8D is found isolated in a southern Paiute tale: there was a beautiful woman Korawini, strikingly like Ishtar, who killed all her lovers in intercourse, since she had *vagina dentata* (which undoubtedly belongs to the most primitive form of the Old-World Venusberg myth); but Coyote outwitted her and survived; Coyote appears as the lecherous pursuer in this myth; see Steward (1936) 365–368.

[42] See Olrik (1922) 253–290, Krappe (1930) 333 f.

These North American myths have cosmogonic features. The story is laid in the world's early days; the monster is connected or identified with water, storm, or darkness. However, a conception of primeval chaos is usually not to be found. It would seem that often the existence of earth, sky, and sea are taken for granted, and that only animals and man had a beginning. The California Maidus, however, among others, had a myth of the world's beginning in darkness and water. But the sky and its divine inhabitants were already in existence above the waters, into which Turtle dived to bring up earth. That is, it is a variant of the Earth-Diver myth.[43]

The fire-theft tales are certainly not variants of the combat myth, though it might be argued that they borrowed themes from it. As for the Maya, Tahoe, and Columbia myths, no decision can really be made. The several correspondences with combat-myth themes are remarkable enough to lead one to suppose that they might have come from the Old World; and the coincidences are remarkable if they are truly indigenous products of the native imagination. But the differences are remarkable too. Certainly the stories are formed on a rather different pattern. If they are derivatives of an imported variant of the combat myth, they have been greatly modified. But one thing is clear: the pattern of the combat myth, as outlined at the end of chapter x, is not found everywhere in the world.[44]

[43] S. Thompson (1929) 24–30, 282 note 47.

[44] In tables 3 to 6 I include the early Chinese creation-and-combat myth (which I label *Kung Kung*), the three Japanese Susanowo myths considered as one, and the myths of Vucub-Caquix and his two sons considered as one, in order to show how many of the themes and plot components of the combat myth are found among them, and how many of them they share with the other myths represented in the tables. Since the themes and components listed account for most that are present in the plots of the Chinese and Japanese myths, the tables tend to show their kinship to the western myths. But since only a part of the Vucub-Caquix myth is represented in the tables, they serve mainly to show just what parts of the combat myth can be found in it.

APPENDIX 4

SAINT GEORGE AND THE DRAGON

It would hardly be proper to write a book on dragon combats without saying something about Saint George and the dragon. It is not a story that will throw much additional light upon our subject; yet a brief discussion of it will not be out of place, because it corresponds closely to the Perseus-Andromeda legend in both themes and locale, and because it allows us to see how an historical or pseudohistorical figure may be cast in the dragon-fighter role. It is a medieval saint's legend that can be traced no farther back than the twelfth century; for the earlier martyrdoms and *Acta* of St. George, which go back to the sixth century at the latest, do not mention any encounter with a dragon.[1]

First of all, the scenes of St. George's legend nearly coincide with

---

[1] There are numerous versions of St. George's dragon combat in hagiography, folktale, and folksong. Earliest is the version of the Greek *Codex Rom. Angel.* 46 of the *Miracula Sancti Georgii*, pt. 12, pp. 113–129 in Aufhauser's edition (Teubner) = pp. 52–69 in Aufhauser (1911). For other versions see Greek *Acta:* Aufhauser (1911) 95–162, and pp. 114–126 in his edition of the *Miracula;* Latin *Acta:* Aufhauser (1911) 180–230, including Jacobus de Voragine, *Legenda Aurea* 58 (pp. 202–206; see Graesse's edition of *Leg. Aur.* pp. 259–262), and pp. 115–129 in his edition of *Mir.;* Greek folktale: Dawkins (1955) 123–128; cf. Lawson (1910) 261; Greek folksong: Hartland (1896) 43 f.; *Laographia* IV (1913) 228–235; South Slavic folksong: Hartland 41–43; English Mummers' Play: Gaster (1950) 441–443. See Baring-Gould (1882) 221–269; Hartland 38–47; Budge (1930) 33–39; Aufhauser (1911) 1–11, 162–180, 230–246. For Coptic and Ethiopian texts of the earlier *Acta*, with translations and summaries, see Budge (1888), (1930); for Greek texts see *Acta Sanctorum*, Aprilis III, Appendix pp. vii–xxxviii; for Latin texts, *ibid.* 119–156; synopses in Baring-Gould 226–229. For representations of St. George's combat in art see Aufhauser (1911) pls. IV–VII; Budge (1930) front. and pls. 1–3, 5, 6.

515

those of the Perseus legend (Th. 2A). George was born in Cappadocia at Melitene or Tarsos. His martyrdom is sometimes placed at Melitene too; but it is also located at Tyre. The site of his tomb is Lydda in Palestine, fifteen miles from Joppa; Lydda is also occasionally the scene of the martyrdom; and Joppa enters the narrative of the early *Acta* as the port to which the saint's body was brought by sea from Tyre, and to which Diocletian's general came with an army on his way to destroy the shrine at Lydda. Furthermore it is sometimes said that while George's father was a Cappadocian, his mother was a Palestinian woman from Lydda; or that George and his mother took refuge in Palestine after his father's martyrdom. The scene of the dragon combat is variously Cappadocia, Palestine, or Libya. In the *Golden Legend* it is a Libyan city, near which the dragon inhabits a lake that is as large as a sea, *stagnum instar maris* (Th. 2E), a survival, perhaps, of the Lake Tritonis of the Perseus legend.[2]

It was a huge, flame-breathing dragon (Ths. 3A, 3B, 3D), who raided the nearby city and region (Th. 4A), seizing and devouring men and beasts (Th. 4D). According to the modern Greek folktale, he had two heads (Th. 3C). The Greek folksongs call him not only dragon, but also lion and ghost (*stoicheio,* Th. 3F). The lion-dragon combination is as old as Asag-Labbu, whose story was told more than four thousand years ago. It is especially noteworthy that it was the Lord who sent this plague against the city because its king and people were pagan persecutors of the Christians. This is the Christian variation on Poseidon's wrath. Like Ketos, the dragon had to be appeased with daily or annual sacrifices of chosen youths and maidens (Ths. 4B, 4C, 7C). According to the *Golden Legend,* he was offered two sheep a day, until sheep ran short; thereafter one sheep and one young human being, until the lot fell upon the king's daughter. Like Andromeda, she was dressed as a bride when she was exposed on the lakeshore (Th. 4E).[3]

---

[2] Birth in Cappadocia: Budge (1888) 205; (1930) 81, 181 f.; Jac. Vor. *Leg. Aur.* 58; at Tarsos "in Western Cappadocia," which seems to be Cilician Tarsos: Budge (1930) 27. Martyrdom at Melitene: *ibid.* 27, 54; Baring-Gould (1882) 228; at Tyre: Budge (1888) 237; (1930) 27, 54, 62. Tomb or martyrdom at Lydda, landing at Joppa: Budge (1888) 238–241; (1930) 115–119, 145–149; *Mir. S. G.* pp. 64, 151, 153, 161 Aufh.; Jac. Vor. *loc. cit.* Palestinian mother: *Mir. S. G.* pp. 2, 148, 150 Aufh. Refuge in Palestine: Baring-Gould 226. Combat in Cappadocia: *Mir. S. G.* 12, p. 120 Aufh.; Aufhauser (1911) 59, 182, 187; in Palestine: *Mir. S. G.* p. 114 Aufh.; Aufhauser (1911) 108, 120; in Libya: Jac. Vor. *loc. cit.* But the scene of combat is "Troyan" in the Bosnian folksong (Hartland 1896: 41), which name points to the Herakles-Hesione legend.

[3] Th. 3A: *Mir. S. G.* pp. 114, 117, 125 f. Aufh.; Aufhauser (1911) 120; Gaster (1950) 443. Th. 3c: Dawkins (1955) 125. Th. 3D: *Mir. S. G.* p. 117 Aufh.; Jac. Vor. *loc. cit.*; Gaster 441, 443. Th. 3F: *Laogr.* IV (1913) 228, 230 f.; he ate his victims only at night

In the modern Greek folktale, though it is more recent than most other versions cited, there persists an ancient feature of the combat myth, the withholding of the waters: the dragon had taken possession of the village spring, the only water supply, and kept the folk from it, unless they offered him a child (Ths. 2D, 4G). Since the earliest known versions do not have this feature, it is possible that it has been taken over from other variants of the combat myth. But it may have been present in the folk tradition, as distinct from hagiography, from the time that St. George first became a dragon fighter. For in the medieval legend the saint caused a spring to burst forth beside the church built in his honor: a vestige of the freeing of the waters.[4]

George was young and handsome when he fought the dragon (Th. 6B); when the exposed princess warned him away, she remarked upon his beauty. The combat is the first act of George's life that the *Golden Legend* mentions, after speaking of his family and birth. It was the Lord who sent him to the afflicted country, that by killing the dragon he might convert the king and people (Th. 7E). As a warrior, armed with sword, spear, and shield, mounted upon a horse, he is Perseus in saint's guise. In the folktales and folksongs he killed the dragon at once with his lance. But in the saint's legend he quelled the dragon with no more than the sign of the cross and an appeal to God to render the creature submissive. Later, after the princess had led the meek dragon into town, he cut off the monster's head (Th. 10A). Then the people rejoiced and were converted (Th. 10B); they built a shrine of St. George in their city and established an annual festival in his honor (Th. 10D).[5]

---

according to Dawkins 125; he is practically identified with death in *Cod. Joas.* 308, *Mir. S. G.* p. 126 Aufh. Th. 4A: *Mir. S. G.* pp. 114, 117, 122, 125 Aufh.; Aufhauser (1911) 120 (*phonikôtatos*); Jac. Vor. *loc. cit.* (*pestifer*, p. 260 Graesse). Ths. 4B, 4C: *Mir. S. G.* pp. 114–123 Aufh.; Aufhauser (1911) 120; Jac. Vor. *loc. cit.*; Dawkins 124; *Laogr.* IV 228. Th. 4D: *Mir. S. G.* pp. 114, 117, 120, 122 Aufh. Th. 4E: *Mir. S. G.* pp. 116–118, 121 Aufh.; Dawkins 124. Th. 4F may be seen in *Cod. Athous Laura* Θ132, fol. 48 (Aufhauser 1911: 120): "in that place lived a dragon who let nobody travel that road without doing him harm." Lord sends dragon: *Mir. S. G.* pp. 113 f., 117 Aufh.; Aufhauser (1911) 53 f., 96, 108, 128, 136, 147, 182; but Satan sent him, *ibid.* 120. As in the myths of Sybaris and Heros of Temesa the people considered abandoning the city.

⁴ Village spring: Dawkins (1955) 124; Hartland (1896) 43. St. George's spring: *Mir. S. G.* pp. 126, 129 Aufh.; Aufhauser (1911) 69, 98, 110, 131, 143, 151, 186, 205, 224; Jac. Vor. *loc. cit.*

⁵ Th. 6B: *Mir. S. G.* pp. 118, 123, 125 Aufh.; Aufhauser (1911) 96, 121; Jac. Vor. *loc. cit.* Th. 7E: *Mir. S. G.* pp. 118 f., 123 f. Aufh.; Aufhauser (1911) 97, 108 f., 129 f., 139 f., 149 f.; Jac. Vor. *loc. cit.*; Hartland (1896) 41; cf. Dawkins (1955) 124, 126 f., where George is helped by his three dogs. For George as a knight in armor see all versions and the art works cited in note 1, p. 515. Ths. 10A, 10B, 10D: *Mir. S. G.* pp. 124, 126, 128 f. Aufh.; Aufhauser (1911) 67–69, 98, 110, 121, 131, 142 f., 151, 185 f., 205, 223 f.; Jac. Vor. *loc. cit.*; Dawkins 125 f. For the festival see Aufhauser (1911) 121.

There is one difference between St. George and Perseus: the saint cannot marry the rescued princess. In this respect the story is like that of Herakles' rescue of Hesione, which is treated in chapter xii. But the memory of the marriage clings to the folktale—the rescued princess wanted to marry her savior, and she was nearly married to a pretender—for the folktale includes the motive of the wretch who falsely claims that it was he who killed the dragon. Then after the saint had vanished from the village, she married a worthy bridegroom, who would have been the victor if this were not a legend of Saint George. Notice that in the English Mummers' Play, St. George has become King George, who by killing the dragon won the King of Egypt's daughter.[6]

It is noteworthy that in a version of the saint's legend which appears in an early fifteenth-century manuscript, the rescued princess is identified with the Queen or Empress Alexandra. Now in the earliest versions of the martyrdom of St. George, Alexandra is the wife of Dadianus, the Persian king who persecuted George and the Christians. At one point in the tedious and detailed narrative of the saint's tortures and sufferings, Dadianus decided to take a different tack and use a more gentle kind of persuasion. Taking George to Alexandra's chambers, he left him there in her company, that she might lead him back to the worship of the pagan gods. But very soon George had converted her to Christianity, and after that she took George's part against Dadianus. Here is a sanctified expression of that form of the Venusberg episode (Th. 8D) in which the demon's mate falls in love with the hero and helps him.[7]

Though George does not fight a literal dragon in the early legends of his martyrdom, yet the tale has its beginnings there. The persecuting King Dadianus is called dragon of the abyss, or simply dragon, though his opposition to George resembles the contendings between Set and Horos rather than the Perseus-Ketos combat. George is killed three times before his final martyrdom, and three times he rises from the dead (Th. 8A). George again and again proves the divine power that backs him; but Dadianus, like Pharaoh of old, remains hard of

---

[6] Dawkins (1955) 126–128; Gaster (1950) 441; cf. S. Thompson MIFL H105.1.

[7] Alexandra as rescued princess: Aufhauser (1911) 120; the writer likens her to the good earth and its germinating power. George and queen: Budge (1888) 226–228, 232 f.; (1930) 96–99, 104–106, 236–241, 248–252. The failure of a temptress before a saint has been seen in the Apsarasas' attempt on Viçvarupa (p. 204). George is also put into the house of a widow in order to bring shame on the Christians: Budge (1888) 221–223, (1930) 91–93.

heart. It is interesting to reflect that the Dadianus legend, which appears six centuries before the earliest record of George's dragon combat, would certainly have been taken for a rationalised form of the combat if it had been later in date. We see here a reversal of the usual sequence: a pseudohistorical narrative has taken a mythical form. It may be that the original tale of George's martyrdom, so much like other martyrdoms, picked up traits of the old Egyptian combat myth among the Copts, and so eventually suggested to the peoples of Syria and Anatolia the familiar dragon combat that had in late pagan times been attached to Perseus (as Baal's successor) and afterwards to Christian saints such as Theodore and Mercurius.[8]

It should also be observed that St. George is a patron of flocks and herds, powerful for their increase and for the protection of the milk, and warder against wolves. He is thus an heir of the ancient Tammuz (p. 247). And like Tammuz he extended his fertilising powers from cattle to crops: he became Green George, a vegetation spirit. So his replacement of Tammuz as the fighter of herd-molesting beasts contributed to the formation of his combat legend.[9]

Though St. George could not win a bride, he was given a large amount of money and riches, which he directed the king to give to the poor. Here we see a hagiographic mutation of the treasure that the hero sometimes finds in the slain dragon's lair. The dragon's treasure, which has its origin in the concept of the withheld waters, the cosmic materials or soma, and its direct antecedents in the apples of the Hesperides and the golden fleece, becomes prominent in the Germanic legends which are reviewed in Appendix 5.[10]

St. George is merely the best known of saintly dragon fighters. He entered into that role, it seems, by much the same processes as did the pagan gods and heroes: i.e., he was assigned the champion role in

---

[8] Dadianus is called dragon: Budge (1888) 206, 223; cf. Budge (1930) 33–44, who likens George against Dadianus to Horos against Set or Ra against Apep. George's deaths: Budge (1888) 207–235, (1930) 57–62, 83–109; see also the Greek and Latin *Acta* cited in note 1. On the origin of George's dragon combat see Aufhauser (1911) 237–246, who because of the six-century interval does not believe that it can have sprung directly from its pagan antecedents, but thinks that George took the combat from earlier saints' legends, e.g., Theodore's. On Mercurius' combat see Budge (1930) 38; cf. Baring-Gould (1882) 254. The actual combat of the amusing Mummers' Play (Gaster 1950: 441–443) is fought between King George and Bold Slasher, a Turkish knight; the dragon combat, having happened previously, is referred to in speeches. George says that he had spent seven years in a cave; thence he went to prison and after that into a rock, where he "laid down (his) grevious bones."

[9] See Frazer (1911 M) II 330–348.

[10] Jac. Vor. *loc. cit.*; Jac. Steph. *ap.* Aufh. (1911) 224.

a familiar plot. The developed legend shows the entire pattern of subtype IV of the combat myth, as can be seen from the tables that follow chapter xii, pp. 362–364.[11]

---

[11] Before leaving St. George, we should observe two more features of his legend that relate it closely to the Herakles-Hesione legend, discussed in chapter xii. The youths and maidens are chosen by lot for the sacrifice; when the princess is chosen, King Selbios, like Laomedon, wants to spare her, but his people force him to keep to his own bargain: *Mir. S. G.* pp. 116, 118, 123 Aufh.; Jac. Vor. *loc. cit.; Laogr.* IV (1913) 228. Again. St. George climbed a wall when the dragon's blood flowed forth: Dawkins (1955) 125; compare p. 347.

I should add that Baring-Gould (1882: 255–264) pointed out the kinship of St. George's dragon legend to the old combat myths of Apollo-Python, Indra-Vritra, Perseus-Ketos, Sigurd-Fafnir, etc., though in ten pages he obviously could make only a sketchy treatment of the subject. His essay is marred by his adherence to Max Müller's meteorological interpretation of myth, so that he saw only a conflict of light against darkness in these combats.

APPENDIX 5

THE COMBAT IN GERMANIC MYTH AND LEGEND

Many legends and folktales of the Germanic peoples tell of combats of god or hero with dragons, ogres, and giants; and gigantomachy is the central theme of their pagan mythology. It may very well be that some of these tales are independent growths, borrowing a few traits at most from the Near-Eastern combat myth. For example, Thor's encounter with the Midgard-Snake from Hymir's boat has very little in common with the pattern outlined at the end of chapter x. But since variants of that pattern and its subtypes have been found around the whole Mediterranean Sea and clear across Asia to Japan, it is not surprising that several should be found in northern and western Europe too. For the northern peoples were never cut off entirely from the more advanced cultures to the south. Myths and folktales were carried with merchandise over the trade routes; and from Greek and Phoenician settlements on the Black Sea and in the far west, from the regions about the Caucasus, where Mesopotamian influences had been felt early, from the northern reaches of Indo-Iranian culture on the steppes of central Asia, tales spread from village to village and from one nomads' camp to another, until they reached the Arctic Ocean and the North Sea.[1]

Though I do not wish to embark now upon a detailed study of any Germanic combat tale, yet something must be said about the legends of Beowulf and of Sigurd-Siegfried as highly important variants of

---

[1] Thor and Midgard-Snake: Poetic Edda, *Hymiskvitha* 17–26; Prose Edda, *Gylfaginning* 48.

the type which can help materially in rounding out our knowledge of the subject. They are the earliest combat tales on record from that part of the world; and the latter became well known over a wide area before the year 1200. Yet before we look at them, we should notice that the Norse myth of beginnings conforms closely to those that we studied in chapter x.

YMIR

Once more chaos is a waste of waters amidst deep darkness; but, as one might expect in these northern lands, the waters have turned to ice. As Snorri Sturluson tells the story in the Prose Edda, there was a world of dark mist, Niflheim (cf. *Caligo*, p. 222), whence flowed twelve rivers, all from a central spring Hvergelmir. Their waters became ice as they flowed out from their source, and the ice piled up in Ginnungagap, which became a mass of ice, frost, sleet, and storm-winds. But there was a fiery region to the south, whence sparks and a hot breath were cast upon the ice pack, quickening it with life; and then the giant Ymir (Aurgelmir) emerged, ancestor of the evil Frost Giants. Soon after his birth the cow Audumla came out of the ice and nourished Ymir with four streams of milk. As she licked salt from the ice, she uncovered Buri, ancestor of the gods.[2]

Ginnungagap means *yawning chasm;* and not only does it designate the Norse counterpart of the Greek *Chaos,* but both parts of the compound are formed on the same Indo-European root as the Greek *chaos, chasmos* (and as English *yawn, gape, gap;* cf. Greek χαίνω). Niflheim, like Tartaros-Erebos, is the outer darkness, and like the Greek names became synonymous with the underworld. Hel's realm is set within Niflheim. It has its rivers, as has been seen, and one of them, Gjöll, separates Hell from the living. The so-called Muspellheim as a fiery land to the south appears to have no warrant in the Poetic Edda, and may be due to Snorri's misunderstanding of his sources. But in the sparks of the southern fire we can see the Norse counterpart of the Hesiodic Eros, the spirit that quickened the chaotic mass with life and generative power.[3]

Now Snorri, as a Christian and Euhemerist, does not report this myth in its truly pagan form, which can be more accurately reconstructed from the rather obscure, yet comprehensible, language of the

---

[2] Prose Edda, *Gylf.* 4–6. See Poetic Edda, *Völuspá* 3–7; *Vafthrúdnismál* 30–33. Cf. de Vries (1937) 386–396.

[3] Niflheim = underworld: Poetic Edda, *Vafthr.* 43; Prose Edda, *Gylf.* 15, 34, 42. Gjöll: *ibid.* 4, 49. On Muspellheim see Olrik (1922) 68–71. De Vries (1937: 388) derives *ginnung* otherwise; but it may be that the folk packed more than one meaning into it.

Poetic Edda. If Snorri's account leads us to suspect that Ymir is himself the living Chaos, the demon that corresponds to Apsu-Tiamat or Vritra, our conjecture is supported by the myth of the creation of the world from his body and by verses of the *Völuspá* (which I shall discuss presently) which say that Ymir lived at the very beginning of time when there was as yet land nor sea nor sky (i.e., they had not yet been separated), but only Ginnungagap. In the *Vafthrúdnismál* it is said that the frozen venom drops of Niflheim's rivers grew in size until Ymir was formed: i.e., his body is the very ice of Ginnungagap. Out of his armpits he begot a two-sexed being, and from the copulation of his two legs a six-headed male monster. Here we can see what may be the earliest form of the creation myth: first there was an hermaphroditic chaos demon who out of himself produced a partner, hermaphroditic also, so that either could enact either sex; then later myth tellers gave the second being a distinct sex, whereupon the original being tended to become endowed with the opposite sex. That is, in Babylonian terms, an hermaphroditic Tiamat appeared first, followed by Apsu, who eventually assumed male sex (an outcome that was perhaps facilitated by the development of grammatical gender); whereupon Tiamat became a woman (see pp. 219–223).[4]

Audumla is surely the Wonder Cow, the Norse Kamaduh or Amaltheia. She with her streams of milk fuses the imprisoned soma cow with the chaos demoness. We have noticed Amaltheia's two-sided nature. The goddess Hel, a Germanic Hekate, who ruled supreme over the dead in Niflheim, also represents the Chaos-Hag. The chaotic pair can be recognised again in Surtr, chief of the giant hosts at Ragnarök, and his spouse Sinmara, who, as Olrik shows, lived not in Muspellheim, but in the depths beneath the earth. Finally, in the Midgard-Snake, who lies at the bottom of the ocean, wrapped clear around Midgard, we can recognise Ocean-Acheloos in his serpent form.[5]

Borr, Buri's son and double, ancestor of the Aesir, had three sons, of whom the greatest was Odin. Odin and his brothers fought and

---

[4] See preceding note. On Snorri's mythology see Olrik (1922) 7 f., 37, 68–80. Be sure to realise that the names Tiamat and Apsu are used here purely for the sake of illustration. See de Vries (1937) 389.

[5] On *Audumla* see de Vries (1937) 389 f. Hel: Prose Edda, *Gylf.* 34. Notice among her surroundings Hunger, Famine, Disease (cf. Virg. *Aen.* 6.273–281; see p. 337, note 24), and that, like the demon Eurynomos (p. 231), she was blue-black in color. See de Vries 399 f. On Surtr's and Sinmara's abode see Olrik (1922) 74–80; cf. Poetic Edda, *Fjölsvinnsmál* 26; Eyvindr *ap. Pr. Edd.*, *Skáldskaparmál* 2. Midgard-Snake: Poetic Edda, *Hym.* 23; Prose Edda, *Gylf.* 34, 48.

killed Ymir, and then fashioned the world out of his corpse, a striking analogue to Marduk's treatment of Tiamat's corpse; but the Norse myth is more specific: his flesh became earth, his blood the sea, his skull the sky, and so forth. That is, his body contained all elements of the ordered world, which remained unseparated and unused until he had been killed. The *Völuspá* says that Borr's sons lifted Midgard, man's earth, from out of Ginnungagap, wherein we see a trace of the earth-diver myth (p. 500, note 18), and also evidence that the world's materials had to be rescued from the confusion of chaos.[6]

Though the gods and Frost Giants wage constant war with each other, the great gigantomachy is projected into the future. On the field of Ragnarök gods and giants battle to mutual destruction. Then Thor faces the Midgard-Snake again, and after killing him dies from the venom that the snake spews upon him. Fenris Wolf swallows Odin, who is avenged by Vidar, Odin's son; Garm, the Norse Kerberos, and Tyr kill each other; so do Heimdall and Loki. As in the Greek Gigantomachy variant tales of god-monster combat have been made into encounters on a battlefield. Vidar and Thor's two sons survive the slaughter; hence these combats belong to subtype II.[7]

But enough has been said to make evident that the familiar themes of combat between the champion of cosmic order and the chaos monster, of gigantomachy, and of the slain god, recur in the Germanic tales of gods. Now we must turn to the great hero legends.[8]

BEOWULF

The reader will remember that the Beowulf epic falls into two parts: Beowulf's combat in his youth with Grendel and Grendel's

---

[6] Poetic Edda, *Völ.* 3 f., *Vafthr.* 21, *Grimnismál* 40 f.; Prose Edda, *Gylf.* 7 f.: notice that the gods extracted sparks and embers from the chaotic mass and made the sun and moon out of them. It is a constant feature of the watery chaos that the sun is buried within it. See de Vries (1937) 390–393.

[7] Poetic Edda, *Völ.* 36–58; Prose Edda, *Gylf.* 51–53. Olrik (1922) has made a thorough and excellent study of Ragnarök. See also de Vries (1937) 410–421.

[8] Worthy of notice too are the northern Zu-bird, the wind eagle Hraesvelgr (corpse swallower): Poetic Edda, *Vafthr.* 37; Prose Edda, *Gylf.* 18; the Rahu-like wolves that pursue sun and moon, causing eclipses: Poetic Edda, *Völ.* 32; Prose Edda, *Gylf.* 12, 51; Naglfar, the boat of the dead, that carries the shades across ocean to join the giants at Ragnarök: *Völ.* 43, *Gylf.* 51; and Thor's combat with the stone monster Hrungnir: Poetic Edda, *Hárbarthsljóp* 15; Prose Edda, *Skáldsk.* 17. In a recent study Wais (1952) has connected the Thor-Hrungnir combat with the Hurrian Ullikummi myth, showing sixteen correspondences (221–228); he also points out themes that they share with the Typhon (235–240) and Alkyoneus-Antaios (240–243) myths and with others, Persian, Caucasian, etc. Themes of Ymir-myth: 1A, 1B, 1C, 2E, 3A, 3C, 3G, 4A (*Gylf.* 5), 5A, 6A, 6B, 7A, 7E, 7G, 10A; of Ragnarök: 1A, 1B, 1C, 2B (Garm), 2D (*Nídhögg*), 2E, 3A, 3B, 3D, 3E (Midgard-Snake as cat, *Gylf.* 46 f.; cf. Loki's changes), 3F, 3G, 4A, 4D, 5A, 6A, 7A, 7E, 7G, 8A.

mother, which with its antecedents and denouement fills about two-thirds of the whole poem; and after a brief transition, in which the poet tells of Beowulf's assumption of the kingship and his long reign of fifty years, the aged hero's combat with a dragon, when, though victorious, he lost his life. Both tales are important variants. For the Grendel story, since its plot fits the Thanatos form of subtype IV and also contains many components of subtype I, bridges the gap between the two, showing clearly how the myth of cosmic combat may be transmuted into a tale of a hero's ridding the land of a monstrous pest. Similarly Beowulf's dragon combat stands between subtypes II and IV. But first Grendel.[9]

A DEATH DEMON CONTROLS AND TERRORISES THE LAND
(Cf. plot components A, B, C, F)

The dragon pair: mother and son (A,2b).—The epic itself makes it clear that Grendel and his mother are infernal fiends, whose underground abode has some relation to the realm of death. It is true that Christianity has imposed upon the epic Grendel's descent from Cain and certain epithets that identify him and his dam with Satan's devils. But in doing so Christianity did no more than give Hebraic-Christian terms to Grendel's original character. And though the epic sees him as one fiend among many, he is, except his mother, the most terrible of all. He is "Death-shadow dark," "ghastly demon-shape," "dread ogre of night," who comes "stalking in the dusky night" to seize men and drag them to the nether shades. In a demon so described we can recognise the Thanatos of German pagans.[10]

More fearful than Grendel himself was Grendel's dam, whom Beowulf had to attack in her underground cavern, and who nearly succeeded in overcoming him, whereas Grendel by comparison was easily destroyed. Here we see the order of *Enuma elish,* wherein after Apsu's death the more dangerous Tiamat remained, whom Marduk had to meet upon her own ground; and of the Vedas, where after Indra killed

---

[9] The reader will learn much about Beowulf from Lawrence (1930), Schneider (1934) 5–51, and Brodeur (1953), (1954). I present the Beowulf-Grendel legend according to the pattern of subtype IV, showing at the same time to what extent it agrees with the archetype (pp. 262–265).

[10] See *Beow.* 86, 100–114, 120, 160, 647–651, 702–713, 850–852, 1257–1266, 1355–1379, 2073 f. The first two quotations are from J. Duncan Spaeth's translation (*Old English Poetry*, Princeton University Press, 1922), and the other two from J. R. C. Hall's (London: Allen and Unwin, 1950). On Grendel as death spirit see Panzer (1910) 258–261, Carpenter (1946) 147, 186; Brodeur (1954) 504. That Grendel is also called ghost (*Beow.* 102, 133, etc.) gives evidence once more that death lord, evil demon, and the dead as ghost (or zombi or dibbuk) become merged in the folk imagination.

Vritra he had to fight Danu (p. 196); and of the Python myth: Apollo had to deal with the dragoness after he had disposed of the dragon. It is probably the original order of the myth, once a male and a female dragon had been distinguished. The more one looks at Grendel's dam, the more she looks like Tiamat: the Anglo-Saxon epic's version of the Beowulf-legend preserves the old Chaos-Hag almost intact.[11]

Chaos and disorder: spirits of primeval chaos, etc. (B,1).—The demon pair haunt moor and fen, but only at night; like vampires they must return to their infernal abode before dawn.

> I have heard my people, the peasant folk
> Who house by the border and hold the fens,
> Say they have seen two creatures strange,
> Huge march-stalkers, haunting the moorland,
> Wanderers outcast. One of the two
> Seemed to their sight to resemble a woman;
> The other manlike, a monster misshapen,
>
> . . . .
>
> Lonely and waste is the land they inhabit,
> Wolf-cliffs wild and windy headlands,
> Ledges of mist, where mountain torrents
> Downward plunge to dark abysses,
> And flow unseen. Not far from here
> O'er the moorland in miles, a mere expands:
> . . . There lives not the man
> Has fathomed the depth of the dismal mere.

The misty fen and dark night of the epic are the primeval chaos of myth. In their midst, moreover, is a wide expanse of water, filled with nickers, the sea monsters, the only path of descent to the demons' abode below. Scholars have debated whether this mere is a marsh-lake, a whirlpool beneath a waterfall, a bay, or the sea itself. It makes little difference: it is all these at once; for the epic has combined the different conceptions of several versions or variants. It is in fact the deep: it is chaos and sea and underworld in one, the haunt of dreadful monsters, whose king and queen are the spawners of them all and the most dreadful.[12]

---

[11] See Brodeur (1954) on the greater terror of Grendel's mother.

[12] Quoted is Spaeth's translation of *Beow.* 1345–1367. See also *Beow.* 103–105, 115–143, 647–651, 710–714 ("Now Grendel came, from his crags of mist / Across the moor; . . . .), 731 f. ("he hoped ere dawn / To sunder body from soul of each"), 820 f., 843–852, 1256–1261, 1368–1378 (the stag turns at bay to face pursuing hounds rather than plunge

The nature of the mere is also revealed in the poet's statement that Beowulf descended for an hour (or a day?) before he touched bottom. There he was attacked both by the Mere-Hag and by the sea monsters that swarmed about him. A doublet of this episode appears in the tale of Beowulf's endurance swim with Breca. After they had been swimming for five days, a storm separated them, and angry sea monsters attacked Beowulf, who fought hard against them. He was wearing his ring-mail corselet; since that is hardly the garb for a long-distance swim, one can safely conclude that in the original tale he had put on armor in order to attack the nickers on descending into the sea. For a monster seized him, much as the Mere-Hag did, and dragged him to the bottom. There, as the monster clutched him, he got his hand free and pierced him with his sword, nearly as in his struggle with the Hag. When day dawned, his victory was won. The equivalence of sea and death realm is nowhere better illustrated than in *Beowulf*.[13]

The poet speaks of a strange light that was seen by night within the waters of the mere. When Beowulf reached the Mere-Hag's cavern, "He saw a light, / A flicker of flame that flashed and shone." And again just after killing her, "A light flashed out from the inmost den, / Like heaven's candle, when clear it shines / From cloudless skies." To the poet it was like the sun; for us it is a memory of the sun that lay hidden in the chaotic waters, as in the Indian and Egyptian cosmogonies, a memory that has clung to the tale as it moved from myth to heroic legend. Then within the inner den Beowulf found heaps of treasures, one of the earliest appearances of dragon-guarded treasure, thereafter a widespread theme. The treasures, we can see, have succeeded to the apples of the Hesperides, the golden fleece, the soma, i.e., the precious cosmic materials which the chaos dragon has withheld. And Beowulf brings back Grendel's head, which corresponds to the Gorgon's head, the potent talisman that the world-

---

into the mere; "wan from its depths the waves are dashed, / When wicked storms are stirred by the wind, / And from sullen skies descends the rain"), 1402–1440 (forest, dark moor, rugged and untrodden ways, high and dangerous cliffs, narrow passes, caves of nickers, dark grove, a gurgling whirlpool of bloodstained waters), 1497–1500 (Grendel's dam appears to rule the watery realms). A variant of the story is found in *Grettissaga* 64–66, though Grettir kills the female monster first and finds her partner in the cave behind a waterfall. Lawrence thinks that Grendel and his dam were originally waterfall trolls, who are certainly one sort of being that the chaos demons might become in folktale. But Lawrence need not think that the *Beowulf* poet has "awkwardly introduced deep-sea beasts into an inland pool." See Lawrence (1912), (1930) 178–200. All translations that follow are Spaeth's.

[13] Beowulf's descent: 1492–1569. Swim with Breca: 506–581 (battle with nickers 549–569).

maker needs: a theme that is enmeshed throughout with the treasure theme.[14]

Giants and monsters (B,3–4).—Both Grendel and his mother had superhuman size. Both were monstrous and frightful to look upon, savage of temper, man eaters; but the poet, perhaps intentionally, leaves their form vague. The pair are called man and woman, but monstrous and misshapen. Grendel's eyes flashed fire; both he and his mother had talons; no other details are given. The only other suggestion of nonhuman form is that his mother is called she-wolf. That the two were considered werewolves can be expected; there was, moreover, something spectral and fiendish about them. Like phantoms and death spirits everywhere, they were invulnerable to ordinary weapons.[15]

Theomachy (C,2).—I have already mentioned the nickers or sea serpents that swarmed about Beowulf as he fought with the Mere-Hag. And when he went out to fight her, he led a band of armed companions to the edges of the mere, where they attacked the nickers that lay basking on the rocks, putting them to flight and killing at least one of them.[16]

THE DEATH DEMON SEIZES THE YOUNG OF MAN AND BEAST
(Plot component F,1: The dragon's reign)

Grendel's first two raids caused the Danes to abandon Heorot. For twelve years Grendel lorded it over the hall, seizing and devouring victims wherever he could—young and old alike, says the poet; but he attacked especially the young thanes who slept in Heorot. He first attacked the hall because he hated the sound of revelry, laughter, and music that echoed there at night. Nothing better illustrates his true nature: he is Thanatos, denying life and joy, eternally at war with Eros. And one recalls Tiamat's and Apsu's dismay at the life-asserting commotion of the younger gods.[17]

---

[14] The light in the mere: *Beow.* 1365 f., 1516 f., 1570–1572. The treasures and Grendel's head: 1612–1615. Notice how Beowulf lifts Grendel's head by the hair in Hrothgar's hall and gives the Danes a gruesome sight (1647–1650), recalling Perseus with Medusa's head in Polydektes' court; but, of course, the tale has been adapted to the requirements of the Beowulf legend. In classical literature a dragon guardian of a treasure of gold is seen in Philostr. *Imag.* 2.17.6, where he appears in the same picture with Etna and Vesuvius, under which, the author says, Typhon and Enkelados lie; and the treasure he expressly likens to the fleece and the Hesperidean apples.

[15] Giants: *Beow.* 1348, 1353. Monstrous and misshapen: 1259, 1266, 1347–1352, 1518 f. Fiery eyes: 726 f. Talons: 984–986, 1501–1505. She-wolf: 1506. Invulnerable: 434, 801–805, 987–990, 1521–1527.

[16] *Beow.* 1400–1441.

[17] *Beow.* 86–169. The poet's Heorot is the myth's world. Though Grendel is said to

THE CHAMPION WANTS TO RID THE LAND OF ITS BANE

(Plot component D)

The gods were panic-stricken (D,1).—The Danes, who replace the gods, not only abandon Heorot to Grendel, but shrink from any attempt to get rid of him.[18]

The young sky-god dared to face the enemy (D,2).—The Geatish hero Beowulf has taken the place of the sky god; but Bearson, as we shall soon see, is a link between god and hero. At any rate, though he had earlier exploits to his credit, the meeting with Grendel occurred early in his career. For it was several years afterwards that he began his reign of fifty years.

THE CHAMPION DESCENDS TO THE LOWER WORLD

(Plot component E,1 *b:* The champion's death: overcome by a dragon)

Beowulf went down to the mere of his own free will in the manner of heroes. At the bottom he was clutched by the Hag's talons and dragged to her cavern: the episode in which the dragon overcomes the hero and then carries him underground (e.g., Typhon and Zeus) has been superimposed upon the hero's voluntary descent. After his sword failed him in the struggle within the cave, she fastened her claws upon him and enfolded him in her arms, so that he fell and lay helpless. If his corselet had not saved him from her knife, he would never have returned from "Under the depths of the ocean vast." When his companions above saw blood rising in the mere, they thought that Beowulf was dead and left the shore to return to Heorot.[19]

THE CHAMPION WAITS AT LAIR OR TOMB

(Plot component E,1*c:* Champion's death: lured by the wiles of dragon or dragoness)

Again the descent can be seen in Beowulf's entry into Grendel-haunted Heorot to await the fiend's attack. It is significant that on

---

rule alone at night in the halls, he still finds victims. His possession of Heorot illustrates Theme 2c as well as 5A. Notice especially the horrifying description of Grendel's eating of Hondscio: 740–745 (Th. 4D).

[18] *Beow.* 590–601, 932–939.

[19] *Beow.* 1492–1553, 1591–1605. Notice 442–451: Beowulf says that if he loses, Grendel will bear his lifeless body to his cave and swallow it. In the earliest form of the myth the hero did lose and this is what happened to him (p. 263; cp. Typhon and the helpless Zeus, p. 73).

entering he is entertained at a feast which Hrothgar holds there, following which he stays to meet Grendel.[20]

THE CHAMPION FIGHTS AND KILLS THE ENEMY,
ACCOMPLISHING HIS PURPOSE
(Cf. plot components G, H, I)

Recovery of the champion: the god's wife, sister, or mother strove to recover him by use of rituals and magic (G,1a).—There is no such goddess in *Beowulf;* but we should notice the encouragement that Hrothgar's queen gave to the hero, as she handed him the mead-cup and spoke of her prayers that a deliverer would come. Since the rituals which were intended to recover the champion often consisted in large part of lamentations, we should also notice the mourning of the Danes and Geats for Beowulf when they thought him dead.[21]

Battle renewed and victory: the god returned to life and renewed the combat (H,1a), *killing the dragon or dragoness* (H,2) *after a hard struggle* (H,3), *in which he had to resort to magic or cunning in order to win* (H,5).—The Hag having failed to kill Beowulf, he sprang to his feet and seized a gigantic sword that hung upon the cavern wall. This was a weapon that could pierce demons' bodies, and the Hag was despatched with a single blow. This was a magical sword, the only trace of Theme 9 present in the narrative. When Beowulf descended, so to speak, into Heorot, taking up the helpless Hrothgar's cause (Th. 7E), he surprised Grendel, who had not expected to meet his peer, by seizing him with his bare hands and with a tremendous effort tearing off an arm. He had to wrestle with Grendel as Herakles with Antaios. Then Grendel ran off to die in his underground cavern; Beowulf found only his corpse when he went thither, as Apollo found Python already dead when he pursued him to Tempe (p. 20).[22]

Restoration and confirmation of order: the god took or recovered the throne (I,1).—Hrothgar recovered Heorot. He told Beowulf that he would ever consider him his own son: a trace of the relation between older and younger god in the myth; for Beowulf cannot liter-

---

[20] *Beow.* 402–646, 669–696. The deadly seductress (Th. 8D) of the Ishtar-Omphale kind appears in a digression: Modthryth was a queen upon whom no courtier might look without being put in bonds and killed; but she became milder after marrying Offa: 1931–1962.

[21] The queen's greeting: *Beow.* 612–641; cf. 1162–1231. Mourning: 1594–1605; cf. 128–131.

[22] *Beow.* 1497–1617, 710–836. It is said that Beowulf is God's agent against the monsters: a vestige of the situation in which Herakles fought for Apollo or Apollo for Zeus (cf. St. George, p. 517); see 478 f., 670, 696–702, 939–945, 1553–1556, 1658–1661; Brodeur (1953) 1187.

ally be Hrothgar's child. He became king of the Geats sometime later, it is true; but the old myth had to be fitted to legendary chronology and genealogy.[23]

He celebrated his victory (I,2). Heorot was very festive on the nights that followed the two victories. Beowulf received greatest honor; his valor was celebrated in song; he received magnificent gifts; he was true lord of the feast. Had the legend allowed it, he would then have been crowned king.[24]

The enemy received postmortem punishment (I,3).—Beowulf cut off the heads of both Grendel and Grendel's dam: a reduced form of the champion's cutting the enemy's body to pieces.[25]

The dragon need not detain us as long as Grendel did; for the tale runs parallel in many respects. Beowulf is now an aged man who dies in the moment of victory, protecting his own Geatish land this time against the destroyer. The *Beowulf* poet's purpose resembles that of the *Gilgamesh* poet: the mightiest hero cannot finally conquer death, but must in the end succumb to destiny. But the poet's creation belongs to literature; the tale that he used belongs to myth. Wiglaf, Beowulf's kinsman, the last of his house, who stood beside the hero in this combat, was truly victor in the fray; for he plunged his sword into the dragon's soft underbelly, delivering a mortal wound; then Beowulf, now near death from poisoned wound, drew his knife and cut the monster in two. Beowulf, dying, gave his armor to Wiglaf as to a son; for he had no sons of his own. Therefore I place this combat under subtype II, wherein it is the slain god's son who fights and kills the monster.[26]

The dragon coincides fairly closely with the Grendel pair, and his tale with theirs, in the following respects. (1) He raided at night, spreading death and devastation far and wide among the Geats, and had to get back to his lair before dawn. (2) He lived in a dark cavern underground, beneath a burial mound on a rocky promontory beside the sea. (3) There he guarded an immense treasure. (4) He was huge of size, fifty feet long, and (5) he breathed forth blasts of flame. (6) Beowulf went to the barrow's rocky mouth to meet Firedrake, as we shall henceforth call him. (7) His companions fled, all except Wiglaf; much as years before his comrades at the mere's edge thought him

[23] *Beow.* 925–956, 991–1017, 2207–2210; cf. 1477–1479.
[24] *Beow.* 856–1250, 1644–1882.
[25] *Beow.* 1566–1568, 1590, 2138–2140; cf. pp. 150, 197.
[26] Combat: *Beow.* 2538–2715. Wiglaf as heir: 2729–2732, 2809–2816. See Brodeur (1953) on the epic's themes.

dead and went back to Heorot. (8) Firedrake was fought and killed, and (9) his body was cut into two parts and cast into the sea. (10) The victor Wiglaf wielded a marvellous sword that giants had forged. Recalling the preceding discussion we can see some correspondence also in that (11) the victor succeeded to the throne, and (12) the Geats mourned the dead Beowulf.[27]

The main difference, aside from Beowulf's death, lies in the monster's form. Firedrake is literally a dragon, and winged at that: he flies through the night. But all three monsters of the epic are enemies of life, who want to keep the treasure from the world's use. The outlaw who first robbed the treasure hoard, when he carried off a golden goblet and thus stirred Firedrake's wrath, has replaced the Indra or Zeus who stole the soma or the needed talisman. That he took a goblet is significant indeed.[28]

Firedrake lived in a tomb, i.e., in Death's realm. Its door was surmounted by stone arches, and its depths lay within a rocky headland (Eagle's Ness). Just outside lay the sea. Through the rocky gate from within the dragon shot out streams of fire, recalling Cacus. Here is a fiery chaos, but a fire amidst the darkness; waters surround it; and ramparts of stone encompass an enchanted hoard. So Firedrake too represents Chaos and Thanatos.[29]

This encounter brought death to Beowulf; but he left this world as Herakles did. A great pyre was made high on a cliff, and his body was laid upon it. Then "High on the headland they heaped a barrow." In another age he would have risen thence to the company of the gods.[30]

Now Panzer has shown convincingly, with careful and sound scholarship, that the Beowulf-Grendel story belongs to the Bearson type.

---

[27] (1) *Beow.* 2210–2214, 2302–2335, 2780–2782; (2) and (3): 2212–2286, 2515, 2545–2549, 2752–2782, 3101–3105, 3123–3135; (4) 3042 f.; (5) 2274, 2333–2335, 2522 f., 2545–2549, 2569, 2582 f., 2671–2677; (6) 2538–2549; (7) 2596–2599; (8) 2550–2707; (9) 2705; (10) 2610–2630; (11) 2813–2816, 2906–2910; (12) 3137–3182. Therefore I disagree with Lawrence (1930: 204–206), when he says that the Firedrake combat does not fit any type story in the way that the Grendel combat fits the Bearson type: "The dragon episode has no analogues of any consequence, because there is so little about it which is distinctive." It is true that Firedrake is not so much an individual as is Grendel; and it is true that not all dragons are derived from a common archetype; but the near agreement of the two legends on the above twelve points is sufficient to show that both are variants of the combat myth under study, though not of the same subtype. It is true that Firedrake does not begin to raid until his hoard has been tampered with; yet it is only an assumption that Grendel raided out of pure malice. Nothing at all is said about his original motive.

[28] *Beow.* 2215–2311.

[29] *Beow.* 2212–2214, 2287–2304, 2542–2558. Notice that the rocky walls of Grendel's cavern hold back the sea: 1514–1516.

[30] *Beow.* 3110–3119, 3137–3182.

And there is much to say for Carpenter's identification of Odysseus with Bearson too, and for seeing in Polyphemos, the Laestrygon king and queen, and Circe, Mediterranean counterparts of Grendel and his dam. The Bearson tale is in essence that of a hero of superhuman parentage, father or mother, who first meets and overcomes a demon, usually male, in a deserted *Waldhaus*, which is nevertheless stocked with food and drink for the enjoyment of the hero and his companions; then either pursues the demon to the underworld or goes down to rescue a princess (or three princesses), meets formidable antagonists, dragons or giants, in particular the demon's terrible mother (in many variants); and finally returns victorious with princess(es) and treasures. Within this frame there is an amazing variety of detail in more than two hundred known variants.[31]

It is evident that the entire Bearson type is a northern form of subtype IV (Thanatos). There is no difficulty in assuming that the combat myth travelled north at an early period and there became influenced by the Sleeping-Bear cult, so that both hero and demon might be assimilated to bears. In the legends of Gilgamesh and Rama, equally as in those of Beowulf and Odysseus, one can discover nearly every feature of the Bearson story.[32]

The Firedrake combat does not fall within the Bearson group, but conforms more closely to the familiar dragon-slayer tales of northern and western Europe. Of the latter Panzer distinguishes three types (which we may now call subtypes): St. George or Andromeda, Sigurd-Fafnir, Thor; and considers the Beowulf-dragon story to be compounded of the latter two. These three subtypes correspond closely to three forms of our subtype IV, distinguished according to the champion's motive (component 3 of the subtype). The St. George-Andromeda plot corresponds to that form in which the champion wants to save the victim out of love (3a) or sympathy (3b). The Sigurd plot is developed from that form in which the hero acts under a superior's

---

[31] Panzer (1910), Carpenter (1946) 136–156; Lawrence (1930) 161–203; Schneider (1934) 19–30; cf. Aarne-Thompson (1928) Type 301; Grimm 91. Carpenter is mistaken in thinking that the Bearson story is purely northern (see next note). Notice that in the Bearson type the opponent's corpse is mutilated or placed under a stone (Th. 10A): Panzer 159.

[32] Notice (1) the powerful beverage that the hero discovers beside the magic sword, and which gives him the strength he needs (Panzer 1910: 156; cf. p. 200), and, conversely, the weakening drink that occasionally appears (Panzer 157; cf. p. 89); (2) that the entrance to the underworld may be spring, shaft, abyss, cavern, grave, cellar (Panzer 116); (3) that the enemy pair may be dragons, giants, fierce mammals, devils, witches, or dwarfs: in the north the demon begins to appear in dwarf form (Panzer 143–150).

order (3c): usually he goes in quest of a treasure or finds one in the dragon's lair. The Thor plot is a special case of the form in which the champion decides on his own to rid the land of a destructive monster (3d). It comprises those members of this class in which the combat ends with the death of both hero and dragon. This group reflects the plot of subtype II, as I have pointed out. Of course, Panzer and others have found the three plots difficult to fix, because any particular story is likely to show features of all three plots. The fact is that all three belong to one subtype of the widespread combat myth and have never been clearly differentiated.[33]

Wagner's *Ring* tetralogy has acquainted so many of us with the tragic tale of the Nibelung gold that I am spared the task of summarising the legend's several versions; for Wagner's narrative is a remarkably good compound of them all. The Eddas, sagas, and epics upon which he drew are not nearly so well known to the average educated reader; though a goodly number of readers are no doubt familiar with two of them, the *Nibelungenlied* and the *Volsunga Saga*. However, the differences that appear among them in the combat and Valkyrie episodes can be left to the discussion that follows and brought forward as occasion demands.[34]

The hero whom we know best as Siegfried is called Sigurd in the Norse Eddas and sagas and Sigmund in the earliest source, a short passage of *Beowulf* that summarises the tale of his great exploit. But nearest to the folk tradition, it seems, is the version which appears in the fifteenth-century *Horn Siegfried Lay,* or perhaps I should say versions, one of which coincides closely with that of the *Thidrekssaga*. In these popular versions, or a combination of them, Panzer sees the Bearson type again, no doubt rightly; but it is obvious that each of the three forms of dragon-combat legend mentioned above has con-

---

[33] Panzer (1910) 293–313; see Lawrence (1930) 204–206, Schneider (1934) 30–35. Significant are the variants of the Thor story adduced by Panzer (309 f.; see also 1912: 88 f.) in which the dragon is the dead owner of the treasure; for they serve to link the dragon more closely to the infernal powers. Themes of Grendel legend: 1A, 1B, 1C, 2B, 2C, 2E, 3A, 3B, 3D, 3F, 4A, 4C, 4D, 4F, 5A, 6A, 6B, 7A, 7B, 7C, 7D, 7E, 7F, 7G, 8A, 8C, 8E, 9, 10A, 10B; of Firedrake-legend: 2B, 2C, 2E, 3A, 3B, 3D, 3F, 4A, 4D, 6A, 6B (Wiglaf), 7A, 7B, 7C, 7E, 8A, 8E, 10A, 10B.

[34] The sources that I rely upon for the relevant parts of the legend are *Beow.* 874–915; *Poetic Edda, Gripisspá, Reginsmál, Fafnismál, Sigrdrifumál, Brot af Sigurðarkviðu, Sigurðarkviða hin skamma;* Prose Edda, *Skáldsk.* 39–41; *Volsunga Saga* 1–27; *Thidrekssaga* 152–168 (hereafter abbreviated *Th.*); *Nibelungenlied* pts. 1–10; *Lied von hürnen Seifrid* (*Horn Siegfried Lay,* hereafter abbreviated HS).

tributed a good deal to the original Nibelung legend and to the several versions thereof.[35]

In particular there is much that recalls the Perseus legend. In the *Thidrekssaga* Sigurd's mother Sisibe was cast out by her husband Sigmund on a false charge of infidelity, and the babe Sigurd was cast in a glass vessel into a stream, which carried him out to sea, whence he was washed ashore and there found by a hind that suckled him. From the dwarf Alberich-Eugel, whose relation to the dragon Fafnir is similar to that of the Graiai to Medusa, Siegfried got the *Tarnkappe*, the cap of darkness, whose original purpose must have been to enable him to approach Fafnir unseen. Or Sigurd won from Fafnir the helm of terror which struck fright into all beholders. It would seem to be Gorgon's head merged with Hades' cap. And like Perseus, Sigurd-Siegfried went into the fray armed with a supernatural sword. Then, as Perseus came upon the sleeping Gorgon, so Sigurd came upon the sleeping Valkyrie, about whom I have more to say presently. A likeness to Herakles can be seen in the hero's lustiness, appetite, and superhuman strength; and in the versions wherein he wrestles with his opponent. A resemblance to the Rama legend appears in the *Horn Siegfried Lay*, when the hero sinks mortally wounded to the ground and is saved by Eugel's *Nebelkappe*, and again when Eugel restores the lifeless Krimhild with an herb.[36]

As in *Beowulf* there is a great treasure of gold which the dragon guards. But Fafnir is a demon who once had human shape. The dragon of *Horn Siegfried* is an enchanted prince who will after a term recover his human form. Or giants guard the treasure, as in the *Nibelung Lay*. In *Horn Siegfried* the giant Kuperan guards the key to the dragonstone, whereby one enters the dragon's lair. His relation to the dragon-prince resembles that of Atlas to Geryon or Ladon. Dwarfs too appear as the dragon's servants or as the hero's enemies.[37]

More significant than the treasure are the potent objects that Sigurd-Siegfried won from Fafnir's lair. I have mentioned the helm

---

[35] Panzer (1912). Sigmund is the name of Sigurd-Siegfried's father in most sources. The folktales and themes that form the Nibelung legend are a subject different from, though related to, what may be called the literary history of the legend, the actual or hypothetical *Sagenkreise*, expressed in lays, ballads, sagas, etc., which merged to form such expressions of the legend as the works listed in note 34. For the latter subject see Schneider (1928) 73–210.

[36] Sisibe: *Th.* 159–162. *Tarnkappe: Nib.* 8, 10; HS 5. Helm of terror: Poetic Edda, *Fafn.* 16–19, 44, *Reg.* 14; Prose Edda, *Skáldsk.* 40; *Vols.* 19. Siegfried's lustiness, etc.: *Nib.* 2; HS 1, 3; *Th.* 164–166. Wrestling: *Nib.* 8, 10; HS 5. *Nebelkappe* and magic herb: HS 5, 7.

[37] *Th.* 3E: Poetic Edda, *Reg.* 9–14; HS 2. Giants and dwarfs: *Nib.* 3, 8; HS 3–5.

of terror; there were also a golden birnie and the sword Hrotti. Sigurd
was bound to find a wondrous sword within the cave. Though in most
Norse sources Sigurd has already killed Fafnir with Sigmund's Gram
when he finds Hrotti, the *Thidrekssaga* and south-German sources
show that originally Gram and Hrotti were one sword, the giant sword
of the dragon's cave. In the *Thidrekssaga* Sigurd gets Gram from
Mimir, the dragon Regin's brother and ally, after he has killed
Regin. Horn Siegfried kills the dragon-prince with the giant sword
that Kuperan has shown him. In the *Nibelung Lay* the Nibelung
princes give Siegfried the sword Balmung, with which he presently
kills them. In the *Volsunga Saga* and Eddas, Gram has been reforged
in the treacherous dwarf's workshop.[38]

Notice too that Sigurd takes the heart (or flesh or blood) of Fafnir
and from them receives supernatural powers. Fafnir's heart corresponds closely to the entrails of the serpent-bull in the Titanomachy
(p. 245). Sigurd came back with Regin's head to Mimir's smithy. Or
Siegfried made himself invulnerable by bathing himself in the dragon's
blood and turning his skin to horn. So every kind of talisman that is
found in Greek myth appears in the Nibelung legend too.[39]

Also present are the soma drink and the imprisoned goddess. In
Horn Siegfried it is of course a princess whom the dragon carried off,
Krimhild, King Gibich's daughter. The dragon held her within a
hollow mountain under heavy guard, intending to marry her after
five years when he should recover his human form. Siegfried had to
get through the dragonstone and fight gigantic and monstrous warders
both before and afterwards to rescue Krimhild. Elsewhere his freeing
of the princess is separate from the dragon combat: he frees Brynhild
from her long confinement after making his way through a wall of
fire or shields. These shields represent armed men, as the *Thidrekssaga*
makes clear. Sigurd first fought and killed seven guards, after breaking
through an iron door; then he fought seven knights, whom Brynhild
finally called off. But in the *Nibelung Lay* Siegfried fought armed
guards and knights to win the Nibelung hoard. It seems clear that

---

[38] Poetic Edda, *Fafn.* 16 f., 27, *Reg.* 14; Prose Edda, *Skáldsk.* 40; *Vols.* 15, 19; *Th.*
167; HS 5; *Nib.* 3. Notice the different names for the dragon and his dwarf brother. The
dragon is usually called Fafnir, but Regin in *Th.* 163, and is nameless in *Nib.* 15 and HS.
The dwarf smith is called Regin in the Poetic and Prose Eddas and *Vols.*, Mimir in *Th.*,
Alberich (Albric) in *Nib.*, Eugel in HS. The princes Nibelung and Schilbung are owners
of the hoard in *Nib.*; but Nibelung is the name of the dwarf Eugel's father in HS; the
Giukings, Siegfried's murderers, are called Niflungs in most sources. The giant attendant
is Kuperan in HS, Eckihard in *Th.*, nameless in *Nib.*

[39] Poetic Edda, *Fafn.* 31–39; Prose Edda, *Skáldsk.* 40; *Vols.* 19; *Th.* 166 f.; *Nib.* 15;
HS 1.

either Krimhild-Gudrun or Brynhild is the captive maiden's name in earlier versions of the tale. But the name Brynhild may come to the legend from the Burgundian story of the killing of Sigurd and Gudrun's revenge. Such episodes as Sigurd's winning of Brynhild for Gunnar-Gunther, the potion that caused him to forget Brynhild, and the tragic quarrel between Brynhild and Gudrun-Krimhild, may be due to the fitting together of Nibelung with Burgundian legend.[40]

But the captive Brynhild has been merged with a quite different character, the sleeping Valkyrie, who is called Sigrdrifa in Eddic poems. Now the Valkyries, who in Edda and saga are warrior maids that hover over battlefields to gather the bodies of slain heroes and carry them to Valhalla, were fearful demons (*Schreckgestalten*) of the battlefield in the earliest folk belief, according to de Vries, when Valhalla was not a hall in Asgard but the gloomy battlefield itself. That is, they were the Keres of the battlefield, whose ghastly shapes and manners are described in Homeric and Hesiodic poems.[41]

We may suppose, then, that Sigurd's Valkyrie was at first the dragon's consort. A direct link appears in the *Thidrekssaga*, where Mimir offers Sigurd the stallion Grani from Brynhild's stud, and to fetch it is Sigurd's motive in going to her fastness. Further evidence may be seen in the character that Brynhild has acquired from the Valkyrie with whom she was identified. In the *Nibelung Lay* she is a dreadful shieldmay, more formidable than any man but Siegfried, and nearly a match for him. She ruled as queen beyond the sea. So great was her beauty that many men wished to marry her; but she had set up a threefold contest that her suitors must enter against herself; and the loser in any one of the three parts lost his head. Or in the Prose Edda and *Volsunga Saga* suitors had to ride to her through the wall of fire that surrounded her. Again in the *Nibelung Lay*, when Gunther married her, "He thought to find joy, but found deep hate" (Margaret Armour). Her husband could win her compliance only by wrestling her to submission. Poor Gunther failed ignominiously: she bound him and hung him from a nail on the wall; and so roughly had she handled him that he almost perished. When Siegfried came in his *Tarnkappe*, pretending to be Gunther, he all but suffered the

---

[40] HS 2–8; *Th.* 168; cf. Poetic Edda, *Grip.* 15 f., *Sigrdr.* praef., *Fafn.* 42–44 (a high wall surrounded by fire), *Helreid Brynhildar* 9–12; Prose Edda, *Skáldsk.* 41; *Vols.* 20, 27. In the Brynhild-Gudrun-Sigurd tale one can see a northern example of triangle tale; see Fontenrose (1948).

[41] For Sigrdrifa see *Sigrdr.* and *Fafn.* 42–44. Valkyries = Keres: de Vries (1937) 384. On the distinction between Brynhild and the Valkyrie see Lehmgrübner (1936), Ellis (1943) 181–183.

same fate. Fearful was the struggle; her strong hands squeezed blood from his fingers; but Siegfried persevered until he overcame her. Whereas in the contest story Brynhild is another Atalanta, here she is Ishtar or Semiramis or Omphale, the deadly bride. Her likeness to Deianeira can hardly escape notice; in fact, her story helps to illuminate the Deianeira legend. And we should observe that in the sequel, though other legends have entered into the Nibelung complex, it is Brynhild who brings about Sigurd's death by inciting the Giukings, who inherited the Nibelung name from the demonic owners of the hoard, to kill him. Finally, it is especially noteworthy that the Valkyrie, like Medusa, was asleep when the hero came upon her.[42]

So in the Nibelung sources every step of the way can be seen, from the beautiful but wicked demoness, the Valkyrie, who lures the hero to his doom, through the demoness who falls in love with the hero, or who is forced by him, the Valkyrie Brynhild, to the dragon-rapt maiden, Krimhild, whom the hero rescues. Notice that the Valkyrie-Brynhild episode follows upon the Fafnir episode; it is the order of the Beowulf legend and of the oldest combat myths.[43]

When Sigurd waked the sleeping Valkyrie, she gave him a horn of mead (or beer), a draught that was "mixed with magic and mighty songs, with goodly spells,—wish-speeding runes" (L. M. Hollander). Here is the horn of plenty and the soma, which some scholars have identified with mead; and Sigurd went through walls of fire and shields to get it, as Garuda went through a ring of fire and a revolving wheel of knives and past two fire-breathing snakes to steal the soma.[44]

Fafnir's heart has a like potency. When Siegfried ate of it he gained strange powers. He tasted it against Regin's wish, much as Indra drank the soma in spite of Tvashtri. It is that early form of Theme 9 in which the champion takes the food or drink of might that the enemy had intended for himself (see p. 201 with note 39). A form of the contrary Theme 8c can be seen in the tale that Mimir gave Sigurd a supply of food and sent him to work in the forest, that the dragon

---

[42] *Th.* 167 f.; *Nib.* 6–10; cf. Prose Edda, *Skáldsk.* 41; *Vols.* 27.

[43] Mimir has a wife in *Th.* 163. In the Prose Edda, *Skáldsk.* 41 and *Vols.* 20, 27, the Sigurd-Valkyrie episode occurs twice (cf. *Nib.* 7, 10), the second time when Sigurd rides through the flames in Gunnar's form (see L. M. Hollander on *Grip.*, *init.*), which story has its southern version in Siegfried's wrestle with the ferocious Brynhild; in this version there is no sleeping Valkyrie. See Lehmgrübner (1936) 41–51. Much apparatus has been added to both forms of the episode in fitting them to the complex Volsung-Nibelung legend.

[44] Poetic Edda, *Sigrdr.* 6; *Vols.* 20. But the drink may have baneful effects, as upon Indra (p. 202). Notice Borghild's horn of ale that poisons Sinfjotli, but cannot harm Sigmund: *Vols.* 10.

Regin might attack him there. Regin attacked just as Sigurd finished his meal.[45]

Like Grendel and his dam, Fafnir and the Valkyrie lived upon moors, Gnita Heath and Hindar Fell. Fafnir had a house dug into the ground, where his treasure lay, protected by door and posts of iron. The Valkyrie lay upon a hill or cliff; since in the *Thidrekssaga* Sigurd had to break through an iron door to reach her, it is probable that her abode was sometimes placed within the mountain. In *Horn Siegfried* the dragon lives in a hollow mountain amidst a dark, uncanny forest. There he ruled over many trolls. In the *Nibelung Lay* we find the Nibelungs' castle on a mountain, in whose side a cave holds the treasure; and we also hear of a mountain on which Siegfried killed a dragon. Especially widespread among the Germans was the belief that the dead lived in mountains. The bridge between hollow mountain and underworld appears to be the grave mound, such as that which appears in *Beowulf*, where the Germans, like many other peoples including the Greeks, thought that the dead man lived as in a house, often in snake form, jealously guarding his possessions.[46]

Important too is Sigurd-Siegfried's relation to a cunning smith, his tutor or fosterfather, Regin or Mimir, who is at first his ally and helper, later his enemy. This is a theme observed before, kinship and conflict between the champion and the artisan god, who is sometimes his father. It is Indra against Tvashtri; it is also Zeus against Prometheus or Hephaistos or Typhon. For Typhon, we should remember, was born of Hera in the same manner as Hephaistos, and is in part a fire demon; and fire deities tend to become divine smiths and artisans. We should recall too that Kronos was a clever god (*ankylomêtês*), who carried a bronze sickle. In Sigurd's killing of his fosterfather, in the strife among Hreidmar, Regin, and Fafnir, in the Giukings' murder of Sigurd, in Siggeir's killing of Volsung and Sigmund's of Siggeir, in Sigmund's desire to destroy the infant Sigurd, in all these episodes and more we hear the echoes of the dynastic strife that fills the creation myths of Mesopotamia, India, Egypt, and Greece.[47]

---

[45] Poetic Edda, *Fafn.* 31–39; Prose Edda, *Skáldsk.* 40; *Vols.* 19; *Th.* 166; cf. HS 6. Another form of Theme 9 can be seen in the ambush that Sigurd laid for Fafnir: *Fafn.* praef.; *Skáldsk.* 40; *Vols.* 18.

[46] Gnita Heath and dragon's lair: Poetic Edda, *Grip.* 11, 13, *Fafn.* praef., *Reg.* 14; Prose Edda, *Skáldsk.* 40; *Vols.* 13, 18 f.; *Th.* 163. Hindar Fell: *Grip.* 15, *Sigrdr.* praef., *Fafn.* 42; *Skáldsk.* 41; *Vols.* 20; *Th.* 168. Hollow mountain: HS 5; cf. *Nib.* 3, 8, 15; see Ellis (1943) 87–96. Forest: HS 3 f. In Böcklin's *Toteninsel* one sees mountain and island as land of death combined with sea passage thither. The name of Nibelungs or Niflungs is probably connected with Niflheim: they are the people of mist or darkness.

[47] Zeus *vs.* Hephaistos: Il. 1.590–594; Apollod. 1.3.5. See Vian (1952) 175 f.

Hence the Sigurd-Fafnir legend has much in common not only with the Bearson, Perseus, and Herakles legends, but also with the fundamental pattern of the combat myth. It is a variant that has been superimposed upon persons and events of the Germanic migrations and invasions of the fifth and sixth centuries. It would not be difficult to show that the pattern recurs in many other medieval legends, in the sagas of Dietrich von Bern and of Wolfdietrich for instance, and in many an Arthurian legend. But it would add nothing to the present study to linger over them.[48]

TANNHÄUSER

Since the Venusberg has been mentioned a number of times in the foregoing pages, and I have given its name to a theme of the combat myth, a few words on the Tannhäuser legend are in order. Again it is Wagner who has made the legend well known among the reading and opera-going public: how Tannhäuser had come upon the hollow mountain where Venus reigned and had spent a year there as her companion in a life of sensual delights; how heartsick at last of this voluptuous life, and mindful of eternal punishment, he had left the mountain and gone to Rome, where he asked Pope Urban for absolution; how the Pope replied that the dry staff which he held in his hand would sooner put forth green shoots than Tannhäuser could be absolved of his sins, so that Tannhäuser went back to the mountain to live with Venus forever; and how three days later the Pope's staff sprouted, so that he sent messengers to call Tannhäuser back, but too late.[49]

With the legend's Christian trappings and the themes of repentance and absolution we are not concerned, but only with the Venusberg and the hero who tarried there. Barto, in his thorough study of the legend, has shown that the Venusberg of this fifteenth-century legend has its antecedent in the Gralsburg, the grail paradise of the Parzival and Lohengrin legends. A direct connection between the Holy Grail and Venus, between Lohengrin and Tannhäuser, may seem strange

---

[48] In the Volsung-Nibelung legend notice Otter, brother of Fafnir and Regin, whose otter shape may recall the seal form of Psamathe and her son Phokos (p. 106); notice too the fish shape of Andvari and the binding of the gods by the warlock *Hreidmar* and his demonic sons: see Poetic Edda, *Reg.* praef.; Prose Edda, *Skáldsk.* 39 f.; *Vols.* 14. The themes present are 1B (*Hreidmar, Atli*), 1c, 2B, 3A (*Vols.* 13, 18), 3B, 3D (HS 6), 3E (*Vols.* 14; HS 2, 6), 3F, 4A (*Vols.* 13 f., *Th.* 163), 4B (HS 6), 4c, 4E, 5A, 5B, 6A, 6B, 7A, 7B, 7c (HS 6), 7E, 7F (*Nib.* 3; *Th.* 167; HS 4), 7G, 8A (*Nib.* 8, 10; HS 5–7), 8c, 8D, 9, 10A (body severed or shattered: *Skáldsk.* 40; *Vols.* 19; *Th.* 166; HS 5, 7), 10B, 10c (*Skáldsk.* 40).

[49] Barto (1916) 155–248 contains 32 versions of the Tannhäuser folksong. For a prose version of the legend see Grimm, *Deutsche Sagen* 170. See Baring-Gould (1882) 207–220.

and incongruous at first sight; but Barto shows that the grail, especially as one finds it in Wolfram's *Parzival*, is a *Wunschding*, i.e., it is an Amaltheia's horn; and the grail paradise of Germanic lore, located within a hollow mountain, is abundantly furnished with food and drink, gold and precious stones, in halls where the grail is served by beautiful women whose queen is the lady Repanse de Joie. It was not without the pleasures of love in any but the most lofty conceptions of it. In fact, a sixteenth-century writer, whom Barto cites, explicitly identifies the grail paradise with the Venusberg. I would only disagree with Barto when he says that "the idea of the grail-realm [deteriorated] into that of a sensual hollow-mountain paradise. . . ." Rather, it seems to me, the pure and heavenly Gralsburg is an exceptional development of the old pagan paradise, whatever the name that it bore at any time. In this Germanic material we have a splendid illustration of how heavenly paradise, earthly paradise, sinners' Hell, and abode of the dead, fade insensibly one into another.[50]

The names Venus and Venusberg in German legend are due either to Italian or to classical-Latin influences. The hostess is really Holda, Holle, Dame Holt, who is the old goddess Hel. In Christianised folklore she is Satan's wife, and the two rule together within the mountain. That the grim underworld queen should be identified with a love goddess need surprise us no longer, now that we have seen the two sides of Ishtar, Anat, and Isis.[51]

Now it should be noticed that Tannhäuser's experience with Venus-Holda repeats Sigurd's with the Valkyrie. Sigurd went within the rampart or castle, built of river gold by cunning craftsmen on a mountain, where lived the Valkyrie who became identified with Brynhild. There he was well entertained with food and drink. In particular he received the aforementioned horn of mead, in which were mingled powerful runes that had been scraped from many potent objects. Sigurd bound himself to her willingly; for not only did he want the wisdom, i.e., power, that she could give him, but he also found her fair. There he tarried for a time, sharing her bed. For many

---

[50] Barto (1916) and authorities cited 249–258; on Gralsburg see 1–17. Johann Fischart identified Gral with Venusberg: Barto 17, 33.

[51] Barto (1913), (1916) 18–57. Venus = Hel: Grimm (1875–78) 780 f.; Barto (1916) 44–46. Remy (1913: 46) does not probe deeply enough when he denies that Venus could be Holda or Berchta on the ground that they are not beautiful and seductive, but have dismal, joyless dwelling places. He has himself just spoken (45) of the Hörselberg as a place of horror and gloom, the abode of damned souls and demons; and nobody can deny that by the nineteenth century the Venusberg had become identified with the Hörselberg in German folklore, where Holda and Satan reigned: see Grimm, *Deutsche Sagen* 7, 173, 313.

are the hints of consummated love between the two; and the sword that Sigurd in Gunnar's shape placed between himself and the maid, as they lay in bed, most likely has a quite different meaning originally from that which the composite legend later gave it. Then Sigurd left, breaking the bond that held him to the Valkyrie. But at last he and she went off to Hel together; for they were laid side by side on funeral pyres. There is also a return to her in the composite legend's doublet, when the wooing of Brynhild was added to the sleeping-Valkyrie episode. The return has no place in the combat myth, but has its beginnings perhaps in just these episodes of the Volsung-Nibelung saga.[52]

Now the *lectulus Brunihildae* is identified by an eleventh-century document with a crag on the Feldberg in the Taunus mountains near Mainz. Though the Venusberg has for the past two centuries been commonly identified with the Thuringian Hörselberg, it has also been identified with other mountains in Germany (and Italy), especially those that are suitably wild or eerie. It is probable that somebody who is equipped to search out all locations of the Venusberg will find that it has also been located in the Taunus. In any case, since "Siren theme" is my alternative name for Theme 8D, it is noteworthy that the Lorelei rock, which is also one of the points on the Rhine where folklore has placed the sunken Nibelung hoard, is situated at the western end of that range.[53]

---

[52] Sigurd's entertainment on Valkyrie's mountain: Poetic Edda, *Sigrdr.*; *Th.* 168; he is bound to her: Poetic Edda, *Grip.* 31, *Sigrdr.* 22 f.; *Th.* 227; he shares her bed: Poetic Edda, *Helr. Br.* 12 f.; Prose Edda, *Skáldsk.* 41; *Vols.* 20, 27; *Nib.* 10; funeral pyres: *Helr. Br.* praef.; *Vols.* 31. The Nibelung mountain castle held gold and all riches without stint; it is certainly a forerunner of the grail paradise: *Nib.* 8. As for the Valkyrie Brynhild notice *Grip.* 29, "Of glee and gladness will the girl rob thee / who is Brynhild hight . . ." (Hollander). Hagen says (*Nib.* 7), "Who is this that Gunther wooeth? Would she were the Devil's bride in Hell!" (Armour). The episode in which she incites Gunnar to Sigurd's murder reflects the original purpose of Th. 8D: she meant to lure the hero to his destruction; and that purpose is not absent from the Tannhäuser legend.

[53] *Lect. Brun.: Cod. Dipl. Nassoicus ap.* Lehmgrübner (1936) 88. On locations of the Venusberg see Baring-Gould (1882) 212 f., Barto (1916) 18–57. For the Lorelei see the poems of Brentano, Eichendorff, and Heine, and Brentano's *Märchen:* see Hertz (1886), who maintains that the Lorelei tale is Brentano's invention and not a genuine German legend. But its principal theme, that of a seductive temptress who entices men to their doom, is little different from the Venusberg theme. Before Brentano's time the rock was called Lorelei (or by such variants as Lurlenberg, Lurlaberg, etc.) and was famous for its echo. And in the first mention of the place by Ruodolf in the *Annales Fuldenses* under the year 858, at which passage *Mons Lurlaberch* is an early gloss, the first record of the name, a ghost story is attached to it. An evil spirit plagued the village, throwing stones, uttering voices, and causing discord; among other acts he caused a priest to lie with the mayor's daughter. In this young lady, perhaps, we have the Lorelei siren in embryo, who finally replaced the male demon. Notice Grimm, *Deutsche Sagen* 221: the *Jungfrau* who haunts the Oselberg (i.e., Hörselberg) and takes the form of a snake with woman's head and breast.

How the historical minnesinger Tannhäuser became the hero of the Venusberg tale has always been a puzzle. Probably the connection is accidental and due to some similarity of name. The Tannhäuser of the tale is a knight (*Ritter*), and Barto is probably right in maintaining that his direct antecedent is Lohengrin or Helyas, the swanknight, who came out of the grail paradise, and went back again to stay forever, after his otherworldly connection was recognised. Once Tannhäuser's relation to Lohengrin is established, we see that he was a knight who performed exploits in this world and, in particular, relieved a lady in distress. And Barto is probably right in connecting the first part of his name with the legendary king Dan, eponym of the Danes, who, like Barbarossa, sleeps within a hollow mountain, sitting at a table, with all his host and rich trappings about him. In fact, Tannhäuser is called Daniel in Dutch and Flemish versions of the folksong; and, as Barto points out, Caspar Abel (early eighteenth century) identified Tannhäuser with King Tanaus, conqueror of Asia and Europe, concerning whom he cites Aventinus (early sixteenth century), who makes it clear that Tanaus is German Dan or Latin Danus. This Dan has entered the Charlemagne cycle as Ogier the Dane, known in Danish folklore as Holger Danske: he conquers cities of Asia and in folklore sleeps within a hollow mountain. In the *chanson de geste,* furthermore, he spent two hundred years in Avalon with Morgan le Fey, returned to the world, and then, after his otherworldly connection was recognised, went back to Avalon to spend eternity with her. Avalon is Arthur's otherworldly kingdom, where he lives with Morgan or the Lady of the Lake; but he also presides over the grail court within a mountain. In the old Babylonian stories of Nergal and Gilgamesh we saw that the champion could become the ruler of the dead.[54]

Another companion of Venus or Holda is Eckhart, who sits before the Hörselberg, or goes before Holda's nightly rout, and warns all mortal men away. One remembers him chiefly as Krimhild's trusty retainer in the *Nibelung Lay;* but he plays a rather different part in the *Thidrekssaga.* There he is the mightiest of Sigurd's twelve apprentice companions who worked in Mimir's smithy. He struck Sigurd with tongs, whereupon the hero thrashed him soundly. Later it was he who saw Sigurd returning from the killing of Regin and ran inside

---

[54] Barto (1916) 58–71, 103–108; Caspar Abel, *Teutsche Alterthümer* 1.8; Aventinus, *Chron.* 1.9; Grimm, *Deutsche Sagen* 534–538. For the Daniel versions see Barto (1916) 155–159; in other versions notice the forms *Danhuser, Danheüser, Danyser,* etc.: *ibid.* 160–213; on Arthur, *ibid.* 11–16. On Ogier see the chanson *Ogier le Danois* and Baring-Gould (1882) 103.

to warn Mimir. So he corresponds to the giant guardsman of the *Nibelung* and *Horn Siegfried* lays, not only as a secondary opponent, but also as a warner. And the Krimhild whom he served so well was the hateful Krimhild, mistress of the Nibelung treasure. As a hero's opponent who later makes warning speeches in the underworld his analogue is Phlegyas, who among the damned of *Aeneid* 6 admonishes everyone of the dire consequences of evil deeds, and who as ferryman in the *Inferno* meets newcomers with menacing words.[55]

More reasons than these can be adduced to connect the Tannhäuser legend with the temptress episode of the combat myth. It appears to be that episode made over into an independent tale. So Germanic legend in manifold ways preserves the several components of the ancient myth pattern.[56]

---

[55] Eckhart with Venus-Holda: Grimm, *Deutsche Sagen* 7, 313; Barto (1916) 42. Mimir's apprentice: *Th.* 165, 167; cf. *Nib.* 8, HS 4. Krimhild's attendant: *Nib.* 19 f., 23. Phlegyas: Virg. *Aen.* 6.618–620; Dante *Inf.* 8.15–21; see pp. 477–479.

[56] Very interesting is the verse of the usual Tannhäuser folksong, stanza 14 or 15: Nehmt Urlaub von dem (*v.l.* den) Greisen. The *Greisen* have usually been interpreted as dwarfs, which may well be true for the fifteenth century and later; and Barto (1913: 296), reading *dem*, refers it to Wodan "der Alte vom Berge." But one thinks of the Graiai.

APPENDIX 6

DRAGONS AND SPRINGS

Norman Douglas, who intimately understood Mediterranean ways of life, discussed the relation of dragons to springs with remarkable insight in *Old Calabria*. He foreshadowed some of the conclusions which have been reached by W. N. Brown, Frankfort, Jacobsen, and the present study after much scholarly labor. Douglas says, "The dragon, I hold, is the personification of life within the earth—of that life which, being unknown and uncontrollable, is *eo ipso* hostile to man." He believes that the primordial dragon is the spring; for, he says, springs are called "eyes" in Italy and Arabia; and the eye must be upon a head, and the head upon a body; the snake suggested the proper animal shape for the spring to take because of his glassy eye, earth-dwelling habit, cold blood, and tenacity of life: hence the dragon. He might have referred also to Hebrew *'ayin*, which means both *eye* and *spring*. Then he points to springs in Greece and Italy that are now called Dragoneria or Dragonara. As springs flow night and day, so the dragons are sleepless. As Earth's children they guard the treasures within her. The spring-dragon easily becomes a river-dragon, who becomes hungry and spreads out over the land in floods. There are heavenly springs, so that he becomes a cloud-dragon that can fall in ruinous thunderstorm upon the fields. A volcanic crater is a spring of fire; so he becomes a fire-dragon that flows forth in lava torrents, or whose poisonous breath becomes the noxious exhalations from volcanic fissures. "In all his protean manifestations, he represents the envious and devastating principle; the spleenful wrath of

545

untamed (untamable) telluric forces." This is not the whole story, and Douglas has neglected the beneficent dragon. But he does perceive a relation between dragon and water, and in particular he realises that popular belief has often identified springs with dragons.[1]

His remarks on the fire-dragon are borne out by Typhon, who, we can be very sure, was identified with the spring and underground river of the Cilician cave. Certainly he was identified with the Orontes River and its source. At the same time he was so often identified with volcanoes that ancient and modern authorities alike have derived his name from the root *typh-* "smoke." The derivation, however, fails to convince me; why should smoke be considered Typhon's salient feature, even if he were primarily a volcano-demon? Wouldn't he more likely be called fire? In fact, his nature was manifold: he was not only river, spring, and volcano, but also sea and wind. His name is very likely not Greek; but, though non-Hellenic etymologies have been suggested, I doubt that its meaning is now recoverable. It was easy, as Norman Douglas shows, for Typhon as a water-dragon to become a rain-dragon, and so a demon of violent storms and winds; then as hurricane-demon he easily became a demon of volcanic eruption and earthquake.[2]

Python and Delphyne were associated with a Delphian spring. The only name given is Castalia, suitably located at the entrance to the Castalian gorge, which must have become Python's lair when the combat scene was moved to Pytho. Though Castalia's water was used in the Pythia's preparation, the mantic spring was Kassotis, just above the temple; and it must be that Python was supposed to have guarded this spring along with Ge's oracular shrine. In fact, there is an outcropping of the same vein of water below the temple at the shrine of Ge and the Muses. Then, to the northwest and higher up the slope is Delphusa, which is the modern village's main water supply. It was obviously as important in ancient times, both because of its resources, and because it is simply called the Delphian spring; though it is mentioned but once in ancient literature (if no other allusion has escaped

---

[1] Douglas (1928 O) 132–138. He shows finally (137) how easily the dragon takes human shape, becoming giant or ogre: in Greece today *dhrakos* means *ogre;* likewise *sdrago* in Calabria, where the ancient dragon is "a mockery of his former self." See Lawson (1910) 280–283.

[2] On Typhon from *typh-:* EM 772; LM 5.1441; Gruppe (1906) 102, 812, 1305; Dornseiff (1933) 18. Gruppe (812) suggests Semitic *siphon* "snake." Some scholars have connected the name with Canaanite *zāphôn* "north": LM *ibid.;* Gruppe 102, 409; Seippel (1939) 137 f.; in fact, Mount Kasios near Ugarit was given that name: see Gaster (1950) 169–171. English *typhoon,* as it happens, has nothing to do with Typhon, but is Chinese *tai fung;* LM 5.1442; Dornseiff 18; Ortiz (1947) 178.

me). It is reasonable to suppose that Delphyne and Delphynes, the Delphian dragons, were imagined to haunt this spring too. Furthermore we have seen the spring Telphusa, Apollo's enemy near Haliartos, whose name is probably a local variation of Delphusa (p. 372). So the spring Delphusa gives us more reason to suppose that the Telphusa of the Hymn to Apollo merely repeats the Delphian dragoness in a different dress.[3]

In the immediate neighborhood of Delphi, down the Papadhia ravine, which carries Castalia's waters to the Pleistos River, and not far above the river, is a springlike pool, out of which in winter there pours a torrent stream. This, called Zaleska in modern times, has been identified with the spring of Sybaris. The identification is almost certain, since on the side of Kirphis across the river is a cave called Krypsana, so that the place fulfils every requirement of the Sybaris story. Here plainly the spring was identified with the Lamia called Sybaris, who probably had a snake form.[4]

The waters of Sybaris rise from underground channels that descend from a sink (*katavothra*) in the southwestern corner of the Arachovite meadows of the Parnassian plateau, where the waters of the winter rains collect, fairly near the Corycian Cave. The cave itself has no spring, as its Cilician namesake has, though its walls and ceiling drip with water, which no doubt was used in the mantic ritual. The Castalia of Lykoreia was probably the spring called Phrias (well), close to the ruins of Lykoreia. There are also two springs in the Arachovite meadows. No doubt the Delphic oracle always made use of springs; and it did not lack them at its old Lycorean site.[5]

In the parallel Theban myth Drakon guarded a spring, which was identified with two Theban springs, as we have seen (p. 311). One spring was identified with the evil Dirke; either was called spring of Ares, Drakon's father; and one, the source of Ismenos, had something to do with the Ismenian oracle. From both Thebes and Delphi we

---

[3] Dragon at Castalia: Stat. *Theb.* 1.565 f.; cf. Eur. IT 1257. Use of Castalia's water: Eur. *Ion* 94–97; Schol. Vet. on Eur. *Phoen.* 224; Heliod. *Aith.* 2.26.4; Lucan BC 5.125. For a possible connection of dragon with Kassotis see Apollod. 1.4.1: Python tried to keep Apollo from the oracular *chasma*. According to Paus. 10.24.7, Kassotis was named after a Parnassian nymph, which may mean a Corycian nymph. Delphusa: Steph. Byz. 150 Holst.; see Ulrichs (1840) 37, 105–110; Amandry (1950) 229, note 5.

[4] See Ulrichs (1840) 26 f., 120. Apparently Krypsana was once a cult site and had its myth of dragon combat. It may be that it once tried to rival Pytho or Lykoreia. The myth is unique in calling the hero Eurybatos; neither Apollo nor Herakles ever took his place; and the fact that the story shows Apollo of Pytho to be spiritless is perhaps due to local rivalry.

[5] See Ulrichs (1840) 120. Also, above Arachova, and beside Apollo's *Lookout* is the source of the north fork of the Pleistos; see Aesch. *Eum.* 27.

have evidence that the local dragon might be identified with any prominent local spring. There was no attempt, it seems, even among the natives, to confine the dragon to only one spring. The Hellenes knew well enough that there are underground streams, that one spring is connected with another. They were wrong in particular instances: Castalia's waters do not come from the Kephisos; the Syracusan spring Arethusa does not flow under sea-bottom from the Alpheios. But the very errors prove their knowledge of the phenomenon. The dragon, being what he was, the living embodiment of underground waters, a creature of dread and wonderful shapes and powers, was seen in the whole system of springs, their underground channels, the issuing streams, and the sea into which they flowed. At every spring one of his eyes looked forth.[6]

But the particular spring may very well be a wife or daughter of the dragon, as the earth from which he rises is his mother. Every spring, we know, had its nymph, who might be beneficent or evil. The good nymph might become distinguished from the bad nymph, and yet both be housed in the same spring: such is the inconsistency that meets us at every turn on this level of thought. So on the scenes of the combat myth the nymph becomes identified with the dragoness: Delphyne, Telphusa, Sybaris, Dirke, Sphinx. In the spring, in the underground waters, dragon and dragoness live together.

Springs rise from the lower depths, the realm of death, and are therefore chthonian powers. It was early in mankind's history that prophecy and divination were associated with underworld powers and the dead. So the spring, a living deity that rises from the lower world, must have prophetic powers. There one can call forth spirits, dream visions, from the deep. So oracular shrines grow up around springs, where men receive visions and responses from the dragon-lord and the dragoness-nymph. The ancient *mantis* of the Corycian oracle could later be called Python, Poseidon, Earth, Night.[7]

The mantic properties of water are one phase of the potency with which men have endowed it. In his essay on the meaning of water in the cult and life of the ancients Martin Ninck has shown that for the ancient Greeks and Italians water had a chthonian nature which was manifested in marvelous powers. It was used in all sorts of ways for magical, divinatory, and religious purposes. In it resided a power that

---

[6] Castalia: Paus. 10.8.10; Arethusa: Strabo 6.2.4, p. 270; Ovid *Met.* 5.494–505, 636–641. Cf. pp. 366–374.

[7] There were men who said that the spring of Ge and the Muses, which belongs to the Kassotis system, flowed with Styx's water, an idea which Plutarch's Boethos didn't like: *Mor.* 402D. For us this is evidence that the ancient goddess was also called Styx.

could change shapes; hence the ease with which spirits of both sea and underworld could change their forms. Ninck's findings have been supported and supplemented by the researches of Onians and of Jacobsen, who shows parallel conceptions of water in Mesopotamia. In water the ancients saw a creative and life-giving power: this was the most marvelous power of all. Powers of life and death were resident in the same substance. It is, of course, easy to see that early man would attribute fertility and life-giving power to the water that is the prime need of all living things. So the water that is the chaos-dragon's body is also the soma, nectar, milk, golden treasure, that the creator-god must win for his world and mankind. In the grand opening lines of the first Olympian ode Pindar said best what all Greeks thought:

Ἄριστον μὲν ὕδωρ, ὁ δὲ χρυσὸς αἰθόμενον πῦρ
ἅτε διαπρέπει νυκτὶ μεγάνορος ἔξοχα πλούτου.

"Best is water, then gold that gleams like fire blazing at night, supreme above proud wealth." [8]

---

[8] Ninck (1921); pp. 47–99 are concerned with the use of water in divination; notice 95–97 on the use of water in lot oracles: of special interest to us is the oracle of the spring Aponina near Padova, which Herakles opened on his way back with Geryon's cattle. See also Onians (1954) 229 f., 288–291; Jacobsen ap. Frankfort (1949) 159–161; Lawson (1910) 281, 333 f., who mentions the immortal water that dragons guard. The Hesperides' garden had *krênai ambrosiai* (Eur. *Hipp.* 742–751), once, no doubt, the object of Herakles' quest; and modern Greek folklore still has "to athanato nero, to athanato votani," as in the folksong *Tragûdhi tû Parnassû*.

APPENDIX 7

LIST OF ART WORKS ILLUSTRATING
THE PYTHON, TITYOS, KYKNOS, AND TYPHON COMBATS

(Numbers in square brackets refer to figures in this volume)

Apollo and Python

1. Bf. lekythos, Bibliothèque Nationale, Cabinet des Médailles, Paris. CVA, France 10, pl. 86. 6–8; LM 3.3408, fig. 4. [1]

2. Coin-type of Croton, ca. 420–380 B.C. HN p. 96, fig. 54; LM 3.3407, fig. 1. [2]

3. Wall-painting in House of Vettii, Pompeii. Accademia dei Lincei, Monumenti Antichi VIII (1898) pl. 11, p. 366; LM 3.3407 f., fig. 2. [27]

4. Tripod base found in Neapolis-Samaria, Palestine: one of six reliefs. LM 3.3407, fig. 3.

5. Roman relief from Gelb am Rhein, now in Berlin. Annali dell' Inst. Arch. XXXII (1860) pp. 201 f.

6. Etruscan mirror. Gerhard, Etruskische Spiegel, pl. 291A; LM 3.3409 f., fig. 5.

7. Rf. Nolan amphora. Lenormant-DeWitte, Elite des Monuments Céramographiques II pl. 1; LM 3.3409 f., fig. 6. [3]

8. Two sculptures in Rome, Capitoline Museum and Mus. Torlonia, representatives of a single original, showing Leto with the twins in her arms. Cat. Pal. Cons. Rome, pl. 85, no. 31; Overbeck, Kunstmyth. pl. 23.17–18.

9. Coin-type of Hierapolis, Phrygia. Philologus LXIX (1910), p. 178, fig. 1.

APOLLO AND TITYOS

10. Rf. amphora, ascribed to Phintias, from Vulci, now in Louvre G42. CVA, France 8, pl. 28.3, 6; FR pl. 112; LM 5.1042, fig. 1; Beazley, Attic Red-Figure Vase-Painters, p. 22, nr. 1.

11. Rf. Attic krater, manner of Polygnotos, Metropolitan Museum, N. Y. Metr. Mus. Studies V (1934) pp. 126 f., figs. 7, 8; Beazley, ARFVP 717, Nekyia-Painter 1.

12. Bf. amphora in Bibl. Nat., Cabinet des Médailles, Paris. CVA, France 7, pl. 31.1–2; LM 5.1046, fig. 3.

13. Gold ring, Louvre. Furtwängler, Antike Gemmen III p. 84, fig. 57.

14. Gold ring, Louvre. Furtwängler, AG III p. 84, fig. 58.

15. Carnelian scarab from Orvieto, Berlin. Furtwängler, AG pl. 8.18.

16. Carnelian scarab from Corneto. Annali dell' Inst. Arch. LVII (1885) pl. GH 34.

17. Etruscan bucchero vase. RE 6A.1600, nr. 8.

18. Relief on bronze tripod from Perugia, Loeb Collection, Fogg Museum, Cambridge, Mass. Am. Journ. Arch. XII (1908) p. 304, pl. 15.

19. Bf. amphora, Musée du Cinquantenaire, Brussels. Ducati, Pontische Vasen, p. 18, pl. 21.

20. Bf. amphora from Caere, Louvre E864. CVA, France 9, pl. 6.4; LM 5.1043, fig. 2. [4]

21. Bf. amphora from Corneto. Antike Denkmäler I 22; JHS LII (1932) 35.

22. Bf. sherd, Acropolis Museum, Athens. Graef-Langlotz, Antike Vasen von der Akropolis I, p. 235, pl. 98.2406; LM 5.1047, fig. 4.

23. Bf. sherd, Acropolis Museum, Athens. Graef-Langlotz, AVA I, p. 76, pl. 39.631b.

24. Bf. amphora, later style, from Vulci, Berlin Mus. 1835. Furtwängler, Vasensammlung im Antiquarium, p. 332.

25. Rf. amphora, severe style, from Vulci, Eucharides painter, British Museum E278. CVA, Br. Mus. 3, pl. 15; Beazley, ARFVP 153, nr. 2. [5]

26. Rf. krater from Agrigentum, Loeb Collection, Fogg Museum, Cambridge, Mass. Lenormant-DeWitte, El. Mon. Cér. II pl. 57.

27. Fragment of rf. lebes gamikos, Tübingen. Watzinger, Griechische Vasen in Tübingen, p. 47, E103, pl. 29.

28. Rf. amphora, severe style, manner of Duris, Berlin Mus. 3189. FR III, p. 279, fig. 128.

29. Rf. amphora pelike from Caere, Louvre G375. CVA, France 12, pl. 42.1, 2, 6, 8; LM 5.1048, fig. 5; Beazley, ARFVP 680, nr. 48. [6]

30. Rf. krater, severe style, from Caere, ascribed to Aegisthus painter, Louvre G161. CVA, France 1, III I c, pl. 10; FR pl. 164; LM 5.1050, fig. 6; Beazley, ARFVP 330, nr. 1. [7]

31. Rf. cup from Vulci, Munich 2689, J 402. FR pl. 55; LM 5.1051 f., fig. 7; Beazley, ARFVP 583, nr. 2.

32. Rf. amphora pelike, late archaic style, Tyskiewicz painter, Villa Giulia. Beazley, ARFVP 187, nr. 38.

See also 54 below.

Herakles and Kyknos

33. Engraved scarab, British Museum. Br. Mus. Catalogue of Engraved Gems 276; LM 2.1692, fig. 1.

34. Rf. kylix from Kameiros, Kleophrades painter, British Museum E73. LM 2.1693 f., fig. 2; Beazley, ARFVP 128, nr. 94.

35. Rf. cup from Corneto, Tarquinia RC 2066. Mon. Inst. XI pl. 24; Pfuhl, Mal. Zeichn. fig. 350; Beazley, ARFVP 101, Cup 2.

36. Bf. amphora, Louvre F36. Pottier, Vases antiques du Louvre II 91, pl. 66.

37. Bf. amphora, Louvre F31. Pottier, VAL II 92, pl. 66. [8]

38. Rf. kylix, painted by Oltos, British Museum E8. AGV pl. 84; Beazley, ARFVP 40, nr. 71. [9]

39. Bf. amphora of archaic style, painted by Amasis, Munich 1379, J 81. CVA, Germany 3, pls. 10.4, 13.2; AGV pl. 121.2; Hoppin, Greek BF Vases, p. 44, nr. 24. [10]

40. Bf. lekythos from Vulci. Annali dell' Inst. Arch. LII (1880) pl. M3.

41. Bf. volute krater, painted by Nikosthenes, British Museum B364 (560). Br. Mus. Cat. Vas. II 18, fig. 27; Hoppin, Greek BF Vases. p. 207, nr. 20.

42. Bf. amphora from Kameiros, painted by Amasis, British Museum B197. CVA, Br. Mus. 3, pl. 38.1b; Hoppin, Greek BF Vases, p. 43, nr. 22.

43. Bf. oinochoe from Vulci, painted by Kolchos, Berlin Mus. 1732. AGV pls. 122, 123; LM 2.1695, fig. 3; Hoppin, Greek BF Vases, p. 157, nr. 1.

44. Bf. amphora, Acropolis Museum, Athens. Graef-Langlotz, AVA I pl. 55.890; Beazley, ARFVP 953, nr. 13.

45. Bf. hydria, Munich 1709. Beazley, Development of Attic Black-figure, p. 83.

46. Bf. column krater, Metropolitan Museum, N. Y. Richter and Milne, Shapes and Names of Athenian Vases, fig. 46.

47. Bf. kylix, Andokides painter, Ricketts and Shannon Collection, Cambridge. CVA, Great Britain 11, III H, pl. 4.1b; Beazley, ARFVP 4, nr. 30.

48. Boeotian lekanis, Louvre. Vian (1945) nr. 39, pl. 2.1; JHS LV (1935) 79, fig. 1.

49. Bf. Etruscan amphora of archaic style, Basseggio, Rome. AGV pl. 121.1 [11]

ZEUS AND TYPHON

50. Bf. Chalcidian hydria, Munich 596, J 125. AGV pl. 237; FR pl. 32; Sieveking-Hackl, Vasensamml. Münch. pl. 24; Vian[1] 4, p. 9 and pl. 1. [13]

51. Mutilated bronze relief from Ptoon with archaic figures. BCH XVI (1892) pl. 10; LM 5. 1452, fig. 4; Vian 3, p. 9 and pl. 1.

52. Bf. Etruscan hydria from Vulci, British Museum B62. LM 5.1452, fig. 3; Vian 6, p. 10 and pl. 2.

53. Rf. prochoos from Canosa, Apulian style, British Museum F237. LM 5.1543 f., fig. 5; Vian 12, p. 11 and pl. 2. [14]

54. Frieze of the great altar of Zeus and Athena at Pergamon: Gigantomachy. H. Winnefeld, Altertümer von Pergamon III 2, pls. 2–5; Vian 38, pp. 19–23 and pls. 11–12. [12, 15]

55. Baldric of shield, Olympia inv. B1636. Vian 1, p. 9.

56. Baldric of shield, Olympia inv. B315. Vian 2, p. 9 and pl. 1.

57. Etruscan sardonyx scarab, Royal Museum, Copenhagen. Vian 5, p. 10 and pl. 2; Furtwängler, Ant. Gemm. I pl. 64.28.

58. Bf. Etruscan amphora, Micali painter, Göttingen. Vian 7, p. 10.

59. Bf. Etruscan amphora, Villa Giulia 18597. Vian 8, p. 10.

60. Etruscan funerary stele, Bologna. Vian 9, p. 10 and pl. 3.

61. Etruscan funerary stele, Bologna. Vian 10, p. 11 and pl. 3.

62. Etruscan urn, once at Museo Guarnacci, Volterra. Vian 11, p. 11.

63. Denarius of C. Cornelius Sisena (102–100). Vian 13, p. 11 and pl. 2; Grueber, Coins of Roman Republic in Br. Mus. III pl. 93.6.

64. Relief from the temple of Baal, Palmyra. Vian 14, pp. 11 f.; Syria XV (1934) pl. 20.

65. Bas-relief, Sueida. Vian 15, p. 12 and pl. 3; M. Dunand, Musée de Soueida, pl. 13.

---

[1] See Bibliography: VIAN (1951)

BIBLIOGRAPHY

BIBLIOGRAPHY

Listed here are those books and articles which are referred to in the notes merely by author's (or editor's) surname and year of publication; a few books listed, however, are more conveniently referred to by initial letters of their titles than by publication date; and articles in RE and LM are referred to by author's name and heading (but only those encyclopaedia articles that have extraordinary importance for the subject of this book are listed).

Antti AARNE, Stith THOMPSON (1928). The Types of the Folk-Tale: A Classification and Bibliography. (Folklore Fellows Comm. 74) Helsinki: Academia Scientiarum Fennica.

M. ADLER. Kyknos. RE 11. 2435–2442.

Pierre AMANDRY (1950). La Mantique Apollinienne à Delphes: Essai sur le fonctionnement de l'Oracle. Paris: Boccard.

Joh. B. AUFHAUSER (1911). Das Drachenwunder des heiligen Georg in der Griechischen und Lateinischen Überlieferung. Leipzig: Teubner.

Janet Ruth BACON (1925). The Voyage of the Argonauts. London: Methuen.

S. BARING-GOULD (1882). Curious Myths of the Middle Ages. Boston.

R. D. BARNETT (1945). The Epic of Kumarbi and the Theogony of Hesiod. JHS LXV 100 f.

Philip Stephan BARTO (1913). The German Venusberg. Journ. of Engl. and Germ. Philol. XII 295–303.

—— (1916). Tannhäuser and the Mountain of Venus: A Study in the Legend of the Germanic Paradise. New York: Oxford University Press; London, etc.: Humphrey Milford.

Edward L. BASSETT (1955). Regulus and the Serpent in the *Punica*. Classical Philology L 1–20.

L. BAYARD (1943). Pytho-Delphes et la légende du serpent. REG LVI 25–28.

Jean BAYET (1921–23). Hercule Funéraire. Mélanges d'Archéologie et d'Histoire, Ecole Française de Rome. I 39 (1921–1922) 219–266, II 40 (1923) 19–102.

—— (1926). Les Origines de l'Hercule Romain. Paris: Boccard.

August BECKER (1883). De Rhodiorum Primordiis. Commentationes Philol. Jenenses II 93–136.

Fernand BENOIT (1950). Les Mythes de l'outre-tombe: Le Cavalier à l'anguipède et l'écuyère Epona. Brussels: Latomus.

J. Theodore BENT (1891). A Journey in Cicilia Tracheia. JHS XII 206–224.

Yves BEQUIGNON (1937). La Vallée du Spercheios des origines au IVe siècle: Etudes d'archéologie et de topographie. Paris: Boccard.

Hans BESIG (1937). Gorgo und Gorgoneion in der archaischen Griechischen Kunst. Berlin: Markert.

A. M. BLACKMAN, H. W. FAIRMAN (1942–44). The Myth of Horus at Edfu: II. C. The Triumph of Horus over his Enemies: A Sacred Drama. Journ. Egypt. Arch. XXVIII (1942) 32–38, XXIX (1943) 2–36, XXX (1944) 5–22.

Chr. BLINKENBERG (1911). The Thunderweapon in Religion and Folklore: A Study in Comparative Archaeology. Cambridge University Press.

Fr. BÖRTZLER (1930). Zu den antiken Chaoskosmogonien. Archiv für Religionswissenschaft XXVIII 253–268.

Helmuth Th. BOSSERT (1932). Šantaš und Kupapa: Neue Beiträge zur Entzifferung der Kretischen und Hethitischen Bilderschrift. Leipzig: Harassowitz. (Mitteilungen der Altorientalischen Gesellschaft VI 3)

Jean BOUSQUET (1951). Observations sur l' "Omphalos archaïque" de Delphes. BCH LXXV 210–223.

Michel BREAL (1863). Hercule et Cacus: Etude de Mythologie. Mélanges de Mythologie et de Linguistique, 2d ed., Paris (1882) 1–161.

Arthur G. BRODEUR (1953). The Structure and the Unity of *Beowulf*. PMLA LXVIII 1183–1195.

—— (1954). Design for Terror in the Purging of Heorot. Journ. of Engl. and Germ. Philol. LIII 503–513.

Frank BROMMER (1944). Herakles und Syleus. Jahrbuch des Deutschen Archäologischen Instituts LIX 69–78.

Norman O. BROWN (1953). Hesiod's Theogony, translated with an Introduction. New York: Liberal Arts Press.

W. Norman BROWN (1941). The Rigvedic Equivalent for Hell. JAOS LXI 76–80.

—— (1942). The Creation Myth of the Rig Veda. JAOS LXII 85–98.

E. A. Wallis BUDGE (1888). The Martyrdom and Miracles of Saint George of Cappadocia. The Coptic Texts edited with an English Translation. London.

—— (1901). The Book of the Dead: An English Translation of the Chapters, Hymns, etc., of the Theban Recension. 3 vols. Chicago: Open Court; London: Kegan Paul, Trench, Trubner.

—— (1911). Osiris and the Egyptian Resurrection. 2 vols. London: Warner; New York: Putnam's.

—— (1912). Legends of the Gods: The Egyptian Texts, edited with Translations. London: Kegan Paul, Trench, Trubner.

—— (1930). George of Lydda the Patron Saint of England: A Study of the *Cultus* of St. George in Ethiopia. [The Ethiopic Texts with translation]. London: Luzac.

—— (1931). Egyptian Tales and Romances Pagan, Christian and Muslim. London: Butterworth.

—— (1934). From Fetish to God in Ancient Egypt. Oxford University Press; London: Humphrey Milford.

Rhys CARPENTER (1946). Folk Tale, Fiction and Saga in the Homeric Epics. (The Sather Classical Lectures, vol. 20) Berkeley, Los Angeles: University of California Press.

Jaroslav ČERNÝ (1952). Ancient Egyptian Religion. London, New York, etc.: Hutchinson's University Library.

Félicien CHALLAYE (1950). Contes et Légendes du Japon. Paris: Nathan.

Ella E. CLARK (1953). Indian Legends of the Pacific Northwest. Berkeley, Los Angeles: University of California Press.

Albert T. CLAY (1919). The Empire of the Amorites. New Haven: Yale University Press.

Gisbert COMBAZ (1945). Masques et Dragons en Asie. (Mélanges Chinois et Bouddhiques VII [1939–1945].) Brussels: Institut Belge des Hautes Etudes Chinoises.

G. CONTENAU (1941). Le Déluge Babylonien, Ishtar aux Enfers. Paris: Payot.

A. B. COOK (1914, 1925, 1940). Zeus: A Study in Ancient Religion. 3 vols. in 5. Cambridge University Press.

Harold P. COOKE (1931). Osiris: A Study in Myths, Mysteries and Religion. London: Daniel.

F. M. CORNFORD (1952). Principium Sapientiae: The Origins of Greek Philosophical Thought. Cambridge University Press.

Johan H. CROON (1952). The Herdsman of the Dead: Studies on some Cults, Myths and Legends of the Ancient Greek Colonization-Area. Utrecht: S. Budde.

Georges DAUX (1936) Pausanias à Delphes. Paris: Picard.

F. Hadland DAVIS (MLJ). Myths and Legends of Japan. New York: Crowell, n.d.

S. DAVIS (1953). Argeiphontes in Homer—The Dragon-Slayer. Greece and Rome XXII 33–38.

R. M. DAWKINS (1953). Modern Greek Folktales, chosen and translated by R. M. D. Oxford: Clarendon Press.

——— (1955). More Greek Folktales, chosen and translated by R. M. D. Oxford: Clarendon Press.

Jean DEFRADAS (1954). Les Thèmes de la Propagande Delphique. Paris: Klincksieck.

A. DEIMEL (1914). Pantheon Babylonicum. Rome: Pontificium Institutum Biblicum.

Edouard DHORME (1949). Les Religions de Babylonie et d'Assyrie. 2nd ed. Paris: Presses Universitaires de France.

Professor DIESTEL in Bonn (1860). Set-Typhon, Asahel und Satan. Ein Beitrag zur Religionsgeschichte des Orients. Zeitschrift für die Historische Theologie XXX 159–217.

Henri DORE (1915). Recherches sur les Superstitions en Chine IX–X. Shanghai: La Mission Catholique.

Franz DORNSEIFF (1933). Die Archaische Mythenerzählung: Folgerungen aus dem Homerischen Apollonhymnos. Berlin, Leipzig: de Gruyter.

Norman DOUGLAS (1928 B). Birds and Beasts of the Greek Anthology. London: Chapman & Hall.

—— (1928 O). Old Calabria. New York: Modern Library.

René Dussaud (1949 A). Les Antécédents orientaux à la Théogonie d'Hésiode. Annuaire de l'Institut de Philol. et d'Hist. Orientales et Slaves IX (= Mélanges Henri Grégoire) 227–231.

—— (1949 R). Les Religions des Hittites et des Hourrites des Phéniciens et des Syriens. 2d ed. Paris: Presses Universitaires de France.

Erich Ebeling (1931). Tod und Leben nach den Vorstellungen der Babylonier. I. Teil: Texte. Berlin, Leipzig: de Gruyter.

—— (1952). Eine Neue Tafel des Akkadischen Zû-Mythos. Rev. d'Assyr. et d'Archéol. Orient. XLVI 25–41.

Wolfram Eberhard (1937). Typen Chinesischer Volksmärchen. (FF Comm. 120) Helsinki: Academia Scientiarum Fennica.

Emma J. and Ludwig Edelstein (1945). Asclepius: A Collection and Interpretation of the Testimonies. 2 vols. Baltimore: Johns Hopkins Press.

Otto Eissfeldt (1939). Ras Schamra und Sanchunjaton. Halle (Saale): Niemeyer.

—— (1951). El im Ugaritischen Pantheon. (Berichte über die Verhandlungen der Sächs. Akad. der Wissensch. zu Leipzig. Phil.-Hist. Kl. XCVIII 4.) Berlin: Akademie Verlag.

Hilda Roderick Ellis (1943). The Road to Hel: A Study of the Conception of the Dead in Old Norse Literature. Cambridge University Press.

R. Engelmann. Kyknos. LM 2. 1690–1699.

Ivan Engnell (1943). Studies in Divine Kingship in the Ancient Near East. Uppsala: Almquist & Wiksells.

H. W. Fairman (1935). The Myth of Horus at Edfu—I. Journ. Egypt. Arch. XXI 26–36.

Lewis Richard Farnell (1896, 1907, 1909). The Cults of the Greek States. 5 vols. Oxford: Clarendon Press.

—— (1921). Greek Hero Cults and Ideas of Immortality. Oxford: Clarendon Press.

R. O. Faulkner (1936). The Bremner-Rhind Papyrus—I. A. The Songs of Isis and Nephthys. Journ. Egypt. Arch. XXII 121–140.

—— (1937). The Bremner-Rhind Papyrus—III. D. The Book of Overthrowing ᶜApep. Journ. Egypt. Arch. XXIII 166–185.

—— (1938). The Bremner-Rhind Papyrus—IV. D. The Book of

Overthrowing ᶜApep. E. The Names of ᶜApep. Journ. Egypt Arch. XXIV 41–53.

T. FISH (1948). The Zu Bird. John Rylands Library Bulletin XXXI 162–171.

Karl FLORENZ (1919). Die Historischen Quellen der Shinto-Religion aus dem Altjapanischen und Chinesischen übersetzt und erklärt (Kojiki, Nihongi). Göttingen: Vandenhoeck & Ruprecht; Leipzig: Hinrichs.

Joseph FONTENROSE (1943). The Garden of Phoebus. American Journal of Philology LXIV 278–285.

—————— (1945). Philemon, Lot, and Lycaon. (Univ. Calif. Publ. in Class. Philol. XIII 93–119.) Berkeley, Los Angeles: University of California Press.

—————— (1948). The Sorrows of Ino and of Procne. Transactions of the American Philological Association LXXIX 125–167.

—————— (1951). White Goddess and Syrian Goddess. (Univ. Calif. Publ. in Semitic Philol. XI 125–148.) Berkeley, Los Angeles: University of California Press.

—————— (1957). Dagon and El. Oriens X 277–279.

—————— Peirithoos. RE 19.114–140.

Henri FRANKFORT (1939). Cylinder Seals: A Documentary Essay on the Art and Religion of the Ancient Near East. London: Macmillan.

—————— (1948). Kingship and the Gods: A Study of Ancient Near Eastern Religion as the Integration of Society and Nature. University of Chicago Press.

—————— (1949), H. A. Frankfort, John A. Wilson, Thorkild Jacobsen. Before Philosophy: The Intellectual Adventure of Ancient Man: An Essay on Speculative Thought in the Ancient Near East. Harmondsworth: Penguin Books.

James G. FRAZER (1911 D). The Dying God. (The Golden Bough III) London: Macmillan.

—————— (1911 M). The Magic Art and the Evolution of Kings. (The Golden Bough I) 3d ed. 2 vols. London: Macmillan.

—————— (1912). Spirits of the Corn and of the Wild. (The Golden Bough V) 3d ed. 2 vols. London: Macmillan.

—————— (1914). Adonis Attis Osiris: Studies in the History of Oriental Religion. (The Golden Bough IV) 3d ed. 2 vols. London: Macmillan.

——————, A. W. VAN BUREN (1930). Graecia Antiqua: Maps and Plans to Illustrate Pausanias. London: Macmillan.

Sigmund FREUD (ID). The Interpretation of Dreams. In the Basic

Writings of Sigmund Freud, translated by A. A. Brill. New York: Modern Library, 1938, pp. 179–549.

—— (BPP). Beyond the Pleasure Principle. Translated by C. J. M. Hubback. New York: Boni & Liveright, n.d.

Paul FRIEDLÄNDER (1907). Herakles: Sagengeschichtliche Untersuchungen. (Philologische Untersuchungen XIX) Berlin: Weidmann.

Johannes FRIEDRICH (1949). Der Churritische Mythus vom Schlangendämon Ḥedammu in Hethitischer Sprache. Archiv Orientální XVII 230–254.

Alan H. GARDINER (1931). The Library of A. Chester Beatty: Description of a Hieratic Papyrus with a Mythological Story, Love-Songs, and Other Miscellaneous Texts. London: Emery Walker, Oxford University Press.

—— (1944). Horus the Beḥdetite. Journ. Egypt. Arch. XXX 23–60.

M. GASTER (1939). Zur Alkestis-Sage. Byzantinisch-Neugriechische Jahrbücher XV 66–90.

Theodor H. GASTER (1950). Thespis: Ritual, Myth and Drama in the Ancient Near East. New York: Schuman.

—— (1952). The Oldest Stories in the World. New York: Viking Press.

Ignace J. GELB (HS). Hurrians and Subarians. University of Chicago Press, n.d.

Delia GOETZ, Sylvanus G. MORLEY (1950). Popol Vuh: The Sacred Book of the Ancient Quiché Maya. Translated by D. G. and S. G. M. from the Spanish translation of Adrián Recinos. Norman: University of Oklahoma Press.

Albrecht GÖTZE (1936). Hethiter, Churriter und Assyrer: Hauptlinien der Vorderasiatischen Kulturentwicklung im II. Jahrtausend v. Chr. Geb. Oslo: Aschehoug (Nygaard); Cambridge, Mass.: Harvard University Press.

Hetty GOLDMAN (1949). Sandon and Herakles. Hesperia, suppl. VIII 164–174 and pl. 18.

—— (1950). Excavations at Gözlü Kule, Tarsus: The Hellenistic and Roman Periods. Vol. I, 2 pts. Princeton University Press.

A. W. GOMME (1913). The Ancient Name of Gla. In Essays and Studies Presented to William Ridgeway. Cambridge University Press, pp. 116–123.

Cyrus H. GORDON (1947). Ugaritic Handbook. Rome: Pont. Inst. Bibl.

—— (1949). Ugaritic Literature: A Comprehensive Translation of the Poetic and Prose Texts. Rome: Pont. Inst. Bibl.

Marcel GRANET (1951). La Religion des Chinois. 2d ed. Paris: Presses Universitaires de France.

Henri GREGOIRE (1934). La Patrie des Nibelungen. Byzantion IX 1–39.

F. Ll. GRIFFITH, Herbert THOMPSON (1904). The Demotic Magical Papyrus of London and Leiden. London: Grevel.

Jacob GRIMM (1875–78). Deutsche Mythologie. 4th ed. 3 vols. Berlin.

Wilhelm GRUBE (1912). Fêng-Shên-Yên-i: Die Metamorphosen der Götter: Historisch-Mythologischer Roman aus dem Chinesischen. 2 vols. Leiden: Brill. [1–46 translated into German by W. G.; 47–100 summarised in German by H. Mueller]

Otto GRUPPE (1906). Griechische Mythologie und Religionsgeschichte. Munich: Beck.

Hans Gustav GÜTERBOCK (1946). Kumarbi: Mythen vom Churritischen Kronos aus den Hethitischen Fragmenten zusammengestellt, übersetzt und erklärt. (Istanbuler Schriften 16) Zurich, New York: Europaverlag.

—— (1948). The Hittite Version of the Hurrian Kumarbi Myths: Oriental Forerunners of Hesiod. Am. Journ. Arch. LII 123–134 and pl. III.

J. HACKIN (AM), ed., et al. Asiatic Mythology: A Detailed Description and Explanation of the Mythologies of All the Great Nations of Asia. Translated by F. M. Atkinson. New York: Crowell, n.d.

W. R. HALLIDAY (1928). The Greek Questions of Plutarch with a New Translation and a Commentary. Oxford: Clarendon Press.

N. G. L. HAMMOND (1931). Prehistoric Epirus and the Dorian Invasion. Annual of the British School at Athens XXXII 131–179.

Ch. de HARLEZ (1893). Le Livre des Esprits et des Immortels: Essai de Mythologie Chinoise d'après les textes originaux. Brussels.

Jane HARRISON (1922). Prolegomena to the Study of Greek Religion. 3d ed. Cambridge University Press.

—— (1927). Themis: A Study of the Social Origins of Greek Religion. 2d ed. Cambridge University Press.

Edwin Sidney HARTLAND (1894–96). The Legend of Perseus: A Study of Tradition in Story, Custom and Belief. 3 vols. London.

Louis HAVET (1888). Le Supplice de Phlégyas: Etude sur un épisode de l'Enéide. Rev. Philol. XII 145–172.

Alexander HEIDEL (1949). The Gilgamesh Epic and Old Testament Parallels. 2d ed. University of Chicago Press.

—— (1951). The Babylonian Genesis: The Story of the Creation. 2d ed. University of Chicago Press.

Kurt HEINEMANN (1913). Thanatos in Poesie und Kunst der Griechen. Munich: Kastner & Callwey.

Robert F. HEIZER (1952). A Survey of Cave Archaeology in California. (Report 15: Papers in California Archaeology 17) Berkeley: Univ. Calif. Arch. Survey, pp. 1–12.

Jules HERBILLON (1929). Les Cultes de Patras. Baltimore: Johns Hopkins Press.

W. HERTZ (1886). Ueber den Namen Lorelei. Sitzungsberichte Akad. Wissensch. München, Philos.-Philol. Kl. (1886) 217–251.

Rudolf HERZOG (1905). Das Panhellenische Fest und die Kultlegende von Didyma. Sitzungsberichte Akad. Wissensch. Berlin, Phil.-Hist. Kl. (1905) 979–993.

Gertrud HERZOG-HAUSER (1930). Tityos und Rhadamanthys. Wiener Studien XLVIII 108–111.

E. L. HICKS (1891). Inscriptions from Western Cilicia. JHS XII 225–273.

Alfred HILLEBRANDT (1927, 1929). Vedische Mythologie. 2d ed. 2 vols. Breslau: Marcus.

A. M. HOCART (1952). The Life-Giving Myth and Other Essays. London: Methuen.

O. HÖFER. Pyrene. LM 3. 3341–3345.

Leicester B. HOLLAND (1933). The Mantic Mechanism at Delphi. Am. Journ. Arch. XXXVII 201–214.

Richard HOLLAND (1900). Mythographische Beiträge. 1. Der Typhoeuskampf. Philologus LIX 344–354.

Fritz HOMMEL (1926). Ethnologie und Geographie des alten Orients. Munich: Beck.

S. H. HOOKE (1953). Babylonian and Assyrian Religion. London, New York, etc.: Hutchinson's University Library.

Clark HOPKINS (1934). Assyrian Elements in the Perseus-Gorgon Story. Am. Journ. Arch. XXXVIII 341–358.

B. HROZNÝ (1936). Les Quatre autels "Hittites" hiéroglyphiques d'Emir Ghazi et d'Eski Kišla, et les divinités Apulunas (?) et Rutas. Archiv Orientální VIII 171–199.

Walter IMMERWAHR (1891). Die Kulte und Mythen Arkadiens. Leipzig.

Hermann JACOBI (1893). Das Râmâyaṇa. Geschichte und Inhalt nebst Concordanz der gedruckten Recensionen. Bonn.

——— (1903). Mahâbhârata. Inhaltsangabe, Index und Concordanz der Calcuttaer und Bombayer Ausgaben. Bonn: Cohen.

Thorkild JACOBSEN (1946). Sumerian Mythology: A Review Article. JNES V 128–152.

——— (1953) and Samuel N. Kramer. The Myth of Inanna and Bilulu. JNES XII 160–188 and pls. LXVI–LXVIII.

George Wharton JAMES (1915). The Lake of the Sky—Lake Tahoe in the High Sierras of California and Nevada. Pasadena: George Wharton James.

H. JEANMAIRE (1939). Couroi et Courètes. Essai sur l'éducation Spartiate et sur les rites d'adolescence dans l'antiquité Hellénique. (Travaux et Mémoires de l'Univ. de Lille XXI) Lille: Bibliothèque Universitaire.

——— (1951). Dionysos: Histoire du Culte de Bacchus. Paris: Payot.

P. JENSEN (1890). Die Kosmologie der Babylonier. Strassburg.

——— (1900). Assyrisch-Babylonische Mythen und Epen. (Keilinschriftliche Bibliothek VI 1) Berlin: Reuther & Reichard.

——— (1906). Das Gilgamesch-Epos in der Weltliteratur. Strassburg: Trübner.

Ernest JONES (1931). Nightmare, Witches, and Devils. New York: Norton.

Arvid S. KAPELRUD (1952). Baal in the Ras Shamra Texts. Copenhagen: Gad.

Karl KERENYI (1949). Ziegenfell und Gorgoneion. Ann. Inst. Philol. et Hist. Orient. et Slav. IX (= Mélanges Henri Grégoire) 299–312.

——— (1951). The Gods of the Greeks. Translated by Norman Cameron. London, New York: Thames & Hudson.

Otto KERN (1926). Die Religion der Griechen I: Von den Anfängen bis Hesiod. Berlin: Weidmann.

Georg KNAACK (1880). Analecta Alexandrino-Romana. Greifswald.

Samuel N. KRAMER (1938). Gilgamesh and the Ḫuluppu-Tree: A Reconstructed Sumerian Text. University of Chicago Press.

——— (1944) Sumerian Mythology: A Study of Spiritual and Literary Achievement in the Third Millennium B.C. (Memoirs XXI) Philadelphia: American Philosophical Society.

Alexandre H. KRAPPE (1930). The Science of Folk-Lore. London: Methuen.

——— (1933). La Légende de Persée. Neuphilologische Mitteilungen XXXIV 225–232.

——— (1938). La Genèse des Mythes. Paris: Payot.

——— (1945). The Anatolian Lion God. JAOS LXV 144–154.

Josef KROLL (1932). Gott und Hölle: Der Mythos vom Descensus-Kampfe. (Studien der Bibliothek Warburg XX) Leipzig: Teubner.

E. KÜSTER (1913). Die Schlange in der Griechischen Kunst und Religion. (Religionsgeschichtliche Versuche und Vorarbeiten XIII 2) Giessen: Töpelmann; New York: Stechert.

Ludwig LAISTNER (1889). Das Rätsel der Sphinx: Grundzüge einer Mythengeschichte. 2 vols. Berlin.

B. LANDSBERGER (1950). Assyriologische Notizen. In Die Welt des Orients, Stuttgart: Koehler, pp. 362–376.

S. LANGDON (1923). The Babylonian Epic of Creation Restored from the recently recovered Tablets of Aššur. Oxford: Clarendon Press.

Emmanuel LAROCHE (1947). Recherches sur les noms des dieux Hittites. Paris: Librairie Orientale et Américaine, G.-P. Maisonneuve.

William Witherle LAWRENCE (1912). The Haunted Mere in *Beowulf*. PMLA XXVII 208–245.

——— (1930). Beowulf and Epic Tradition. Cambridge, Mass.: Harvard University Press.

John Cuthbert LAWSON (1910). Modern Greek Folklore and Ancient Greek Religion: A Study in Survivals. Cambridge University Press.

James LEGGE (1879), translator. The Sacred Books of China: The Texts of Confucianism. Part I: The Shû King, The Religious Portions of the Shih King, the Hsiâo King. Oxford.

Emile LEGRAND (1899), Hubert Pernot, editors. Chrestomathie Grecque Moderne. Paris.

Wilhelm LEHMGRÜBNER (1936). Die Erweckung der Walküre. (Hermaea XXXII) Halle: Niemeyer.

William Ellery LEONARD (1934). Gilgamesh, Epic of Old Babylonia, translated into English from Hermann Ranke's German translation. New York: Viking Press.

Albin LESKY (1925). Alkestis, der Mythus and das Drama. Sitzungsb. Akad. Wissensch. Wien, Phil.-Hist. Kl., 203, Abh. 2.

——— (1950). Hethitische Texte und Griechischer Mythos. Anzeiger Akad. Wissensch. Wien, Phil.-Hist. Kl., 87, 137–159.

G. Rachel LEVY (1934). The Oriental Origin of Herakles. JHS LIV 40–53 and pl. II.

——— (1953). The Sword from the Rock: An Investigation into the

Origins of Epic Literature and the Development of the Hero. London: Faber.

Ivan M. LINFORTH (1941). The Arts of Orpheus. Berkeley, Los Angeles: University of California Press.

F. LØKKEGAARD (1953). A Plea for El, The Bull, and Other Ugaritic Miscellanies. In Studia Orientalia Joanni Pedersen D., Copenhagen: Munksgaard, pp. 219–235.

André LOYEN (1940). Hercule et Typhée à propos de Virgile, Enéide VIII, 298. In Mélanges . . . offerts à Alfred Ernout, Paris: Klincksieck, pp. 237–245.

Ernst MAASS (1906). Die Griechen in Südgallien. Jahreshefte Österreich. Arch. Inst. Wien IX 139–182.

―――― (1907). Der Kampf um Temesa. Jahrbuch Deutsch. Arch. Inst. XXII 18–53.

A. A. MACDONELL (1897). Vedic Mythology. (Grundriss der Indo-Arischen Philol. und Altertumsk. III 1A) Strassburg.

L. A. MACKAY (1948). The Wrath of Homer. Toronto: University Press.

Donald A. MACKENZIE (EML). Egyptian Myth and Legend. London: Gresham, n.d.

―――― (IML). Indian Myth and Legend. London: Gresham, n.d.

―――― (MBA). Myths of Babylonia and Assyria. London: Gresham, n.d.

Ludolf MALTEN (1914). Das Pferd im Totenglauben. Jahrbuch Deutsch. Arch. Inst. XXIX 179–256.

Wilhelm MANNHARDT (1884). Mythologische Forschungen aus dem Nachlasse. Strassburg, London.

―――― (1904–05). Wald- und Feldkulte. 2d ed. 2 vols. Berlin: Borntraeger.

Henri MASPERO (1924). Légendes Mythologiques dans le Chou King. Journ. Asiatique CCIV 1–100.

Maximilian MAYER (1887). Die Giganten und Titanen in der antiken Sage und Kunst. Berlin.

G. MEGAS (1933). Die Sage von Alkestis. Archiv für Religionswiss. XXX 1–33.

Isaac MENDELSOHN (1955), editor. Religions of the Ancient Near East: Sumero-Akkadian Religious Texts and Ugaritic Epics. New York: Liberal Arts Press.

Samuel A. B. MERCER (1942). Horus Royal God of Egypt. Grafton: Society of Oriental Research.

A. von MESS (1901). Der Typhonmythus bei Pindar und Aeschylus. Rhein. Mus. LVI 167–174.

Karl MEULI (1921). Odyssee und Argonautika: Untersuchungen zur Griechischen Sagengeschichte und zum Epos. Berlin: Weidmann.

Eduard MEYER (1875). Set-Typhon. Eine Religionsgeschichtliche Studie. Leipzig.

August MOMMSEN (1878). Delphika. Leipzig.

Anton MOORTGAT (1949). Tammuz: Der Unsterblichkeitsglaube in der Altorientalischen Bildkunst. Berlin: de Gruyter.

Karl Otfried MÜLLER (1825). Prolegomena zu einer wissenschaftlichen Mythologie. Göttingen.

——— (1844). Orchomenos und die Minyer. 2d ed. Breslau.

J. MUIR (1870). Original Sanskrit Texts on the Origin and History of the People of India, Their Religion and Institutions. Vol. V. London.

J. A. R. MUNRO (1934). Pelasgians and Ionians. JHS LIV 109–128.

Edouard NAVILLE (1870). Textes relatifs au Mythe d'Horus recueillis dans le temple d'Edfou. Geneva, Basle.

Ditlef NIELSEN (1936). Ras Šamra Mythologie und Biblische Theologie. (Abhandl. für die Kunde des Morgenlandes XXI 4). Leipzig: Deutsche Morgenländische Gesellschaft.

M. P. NILSSON (1932). The Mycenaean Origin of Greek Mythology. (Sather Classical Lectures, vol. 8). Berkeley: University of California Press.

Martin NINCK (1921). Die Bedeutung des Wassers im Kult und Leben der Alten: Eine Symbolgeschichtliche Untersuchung. (Philologus, suppl. XIV 2). Leipzig: Dieterich.

Axel OLRIK (1922). Ragnarök: Die Sagen vom Weltuntergang. Translated into German by Wilhelm Ranisch. Berlin, Leipzig: de Gruyter.

Richard Broxton ONIANS (1954). The Origins of European Thought about the Body, the Mind, the Soul, the World, Time and Fate. 2d ed. Cambridge University Press.

A. Leo OPPENHEIM (1947). Mesopotamian Mythology I. Orientalia N.S. XVI 207–238.

——— (1948). Mesopotamian Mythology II. Orientalia N.S. XVII 17–58.

——— (1950). Mesopotamian Mythology III. Orientalia N.S. XIX 129–158.

570 BIBLIOGRAPHY

Fernando ORTIZ (1947). El Huracán: Su Mitología y sus Símbolos. Mexico City, Buenos Aires: Fondo de Cultura Económica.

Heinrich OTTEN (1950). Mythen vom Gotte Kumarbi: Neue Fragmente. (Deutsche Akad. Wissensch. Berlin: Inst. für Orientforschung, Veröff. 3). Berlin: Akademie-Verlag.

Svend Aage PALLIS (1926). The Babylonian *akîtu* Festival. (Kgl. Danske Vidensk. Selskab, Hist.-Filol. Medd. XII 1). Copenhagen: Høst.

Friedrich PANZER (1910). Studien zur Germanischen Sagengeschichte I. Beowulf. Munich: Beck.

—— (1912). Studien zur Germanischen Sagengeschichte II. Sigfrid. Munich: Beck.

H. W. PARKE (1956) and D. E. W. Wormell. The Delphic Oracle. 2 vols. Oxford: Blackwell.

Rudolf PFEIFFER (1949). Callimachus edidit R. Pf. I. Oxford: Clarendon Press.

Paula PHILIPPSON (1936). Genealogie als mythische Form: Studien zur Theogonie des Hesiod. (Symbolae Osl., suppl. 7). Oslo: Brøgger.

—— (1944). Thessalische Mythologie. Zurich: Rhein-Verlag.

Alexander PIANKOFF (1934). The Sky-Goddess Nut and the Night Journey of the Sun. Journ. Egypt. Arch. XX 57–61.

J. C. POESTION (1884). Isländische Märchen. Vienna.

W. PORZIG (1930). Iluyankas und Typhon. Kleinasiatische Forschungen I 379–386.

James B. PRITCHARD (1950), editor. Ancient Near Eastern Texts Relating to the Old Testament. Princeton University Press.

L. RADERMACHER (1903). Das Jenseits im Mythos der Hellenen. Untersuchungen über antiken Jenseitsglauben. Bonn: Marcus & Weber.

—— (1938). Mythos und Sage bei den Griechen. Baden bei Wien, Leipzig: Rohrer.

—— (1949). Das Meer und die Toten. Anzeiger Österreich. Akad. Wissensch. Wien, Phil.-Hist. Kl., LXXXVI 307–315.

Lord RAGLAN (1936). The Hero: A Study in Tradition, Myth, and Drama. London: Methuen.

W. M. RAMSAY (1890). The Historical Geography of Asia Minor. (Royal Geographical Society, Suppl. Papers IV). London.

—— (1926). Studies in the Roman Province Galatia. Journ. Roman Studies XVI 102–119.

Arthur F. J. REMY (1913). The Origin of the Tannhäuser-Legend. Journ. Engl. and Germ. Philol. XII 32–77.

Carl ROBERT (1879). Thanatos. (Winckelmannsprogramm 39) Berlin.

G. ROEDER. Set. LM 4. 725–784.

———. Thuëris. LM 5. 878–908.

Robert William ROGERS (1912). Cuneiform Parallels to the Old Testament. London, etc.: Henry Frowde, Oxford University Press.

Erwin ROHDE (1925). Psyche: The Cult of Souls and Belief in Immortality among the Greeks. Translated by W. B. Hillis from the 8th ed. London: Kegan Paul, Trench, Trubner; New York: Harcourt, Brace.

Géza ROHEIM (1940). The Dragon and the Hero. American Imago I 2, 40–69; I 3, 61–94.

Wilhelm ROSCHER (1873). Apollon und Mars. Leipzig.

——— (1879). Die Gorgonen und Verwandtes. Eine Vorarbeit zu einem Handbuch der Griechischen Mythologie vom vergleichenden Standpunkt. Leipzig.

——— (1900). Ephialtes, eine pathologisch-mythologische Abhandlung über die Alpträume und Alpdämonen des klassischen Altertums. Leipzig: Teubner.

———. Andromeda. LM 1. 345–347.

———. Lapithen. LM 2. 1851–1865.

———. Phorbas. LM 3. 2424–2430.

H. J. ROSE (1928). A Handbook of Greek Mythology Including Its Extension to Rome. London: Methuen.

——— (1954). Chthonian Cattle. Numen I 213–227.

Francesco SBORDONE (1941). Il Ciclo Italico di Eracle. Athenaeum di Pavia N. S. XIX 72–96, 149–180.

Fritz SCHACHERMEYR (1950). Poseidon und die Entstehung des Griechischen Götterglaubens. Bern: A. Francke Ag. Verlag.

Konrad SCHAUENBURG (1953). Pluton und Dionysos. Jahrbuch Deutsch. Arch. Inst. LXVIII 38–72.

K. SCHERLING. Tityos. RE 6A. 1593–1609.

Hans SCHLOBIES (1925). Der Akkadische Wettergott in Mesopotamien. (Mitt. Altorient. Gesellsch. I 3). Leipzig: Pfeiffer.

Johanna SCHMIDT. Phorbas. RE 20. 528–532.

Johannes SCHMIDT. Typhoeus, Typhon. LM 5. 1426–1454.

Hartmut SCHMÖKEL (1928). Der Gott Dagan: Ursprung, Verbreitung und Wesen seines Kultes. Borna-Leipzig: Universitätsverlag von Robert Noske.

Paul SCHNABEL (1923). Berossos und die Babylonisch-Hellenistische Literatur. Leipzig, Berlin: Teubner.

Hermann SCHNEIDER (1928). Germanische Heldensage I: Einleitung: Ursprung und Wesen der Heldensage; I. Buch: Deutsche Heldensage. Berlin, Leipzig: de Gruyter.

———— (1934). Germanische Heldensage III: Englische Heldensage. . . . . Berlin, Leipzig: de Gruyter.

Jacques SCHNIER (1947). Dragon Lady. American Imago IV 3, 78–98.

Albert SCHOTT (1934). Das Gilgamesch-Epos, neu übersetzt und mit Anmerkungen versehen. Leipzig: Reclam.

Theodor SCHREIBER (1879). Apollon Pythoktonos: Ein Beitrag zur Griechischen Religions- und Kunstgeschichte. Leipzig.

L. von SCHROEDER (1914). Herakles und Indra. Eine Mythenvergleichende Untersuchung. (Denkschriften Akad. Wissensch. Wien, Phil.-Hist. Kl., LVIII 3). Vienna: Hölder.

August SCHULTZ (1882). Phlegyersagen. Jahrb. Class. Philol. CXXV 345–350.

Bernhard SCHWEITZER (1922). Herakles: Aufsätze zur Griechischen Religions- und Sagengeschichte. Tübingen: Mohr (Siebeck).

Gerhard SEIPPEL (1939). Der Typhonmythus. Greifswald: Dallmeyer.

Kurt SETHE (1928). Dramatische Texte zu Altaegyptischen Mysterienspielen. (Untersuch. Gesch. und Altertumsk. Ägypt. X, 2 pts.) Leipzig: Hinrichs.

Katharine SHEPARD (1940). The Fish-Tailed Monster in Greek and Etruscan Art. (Bryn Mawr thesis) New York: Privately printed.

Ernst SIECKE (1907). Drachenkämpfe: Untersuchungen zur Indogermanischen Sagenkunde. Leipzig: Hinrichs.

G. Elliot SMITH (1919). The Evolution of the Dragon. Manchester: University Press; London, New York, etc.: Longmans, Green.

Kirby Flower SMITH (1902). The Tale of Gyges and the King of Lydia. Am. Journ. Philol. XXIII 261–282, 361–387.

Friedrich SOLMSEN (1949). Hesiod and Aeschylus. Ithaca: Cornell University Press.

Lewis SPENCE (1913). The Myths of Mexico and Peru. London: Harrap.

John STEINBECK (1941). The Forgotten Village. New York: Viking Press.

Julian H. STEWARD (1936). Myths of the Owens Valley Paiute. (Uni. Calif. Publ. Am. Arch. & Ethn. XXXIV 355–439.) Berkeley: University of California Press.

Franz STOESSL (1945). Der Tod des Herakles: Arbeitsweise und Formen der antiken Sagendichtung. Zurich: Rhein-Verlag.

Joh. SUNDWALL (1913). Die Einheimischen Namen der Lykier nebst einem Verzeichnisse Kleinasiatischer Namenstämme. (Klio XI) Leipzig: Dieterich.

Joseph TEIPEL (1922). Typhoei fabula qualis usque ad Pindari et Aeschyli aetatem fuerit. Münster: Theissing. [Seen in abstract only.]

D'Arcy Wentworth THOMPSON (1947). A Glossary of Greek Fishes. Oxford University Press, Geoffrey Cumberlege.

Stith THOMPSON (1929). Tales of the North American Indians. Cambridge, Mass.; Harvard University Press.

———— (MIFL). Motif-Index of Folk-Literature. 2d ed. 6 vols. Bloomington: Indiana Univ. Press, 1955–1958.

George THOMSON (1949). Studies in Ancient Greek Society: The Prehistoric Aegean. London: Lawrence & Wishart.

Johannes TOEPFFER (1890). Theseus und Peirithoos. In Aus der Anomia: Archaeologische Beitraege Carl Robert zur Erinnerung dargebracht, Berlin, pp. 30–46.

Karl TÜMPEL (1888). Die Aithiopenländer des Andromedamythos: Studien zur Rhodischen Kolonisation. Jahrb. Class. Philol., Suppl. XVI 127–220.

G. TÜRK. Phlegyas. LM 3. 2378–2383.

————. Python. LM 3. 3400–3412.

H. N. ULRICHS (1840). Reisen und Forschungen in Griechenland I: Reise über Delphi durch Phocis und Boeotien bis Theben. Bremen.

Hermann USENER (1899). Die Sintfluthsagen. Bonn.

———— (1901). Eine Hesiodische Dichtung. Rhein. Mus. LVI 174–186.

———— (1904). Heilige Handlung. Archiv für Religionswiss. VII 281–339.

E. Douglas VAN BUREN (1946). The Dragon in Ancient Mesopotamia. Orientalia N.S. XV 1–45 and pls. I–VIII.

———— (1950). Akkadian Sidelights on a Fragmentary Epic. Orientalia N.S. XIX 159–174 and pls. IX–XII.

Francis VIAN (1945). Le Combat d'Héraklès et de Kyknos d'après les documents figurés du VIᵉ et du Vᵉ siècle. Rev. Et. Anc. XLVII 5–32.

———— (1951). Répertoire des Gigantomachies figurées dans l'art Grec et Romain. Paris: Klincksieck.

——— (1952). La Guerre des Géants: Le Mythe avant l'époque Hellénistique. (Etudes et Commentaires XI). Paris: Klincksieck.

M. W. de VISSER (1913). The Dragon in China and Japan. Amsterdam: Müller.

Jan de VRIES (1937). Altgermanische Religionsgeschichte II: Religion der Nordgermanen. Berlin, Leipzig: de Gruyter.

G. A. WAINWRIGHT (1935). Some Celestial Associations of Min. Journ. Egypt. Arch. XXI 152–170.

Kurt WAIS (1952). Ullikummi, Hrungnir, Armilus und Verwandte. In Edda, Skalden, Saga: Festschrift Felix Genzmer, Heidelberg: Winter, pp. 211–261, 325–331.

William J. WALLACE (1951). The Mortuary Caves of Calaveras County, California. Archaeology IV 199–203.

Otto WASER (1898). Charon. Archiv für Religionswiss. I 152–182.

Leo WEBER (1910). Apollon Pythoktonos im Phrygischen Hierapolis. Philologus LXIX 178–251.

——— (1936). Die Alkestissage. Rhein. Mus. LXXXV 117–164.

E. T. C. WERNER (1922). Myths and Legends of China. London, Calcutta, Sydney: Harrap.

Konrad WERNICKE (1890). Zur Geschichte der Heraklessage. In Aus der Anomia, Berlin, pp. 71–85.

E. W. WEST (1882). Pahlavi Texts, II. Oxford.

Post WHEELER (1952). The Sacred Scriptures of the Japanese. New York: Schuman.

Ulrich von WILAMOWITZ-MOELLENDORF (1895). Euripides Herakles erklärt. 2d ed. Berlin.

——— (1925). Die Griechische Heldensage II. Sitzungsb. Akad. Wissensch. Berlin, Phil.-Hist. Kl., (1925) 214–242.

——— (1931–32). Der Glaube der Hellenen. 2 vols. Berlin: Weidmann.

John Garrett WINTER (1910). The Myth of Hercules at Rome. (Univ. Michigan Studies, Humanistic Ser., IV 171–273) New York, London: Macmillan.

P. Maurus WITZEL (1920). Der Drachenkämpfer Ninib. Fulda: Privately printed.

——— (1948). Zur Sumerischen Mythologie. Orientalia N.S. XVII 393–415.

Jocelyn WOODWARD (1932). Bathycles and the Laconian Vase-Painters. JHS LII 25–41.

———— (1937). Perseus: A Study in Greek Art and Legend. Cambridge University Press.

Friedrich WORMS (1953). Der Typhoeus-Kampf in Hesiods Theogonie. Hermes LXXXI 29–44.

K. ZIEGLER. Theogonien. LM 5. 1469–1554.

Heinrich ZIMMERN (1926). Das Babylonische Neujahrsfest. (Der Alte Orient XXV 3). Leipzig: Hinrichs.

INDICES

INDEX A

THEMES AND MOTIFS
(In Three Parts)

Part I is an index of the forty-three Themes of the combat myth, the full statements of which are found on pages 9–11; for each Theme it refers not only to page numbers but also, in parentheses, to motifs of Stith Thompson's *Motif-Index* which are identical with or very similar to the Theme or part of it (however, none of Thompson's motifs corresponds to Themes 2A, 6B, 7D, 7E, 10B, 10D).

Part II is an index of motifs according to Thompson's index. It includes (*a*) the motifs which are referred to in part I—for many of these reference to the corresponding Theme of part I is sufficient, others require page references in addition, since they represent an interesting or significant phase or section of the Theme; (*b*) other motifs which either recur among the myths and legends discussed or which have a special interest, though the particular motif may be represented only once.

Part III is an index of motifs which are not represented in Thompson's index, although for most of them I can refer to a somewhat similar motif that Thompson lists.

PART I

THEME

1A. The Enemy was son of chaos demoness or earth goddess. (A111.1, A115.1–3, A401, A625, G303.11.3.) 16, 22, 47–49, 71–73, 77 f., 132, 151, 165, 169, 178, 188, 194, 196, 214, 240 f., 244, 256 f., 262, 308, 316, 330, 334, 342, 345 f., 351, 356, 470, 497, 525 f.

579

THEME

1B. He was son of a father god. (A625, F531.6.1.1., G303.1.1, A115.1, A115.3–4.) 49–51, 71, 73, 78, 132, 152, 178, 191, 194, 201, 211, 214, 262, 282, 308, 328, 330, 334, 339 f., 345 f., 347 f., 351, 356, 395 f., 470, 489, 501, 522 f., 525, 540 n.48.

1C. He had a wife or female companion. (B11.2.0.1, G303.11.1; cf. G200, G303.11.3.) Chapter vi, 13 f., 72 f., 78, 122, 133, 138, 141 f., 152, 165, 171 f., 178, 189, 204, 206 f., 210 n.54, 231, 243-246, 255–260, 262, 282 f., 308–310, 313–316, 326 n.6, 329, 331–333, 337 f., 341 f., 345 f., 350 n.44, 353–356, 358, 366–374, 395–397, 470, 497, 505, 507, 509, 512, 518, 523, 525 f., 537.

2A. Feature of geographical correspondence. 51–54, 78 f., 110, 122, 133, 141, 145, 173, 177, 212, 214, 231, 242, 244, 276–281, 286, 307, 310, 315, 322 f., 325, 331, 337 n.24, 344 f., 351 f., 407–412, 468 f., 489, 515 f.

2B. The enemy lived in a cave, etc. (B11.3.5, F531.6.2.1, G637; cf. F164.) Chapter xiv; 19 f., 45, 54, 72 f., 79, 94 f., 97, 100, 122, 168, 172, 186, 202, 206, 208, 262 f., 286, 298, 311, 331, 342, 346, 356, 470, 489, 496 n.12, 503, 505 f., 510, 513 n.40, 524 n.8, 525–527, 531, 535 f., 539.

2C. He occupied a temenos. (Cf. B11.3.4, D950.0.1, F771.5.1-2.) 15, 29, 35, 39, 54, 129 n.14, 167, 171 f., 208 n.50, 263, 290, 311, 332, 339, 346, 501, 528.

2D. He guarded a spring. (B11.7.1.) Appendix 6; 45, 79, 120, 143 f., 195 n.30, 262 f., 307, 311, 315 f., 341 n.30, 342, 354 n.52, 356, 366–374, 408, 470, 489, 510, 517, 524 n.8, 546–548.

2E. He lived in the water. (B11.3.1, B11.7.2, B91.5, G303.8.8, G308; cf. G303.17.2.2, G311.) 97, 106 f., 120, 122, 142–144, 152, 168 n.48, 172, 175, 182–184, 190 f., 193 n.26, 194, 206, 209 f., 212, 218–222, 229–239, 262 f., 277 f., 283 f., 303 f., 311, 328, 330, 335, 346, 347 f., 351, 356, 470, 489, 493–495, 497, 501, 503, 506, 510–512, 514, 516, 523, 526–529, 531 f., 546.

3A. He was gigantic. (B11.2.12, B16.5.1, B31, B870–875, B875.1, B877.1, F531, F531.2, F531.2.1.5, F533, G100; cf. B871.1.1.2, B871.1.2, B871.2, B871.2.4–5, B875.2–4, B873.2, F.167.3.) 54 f., 70, 79 f., 97 n.8, 106, 147, 152, 167 f., 174, 182 f., 186, 194, 203, 205 f., 209 n.52, 210, 212, 214, 239–247, 263, 290, 311, 327 n.8, 330 n.15, 339, 347, 350 n.44, 356, 416 n.13, 489, 493, 496, 500, 504 f., 510–513, 516, 522 f., 528, 531, 540 n.28.

3B. He had nonhuman form. (B11, B11.2.1, B11.4.1, B16.1.4.1, B29.2, B42, B56, B61, B70, B91, B91.1, B91.3, B91.5, D113.1.1, F401.3, F526.1, F526.6, F531.1.3.1, G211, G301, G303.3.3.6.1, G308, G354.1; cf. A671.2.1, A673, B11.2.5–7, B11.2.10, B14.1, B15.7.1, B21–24, B43, B51, B52, B80, B82, B99, E423.5, F526.2–3, G303.4.1.6, G303.4.2, G303.4.4, G303.4.6.) Chapters i, iv, vi; appendix 4; 44, 55–57, 80–82, 121 f., 129, 131, 134, 138–140, 146 f., 149, 152 f., 166, 168 f., 171 f., 174 f., 178 f., 182–190, 192, 194–208, 209 f., 230, 242–247, 262 f., 281–283, 286, 288 f., 307–309, 311, 324, 328, 331 n.15, 336, 342 n.33, 346, 347 f., 350 f., 354, 356–358, 470, 481, 483 f., 493–498, 500–504, 510–513, 523 f., 526–528, 531 f., 535–539.

3C. He had several heads, arms, legs, etc. (B11.2.3, B.11.2.3. 1–4, B15.1.2, B15.1.2.6–10, B15.6.3, F515.0.2.1, F531.1.2.2, G303.4.1.1, G361.1, G361.1.1–5; cf. B15.1.2.2, B15.7.1, F512.2, F512.2.2.) 71, 82 f., 97, 134, 154, 192, 202, 206, 209 n.52, 210, 243, 263, 311, 334, 336 n.22, 343 n.33, 346, 350 n.44, 356, 470, 484, 487, 500, 502, 516, 523.

3D. He sent death by fire or glance. (B11.2.11, B742, D581, D2061.2.1, D2071, F531.1.1.2, F541.1.1–4, G303.4.1.2.2–3, B11.12.3; cf. B15.4.2, B19.1, F541.3.1, G264.1, G363.1.) 73, 83, 97 n.8, 106, 110, 118, 134, 150, 167–169, 171, 186 f., 203, 205 n.48, 206, 210, 235, 244 f., 263, 284–286, 288, 311, 339, 342, 356, 432 n.38, 470, 489, 498, 501, 504, 505, 511, 513, 516, 524, 528, 531 f., 540 n.48.

3E. He could change his shape. (B11.5.1, D102, D113.1, D152.1–3, D191, D199.2, D391, D399.1, D419.1, D610, D630, F420.4.1.1, G211, G303.3; cf. D112.1, D112.4, D113.2, D127.1-2, D133.2, D134, D161.1, D162, D185.1, D194, D215, G211.1.8.)

THEME

118, 138, 141, 176 n.62, 179, 184–186, 192, 203, 206, 234, 263, 328, 331, 432 n.38, 471, 493, 498 n.15, 504, 524 n.8, 535, 540 n.48.

3ꜰ. He was a death spirit. (A310, E261, E272, G302, G303; cf. A311, B15.6.2, B29.1, D113.1.1, E251, E271, E422, E423.5, E501, E501.1, E501.1.8.2–3, F470, F471.1, F526.3.) Chapter xii, appendix 1; 101–120, 126 f., 130 f., 134, 142, 144 f., 154 f., 165, 170–173, 175 f., 180 n.5, 188, 191 f., 194, 197, 206, 208, 210, 215 n.58, 263, 283–291, 304–306, 309 f., 471, 489 f., 497 f., 500–503, 507–509, 512, 516, 518, 524 n.8, 525–533, 537.

3ɢ. He was wind, flood, etc. (A282.1, A284.2, A289.1, B11.7, F432–434, F436, F493, F531.3.8, A255; cf. A1010, D429.2.1, D2141.0.3, D2142.0.1, G242.2, G283.) 83, 105, 118, 125–127, 147, 149, 155, 165 f., 182, 187, 203, 208 n.50, 210, 219–222, 248, 263, 277, 291, 311, 327, 347 f., 351, 420 f., 459, 471, 493, 495–497, 500 f., 505, 512 n.40, 513 f., 522–524, 545 f.

4ᴀ. He plundered, murdered, etc. (B11.9, B16.1.4.1, E266, G260, G262, G302, G303.20, G346, S110–112; cf. G262.0.1.) 58, 83 f., 97 f., 125–127, 134, 138 f., 141, 155, 164–166, 167, 174, 175 n.59, 178, 187, 194, 206, 208 n.49, 209 n.52, 210, 214, 247 n.43, 248, 263, 286, 299, 310, 326 n.6, 331, 338–341, 345, 347 f., 351, 356, 471, 489, 493 f., 501, 503, 505, 507, 510 f., 513, 516, 525, 528, 531, 540 n.48.

4ʙ. He was a despot, imposed tribute. (M2, P12.3, S262, S262.2; cf. E433, S265.) 42, 44 f., 67, 103, 130, 137, 174, 191, 205, 248, 263, 265, 286, 297, 299, 340, 347 f., 350, 471, 489, 497, 500 f., 516, 518, 528, 540 n.48.

4ᴄ. He carried off the young. (B11.10.3, F321, G261, G262.0.1, S302, G442; cf. S262.2.) 44, 100–102, 104 f., 114, 116, 190, 210, 263, 265, 309, 326 n.6, 347 f., 471, 489, 494, 497, 500 f., 503 f., 506 f., 510, 516 f., 528, 536.

4ᴅ. He was gluttonous, voracious, a maneater. (B11.10, B16.0.3, B16.4.1, F531.3.4, F531.3.4.1, G10, G11.2–3, W125; cf. A928, E251, G262.0.1.) 84, 97, 100, 104–107, 114, 116, 122, 126, 134, 156, 175 n.59, 193 n.28, 194, 203, 206 f., 210 f., 247 n. 43, 248, 261, 263, 299, 304, 309, 331 n.15, 342, 345, 347 f., 356, 393 n.36, 416 n.13, 471, 489, 494, 497, 500, 503 f., 510–512, 516, 528.

4ᴇ. He was lecherous, raped. (G303.9.5.1, R11.1, S262.1, B82.1.1, T118, T471, T471.2; cf. G440, R111.1.1, R111.1.3–4.) 22 f., 44, 58 f., 68, 84, 102 f., 120, 126, 143 n.46, 174 f., 178–180, 190–192, 205 f., 208 n.49, 210, 212, 242, 260, 263, 265, 292, 300, 303 f., 307 n.59, 313 f., 326, 334, 347 f., 354 f., 368 n.5, 471, 483 n.10, 488 f., 497, 500, 504, 510, 516, 536.

4ꜰ. He commanded a road, killed travellers, forced them into contests. (F402.1.2; cf. E272, G317, H541.1.1.) 25, 29, 31, 39 f., 43 f., 59 f., 95, 97, 112 f., 134, 168 n.48, 188, 195 n.30, 215 n.58, 263, 265, 310, 329, 330, 356 nn.54 & 55, 471, 482, 486, 498 n.15, 503, 511, 517 n.3, 528.

4ɢ. He blockaded or drained rivers, springs. (A1111, B11.7.1, A928, F531.3.4.2.) 84, 126 f., 169, 194, 203, 263, 471 f., 489, 501, 517.

5ᴀ. He wanted to rule the world. (Cf. A60, A63, A106.0.1.) 60, 71–73, 84, 126, 130, 134 f., 147–150, 156, 178 f., 181, 188, 195, 205, 207, 210–214, 230 f., 240 f., 250, 263, 291–295, 299, 311 f., 350 n.44, 472, 489, 493, 502, 505, 513, 524, 528, 539.

5ʙ. His consort incited him. (Cf. S322.3.1.) 18, 60 f., 72 f., 84, 119, 138, 141, 156, 168 f., 188, 192, 207, 208 n.50, 214, 244, 256, 263, 296, 308, 316, 329, 356 f., 472, 538.

6ᴀ. The weather god went forth to fight him. (A162.2–3.) 25, 61 f., 70–74, 84, 121 f., 126 f., 130, 135, 148, 150, 156–158, 166, 178, 182, 195, 210, 212, 242, 248, 263, 296 f., 312, 337, 344, 357, 406, 472, 496 n.12, 498, 511, 512 n.40, 524, 529, 535.

6ʙ. It was his first exploit. 15–18, 23 f., 62, 84, 135, 141, 149 f., 158, 167, 169, 172, 178 f., 195, 206, 209 n.52, 215 n.58, 242, 263, 297, 312 n.70, 327, 357, 406, 472, 493, 498, 501, 505, 507, 517, 523 f., 529, 534 n.33, 535.

7ᴀ. He fought and killed the enemy. (B11.11, G303.8.1, G500, G510, G512, G512.1, G514, A50, A162.2–3, A531, H1161, A106; cf. A255, C54, G512.1.1.) Chapters i, ii,

THEME

iv, vii, viii, ix, xi, xii; appendices 3, 4, 5; 62–64, 84 f., 90 f., 95, 97, 101–103, 105, 108–110, 112 f., 243, 252, 263–265, 390–392, 472, 489 f.

7B. He had to use numerous missiles against a formidable or invulnerable enemy. (Cf. B11.12.1.) 15, 73 f., 85, 135 f., 176 n.62, 183, 195, 210, 264, 311, 330, 343 n.33, 350 n.44, 356, 472, 510, 512, 530.

7C. The gods fled or appeased the Enemy. (R220; cf. D671, S262.1.) 73, 75, 102, 123, 125–127, 129, 130, 136 f., 141, 147–149, 159, 168, 175 f., 179, 191, 197, 210, 215 n.58, 250, 263, 297, 313 n.71, 326 n.6, 347 f., 355, 489, 494, 501, 512 n.40, 513, 516, 529, 531, 540 n.48.

7D. The champion's sister, wife, or mother helped him. 23, 29, 37, 64, 85, 121, 123, 125 f., 129, 136, 139, 141, 159, 165, 175, 178 f., 183 f., 187, 205, 244 f., 257, 263–265, 301, 316, 328 f., 333 n.18, 335 n.21, 347, 356, 489, 494 f., 501, 511, 530.

7E. He was helped by another god or hero. 28, 36, 61, 73–75, 85, 109, 121–124, 125 f., 129, 136, 160, 166, 167–169, 175, 178 f., 181, 183–185, 187, 193, 197, 201 f., 210, 212, 242, 251 f., 263 f., 301, 329, 333 n.18, 335 n.21, 343 n.33, 345 f., 348, 356 n.54, 493–496, 500 f., 505–508, 513, 517, 523 f., 530 f., 537, 539.

7F. The Enemy fled during the combat. (R220.) 20, 73–75, 85, 169, 172, 183 f., 264, 302 n.51, 313 n.71, 343 n.33, 493, 502 n.25, 511, 530, 540 n.48.

7G. Gigantomachy. (A162, A162.1, A162.8, A106, A106.1-2.) 58, 84, 149–151, 160, 166, 181, 183, 187, 197, 207, 210, 230 f., 239–247, 263 f., 291–296, 316, 328, 337, 343 n.33, 344, 348, 351 f., 356 n.55, 393, 490, 492 n.2, 495, 501, 523 f., 528, 536.

8A. The Champion suffered temporary defeat or death. (A173, A192, A535, A565; cf. R45, S322.) 73–75, 85–89, 91, 105 n.25, 108 f., 121 f., 124, 127, 130 f., 136, 138–140, 148, 161 f., 164 f., 168 f., 171, 173, 175, 178, 180 f., 184 f., 188 f., 191 f., 197–200, 202–204, 206 f., 212, 248–250, 263, 297–299, 313, 326 f., 336 n.22, 341, 347–349, 354, 357 f., 381–389, 472, 488 f., 493, 498, 501 f., 503 n.26, 505, 507 f., 511 f., 518, 524, 527, 529, 531 f., 535.

8B. He lost a potent organ or object. (A128, A153.1, A1417, A162.3.1, E765.3; cf. E761, E781, S165.) 73–75, 91, 122, 124, 140, 162, 168, 172, 180 f., 184–188, 191 f., 202 f., 244–246, 249, 263, 348, 401–404, 422, 472, 497 f., 500 n.19, 505, 507.

8C. The Enemy lured him to a feast. (G412, K811.1; cf. K714.2.) 112 f., 126, 130, 137, 138, 140, 175, 178, 215 n.58, 263, 299, 316, 326 n.6, 341, 393 n.36, 403, 472, 530, 533, 538 f.

8D. Venusberg or Siren theme: [i] To Champion's disadvantage. (G264, F131.1, F302.3.4, F585.1, T173, B15.6.2, B53; cf. F547.1.1, G262.0.1.1, G264.1.) 138, 141, 188, 192, 206, 263, 304, 309, 314 f., 352–356, 366, 368 n.5, 371 f., 472, 497, 502, 504, 513 n.41, 530 n.20. [ii] To Champion's advantage. (G530.1-2; cf. T91.1.) 97–99, 107–110, 113, 171, 175, 178, 189, 191, 237 n.27, 313–316, 331, 342, 347, 429, 486, 502, 507, 509, 518. General. (F131.1; cf. F300, F302, F531.1.0.1.1.) 116, 122, 124 f., 168–170, 174, 185 n.14, 190, 257–259, 299, 333, 466, 486, 488 f., 537 f., 540–544.

8E. The dead Champion was lamented. (E58, E58.1.) 86 f., 89, 130, 137, 138, 141, 162, 165, 171, 173, 178, 181, 184, 191, 263, 299, 386 f., 472, 488, 502, 530, 532.

9. The Enemy was outwitted, deceived, bewitched: (a) Lured by food. (K811.1, K913, G521, K776, K871.) 73 f., 89, 121, 124, 127, 129, 139 f., 162 f., 180, 193 n.26, 201 n.39, 215 n.58, 327 n.7, 489, 496 n.11, 500, 503, 505 f. (b) By sex. (K872.) Appendix 2; 139, 175, 180, 191, 205, 212, 215, 242, 259 f., 263, 466, 472, 488 f., 504. (c) Taken in by disguise. (K1810, K2357, D651; cf. K913.) 75, 89, 113, 122, 124, 139 f., 180 f., 193, 489, 505 f., 511. (d) Overcome by magic. (D1080, D1081, D1094, D1381, D1383.2, D1400.1.4, D1710; cf. D1101, D1273, D1344.5.) 130, 136, 147, 149, 163, 180, 184, 186 f., 193, 200, 263 f., 301, 506. General. 150, 163, 261 f., 263 f., 301, 317, 343 n.33, 356, 502 f., 507–511, 513 n.40, 538.

10A. Punishment of Enemy. (A1071, A106.2.1, G303.8.3.1, G303.8.5, G512.1.2, Q421, Q433.2, Q451, Q491, Q560, R45; cf. D231, Q456, Q511, Q552.2.3.) 64 f., 70–74,

THEME
90, 150, 163, 165, 179, 181, 183, 187, 195 f., 205, 209 f., 231, 241 f., 244, 264, 303 n.54, 331 n.15, 345, 350, 354 n.52, 356, 472, 477 f., 490, 493, 496, 500, 503 f., 505 f., 508, 511, 512 n.40, 517, 524, 531 f., 540 n.48.

10B. Celebration of victory. 19, 90, 129, 136 f., 150, 163 f., 168 n.48, 169, 182 f., 208 n.50, 262, 264, 302, 317, 335 n.21, 347, 472, 490, 510, 517, 531.

10C. Purification and expiation. (Cf. A181, Q431, Q431.3, Q482, Q520.1.) 15, 20, 86 f., 104, 107, 137, 169, 198–200, 264, 302, 317, 326 f., 343 n.33, 386, 490, 540.

10D. Institution of cult, ritual, etc. Chapter xv; 13–16, 19 f., 37 f., 65, 86–89, 105, 125 f., 129, 137 f., 142, 150, 164, 181, 184, 208 n.50, 245, 263 f., 280 f., 303, 317, 334 n.19, 337 n.24, 339, 349, 357 f., 366, 469, 472, 498 n.15, 512, 517.

PART II

(In the following statements of motifs I have often translated Thompson's terms into those that have been used in this book.)

A50. Conflict of good and evil creators. *See* Ths. 7A, 7G.

A60, 63. Evil demon as marplot at creation. *See* Th. 5A.

A106, 106.1–2. Conflict of good and evil gods; revolt of evil gods. *See* Th. 7G.

A106.0.1. Gods and demons fight for sovereignty. *See* Th. 5A.

A106.2.1. Revolting god banished to hell. *See* Th. 10A.

A111.1. Mother of the gods. 132, 149, 151, 178, 196, 256 f., 318, 369, 481, 494 f., 497. *See* Th. 1A.

A115.1–4. First deity grows out of primeval chaos or earth. 149, 151, 212 f., 221–223, 225 f., 232, 234, 473, 522 f. *See* Ths. 1A, 1B.

A128. Mutilated god. *See* Th. 8B.

A153. Ambrosia. *See* A154.

A153.1. Theft of ambrosia. *See* Th. 8B.

A154. Nectar, soma. 194, 198, 200–204, 430 f., 538, 549.

A162, 162.1. Theomachy, gigantomachy. *See* Th. 7G.

A162.2–3. Sky-god fights dragon of the waters or evil demon. *See* Ths. 6A, 7A.

A162.3.1. Evil demon steals thundergod's weapons. *See* Th. 8B.

A162.8. Rebellion of gods against their ruler. *See* Th. 7G.

A164.1. Brother-sister marriage of the gods. 130, 141, 149, 178, 257, 488.

A173. Gods deposed for a time. *See* Th. 8A.

A181. God serves as menial on earth. 87, 325, 347, 350, 357. *See* Th. 10C.

A192. A god dies. 111 f., 125–127, 130, 164 f., 176, 192, 247–255, 329 n.12, 375–377, 379–381, 387–389, 393, 420, 439–441, 448 f., 468, 480 f., 488, 503. *See* Th. 8A.

A193. Resurrection of god. 127, 131, 161, 192, 263, 300, 357, 377, 420, 439 f., 480, 498, 501, 508, 530.

A255. Contest with drought demon. 125 f., 196, 471. *See* Ths. 3G, 7A.

A282.1. Spirit of whirlwind, typhoon. 472, 491 f., 499, 505, 546. *See* Th. 3G.

A284.2. Thunderbird. 147 f., 152, 154 f., 166, 203 f., 496 f., 510, 524 n.8. *See* Th. 3G.

A289.1. Frost-spirit. 125, 379–381, 522 f. *See* Th. 3G.

A310. God who rules lower world. *See* Th. 3F.

A311. Conductor of the dead. Appendix 1. *See* Th. 3F.

A401. Mother Earth. *See* Th. 1A.

A525.1. Culture hero fights with brother. 130 f., 178, 182, 184, 319, 387–390, 501 f., 507. Cf. Th. 7A.

A531. Culture hero, demigod, overcomes monsters. *See* Th. 7A.

A535. Culture hero swallowed and recovered from animal. 138, 161 f., 198, 206 f., 248, 298, 313, 347, 510–512. *See* Th. 8A.

A565. Dying culture hero. *See* Th. 8A and A192.

A605. Primeval chaos. 149, 194, 196 f., 213, 218–239, 262 f., 283 f., 343 f., 351 f., 465 f., 469, 473, 492–496, 499, 504, 522–524, 526 f., 532.

A625. Sky-father and earth-mother are parents of the world. *See* Ths. 1A, 1B.

A642. World was made from body of slain giant. 150, 196 f., 220, 511, 523 f.

A671.2.1. Snakes in hell. 117, 154, 208, 502, 539. *See* Th. 3B; cf. 3F.

A672, 672.1. River in lower world with ferryman. Appendix 1; 144, 154, 171, 180 n.5, 221, 228 f., 524 n.8.

A673. Hound of hell. 72, 95, 117 f., 155, 208, 336, 479 n.3. *See* Th. 3B; cf. 3F.

A692. Islands of the Blest; Elysium in west. 171, 337 n.24, 543.

A721.1. Theft of sun. *See* A1415.

A737.1. Eclipse demon swallows sun or moon. 162 n.34, 186 f., 208, 221, 524 n.8.

A810. Primeval water. *See* A605.

A811, 812. Earth-diver. 500 n.18, 514, 524.

A816. Earth rises from the sea. 218, 220 f., 222 n.6, 500 n.18.

A816.1. Stone rises from primeval water. 212, 222, 229 n.15.

A831.2. Earth from giant's body. *See* A642.

A876. Midgard snake that surrounds earth. 234 f., 523.

A928. Giant drinks up sea. *See* Ths. 4D, 4G.

A1010. Deluge, inundation of world. 171, 210, 236 f., 277, 291, 347 f., 401, 403, 414, 417, 419–421, 455 n.20, 471 f., 492–497. *See* Th. 3G.

A1071. Dragon fettered. *See* Th. 10A.

A1111. A monster keeps water from mankind until a hero defeats him and releases it. 194–196, 201, 220, 253, 278 n.5, 466, 489, 494 f., 517. *See* Th. 4G.

A1411, 1415. Theft of light, fire. 513.

A1417. Theft of tablet of destinies. 147–149, 162, 246, 402. *See* Th. 8B.

B11. Dragon. Appendix 6; 13–22, 70, 80 f., 94–97, 152 f., 208, 230–235, 491–493, 496, 499 f., 504. *See* Th. 3B.

B11.2.0.1. She-dragon. *See* Th. 1C.

B11.2.1. Dragon as compound animal. 70, 80–82, 94 f., 97–99, 104, 147, 152, 166, 167, 203, 207, 234, 242 f., 245, 308, 493 f., 496 f., 504, 510. *See* Th. 3B.

B11.2.2. Dragon has bright colors. 81, 184–187, 210, 309, 493, 504.

B11.2.3, 11.2.3.1–4. Dragon has many heads. 71, 80 f., 154, 202, 206, 209 n.52, 210, 243, 311, 346 n.39, 356, 500. *See* Th. 3C.

B11.2.5–6. Dragon has horns, wings. 82, 138–140, 152 f., 190, 203, 210, 234, 244, 287, 308 f., 430 n.35, 491, 494, 496 f., 504, 532. *See* Th. 3B.

B11.2.7. Snakes grow from dragon's shoulders. 71, 80; cf. 285. *See* Th. 3B.

B11.2.10. Dragon has scales. *See* Th. 3B.

B11.2.11. Dragon breathes fire. 73, 83, 167, 169, 187, 203, 210, 244, 339, 342, 498, 516, 531 f., 545 f. *See* Th. 3D.

B11.2.12. Dragon has enormous size. *See* Th. 3A.

B11.3.1. Dragon lives at bottom of sea. *See* Th. 2E.

B11.3.4. Dragon lives under castle. Cf. 539. *See* Th. 2C.

B11.3.5. Dragon lives underground. 95, 372, 531 f., 539, 545. *See* Th. 2B.

B11.4.1. Dragon can fly. *See* B11.2.6.

B11.4.3. Dragon never sleeps. 100, 285 f., 545.

B11.5.1. Dragon has power of transforming himself. *See* Th. 3E.

B11.5.3. Dragon has miraculous vision. 285 f.

B11.5.5. Self-returning dragon's head. 206, 356.

B11.6.2. Dragon guards treasure. 202 f., 313 n.72, 346, 519, 527 f., 531 f., 535, 545.

B11.7. Dragon is rain-spirit. 491 f., 499, 504 n.28, 545 f. *See* Th. 3G.

B11.7.1. Dragon controls water-supply. *See* Ths. 2D, 4G.

B11.7.2. Dragon guards lake. 496, 510 f., 512 n.40. *See* Th. 2E.

B11.9. Dragon as power of evil. *See* Th. 4A.

B11.10. Human beings sacrificed to dragon. *See* Th. 4D; cf. 4E.

B11.10.3. Dragon devours children. *See* Th. 4c.

B11.11. Fight against dragon. *See* Th. 7a.

B11.11.7. Woman as dragon-slayer. 131, 133, 136, 139, 159, 165, 193 n.26, 244 f., 263 f., 300 f., 494. *See* Th. 7d.

B11.12.1. Dragon cannot be killed with weapons. 153, 330, 510, 528. *See* Ths. 7b, 9.

B11.12.3. Fiery dragon. *See* Th. 3d.

B14.1. Chimera. 72, 244 n.37, 308 f., 371. *See* Th. 3b.

B15.1.2. Many-headed animal. *See* Th. 3c.

B15.1.2.6–10. Monster, snake, of seven or more heads. *See* Th. 3c.

B15.4.2. Beast with fiery eyes. 106, 118, 505, 511. *See* Th. 3d.

B15.6.2. Empusa. 115–118, 186, 188, 257, 287 f., 310, 504. *See* Ths. 3f, 8d.

B15.6.3. Many-legged animals. *See* Th. 3c.

B15.7.1. Kerberos. *See* Ths. 3b, 3c (cf. 3f); A673.

B16.0.3. Maneating monster. *See* Th. 4d.

B16.1.3.1. Maneating mares. 345.

B16.1.4.1. Giant devastating boar. *See* Ths. 3b, 4a; B871.1.2.

B16.4.1. Devastating fish carries off victim. *See* Th. 4d.

B16.5.1. Giant devastating serpent. *See* Th. 3a.

B19.1. Fire-breathing bulls. 169. *See* Th. 3d.

B19.2. Wonder cow. 350, 523.

B21. Centaur. 186, 288 n.23, 354 f., 387. *See* Th. 3b.

B22. Human-asinine compound. *See* Th. 3b; B15.6.2.

B23, 23.1. Man-bull, Minotaur. 81 f., 234, 247, 313 f., 328, 350 f., 354, 405. *See* Th. 3b.

B24. Man-goat. 20, 73, 353 f., 378 f., 387 n.30, 418. *See* Th. 3b.

B29.1. Lamia. Chapter vi; 206, 208, 284–288, 309, 332, 416, 498 n.15, 500 n.20. *See* Th. 3f.

B29.2. Echidna. 72, 94–97, 110, 310, 338, 356, 404, 542 n.53. *See* Th. 3b.

B31. Giant bird. *See* Th. 3a; A284.2.

B41.1–2. Pegasos, flying horse. 370 f.

B42, 43. Griffin, winged bull. *See* Th. 3b; A284.2, B19.1.

B51. Sphinx. 59, 79, 308–310. *See* Th. 3b.

B52. Harpy. 140, 352 f., 371, 486. *See* Th. 3b.

B53. Siren. 188, 257, 352-354, 366, 486, 542. *See* Th. 8d.

B56. Garuda-bird. *See* Th. 3b; A284.2.

B61. Leviathan. 209 f., 222. *See* Th. 3b.

B70, 80, 82. Compounds of fish with beast or man. *See* Th. 3b; G308.

B82.1.1. Sea monster demands princess. *See* Th. 4e; S262.1.

B91, 91.1. Mythical snake, snake-demon. *See* Th. 3b.

B91.3. Horned snake. *See* Th. 3b; B11.2.5.

B91.5. Sea serpent. *See* Ths. 3b, 2e; G308.

B184.2.1. Magic cow. *See* B19.2.

B576.2. Animal guards treasure. 387; cf. 535 f., 539.

B742. Animal breathes fire. *See* Th. 3d; B11.2.11.

B870, 871. Giant animals, beasts. *See* Th. 3a.

B871.1.1.2. Giant bulls. *See* Th. 3a; B19.1.

B871.1.2. Giant boar. 56 f., 186, 194, 202, 234, 254, 289, 329 n.12, 384, 432 n.38, 480 f., 496, 501. *See* Th. 3a.

B871.2.4. Giant hippopotamus. 179, 182–187, 189 f., 209 f. *See* Th. 3a.

B871.2.5. Giant lion. 147, 149, 152, 164, 207, 308, 357 f., 516. *See* Th. 3a.

B872. Giant bird. *See* Th. 3a.

B873.2. Giant scorpion. 149, 171, 184 f.; cf. 504. *See* Th. 3a.

B874. Giant fish. *See* Th. 3a; G308.

B875, 875.1–4. Giant reptile; snake, etc. *See* Th. 3a.

B877.1. Giant sea monster. *See* Th. 3a; G308.

C54. Contest between god and mortal. 25, 43, 89, 111, 384. *See* Th. 7A.

D102. Transformation of evil demon to animal. *See* Th. 3E.

D112.1, 4. Transformation to lion, panther. 176 n.62, 328, 334 n.19, 378; cf. 166. *See* Th. 3E.

D113.1, 113.1.1. Transformation to wolf, werewolf. 116–118, 120, 184, 254, 421 f., 432, 528. *See* Ths. 3E, 3F, 3B.

D113.2. Transformation to bear. 207, 495, 533. *See* Th. 3E.

D127.1–2. Transformation to seal, otter. 106, 540 n.48. *See* Th. 3E.

D133.2, 134. Transförmation to bull, goat. 192, 313 f., 378. *See* Th. 3E.

D152.1–3. Transformation to hawk, eagle, vulture. 138 f., 176 n.62, 328, 421, 470 f.; cf. 190. *See* Th. 3E.

D161.1, 162. Transformation to swan, crane. 57, 101, 286 f. *See* Th. 3E.

D185.1. Transformation to fly, bee. 328, 484. *See* Th. 3E.

D191, 194, 199.2. Transformation to snake, crocodile, dragon. *See* Th. 3E.

D215. Transformation to tree. 192, 511; cf. 423. *See* Th. 3E.

D231. Transformation of person to stone. 106, 179, 284, 286, 292, 294. *See* Th. 10A; D581.

D391. Transformation of snake to man. *See* Th. 3E.

D399.1, 419.1. Transformation of dragon to man or other animal. *See* Th. 3E.

D429.2.1. Dragon king as wind. *See* Th. 3G; A282.1.

D581. Petrefaction by glance. 245, 284, 286, 294. *See* Th. 3D.

D610, 630. Repeated transformation or at will. *See* Th. 3E.

D651. Transformation to defeat enemies. *See* Th. 9, *c*.

D658.1. Transformation to animal to seduce woman. 57, 101 n.20, 314 f., 367, 378, 396, 422 n.23.

D671. Transformation flight. 73, 75, 190, 207, 378, 493. *See* Th. 7C.

D830. Needed object or information acquired by a trick. 75, 138, 203 f., 301, 513. Cf. Th. 9.

D838.2, 859.2. Magic object taken from ogre's house or from lower world. 200–204, 502, 530, 535 f.

D950.0.1. Magic tree guarded by snake. 313 n.72, 346. *See* Th. 2C.

D1030. Magic food. *See* A154.

D1030.1. Food supplied by magic. *See* D1472.

D1040. Magic drink. *See* A154.

D1080, 1081, 1094, 1101.1–4. Magic weapons, armor. *See* Th. 9, *d*.

D1171.6. Magic cup, Grail. *See* D1472.

D1242.1. Magic water. *See* E80, A154.

D1273. Magic formula. *See* Th. 9, *d*.

D1335. Potency index. 75, 147 f., 162, 200–204, 244–246, 249, 301, 350–354, 402, 497 f., 535 f., 538. Cf. Th. 8B.

D1335.1–2, 1335. 2.2. Magic strength-giving food, drink, water. *See* A154.

D1336. Ephemeral fruits. 74, 89, 180, 506, 533 n.32.

D1344.5. Magic ointment renders invulnerable. 147, 153. *See* Th. 9, *d*.

D1346.2. Fountain of immortality. *See* E80.

D1346.3. Food of immortality. *See* A154.

D1346.5–6. Plant, fruit of immortality. 172, 497, 535, 549 n.8. *See* A154.

D1361.15. Cap of invisibility. 301, 535, 537.

D1381, 1383.5. Magic object, charm, protects against attack, poison. *See* Th. 9, *d*; D1344.5.

D1400.1.4. Magic weapon defeats enemy. 135, 158f., 184, 200–202, 301, 517, 530, 535 f. *See* Th. 9, *d*.

D1470.1.18. Magic wishing-cup. *See* D1472.

D1470.2.3. Horn of plenty. 350–354, 380, 538. *See* D1472.

D1472, 1472.1.9–19. Wunschding, magic cup, Grail. 350, 430 f., 540 f.

F134. Otherworld on island. *See* E481.2.0.1.

F141.1. River as barrier to otherworld. *See* A672.

F145. Mountain at boundary of otherworld. *See* F131.

F164. Habitable cave in otherworld. 54, 208, 478, 527. *See* Th. 2B.

F167.3. Giants in otherworld. *See* Th. 3A.

F300, 302. Marriage or liaison with fairy, demoness. *See* Th. 8D.

F302.3.4. Fairy, demoness, entices men to harm them. *See* Th. 8D [i].

F321. Demoness steals children from cradles. *See* Th. 4C.

F401.3. Spirit in animal form. *See* Th. 3B.

F402.1.2. Spirit blocks person's road. *See* Th. 4F.

F420.4.1.1. Protean transformations of water-deity. *See* Th. 3E.

F432, 433, 434, 436. Spirits of wind, storm, thunder, cold. *See* Th. 3G; A282.1–2, A289.1.

F451. Dwarf as underground spirit. 207, 533 n.32, 535, 539. Cf. Th. 3F.

F470, 471.1. Night spirits, nightmare. 116–119, 120, 144, 186, 288 n.23, 309 n.63, 341 n.31, 345 n.38, 426, 479, 485; cf. 371. *See* Th. 3F.

F493. Spirit of plague. 105, 118, 193 n.26, 235, 291, 459, 471. *See* Th. 3G.

F511.1.1. Two-faced person. 154, 470.

F512.1, 1.1. One-eyed person, Cyclops. 180 f., 206 f., 285 f., 288, 301, 326 f., 387.

F512.2, 2.2. Many-eyed person, Argos Panoptes. 50, 95, 154, 338, 385, 405, 483 f. *See* Th. 3C.

F515.0.2.1. Giants have hundred hands or arms. 82, 97, 202, 227 f., 470. *See* Th. 3C.

F526.1. Typhon. *See* Th. 3B; A282.1.; index C.

F526.2. Skylla. 97–100, 117. *See* Th. 3B.

F526.3. Gorgon. 117, 244 f., 280–291, 309, 353 f., 370 f. *See* Ths. 3B, 3F; index C, Medusa.

F526.6. Snake-man compound. *See* Th. 3B.

F531. Giant. *See* Th. 3A.

F531.1.0.1.1. Beautiful giantess. *See* Th. 8D.

F531.1.1.2. Giant with large gleaming eyes. *See* Th. 3D.

F531.1.2.2. Many-headed giant. 154, 202, 204, 206, 334, 523. *See* Th. 3C.

F531.1.3.1. Giant with snake-feet. 70, 80, 117, 242 f. *See* Th. 3B.

F531.2. Size of giant. *See* Th. 3A.

F531.2.1.5. Giant reaches to sky. 80, 212, 214, 290, 311, 523 f. *See* Th. 3A.

F531.3.4, 3.4.1. Giant eats prodigious amount: a thousand cattle. 84, 156, 194, 203, 206, 511. *See* Th. 4D.

F531.3.4.2. Giants drink up a river. *See* Th. 4G.

F531.3.8. Giants' shouts are storms. *See* Th. 3G.

F531.6.1.1. Giants begotten by god on women. *See* Th. 1B.

F531.6.2.1. Giants live in caves. *See* Th. 2B.

F531.6.7, 6.7.1. Giant's treasure. 201 f., 290 f., 332, 527 f., 535, 539.

F533. Remarkably tall man. *See* Th. 3A.

F541.1.1–3. Eyes flash fire, lightning; are live coals. 83, 106, 118, 203, 206, 235, 244, 311, 432 n.38, 528. *See* Th. 3D.

F541.1.4, 541.3.1. Serpent-eye, eyes with two pupils. 237 n.27, 285, 545. *See* Th. 3D.

F547.1.1. Vagina dentata. 513 n.41. *See* Th. 8D [i].

F557. Removable organs. 73, 122, 505, 507. *See* E781.

F611.3.2. Hero has full strength when very young. *See* T615.

F615.2. Strong hero sent for wild animals. *See* H1325.

F701. Land of plenty. *See* A692.

F721. Subterranean world. *See* E481.1.

F721.1. Underground passages. 144, 208, 415, 431, 548.

F721.2. Habitable hill. *See* F131.

F725. Submarine world. *See* F133.

F755.2. Plain that is earthly paradise. *See* A692.

F771.1.9. House of skulls as murderer's abode. *See* G315.

F771.5.1–2. Castle, palace guarded by beasts, giants, ogres. Cf. 536, 539. *See* Th. 2c.

F841.1.1. Stone boats. 181, 487.

F1022. Descent into the sea. 190, 212, 298, 473, 484, 527, 529.

G10. Cannibalism. *See* Th. 4d; G11.2.

G11.2. Cannibal giant. 134, 198 f., 203, 206 f., 210, 299, 304, 393 n.36, 416 n.13, 496, 498 n.15, 500, 503 f., 510–512, 516 f., 524, 528. *See* Th. 4d.

G11.3. Cannibal demoness. 97, 100, 104 f., 116, 199, 206 f., 304, 309. *See* Th. 4d.

G100. Giant ogre. *See* Th. 3a.

G200. Witch, demoness. *See* Th. 1c.

G201. Three demon-sisters. 280 f., 285–287, 301, 331 f., 352 f., 426–432, 511 f.

G211. Demoness in animal form. Chapter vi; 44, 189 f., 206 f., 208, 220, 243 f., 286, 288 n.23, 353 f., 528. *See* Ths. 3b, 3e.

G211.1.8. Demoness in dog form. 97, 118, 207, 309 n.62, 371. *See* Th. 3e.

G242.2. Demon flies as whirlwind. *See* A282.1.

G260. Demoness commits evil deeds. *See* Th. 4a.

G261. Demoness steals children. *See* Th. 4c.

G262. Demoness commits murder. *See* Th. 4a.

G262.0.1. Lamia, demoness who eats children. *See* Ths. 4a, 4d; B29.1.

G262.0.1.1. Lamia devours her lover. *See* Th. 8d [i]; B15.6.2.

G264. La belle dame sans merci: demoness seduces men to destroy them. *See* Th. 8d [i].

G264.1. Woman brings death to all who behold her. 284, 286, 530 n.20. *See* Ths. 3d, 8d [i].

G283. Demons have control over weather. *See* Th. 3g.

G301. Monsters. *See* Th. 3b.

G302. Malevolent demon. *See* Ths. 3f, 4a.

G303. Devil, Satan. 210, 518, 525, 541. *See* Th. 3f.

G303.1.1. Evil demon is god's son. *See* Th. 1b.

G303.3. Evil demon takes various forms. *See* Th. 3e.

G303.3.3.6.1. Evil demon in form of snake. *See* Th. 3b; cf. 3f.

G303.4.1.1. Evil demon has ninety-nine heads. Cf. 202 (99 arms), 197, 203 (99 rivers). *See* Th. 3c.

G303.4.1.2.1. Evil demon has one eye in middle of forehead. *See* F512.1.1.

G303.4.1.2.2, 4.1.2.3. Evil demon with glowing eyes; two beams of fire shoot from his eyes. *See* Th. 3d; F541.1.1–3.

G303.4.1.6, 4.2, 4.4, 4.6. Evil demon has horns, wings, claws, tail. *See* Th. 3b; B11.2.5–6.

G303.8.1. Evil demon driven from heaven. *See* Th. 7a.

G303.8.3.1, 8.5. God thrusts evil demon into hell as punishment. *See* Th. 10a.

G303.8.8. Evil demon lives in the water. *See* Th. 2e.

G303.9.5.1. Evil demon abducts girl. *See* Th. 4e.

G303.11.1. Evil demon has wife. *See* Th. 1c.

G303.11.3. Evil demon has mother. *See* Ths. 1a, 1c.

G303.13. Stupid demon. *See* G501.

G303.17.2.2. Devil disappears in a whirlpool. Cf. 102, 120, 493, 530. *See* Th. 2e.

G303.20. Evil demon kills people. *See* Th. 4a.

G308. Sea monster. 96, 97, 117, 142–144, 147, 175, 190 f., 208, 209 f., 230–238, 282 f., 288 f., 303, 347–349, 356, 492, 495, 498 n.15, 503, 504, 511. *See* Ths. 3b, 2e.

G311. Old man of the sea. 106, 236 n.25, 238, 331 f., 337, 484. *See* Th. 2e.

G315. Demon cuts off men's heads to build with them. 25, 29, 330 f., 333; cf. 504 n.27.

G317. Wrestling ogre. 330–333, 336, 352, 432 n.38, 492, 530. *See* Th. 4f.

G346. Devastating monster. *See* Th. 4a.

G354.1. Snake as ogre. *See* Th. 3B.

G361.1, 1.1–5. Many-headed ogre. *See* Th. 3C.

G363.1. Ogre with flaming mouth. *See* Th. 3D.

G371. Stone giants. 147, 171, 211–215, 290, 303 n.54, 392, 416 n.13, 501, 503 n.25, 506, 524 n.8; cf. 423.

G412. Ogre's food lures victim. *See* Th. 8C.

G440. Ogre abducts person. *See* Th. 4E.

G442. Ogre steals children. *See* Th. 4C.

G465. Ogre sets impossible tasks. 486, 502, 507 f.

G500. Ogre defeated. *See* Th. 7A.

G501. Stupid ogre. 122, 181.

G510, 512, 512.1, 512.1.1, 1.2. Ogre killed, maimed, decapitated, with sword or knife. *See* Ths. 7A, 10A.

G514. Ogre captured. *See* Th. 7A.

G521. Ogre made drunk and overcome. *See* Th. 9, *a.*

G530.1–2. Hero helped by ogre's wife or daughter. *See* Th. 8D [ii].

G637. Ogres live in trees. 54, 168, 172. *See* Th. 2B.

G691. Bodies of victims in front of ogre's house. 284, 331, 342, 352.

H331. Suitor contest, bride offered as prize. 327 n.7, 333, 350, 354, 537 f.

H331.4.1. Suitor contest: with bride's father in shooting. 43.

H331.5.0.1, 5.1. Suitor contest: race with princess for her hand; loser dies. 333, 537.

H331.5.2. Suitor contest: race with bride's father. 333.

H331.6.1. Suitor contest: wrestling with bride. 537 f.

H332.1. Suitor in contest with bride. *See* H331.5.1., 6.1.

H541.1.1. Sphinx propounds riddle on pain of death. 309 f. *See* Th. 4F.

H901.1. Heads placed on stakes for failure. *See* S110.3.

H931. Tasks assigned to hero to get rid of him. 292.

H1161. Task: killing ferocious beast. *See* Th. 7A.

H1211. Quests assigned to hero to get rid of him. See H931.

H1250, 1270, 1273, 1275. Quest to otherworld for object or treasure. Appendix 1; 171–173, 293, 304 f.

H1321.1. Quest for water of life. *See* E80.

H1331, 1332, 1332.1, 3. Quest for remarkable animal or part of animal: e.g., golden fleece, Gorgon's head. 297, 301, 330, 486.

H1333.2.1. Quest for plant of immortality. *See* D1346.5–6.

H1333.3.1. Quest for marvelous apple. 331, 345 f.

H1385.2, 4. Quest for vanished child, husband. 130 f., 161, 165, 178, 185, 338, 367, 439 f.

J218. Reconciliation between enemies ends combat. 131, 174 f., 181, 193 n.26, 203, 388 f., 401, 404, 502.

K12.3. Demon's strength is renewed from contact with earth. 330, 333.

K714.2. Victim tricked into entering box. 178, 501. *See* Th. 8C.

K776. Enemy captured when drunk. *See* Th. 9, *a.*

K811.1. Opponent lured to a banquet. *See* Ths. 8C. 9, *a.*

K871. Enemy killed when drunk. *See* Th. 9, *a.*

K872. Judith and Holofernes. Appendix 2. *See* Th. 9, *b.*

K913. Disguised hero attacks enemy at feast. *See* Th. 9, *a, c.*

K917. Treacherous murder during hunt. 501, 506, 538 f.

K1810. Deception by disguise. *See* Th. 9, *c.*

K1844.1. Siegfried-Gunther theme. 327 n.7, 537 f.

K1913.3. Brothers kill hero. *See* K917.

K2357. Disguise to enter enemy's camp. *See* Th. 9, *c.*

M2. King makes inhuman decisions. *See* Th. 4B.

M343, 343.2. Oracle predicts death from son or grandson. 291, 481.

M372. Confinement in tower to avoid fulfilment of prophecy. 292 n.31.

P12.3. Usurper imposes burdensome taxes. 191, 516; cf. 67. *See* Th. 4B.

Q53. Hero receives reward for rescue. 102, 347–349, 510, 519. *See* T68.1.

Q421. Punishment: beheading. 112, 168, 179, 181, 440, 463, 500, 503 f., 517, 531. *See* Th. 10A.

Q431. Banishment, exile. 37, 195 f., 207, 312, 319 n.85, 382 f., 540. *See* Th. 10C.

Q431.1. Voluntary exile as punishment for murder. 87, 198–200, 302.

Q431.3. Banishment for disobedience. 382 f. *See* Th. 10C.

Q433.2. Defeated giants imprisoned in netherworld. *See* Th. 10A.

Q451. Punishment: mutilation. 65, 150, 163, 169, 179, 181, 183, 185, 187, 196 f., 206, 244, 511 f. *See* Th. 10A.

Q456. Punishment: burial alive. *See* Th. 10A.

Q467. Casting into water as punishment. *See* S141, 142.

Q482. Noble person must do menial service. *See* Th. 10C; A181.

Q491. Punishment: indignity to corpse. *See* Th. 10A; Q451.

Q511. Punishment: carrying corpse of murdered man. 181, 447 f. *See* Th. 10A.

Q520.1. Murderer does penance. 15, 86f., 198–200, 302, 317, 326 f. *See* Th. 10C.

Q552.2.3. Punishment: swallowed up in earth. *See* Th. 10A.

Q560. Punishment in hell. 64 f., 90, 150, 163, 187, 224, 234, 477 f., 544. *See* Th. 10A.

R11.1. Princess abducted by monster, ogre. *See* Th. 4E.

R41.3.1. Hero confined in houses of snakes, scorpions, etc. 502, 507.

R45. Captivity in mound, cave, hill. 73, 161, 163, 438 f. *See* Ths. 8A, 10A.

R111.1.1, 1.3–4. Rescue of princess from ogre, dragon, giant. *See* Th. 4E.

R185. Hero fights Death to save somebody. 102 f., 105, 112, 114, 260, 265, 303–306, 324–326, 334, 347 f., 500, 529 f., 533. Cf. Th. 7A.

R220. Flight. *See* Ths. 7C, 7F.

S110. Murder. *See* Th. 4A.

S111, 112. Murder by poisoning, burning to death. 109, 188, 354, 501, 506, 512, 538 n.44. *See* Th. 4A; cf. Th. 3D.

S141, 142. Exposure in boat; person thrown into water and abandoned. 178, 298, 535.

S165. Mutilation: putting out eyes. *See* Th. 8B; E781.

S262. Periodic sacrifices to a monster. 102, 347–350, 497, 500, 516 f., *See* Th. 4B.

S262.1. Woman given as wife to monster to appease him. 102 f., 120, 260, 303 f., 497, 504, 516. *See* Ths. 4E, 7C.

S262.2. Tribute of youths regularly sent to enemy. *See* Ths. 4B, 4C; S262.

S265. Sacrifice of strangers. 334, 340, 352. *See* Th. 4B.

S302. Murder of children. *See* Th. 4C.

S313. Child of supernatural birth is exposed. 104, 115, 291, 298.

S322. Children driven out by hostile parents. 298, 312, 535. *See* Th. 8A.

S322.3.1. Jealous wife wants rival's children killed. 100, 185, 207, 316 n.76, 357. *See* Th. 5B.

S331, 431.1. Exposure of child (and mother) in boat or chest. *See* S141, 142, 313.

T68.1. Princess offered as prize to rescuer. 293 f., 326, 347–349, 500, 518.

T91.1. Giant's daughter loves hero. *See* Th. 8D [ii].

T118. Girl married to monster, *See* Th. 4E; S262.1.

T173. Murderous bride. 108, 116, 141, 168–170, 237 n.27, 257 f., 285, 304, 486, 513 n.41, 537 f. *See* Th. 8D [i].

T381. Father imprisons daughter to keep her from men. *See* M372.

T410, 411, 412, 415. Incest: father-daughter, mother-son, brother-sister. 189, 255–257, 300, 353 n.49, 367 f., 420.

T455. Woman grants favors for performance of request. 121, 138, 141, 504.

T471. Rape. 23, 42 f., 58 f., 67 f., 102, 174, 189, 206, 242, 259 f., 265, 293 f., 313 f., 315 n.75, 334, 367, 536. *See* Th. 4E.

T471.2. Wild man as ravisher of women. *See* Th. 4E.

T511, 533. Impregnation from eating or swallowing or from spittle. 180, 192, 211, 213, 507, 513.

T585.1. Child born full-grown or nearly so. *See* T615.
T615. The god grows up in a few days. 18, 149, 195, 212, 215 n.58.
W125. Gluttony. *See* Th. 4ᴅ; F531.3.4.

Part III

Bird-messenger to absent god (cf. A165.2.2: Birds as gods' messengers) . 127, 502 f.
Bird steals potent object (cf. Th. 8ʙ) . 147 f., 203 f., 245 f.
Box and Cox. 253, 388 f., 466, 468.
Brawl at wedding-feast. 293, 355, 483.
Building of temple or palace after god's victory (cf. Th. 10ᴅ) . 130 f., 138 n.36, 150, 164, 184.
Control of waters by damming or channeling (cf. A533: Culture hero regulates rivers) . 343 f., 351, 402, 492–495, 497.
Cows as water or clouds (cf. A1421: Hoarded animals released). 200, 343 f., 346, 349, 403.
Death-lord as cattle baron or herdsman. 326 n.6, 335 f., 341, 343, 345 f., 350, 403, 432.
Death-lord as host (cf. E499.1: Banquet of the dead) . 112 f., 130, 293, 325 f., 340, 356 n.54, 403, 486 n.15, 502.
Eagle or hawk fights snake (cf. A2494.16: Enmity between reptiles and other animals) . 203 f.
Earth and heaven joined when emerging from chaos (cf. A625.2: Raising of sky) . 196, 212, 218, 220 f.
Earth-mother and heaven-father are separated forcibly by their son (cf. A625.2) . 213, 221, 259 n.51.
Emasculation of father-god by son (cf. S176.1: Emasculation, and A192.1.1: Old god slain by young god) . 211, 213.
Enemy's daughter captured by hero (cf. R10.1: Princess abducted) . 42 f., 67, 113, 259, 313, 348 f.
Failure of several gods before one succeeds (cf. H1242: Youngest brother alone succeeds on quest) . 125 f., 147–150, 492 f., 502 f.
Failure of test by enemy (cf. Th. 9) . 503.
Harpe, sickle-shaped sword, usually bronze (cf. D1081 above) . 73, 85, 212 f., 278, 296 f., 301, 539.
Harrowing of Hell (cf. H1270 above) . 175, 327–330, 343, 466, 507–509.
Hero as herdsman (cf. L113.1–6: herdsmen as heroes) . 164 f., 174, 176, 341 n.30, 348, 432, 519.
Hibernation in a cave (cf. A2481: Why animals hibernate) . 97, 341, 470, 533.
Homage is refused by young god (cf. P12.12: King avenges lack of homage) . 130, 175, 297.
Husband is bound to fulfill wife's destructive request (cf. M223: Blind promise). 192, 207.
Imitation dragon receives worship (cf. K1972: Sham oracular images) . 498 n.15, 503 n.26.
Interrex (cf. J711.3: King for a year provides for future, and A173 above) . 130, 205, 393, 440 n.6, 445 n.11.
Net is used to catch enemy (cf. D1196: Magic net) . 74, 150, 158, 180 n.3, 183, 196 n.32, 209, 404 n.56.
Noise made by younger gods bothers older gods (cf. S40–42: Cruel grandparents). 149, 507.
Plague sent by god (cf. Q552.10: Plague as punishment) . 25 f., 86 f., 105, 347 f., 459, 471, 483 n.10, 516.
Receiver of daughters or maidens for execution or slavery (cf. S210.1–2: Children sold into slavery or to be killed) . 350, 481 f.
Rivalry in beauty with a goddess (cf. C54 above) . 100 f., 285, 295.

Rivalry in love between hero and enemy (T92.7: Rival lovers fight for girl). 25, 102, 189–192, 205–207, 242, 258–261, 293 f., 300, 318 f., 350, 354 f., 398, 536.

Seductress fails. 168, 204, 206, 212, 258, 260, 299, 518.

Skulls hung on tree (cf. G315 above). 25, 51 n. 19, 507.

Sleeping enemy caught, 284, 331 f., 404 n.56, 421, 502, 535, 538.

Sun and world materials are hidden in the waters of chaos (cf. A719.1: Sun emerges from lake). 194–197, 220 f., 397 n.43, 504, 522–524, 527, 532.

Treasure is won by hero from dragon (cf. H335.3.2: Suitor kills treasure-guarding snake that encircles princess' chamber). 311, 345 f., 402–404, 519, 527, 535 f.

INDEX B

INDEX LOCORUM

Only the more important passages from texts consulted in the original languages (Greek, Latin, Hebrew, Sanskrit, west European) are listed here. The titles of Hittite, Ugaritic, Babylonian, Egyptian, Norse, and other texts, for which I have had to rely mainly or entirely upon translations, are entered in index C.

INDEX C

GENERAL INDEX

ADDENDA

Pp. 226 f. Tethys, like Tiamat, seems to have been both the salt waters and the earth. See Hesychios Θ418: *Thetis* is the sea, and the earth is called *Téthys*. Though the lexicographer makes a distinction here between Thetis and Tethys, the two deities are originally the same: they have the same name and the same province.

Pp. 372 f. Marie Delcourt's *L'Oracle de Delphes* (Paris: Payot, 1955) reached me after this book had gone to press. She accepts the derivation of the names Delphusa, Delphyne, and Telphusa from a common base (pp. 137–139), although like her predecessors she thinks that the dragoness Delphyne is simply an earlier version of the Delphic dragon, giving place in the tradition to the male dragon called Python.

Pp. 374 f. A silver coin of Delphi, dated 346–339, shows a snake coiled around the omphalos. See BCH XX (1896) 30, no. 34, pl. 26.37 = HN 342 = BMCC, Central Greece, *Delphi* no. 30, p. 29, pl. 4.20. On the omphalos as Python's tomb see also Jane Harrison, "Delphika," JHS XIX (1899) 205–251.

ADDENDA ET CORRIGENDA

Pp. 3–4. I would not now say that a myth necessarily accompanies rituals or that all myths tell of supposed primeval events commemorated in religious institutions. It is sufficient to define myth as a traditional tale of the deeds of supernatural beings, or simply a tale of supernatural events. See my *The Ritual Theory of Myth* (Berkeley, Los Angeles: University of California Press, 1966 [1971]), p. 54.

P. 11, line 23. By "father god" I do not mean any god that had a son, but a primal or supreme father of gods or all creatures, e.g., Chaos, Kronos, Zeus.

Pp. 164–166. There is no evidence so far that Tammuz was killed by a lion: he was killed (or removed to the death realm) by infernal demons. Furthermore there are uncertainties in the interpretation of the Bilulu text, so that Bilulu cannot confidently be taken as a Tiamat-like figure or this story as a variant of the combat myth.

P. 198, top. Since *yátrānam* is masculine in form it is not likely to refer to Danu.

Pp. 414–418. My suggestion that the Delphians had an Oracle at Lykoreia before moving to Pytho must apparently be given up, since recent excavations show that the Corycian Cave was unused between Mycenaean times and the sixth century B.C. See my *The Delphic Oracle* (Berkeley, Los Angeles, London: University of California Press, 1978), p. 4, note 4, for citations. The Delphic Oracle was founded at Pytho in the eighth century, and we cannot suppose that there were any oracular establishments in Greece or elsewhere before 1000 B.C., (except perhaps divinatory shrines in the late second millennium, such as that of the Apis-bull at Memphis). Nevertheless the Delphic cult of Apollo may have been first established at Lykoreia; and certainly the Corycian Cave and Parnassian plateau were the scene of the Apollo-dragon combat in the earliest myth. Moreover the Homeric Hymn to Hermes attests a divinatory Oracle on the slopes of Parnassos (see pp. 426–433), perhaps situated at Lykoreia and perhaps making use of the Corycian Cave in the sixth century.